FOURTH EDITION

Teaching and Learning with Technology

Judy Lever-Duffy
Miami Dade College

Jean B. McDonald
Lambuth University

PEARSON

Boston Columbus Indianapolis New York San Francisco Upper Saddle River
Amsterdam Cape Town Dubai London Madrid Munich Paris Montreal Toronto
Delhi Mexico City Sao Paulo Sydney Hong Kong Seoul Singapore Taipei Tokyo

Acquisitions Editor: Kelly Villella Canton
Development Editor: Amy J. Nelson
Editorial Assistant: Annalea Manalili
Vice President, Director of Marketing: Quinn Perkson
Senior Marketing Manager: Darcy Betts
Production Editor: Gregory Erb
Editorial Production Service: Nesbitt Graphics, Inc.
Manufacturing Buyer: Megan Cochran
Electronic Composition: Nesbitt Graphics, Inc.
Interior Design: Carol Somberg
Photo Researcher: Annie Pickert
Cover Designer: Elena Sidorova

Library of Congress Cataloging-in-Publication Data

Lever-Duffy, Judy.
Teaching and learning with technology / Judy Lever-Duffy. -- 4th ed.
p. cm.
Includes bibliographical references and index.
ISBN 0-13-800796-9
1. Educational technology. 2. Computer-assisted instruction. 3. Computer network resources. 4. Audio-visual materials. I. Title.
LB1028.3.L49 2011
371.33'4--dc22

2010000166

All photos are credited on the page where they appear except for the following: Figure 1, page 6 a, m, Jupiter Unlimited; 6 b, Shutterstock; 6 n, David Frazier/The Image Works; Interchapter 5, pages 142 a, Courtesy of Kingston Technology; 142 b, c, d, g, Courtesy of Acer America Corporation; 142 e, Courtesy of Seagate Technology; 142 f, © Royalty-Free/Corbis; 142 h, j, Courtesy of Sony Electronics; 142 i, Courtesy of Iomega Corporation. Copyright © 2004 Iomega Corporation. All rights reserved. Zip is a trademark in the United States and/or other countries. Iomega, the stylized "I" logo, and product images are property of Iomega Corporation in the United States and/or other countries; 142 k, Courtesy of Lexmark International; 131 a, c, d, e, Courtesy of Logitech; 143 b, Courtesy of Sony Electronics; 143 f, Courtesy of EPSON America, Inc.; 143 g, Courtesy of Casio, Inc.; 190 (students with school bus) David R. Frazier Photolibrary; (red school) The Image Works; (teacher with students) © Royalty-Free/Corbis; (school bus) Index Stock Imagery; Table 8.3 page 216 a, Courtesy of Knowledge Adventure, Inc.; 216 b, Where in the World Is Carmen Sandiego © Riverdeep Interactive Learning Limited, and its licensors; 216 c, © Riverdeep Interactive Learning Limited. All rights reserved. Used with permission; 330 (TV, CD, iMac), Jupiter Unlimited.

10 9 8 7 6 5 4 3 2 1 WEB 14 13 12 11 10

www.pearsonhighered.com

ISBN-10: 0-13-800796-9
ISBN-13: 978-0-13-800796-6

ABOUT THE AUTHORS

Dr. Judy Lever-Duffy, Professor of Computer Science and Education at Miami Dade College, Miami, Florida, teaches computer and education courses on campus and in MDC's Virtual College. She holds a B.A. degree in Education from Florida Atlantic University, Boca Raton, Florida, and an M.S. in Computer Studies and Ed.D. in School Management and Instructional Leadership from Nova Southeastern University, Ft. Lauderdale, Florida. Dr. Lever-Duffy enjoys teaching, writing, traveling, and living in the Florida Keys.

Dr. Jean B. McDonald, Associate Professor of Education at Lambuth University, Jackson, Tennessee, teaches educational technology and methods courses for middle school and high school pre-service teachers. She holds a B.S. degree in English and an M.A. in English from Bradley University, Peoria, Illinois, and an Ed.D. from the University of Memphis, Memphis, Tennessee. Dr. McDonald enjoys international travel, reading, and classical music.

BRIEF CONTENTS

PART THREE Technology in Schools: Changing Teaching and Learning 316

CONTENTS

CHAPTER 5

Computers in the Learning Environment 110

CHAPTER 6

Digital Technologies in the Classroom 144

CHAPTER 7

Administrative Software 168

CHAPTER 10

Using the Web for Teaching and Learning 260

CHAPTER 14

PREFACE

Introduction

Educational technology can enrich and enhance instructional experiences for both the teacher and the learner. *Teaching and Learning with Technology* explains, on many levels, how educational technology can provide resources for teachers and students and open the door to more comprehensive learning as well as extend the learning process.

The power of the Internet can put the world's body of knowledge quite literally at one's fingertips. A computer in a classroom can be an endlessly patient and positive tutor. An audio recording of a children's story can encourage the development of good listening skills and meet the needs of auditory learners. A nature video can bring the most remote corner of the world into the classroom. These technologies, from the commonplace to the newest digital technologies, provide powerful tools for creative teachers and support diverse learners.

However, educational technology remains underutilized in many classrooms. Too often, teachers have not learned how to work effectively with educational technologies in teaching and learning. Current and future teachers need exposure to and experience with the many and growing number of technologies that exist in schools and that schools are likely to acquire. Teachers also need a basic understanding of the technologies. They need hands-on practice with the technologies, and they need to explore how the technologies fit into the teaching and learning process.

In response to these needs, courses in educational technology have become a vital part of teacher preparation programs. Some are computer courses adapted for educators. Others are focused on the historical and theoretical aspects of educational technology. Each approach has merit, but perhaps the most effective and pragmatic solution is a balance that includes components of both. Finding the points at which these approaches intersect has been challenging. This text is a result of that challenge.

New to This Edition!

This text provides a robust view of all technologies, including the most current and engaging technologies that are available to teachers, while focusing on the educational application of each. You will find a full range of in-text activities, including group, critical thinking, and hands-on experiences as well as marginal references to the robust MyEducationKit online course. The fourth edition addresses the needs of today's teachers and students in the following ways:

- **Chapter 1, *Teaching, Technology, and You*,** previously Chapter 12, has been moved forward in response to reviewer feedback. It offers additional pragmatic information on how current and future educators can use technology in their professional lives to address administrative and instructional tasks, achieve national and content area standards, and teach more effectively.
- **Chapter 4, *Technology for Diverse Learners*,** highlights and explores technologies that are available to support learning for students with special needs, English Language Learners, and gifted students as well as addressing diverse learning styles.
- **Chapter 14, *Emerging Technologies and Schools*,** focuses on new trends and changes in technologies that are particularly relevant to today's educators. Emerging technologies are introduced and explained, and their application is reviewed to provide future educators with the knowledge they need to apply these changing systems to teaching and learning.

- **Updated topics** include cyberbullying, Internet security, netiquette, and more.
- Coverage of **Web 2.0** has been enhanced to include an exploration of the most popular social networking sites including Facebook, MySpace, and Twitter and their impact on students in and outside of the classroom. Virtual social interaction sites such as Second Life are also examined for their potential for educational application. The current impact and possible evolution of Web 2.0 is reviewed with an eye to its implication for educators and their students.
- **ISTE NETS•T and NETS•S** standards are matched with chapter content and are called out in the margins to raise students' awareness of relevant standards and to directly connect these standards to chapter topics.
- **Teaching with Technology Integration Ideas Web Quests** are located at the end of every chapter. Teacher candidates are able to search and review specific annotated web links for best practices, sample lessons, and educational resources across all content areas. They are prompted to do web research on the chosen topic and then write a summary of their findings.
- **MyEducationKit, an online extension of this text,** offers ready-made assignments and activities set in the context of real classrooms. Fully integrated with the text, it provides opportunities for reflection and practice in an easy-to-assign format. MyEducationKit for this text includes the following:
    - **Assignments and Activities**—These assignable exercises are connected to chapter objectives and present content in an active format. Both video and web activities provide questions that probe students' understanding of a concept or strategy.
    - **Study Plan**—These quizzes assess mastery of chapter content. These assessments are mapped to chapter objectives, and students can take each multiple-choice quiz as many times as they want. Not only do these quizzes provide overall scores for each objective, but they also explain why responses to particular items are correct or incorrect.
    - **Rubrics**—Located throughout the text, rubrics offer students pragmatic tools and myriad opportunities to evaluate and study technologies discussed in the text.
    - **Video Tutorials**—These twenty unique tutorials include step-by-step, hands-on exercises that develop proficiency with a variety of current educational technology tools. Tutorials include, but are not limited to, Inspiration, Kidspiration, Dreamweaver, iMovie for Macs, and MovieMaker for PCs.
    - **Podcasts**—Students can download ten podcasts that address key educational technology topics that expand on the text content in an audio format. Topics include, but are not limited to, meeting students' needs, professional development, selecting software, and writing technology grants for funding.
    - **Web Sites**—Students can access this section to explore other resources and readings on chapter topics.

Organization of This Text

Teaching and Learning with Technology was designed to combine theoretical, technical, and experiential components into a single pragmatic approach that is suitable for current and future teachers using educational technology in the classroom.

In creating the text, we followed three basic principles:

1. Ground the study of educational technologies in effective teaching and learning and in the real-world classroom.
2. Explore all technologies that are likely to be found in the classroom.
3. Offer pragmatic tools and activities throughout the text that prepare students to use educational technology effectively.

We present technology throughout this text within the framework of education and from a classroom perspective. We follow our principles in three parts. **Part One** offers an exploration of the role technology has for the teacher, especially given the standards that he or she must address. It then provides an overview of learning theories and instructional design, maintaining a focus on teaching and learning as the force that drives the selection and implementation of technology.

Part Two begins with a focus on diverse learners and using technology to meet their unique needs. It continues with a thorough study of the major categories of educational technologies that are likely to be found in schools, from traditional audiovisual technologies to the current and emerging digital technologies. These technologies are examined both as objects of instruction to be mastered by technology-literate educators and, more important, as tools within the broader framework of teaching and learning.

As an outgrowth of this technological exploration, we then present distance learning as an instructional model in **Part Three.** We examine these approaches both as professional development tools and as delivery systems that have the potential to redefine the classroom. This part also offers an in-depth consideration of the issues associated with implementing technologies in education, including the teacher's role in strategic planning for technology and the ethical, legal, and social issues resulting from its implementation. The final chapter focuses on emerging technology and its impact on teaching and learning in the Digital Age. These topics converge to provide a powerful and complete experience for those who must soon face the challenges of the effective application of technology to their own classrooms and in their schools.

Text Features

In this fourth edition, this text's popular chapter features illustrate how real teachers are using technology to enhance learning, help readers to consider technology applications and implications, and provide opportunities for hands-on practice.

REAL TEACHERS, REAL STORIES provide an exemplary case, interview, or personal story by an educator to introduce readers to an educational technology topic in each part opener. ▶

REAL TEACHERS REAL STORIES

Liz Brennan

Stacy Still

Meet Liz Brennan and Stacy Still. To build an effective learning environment requires planning. While planning may not be as exciting as delivering the instruction, careful and systematic planning is what makes effective teaching and learning. When Liz Brennan and Stacy Still recognized the problems their teachers were experiencing incorporating technology into their plans, they sat down with them and met the challenge together.

University School of Nova Southeastern University is a campus-based, independent college preparatory day school located in Fort Lauderdale, Florida. I am Liz Brennan, Associate Head of the University School of Nova Southeastern University. I would estimate that at least 75 percent of the "work" I do each day involves curriculum design and development. Whenever we think of curriculum, we are also thinking planning; and, one cannot think planning without thinking learning. On a daily basis working with my faculty, I can see that issues with student learning can, many times, be connected to breakdowns in classroom curriculum design planning.

My name is Stacy Still. I am the Technology Facilitator at the Lower School. There are many aspects to my job as Technology Facilitator, but one of the most important functions is to assist faculty in the planning of lessons that tie technology into the learning process.

Our problem involves a condition where, despite the knowledge and skills for generic lesson planning, the teacher is unable to effectively or consistently "fit" appropriate uses of computer-based learning experiences into a previously developed lesson plan. In addition, either she may lack the personal technical skills to feel comfortable with available hardware or she lacks an understanding of software options available either within the school or via the Internet.

Liz: To get the most from a planning experience, Stacy often sits with an individual teacher, and together they plan the lesson in

study it together and make decisions as to how and where to use technology effectively. This empowers the teacher to determine if the technological ideas that Stacy suggests, or the ones that they find together, are appropriate for the lesson, connect to the outcome objectives, address various learning styles of their students, and match the students' current performance levels. During their collaborative planning process, teachers can practice the lesson with the selected technology to simulate how it will work in their classrooms. This pre-instructional step helps the teacher feel more comfortable and confident in the quality of the plan and in his or her use of technology.

Stacy: I worked with one of our teachers in planning a lesson. Through our discussion, the teacher determined that her plan was sound in most of the steps of the planning process. We identified and listed the areas of strength: clearly stated objectives, an appropriately established learning environment, and a well-targeted summative evaluation. However, given the large number of students for whom the lesson was intended, it was difficult for her not only to identify but to manage the learning styles and specific learning needs of all of these students. We decided to strengthen several areas: knowing the learner, identifying teaching and learning strategies, and identifying and selecting technologies to be used to enhance and extend the lesson to be meaningful to more students.

Our first planning collaboration was to go online and find instructional plans that effec-

www.google.com. We found hundreds of sites that included well-planned technology-enhanced lesson plans. I suggested that we try to use a kid's search engine, such as www.yahooligans.com, sunsite.berkeley.edu/KidsClick!/, or www.ajkids.com to look for other resources and lesson plan sites that would be more limited or controlled by age level and content. She was able to incorporate both audio and video experiences from sites such as

www.rainforesteducation.com/FunNGames/canuseethem.htm
www.exploratorium.edu/frogs/rainforest/
www.christiananswers.net/kid/vidclips.html
http://schools.pinellas.k12.fl.us/educators/tec/templ1.htm

The next step was to determine how to incorporate these links and the other information into a PowerPoint presentation. Having me there as a guide enabled her to learn, in a hands-on mode, how to do these things, yet she was not "afraid" of the task or the technology. The final step in the plan then was to determine the best way to display this presentation. We decided to use a portable smart board to deliver the instruction and present the PowerPoint project.

This was a tremendous experience for both of us. The teacher gained confidence in herself, as a professional, and in her own ability to use the technology effectively, and I was able to see the lesson plan implemented and use its outcome as a reference later with other teachers.

For further information, you may contact the writers at the following:

th C. Brennan's email:
an@nova.edu
: 954-262-4484
email: **stacy@nova.edu**
: 954-262-4500

85

IN THE CLASSROOM stories throughout the text demonstrate real-world implementation of various technologies across the content areas by highlighting particular teachers and their lessons. ▶

In the CLASSROOM

Digital Cameras in Schools

Ideas for using digital cameras to enrich and enliven learning abound on the Brunswick, Maine, "Teacher to Teacher" handbook webpage. **Patti Irish,** seventh-grade science teacher, along with her students, is creating an online field guide for insects. They collect insects (live if possible), identify them, photograph them, and research their habitats and habits. With this information, they write a field guide that they publish online. Check it out at **http://www.brunswick.k12.me.us/lon/lonlinks/digicam/teacher/ home.html.**

Dorothy Small, technology integration specialist in MSAD#54 (Maine School Administrative District #54), points out how art teachers showcase student art by posting digital photos on the district's web site. **Matthew Charland** and **Mr. Chin,** both art teachers, use the District Wide Art Program web pages to share their students' work by keeping updated displays available online. You can see them at **http://www.msad54.org/.**

Liz Sheldon, K–5 teacher in Framingham, Massachusetts, has students present reports on books and/or famous people that include the students dressed in era appropriate character costume. Their image is captured and put into a KidPix slide show, and a voiceover tells who they are and why they are famous. Or they may document the steps of a science experiment in a slide show to share with other classes. In first grade, shapes are taught by using pictures taken of familiar objects around the school. The students then draw the shapes they saw in KidPix (using the pencil tool). Fifth graders took pictures during a field trip to an aquarium and placed them in a presentation. Each student was responsible for a picture and adding a brief description, which included new highlighted vocabulary words. Upon completion, the presentations are added as additional examples of digital cameras in the classroom on Ms. Sheldon's web page, at **www.framingham.k12.ma.us/k5.**

For students with special needs, **Katie Tyrrell** in Yarmouth, Maine, takes pictures of items around the room that a student with autism may want or need. The student can learn to communicate using symbol-size photos when the Mayer-Johnson symbols have not been successful.

Source: Dollof, K. *Teacher to teacher.* Retrieved August 13, 2006, from **http://www.brunswick.k12.me.us/lon/lonlinks/digicam/teacher/home.html.**

COOL TOOLS

The Scantron

Optical Mark Recognition (OMR) technology for scanners is the basis for a cool tool that helps you grade tests and analyze results. The Scantron, one of the most popular OMR scanners used in schools, lets your students respond to test questions by filling in bubbles on preprinted answer sheets. The Scantron scanner will then compare their marks on the answer sheet with your key and grade all of the tests for you. Results can then be automatically imported into grading software to be posted to your computer-based grade book and even analyzed to give you a graphical picture of class and individual results. This dedicated scanner can save busy teachers time when grading and tracking student progress. For more information about Scantrons, visit the company web site at **www.scantron.com.**

Source: Photo from **www.scantron.com.**

COOL TOOLS highlights particularly useful technology tools for educators.

YOU DECIDE! offers a deep examination of critical issues related to using or implementing technology. This feature presents contrasting opinions on important technological issues in education.

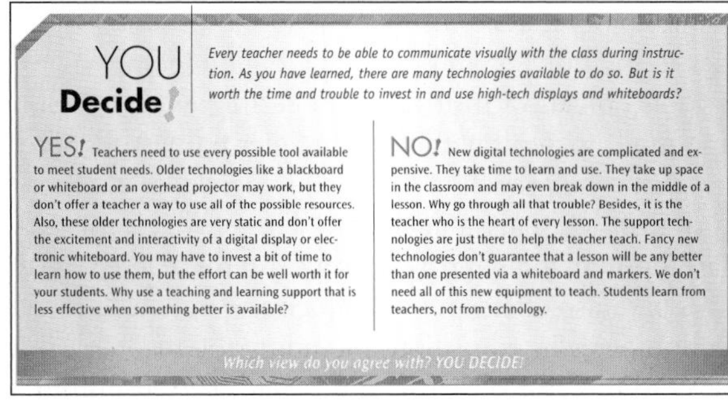

YOU Decide!

Every teacher needs to be able to communicate visually with the class during instruction. As you have learned, there are many technologies available to do so. But is it worth the time and trouble to invest in and use high-tech displays and whiteboards?

YES! Teachers need to use every possible tool available to meet student needs. Older technologies like a blackboard or whiteboard or an overhead projector may work, but they don't offer a teacher a way to use all of the possible resources. Also, these older technologies are very static and don't offer the excitement and interactivity of a digital display or electronic whiteboard. You may have to invest a bit of time to learn how to use them, but the effort can be well worth it for your students. Why use a teaching and learning support that is less effective when something better is available?

NO! New digital technologies are complicated and expensive. They take time to learn and use. They take up space in the classroom and may even break down in the middle of a lesson. Why go through all that trouble? Besides, it is the teacher who is the heart of every lesson. The support technologies are just there to help the teacher teach. Fancy new technologies don't guarantee that a lesson will be any better than one presented via a whiteboard and markers. We don't need all of this new equipment to teach. Students learn from teachers, not from technology.

Which view do you agree with? YOU DECIDE!

HANDS ON LEARNING

Multimedia helps to address the diverse learning styles of your students. Input and output devices let you create and use multimedia by capturing text, audio, still images, and video clips that might be just the added extra to help that unique student learn. Consider a topic you will be teaching at the grade level or in the content area of your choice. Using the available multimedia capture technology, including scanners, digital cameras, graphics tablets, and microphones, create images and audio and video elements that you feel could enhance a lesson on that topic. Share the multimedia elements with your peers and explain how you would use each

HANDS-ON LEARNING features offer students an opportunity to utilize the Internet or another technology to experience and apply the content that has been introduced in the text.

TECH TIPS for Teachers

Selecting the right digital camera for your classroom is a challenge. One of the most significant features to consider is the possible image quality or resolution that you need. The megapixel number for a camera identifies how many millions of pixels (picture elements) the camera is capable of. The table below will give you an idea of how many megapixels you want to do the job.

Camera's Megapixels	Image Quality and Size
2–3 megapixels	Good, detailed screen images; excellent 4 × 6 and very good 5 × 7 prints; some cameras may produce reasonable 8 × 10 prints
4–5 megapixels	Equal to 35-mm photos; able to print high-quality 8 × 10 images
6 or more megapixels	Allow you to crop and blow up portions of photos without losing clarity; able to produce high-quality images greater than 8 × 10

TECH TIPS FOR TEACHERS throughout the text offer educators practical tips and best practices for utilizing the technology under study to enhance teaching and learning.

MYEDUCATIONKIT, this text's online course, offers multiple opportunities to practice using new technologies, applying content, and extending student learning.

PEARSON myeducationkit

Go to the *Assignments and Activities* section of Chapter 6 in MyEducationKit and complete the video activity entitled *Cooperative Learning with Handhelds.*

RUBRICS offer students pragmatic tools and myriad opportunities to evaluate and study technologies throughout the text. They are also available for download from the text's MyEducationKit. ▶

162 PART TWO Applying Technologies for Effective Instruction

Classroom Equipment Evaluation **Rubric**

EQUIPMENT:
DESCRIPTION:
VENDOR: COST:
NOTES ON USE:

Please rate the features below for each piece of hardware. Next to each of the items in the rubric, mark the box that best reflects your opinion.

	EVALUATION CRITERIA				
HARDWARE FEATURE	**1 Poor**	**2 Below Average**	**3 Average**	**4 Above Average**	**5 Excellent**
Ease of Setup	☐ No or minimal setup instructions; poor or missing summary list of hardware components	☐ Instructions poorly written and somewhat difficult to follow; minimal description of equipment components	☐ Instructions complete and adequately user-friendly; necessary equipment	☐ Clear and complete instructions; parts identified by letter or code to correspond to instructions	☐ Pictorial or video guide showing step-by-step assembly with clear, easy-to-follow instructions; equipment goes together easily and smoothly
Ease of Use	☐ Equipment complex and difficult for students to use alone; time consuming and complex for teachers	☐ Students can use with minimal support by teacher; teachers can use with some difficulty	☐ Students can use without support after initial orientation; teachers can use with minimal practice	☐ Students can use with brief orientation; teachers can use with little or no practice	☐ Students can use without orientation or supports; teachers can use with no practice
Space	☐ Space required may exceed maximum available	☐ Space required somewhat large, but available room could be adjusted to accommodate equipment	☐ Space required by equipment is appropriate to available space with current room configuration	☐ Space requirement is appropriate and equipment will fit comfortably in the room	☐ Space requirement is equal to or less than the space available; equipment adds to the look and usefulness of the room without crowding
Tutorials/ Training Available	☐ No tutorials packaged with equipment; no online or other training available	☐ Minimal tutorials packaged with equipment; few free or inexpensive optional tutorials or training available	☐ Brief tutorial provided on CD-ROM with equipment; some additional tutorials or training available at minimal cost	☐ CD and online tutorials readily available for free or minimal cost; some in-house training available for a reasonable fee	☐ CD and online tutorials and training materials available without charge; in-house training provided for free or minimal cost
Other Criteria (List your own					

***INTER*CHAPTERS** follow each chapter and expand on topics of special interest in education technology, including writing grants to fund technology purchases, copyright and fair use, social networking, universal design for learning, and a teacher's buying guide for classrooms. ▶

interchapter 6

The Technology-Rich Classroom

What exactly would the ideal technology-rich classroom look like? Take a look in the table below at one teacher's description of the technology that she would like to have in a middle school classroom. Which of the technologies do you feel are must-have technologies for you? Which would you do without? Are there any that make little difference to you? Enter a checkmark next to each item to develop a profile of your ideal technology-rich classroom.

MY TECHNOLOGY-RICH CLASSROOM SPECIFICATIONS AND RATIONALE	Check which you prefer. MUST HAVE	DON'T NEED	NO PREFERENCE
TEACHER'S COMPUTER SYSTEM:			
3-gigahertz CPU: This is enough speed for editing video and graphics, and more than enough for common office tasks.	○	○	○
4-GB RAM: I'll need the RAM for multitasking and for graphics and video applications.	○	○	○
500-GB hard drive: I'll need a lot of space for multimedia applications, video, and pictures of my classroom activities.	○	○	○
DVD+/-RW drive: For reading and backup with any type of optical media, and to create my own instructional DVDs.	○	○	○
22" LCD monitor: Takes up less desk space, and I need that much viewable space for graphics and video editing programs, which tend to have cluttered interfaces.	○	○	○
Six or more USB 2.0 ports: Almost everything connects to USB ports these days. I'll need several of them or a USB hub to keep all my high-tech gear connected!	○	○	○
Upgraded speaker system: I'll need a relatively powerful speaker system so that when I'm using a CD-ROM or DVD for classroom instruction, all the students can hear clearly and without distortion.	○	○	○
Bluetooth connectivity: This new wireless standard for computers will be used for many of my high-tech devices.	○	○	○
Approximate cost: $900–$1,200			
5 STUDENT COMPUTER SYSTEMS			
3-gigahertz CPU: Going slower here probably wouldn't save me much money, so I wouldn't sacrifice the speed. It would be expensive to update later.	○	○	○
512-MB RAM: Additional RAM is inexpensive and easy to upgrade later; I'll wait until it looks as though I'll need more.	○	○	○
120-GB hard drive: Also easy and inexpensive to upgrade later. There are also some good reasonably priced external options that students could share when working on multimedia or video projects.	○	○	○
DVD+/-RW drive: This will make sure students can write to whatever media they bring in from home.	○	○	○
17" flat-panel monitor: Less expensive than 19" monitor. I'd go to a CRT before going to something smaller than 17" since so many programs require higher resolution than a 15" LCD can display.	○	○	○
Six or more USB 2.0 ports: Same as teacher station.	○	○	○
Headphones: This helps keep the noise down when students are working individually with multimedia applications.	○	○	○
Approximate cost: $600–$1,000 each			

166

Using a Pragmatic Approach

A constant aspect of our pragmatic approach in *Teaching and Learning with Technology* is the reader-friendly style of the text. To maintain interest and readability in a content area that tends toward jargon and technical detail, we deliberately engage students with a conversational tone and easy-to-use definitions and tools. Together, these elements present the complexities of educational technology in the most readable and engaging format possible.

Teaching and Learning with Technology provides current and future educators with a pragmatic survey of educational technology and an exploration of the applications and issues related to its use. This approach and style present key technological content while remaining well grounded in the theoretical foundations of teaching and learning

PEARSON
myeducationkit™

Dynamic Resources Meeting Your Needs

MyEducationKit is a dynamic web site that connects the concepts addressed in the text with effective teaching practice. It is easy to use and integrate into assignments and courses. Whenever the MyEducationKit logo appears in the text, follow the simple instructions to access a variety of multimedia resources geared to meet the diverse teaching and learning needs of instructors and students. Here are just a few of the features that are available:

- **Self-assessment quizzes**
- **Gradetracker, an online grade book**
- **A wealth of multimedia resources, including classroom video, expert video commentary, student and teacher artifacts, case studies, and strategies**
- **Web links to important national organizations and sites in your field**

Study Plan

A MyEducationKit Study Plan is a multiple-choice assessment with feedback tied to chapter objectives.

- *Chapter Objectives* identify the learning outcomes for the chapter and give students targets to shoot for as they read and study.
- *Multiple-Choice Assessments* assess mastery of the content. These assessments are mapped to chapter objectives, and students can take the multiple-choice quizzes as many times as they want. Not only do these quizzes provide overall scores for each objective, but they also explain why responses to particular items are correct or incorrect.
- *Study Material: Review and Enrichment* give students a deeper understanding of what they do and don't know related to chapter content, with text excerpts connected to chapter objectives.
- *Flash Cards* help students to study the definitions of the key terms within each chapter.

Assignments and Activities

Designed to save instructors preparation time and enhance student understanding, these assignable exercises show concepts in action (through videos, cases, and/or student and teacher artifacts). They help students to synthesize and apply concepts and strategies they read about in the book.

Multimedia Resources

The rich media resources that you will encounter throughout MyEducationKit include the following:

- *Videos:* The authentic classroom videos in MyEducationKit show how real teachers handle actual classroom situations. The process of discussing and analyzing these videos not only deepens understanding of concepts presented in the text, but also builds skills in observing children and classrooms.
- *Student & Teacher Artifacts:* Real K–12 student and teacher classroom artifacts are tied to the chapter topics in the text and offer practice in working with the different materials that teachers encounter daily in their classrooms.
- *Web Links:* On MyEducationKit, you don't need to search for the sites that relate to the topics that are covered in the chapter. Here, you can explore web sites that are important in the field and that give you perspective on the concepts that are covered in your text.

General Resources on MyEducationKit

The Resources section on MyEducationKit is designed to help students pass their licensure exams; put together effective portfolios and lesson plans; prepare for and navigate the first year of their teaching careers; and understand key educational standards, policies, and laws. This section includes the following:

- *Licensure Exams:* Contains guidelines for passing the Praxis exam. The *Practice Test Exam* includes practice multiple-choice questions, case study questions, and video case studies with sample questions.
- *Lesson Plan Builder:* Helps students to create and share lesson plans.
- *Licensure and Standards:* Provides links to state licensure standards and national standards.
- *Beginning Your Career:* Offers tips, advice, and valuable information on:
  - Resume Writing and Interviewing: Expert advice on how to write impressive resumes and prepare for job interviews
  - Your First Year of Teaching: Practical tips on setting up a classroom, managing student behavior, and planning for instruction and assessment
  - Law and Public Policies: Includes specific directives and requirements educators need to understand under the No Child Left Behind Act and the Individuals with Disabilities Education Improvement Act of 2004

Visit **www.myeducationkit.com** for a demonstration of this exciting new online teaching resource.

Student Resources

Activity reproducibles are included in the Instructor's Resource Manual and are available for download. Activities include puzzles, projects, reflections questions, tutorials, and field experience activities. These hands-on assignments are ready to copy and offer students practical applications and practice with the content being presented.

Instructor Resources

The text has the following ancillary materials to assist instructors as they strive to maximize learning for all students. These instructor supplements are located at the Instructor Resource Center at www.pearsonhighered.com/irc.

Instructor's Resource Manual and Test Bank

The Instructor's Resource Manual provides concrete chapter-by-chapter instructional and media resources with full integration of MyEducationKit. Each chapter includes chapter objectives, classroom activities, evaluation suggestions, supplemental readings, additional research, reproducibles of student activities, web site URLs, and answer keys to chapter review questions.

MyTest

Pearson MyTest is a powerful assessment generation program that helps instructors to easily create and print quizzes and exams. Questions and tests are authored online, allowing ultimate flexibility and the ability to efficiently create and print assessments anytime, anywhere. Instructors can access Pearson MyTest and their test bank files by going to www.pearsonmytest.com to log in, register, or request access. Features of Pearson MyTest include the following:

Premium assessment content

- Draw from a rich library of assessments that complement your Pearson textbook and your course's learning objectives.
- Edit questions or tests to fit your specific teaching needs.

Instructor-friendly resources

- Easily create and store your own questions, including images, diagrams, and charts, using simple drag-and-drop and Word-like controls.
- Use additional information provided by Pearson, such as the question's difficulty level or learning objective, to help you quickly build your test.

Time-saving enhancements

- Add headers or footers, and easily scramble questions and answer choices—all from one simple toolbar.
- Quickly create multiple versions of your test or answer key, and when ready, simply save to MS Word or PDF format and print.
- Export your exams for import to BlackBoard 6.0, CE (WebCT), or Vista (WebCT).

PowerPoint™ Presentations

Ideal for lecture presentations or student handouts, the PowerPoint™ Presentation for each chapter includes key concept summaries.

Online Course Management

Contact your local Pearson representative to learn how the online and instructor resources available with this book can be customized for delivery through today's popular learning management systems, including BlackBoard, WebCT, and more.

A Note from the Authors to Instructors

The authors of this text understand the challenge of teaching and learning about how best to use our ever-changing technology resources to help people learn. With so many technological resources changing so quickly and so many diverse pressures affecting teachers and schools, it is difficult to determine what needs to be included in a first course in educational technology. In preparing this text for your use, we have used as our barometer the ongoing question, "What do teachers really need to know about this technology to help them use it effectively in teaching and learning?" The result of our continuous response to this question is this text, which we hope will offer you an inclusive, focused, and practical survey of educational technology.

With this fourth edition, we have tried to streamline content while updating the text to reflect the latest technologies that are currently available or on the horizon. With support from the resources on MyEducationKit, we hope that we have provided both faculty and students with an abundance of useful and practical tools with which to teach and learn about technologies for education. With the electronic Instructor's Resource Manual, assessment generation software, and PowerPoint™ Presentation, we hope that we have offered our colleagues the full array of tools they might require when teaching this course. However, we know that we can always do more for both the faculty and students who use this text. We encourage both faculty adopting this text and students using it to share with us your thoughts about whatever might be done to make this text and MyEducationKit more useful to you. We look forward to hearing from you!

Acknowledgments

When we created the first edition of our text, we discovered how essential the help, encouragement, and support of those with whom we live and with whom we work are. It was a critical component of our very successful first edition, and we continue to be very grateful to all. As we prepared this fourth, greatly improved edition, we found the support of our families and colleagues to be critical once again. First, we would like to thank our families for their continued encouragement and for their patience and tolerance of the time spent away from them during the creation of this edition. Special thanks to Judy's son, Jonathan Lever, for his suggestions, contributions, and patience; to Dewayne Roos, editor, contributor, colleague, and husband, without whom this edition would not have been as well conceived, well executed, or anywhere near on time; to Jean's sons and daughters-in-law, Mike and Mary and Tom and Jenny; to her daughter, Melany; and to her son, Mark, and his friend, Lori; as well as to Jean's grandchildren.

At Pearson, we gratefully acknowledge the patience, hard work, creativity, and support of all those known and unknown to us who made our fourth edition a reality. Special thanks to Kelly Villella Canton for her support and advice and for championing our cause; to Amy Nelson, development editor, who shepherded this edition to completion; and to our production team. We thank Greg Erb, production editor; Carol Somberg, text designer; and Annie Pickert, photo researcher, who together made this edition better than we had hoped. We also thank Nesbitt Graphics, including Jude Bucci and especially Susan McNally, whose patience and artful requests made the process flow.

We gratefully acknowledge the many reviewers of the text, including

> Dionne Clabaugh, Gavilan Community College; Russell L. Lee, University of West Florida; and James E. Betts, Monmouth College. Thanks also to the reviewers of the previous edition: Temba Bassoppo-Moyo, Illinois State University; Tanaka Gaines, San Francisco State University; Denis Hlynka, University of Manitoba; Craig Kami, Western Michigan University; Donna Kitchens, University of Wisconsin, Stevens Point; Sandra Leslie, Belmont Abbey College; Cynthia Rich, Eastern Illinois University; Rick Richards, St. Petersburg College; and Locord D. Wilson, Jackson State University. Their suggestions and comments helped us to improve and refine this text and make it a more meaningful instructional support.

Finally, thanks to our many colleagues who offered suggestions, advice, and support. At Miami-Dade College, we offer special thanks to Judy's Homestead Campus colleagues, all of whom offered continuous encouragement and support, and to Judy's technowizard nephew, Rob Schwartz, who made our e-supplements a reality.

At Lambuth University, a sincere expression of gratitude to Don Ashton, Provost; Paula Brownyard, Head of the School of Education; Beth Davidson, Assistant Professor of Education; Linda Long, Instructional Assistant in the Education Department; Donna Overstreet, Instructor of Education; Matthew Collins, Bryan Steinfeld, and James Frommeyer, secondary education students; Sammy Chapman, Assistant Professor of Library Science and Reference Librarian; and Jan Kelley, Administrative Assistant for the Education Department, for the encouragement, advice and assistance they unfailingly and competently have given Jean.

Thank you all. Surely, this new, very improved edition could not have come into existence without you!

—Judy Lever-Duffy (jlever@mdc.edu)

—Jean B. McDonald (mcdonald@lambuth.edu)

PART ONE

Technologies for Teaching and Learning

All too often, prospective teachers who begin the study of educational technology expect to spend all their time learning how to use a computer and perhaps some of the other equipment available in a typical classroom. After all, isn't a course on educational technology (and its textbook) supposed to focus on the technology—the audiovisual and electronic equipment—that helps teachers teach and students learn?

The equipment is a primary concern, of course. However, equipment is simply a tool. It extends the reach of the teacher and of the learner. We can do more, and we can do it better, by using these tools—if we use them at the right time, in the right way, and for the right purpose. You can expect this text to help you explore, with great enthusiasm, the many kinds of materials and equipment that can be used to support teaching and learning. But you can also expect this text to encourage you to conduct this exploration from the perspective of, and with emphasis on, the professional and educational processes these technologies serve.

Educators who want to understand how to use technology effectively in instruction must do so within the context of sound educational theory and practice. What is the point of knowing what a technology can do if you aren't sure where and how to use it to help teach a lesson or support a learner?

The chapters in Part One begin with an examination of educational technology and a review of its role in the profession. Chapter 2 will then take a closer look at the teaching and learning process itself, from its theory to its application. You will examine learning and the factors that help or hinder it. In Chapter 3, you will explore designing effective instruction and the development and implementation of an instructional planning system that you can use when teaching. These chapters will help you build the educational framework you need as you begin your in-depth exploration of educational technologies. Without this framework, you would be learning only about how a variety of equipment works. With this framework, you will understand when, where, and why to use this equipment to help you teach and your students learn. This broader understanding is the goal of this text and the purpose for taking a course in educational technology.

REAL PEOPLE REAL STORIES

Sandra Burvikovs

Meet Sandra Burvikovs. A growing challenge in education is to find a way to meet the needs of a wide variety of youngsters in overcrowded schools with limited resources and expertise. Teachers have heard that they need to find ways to reach students with differing ways of cognitive processing, including different learning and cognitive styles and multiple intelligences.

We are pleased to introduce Sandra Burvikovs, a teacher of gifted students in a crowded elementary school in Illinois. Sandra tells about the challenges of meeting the diverse needs of her students and how she used technology to help her succeed.

I teach a gifted education pilot program for grades 3–5 replacement classes. My school, May Whitney Elementary, is located in the center of Lake Zurich, Illinois; it is one of the oldest elementary schools in the district and has a very diverse student population. The school has approximately 500 students, significantly over its capacity. I taught my groups in the hallway for three months and then was moved to the stage in the gym because there were no other locations available. The district was in the process of building a new elementary school to accommodate the increased enrollment. Regardless of the overcrowding while we waited for our new school, the staff and administration at the school were very dedicated, innovative, and committed to providing students with a positive learning experience.

About 7 percent of the students in the Lake Zurich Elementary School District take part in the district's gifted education programs. As the teacher of the gifted pullout program, I met with my students for two hours per week, with classes varying in size from seven to eighteen students. These students displayed a wide range of strengths, weaknesses, and individual learning styles. I met with my groups on the gym stage; my classroom equipment consisted of two large tables, chairs, a metal storage cabinet, an old TV and VCR, and a filmstrip projector. I knew that I had to find a way to accommodate the large variety of learning styles and still meet all of the learning objectives for these students in spite of the teaching location or the difficulties involved in finding ways to meet their unique needs.

The district had just purchased a computer cart with laptop computers and wireless Internet connections. One of the curricular goals for this group of students was to complete a long-term project. I knew that my students' parents had very high expectations about the quality of the long-term project. All the projects were to be displayed at a district wide fair.

I believed I could use technology to meet my students' needs and thus help them meet their learning objectives. Therefore, I asked about the availability of the district's laptop computers. I found that after a simple sign-up procedure, the computers were mine for a few hours each day. Even though there were only eight computers and my largest class had eighteen students, I felt the addition of the computers would help me meet student needs. But to use the computers, I needed both power and Internet connections, and I didn't have these on the gym stage. I discovered that if I placed the carts near the stage door, I had access to the Internet connection in the gym office.

I know that an essential aspect of working with gifted students is addressing their social and emotional needs. As part of our curriculum, students work to identify their strengths and weaknesses and even address their passions. To accommodate these individual differences, the long-term project was developed with both required elements and multiple options.

The students decided what elements they wanted to include with their technology component of the project, in addition to the computers. To accommodate different learning styles, students were given options that included videotaping their construction of models, conducting interviews, building models, designing booths in which to display their products, and recording informational audiotapes about their topics.

I developed technology goals for each grade level. Most of my second-grade students had a great deal of difficulty using a keyboard, so they were required to type only part of the information that would be displayed on their posters. The third-grade students, who were ready to explore additional programs, used Inspiration, TimeLiner, and Kidspiration to help them display their information. I felt that the fourth- and fifth-grade students were capable of a more challenging project. My fourth-grade students loved seeing pictures of themselves, so I borrowed a digital camera from the library media center and had the students take pictures of each other. The students then copied the images to Microsoft Word and, using Word-Art, added thought bubbles to express the most important thing that they had learned while researching. Because this was one of my larger groups, the use of the digital camera allowed the class to work on different segments of the project at the same time and decreased the wait time for the computers.

I knew that my greatest challenge was going to be my largest group, the fifth graders. I had the students work in small groups to develop PowerPoint presentations to share their research results. The final projects were well received by the parents; some were amazed at the creativity and level of proficiency that the students displayed in the projects.

Overall, technology has enabled my students to advance at a more appropriate pace for their intellectual development and to find greater interest in their schoolwork, because the use of technology gave me a greater number of options, enabling me to match the students' learning activities with their individual learning styles.

For further information, contact Sandra Burvikovs at:

May Whitney Elementary School
120 Church Street
Lake Zurich, IL 60047
Email: sburvikovs@lz95.org

SOURCE: Online interview with Sandra Burvikovs conducted by Al P. Mizell.

CHAPTER 1

Technology, Teaching, and You

Jupiter Unlimited

CHAPTER OVERVIEW

This chapter addresses these ISTE National Educational Technology Standards:
•NETS•T Standard 3
•NETS•T Standard 5

- **What Is Educational Technology?**
- **Why Study Educational Technology?**
- **Educational Technology Skills**
- **Professional Educational Technology Requirements**
- **Technology Standards**
- **Teacher Professional Preparation for Educational Technology Literacy**
- **Technology Training for Other Educators**
- **Achieving and Expanding Your Educational Technology Literacy**

Technology has become ubiquitous. It assists us in our personal life, our academic life, and our professional life. As a result, technology literacy has become an essential skill for everyone. From getting information through the Internet to making purchases to paying bills, or communicating with others, technology has become a critical tool. Being conversant in all aspects of technology gives us the ability to function in the Information Age today and will be increasingly important in the future.

For educators, the professionals charged with ensuring that our students are prepared for their place in a technology-intensive society, technological literacy becomes even more critical. We cannot imagine a teacher unable to read and write. We should no more be able to imagine a teacher unable to use technology. Educational technology skills are, for today's educators, essential skills. They are necessary for the many administrative and instructional tasks a teacher faces each day. But how does one gain these skills and maintain them? That is the focus of this chapter.

In Chapter 1 you will:

- Examine differing views of educational technology
- Explore the role of educational technology literacy as a teacher or other educator
- Investigate licensure and certification requirements in terms of technology literacy
- Review the evolution and application of standards and the role of educational technology within them
- Explore how educational professionals achieve and maintain educational technology literacy

What Is Educational Technology?

The definition of educational technology often varies depending on whether the term is used by educators or by technologists. Some use the term **educational technology** very broadly. For those educators, educational technology includes any **media** that can be used in instruction. Other, more computer-oriented educators take a narrower view. Those individuals confine educational technology to computers, computer peripherals, and related software used in teaching and learning. For **technologists,** those whose primary responsibilities relate to the management of equipment, educational technology is often defined as any hardware that is used in the classroom. As you can see, the body of knowledge broadly defined as educational technology varies.

Media refers to different formats of communication.

A technologist manages and implements technological materials, tools, and equipment to improve or enhance operations.

The field, like our society in general, is in a state of rapid change as a result of the influences of the Information Age. Therefore, to begin our exploration of educational technology, we must first define its scope. For the purposes of this text, our definition of technology is based on the definition provided by the **Association for Educational Communications and Technology (AECT).** The AECT has been prominent in the area of design and implementation of educational technology for more than seventy-five years. As described in the AECT's publication *Educational Technology: A Definition with Commentary*, "Educational technology is the study and ethical practice of facilitating learning and improving performance by creating, using and managing appropriate technological processes and resources." This definition takes the broadest view possible and allows us to explore the full range of media that a teacher might use to enhance his or her instruction and augment student learning. Our definition of educational technology, then, is *any technology used by educators in support of the teaching and learning process* (see Figure 1.1 on page 6).

PEARSON myeducationkit™

Go to the *Assignments and Activities* section of Chapter 1 in MyEducationKit and complete the web activity entitled *Educational Technology Organizations.*

Why Study Educational Technology?

The **International Society for Technology in Education (ISTE)** has led a federally funded initiative to develop standards for technology for both teachers and students. This initiative has been instrumental in defining what you need to know about educational technology. ISTE's project is called the National Educational Technology Standards for Teachers

FIGURE 1.1

Educational Technology: What Is Your Definition?

What do you think of when you think of educational technology? Check all that you think apply to educational technology in this figure. How many did you choose? In fact, educational technology can include all of these and much more! Anything used to help you teach or your students to learn can be considered an educational technology.

(NETS•T) Project. It is part of the Preparing Tomorrow's Teachers to Use Technology (PT3) grant program sponsored by the U.S. Department of Education. The NETS•T Project states, "The world is different. Kids are different . . . learning is different . . . and teaching must be different too. Today's classroom teachers must be prepared to provide technology-supported learning opportunities for their students" (NETS•T, 2002). NETS•T describes what a technology-using teacher should be able to do and provides rubrics to determine one's technology level. The NETS•T standards assume that teachers have already met the NETS standards for students (NETS•S). These student standards (Figure 1.2) articulate not only the basic technology competencies for students but also their application. Together, these two sets of standards provide current and future educators direction for effective and appropriate goals for the implementation of educational technology.

Like ISTE, AECT has also developed guides for current and future teachers in their educational technology competencies. AECT's approach to defining necessary competencies, like its definition of educational technology, takes a broad view that incorporates design and development as well as the areas of utilization, management, and evaluation typically included in most standards.

The AECT and ISTE standards contribute to and have been folded into the professional preparation requirements for all teachers as defined by the National Council for Accreditation of Teacher Education (NCATE). These requirements and their impact on current and future educators have changed the way future educators prepare for their profession. Within the framework of student technology literacy, it is clear that compe-

FIGURE 1.2

ISTE National Educational Technology Standards for Students (NETS•S) and Teachers (NETS•T) summarize what teachers should know about and be able to do with technology.

The ISTE National Educational Technology Standards (NETS•S) and Performance Indicators for Students

1. **Creativity and Innovation**
   Students demonstrate creative thinking, construct knowledge, and develop innovative products and processes using technology. Students:
   a. apply existing knowledge to generate new ideas, products, or processes.
   b. create original works as a means of personal or group expression.
   c. use models and simulations to explore complex systems and issues.
   d. identify trends and forecast possibilities.
2. **Communication and Collaboration**
   Students use digital media and environments to communicate and work collaboratively, including at a distance, to support individual learning and contribute to the learning of others. Students:
   a. interact, collaborate, and publish with peers, experts, or others employing a variety of digital environments and media.
   b. communicate information and ideas effectively to multiple audiences using a variety of media and formats.
   c. develop cultural understanding and global awareness by engaging with learners of other cultures.
   d. contribute to project teams to produce original works or solve problems.
3. **Research and Information Fluency**
   Students apply digital tools to gather, evaluate, and use information. Students:
   a. plan strategies to guide inquiry.
   b. locate, organize, analyze, evaluate, synthesize, and ethically use information from a variety of sources and media.
   c. evaluate and select information sources and digital tools based on the appropriateness to specific tasks.
   d. process data and report results.
4. **Critical Thinking, Problem Solving, and Decision Making**
   Students use critical thinking skills to plan and conduct research, manage projects, solve problems, and make informed decisions using appropriate digital tools and resources. Students:
   a. identify and define authentic problems and significant questions for investigation.
   b. plan and manage activities to develop a solution or complete a project.
   c. collect and analyze data to identify solutions and/or make informed decisions.
   d. use multiple processes and diverse perspectives to explore alternative solutions.
5. **Digital Citizenship**
   Students understand human, cultural, and societal issues related to technology and practice legal and ethical behavior. Students:
   a. advocate and practice safe, legal, and responsible use of information and technology.
   b. exhibit a positive attitude toward using technology that supports collaboration, learning, and productivity.
   c. demonstrate personal responsibility for lifelong learning.
   d. exhibit leadership for digital citizenship.
6. **Technology Operations and Concepts**
   Students demonstrate a sound understanding of technology concepts, systems, and operations. Students:
   a. understand and use technology systems.
   b. select and use applications effectively and productively.
   c. troubleshoot systems and applications.
   d. transfer current knowledge to learning of new technologies.

tence in educational technology and its application in education are now considered a national mandate.

But beyond professional standards, the need to be able to use educational technologies effectively is urgent. Think about the last time you sat in a K–12 classroom taking a course. Chances are that your teacher presented information to you primarily by talking to you about the course content. This familiar teaching **method,** called *lecture* or

Teaching methods include the strategies and techniques used to communicate content.

FIGURE 1.2 *(continued)*

The ISTE National Educational Technology Standards (NETS•T) and Performance Indicators for Teachers

Effective teachers model and apply the National Educational Technology Standards for Students (NETS•S) as they design, implement, and assess learning experiences to engage students and improve learning; enrich professional practice; and provide positive models for students, colleagues, and the community. All teachers should meet the following standards and performance indicators. Teachers:

1. Facilitate and Inspire Student Learning and Creativity

Teachers use their knowledge of subject matter, teaching and learning, and technology to facilitate experiences that advance student learning, creativity, and innovation in both face-to-face and virtual environments. Teachers:

a. promote, support, and model creative and innovative thinking and inventiveness.

b. engage students in exploring real-world issues and solving authentic problems using digital tools and resources.

c. promote student reflection using collaborative tools to reveal and clarify students' conceptual understanding and thinking, planning, and creative processes.

d. model collaborative knowledge construction by engaging in learning with students, colleagues, and others in face-to-face and virtual environments.

2. Design and Develop Digital-Age Learning Experiences and Assessments

Teachers design, develop, and evaluate authentic learning experiences and assessments incorporating contemporary tools and resources to maximize content learning in context and to develop the knowledge, skills, and attitudes identified in the NETS•S. Teachers:

a. design or adapt relevant learning experiences that incorporate digital tools and resources to promote student learning and creativity.

b. develop technology-enriched learning environments that enable all students to pursue their individual curiosities and become active participants in setting their own educational goals, managing their own learning, and assessing their own progress.

c. customize and personalize learning activities to address students' diverse learning styles, working strategies, and abilities using digital tools and resources.

d. provide students with multiple and varied formative and summative assessments aligned with content and technology standards and use resulting data to inform learning and reaching.

3. Model Digital-Age Work and Learning

Teachers exhibit knowledge, skills, and work processes representative of an innovative professional in a global and digital society. Teachers:

a. demonstrate fluency in technology systems and the transfer of current knowledge to new technologies and situations.

b. collaborate with students, peers, parents, and community members using digital tools and resources to support student success and innovation.

c. communicate relevant information and ideas effectively to students, parents, and peers using a variety of digital-age media and formats.

d. model and facilitate effective use of current and emerging digital tools to locate, analyze, evaluate, and use information resources to support research and learning.

4. Promote and Model Digital Citizenship and Responsibility

Teachers understand local and global societal issues and responsibilities in an evolving digital culture and exhibit legal and ethical behavior in their professional practices. Teachers:

a. advocate, model, and teach safe, legal, and ethical use of digital information and technology, including respect for copyright, intellectual property, and the appropriate documentation of sources.

b. address the diverse needs of all learners by using learner-centered strategies and providing equitable access to appropriate digital tools and resources.

c. promote and model digital etiquette and responsible social interactions related to the use of technology and information.

d. develop and model cultural understanding and global awareness by engaging with colleagues and students of other culture using digital-age communication and collaboration tools.

5. Engage in Professional Growth and Leadership

Teachers continuously improve their professional practice, model lifelong learning, and exhibit leadership in their school and professional community by promoting and demonstrating the effective use of digital tools and resources. Teachers:

a. participate in local and global learning communities to explore creative applications of technology to improve student learning.

b. exhibit leadership by demonstrating a vision of technology infusion, participating in shared decision making and community building, and developing the leadership and technology skills of others.

c. evaluate and reflect on current research and professional practice on a regular basis to make effective use of existing and emerging digital tools and resources in support of student learning.

d. contribute to the effectiveness, vitality, and self-renewal of the teaching profession and of their school and community.

presentation, is one of several available to your instructor. Like most methods of teaching, it can be enhanced through the use of educational technology. Let's consider how technology might improve this common teaching strategy.

Lecture or oral presentation, when used alone, can be challenging for many students. If a teacher using this method did not occasionally stop to write a key word on the board or perhaps show a graphic using an overhead or digital projector, most people would find it fairly difficult to follow the presentation, much less take adequate notes on what was said. Because of our accumulated experiences, we understand that common technologies, such as a whiteboard, a chalkboard, and a projector, can enhance a lecture substantially and significantly improve communication. Beyond the familiar and obvious media, many different types of strategies and technologies can contribute substantially to the teaching and learning process. The NETS•T Project reminds us that educators must acquire a broad range of methods and skills to enhance teaching and support learning with technology effectively.

For those who want to teach, it is therefore essential to first have a thorough working knowledge of the many kinds of educational technologies available that might assist in teaching and in enhancing learning. Educational technologies become the tools that a teacher might use to create an effective instructional event. This text will assist you in discovering the tools that are now available and those on the technological horizon. You will learn how to use these tools and explore their application to the teaching and learning process to make it as effective and meaningful as possible.

Educational Technology Skills

Just as teachers need to be able to read and write, so too do they need to be technologically skillful. Just being able to use technology is not enough. Teachers must also be able to apply the technologies in ways that will enrich their teaching and enhance their students' learning. This unique **educational technology literacy** is an essential skill set that not only must be acquired but also must be continually updated. The recognition of this necessity is demonstrated by the extent to which states have adopted the NETS standards. Figure 1.3 summarizes the extent of standards adoption.

Educational technology literacy is the ability to use and apply technologies to training and learning.

In a continued response to the technological imperative created by the unfolding Information Age, additional educational standards reflecting the new emphasis on educational technology have become evident at every level. From the federal **No Child Left Behind (NCLB) Act** to national organizational standards to individual state professional preparation requirements, the thrust toward required educational technology literacy is evident. As educators, you need to understand and accept this expectation and to plan how, during your preservice and in-service years, to meet this escalating professional requirement.

ISTE NETS are technology standards for teachers, students, and administrators.

Professional Educational Technology Requirements

The current emphasis on technology literacy for teachers and students is grounded in the No Child Left Behind Act (NCLB). NCLB requires that by the time students finish the eighth grade they should be technology literate. This mandate has created a series of action steps for states, districts, and schools to use to evaluate their use of technology in improving student achievement. In response to NCLB, most states have developed technology standards for students. Consequently, states have also developed associated technology standards for teachers and have included these, directly or indirectly, within their certification and licensing requirements.

FIGURE 1.3

National Educational Technology Standards (NETS) and the States

The *NETS for Students* were released in June 1998, *NETS for Teachers* in June 2000, and *NETS for Administrators (TSSA)* in November 2001. At the state level, forty-nine of the fifty states have adopted, adapted, aligned with, or otherwise referenced at least one set of standards in their state technology plans, certification, licensure, curriculum plans, assessment plans, or other official state documents. States that have adopted, adapted, aligned with, or referenced the NETS in state department of education documents are shown here.

http://cnets .iste.org/docs/states_using_nets.pdf

STU (A=adopted, adapted, or aligned with; R=referenced)	TCH	ADM	STATE	STU (A=adopted, adapted, or aligned with; R=referenced)	TCH	ADM	STATE
A	A	A	Alabama	A	A	A	Nebraska
R	R	R	Alaska		A		Nevada
A	A	A	Arizona	R	A	A	New Hampshire
A	A	A	Arkansas	A	A	A	New Jersey
		R	California		A		New Mexico
A	A		Colorado	A	A	A	New York
A	A	A	Connecticut	A	A		North Carolina
A	A	A	Delaware	A		A	North Dakota
	A		District of Columbia	A		A	Ohio
A	A		Florida	A			Oklahoma
	A	A	Georgia	A		A	Oregon
A			Hawaii			A	Pennsylvania
	A		Idaho	A			Rhode Island
A	A	A	Illinois	A	A		South Carolina
	R	R	Indiana		A	A	South Dakota
A	A	A	Kansas		A	R	Tennessee
A	A	A	Kentucky	R	A	R	Texas
A	A	A	Louisiana	A			Utah
		R	Maine	A	A	A	Vermont
R	A	A	Maryland	A	R	R	Virginia
A	A		Massachusetts	A	A	A	Washington
A	A	A	Michigan	A	A	A	West Virginia
A	A	A	Minnesota	A		A	Wisconsin
A	A	A	Mississippi			A	Wyoming
A	A	A	Missouri				

State Certification and Licensure Technology Requirements

In all states, teachers must be licensed or certified by the state to be employed as educators. The requirements for **teacher licensure/certification** are set by each state's Department of Education. While the state licensing requirements differ among states, teachers must fulfill certain basic requirements. These state certification requirements typically include specific technology requirements, most often met through an undergraduate course in educational technology. For teachers who graduated before such specific technology requirements were instituted, courses in educational technology are often a recommendation for certificate renewal.

Awareness of licensure or certification requirements is every educator's individual responsibility. While districts and colleges may provide support, the ultimate resource is the agency that grants the license, the state Department of Education. Reviewing your state's requirements is strongly recommended to be sure you are meeting all licensure provisions for the area in which you plan to teach. The Tech Tips for Teachers on page 12 will provide you with certification information for your state.

The National Board for Professional Teaching Standards has established national certification.

National Certification and Educational Technology

In addition to state licensure, the National Board for Professional Teaching Standards (NBPTS at **www.nbpts.org**) offers **national certification** recognition. The NBPTS is a nonprofit, nongovernmental agency governed by a sixty-three-member board of directors, the majority of whom are classroom teachers. This board was created in 1987, influenced by the release of *A Nation Prepared: Teachers for the 21st Century*, a report of the Carnegie Forum on Education and the Economy's Task Force on Teaching as a Profession. The purpose of NBPTS is to improve teaching and learning by encouraging teachers to become nationally certified through a voluntary system. This certification is awarded to teachers who can demonstrate that they have achieved high and rigorous standards in what they know and what they do (Figure 1.4). NBPTS also promotes educational reform by guiding this voluntary certification process, and it uses the expertise of already National Board–certified teachers to promote the process and assist others to attain certification.

While there are currently no directly stated technology requirements for national certification, diversity of teaching methodology is a requirement. Teachers who obtain National Board certification must use multiple methods and pathways in their approach to teaching. In addition, National Board–certified teachers employ multiple methods to measure student growth and the depth of understanding students have achieved in the subject matter. Educational technology literacy assists teachers in reaching the level of competence in multiple methods to be granted this prestigious national certification.

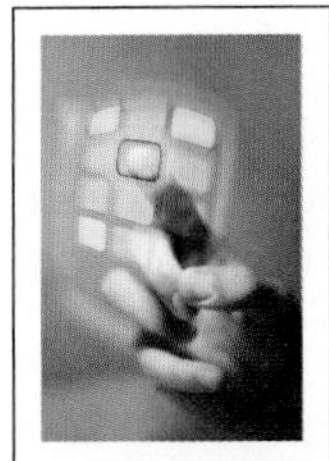

HANDS ON LEARNING

Before the twentieth century, teacher certification could have included any number of requirements: formal examinations, interviews of moral decency, and even a spelling test. Since 1867, though, almost all states have required teachers to pass a test to obtain a state teaching license. Into the twentieth century, new laws emerged requiring all public school teachers to hold a state teaching license, and institutions of higher education became increasingly responsible for the preparation of professional teachers. However, among states, there are many variations in the types of licenses and the requirements to obtain and maintain a state teaching license. In addition, as school districts struggle to meet the demands for more teachers, alternative teaching certifications have emerged. Alternative certification methods allow those who have already graduated from college but want to change careers to enter the teaching profession without having to return to four years of full-time coursework on a college campus.

Find your state's Department of Education web site and compile a checklist of the requirements of your state. Develop your own timeline of necessary coursework, required examinations, and other requirements for you to become certified or to extend an existing certificate. You might want to begin your search with **http://www.alleducationschools.com/faqs/statedepartment.php** to find a quick link to your state.

FIGURE 1.4

National certification is awarded to outstanding teachers able to demonstrate that they meet the highest standards in their discipline.

Technology Standards

Discipline-specific and other education standards provide teachers and administrators with direction and guidance for creating programs that meet the needs of students. Well-written standards have measurable outcomes so that educators can assess student learning, the level of learning achieved, and how the learning is demonstrated. Typically, state and national educational associations have created standards in their content area or discipline. Often, these standards address or incorporate educational technology requirements, particularly those set forth by ISTE. ISTE's NETS standards, then, have established their place at the core of national and state educational technology literacy requirements. For that reason, an in-depth examination of the history, organization, and implication of these standards is useful for educational professionals.

TECH TIPS for Teachers

The College of Education at the University of Kentucky provides a web site that links to the teacher certification requirements for all fifty states. While this web site is a very rich resource, please be aware that states continually revise their teacher certification or licensure rules and requirements. To gain access to the web site and linked state certification requirements, go to **www.uky.edu/Education/TEP/usacert.html.**

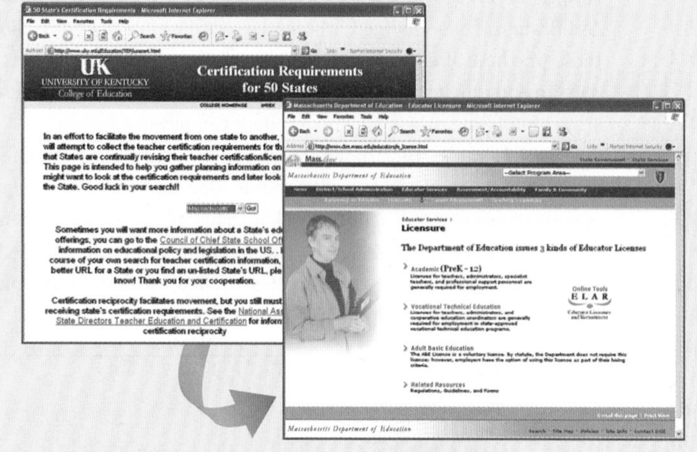

Left: Screen capture from www.uky.edu. Constructed and maintained by Stuart C. Reedy, M. Daniel Vantreese and William E. Stilwell III. Used with permission. Right: Reproduced by permission of the Massachusetts Department of Education. All of the Massachusetts Department of Education websites are revised periodically. For periodic updates please consult http://www.doe.mass.edu/.

ISTE National Educational Technology Standards

As you have learned, ISTE is the national educational technology organization that has led to the development of the nationally recognized technology standards for both teachers (**NETS•T**) and students (**NETS•S**). The NETS project was initiated to create a series of national standards that could be used to facilitate the use of educational technology by students, teachers, and administrators to promote school improvement in the United States. These standards as created by the NETS project have been widely used to benchmark student achievement in specific technological areas proven to be critical for success in society and industry and to measure teacher technology preparedness.

Many school districts use the NETS standards to guide their efforts to ensure that their teachers (NETS•T) and students (NETS•S) achieve technology literacy. According to NETS, a technologically literate student is one who is deemed to be proficient in six broad areas or categories. Teachers can use these standards and profiles as guidelines for planning technology-based activities in which students achieve success in learning, communication, and life skills. Further, NETS teaching standards not only include the student standards but also extend beyond them to ensure that teachers can use technology appropriately and effectively in both academic and administrative tasks. The inside front cover of your text includes both NETS•T (on the left-hand side) and NETS•S (on the right-hand side) for your review.

In addition to NETS•T and NETS•S, ISTE has recently created Technology Standards for School Administrators (**NETS•A**). These new standards are based on a national consensus among educational stakeholders about what best indicates effective school leadership for comprehensive and appropriate use of technology in schools. An underlying assumption of these standards is that administrators should be competent users of information and technology tools common to Information Age professionals.

PEARSON **myeducationkit**™

Go to the *Assignments and Activities* section of Chapter 1 in MyEducationKit and complete the web activity entitled *National Standards*.

NETS standards for teachers, students, and administrators have become foundational in the development of technology standards for other professional entities. For example, the National Council for Accreditation of Teacher Education (**NCATE**), the official body for accrediting teacher preparation programs, changed their teacher preparation guidelines in response to NETS. These changes support the use of technology in teacher preparation

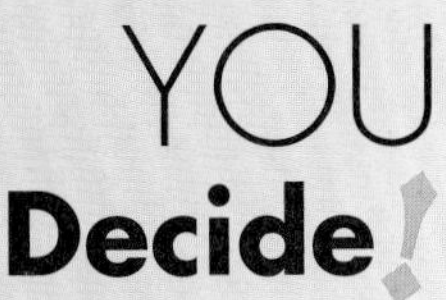

Educational standards offer measurable outcomes for student achievement and for professional competency. Whether standards are discipline based or generic standards that cross multiple disciplines, they are important guideposts for educators. Without standards, there would be no consistency as to what is taught or what skills students should achieve in any given area. In terms of technology literacy, standards are all the more important, as baseline technology competencies are often prerequisites for achieving content-area requirements. Standards are essential for education.

YES! Without standards, each state, each district, and even each school could have different requirements for their students and for professional educators. A grade of A in one school might not be equivalent to the same grade in another school. Standards give everyone the same requirements to teach toward. Without them, required competencies could be very different in whatever school you happened to be in. That would make it difficult or impossible for students to be ready if they change schools or when they graduate and prepare for college.

NO! Standards are just more unnecessary and time-consuming paperwork for teachers. When lesson plans require that standards be addressed, it just takes too long to review and select which of the hundreds of standards should be addressed by a lesson. For teachers already buried in too much paperwork and with too little planning time, it is a waste of what little valuable time is available. Standards are fine to learn about in college, but once a teacher is working in the field, standards are extraneous.

Which view do you agree with? YOU DECIDE!

programs. The result of the adoption of the NETS standards within NCATE has been that teacher preparation programs must now include courses and/or experiences to develop an understanding of the use of technology for the subjects those taking the program plan to teach, the impact of technological changes on schools, and the use of computer and other technologies in instruction, assessment, and professional productivity. This change has had a profound positive impact on educational technology literacy for preservice teachers.

State Responses to NETS

States use NETS in standards and in strategic planning.

Many states have utilized NETS not only in adopting standards (see Figure 1.3) but also in developing accomplished practices for teachers and in strategic planning for technology. With the NCLB requirement that students be technologically literate by the end of the eighth grade, states have felt the pressure to find appropriate technological benchmarks for teachers and students. Since NCLB requires technology literacy without specific mandates on how to achieve this or how to assess the level of success, states have taken a variety of approaches to achieving technology requirements. For example, Indiana's K–12 Plan for Technology requires that students have access to appropriate technologies, including hardware and connections, and teachers who are highly skilled in the uses of technology. It further recognizes the need for ongoing professional development for teachers. These two mandates within the Indiana Technology Plan affect district decision making as to technology acquisition and implementation. Other states vary widely as to how NETS is incorporated, from designating additional certification requirements to identifying student technology competencies within the curriculum to inclusion of mandates within a strategic plan. Regardless of how the state addresses the standards, it is clear that technology literacy is now a critical component of education across all states. ISTE NETS can often be found at the heart of state solutions to achieving technology literacy.

Go to the *Podcasts* section of Chapter 1 in MyEducationKit and click on *Professional Development and Technology*.

Frank Siteman/PhotoEdit

Educators participate in workshops and training to develop the skills needed to meet NETS•T standards.

Once a state adopts, adapts, or aligns with NETS, these technology standards typically become part of the state's "accomplished teacher" requirements. Also known as "accomplished practices," these requirements dictate the expectations for educational professionals. Once accomplished practices are determined, institutions that are preparing future teachers and local school districts within that state must demonstrate how they ensure that teachers meet these practices. Teachers who meet accomplished practices requirements are well prepared to include and apply technology standards to their local schools and individual classroom.

Teacher Professional Preparation for Educational Technology Literacy

NCATE guidelines have been adjusted for educational technology.

Ultimately, the national and state standards that are adopted have a direct impact on current and future teachers. These standards and requirements reverberate in colleges and universities where preservice teachers are educated. National Council for Accreditation of Teacher Education (NCATE) guidelines require that colleges of education include courses or experiences in the use of technology for instruction, assessment, and professional productivity. While some programs have added an educational technology course in the first two years of preservice teacher education programs, other programs require alternative technology-focused coursework. These required courses provide information about and practice in integrating technology into unit and lesson plans. This is also a mandate from NCLB (Title II, Part D—Enhancing Education through Technology) whose primary goal is to improve student academic achievement through the use of technology in elementary and secondary schools. As current and future preservice teachers complete their professional education requirements, educational technology literacy will play an increasingly significant role.

For in-service teachers, educational technology standards and requirements are often included directly or indirectly into annual professional evaluations. For teachers who need to ensure that they are prepared to demonstrate required skills, two options are commonplace. Teachers can either return to a college or university to take credit courses in educational technology or other targeted technology skills or can participate in district workshops to achieve the same competency. For those who wish college credit, the additional value in doing so may include meeting requirements to add additional endorsement areas to their teaching certificate or meeting certificate renewal requirements. In any case, an expectation of educational technology literacy has come to be at the core of professional preparation and ongoing development.

States and districts typically also provide ongoing professional development activities to support continuous improvement in technology skills and curriculum integration. The professional development ranges from individually attended or accessed opportunities to group or grade-level options. School districts typically provide these training opportunities free of charge to in-service educators. Further, to meet the requirements of the federal NCLB legislation, many states provide valid third-party assessment of workshop outcomes to document the numbers of teachers who are meeting state standards in technology.

Many state education associations, under the auspices of the National Education Association (NEA), also give workshops for professional development in technology-related content at local locations and without charge. Technology curriculum integration is one of the most popular topics for these sessions. Collaborative agreements with local colleges, universities, and training companies also give rise to in-service workshops for PreK–12 teachers with technology skills updates and curriculum integration of technology being high on the lists of preferred topics. All of these options provide the in-service teacher an opportunity to achieve the skills necessary to meet NETS•T and NCLB requirements.

PEARSON myeducationkit™

Go to the *Assignments and Activities* section of Chapter 1 in MyEducationKit and complete the video activity entitled *Collaborative Approach to Professional Development*.

But perhaps one of the most convenient opportunities for achieving technology literacy results from the application of distance education methods to educational technology training. Online training opportunities are rich and varied. Many sites offer professional development courses and workshops, including some of the premier technology vendors. For example, Apple offers professional development at **www.apple.com/education/apd** (Figure 1.5). This rich site offers teachers many options for professional development.

While many of the major technology vendors charge for their technology training, Annenberg Media's Learner.org offers free video-based online professional development training for K–12 teachers (Figure 1.5). This online resource offers training in a wide variety of discipline-specific topics as well as educational technology training.

These online examples are just a few of the many training opportunities offered to teachers. Table 1.1 summarizes additional opportunities.

PEARSON myeducationkit™

Go to the *Assignments and Activities* section of Chapter 1 in MyEducationKit and complete the video activity entitled *Professional Development for Virtual Schools*.

TABLE 1.1 Sampling of Online Training Opportunities for Educators

VENDOR	DESCRIPTION
ADOBE	Self-paced courses, instructor-led courses, certification, professional development workshops, books, events and seminars, additional learning resources in text, audio, video, live, and on-demand format. **www.adobe.com/training/**
APPLE	Instruction in technologies such as Mac OS X or the iLife applications (iMovie, iPhoto, iTunes, and iDVD) to understand how better to employ computers in education; technology integration opportunities for teachers to develop units or lessons for their classrooms. **www.apple.com/education/services/training/**
INSPIRATION SOFTWARE	There are Quick Tours of the software products, Quick Start Tutorials, Training CD, and Classroom Project Tours. **www.inspiration.com/prodev/index.cfm?fuseaction=training**
MICROSOFT	Product tutorials, lesson plans for K–12 educators, and how-to articles. **www.microsoft.com/education/schools.mspx**

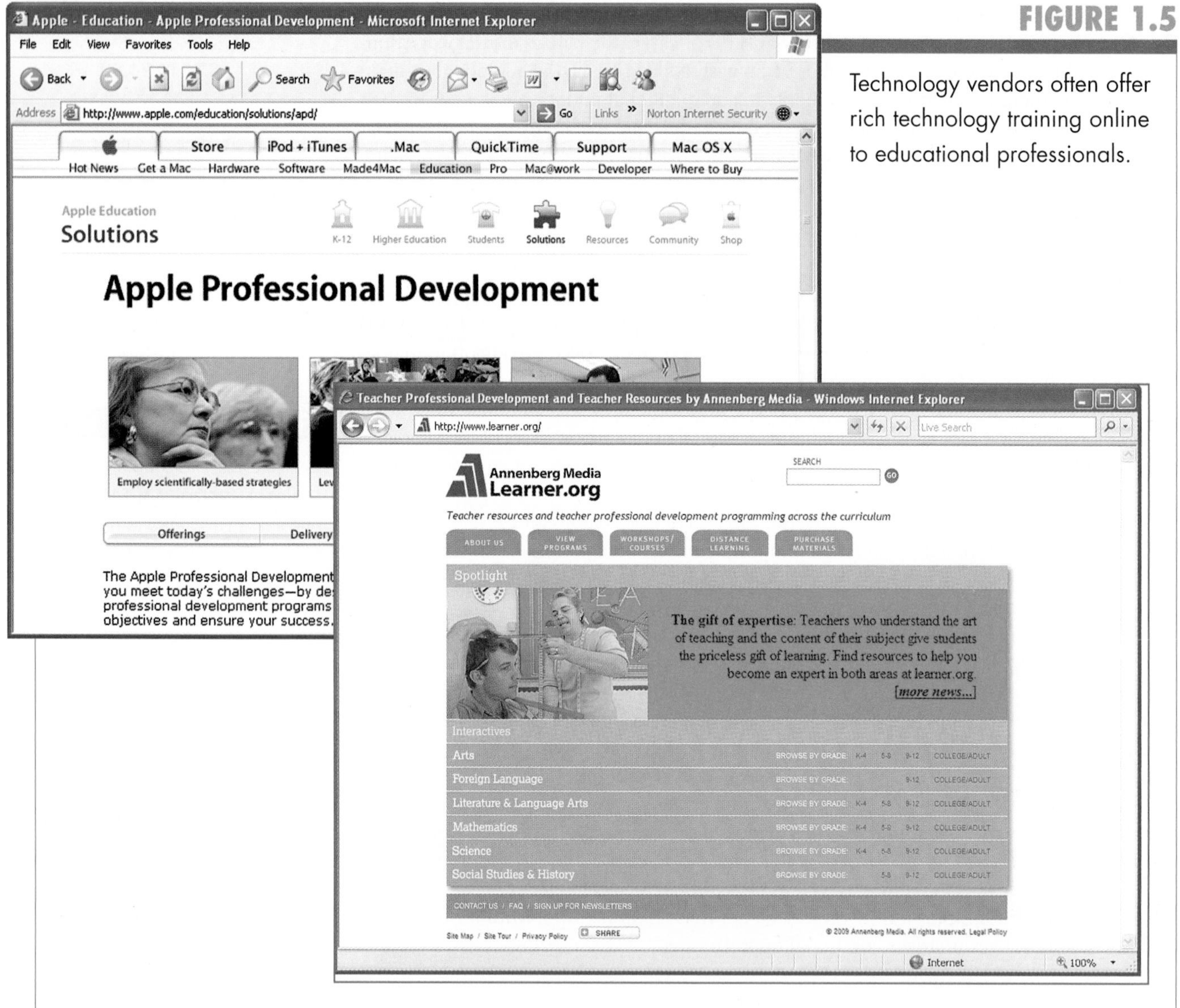

FIGURE 1.5

Technology vendors often offer rich technology training online to educational professionals.

Left: Courtesy of Apple Inc.; Right: Used by permission of Annenberg Media, a division of The Annenberg Foundation

Technology Training for Other Educators

Technology literacy is no less important for noninstructional educators. Each professional serves unique student needs and contributes to the school community. For technology to succeed in enriching the instructional environment, all educators need to achieve their own technology competencies. While these may vary from one noninstructional professional to another, all are critical to achieving successful technology implementation in the school.

Media Specialists

Media specialists must have unique technology competencies.

Media specialists are the current evolution of librarians in the Information Age. As a result of the Internet, library information is no longer bounded by the four walls of the media center. **Media** specialists must be able to assist students with seeking information beyond the books on the shelf in order to complete a research assignment. Keeping up with the latest developments in the scholarly research students will need is a part of the media specialist's responsibility. Professional publications for media specialists are dominated by the technology they must use to obtain information for students and teachers. *Library Journal* and *School Library Journal* feature in each issue articles largely devoted to technology literacy in the context of media centers. In addition, Google has introduced a librarian newsletter, *Newsletter for Librarians*. Media specialists, like teachers, have access to credit courses and workshops to hone their technology skills. Technology literacy is just as critical for the media specialist as for teachers, since this is the group of educators most often asked to schedule, organize, and provide technology training to their peers. Like all educators, for media specialists, current and comprehensive educational technology literacy is a necessity.

Administrators

For future **administrators**, the acquisition of technology literacy is a key skill not just for administrative use but also for effective decision making. *Technology Standards for School Administrators* (**TSSA**) were developed by a collaborative effort of several school administrators' professional organizations, the Departments of Education of Mississippi and Kentucky, several regional educational organizations, and ISTE. This group recognized that administrators are essential in how effectively technology will be used in schools. It took into consideration the varied responsibilities assumed by administrators in diverse school systems, such as the size of the school system, the type of governance the system employs, the prevailing culture of the community, and the characteristics of the administrators themselves. The TSAA further stressed that administrators have a professional obligation to further the potential for technology literacy from their position of leadership by pointing out the positive influence they can bring about for digital equity in the schools. The TSAA was the foundational document for the establishment of ISTE's NETS•A standards.

To achieve and maintain educational technology literacy, administrators participate in university or college credit courses and targeted leadership workshops. In particular, the American Association of School Administrators offers numerous publications as well as a comprehensive program of workshops through its Center for System Leadership and through professional development conferences (Figure 1.6). Many of these focus on technology.

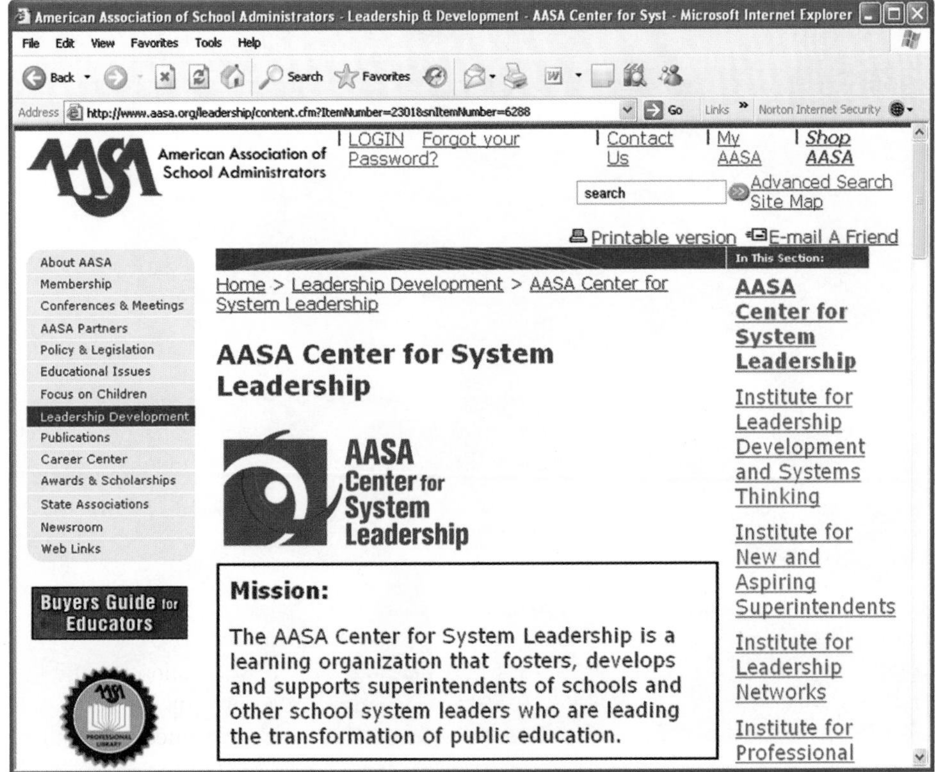

FIGURE 1.6

Administrators, like all educators, maintain currency in technology through training offered by their professional associations.

Screen capture of the AASA, www.aasa.org. Reproduced with permission of the American Association of School Administrators.

Other Educational Professionals

For future guidance counselors or those in instructional support fields, such as speech therapists and reading specialists, technology literacy is as important as it is for the classroom teacher. In addition to accomplishing the many administrative tasks associated with an education support role, technology literacy is required to make the most of available online resources for the benefit of students. Training opportunities to achieve appropriate technology literacy are typically offered through college credit courses, district technology workshops, and professional organizations and conferences. Like all other educators, educational support personnel must acquire and maintain their technology skills to perform professionally.

Achieving and Expanding Your Educational Technology Literacy

Every teacher is responsible for maintaining his or her technology literacy.

In your role as a professional, you will have the responsibility to continuously update the educational technology skills this text introduces. It is clear that the future of education rests on assuring that each child has teachers with a depth of knowledge involving more than the key facts they learned while getting their professional degree. Teachers need to be able to continually expand both their knowledge base and their technology skill set. Busy teachers often have little time for formal classes. Yet, it has become clear that teachers will need to keep up with the emerging technologies available to them as professionals and to their students. Educational technology literacy is a dynamic and fluid requirement. Whether achieved through this text, college courses, in-service workshops, vendor training, or personal research, this requirement is a core component and expectation of today's educational professional.

DGV-1682013/Age Fotostock

Technology literacy is an essential skill for twenty-first century teachers that is typically achieved through continuous professional development.

This text will help you to meet this expectation. Through these pages, you will be introduced to the learning theories that inform instruction; you will examine and practice the techniques to plan effective instruction; and you will explore the many and varied technologies that will ensure your instruction is relevant to the Information Age. Ultimately, this text will prepare you to achieve the NETS•T standards.

Fortunately, teachers as a group are typically intellectually curious. They seek out the knowledge they need to help their students learn. For success in this profession, you too must have the initiative and energy to be a **lifelong learner.** You too must embrace the technology our society has placed at the core of its twenty-first century life. As a teacher, when you address and support the learners in your classroom, you hold the society's future in your professional hands. You are bound to use the best instructional means to achieve the end of shaping the lives and actions of the young people who are entrusted to you. Without doubt, that will include technology.

Professionally you should expect that this text will provide a foundation for your educational technology literacy. The knowledge gained gives you a basis from which you can expand your technological skills and your ability to use technology for teaching and learning. The Information Age is an exciting and dynamic time to be an educational professional. While the demands may be daunting, the outcomes in terms of our students' ability to succeed are without measure. Technology will help you achieve these professional goals and, further, will assist you in helping your students achieve theirs.

PEARSON myeducationkit™

To check your comprehension on the content covered in this chapter, go to the MyEducationKit for your book and complete the Study Plan for Chapter 1.

Key Terms

Student Activities

CHAPTER REVIEW

1. What is educational technology? How is it different when perceived by educators versus technologists?
2. What is educational technology literacy? Why is it important for educators?
3. What impact does NCLB have on educational technology standards?
4. What is certification? What role does technology literacy play in certification and licensure?
5. What is the difference between state and national certification? How is technology literacy incorporated in each?
6. How and for what purpose did ISTE establish NETS? What standards are currently in place?
7. What is NCATE? How have NETS standards changed college programs through NCATE adoption?
8. What options do preservice teachers have to achieve technology standards? How do they differ from options offered to in-service teachers?
9. How do corporations provide training resources for teachers? Give examples.
10. What unique technology training is required for noninstructional educators? Why are they different?

WHAT DO YOU THINK?

1. Standards have altered teacher preparation programs and the curriculum requirements in schools. The intention behind standardization is to ensure equivalent and consistent instruction and to provide measurable outcomes. Do you feel the implementation of standards by national, state, and curriculum organizations has accomplished their intent? Explain why or why not.
2. Lifelong learning is not just a preference of most teachers, it is a requirement to maintain state certification. Technology literacy courses and workshops are some of the most popular experiences for certificate extension and renewal. Do you feel that technology literacy is as important as taking additional courses in your content or discipline? Is too much emphasis being placed on developing and maintaining technology competency? Defend your view.
3. NCLB has altered education in innumerable ways. In particular, the call for high-stakes testing in every state, mandated standards in multiple areas, and the requirement of employing highly accomplished teachers have all changed state and district approaches to teacher preparation and training. Has the implementation of NCLB helped or hurt education? Do you feel it has had a positive or negative impact on technology literacy in particular? Research NCLB if necessary and be prepared to explain your views.

LEARNING TOGETHER!

The following activities should be done in small groups.

1. Join a group interested in teaching the same grade level or content area as your own preference. Research the standards on the Internet for your discipline or grade. Identify the specific standards that relate to educational technology. Prepare a summary to share with your class.
2. Brainstorm the technology training that you would find most useful during your first three years of teaching. Make an annotated list of the top ten technology-related workshops you would most like to attend. Be prepared to share your list with your peers.
3. Create a visual that represents the impact of the NETS•S, NETS•T, and NETS•A or other national and or state technology standards. Incorporate the visual into a PowerPoint presentation. Include specific examples of how NETS has altered technology planning and/or training.

TEACHING WITH TECHNOLOGY: INTEGRATION IDEAS WEB QUEST

The Internet offers educators a great variety of resources to support the integration of technology into the classroom and to offer online teacher training to facilitate the use of technology. Let's take a look at some specific resources to help prepare you for using technology in teaching and learning using the links that follow.

ACTIVITY: After you explore the links that interest you, complete a web search to discover at least three places you can find the ideas or training you feel you need to effectively use technology in your classroom. Write a one-page summary of your web quest that includes (1) the training or ideas that you feel you need, (2) a description of which NETS•T standards you will address by meeting these needs, and (3) a description of the links you used and the resources you found.

Internet Educational Technology Resources

Tech & Learning is a free online comprehensive resource for educators to find information on technology and teaching. Topics covered include Best Practices, From the Classroom, Leadership, Professional Development, Product Reviews, Blogs, Tips, How to, News, IT Guy, and many more. Review the resources offered by Technology & Learning—The Resource for Education Technology at **http://www.techlearning.com.**

Edutopia is a premier publication produced by the George Lucas Educational Foundation that appears both in print and digital formats. Its subtitle, "What Works in Public Education," is an apt description of its contents. The articles cover all areas of education, with technology occupying a major presence in each edition. Stories highlight actual teachers in the classroom and the ways in which they use technology innovatively. Regular features include "Teacher Tools and Teacher Events," "Up-Front: Digital Generation Project," "Sage Advice," "Video," "Blog," "Poll," pages devoted to core subjects for technology-based activities along with web sites for research to support the activities, and themed feature articles. Review this resource at **www.edutopia.org.**

For planning to integrate technology into lessons, the **EduHound: Everything for Education K12** web site offers a wealth of resources. It features Site Sets for teachers to tour with "Technology Planning," "Technology Research & Reports," "PowerPoint Templates," "Cyberbullying," "Acceptable Use Policies," "Cyber Safety," and "WebQuests" devoted entirely to technology in the classroom and the other 134 containing uses for technology in support of teaching the topics. "Browse by EduHound Categories" is another list that has many links, as does "Browse by EduHound Lesson Plans." The "Lesson Plan Resources" link gives twenty-four addresses with brief annotations of other sites where lesson plans are to be found. For example, the annotation for MiddleSchool. Net points out that the site is for teachers by teachers and has "terrific technology resources." EduHound also has a link to *T.H.E. Journal* and to "Classrooms on the Web," classroom web sites posted by teachers from across the nation. To explore eduhound, go to **http://www.eduhound.com.**

Internet Educational Technology Training

Teacher Tap offers educators and librarians easy access to online resources and activities related to educational technology. This professional development resource provides quick links to a wide variety of technology tutorials on software, educator training, and vendor training sites. To begin a review of the many training opportunities of the Internet, begin with a visit to the Teacher Tap at **http://eduscapes.com/tap/topic76.htm.**

The U.S. Department of Education funded the **Regional Technology in Education Consortia** (**R*TEC**) program. Its objective was to help states, schools, districts, and other educational institutions use technologies to improve teaching and student achievement. Its web pages include extensive resources for professional development, technical assistance, and support technology for integration. Review these resources at **http://www.rtec.org/.**

For educators interested in using Virtual Worlds for teaching and learning, **Edtech Island** is a fascinating option. Started in 2007 by faculty and graduate students in the Department of Educational Technology at Boise State University, this space exists as a part of Second Life, a virtual world created by its participants. On Edtech Island, you will find diverse resources for educators and even an opportunity to take a graduate course via the virtual space. To explore the island, go to **http://edtechisland.wetpaint.com/.**

Rate Your Educational Technology Literacy

You will learn much about educational technology as you read through this text. Take the self-assessment below to determine your level of educational technology literacy at the beginning of this course. Return to this self-test at the end of the course and retake it to determine which competencies have been achieved and which need further work.

EDUCATION TECHNOLOGY COMPETENCIES	*Check Achieved Competencies* START OF COURSE	END OF COURSE
I am aware of what comprises educational technology and the professional standards associated with it.		
I am aware of my professional requirement and responsibilities related to technology.		
I am aware of the ways technology will help me to engage in lifelong learning and professional development.		
I am aware of learning theories and their impact on implementation of educational technology.		
I can prepare a comprehensive instructional plan that uses technology effectively.		
I can use a stand-alone and networked computer system.		
I can use most traditional and digital classroom technologies to support teaching and learning.		
I can use administrative software for my administrative tasks.		
I can use academic software to reinforce student learning.		
I can use technology for communication and collaboration.		
I can use technology to improve my professional productivity.		
I can creatively integrate technology for more effective lessons.		

EDUCATION TECHNOLOGY COMPETENCIES	*Check Achieved Competencies* START OF COURSE	END OF COURSE
I can use a variety of technologies for precise and clear presentation of ideas.		
I can use technology to help manage my classroom.		
I can use the Internet for global communication and research.		
I can use World Wide Web and Web 2.0 tools to support teaching and learning.		
I can use technology to accurately assess student progress in a variety of ways.		
I can use technology to support learner-centered strategies and meet content standards.		
I can organize data via technology for reporting for both administrative and academic purposes.		
I am aware of social, ethical, and legal issues associated with technology.		
I can use technology to address special needs students' unique requirements.		
I can use technology to address student diversity.		
I am aware of how to use technology in a manner that ensures my students' safety.		
I can use technology in a manner that ensures equity in my classroom.		
I am aware of emerging technologies that will affect education in the future.		

CHAPTER 2

Theoretical Foundations

Creatas/Age Fotostock

CHAPTER OVERVIEW

This chapter addresses these ISTE National Educational Technology Standards:
- •NETS•T Standard 1
- •NETS•T Standard 2
- •NETS•T Standard 5

To understand the role of educational technology in the teaching and learning process, it's best to begin with a solid understanding of what teaching and learning really are. To be effectively used, educational technology should not be segregated from the teaching and learning that it supports. It is therefore critical to begin our examination of educational technology with a closer look at the teaching and learning process and technology's role in that process.

This chapter will help you develop the conceptual groundwork for the remaining chapters in this text. In Chapter 2, you will:

- Explore learning within the framework of communication
- Review key learning theories
- Examine the learner characteristics that affect learning
- Investigate teaching styles and their impact on learning
- Explore teaching, learning, and technology from a holistic view
- Briefly review educational technology within a historical perspective
- Synthesize your own view of the relationships among teaching, learning, and technology

Teaching and Learning: A Closer Look at the Instructional Event

To understand how technology fits into instruction, you must first have a very clear picture of the nature of teaching and learning. Teachers create **instructional events** to transfer knowledge and skills to their students. Technology is a key tool in this process. For a teacher, this conceptual framework of teaching, learning, and the role of technology is important. A clear and precise grasp of key teaching and learning theories provides a solid base for development of this framework and is therefore a logical place to begin your exploration of technology in teaching and learning.

An instructional event includes all the teaching methods and learning experiences created to support the learning process.

What Is Learning?

We teach so that our students will learn the concepts or skills we have identified as critical. Teachers want to transfer the knowledge and skills they currently possess to their students so that they too can embrace, enjoy, and use that knowledge academically, personally, and professionally. It is imperative that teachers begin the transfer process with a full understanding of learning so that they can plan and implement appropriate instruction that will result in learning success. Just as an architect must understand the properties of wood, steel, and glass and the purpose of a building before designing it, so too must a teacher understand the essential components of the teaching and learning process.

How Do We Learn?

The human mechanism of incorporating new knowledge, behaviors, and skills into an individual personal repertoire broadly defines learning. For a deeper understanding of how learning occurs, you must first examine the underlying psychological views of human behaviors. Psychologists are not unanimous in these views. There are, in fact, a variety of **theories** to explain how and why people do what they do. Most of these theories, however, fall within a few prevailing schools of thought. Each school has its own perspective on human behavior. To understand learning, then, you must examine the prevailing views and the learning theories that result from each.

A theory is an idea or concept that offers an explanation for observed phenomena.

As an educator, awareness of these differing views helps you understand the options you have in approaching the design of an instructional event and, indeed, the entire learning environment. Examining these sometimes opposing views of learning will help you to determine the position with which you personally most agree. In turn, this will help you to design instruction that is consistent with your own view of the teaching-learning process and its principles.

Understanding learning is even more critical when a teacher integrates technology into an instructional event. Technology is best viewed as a robust set of instructional tools that help you accomplish the objectives of the teaching-learning process. Technology is a means to an instructional end, not an end in itself. To use technology effectively, the teacher must have a clear understanding of learning and the teaching strategies that will result in the intended knowledge transfer. The teaching strategies you select will then determine the appropriate types of technological tools necessary to carry them out.

Perspectives on Learning

Different people can look at the same thing and see it in very different ways. This describes the concept of **perspective.** Learning is a complex activity that can be explained differently depending on one's perspective on how and why people do what they do. Each of the different schools of psychology has its own view or perspective of learning.

In the next few sections, you will be introduced to differing, sometimes contrary views of learning. Each is correct from the perspective of the theorists presenting it. As you read about each of these perspectives on learning, consider which most closely coincides with your views on learning. As you consider these different viewpoints, you might find that you agree with one of these theories part of the time and prefer a different theory at other times or for different learners. If that is the case, you have an eclectic approach that takes key ideas from multiple theories.

Learning as Communication

One of the earliest approaches to understanding learning was to examine the phenomenon as a communication process. The teacher was the sender of a message, and the student was the receiver of the message. Within this framework, learning was considered to have occurred when the information was accurately transmitted to the receiver. To be sure that this had indeed happened, the sender checked returning messages (**feedback**) from the receiver to confirm that accurate communication had taken place. This **communications cycle** is diagrammed in Figure 2.1.

As you know from your own personal experiences, clear and precise communication does not always occur. There are three general types of variables that can interfere with the communication cycle: (1) environmental factors, (2) psychological factors, and (3) personal filters (see Figure 2.2). It is important for those who are trying to communicate to have an awareness of the nature and impact of each of these.

Environmental factors include physical conditions that may impede the message.

Environmental factors that may interfere with the communication process include environmental conditions that cause the message to be distorted or even blocked. In a classroom, as the teacher (sender) engages in the communication process, loud, incessant noise from outside the classroom may interrupt communication or cause environmental static that interferes with the clarity of the message the student receives. Dim lighting, excessive movement, and uncomfortable temperatures inside the classroom are among other physical distractions that can cause the participants to lose focus and thus add a different but equally disruptive static to the process. Any factors emanating from the environment that cause a learner to lose focus and disengage from active participation in the communication process may be included in environmental factors. Some environmental factors affect some learners but not others. This can be the result of those environmental factors interacting with individual psychological factors.

Psychological factors are the internal psychological conditions that affect communication.

Psychological factors are the unique individual psychological differences that define and affect the reception of a communicated message. Psychological factors can include the receiver's emotional state at the time the message is transmitted. For a receiver who entered

FIGURE 2.1

The Communications Cycle

An analysis of the components of the communication process.

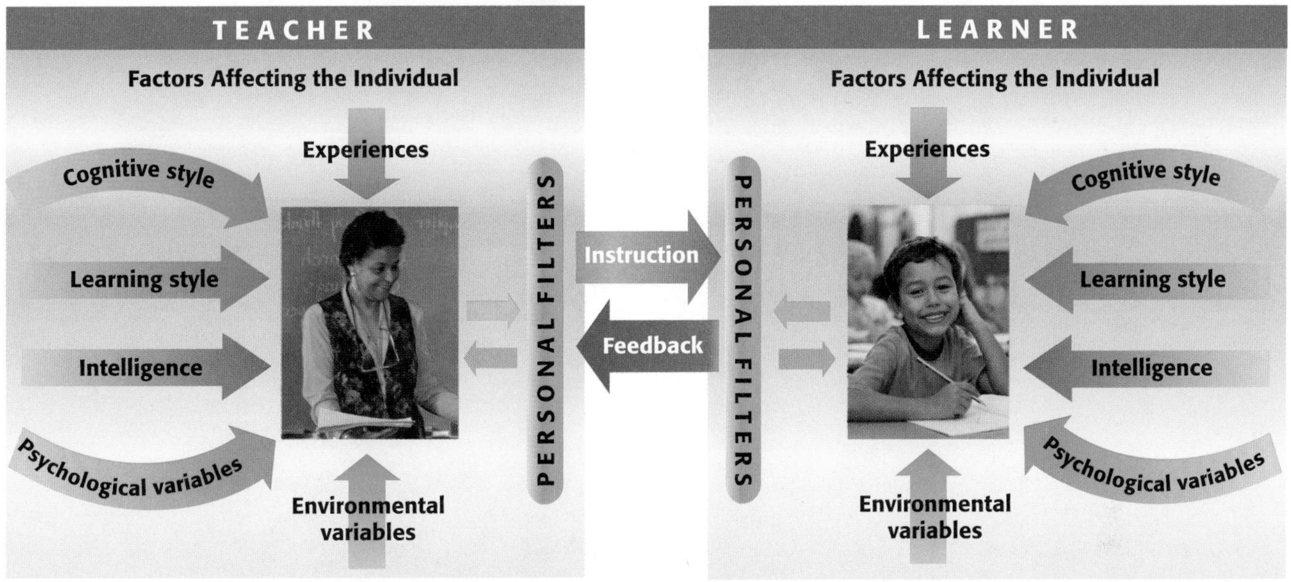

the communication process immediately after a highly emotional or traumatic event, internal emotional turmoil may be the source of static that distracts the individual from the message. Sometimes, it is the manner in which the message is transmitted that causes the static. Individuals all have preferences as to how they best receive information. Each of us has a preferred sensory gateway, that is, the sense that is most effective for receiving and decoding information. This collection of preferences, or **learning style,** when not addressed by the sender, can cause frustration as the learner tries to grasp the content. This frustration in turn garbles the message. If one learns best through careful examination of pictures and diagrams, then a message that is transmitted orally can be difficult and frustrating to understand and may therefore not be clearly received. If one's dominant sensory gateway is touch, then verbal or visual communication is less effective than tactile-kinesthetic experiences.

Learning styles are the sensory preferences that impact learning.

Learning styles may act as a barrier to communication when the sender does not address the receiver's preferred learning style. Thus, one's unique physiological and psychological predisposition to the way in which a message is delivered is another example of the psychological factors that may disrupt communication.

The final factor that may interfere with the communication process is the **personal filter** through which the message must pass. Both sender and receiver have a number of personal filters. These include the individual's personal values, cultural heritage, and social belief system. The pure message, that is, the objective set of data that is to be transferred, may be distorted by the belief system held by the sender or the receiver. For example, if the sender or the receiver comes to the process with a predisposition toward the message content, that predisposition may distort the message itself. A negative attitude toward the message or toward the participants in the communication process may cause the intended message to be distorted on delivery. This type of filter may be referred to as having a closed mind with reference to the message. Cultural beliefs can also act as filters by distorting the message content. If one holds a belief that is directly opposed to the content of the message, then the filter may distort the information to be more consistent with the belief or reject it because it is in conflict with the belief. In teaching, awareness of potential filters, both your own and those of the receiver, will help you overcome the potential for distortion.

Personal filters include values, cultural heritage, and beliefs.

FIGURE 2.2

Variables Affecting Learning

Environmental factors, psychological factors, and personal filters are among the many variables that affect learning.

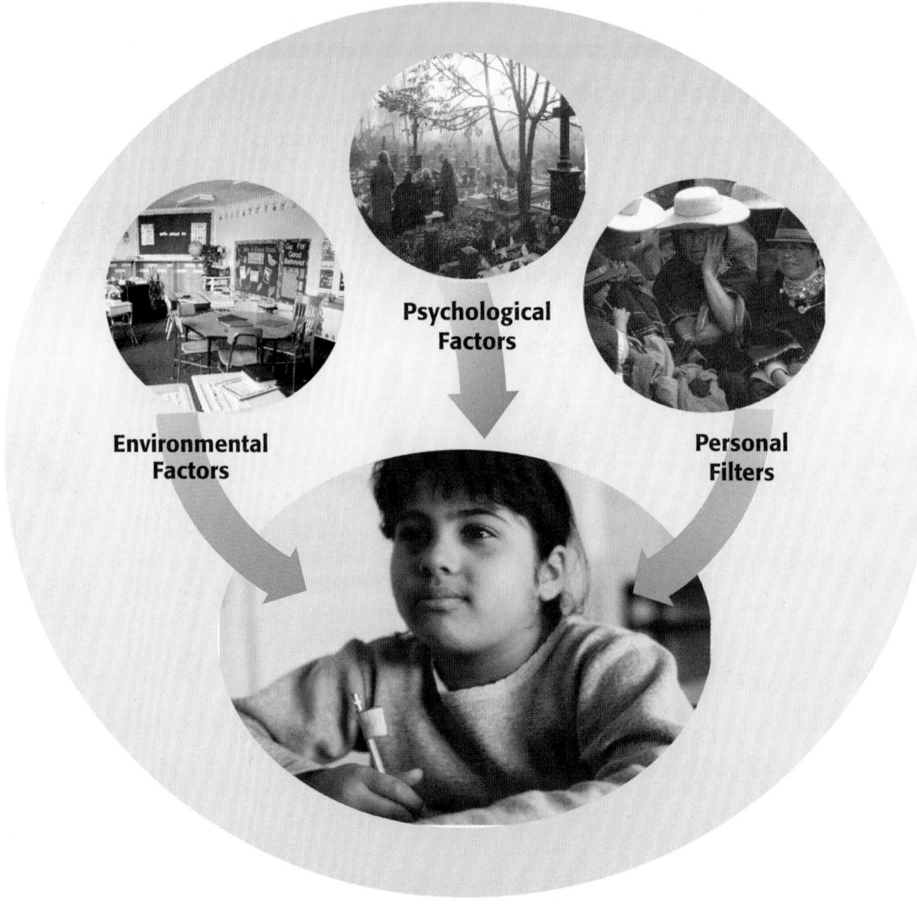

Review the communications model diagrammed in Figure 2.1. Note each of the unique elements that affect communication, from the message itself to the filters through which it must pass. Together, these components interact to determine the success of the teaching-learning process.

Whether the message was the original content sent from sender to receiver or the feedback from receiver to sender, you can see that many factors can help or hinder communications. With an understanding of the nature of communication as a foundation, you can begin to see the complexity of successful teaching. The teaching-learning process embraces the entire component of the communication process but then continues a step further. Understanding the teaching-learning process also requires understanding what happens once the message has been correctly transmitted. Is receipt of the message learning, or is there more to it? How do understanding and learning take place? To answer these questions, we must delve deeper into theories about how we learn. Thus far, we have examined teaching and learning from a macro view, that is, from the larger perspective of communication. Now it is time to consider the process from a micro view, the narrower perspective of the internal processes that determine how one learns.

AP Images

B. F. Skinner (1904–1990) was the father of modern behaviorism.

The Behaviorist Perspective

Behaviorists, that is, those who see learning from a behaviorist perspective, view all behavior as a response to external stimuli. A stimulus is the initial action directed to the organism, and a response is the organism's reaction to that action. According to behaviorists, the learner acquires behaviors, skills, and knowledge in response to the rewards, punishments, or withheld responses associated with them. A reward includes all positive, negative, or neutral reinforcement to a behavior. Rewards determine the likelihood that the behavior will be repeated. Such reinforcing responses can include rewards (positive reinforcement), punishments (negative reinforcement), or withheld responses (no reinforcement). For behaviorists, learning is essentially a passive process, that is, one learns as a response to the environment, not necessarily because of any specific mental activity. Key theorists in this perspective include **Ivan Pavlov, John Watson,** and **B. F. Skinner.**

Behaviorism sees learning as the response to an external stimulus.

The Cognitivist Perspective

In contrast to the behaviorist view, **cognitivists** focus on learning as a mental operation that takes place when information enters through the senses, undergoes mental manipulation, is stored, and is finally used. Unlike behaviorism, with its exclusive focus on external, measurable behaviors, this theory makes mental activity (cognition) the primary source of study. Although behavior is still considered critical, it is viewed as an indicator of cognitive processes rather than just an outcome of a **stimulus-response** cycle. Cognitive theorists attempt to explain learning in terms of how one thinks. Cognitivists believe that learning is more complex than a simplistic behaviorist view. Learning and problem solving, according to cognitivists, represent mental processes that are undetectable by mere observation. Key theorists in this perspective include **Jerome Bruner** and **David Ausubel.** The early works of constructivist **Jean Piaget** also significantly contributed to the cognitivist perspective. Each brings a unique perspective to the view of learning as a function of thinking.

Corbis

Jean Piaget (1896–1980) offered a constructivist view suggesting children develop cognitive structures during specific developmental stages.

The Constructivist Perspective

For **constructivists,** knowledge is a constructed element resulting from the learning process. Further, knowledge is unique to the individual who constructs it. Mahoney (1994) places constructivism on the cognitive family tree because it relies on the cognitive concepts of inquiry-based learning and social interaction. However, it differs from the cognitivist view in that learning is not seen as just the product of mental processes; it is an entirely unique product for each individual based on the experiences within which those mental processes occurred. Constructivism is at present the most influential force in shaping contemporary education.

Perhaps the most notable early constructivist was Jean Piaget. Piaget theorized that children construct mental maps as they encounter information. New knowledge is either assimilated (fitted into existing maps) or accommodated (existing maps are adjusted to accommodate

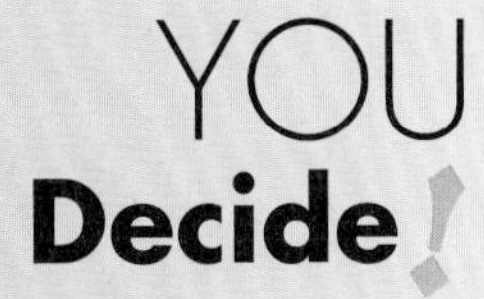

Learning theories attempt to explain how we learn. Each explanation focuses on different attributes, conditions, and outcomes. Sometimes the theories seem to contradict each other; at other times, they may resonate with us and help us to grasp how we can best help our students learn. Is becoming familiar with learning theories useful to current and future teachers?

YES! Learning is very difficult to understand. Is it physical? Is it psychological? How does it really happen? Theories help you create your own mental model of learning. You consider alternative theories; and whether you agree with them or not, becoming familiar with them helps you to come to your own conclusion about what learning is and how best you can promote it in your own classroom.

NO! A theory is just a hypothesis or guess about reality. Learning theories are just someone's idea of what learning actually is. Spending time becoming familiar with guesses, even those of famous educators and scientists, does not help you to decide anything concrete enough to use in the classroom. The different and sometimes conflicting views of learning too often confuse the issue and offer no practical solutions for teachers.

Which view on learning theories do you agree with? YOU DECIDE!

> Cognitivists and constructivists both recognize learning as a mental process.

the new information). Thus, children maintain a type of mental equilibrium. In the area of educational technology, **Seymour Papert** adapted Piaget's perspective and applied it to children engaged in using technology. Papert's application of this approach resulted in the development of Logo, a graphical programming language that, when used by children, effectively transferred complex mathematical skills. Papert, a founding faculty member of MIT's Media Lab, continues to develop constructivist educational software and to research learning.

Within the constructivist school of learning, two views dominate. The first is a cognitive-constructivist view championed by **Robert Gagné.** In this perspective, learning is a result of an individual's cognitive efforts to construct his or her personal knowledge. The other view, that of social constructivism, was well articulated by **Lev Vygotsky** and **Albert Bandura.** In this view, learning is considered a result of the collaboration of a group of learners in an effort to construct a common core of knowledge. Cognitive constructivism is an outgrowth of the cognitivist view of learning. However, it differs in that the emphasis is placed on the constructs that the individual creates as a result of his or her own cognitive processes. Table 2.1 compares several important constructivists.

TABLE 2.1 Key Theorists and Their Differences

THEORIST	DEFINING CHARACTERISTICS	TEACHER ROLE
JEAN PIAGET (developmental theorist)	Identified key developmental stages that may affect learning; children either assimilate or accommodate knowledge based on existing schemas.	Be aware of child's developmental stage when presenting content; help child construct schemas.
ROBERT GAGNÉ (bridge theorist between behaviorism and cognitivism)	Controlled, external, sequential instructional events with eight conditions for learning determined by developmental stage of learner and by subject matter.	Create systematic design to address student's needs; individualize instructional events.
LEV VYGOTSKY (social learning theorist)	Zone of proximal development recognizes students' readiness to bond with the community; speech and language are keys to intelligence.	Arrange for tutoring by skilled and learned adults as a means of student enculturation.
ALBERT BANDURA (social learning theorist)	Concern with the way people acquire socially appropriate behavior; builds on Skinner to form social learning theory; agrees with Gagné that subject matter is central to learning stages.	Outcome expectancies (prediction of results of a behavior) motivate students to imitate the behavior, "modeling."
SEYMOUR PAPERT (mathematician and educational technologist)	Technology should help children experience knowledge and construct meanings; developed Logo and constructivist software based on this perspective.	Provide opportunities for children to develop constructs through experience; use technology to support experiences.
HOWARD GARDNER (multiple-intelligences theorist)	Nine innate capabilities (with more under study): linguistic, spatial, bodily-kinesthetic, logical-mathematical, and others; every child is smart in his or her own way and possesses combined intelligences that should be encouraged to develop.	Gear curricula and instructional approaches to individual intelligences and their dominant ways of knowing, for the successful pursuit of knowledge, both vocational and avocational, by all.
B. F. SKINNER (stimulus-response)	Described learning as a response to events or stimuli and the result of the reinforcement of the response.	Responses should be reinforced with immediate and appropriate feedback.
JEROME BRUNER (constructivist theorist)	Finds learning to be an active process in which learners build new ideas or concepts based on their current/past knowledge.	Try to encourage students to discover knowledge with instruction organized in a spiral manner so students continually build on what they have already learned.
DAVID AUSUBEL (subsumption theorist)	Suggests that learning is based on cognitive processes that occur during the reception of information.	General information should be presented first; use preorganizers to best prepare for information integration.

SOURCE: Theory into Practice (TIP) Database. Retrieved 12/15/05. Reproduced with permission of Greg Kearsley.

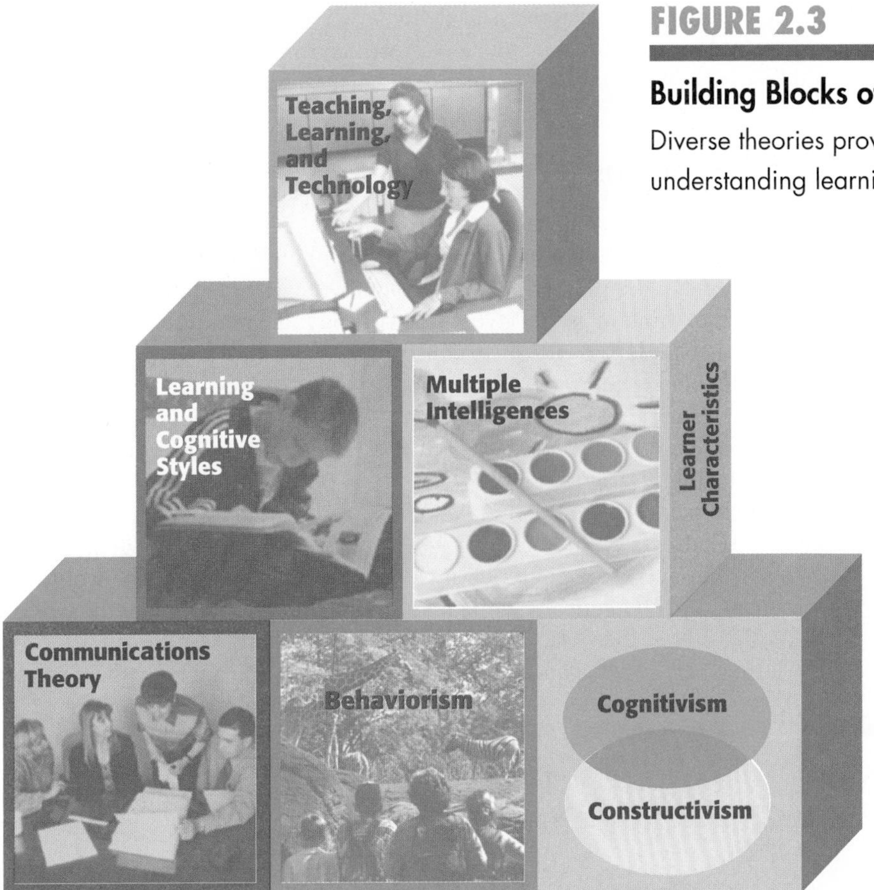

FIGURE 2.3

Building Blocks of Effective Teaching

Diverse theories provide the foundation for understanding learning.

Toward an Integrated View of Learning

All of the theoretical perspectives described in this section attempt to explain the complex process called learning. Depending on the psychological framework that you believe best explains why people behave the way they do, you may find one of these perspectives more attractive than the others. Still, it is best to think of all of them together as the range of possible explanations of learning and to think of each individual approach as a unique and special addition to your own view of learning (see Figure 2.3). Then, as an eclectic instructor, you can choose to implement those parts of the theories that best match your learners' needs and the characteristics of a particular lesson's specific objectives.

Which theory is correct? To determine an answer to this question, you would probably read a variety of resources and investigate a number of web sites to get an idea of the possibilities. After reviewing these possibilities, you would ultimately form your own personal answer. Perhaps that, too, is the best approach to learning theory. To create the best possible **learning environment** for your students, you need a working knowledge of learning theory. Then, once this knowledge base is in place, you can examine all the options and let your own mental model of learning develop.

> The learning environment refers to all the elements that make up the design and implementation of the instruction.

A View of the Learner

Understanding learning is just the first step a teacher must take in planning effective instruction. Learning theory tells us how learning might occur. The next area for consideration is to examine characteristics that might have an impact on an individual's attempt to learn.

Each learner in a classroom is likely to have a unique cognitive style, a unique learning style, and some parameters related to intelligence. This section will help you understand how each of these relates to the teaching-learning process.

Cognitive Styles

Cognitive styles refer to how one thinks.

Cognitive style refers to how one thinks. Each person has his or her own tendencies and preferences when it comes to cognition (thinking). Such preferences can even be measured. One of the most widely used cognitive style instruments to determine one's own patterns of thinking is the Myers-Briggs Type Indicator (MBTI). The Myers-Briggs instrument is based primarily on a constructivist view of learning. In it, a learner answers a series of questions about his or her own preferences. The responses are then totaled and categorized. The clustering of responses points to one of four sets of opposing cognitive preferences: extrovert (E) or introvert (I), sensing (S) or intuitive (N), thinking (T) or feeling (F), and judging (J) or perceiving (P). Everyone has a preference in each of these pairs of opposites. Thus, a person's cognitive type may turn out to be the ENFP type (Extrovert, Intuitive, Feeling, Perceiving). Such an individual would be likely to be excited by and involved in new ideas and possibilities. He or she would join in enthusiastically and energetically while maintaining a deep concern for the world and others (Martin, 2002). Everyone has preferences in each of these four pairs of opposites, and each combination of types results in a noticeably different cognitive style. These cognitive characteristics are also likely to influence how the individual might successfully learn. Awareness and understanding of students' cognitive preferences can help a teacher design instruction that is consistent with these preferences and therefore more palatable to those students. Figure 2.4 gives you a sense of the cognitive types that the MBTI identifies.

Learning styles are based on sensory preferences.

FIGURE 2.4

Summary of Myers-Briggs Types

Cognitive types as measured by the MBTI.

Learning Styles

Learning style is another factor influencing how an individual learns (Figure 2.5). Unlike the broader concept of cognitive style—that is, how we think—learning style refers to those conditions under which we best learn. Most learning style theorists identify three primary modalities for learning: auditory, visual, and kinesthetic. Some individuals learn best by listening; thus, they may be said to have a predominantly auditory learning style. Others may learn best by seeing, thus having a visual learning style. Yet others learn best by doing, which suggests a kinesthetic learning style. Although everyone can learn using each of these modalities, learning style theorists suggest that each person has a preference, a dominant sensory gateway. It is easiest for the individual to learn when information is presented in a manner consistent with her or his personal learning modality preference. Learning styles are therefore of considerable importance to those who are constructing the learning environment.

Learning style is consequently another individual factor that affects learning regardless of the psychological perspective with which you agree. Understanding the

FIGURE 2.5

What Is Your Learning Style?

A number of learning style instruments are available online. The Index of Learning Styles (ILS), developed by Richard M. Felder and Linda K. Silverman of North Carolina State University, assesses preferences on four dimensions based on a learning styles model they developed. Here is a sampling of the forty-four questions included in the ILS. To read more about learning styles and to try the instrument yourself, go to Dr. Felder's web site at **www.ncsu.edu/felder-public/ILSpage.html**

ILS Sample Questions

When I start a homework problem, I am more likely to

a. try to fully understand the problem first.

b. start working on the solution immediately.

I understand something better after I

a. try it out.

b. think it through.

When I think about what I did yesterday, I am most likely to get

a. a picture.

b. words.

When I am learning something new, it helps me to

a. talk about it.

b. think about it.

I prefer to get new information in

a. pictures, diagrams, graphs, or maps.

b. written directions or verbal information.

Once I understand

a. all the parts, I understand the whole thing.

b. the whole thing, I see how the parts fit.

In a book with lots of pictures and charts, I am likely to

a. look over the pictures and charts carefully.

b. focus on the written text.

Learning style instruments such as this one include questions that help students identify various aspects of their personal learning styles. Try the ILS and other online instruments to determine your own learning style and to see whether the results you get from various instruments provide you with a reasonably consistent and accurate description of your personal style.

SOURCE: Reprinted with permission from the Index of Learning Styles by B. A. Soloman and R. M. Felder, **www.ncsu.edu/felder-public/ILSpage.html.**

dominant learning styles of the students you are trying to teach and then designing the components of the instructional event to be consistent with their styles will make instruction significantly more effective for those learners.

Intelligence

A final factor affecting learning is **intelligence,** or the inherent capability of the learner to understand and learn. Intelligence quotient (**IQ**), a quantitative measure of intelligence, was once thought to be a definitive way to measure this capability within a specified range. Extensive research was done to develop an instrument that would provide a snapshot of a person's intelligence without regard to cultural or other bias. Bias is any tendency or prejudice that might distort a view. An example of cultural bias in intelligence testing would be the inclusion of questions that rely on a framework that is outside the test taker's cultural experience, thus potentially distorting the results.

Intelligence is the inherent capacity to understand and learn.

TECH TIPS for Teachers

Many web sites offer online cognitive style, learning style, and multiple intelligence tests that you can have your students take to get an idea of their styles. While not as accurate as the validated and tested instruments developed by Dunn and Dunn, Myers-Briggs, and Howard Gardner, these brief online tests can give busy teachers some indication as to their students' styles. Often, these instruments will score the tests and provide results instantaneously. And there are instruments available for almost any grade level. For an example of this type of online style resource, visit the Learning Disabilities Pride web site at **www.ldpride.net/learningstyles.MI.htm.**

One of the most commonly used IQ tests is the Stanford-Binet. Alfred Binet, a French psychologist, initially developed the test in 1905 for the French Ministry of Education to help predict which students would succeed in school. Binet's test was later adapted for the United States by Louis Terman of Stanford University. The Stanford-Binet or a similar test is typically given to students several times during their academic careers. Teachers can easily get an idea of their students' potential by reviewing student records—or can they? Increasingly, this traditional means of measuring intelligence based on verbal and mathematical abilities has come under attack. In fact, the very definition of intelligence is being debated.

How to measure intelligence and the value system we attach to it are variables that are being given scholarly consideration. McLuhan (1998) asserts, "It is in our IQ testing that we have produced the greatest flood of misbegotten standards. Unaware of our typographic cultural bias, our testers assume that uniform and continuous habits are a sign of intelligence, thus eliminating the ear man and the eye man." As a result of the inadequacies of traditional intelligence testing, extensive research is being done to develop instruments that will provide a more accurate result.

Howard Gardner, Professor of Education at Harvard, developed the theory of Multiple Intelligences, which offers a diverse view of abilities.

Howard Gardner provided a new view of intelligence, the **theory of multiple intelligences.** He theorized that there is more to intelligence than what was historically measured by IQ tests. Gardner suggested that these objective tests did not go far enough in representing intelligence. He suggested instead that each individual has multiple types of intelligences, only a few of which can be measured by IQ tests. In Gardner's theory of multiple intelligences, he describes nine different aspects or types of intelligences that every person possesses (see Figure 2.6). These intelligences (or talents) include the following:

Gardner theorizes that multiple intelligences exist.

- Linguistic intelligence (verbal skills and talents related to sound, meanings, and rhythms)
- Logical-mathematical intelligence (conceptual and logical thinking skills)
- Musical intelligence (talents and abilities related to sound, rhythm, and pitch)
- Spatial intelligence (skill in thinking in pictures and visioning abstractly)
- Bodily-kinesthetic intelligence (skill in controlling body movements)
- Interpersonal intelligence (responsiveness to others)
- Intrapersonal intelligence (high degree of self-awareness and insight)
- Naturalist intelligence (skills in recognizing, categorizing, and interacting with the natural world)
- Existential intelligence (ability to consider and deal with questions of human existence)

According to Gardner's theory, every individual possesses some degree of each of the intelligences he details, but one or more of the intelligences dominates. If any one of the intelligences is of significant capacity, the result is a prodigy in that area. Gardner's view equally recognizes the unique abilities of Mozart (musical intelligence), Frank Lloyd Wright (spatial intelligence), and Babe Ruth (bodily-kinesthetic intelligence), whereas standard IQ tests might recognize only Albert Einstein (logical-mathematical intelligence) and William Shakespeare (linguistic intelligence). This broader view of individual capacities changes the assumptions a teacher might make about a student's potential and capacities. Such reevaluation, in turn, should change that teacher's plan for instruction. If one adopts the multiple-intelligences approach, then learning will be affected by the dominance of one or more of the intelligences in each individual student. Teaching then would have to accommodate these various propensities to maximize student learning.

PEARSON myeducationkit™

Go to the *Assignments and Activities* section of Chapter 2 in MyEducationKit and complete the video activity entitled *Teaching to Multiple Intelligences*.

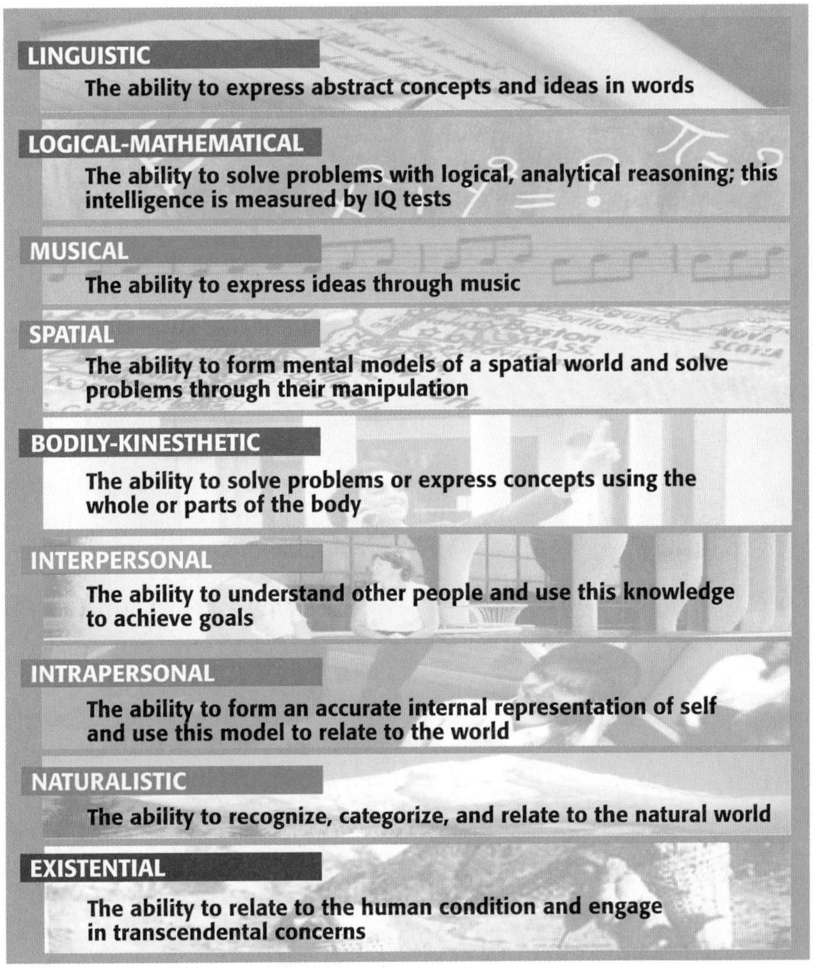

FIGURE 2.6

Howard Gardner's Theory of Multiple Intelligences

Multiple forms of intelligence as theorized by Howard Gardner.

LINGUISTIC
The ability to express abstract concepts and ideas in words

LOGICAL-MATHEMATICAL
The ability to solve problems with logical, analytical reasoning; this intelligence is measured by IQ tests

MUSICAL
The ability to express ideas through music

SPATIAL
The ability to form mental models of a spatial world and solve problems through their manipulation

BODILY-KINESTHETIC
The ability to solve problems or express concepts using the whole or parts of the body

INTERPERSONAL
The ability to understand other people and use this knowledge to achieve goals

INTRAPERSONAL
The ability to form an accurate internal representation of self and use this model to relate to the world

NATURALISTIC
The ability to recognize, categorize, and relate to the natural world

EXISTENTIAL
The ability to relate to the human condition and engage in transcendental concerns

A View of the Teacher

Teaching is a systematic, planned sequence of events that facilitates the communication of an idea, concept, or skill to a learner. The act of teaching requires an understanding of learning and an understanding of the individual and environmental factors that affect the learner. It also requires an understanding of yourself and the individual and environmental factors that affect you. Every teacher has his or her own learning style, cognitive style, and dominant intelligence. Given these variables, teachers also differ in their styles of teaching. **Teaching style** is typically a function of one's personal preferences. Research has shown that we teach in the way we like to learn, think, or do. Although that is unavoidable and often positive, a teacher must have an awareness of his or her own teaching style to be able to adjust it to meet the needs of the learners. Have you ever had instructors who were difficult to learn from? Did they lecture too much, or were they too unorganized for you? Did you notice that some of your peers did not seem to have difficulty with those instructors' teaching styles? This may result from a conflict between learning and teaching styles.

Teaching styles are preferred teaching methods that mirror a teacher's learning styles.

A well-developed and well-articulated teaching style can be a positive trait that separates the master teacher from the average teacher. Yet one must always maintain awareness of how effective one's style is with reference to the goal of teaching: learning. An understanding of learning theory, cognitive styles, learning styles, and intelligence will serve you well in understanding and improving your own teaching style.

FIGURE 2.7

A Holistic View of Teaching, Learning, and Technology

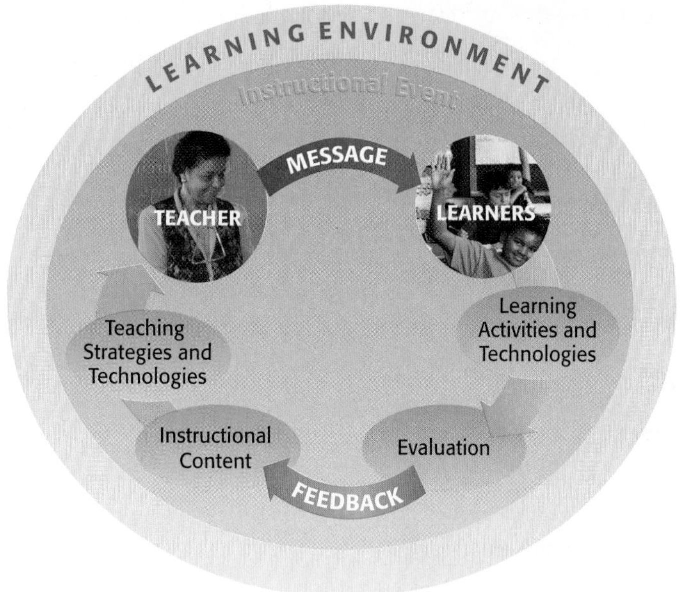

Toward a Holistic View of Teaching, Learning, and Technology

Teaching, learning, and technology work together to achieve the ultimate goal of effective knowledge transfer. When you consider the process of teaching and learning as a holistic system, you can begin to sense how all of the elements of the process, from the learning environment to teaching strategies, to learning activities, to support technologies, interact in support of the learner. (These relationships are diagrammed in Figure 2.7.) When you take the time to carefully examine each component and its interaction with other components, you are better able to design an effective process that will help you teach and help your students learn. Using such a holistic **systems approach** helps to give you the perspective needed to effectively apply each aspect of instruction to the creation of a meaningful teaching and learning process.

A systems approach specifies a methodical process for teaching and learning.

Once the teaching-learning process has been defined, it is much simpler to see the role technology plays in it. Technology supports teaching, and it supports learning. However, educational technologies cannot be selected or implemented until the teaching and learning process they support has been planned and detailed by an educator.

At this point, you have already explored many theoretical foundations of the teaching and learning process. The next step is to consider how technology fits into the instructional system we have created.

Why Use Technology?

You have explored communication. You have examined learning theories. You have reviewed cognitive and learning styles. You have explored another way of looking at intelligence. You have been encouraged to find out how your students process information. You have applied these concepts to yourself to begin to understand the personal characteristics that will define your teaching style. You have viewed the whole of the teaching-learning process as a system. But what does all this have to do with the focus of this text, educational technology?

Technology is an Information Age teaching tool.

To see the relationship, it is appropriate to remember the definitions and standards offered by the AECT and ISTE. These organizations suggest that the concept of educational technology is more than a certain type of computer or a specific brand of camera. It is, instead, a wide variety of theories and practices associated with designing, developing, using, managing, and ultimately evaluating both the teaching-learning process and the technological resources used to implement that process. Professional standards articulate the minimum levels of technology knowledge and performance for teachers. These reflect the need for every teacher to have a solid command of the educational technology skills necessary for integrating appropriate and meaningful technologies into teaching and learning.

Educational technology can include any resource and any process that facilitates learning. A teacher might use educational technology to enhance the quality and clarity of communication. A teacher might employ a particular process or a specific technology to increase

Bob Daemmrich Photography

Technology serves both learners and teachers in a variety of settings.

the likelihood that a presentation addresses a specific learning style or intelligence. Or a learner might select a process or technology because it organizes and presents content in the manner that is most comfortable for his or her personal cognitive style. Some educational technologies can be employed to ensure the rewards and feedback that are critical to a behaviorist approach. Other technologies help a learner to construct and test the mental models suggested by cognitivists. Still others encourage and support social exchange to construct new knowledge through social interaction. Educational technologies can be used to enhance and support the teaching-learning process at any number of points in the process. Educational technology is one of the supports for teaching and learning that both teacher and learner can call on to help ensure the opportunity for optimum performance.

PEARSON myeducationkit™

Go to the *Assignments and Activities* section of Chapter 2 in MyEducationKit and complete the video activity entitled *Steps to Successful Technology Integration*.

This holistic approach to educational technology has not always been the accepted model. For many years, educational technology had a very narrow, technical definition. The evolution from an equipment-based view of educational technology to a teaching-and-learning-based view may cause confusion for those who are new to education. A brief review of this evolution may help to clarify the change in emphasis and influences of technology on instruction.

Educational Technology: The Past

For many people, the term *educational technology* conjures up images of audiovisual equipment such as a tape recorder or videocassette player. This audiovisual movement as we define the term today came into existence in the early 1900s with the advent of the first form of motion media: early movies. So strong was the belief in this new educational technology that Thomas Alva Edison (1913) suggested, albeit incorrectly, that "Books will soon be obsolete in schools." Although books have not become obsolete even today, motion media have indeed made their influence felt in schools, as they have in society in general. It was soon discovered that films incorporating sound and images could be used to teach as well as to entertain. Thus, the movie projector became an important addition to a teacher's arsenal of teaching tools. Thomas Edison also predicted that the movie projector would replace teachers. As far-fetched as this might sound, it was a widely believed and sometimes feared idea. By now, we have learned that predictions suggesting that any particular technology will replace professional educators or be the ultimate answer to improving teaching are not realistic.

Teachers have historically sought technology to support instruction.

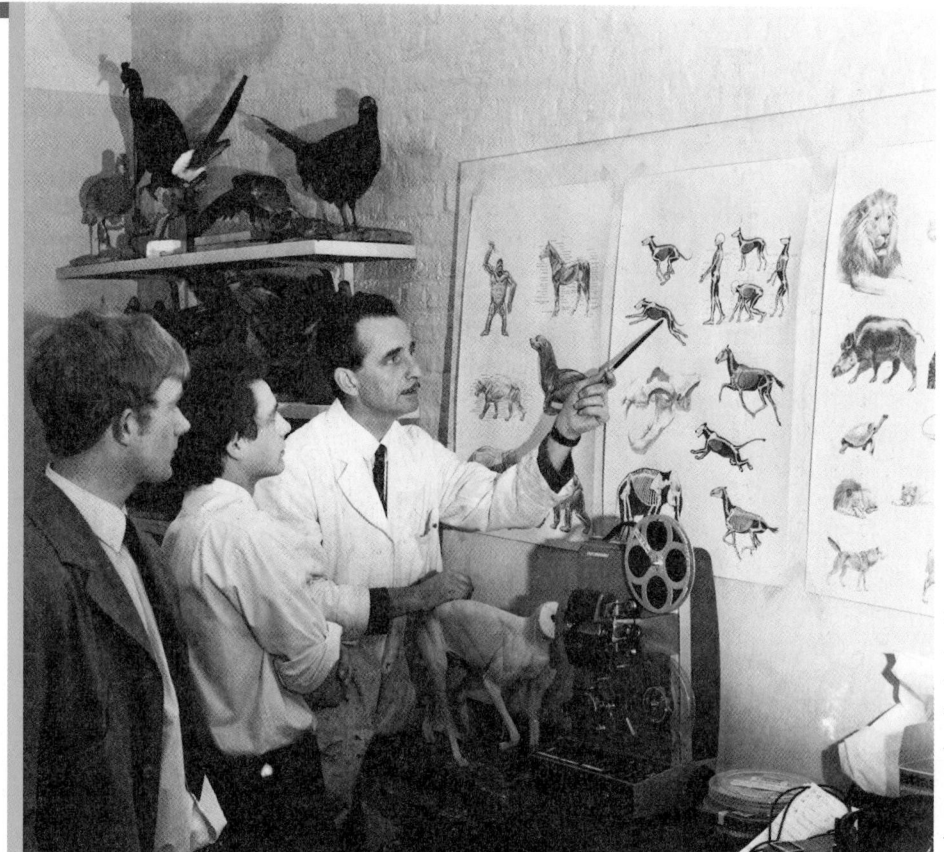

Hulton Deutsch Collection/Corbis

During the 1920s and 1930s, both audio and visual educational technology evolved steadily. Technological advances in slides, radio, and sound recordings and continuing improvement in the quality of motion pictures all contributed to this evolution. With World War II and the use of audiovisual instruction by the military, a surge in the development of audiovisual equipment occurred. To the array of technologies used in training and instruction, the military added the overhead projector, slide projector, simulator, and audio equipment for teaching foreign languages.

After World War II, research on the use of audiovisual tools supporting instruction was begun so that the training successes that evidently resulted from audiovisual-intensive military training could be better understood. This was followed in the 1950s by a greater articulation of the theories and models of communication and an exploration of how audiovisual technologies fit in with them.

The audiovisual movement gained further momentum with the spread of television in the 1950s. Many people assumed that instructional television would revolutionize education. Although the Federal Communications Commission (FCC) set aside television channels for educational purposes and the Ford Foundation and other organizations made serious investments in educational programming, instructional television (ITV) had slid into decline by the mid-1960s. The factors that led to this decline included teacher reluctance to use television programming in the classroom, the high cost of production of good-quality programming, and the passive nature of television viewing, which did not adequately meet students' learning needs.

The advent of ITV changed the role of TV in schools.

Although not the revolutionary technology it was expected to be, broadcast television and its counterpart, videotapes, have indeed changed the face of education. Further, ITV did not disappear from the education scene. Dollars from various sources continued to flow into the Public Broadcasting System, and much fine-quality educational programming emanated from it. Much of this programming, in videotape and DVD form, is still a mainstay of school video libraries.

Educational Technology: A Modern View

The 1960s saw a change in the concept of audiovisual instruction as a model closer to our current views of educational technology began to evolve. Although audiovisual equipment remained a component of the educational technology concept, the technology was no longer limited to just equipment—audio, visual, or otherwise. By the 1970s, AECT's broader view dominated. Instructional technology came to be seen as all types of learning resources and the systems necessary to place them in service to teaching and learning.

The first broadly implemented educational technology appeared in the mid-1950s as an outgrowth of the popularity of B. F. Skinner's work and behaviorist views of learning. **Programmed instruction** was an instructional system in which material was presented in a series of small steps. Each step required an active learner response, to which there was immediate feedback as to the correctness of the response. Programmed instruction emphasized individualized learning materials that would require students to interact with the information presented. In keeping with Skinner's behaviorist approach, immediate feedback to student responses was a key feature. Additional features of programmed instruction included self-paced, self-selected sequencing of the materials resulting from the learner's responses. Although popular at its inception, programmed instruction faded quickly. By the late 1960s, interest in this technology had declined. Research on programmed instruction indicated that it did not significantly improve learning. This finding, combined with negative feedback from students and teachers who found the format unstimulating, moved programmed instruction to the background of the educational landscape.

However, during its short term as an educational innovation, the programmed instruction movement did manage to have a lasting impact on educational technology. It has, in fact, turned out to be the grandfather of subsequent approaches. Its methodical approach to the analysis of instruction, its rigorous statement of observable learning objectives, and its use of a systematic development process made it a forerunner to current systems approaches to designing instruction and selecting educational technologies. Programmed instruction empirically analyzed the data related to content and learner, identified strengths and weaknesses, adjusted the system accordingly, evaluated the resulting learning, and revised the system in accordance with the evaluation data. The logic and organized approach embodied in these steps ultimately gave rise to other individualized educational technology systems.

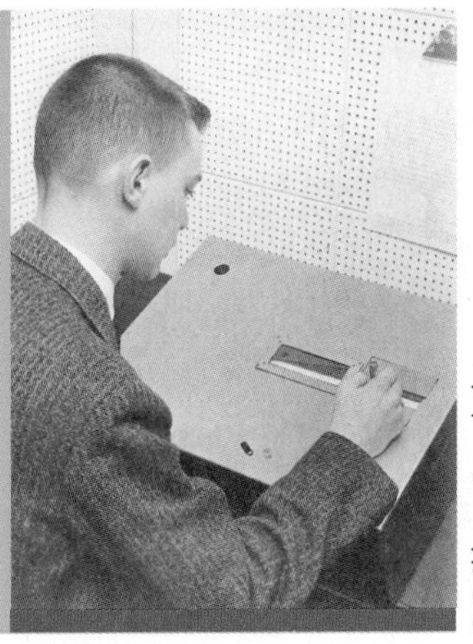
B. F. Skinner Foundation

The Skinner teaching machine was the precursor to the programmed instruction materials popular in the 1960s.

Educational technology encompasses all resources that support teaching and learning.

Multimedia Software

Early computer-assisted instruction (CAI) has given way to a variety of engaging and exciting educational software that helps students learn in fun and novel ways. With online educational resources ever expanding, many programs are now available at little or no cost to educators. Computer games, CAI software and content specific reviews have evolved into very cool teaching and learning tools. Discovery Education is one example of a multimedia online educational resource. As noted on their website, "through solutions like Discovery Education streaming, Discovery Education Science, Discovery Education Health and more, Discovery Education helps over one million educators and 35 million students harness the power of broadband and media to connect to a world of learning." For multimedia educational games, FunBrain offers an array of K-8 games in every subject area. It also offers companion teacher resources that include game finders that matches activities to McREL standards and flash cards for additional practice. You can experience these very cool online multimedia tools by going to **www.discoveryeducation.com** and to **www.funbrain.com**.

CAI software can provide interactive learning experiences.

Zigy Kaluzny/Stone/Getty Images

It was not until the advent of the microcomputer in the late 1970s that the concept of interactive individualized instruction that was introduced by programmed instruction could be fully realized. Because computers could be programmed to be interactive, to provide immediate feedback, and to allow students to navigate the material according to their own learning inclinations, educational technology entered a new era.

Computers made interactive, individualized instruction possible.

Computer-assisted instruction (CAI) broadly refers to the body of computer software that is the digital equivalent of the programmed instructional packages of the 1950s and 1960s. Early CAI was primarily text-based, drill-and-practice software; but as computing power expanded, so too did the capabilities of CAI. Today's CAI typically contains colorful graphics, easy navigation, and many instructional management features. Overall, however, the basic concepts of a systematic, organized, and responsive instructional system remain intact.

Since the advent of powerful and inexpensive computers, early CAI programs have evolved into the powerful, multimedia programs available today that entice students to learn and support teachers' instructional efforts. Although still based on the theoretical foundations you have been introduced to in this chapter, today's educational technologies offer teachers an amazing array of teaching and learning support media from which to choose. This text is designed to introduce you to the full array of technologies you might select to help you teach and to help your students learn. How you choose to use these many and varied technologies will be your personal and professional decision.

Teaching, Learning, and Educational Technology: A Personal Synthesis

To understand educational technology, you need to understand its role in support of the teaching-learning process. To understand the teaching-learning process, you need to understand teaching. To understand teaching, you need to understand communication and the participants in the communications cycle. To understand the participants, you need to understand the learner. To understand the learner, you need to understand learning theory and the factors that affect individual learning. This chapter has presented information related to each of these layers of understanding to help you lay a solid foundation on which to build your own personal framework for using educational technologies.

You must now synthesize the knowledge you have gained from this chapter into your own personal view of the teaching and learning process. You must decide how technology will fit into your teaching-learning model. You must consider what you have learned thus far and synthesize the following:

- Your own view of how students learn and how you should best communicate with them
- How best to assess the learning characteristics of your students
- How best to adapt your teaching style to your students' needs
- What you need to know to develop systematic and effective instruction
- How educational technology fits into your synthesized view of teaching and learning

Thinking about how you will apply these concepts is the first step toward really understanding what you need to do to be an effective educator.

Chapter 3 takes this process to its logical conclusion. Once you have developed your personal synthesized view of teaching, learning, and technology, you will be ready to explore the techniques that can make the job of designing effective instruction easier. Chapter 3 teaches you how to design effective instruction to focus your instructional efforts on making your teaching as meaningful as possible for your students. Further, the instructional design principles and skills that you will explore will enable you to incorporate educational technology in a manner that will be appropriate and effective for the learners you serve.

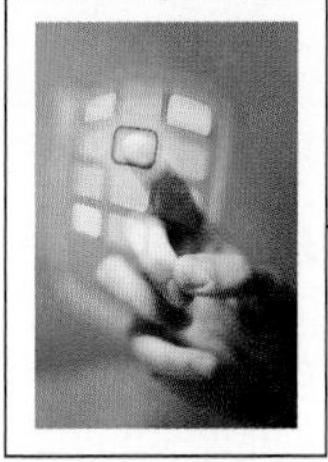

HANDSON LEARNING

After examining the role of technology in teaching and learning and after reviewing the foundational concepts presented in this chapter, you should be able to synthesize your own view of technology integration. It is a much discussed and explored topic. Some of the best educational minds in the nation have carefully articulated and defended sometimes contradictory positions. Reviewing some of their views will help you better clarify your own thinking.

Using online or library resources, research the role of technology in teaching and learning. Examine articles by those who agree with your personal view on using technology in your classroom as well as articles by those who hold opposing views. Summarize what you find on both positions and include the appropriate references. Conclude with your own position and explain what impact your reading had on it.

PEARSON myeducationkit™

To check your comprehension on the content covered in this chapter, go to the MyEducationKit for your book and complete the Study Plan for Chapter 2.

Key Terms

behaviorists, 26
cognitive style, 32
cognitivists, 29
communications cycle, 26
computer-assisted instruction (CAI), 40
constructivists, 29
environmental factors, 26
feedback, 26
instructional events, 25
intelligence, 33
IQ, 33
learning environment, 31
learning style, 26
personal filter, 26
perspective, 26
programmed instruction, 39
psychological factors, 26
stimulus-response, 29
systems approach, 36
teaching style, 35
theories, 25
theory of multiple intelligences, 34

Key Learning Theorists

David Ausubel, 29
Albert Bandura, 30
Jerome Bruner, 29
Robert Gagné, 30
Howard Gardner, 34
Seymour Papert, 30
Ivan Pavlov, 29
Jean Piaget, 29
B. F. Skinner, 29
Lev Vygotsky, 30
John Watson, 29

Student Activities

CHAPTER REVIEW

1. What is the relationship between the teaching-learning process and educational technology?
2. What factors can affect effective communication? Explain how each can interfere with the sender's message.
3. Contrast the three perspectives on learning. How are they the same? How are they different? With which do you most agree?
4. Explain the difference between cognitive styles and learning styles. How might each affect learning?
5. Describe the theory of multiple intelligences. How might this theory affect teaching?
6. What is a holistic approach to education? How might educational technology be viewed as a system?
7. How does the current view of educational technology differ from earlier views?
8. What is programmed instruction? What has been its impact on the current approach to educational technology?
9. What is computer-assisted instruction? How might it support student learning?
10. Describe your synthesized view of teaching, learning, and technology.

WHAT DO YOU THINK?

1. Imagine that you are going to teach a unit on Christopher Columbus to the grade level of your choice. What immediately comes to mind as you consider how you might teach this unit? Is there any relationship between how you might want to teach this unit and your own learning or cognitive style? Describe how you think your own personal style might affect your teaching style.
2. Cultural filters can make a difference as to whether your message is communicated clearly. Considering the potential diversity of the students you will teach, imagine teaching a unit on how the U.S. president is elected. Analyze the possible cultural filters that you need to address to ensure that the lesson is communicated accurately. List these filters and suggest how you would overcome each.
3. You have learned about a variety of learning theories in this chapter. Which one of the theoretical frameworks are you most comfortable with? Explain why the theory you selected is most appealing to you.
4. For this course, the study of educational technology begins with a very close look at the teaching-learning process. Why do you think this is an important place to start?
5. Some educators believe that having computers in the classroom is just another educational fad, like the emphasis in the 1950s and 1960s on television in the classroom. Do you agree or disagree? Defend your answer.

LEARNING TOGETHER!

The following activities should be done in small groups.

1. Describe to your peers the teachers you have had that seem to fit into the theoretical frameworks described in this chapter. After each member of the group shares her or his experiences, select a single teacher from your collective experiences who best represents each learning theory. Summarize the teachers and the reasons they were selected. Be prepared to share your group's views with the class.
2. Select a single theorist to study in greater depth. In your group, explore the theorist's life, work, and theories. Prepare a summary of key points of interest to share in a group oral report to the rest of the class.
3. Visit a school classroom and media center to observe the technologies that are available in these areas. Considering the historical trends in technology described in this chapter, where would you place the school in terms of its level of technological innovation? Share your observations with your group and together build a snapshot of the state of technology in the average school today.

TEACHING WITH TECHNOLOGY: INTEGRATION IDEAS WEB QUEST

This chapter introduced you to the foundational theories and concepts necessary to make effective use of technology. Examine the links below to review some of the ways in which this knowledge affects classroom teachers.

ACTIVITY: After you explore the links that interest you, select the one learning theory with which you most agree. Complete a web search on the theory and on some classroom practices that exemplify the theory in action. Write a one-page summary of your web quest that includes (1) the theory you explored, (2) a summary of at least three classroom practices that show how that theory is applied, and (3) a description of how you will apply the theory in your own classroom.

Effects of Using Instructional Technology in Elementary and Secondary Schools

James Kulick conducted a review of eight meta-analyses on the effect of instructional technology in elementary and secondary schools. In this review, he examines how the use and effectiveness of technology integration have changed since earlier studies in the 1990s. He addresses critical questions including how technology affects academic performance, what effect it has on higher-order thinking, and what strategies result in effective technology application. To learn more about the fascinating study, visit **http://caret.iste.org/index.cfm?fuseaction=studySummary&studyid=1044.**

Standards in the Elementary Classroom

In *The Goal Is Excellence*, Luana Ellison describes how she successfully creates an engaging learning environment that remains focused on the standards her students must achieve. Far from teaching to the test, Ms. Ellison has found innovative ways to "weave student's interests and learning style needs with larger themes surrounding the individual standards." For more on teaching to standards without sacrificing innovation, visit **www.newhorizons.org/strategies/assess/ellison.htm.**

Multiple Intelligence in the Classroom

In this article, elementary teacher Bruce Campbell describes how he sets up learning centers in his classroom so that each center supports one of Gardner's identified intelligences. Using this approach, each day every student has an opportunity to work within the framework of his or her dominant intelligence. For specifics on how this innovative strategy was achieved, visit **www.newhorizons.org/strategies/mi/campbell3.htm.**

Addressing Diversity in Math and Science Education

In "An Interview with Sheila Tobias on Re-Thinking Teaching Math," Science Education World interviews author and educator Sheila Tobias as she explores how best to teach math and science to diverse students. Ms. Tobias discusses a broad range of topics, from teaching math and science to diverse learning to handling math phobia. For more on these educational concerns, visit **www.educationworld.com/a_curr/profdev026.shtml.**

Learning Styles

In *Your Students: No Two Are Alike*, middle school math teacher Brenda Dyck discusses how she helps her students discover their own learning strengths while developing a learner profile she can refer to. She provides links to online styles instruments that teachers can use to better target instruction to their students' learning needs. For more, visit **www.educationworld.com/a_curr/voice/voice061.shtml.**

Multiple Intelligences

Tapping into Multiple Intelligence is a free online teacher workshop, one of several offered by Concepts to Classrooms, that provides visitors with eight multimedia pages exploring multiple intelligence theory and its application to the classroom. To take the workshop and discover more about multiple intelligence, visit **www.thirteen.org/edonline/concept2class/mi/index.html.**

History of Educational Technology

The Association for Educational Communications and Technology offers an interactive history of educational technology in the twentieth century. Review each period of educational technology evolution and see historical photos of each. Exploring these web pages will add depth to your understanding of how educational technology has evolved and become a vital component of instruction. To learn more, visit **www.aect.org/About/History/.**

For these and many more *Integration Ideas* for understanding the role of technology in learning, visit the text web site at **www.ablongman.com/lever-duffy3e.**

Integration Ideas: The Learning Environment in the Primary Classroom

In *The Multi-Cultural Primary Classroom,* Jo Bertrand discusses the establishment of a multicultural environment in the primary-grade classroom by pointing out that children should recognize the cultural differences of their classmates and be encouraged to feel good about being in a richly diverse environment. She suggests using maps to help the children visualize the location of different countries and includes tips on how to help students identify where other children's families come from. She provides tips on how to create a classroom community that will engage all the children as participants, such as making the classroom language accessible to all the children through "say and do" demonstrations, playing the game known as Chinese whispers (also known as gossip and telephone) to teach greetings, and observing festivals from the various cultures represented in the student population. To read about the suggested activities, visit **http://www.teachingenglish.org.uk/print/4383.**

interchapter 2

The Evolution of Educational Technology

1600s

Quill Pens and Slates
Early one-room schoolhouses in the 1700s and 1800s used these materials to teach students how to write and cipher.

1700s

Primers
The New England Primer remained the basic school text for 100 years after its publication.

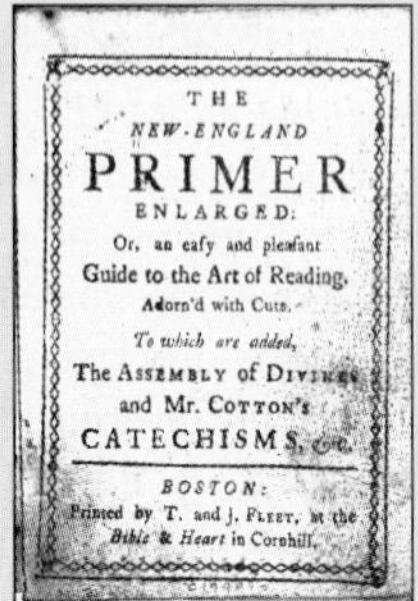

THE
NEW-ENGLAND
PRIMER
ENLARGED:
Or, an easy and pleasant Guide to the Art of Reading.
Adorn'd with Cuts.
To which are added,
The ASSEMBLY of DIVINES, and Mr. COTTON's CATECHISMS, &c.
BOSTON:
Printed by T. and J. FLEET, at the Bible & Heart in Cornhill.

Bettmann/Corbis

1826

Wall Charts
To save the cost of individual books, passages were sometimes printed in large letters and hung for all to see in Lancastrian schools.

Bettmann/Corbis

1855

Models
With the introduction of kindergarten in Wisconsin, models and materials were given to students to manipulate and to learn from.

Hulton Archive/Getty Images

1901

Manipulatives
Maria Montessori's kinesthetic approach offered a variety of manipulatives from which students could learn.

Jennie Woodcock Reflection/Corbis

1904

Educational Museums
The visual-education movement resulted in educational museums with abundant visual displays.

1910

Films
Edison declared after inventing motion pictures that books would soon be obsolete. Public schools in New York City implemented films for instruction for the first time.

Education as a Science
Edward Thorndike helped establish education as a science.

SOURCES: A Hypertext History of Instructional Design. Retrieved October 3, 2003, from **www.coe.uh.edu/courses/cuin6373/idhistory/idex.html**; P. Saettler. 1968. A history of instructional technology. New York: McGraw-Hill.

1914

Behaviorism Theory
John Watson helped establish behaviorism, which became one of the theoretical foundations for learning.

1923

AECT
The Association for Educational Communications and Technology was created to help improve instruction through technology.

1929

Radio
The Ohio "School of the Air" broadcast instruction to homes.

1933

Objectives in Education
Ralph Tyler at Ohio State University developed and refined procedures for writing objectives.

1940–1945

Instructional Technologists
With the role of technology in learning increasing, the need for expertise in both education and technology grew, and professional instructional technologists emerged.

Bettmann/Corbis

1945

Multiple Media Used by Military Armed Forces
Training used films, sound, graphics, models, and print to help prepare recruits for war.

1953

ITV
The University of Houston launches KUHT, the first noncommercial education station.

Bettmann/Corbis

1956

Bloom's Taxonomy
A team led by Benjamin Bloom identified and articulated levels of cognition.

1957

Programmed Instruction
Programmed instruction materials based on Skinner's behaviorism were used at the Mystic School in Winchester, Massachusetts.

The Evolution of Educational Technology *(continued)*

1965

Instructional Design System
Robert Gagné introduced a model for a systems approach to designing instruction.

1967

PBS and NER
The Public Broadcasting Act established the Public Broadcasting Service and National Educational Radio.

1970

Cognitive Approach
Cognitivists including Ausubel, Bruner, Gagné, and others dominated thinking about learning.

1977

Personal Computers
The first microcomputer, the Apple, was created by Steve Wozniak and Steve Jobs.

Bettmann/Corbis

1980s

CAI
Computer-assisted instruction on personal computers reached its peak of popularity.

1990s

Constructivist Approach
The influence of Dewey, Piaget, Vygotsky, and others led to the emergence of the constructivist view of learning.

Computer-Based Technologies
Video discs, CD-ROMs, multimedia, digital presentations, interactive video, teleconferencing, compressed video, and the Internet combined to greatly increase the technologies available to enhance teaching and learning.

Virtual Reality
Digital representations of a given reality let teacher and student "experience" it; e.g., the inside of a volcano erupting.

Digital Assistants
Intelligent agents help you interact with your equipment and cyberspace.

1991

World Wide Web
The Internet became accessible to all with the creation of the Web by Tim Berners-Lee.

2003

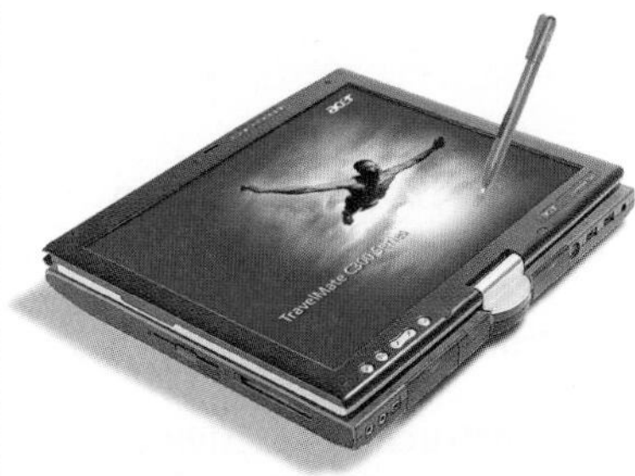

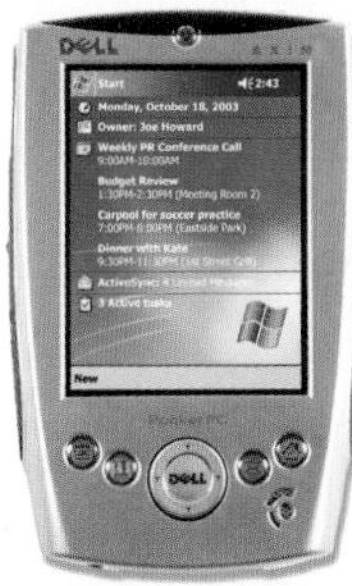

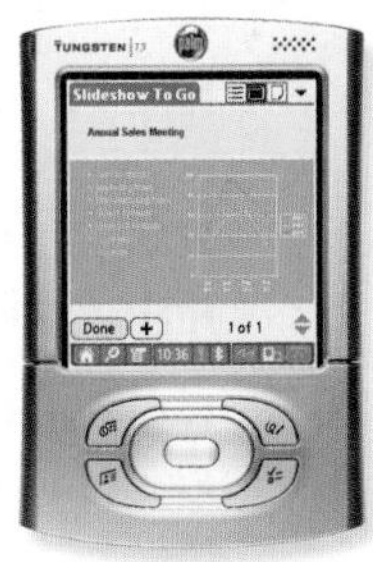

Mobile Devices
Smart phones, netbooks, and hand-held PCs joined with wireless networking to make mobile computing commonplace everywhere, including in the classroom.

2008 and beyond

Online Life
The Internet expands to include the Web 2.0, featuring social networking, audio and video streaming and options, for interaction leading to instruction anytime, anywhere.

The Grid
Using distributed computing technology, the Grid will make it possible to dynamically pool and share computer resources, making unprecedented computing power available to everyone on the Grid.

CHAPTER 3

Designing and Planning Technology-Enhanced Instruction

Frank Siteman

CHAPTER OVERVIEW

This chapter addresses these ISTE National Educational Technology Standards:
- NETS•T Standard 1
- NETS•T Standard 2

- **Planning for Effective Instruction**
- **Using an Instructional Planning Method**
- **The Dynamic Instructional Design Model**
- **Using the DID Model to Plan Instruction**
- **Creating Lesson Plans from the DID Model**
- **Instructional Action Planning**
- **The Instructional Action Planner: Getting Ready to Teach**
- **Linking Planning, Teaching, Learning, and Technology**

In Chapter 3, you will begin your exploration of the way in which effective teachers design and plan instruction enhanced and supported by technology. In Chapter 2, you learned a great deal about the teaching and learning process. Chapter 3 will help you discover how to apply what you have learned as you plan and carry out effective instruction.

In this chapter, you will examine learning environments, beginning with the physical aspects of the environment such as classroom layout and facilities. You will then have the opportunity to explore the less tangible, more critical aspects of the environment: the instructional design that drives instruction and the teaching strategies that might be incorporated in the design. You will then explore the planning of day-to-day lessons for use in your classroom. Finally, you will learn to create an instructional action plan to help ensure that your lessons are implemented just as you planned them.

In Chapter 3, you will:

- Examine classroom facilities and their impact on the teaching and learning process
- Explore instructional design and how design affects instruction
- Examine performance objectives and their role in targeting learning outcomes
- Review the instructional design process and the pedagogical cycle incorporated therein
- Examine the process of lesson planning
- Review the components of an instructional action plan and examine its role in the teaching and learning process
- Explore the role of planning in the selection and implementation of instructional technology

Planning for Effective Instruction

Go to the *Assignments and Activities* section of Chapter 3 in MyEducationKit and complete the web activity entitled *Planning for Instruction*.

The foundation in learning theory and educational technology you gained from Chapter 2 can now be used to build an approach for the creation of effective instruction. Instruction can be broadly defined to include all of the components of teaching and learning from the instructional environment to the actions taken by both teacher and students to evaluating instructional success. To be effective in creating effective instruction, a teacher must carefully consider everything that needs to occur in the classroom and during the lesson. Questions that need to be answered through reflection and planning include the following:

- What are my students like, and what special needs do they have that should be addressed via instruction?
- What exactly should my students to be able to do when I am done with the instruction?
- What do I need to do in my classroom to get everything ready for instruction?
- What strategies am I going to use to teach the content?
- What should I have my students do to learn the target skills and content?
- What technologies do I need to support instruction?
- How will I know whether instruction was successful, and what is the process for changing it if it was not?

These questions offer a framework for the systematic process that will lead to the creation of effective instruction. These questions are the core of the planning process engaged in by every effective teacher. Initially, a carefully articulated planning process seems long and cumbersome. But ultimately and with years of practice, it becomes inherent in the way a teacher approaches instruction. The essential skill of instructional planning eventually becomes a way of thinking in the classroom. This chapter introduces you to systematic instructional planning; subsequent chapters provide you with the technology tools to enhance your plans. This approach allows instruction to drive technology selection and implementation, which in turn keeps the focus on teaching and learning.

Using an Instructional Planning System

D-P-A is a systematic approach to effective instruction.

Effective instruction is instruction that has been thoroughly thought out and articulated by a skillful and creative educator. To ensure that every moment of a learner's educational time is productive, an educator must envision all aspects of instruction, from what will be covered in an instructional unit to what needs to be done each day. The notion of a carefully planned, step-by-step process to design, create, evaluate, and revise instruction is called a **systems approach** to instruction. In this chapter, you will explore a comprehensive three-part system that will help you maximize the quality of your teaching. The system, called the **design-plan-act! (D-P-A) system**, includes the following three planning processes (see Figure 3.1):

1. Design: Designing the instructional unit
2. Plan: Articulating specific daily lesson plans within the unit
3. Act: Developing an instructional action plan for each day of instruction

Together, these three system elements will help you effectively plan and implement all aspects of effective instruction. The design phase of the D-P-A system helps you to envision your unit of instruction in its entirety. During this phase, you determine what must be done to accomplish all of the learning goals of the unit and how each day of instruction will fit with the others to do this. You also identify, in broad strokes, each step of the planning process that will be used to guide you through the unit. The planning phase addresses the daily lesson plans that will result from the design you have created. While your design organizes your multiday unit, the daily lesson plans articulate what needs to happen each day to carry out your design. Finally, for each day of the daily lesson plan, it is a good idea to organize the action you must take for the lesson to run smoothly. That is the purpose of the action plan: to be a detailed organizer for each lesson.

The Design Phase

At this most comprehensive and strategic level of the instructional planning system, the educator envisions the delivery of the targeted curriculum as a complete instructional unit. The unit includes a clearly identified series of competencies that the students will achieve as the unit is presented. The instructional design articulates all of the broad steps that must be taken to ensure that the intended instruction occurs. Typically, an **instructional design model,** a design template, is used to help educators in the first phase of the system to envision the unit of instruction. Using such a model as a foundation will result in coordinated and focused daily lesson plans and subsequent instructional action plans.

FIGURE 3.1

The Design-Plan-Act! (D-P-A) System

D-P-A's three system components work together to create effective instruction.

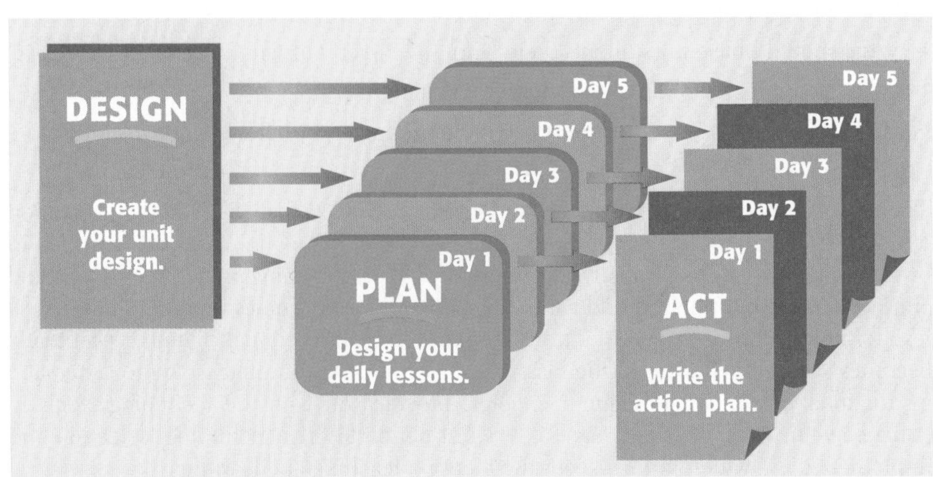

The instructional design model must be flexible and adaptable to accommodate continual changes in strategies to meet learner needs. To that end, on the following pages, the **dynamic instructional design (DID) model** is presented. It will serve as the basis for designing technology-rich instruction and as a practical guide as you conceptualize how you will create an effective unit. The DID model will serve as the foundation for the creation of lesson planners and instructional action planners to effectively and successfully develop instruction for each day.

Design identifies overall goals and the steps to achieve them.

The Plan Phase

The second phase of the D-P-A system is daily lesson planning. During this phase, the unit design is broken down into daily lesson plans, which detail what needs to be done each day. During this phase, the teacher considers which components of the design should be presented during each day of instruction and describes precisely how the lesson will unfold. For many experienced teachers who have already learned to think about instruction systematically, it is this phase that is typically noted in lesson plan books.

The Act Phase

Once daily lesson plans have been articulated, a teacher needs to remember the many small but critical details necessary for instruction. These many details need to be noted and acted on so that instruction can move forward smoothly and without incident. This is the action phase of planning. For an experienced teacher, this phase may be as informal as jotting down a to-do list. In completing a systematic plan, however, this phase is fully articulated to be sure no critical element is forgotten.

ISTE Standard

Learning about instructional Planning will help you address **NETS•T STANDARD 2:**

DESIGN AND DEVELOP DIGITAL-AGE LEARNING EXPERIENCES AND ASSESSMENTS Teachers design, develop, and evaluate authentic learning experiences and assessments incorporating contemporary tools and resources to maximize content learning in context and to develop the knowledge, skills, and attitudes identified in the NETS•S.

D-P-A Systematic Planning

In a systematic instructional design process, then, the teacher considers instruction as a series of planning steps from the broadest components of the sequence to the most detailed. A unit may cover multiple weeks, so the design model takes into account all necessary steps. On a day-to-day basis, daily lesson plans for each of the days the unit will be taught offer the teacher guidelines as to what must be completed each day to meet unit goals. In the final planning step, the action plan, each detail needed for successful daily instruction to occur is articulated. Together, reflecting on and planning each phase result in smoothly executed, comprehensive, and effective instruction.

The Dynamic Instructional Design Model

The DID model includes all of the critical elements necessary to design effective instruction. Every step of the model is crucial to the process and must be considered carefully. Just as the architectural process must begin with an understanding of the qualities of the land on which a building will be built and must proceed through discussions of the purpose and use of the building before any plans are made, so too must educators think broadly and strategically about their intended instruction.

The dynamic instructional design (DID) model is a flexible system for designing instruction.

A number of instructional design systems models are available for educators to follow. The most pervasive and influential of these is the systems model originally developed by **Robert Gagné.** Known for the application of systems thinking to instructional design, Gagné is perhaps the leading figure in instructional design systems. He was the first to promote and develop a comprehensive systems view of instructional design, that is, a system of steps that provide a logical systematic foundation for designing instruction. His definitive work is the foundation for many subsequent models.

Gagné's model and the others that were developed as a result are the foundation for today's instructional systems. The DID model, which builds on these definitive systems models, differs primarily in its emphasis on a dynamic design, which is necessary to represent the capability for continuous adjustment and change. The instructional design must be flexible enough to embrace and use data provided by ongoing feedback from learners. The DID model is specifically designed to ensure that responsiveness while maintaining the logical sequencing of the design process.

Feedback is the return of information regarding the success of each step.

The DID model is therefore built around a continuous internal and external **feedback loop** to ensure that each step of the process is functioning at its maximum effectiveness. Internal feedback loops occur within each step of the process. External loops are built between all steps of the process. Continual self-examination, feedback, and correction are built into the model to emphasize its flexibility while maintaining its system integrity. Although each step of the process includes the classic elements articulated initially by Gagné, the DID model is designed to help educators envision instruction as a changing and dynamic process.

Teachers who embrace a systems approach such as the D-P-A system better understand and are better able to envision the instructional big picture. They start with a conception of all the instructional elements necessary for teaching an instructional unit. From this strategic beginning, they can then narrow and refocus their efforts on daily lesson planning, through which they can specify the instructional events on a day-to-day basis. Finally, they reach the pragmatic stage, during which they articulate an instructional action plan or to-do list for making the instructional events flow flawlessly. The DID model is the first step in this process: the design step.

Formative feedback occurs while the learning event is in progress.

As you review the DID model illustrated in Figure 3.2, note that a formative feedback process is a component of each step. **Formative feedback** occurs during an event or process. Formative feedback ensures a way to facilitate the continuous flow of information as a system is implemented so that corrections and adjustments can be made while the process unfolds. The DID model includes a formative feedback loop during every step of the process

FIGURE 3.2

The Dynamic Instructional Design (DID) Model

The DID model emphasizes flexibility and responsiveness in the instructional design process.

so that feedback can be gathered and midcourse corrections can be made. In implementation of the model, this would mean that the design includes strategies to respond quickly to feedback during implementation. Thus, each step is dynamic and flexible; that is, each step remains a work in process throughout and after the design phase.

Additionally, summative feedback is built into the DID model. **Summative feedback** is returned at the end of a process. In the DID model, the summative feedback loop can return information to help revise each step of the process once the entire process is completed. Because formative feedback is continuous throughout all steps of the process, the summative feedback loop serves as a final check once all steps are completed.

Summative feedback occurs at the conclusion of the learning event.

The feedback loops of the DID model encourage you to create a dynamic instructional process that remains responsive even as you are actively engaged in planning and implementing the instruction. In this model, you are encouraged to think about how you intend to continuously correct and improve each step in response to your students. Such a continuous improvement process is at the core of high-quality instruction. Table 3.1 on page 54 shows how formative feedback and summative feedback are used at each step in the DID model. Let's examine how each step of the model contributes to the design phase.

Step 1: Know the Learners

To begin the process of designing a unit of instruction, you must first have a clear picture of those for whom the instruction is being created. Instruction must be adjusted to ensure that it is the most appropriate sequence of events for the target audience. To successfully focus instruction, you must begin by carefully reviewing the characteristics of your learners. To do so, you should ask yourself a number of questions about your learners. You may also have additional questions based on the instructional setting in which you are teaching. A few of the most common questions that lead to careful examination of your learners are the following:

- What are their developmental stages, both physically and cognitively?
- What in their cultural or language backgrounds may affect how instruction is received?
- What are their incoming skills and knowledge base relative to the intended instruction?
- What are their individual characteristics, such as learning styles, cognitive styles, and types of intelligence?
- As a group, how are the learners the same, and how are they different?
- How might these similarities or differences affect the design of the intended instruction?

Each of these questions must be answered to establish a clear picture of the learners for whom you are designing instruction. Your answers may be informal, that is, based simply on your observations of your students or discussions with them, or your answers may be formal, that is, derived from objective data. Such data may be from student records kept by your school or gathered by you using assessment tools such as the learning style inventories you learned about in Chapter 2. The more information you gather, whether formal or informal, the more likely it is that your instruction will be targeted correctly to meet the needs of your students.

Use formal and informal methods to profile students.

Step 2: State Your Objectives

Objectives are statements of what will be achieved as a result of the instruction you are designing. **Performance objectives** are objectives that specify what the learner will be able to do when the instructional event concludes. To keep your instructional design focused, it is critical that you take the time to state your instructional objectives in terms of student performance so that all subsequent steps will be tightly targeted on student outcomes.

Performance objectives detail expected competencies.

TABLE 3.1 DID Formative and Summative Feedback Loops

DID STEP	FORMATIVE FEEDBACK QUESTIONS Questions to Ask during the Design Process	SUMMATIVE FEEDBACK QUESTIONS Questions to Ask at the End of the Design Process
1. KNOW THE LEARNERS.	• Am I responding to all learning styles? • Am I accurately depicting the students' developmental stages? • Am I correctly assessing student skill levels?	Did the design successfully meet the needs of the learners?
2. STATE YOUR OBJECTIVES.	• Are my objectives targeting the performances I intended? • Are my objectives stated in a format that makes it possible to accurately measure performance? • Do my objectives include multiple levels of critical thinking?	Did my objectives accurately capture, in performance terms, the essence of the content the students needed to learn?
3. ESTABLISH THE LEARNING ENVIRONMENT.	• Does the physical space I am planning offer sufficient diversity to meet learner needs? • Is the environment nurturing and secure for all students? • Does the class management system promote positive and productive interaction? • Am I planning student and teacher exchanges that support and enhance learning?	Was the learning environment that I established effective in promoting learning?
4. IDENTIFY TEACHING AND LEARNING STRATEGIES.	• Am I addressing all of the steps of the pedagogical cycle? • Does each step make sense in terms of the cycle and the student learning it is intended to promote? • Am I including sufficiently varied teaching strategies and learning activities to meet the needs of my diverse students?	Are the teaching and learning strategies sufficient for and effective in meeting the objectives I identified?
5. IDENTIFY AND SELECT TECHNOLOGIES.	• Are the technologies I have selected appropriate to the content and pedagogy? • Am I selecting a variety of technologies that will meet the diversity of learning styles? • Are the technologies and support materials readily available?	Were the technologies I selected successful in supporting the targeted teaching and learning?
6. PERFORM A SUMMATIVE EVALUATION.	• Am I identifying a method of assessment that will measure achievement of objectives? • Is the data to be gathered from the assessment useful to determine necessary revisions? • Are the evaluation techniques valid and reliable with reference to the design?	Does the summative evaluation provide the data I need to determine whether the objectives were achieved? Was the data sufficient for effective revision?

Performance objectives typically are concise single sentences that include a stem plus three key components: targeted student performance, a description of the method for assessing the intended performance, and a criterion for measuring success. Let's examine a performance objective for a grammar unit in a middle school language arts class:

Objective: The student will be able to identify, with 95 percent accuracy, the subject and the verb in sentences contributed by peers and written on the board.

- *Stem:* The student will be able to
- *Target performance:* identify the subject and verb
- *Assessment method:* in sentences contributed by peers and written on the board
- *Criterion for success:* with 95 percent accuracy.

Michael Newman/PhotoEdit

To teach effectively, you must know and address the diverse characteristics of your students.

Notice that in this objective, the critical factor is the performance expected of the *student* as a result of the anticipated instruction, not the performance of the teacher. In our example, the student is going to be able to perform a measurable action (*identify* subject and verb). Furthermore, the objective indicates the method that will be used to assess performance. Again in our example, success in identifying the target concepts will be measured by the student's correctly identifying the subject and verb in sentences contributed by peers and written on the board. Finally, the criterion that indicates success in achieving that objective is articulated: performing the action correctly 95 percent of the time. In our example, a student who mistakes the subject and verb 5 percent of the time would still be considered to have sufficiently achieved the objective. Objectives written in this format leave no doubt about what performance is expected of the student. This, in turn, leaves no doubt about what the teacher needs to teach for the designated outcomes to occur. Figure 3.3 illustrates another performance objective.

This focus on student outcomes is the purpose of fully articulated performance objectives. These objectives not only detail precisely what the student is supposed to learn and how such learning is to be measured, they also require that

HANDSON LEARNING

Instructional planning is required at every level of education from kindergarten through college level. Many tools and templates have been developed to help teachers plan. Whether a formal instructional design model is required or a more concise daily lesson plan is used, every teacher can find a template that makes sense to him or her.

Investigate your options by completing a web search with the key words *lesson plan template*. From the results of your search, explore at least three different types of templates. Compare the steps of each of the templates you review to the D-P-A templates. Describe how they differ and how they are the same. What did you like best about each?

FIGURE 3.3

The Components of a Performance Objective

The student will be able to	identify latitude and longitude lines	on a map	with 100% accuracy.
STEM	TARGET PERFORMANCE	ASSESSMENT METHOD	CRITERION FOR SUCCESS

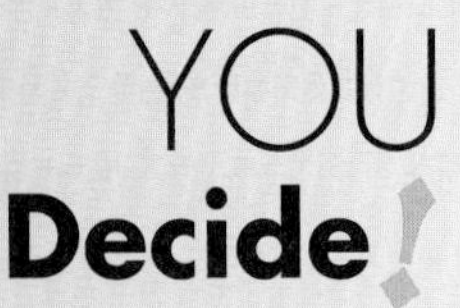

Planning can be a cumbersome process. It takes time to think through exactly what you want your students to be able to do when you are done teaching. It takes a great deal of thought to consider all aspects of content that you want to include in the unit. It takes time to research what other teachers have done to see whether you are including the most innovative ideas and the best technology available. It takes creativity to consider how the content can be best delivered in a manner that meets the needs of all of your learners. Is it worth the time and effort to create comprehensive plans?

YES! Teaching isn't an easy profession. It takes time, effort, and dedication to create lessons that really work. Everyone has been in a class where the teacher seemed to be unprepared. The instruction came off as disjointed and confusing. It wasted everyone's time. But when a teacher comes to class with a clear idea of what he or she wants to accomplish, a good plan as to how to teach the content, and activities that help students to learn the content, that teacher makes instructional time worthwhile. It may be hard, but planning is essential.

NO! Teaching just has too many requirements to make it possible to write out detailed lesson plans. Between all of the administrative tasks, the paperwork, and grading, planning just can't be done at the level everyone seems to expect. Something has to give. Thinking about what you want to do for a lesson and jotting down brief notes in a lesson plan book are enough. Writing down objectives, strategies, and assessments and relating it all to standards are just more than can be reasonably expected.

Which view do you agree with? YOU DECIDE!

teachers stay centered on outcomes in their teaching. Generic objectives such as "The student will have an understanding of grammar" do little to assist the teacher in deciding what and how to teach. Furthermore, it is difficult to accurately measure something as broad as "understanding." Such overly broad objectives help neither teacher nor student to engage in a meaningful exchange and do little to direct what needs to happen in the teaching-learning process.

Use action verbs to describe expected performance.

Another role of performance objectives is to ensure that the teaching and learning experience includes a full range of cognitive levels, from simple recall of facts to higher-end critical thinking. Writing down performance objectives helps to identify exactly which skills and related cognition the teacher is targeting. If all objectives are recall objectives, that is, their outcome is the memorization of facts, it is clear before instruction begins that critical thinking and higher cognitive skills are being ignored. This is a significant loss in terms of student growth, although it is admittedly sometimes easier for a teacher to plan when the goal is to achieve lower-level objectives. However, the benefit to learners of engaging in critical thinking far outweighs the instructional costs involved in creating them.

Several theorists have developed methods for categorizing differences in thinking skills. One of the most prominent was developed in 1956 by a group of researchers led by **Benjamin Bloom.** The categories of cognition that resulted from their efforts have come to be called **Bloom's taxonomy.** Bloom's taxonomy (Bloom, 1956) provides a very useful delineation of the levels of thinking that should be included in creating objectives. These levels do not interfere with the knowledge outcomes of the objectives. Instead, they help you identify the level of thinking desired from the learner with regard to that knowledge.

Bloom's taxonomy describes levels of cognition. A taxonomy is a system of levels to better organize a concept.

Bloom's taxonomy includes six levels of cognition ranging from recall of knowledge to evaluation of knowledge (see Figure 3.4 on page 57). Each of these levels is described in the following list, along with action verbs that might be used in objectives that are aimed at that level of thinking:

FIGURE 3.4

Bloom's Taxonomy and Action Verbs

Use Bloom's taxonomy to step up to higher levels of thinking.

Loosely adapted from Bloom's wheel at www.vacadsci.org/teaching/bwheel.htm.

- *Knowledge:* This level of cognition includes memorizing, recognizing, or recalling factual information. Objectives at the knowledge level would include verbs such as *list, identify, name, recite, state,* and *define* with reference to the material.
- *Comprehension:* At this level of cognition, the emphasis is on organizing, describing, and interpreting concepts. Verbs used in objectives at the comprehension level might include *explain, illustrate, summarize, restate, paraphrase,* and *defend* concepts or information. You can see that the thinking required at this level extends beyond rote learning.
- *Application:* The application level of cognition requires that the student apply the information presented, solve problems with it, and find new ways of using it. Objective verbs that would represent outcomes at this level of thinking would include *apply, classify, demonstrate, discover, predict, show, solve,* and *utilize.*
- *Analysis:* This level of the taxonomy requires higher-level thinking skills such as finding underlying structures, separating the whole into its components, identifying motives, and recognizing hidden meanings. Verbs used in objectives at this level might include *analyze, ascertain, diagram, differentiate, discriminate, examine, determine, investigate, construct,* and *contrast.*
- *Synthesis:* The synthesis level raises desired outcomes to significantly higher levels of cognition. At this level, the student is expected to create an original product based on the knowledge acquired, combine the ideas presented into a new whole, or relate knowledge from several areas into a consistent concept. Action verbs in objectives at the synthesis level would include *combine, compile, create, design, develop, expand, integrate, extend, originate, synthesize,* and *formulate.*
- *Evaluation:* The highest level of cognition in Bloom's taxonomy is the evaluation level. At this level, the learner is expected to make thoughtful value decisions with reference to the knowledge; resolve differences and controversy; and develop personal opinions, judgments, and decisions. Objective verbs at this level would include *assess, critique, judge, appraise, evaluate, weigh,* and *recommend.*

As you can see from the taxonomy, each level ratchets up the cognition level required for successful achievement of the objective. Outcomes at the highest levels require significant levels of critical thinking. At the lowest level, knowledge, simple memorization is all that is required. However, after examining Table 3.2, you will see that the lower levels are a necessary prerequisite as you move up the taxonomy. One must know the facts to comprehend, apply, analyze, synthesize, or evaluate them. Although some performance objectives may reasonably target the lowest levels, too often a majority of objectives aim only at these levels. Awareness and application of Bloom's taxonomy in writing performance objectives will help you to create instruction that encourages and emphasizes a broad range of thinking skills for your students.

When creating objectives, in addition to clearly identifying intended student performance and levels of critical thinking targeted, it is also necessary to determine how your objectives align with the curriculum standards of your state and school system. As you learned in Chapter 1, standards are developed to help teachers and students stay consistent nationally, statewide, and locally in their teaching and learning goals. Each state develops standards that align with national goals, and each district develops curriculum standards consistent with the state standards to ensure that every student in the state receives equal and appropriate instruction. As each teacher develops objectives, then, the district and state standards must be kept in mind as the guidepost for instruction. Curriculum standards determine the student outcomes that will result from a unit of instruction. So in developing performance objectives for that unit, it is necessary that they be in line with the standard they are intended to achieve.

To accomplish this alignment with standards, different states and districts use somewhat different approaches. A common practice is to ask teachers to create objectives with a notation that references the standards to be achieved. Therefore, when examining objectives, you may see a parenthetical comment with abbreviations following the objectives. For example, for our sample objective in a school district in Florida, the following references might be required: "*The student will be able to identify the subject and verb in sentences contributed by peers and written on the board with 95% accuracy* (211–7.3)." In this example, the "2ll" refers to curriculum competency numbering system, with the 2 referring to second grade and the ll referring to the language arts section. The "7.3" reference relates to the third subitem under the seventh item in the list of numbered competencies.

The DID's formative feedback loop ensures performance objective validity.

TABLE 3.2 Bloom's Taxonomy and Performance Objectives

LEVEL	DESCRIPTION	PERFORMANCE OBJECTIVE
KNOWLEDGE	Student recalls or recognizes information, ideas, and principles in the approximate form in which they are learned.	On an unlabeled diagram, the student will be able to label the parts of the human eye with 85 percent accuracy.
COMPREHENSION	Student translates or comprehends information based on prior learning.	In an oral presentation, the student will be able to summarize the plot of *The Lion, the Witch, and the Wardrobe* mentioning at least five of the seven major events with 85 percent accuracy.
APPLICATION	Student selects, transfers, and uses data and principles to complete a problem or task with a minimum of direction.	On a test, the student will be able to solve word problems with two variables with 90 percent accuracy.
ANALYSIS	Student differentiates or examines the assumptions, hypotheses, evidence, or structure of a statement or question.	The student will be able to contrast the causes of the Korean War and the Vietnam War in an oral report with 80 percent accuracy.
SYNTHESIS	Student originates, integrates, and combines ideas into a product, plan, or proposal that is new to him or her.	The student will be able to design a science experiment that includes each step of the scientific method in a written activity with 90 percent accuracy.
EVALUATION	Student appraises, assesses, or critiques a work or works using specific standards or other criteria.	Using a rubric created by the students, the student will be able to critique sample media on the basis of five criteria with 90 percent accuracy.

Some districts may require that teachers reference state standards in a similar manner. Regardless of the system in place for standards referencing, teachers typically are required to note the state, district, and sometimes national competencies their objectives address. Since your target performance objectives drive your instruction and provide the foundation for all subsequent teaching and learning strategies, it is important to ensure that the intended instructional experience is aligned with similar experiences in other classrooms throughout the district and state. For that reason, the process of aligning to and stating standards is quickly becoming a mandatory component of planning.

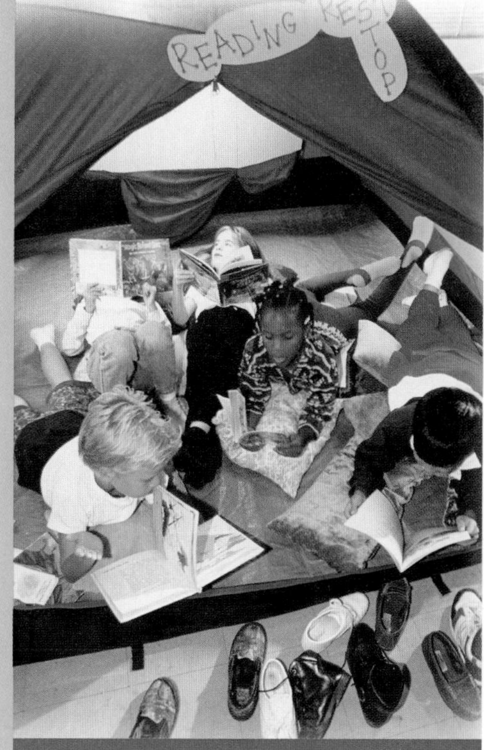

Bob Daemmrich/Getty

Alternative instructional spaces within a classroom meet diverse learner needs.

Step 3: Establish the Learning Environment

As you learned in Chapter 2, a **learning environment** includes all conditions, circumstances, and influences that affect the learner's development. Every aspect of the milieu in which teaching and learning take place is an element in the learning environment, from the physical surroundings to the instructional events that occur within those surroundings. So let us begin our exploration of the learning environment with an examination of how physical space affects learning.

The learning environment includes the space and facilities in which instruction occurs. The classroom or learning space itself, the student furniture and its arrangement in the instructional space, and the teaching facilities built into the classroom are all essential elements of the learning environment. Each can have a significant impact on the teaching-learning process. By adjusting these elements to be consistent with the students' learning styles and the educator's teaching style, the effectiveness of the instructional space can be maximized.

Rita and Kenneth Dunn have done extensive research on matching the physical environment to individual learning styles (Dunn and Dunn, 1992). Their learning styles research indicates that changes in lighting, seating, and other physical accommodations in the classroom can reduce distractions to the learning process by providing a sensory environment that accommodates individual preferences. They suggest that a teacher can readily improve the learning environment for students by making simple physical adjustments to the classroom. Such adjustments might include creating well-lit reading areas, arranging for areas of the classroom to be warmer or cooler than normal, establishing classroom sections in which students can work with a peer or a group, providing informal seating such as beanbags or a couch, and setting up quiet or screened study areas for individuals or pairs. These adjustments can be accomplished through creative use of the floor space and traditional furniture found in most classrooms.

To be effective in establishing the learning environment, you should first take inventory of the physical space in which learning occurs. The Learning Environment Rubric on page 60 will help you evaluate the learning space. It is important to provide, whenever possible, alternatives in terms of learners' sensory preferences. It might not be feasible to make all the adjustments you desire, but if you make every possible effort to become aware of and adjust your teaching and learning space, you will help to optimize the conditions for your students' learning. As always, the dynamic nature of the DID model requires that you remain vigilant in assessing the effectiveness of your arrangement of the physical space so you can continually monitor and adjust the learning environment.

Courtesy of Rita and Kenneth Dunn

Rita and Kenneth Dunn focused their research on articulating the elements that either stimulate or inhibit learning based upon a student's unique learning style.

Nonphysical aspects of the learning environment include the general academic climate of the classroom, the dominant attitudes of learners and the instructor, and the quality of instructional organization provided by effective planning. The general climate of the classroom

Learning Environment **Rubric**

HARDWARE:
DESCRIPTION:
VENDOR: **COST:**
NOTES ON USE:

Using the criteria below, evaluate the effectiveness of the learning environment across each dimension. Highlight the box that best reflects the learning space with reference to the evaluation dimension. Effective learning environments are those that score 4 or higher in most dimensions.

EVALUATION CRITERIA

DIMENSION	1 Poor	2 Below Average	3 Average	4 Above Average	5 Excellent
PHYSICAL SPACE	Space is not arranged in an orderly manner and does not promote active learning and positive interaction.	Space is arranged neatly and safely but does not address individual learner needs.	Space is adjusted to the learning style of some but not all learners. Space arrangement promotes safety and some interaction.	Space meets the needs of most learners. Arrangement clearly promotes safety and positive interaction.	Space has been maximally adjusted to meet learner diversity. Space arrangement promotes interactivity, active learning, and positive interaction.
CLASSROOM CLIMATE	Climate is not flexible and responsive to learners. Climate promotes strong competitiveness and does not sufficiently foster cooperation or active learning.	Climate is somewhat flexible to learners. Learner is somewhat nurtured. Competitiveness exceeds cooperation. Active learning is insufficiently emphasized.	Climate is sufficiently flexible. Learner is nurtured to a moderate degree. Competitiveness is equaled by co-operation. Active learning is present.	Climate is flexible and meets most learners' needs. Minimal competitiveness is in evidence. Active learning is supported.	Classroom climate is flexible and meets diverse learners' needs. Cooperation is emphasized without loss of healthy competition. Active learning is emphasized.
ATTITUDES	Teacher attitude is usually cold and tends toward criticism and negativity. Learners typically demonstrate lack of self-confidence and self-criticism.	Teacher attitude is inconsistent and is often negative. Learners demonstrate inconsistency and ambivalence about their capability and self-worth.	Teacher attitude includes both positive and negative components. Learners demonstrate some confidence and self-worth.	Teacher attitude is mostly positive, friendly, and nurturing. Students appear confident and are usually risk takers.	Teacher attitude is consistently positive and encouraging. Teacher is always friendly and nurturing. Students demonstrate confidence and are clearly willing to be risk takers.

Go to the *Rubrics* section of Chapter 3 in MyEducationKit to download the *Learning Environment Rubric* for your use.

The learning environment includes all aspects of the environment that affect the learner.

A rubric is a detailed rating scale that can help you make objective evaluations and assessments.

refers to the tone of the psychological environment in which the teaching and learning process occurs. For effective instruction, learners need a safe, nurturing environment that offers opportunities to engage in learning and to excel. Awareness of the nature of the classroom climate will help you continually monitor and adjust it to maximize its support of teaching and learning.

Research has demonstrated that the attitudes of learners and of the teacher directly affect student performance (Dunn, 1999). Therefore, a component of designing instruction must be a deliberate effort to ensure that the learning environment fosters positive, confident attitudes on the part of the learner. Furthermore, it is important to ensure that the teacher's words and actions reflect a positive, caring attitude toward student achievement rather than a rigid focus on completing the planned lesson. To create an effective learning environment, it is important to stay aware of the steps you are taking to encourage attitudes that nurture learning rather than hinder it. The learning environment rubric will assist you in maintaining the level of awareness necessary to implement this step.

The final aspect of the nonphysical learning environment relates to the organization of the learning process itself. Well-conceived and clearly articulated instructional plans will create an organized, cohesive environment that fosters learning. Although this might seem to be common sense, all too often the pressures of time and tasks cause teachers to skip steps that are necessary for instructional success. Teachers who do not apply instructional design principles and who do not carry these through to sound lesson plans often find the learning environment turning chaotic and frustrating to both learner and teacher. Just as you would plan a house before you begin building, you must plan instruction before implementing it. Taking the time and energy to carefully plan instruction will make the teaching-learning process smooth and effective.

PEARSON **myeducationkit**

Go to the *Assignments and Activities* section of Chapter 3 in MyEducationKit and complete the video activity entitled *Authentic Learning with Technology*.

Teaching strategies are the methods carried out by the teacher. Learning strategies are activities carried out by students.

Step 4: Identify Teaching and Learning Strategies

At this point in the process, you have a high degree of awareness of your learners and their needs, your instructional objectives are clear and stated in terms of the desired student outcomes, and you have taken steps to achieve a positive learning environment. Now it is time to decide on your teaching strategies. **Teaching strategies** are the methods you will use to assist your students in achieving the objectives. As you learned in Chapter 2, both teacher and learner are involved in this process, so it is important to consider both the teaching strategies and the learning strategies you intend to employ. **Learning strategies** are the techniques and activities that you will require your students to engage in to master the content.

When identifying teaching strategies, it is important to clearly understand the difference between methods and the media that support them. **Methods** are the actions and activities that a teacher uses to communicate a concept. The methods you select should address the needs and learning styles of your students. They should offer alternative ways of explaining and exploring the information presented. The methods you select should keep your learners active and engaged in learning. Selecting the right teaching method for the type of knowledge presented is one of the most creative activities in which a teacher engages. The right method or combination of methods is one of the keys to achieving the lesson objectives.

Media are the technologies that are used to facilitate the method (see Table 3.3). For example, lecture may be the method, but the PowerPoint slides used by the teacher are the media used to support and enhance the teaching method selected. Various technologies and media are simply tools to enhance and facilitate instructional delivery. The teaching method that a creative teacher chooses is at the core of the teaching process. Instructional media and technologies play a supporting role, not a starring one. It is unfortunate that method and media are sometimes confused. This can lead to a teacher's use of a technology just because it is interesting or fun to use even when it does not directly support the intended method. The appropriate use of technology can add excitement and interest to many methods, but the key to its use is its role as a support to teaching methodology. This differentiation is the reason that the identification of teaching and learning strategies and the selection of instructional media are two distinct steps in the DID model.

ISTE Standard

Learning about teaching media and methods will help you address **NETS•T STANDARD 1:**

FACILITATE AND INSPIRE STUDENT LEARNING AND CREATIVITY Teachers use their knowledge of subject matter, teaching and learning, and technology to facilitate experiences that advance student learning, creativity, and innovation in both face-to-face and virtual environments.

Media are the technologies that support methods.

Step 5: Identify and Select Technologies

Instructional technologies are the tools used to enhance and support the teaching and learning strategies planned by the teacher. Once strategies have been mapped out, the tools needed to build the experience become evident. In this step of the instructional design process, you will identify the types of technological tools you need and select from those available to you.

As you will learn throughout this text, different technological tools have different uses, advantages, and disadvantages. Knowing what a technology can do in support of instruction, how to use it, and when it is appropriately used are the focus of this course. At this point, it is sufficient to differentiate between teaching and learning strategies and instructional

Support technologies enhance teaching and learning strategies.

TABLE 3.3 Methods versus Media

Methods are . . .
The strategies you use to achieve the lesson objective(s).

Methods include . . .
Teacher-Centered Strategies:

- Presentation
- Lecture
- Demonstration
- Class discussion

Student-Centered Strategies:

- Research projects
- Oral reports
- Cooperative learning groups
- Simulations
- Role playing
- Games

Media are . . .
All audio, visual, video, or digital resources you use to carry out your methods.

Media Include . . .

- Nonprojected visual media (posters, charts, bulletin boards, models, dioramas)
- Projected visuals (overhead transparencies, slides, computer displays)
- Audio media (tapes, CDs, MP3s, audio broadcasts, podcasts, and webcasts)
- Video media (videocassettes, DVDs, broadcasts, webcasts)
- Digital media (anything generated via computer technologies)

Materials and media differ in that materials are any supplies you or your students use during a lesson.

We select media and materials that support our methods to achieve our objectives.

technologies and to understand that technology's primary role is in support of the strategies you select for yourself and your students. The remainder of this text will familiarize you with the many technologies available to support teaching and learning, some of which are listed in Table 3.4.

Step 6: Summative Evaluation and Revision Plan

No design is ever perfect. However, a systematic process for continuous improvement will maximize quality. Therefore, it is important to end your instructional design with a plan to evaluate its effectiveness and to make appropriate revisions. The results from this summative evaluation can then be used to improve the design. Building this final evaluative step into the process ensures that a continuous improvement process will be in place and that the design will undergo positive revision with each use. Ultimately, through multiple implementations, evaluations, and revisions, your instructional design will come ever closer to your ideal.

Instructional design evaluation can take many forms. You can develop a success rubric (evaluation matrix) that can help you quantitatively self-evaluate the effectiveness of your lesson, or you may ask students to complete student feedback forms that

TABLE 3.4 Sampler of Support Technologies

AUDIO	VISUAL	DIGITAL
Cassette tapes	Videotapes	Computer hardware
Radio	DVDs	Productivity software
Music CD-ROMs	Overhead projector	Educational software
Talking books	Slide projector	Presentation software
Multimedia CDs	Other projection devices	Streaming audio
Recordings: Rhymes and reading	Models, real objects	Streaming video
Recordings: Musical instruments	Boards (bulletin, white, chalk, etc.)	Webcasts
MP3s	Digital-analog converter	Internet resources
Podcasts	Cartoons and drawings	Electronic whiteboards
	Document camera	

you create to determine their perception of the effectiveness of the various components of the design. Regardless of the method you use for the specific evaluation of the design components, the ultimate evaluation is in the students' performance. Your instructional objectives identify very specific criteria and methods for measuring student success. Your students' achievement of your instructional objectives, then, is the most significant evaluation of your design. Student achievement combined with results from other summative feedback efforts will give you the information you need to make future improvements to your design.

The summative evaluation is a final review of the entire process.

If you find that your design did not work as effectively as you intended, this step of the design can suggest remedial follow-up strategies. While summative feedback will ultimately cause you to revise the design for the next time it is used, you must also consider what you can do for the students currently being taught lesson derived from this design. Remediation strategies that could follow design implementation might include additional review activities, small-group instruction, or technology support. When you are articulating this step, while the design is fresh in your mind, it is appropriate to note possible remediation strategies should you need them.

Owen Franken/Corbis

Instructional designs that include a variety of educational technologies engage students in active learning.

Using the DID Model to Plan Instruction

Now that you have reviewed all of the steps of the DID model, you can begin to see how they create a blueprint for the teaching-learning process. The model helps you ask yourself the critical questions that will help you build high-quality instructional experience for both you and your students. Using the model is an important first step before the instructional event and a skill that needs to be acquired through practice. Table 3.5 summarizes each step of the DID model and provides a template with a series of prompts to help you build your own design.

You will also find downloadable templates of MyEducationKit. These templates are Word forms are formatted to fill in to help you build a Dynamic Instructional Design. You can find the DID Designer template in MyEducationKit.

TABLE 3.5 DID Model Template with Examples for a Unit on Money and Banking

STEP 1: KNOW THE LEARNERS	EXAMPLE ANALYSIS OF LEARNERS
Summarize the characteristics of the learners for whom you are creating the lesson. • What are the personal demographics (ethnicity, socioeconomic level, cultural background) that might affect learning? • What is the developmental stage of the student relative to the content? • What is the cognitive/learning style of each student? • What are the student's strengths in terms of multiple intelligences? • What group dynamics might help or hinder the teaching-learning process? • What are the student's entry skills with reference to the content? • What feedback can I use to ensure that I have accurately assessed the learner's skills?	The students are seventh-grade middle-class students with an ethnic mix of 43 percent white non-Hispanic, 26 percent Hispanic, and 31 percent black. Five students are ESL students with a good command of English but who occasionally need an assist with spelling. Twenty-three students are predominantly kinesthetic learners, six show some preference for visual learning, and two show a preference for auditory learning. The two auditory learners need a quiet area in which to work. The kinesthetic learners need multiple spaces in which to move and experience the content. The visual learners need screened areas for studying. One student has strong musical intelligence, ten have strong logical intelligence, and all have good verbal intelligence. The students are generally friendly, noncompetitive, and cooperative. Working in teams is a preferred strategy for all but three students. Entry skills for this unit include only a limited understanding of money and banking.
STEP 2: ARTICULATE OBJECTIVES	**SAMPLE OBJECTIVES**
State the behaviors that you expect your students to be able to demonstrate at the conclusion of the unit. • What performance will result from the unit? • What criteria for success are necessary to ensure mastery? • How will you assess the performance? • Have you included all the levels of Bloom's taxonomy that are appropriate for the content?	On a written test, the student will be able to explain the difference between a checking and a savings account with 90 percent accuracy. (VI 7.3, SS6.13) The student will be able to define interest with 95 percent accuracy on a written test. (VI 7.4, SS6.13) Given a matching exercise, the student will be able to distinguish between credit cards, debit cards, and ATM cards with 90 percent accuracy. (VI 7.1, SS6.15) The student will be able to contrast, with 85 percent accuracy, cash spending and credit spending on a written test. (VI 7.3, SS6.17) In a simulated checking account, the student will be able to deposit money, write checks, and balance the account with 95 percent accuracy.
STEP 3: ESTABLISH THE LEARNING ENVIRONMENT	**EXAMPLES**
Clarify what you plan to do to create an environment for this unit conducive to learning. • What changes need to be made to the classroom space? • What reinforcers are needed for this unit to motivate and build learning success? • How can learning be made active? • How should students be grouped for positive interaction? • How will I know the environment is effective?	For the duration of this unit, a corner of the classroom will become a banking center in which all transactions will take place. As closely as possible, the center will be arranged to emulate the lobby of a bank. A screened quiet corner with additional lighting will be set up adjacent to the banking center. Students will be rewarded with classroom currency for sound banking practices and for maintaining a balanced checkbook. Practices and checkbook will be evaluated weekly. Interim spot checks will be rewarded with game center time. Audit teams will be used to check each other's progress and to assist students who need peer support to complete the unit.
STEP 4: IDENTIFY TEACHING AND LEARNING STRATEGIES	**SAMPLE STRATEGIES FOR UNIT OBJECTIVES**
Given the objectives, describe the teaching and learning strategies that need to be implemented to meet the objectives. ***Teaching Strategies:*** • How will you introduce the unit? • How will you determine levels of entry skills with reference to the topics?	*Teaching Strategies:* To motivate learners, students will estimate and add up all the money a typical family spends in one month. Given the amount, they will be asked to consider the challenges of carrying that much cash for all necessary transactions. Checks and credit cards will be introduced as an alternative.

TABLE 3.5 Continued

STEP 4: IDENTIFY TEACHING AND LEARNING STRATEGIES (continued)	SAMPLE STRATEGIES FOR UNIT OBJECTIVES (continued)
• How will you present new information? • How will you reinforce the information presented? • What formative feedback will you use to ensure that students understand? • What summative feedback will you use to ensure that the objectives have been achieved?	To introduce banking, scanned bank forms and bank statements will be displayed. Students will be asked whether they can identify what the form is and how it is used. This unit's presentations explaining types of accounts and their uses will introduce content. Forms and statements will be reviewed. An explanation and sample calculation of interest will be demonstrated. The purpose of interest will be explained. Banking methods and access points will be presented. During the presentations, students will be called upon to complete an ongoing class diagram of the pros and cons of cash versus checks and credit as a formative review. The completed diagram will be used as a format to review key concepts at the conclusion of the presentations. As a summative review, students will be called upon to explain which method of transaction they prefer and why.
Learning Strategies: • What activities will you have students engage in to practice mastery of the content? • What activities will you provide that encourage active and engaged learning? • What experiences with reference to the content will ensure higher-order critical thinking skills? • What culminating review activities will be provided to ensure students have achieved the objectives?	*Learning Strategies:* Students will complete a personal version of the class diagram completed throughout the unit. Students will be asked to interview their parents to determine when cash versus credit is used in their household. They will then reflect on these uses based on the presentations in class. Students will complete a simple interest worksheet to determine the value of saving and using credit cards. Students will roll play teller–customer transactions after a banking guest speaker explains a day at the bank. Students will explore local bank web sites to determine services and interest rates. Using a rubric, they will evaluate which bank is best. Throughout the unit presentation, students will use model banking forms and will open and use practice accounts and practice credit cards to purchase goods from the class goodie box. Students will examine their spending habits, assets, and indebtedness at the end of the unit.
STEP 5: IDENTIFY AND SELECT TECHNOLOGIES	**EXAMPLES**
Given the strategies selected, identify the technologies that will be needed to support those strategies. • What technologies and related materials are needed for this unit? • Which technologies are required for each strategy? • What feedback will help me determine whether I have selected the best technology?	*Strategies for this unit will require the use of:* Scanner, printer, and copier to create bank center forms Overhead projector for guest speaker Computer connected to the Web LCD display for large-group projection of computer image
STEP 6: MAKE A SUMMATIVE EVALUATION	**EXAMPLES**
Describe the summative feedback process you will use to evaluate the design and how the results of the evaluation will be used to revise it. • How will you know whether the design is effective? • What assessment instruments are needed to measure effectiveness? • What should I do to remediate if the feedback shows that students did not achieve the objective? • What is the revision process once you have the results from your evaluation?	The design will be evaluated on the basis of student achievement of outcomes and student satisfaction. Evaluation will be completed through objective measures (tests and quizzes) and through performance assessment (observation of the performance of each student in the bank center). A summative student feedback form will assess student satisfaction with the unit and provide self-evaluation of mastery of the content.

Creating Lesson Plans from the DID Model

The DID model helps you to see the instructional big picture. With it, you can plan an effective instructional unit experience that carefully details each step of instruction. However, you might wonder how busy teachers manage to use instructional design models on a day-to-day basis. Essentially, even busy teachers know that to teach effectively, they must have formulated an instructional design, either fully articulated on paper or, at the very least, jotted down in brief notes to themselves. Just as artists plan the elements of their artwork or architects create blueprints for their building, teachers use instructional design to create their personal overview of instructional units. Over time and with experience, such planning becomes intuitive. Very experienced teachers can create complex designs with just a few notes on each of the steps, just as an experienced and talented artist paints a powerful picture with just a few brushstrokes. Beginning teachers need to practice their instructional design technique until it becomes a skill that is second nature to them. Whether you are a new teacher who must fully articulate the design or an experienced teacher who needs only a list of summary ideas, the systematic planning of instruction remains the foundation of effective teaching and learning.

Go to the *Templates* section of Chapter 3 in MyEducationKit and select the *DID Designer Template* to work through the process of creating lessons using the model.

From a day-to-day perspective, the instructional outline provided by the unit design is often too broad for pragmatic use. For daily lesson planning, you must narrow the focus to more specific topics or targeted daily objectives. An instructional design frequently includes content that will take several days of instruction to complete. The lesson plan focuses on what must be done each day in each class to implement the instructional activities outlined in the design. The relationship of the DID model to lesson plans is illustrated in Figure 3.5.

Lesson Planning

While the instructional design provides the overview of the planned unit of instruction, it is the lesson plan that provides a day-to-day snapshot of what will happen in the classroom. The design is the foundation for the daily lesson plans that will emerge from it. For that reason, the lesson plan follows the same general organization as the instructional design but offers more daily detail. Let's look now at the essential components of the lesson plan.

> The lesson plan provides a daily guide for teachers.

Readying the Learners

In the instructional design, you have already carefully analyzed the characteristics of your learners and their specific needs. When beginning the lesson plan, you should review learner characteristics and update any information about your students that has changed. Once you feel confident that you have a clear picture of those you will teach, it is then necessary to evaluate their current level of skills, called entry skills, with respect to the targeted lesson. Such evaluation can be done formally through a pretest or informally through select verbal questions. In the lesson plan, you should articulate how you plan to assess these skills.

Once you are clear on the learners' needs and on how you will determine their entry skills, you are ready to plan the lesson itself.

Targeting Specific Objectives

Your lesson plan may include one or more objectives from your DID model. Your lesson plan should identify the specific objectives the daily lesson is targeting. You should review the objectives in your design and then select one or two target objectives for that day's lesson plan. To maintain accountability, standards references should be carried over to and be included in the lesson plan's target objectives.

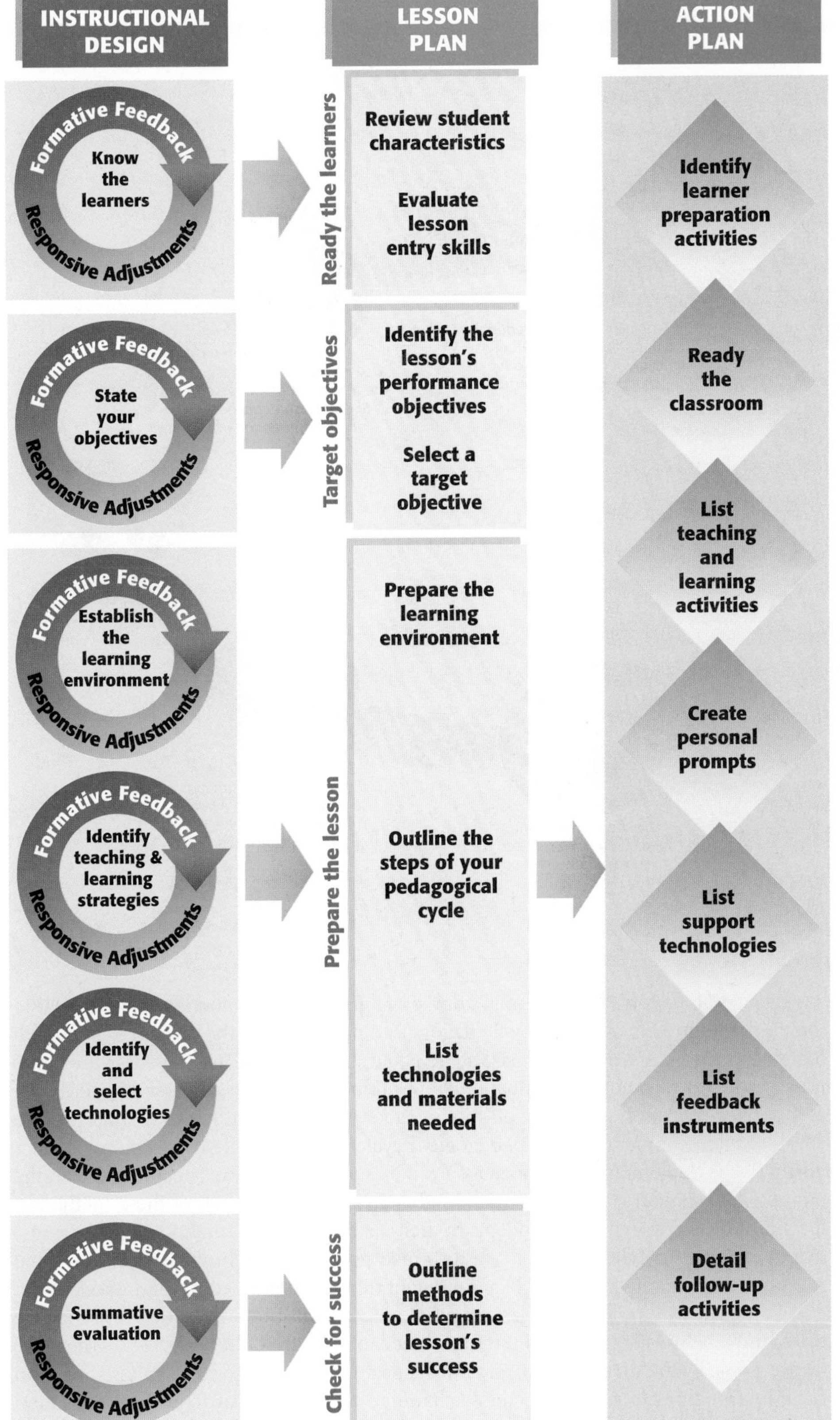

FIGURE 3.5

Relationship of Design-Plan-Act! Elements

All phases of the D-P-A system work together to create and implement high-quality instruction.

FIGURE 3.6

The Pedagogical Cycle

Each step in the cycle contributes to successful student learning.

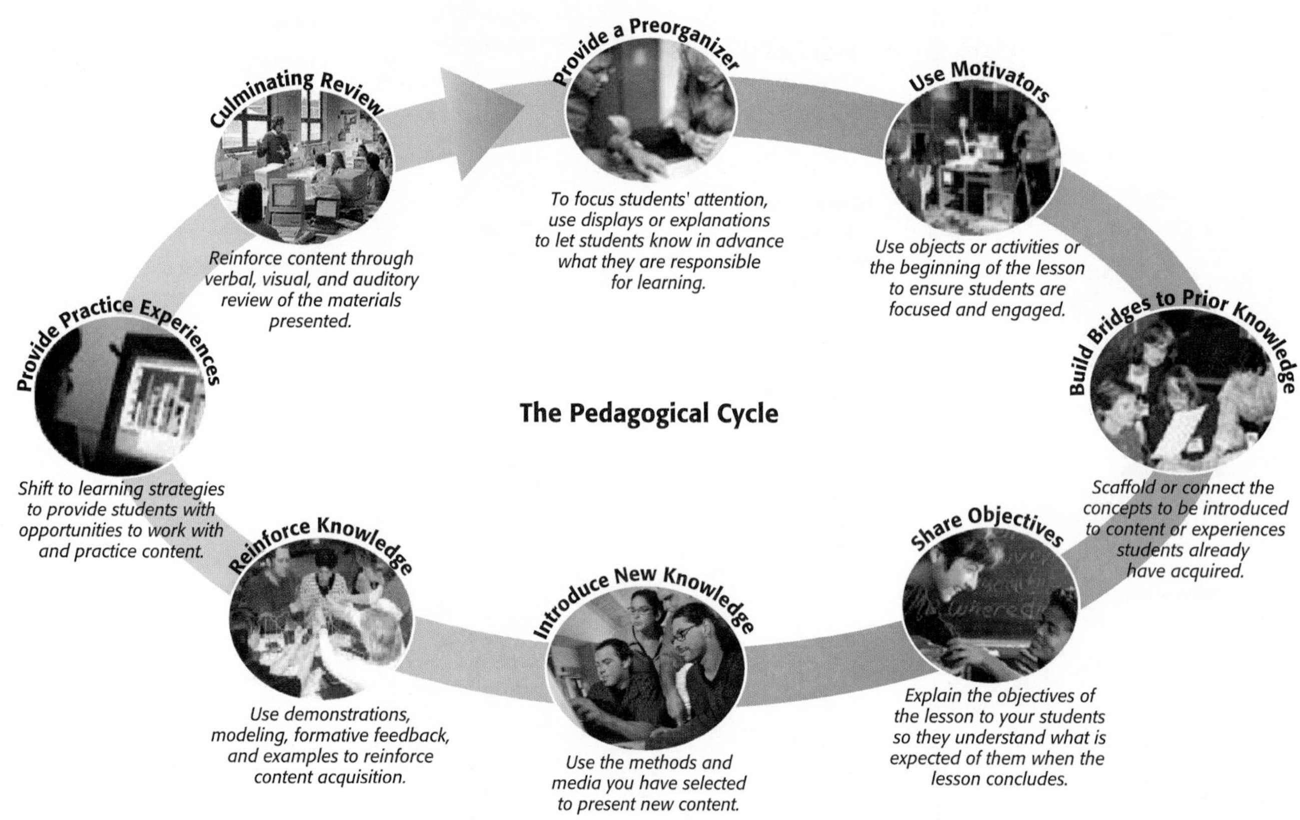

> The pedagogical cycle is a sequence of methods that promote effective instruction.

The combination and implementation of planned teaching and learning strategies is sometimes referred to as pedagogy. **Pedagogy** can be defined as the principles and methods of instruction. A series of events that are pedagogically sound are those that are appropriate to the learning environment and that result in the students' successful achievement of the stated objectives. One way of thinking about teaching and learning strategies is to consider them components of a **pedagogical cycle** that is played out again and again as instruction is implemented. The pedagogical cycle is a sequence of specific methods that promote and support effective instruction. Teachers engage in each of these methods as they introduce new skills and concepts in their classroom. Each methodology becomes a unique step within the cycle. These in turn incorporate the teaching and learning strategies to be implemented. This cycle and its eight steps are described in Figure 3.6.

The quantity of information provided in a lesson must be subdivided into manageable chunks before the information is introduced to students. Otherwise, the learners may be overcome by the sheer quantity of knowledge and may shut down or suffer confusion. Each information chunk may need to be handled in a distinct way to be effectively communicated to students. One cycle is required for the introduction of each chunk. Once the learners have absorbed it, the next chunk is introduced. Thus, the cycle is repeated again and again in the classroom. Planning what to do at each step of the cycle is the way you determine the teaching and learning strategies you intend to use. Examine carefully the pedagogical cycle illustrated in Figure 3.6 to help you complete the fourth step of the DID model.

Preparing the Lesson

You are now ready to write out the lesson you plan to implement. This component closely parallels and expands on its parent instructional design. The lesson plan should include each of the following sections, fully articulated and focused on the specific knowledge and/or performance detailed in the objective:

- *Prepare the classroom:* Describe what you need to do to create a physical environment that meets learners' needs and supports the lesson's teaching and learning strategies.
- *Summarize your plan using the pedagogical cycle steps:* Articulate exactly how you will carry out the lesson in terms of the teaching and learning strategies you intend to use. To ensure that all steps are included, use the pedagogical cycle as your guide.
- *Identify and list required technologies and materials:* Once you have planned each step in the cycle, you will need to identify and make a list of the technologies and materials you will need to carry out the strategies you have planned. This component of the lesson plan helps you organize the technologies and materials you will need.
- *Check for success:* You have your lesson ready and well planned out. The last step in the lesson planning process is the plan for summative feedback. In this section, you should identify the assessment strategies you will use to ensure that the lesson was successful. The assessment plan should provide you and your students with the feedback necessary to decide whether to go on to the next chunk of knowledge or stop and review or reinforce the current lesson.

PEARSON myeducationkit™

Go to the *Assignments and Activities* section of Chapter 3 in MyEducationKit and complete the web activity entitled *Lesson Planning Ideas.*

PEARSON myeducationkit™

Go to the *Assignments and Activities* section of Chapter 3 in MyEducationKit and complete the video activity entitled *Planning for Computer Use.*

The Lesson Planner: Practical Application of the DID Model

Just as the DID template provided you an assist in building an instructional design, the sample **lesson planner** (Table 3.7 on page 70) will help you create a fully articulated lesson plan. The lesson planner is the pragmatic product of the instructional design process. With it, you will be able to narrow your focus of the daily lesson to create powerful and effective instructional experiences. You will also find downloadable lesson plan templates on MyEducationKit. The Lesson Planner templates are Word forms are formatted to fill in to help you build a daily plans. You can find the Lesson Planner template in the *Template* section of MyEducationKit.

The lesson plan itself is followed by one last step in the instructional planning process. Although less formal than the previous steps in the process, this last step—action planning—is a necessary culmination to the process.

PEARSON myeducationkit™

Go to the *Template* section of Chapter 3 in MyEducationKit and select the *Lesson Planner Template* to work through the process of creating lessons using this template.

While many web sites offer a library of lesson plans, the Lesson Architect located at **www.ibinder.uwf.edu/steps/welcome.cfm** offers a tool that helps you to build an instructional unit, plan lessons, and align your lesson to appropriate standards. This online tool was designed for Florida teachers and therefore uses the Florida standards, but the planning tool is useful for all teachers. The Lesson Architect has been integrated with a lesson planning tutorial called STEPS that can help you learn to plan while creating your own plan. This site also provides a feature called ANDIE that guides you through each step of a lesson plan and provides you with questions you may not have considered. While not identical to the steps in the D-P-A system, like all systematic planners, the Lesson Architect is similar in its approach. Try it to experience online planning, to gain access to its database of plans, and to try aligning lessons to standards.

TABLE 3.6 The Lesson Planner Template with Examples for Money and Banking Unit

STEP 1: READY THE LEARNERS	EXAMPLES
Describe how you will prepare the students for the lesson. • Have any of the characteristics previously recognized changed? • Do any assumptions about learners need to be corrected? • What techniques will you use to gauge entry skills?	***Unit on Money and Banking*** Most student characteristics have not changed; however, an ESE (exceptional student education) student has now been mainstreamed into this class. This student will need additional support, so a copy of all work relating to this lesson must be given to the ESE team. A money and banking pretest will be created and administered at the start of the lesson. The same test will be given as a posttest to measure progress.
STEP 2: TARGET SPECIFIC OBJECTIVES	EXAMPLE
State the instructional design objective that will be addressed by this lesson. • To which of the design's objectives does this lesson relate? • How, if at all, does this lesson relate to the other design objectives?	This lesson targets design Objective 1: On a written test, the student will be able to explain the difference between a checking and a savings account with 90 percent accuracy. (VI 7.3, SS6.13)
STEP 3: PREPARE THE LESSON	EXAMPLES
Describe what you need to do to prepare for the lesson. • What needs to be done in the classroom to get it ready? • What must be accomplished for each step of the pedagogical cycle? How will it be accomplished? • What materials, media, and technologies are needed, and how will they be used? • What needs to be done to implement the intended assessments?	***Classroom Preparation*** The banking center will consist of a refrigerator box with a cutout as the teller window and a small table behind it with a desk organizer for managing forms and transactions. The rolling bookcase will serve as a forms counter. A table on the other side of the bookcase with a study carrel next to it will provide quiet space. ***Lesson Preparation Using the Pedagogical Cycle*** *Preorganizer:* Gather bank forms from a local bank, cover identifying numbers, enlarge and laminate the forms, and hang them on the front board. *Bridge to prior knowledge:* Use PowerPoint slides and play money to compare paper and coin equivalence. *Introduce new knowledge:* Show students a bank process PowerPoint presentation. Give a blank version to students to fill in as the information is presented. 1. Present and explain each banking form to students, filling out an enlarged version while they complete their paper versions. 2. Prepare a checklist of the steps in a customer–teller interaction for depositing, withdrawing, and checking balances to review with students. Give some example transactions and have students role-play the key steps. *Reinforce knowledge:* Open a class checking and savings account for the teacher, perform a series of correct and incorrect transactions, and let the class decide whether the teacher is doing it right or wrong. *Provide practice:* Have students open a checking and savings account and give them $100 in class "dollars." Have them deposit half in each of their accounts at the bank center, filling in the correct forms for the transactions. Then ask them to write a check for $10 to move this amount from checking to savings, filling in the correct forms. Ask students to use a check to make a $5 purchase from the class store. *Culminating review:* Have each student request a bank statement at the end of the activity. Review each for accuracy. When they have been done correctly, give each student a personal bankbook to store transactions and documents. ***Technology/Media Preparation*** Scan, print, and make copies of bank center forms. Enlarge one of each and laminate them. Prepare money equivalence PowerPoint slides. Create a bank process PowerPoint presentation. Locate a suitable bank web site to share. ***Assessment Preparation*** Prepare and administer a quiz asking students to fill in each type of form and to compute their account balances.

Instructional Action Planning

Instructional action planning helps you articulate your lesson's to-do list. It is the detailing of all of the preparations that need to be made to successfully carry out your lesson plan. The **instructional action plan (IAP)** includes the following steps:

- *Identifying learner preparation activities:* This component describes the preparations that are necessary to assess and prepare the learners before the lesson. It should list the materials, props, and assessment instruments you will need.
- *Getting the classroom ready:* When action planning for the physical space, you should describe the steps you have to take in the classroom to prepare it for the lesson implementation. Be sure to list any changes to the classroom furniture or fixtures that need to be made before the lesson.
- *Listing teaching-learning activities:* In this component of the IAP, you should list the materials that need to be created, gathered, copied, or assembled for the teaching and learning strategies you have identified. Be specific about these needs so that your list can serve as a last-minute checklist before the lesson. You might also include in this section of the IAP alternative activities that could be used if unexpected circumstances interfere with the lesson plan's scheduled activities.
- *Creating personal prompts:* Personal prompts are reminders of the things you want to do and/or say as you implement the lesson. They are personal cues to remind you in case you forget to include something you had planned to do. Listing them in the IAP gives you a single point of review that you can use just before the lesson.
- *Listing support technologies:* This section of the IAP provides you with an opportunity to identify the technologies you will need and any associated materials that are required. Here you should list the technologies, what you need to do to get them into your classroom, and what preparation or practice sessions you need to successfully use the technologies you selected.
- *Listing feedback instruments:* Formative and summative feedback are a part of your lesson plan and your design. In the IAP, you should list any instruments or techniques that you need to develop or use to accomplish the feedback you have planned. You should also indicate what you need to do to use the feedback from the instruments. This list will serve as a feedback checklist to use before you implement your lesson.
- *Detailing follow-up activities:* Once you have collected formative and summative feedback, the data that result will prompt you to go on to the next lesson or to review and reinforce the current lesson. In this section of the IAP, you should detail what you need to do as a follow-up to a less successful lesson, what you might want to do to reinforce a successful lesson, and/or what you need to do to improve the lesson.

The Instructional Action Planner: Getting Ready to Teach

To help you create a useful instructional action plan, a template, similar to the previously presented lesson planner, is provided in Table 3.7. The instructional action planner provides a format in which you are prompted to list your lesson requirements and to detail what you will need for successful implementation. The action planner is your last step in the planning process. With its completion, you are finally ready to teach and to help your students learn. You will also find downloadable action plan templates on MyEducationKit. These templates are Word forms are formatted to fill in to help you build a complete instructional to-do list.

Go to the *Template* section of Chapter 3 in MyEducationKit and select the *Action Planner Template* to work through the process of creating lessons using this template.

TABLE 3.7 The Action Planner Template with Examples for Money and Banking Unit

TO-DO #1: IDENTIFY LEARNER PREPARATION ACTIVITIES	EXAMPLES
Describe what action needs to be taken to prepare the learners. • What steps need to be taken to prepare the learners? • What props are needed?	***Learner Checklist*** ______ Contact ESE teacher and review unit plan for inclusion student. ______ Review prerequisite vocabulary with ESL students. ______ Obtain bank forms, bankbook covers, bank signs, and customer "goodies" from local bank.
TO-DO #2: READY THE CLASSROOM	EXAMPLES
Describe what you need to do to get the classroom ready for the lesson. • What furniture needs to be acquired or moved? • What additional materials are needed? • Whom do you need to contact to assist in making the intended adjustments?	***Classroom Checklist*** ______ Stop by an appliance store for refrigerator box. ______ Borrow a rolling bookcase from the library. ______ Move the reading center temporarily to make room for the bank center. ______ Purchase or borrow three desk organizers for the teller.
TO-DO #3: LIST TEACHING AND LEARNING ACTIVITIES	EXAMPLES
List the materials you need to prepare and/or tasks that need to be done for the intended activities • What materials are needed by teacher and students? • What tasks need to be completed for these activities?	***Materials Checklist*** ______ Money equivalence PowerPoint slide ______ Process PowerPoint presentation ______ Deposit/withdrawal forms for checking accounts ______ Deposit/withdrawal forms for savings accounts ______ Poster-size laminates of each form ______ Blank bank statement forms for reconciliation ______ Blank bankbooks ***Task Checklist*** ______ Contact a potential guest speaker to discuss lesson requirements. ______ Scan and print copies of forms if necessary. ______ Bookmark bank web sites. ***Activity Backup Plan*** Locate a banking video, preview it, and prepare a related activity in case the guest speaker cancels or web access is unavailable.

Linking Planning, Teaching, Learning, and Technology

Go to the *Podcasts* section of Chapter 3 in MyEducationKit and click on *Meeting Student Needs.*

As you learned in Chapter 2, teaching and learning are, at their core, processes of effective and successful communication. Just as you would carefully plan and rehearse an important speech before giving it, so too must you carefully plan and rehearse the important communication process that takes place between teacher and learner. This chapter has reviewed the many components of this planning process and has provided specific planning tools for effective teaching and learning. Each step of the systematic instructional process is a critical one, and each offers a unique contribution to the process. Now that you are aware of all of the planning components, let's take a moment to see how they fit together to help you effectively plan your teaching and your students' learning experiences.

TABLE 3.7 Continued

TO-DO #4: CREATE PERSONAL PROMPTS	SAMPLE PROMPTS FOR OBJECTIVE 1
List the prompts you want to remember to use to cover all points of the lesson. • What specifics do you want to remember to do? • What specifics do you want to remember to say?	***Talking Points*** • Why do we save? • What is a budget? • Advantages and disadvantages of checks versus cash. • How banks make their money. ***Don't Forget To*** • Close the teller window at the end of the class session • Monitor the location of the class cash supply.
TO-DO #5: LIST SUPPORT TECHNOLOGIES	**EXAMPLE**
Describe the things you need to do to ensure that the technologies you have selected are available and working. • What technologies and related materials need to be acquired for another source? From where? • What hardware or software adjustments need to be made? • Which technologies need to be checked to be sure they are functioning?	***Technology Checklist*** ______ Make sure the scanner is working. ______ Check the printer cartridge. ______ Get colored paper from the art room. ______ Bookmark the home pages of banking web sites. ______ Check the LCD display for all cables and to be sure it is working.
TO-DO #6: LIST FEEDBACK INSTRUMENTS	**EXAMPLE**
Describe the feedback instruments you need to have ready for this lesson. • What do you need for formative feedback? • What do you need for summative feedback?	***Feedback Checklist*** ______ Rubric for assessing performance while at the bank center. ______ Quiz on filling in forms and determining balances. ______ Lesson objective test on terms and concepts. ______ Student satisfaction questionnaire.
TO-DO #7: DETAIL FOLLOW-UP ACTIVITIES	**EXAMPLE**
Given the feedback, describe the follow-up activities. • If the lesson was not successful, what remediation is planned? • If the lesson was successful, what reinforcement is planned?	*Remediation:* PowerPoint self-paced review of key terms followed by a quiz on key points; direct tutoring or peer mentoring if mastery is not demonstrated on quiz. *Reinforcement:* Continued use of the bank center for a token-economy reward system.

Design

Instructional design is the component of the process that helps you think strategically about the teaching and learning experience as a multiple-day instructional unit. It offers you, through the DID model, a way to plan for and articulate every essential ingredient in the unit you are planning. Instructional design paints the big-picture version of instruction during the unit and a precise blueprint of what should happen and how.

Plan

The lesson plan brings the instructional design down to earth. It moves the planning process from a systems model to a mainstream, day-to-day lesson plan. While never deviating from the elements of the instructional design model, the lesson plans that result from it narrow

Michael Newman/PhotoEdit

Teachers must plan for, select, and effectively use the best technologies to support teaching and learning.

the focus of planning to a specific objective and knowledge segment. Using the lesson planner template, you are able to clarify precisely what you need to do to successfully complete each day's lesson.

Act

Design-plan-act! completes the Instructional systems cycle.

Action planning is the final step in the three-part planning process. The action plan specifies everything you need to do to make learning happen in the classroom. Through the action planning step, you review the lesson plan and stop to create your lesson plan to-do list. By completing the instructional action planner, you culminate the planning phase of instruction and are ready to begin implementation.

PEARSON myeducationkit™

Go to the *Assignments and Activities* section of Chapter 3 in MyEducationKit and complete the video activity entitled *Why Use Technology?*

Planning for Technology in Teaching and Learning

All aspects of instruction benefit from careful planning, but for using technology in instruction, planning is especially critical. Technology-enhanced teaching and learning must be well thought out, with appropriate technologies identified and justified within the framework of the instructional event. Adding a technology to your instruction just because it is available can detract from the instruction and even hamper the teaching-learning process. Technology should be employed only when instructional planning has been completed and it is clear that a technology in support of instruction is called for. A general rule of thumb suggests that a technology included in a lesson should make it possible for something that was done before to be done better or make it possible for something that couldn't have been done before to happen. A fully implemented plan, with its emphasis on carefully thought-out instructional events, helps to ensure such appropriate selection and utilization of technology.

As you proceed through this text, you will have the opportunity to learn about a wide variety of technologies that will assist you in effective teaching. Although each of these technologies will serve you well as a tool with which you can build a sound learning environment for your students, none should be used until you have fully planned the intended instruction. The old axiom in carpentry, "Measure twice, cut once," suggests that we should be careful to take the time to plan before taking action in order to avoid irreversible, costly mistakes. The instructional mistakes of teachers affect the students who are in our charge. No mistakes can be more costly than those that affect our students. Careful instructional planning helps us avoid instructional errors and maximize the effectiveness of our teaching time and our students' learning time. So when time pressures cause you to consider shortcutting the planning component of the teaching-learning process, remember this modified axiom: "Plan well, teach well."

PEARSON myeducationkit™

To check your comprehension of the content covered in this chapter, go to the MyEducationKit for your book and complete the *Study Plan* for Chapter 3.

Key Terms

Bloom's taxonomy, 56
design-plan-act! (D-P-A) system, 50
dynamic instructional design (DID) model, 51
feedback loop, 52
formative feedback, 52
instructional action plan (IAP), 71
instructional design model, 50
learning environment, 59
learning strategies, 61
lesson planner, 69
media, 61
methods, 61
pedagogical cycle, 68
pedagogy, 68
performance objectives, 53
summative feedback, 53
systems approach, 50
teaching strategies, 61

Student Activities

CHAPTER REVIEW

1. What is an instructional planning system? What are the components of the D-P-A system?
2. How can an instructional design model help you develop your instructional plan? Identify the steps of the DID model and briefly explain each.
3. What is the difference between formative feedback and summative feedback?
4. What is a performance objective? How does it differ from more generic objectives?
5. Name and briefly describe the six levels of Bloom's taxonomy.
6. What components constitute a learning environment?
7. Name and briefly describe each step of the pedagogical cycle.
8. What role do educational technologies play in teaching and learning?
9. What is the difference between an instructional design and a lesson plan?
10. What is an instructional action plan? How does it help a teacher prepare for the instructional event?

WHAT DO YOU THINK?

1. Assume that you have been asked to assist a fellow teacher in writing objectives in performance terms. He shares with you the following objective for his sixth-grade science class: "*When I complete my instruction, my students will understand and appreciate the ecology of the rainforest.*" What would you say to your colleague to explain why his objective as written would not help him decide what to teach and what his students should learn? Help him rewrite this objective in performance terms.
2. Many teachers write objectives and focus their instruction at the three lowest levels of Bloom's taxonomy. Why do you think this happens? Do you believe it is an appropriate emphasis? How might it help or hurt the learners?
3. You are about to teach a lesson on the importance of the Nile in ancient Egypt at the grade level you would prefer to teach. Describe the steps you would take to effectively prepare for teaching this instructional unit.
4. Observe a teacher presenting a lesson and note which of the steps of the pedagogical cycle he or she includes. Critique the lesson in terms of the cycle. Be sure to include how the lesson might have been improved through application of the pedagogical cycle's components.
5. Assume that the teacher in the next classroom is a computer enthusiast. She creates most of her lessons around the use of computers and software she has available in her classroom. Do you believe this is an appropriate approach to instruction? Why or why not?

LEARNING TOGETHER!

The following activities are designed for groups of three to five students:

1. Lay out an ideal classroom space that would meet the needs of a variety of learners. Include the number and placement of desks, tables, teacher's desk, file cabinets, bookcases, bulletin boards, chalkboards or whiteboards, and any less traditional fixtures and furniture you would like to include. Draw your group's ideal classroom to share with your class.
2. Select a teaching unit of your choice at the grade level you would like to teach. Together, write ten performance objectives related to the unit, with at least one at each of the levels of Bloom's taxonomy. Be prepared to share your objectives with the class.
3. Use all three components of the D-P-A system to complete a hypothetical instructional unit plan. Use as the instructional-unit content a topic appropriate to the grade level you would like to teach.

TEACHING WITH TECHNOLOGY: INTEGRATION IDEAS WEB QUEST

Planning is at the heart of effective instruction. The web offers teachers abundant planning resources and examples. Below you will find a sampling of some of the planning resources available on the Web.

ACTIVITY: Explore the links that below and the web resources you have learned about in this chapter, and select three resources of most interest to you to explore. On each of the resources, search for an innovative plan that you might consider using at the grade level or content area you plan to teach. Write a one-page summary of your web quest that includes (1) the links you explored and the plans you found briefly describing the idea presented, (2) a brief summary of how each plan differs from the elements of the DPA system, and (3) a pro and con summary of using each of the plans you found in your classroom

All Grade-Level Lesson Plans

Apple Learning Interchange, sponsored by Apple Computers, provides a powerful and innovative web-based collection of lesson plans that use Apple computers. This site provides in-depth plans aligned to standards. **http://ali.apple.com/ali_sites/ali/.**

Discovery Schools offers a Lesson Plan Library featuring original lesson plans, written by teachers for teachers. The web site offers a searchable database with pull-down menus so teachers can browse plans by subject, grade, or both. Most content areas and grade levels are included. Review this site for innovative plans. **http://school.discovery.com/lessonplans/k-5.html.**

Education World is a highly popular resource for teachers. Its lesson planning center provides teachers with field-tested teacher-contributed plans at every grade level and for every content area. Review this site frequently, as new plans are added daily. **www.educationworld.com/a_lesson/.**

The Educator's Reference Desk offers numerous resources, including a teacher's guide to writing lesson plans as well as their Lesson Plan Collection. Resources at this site include more than 2,000 lesson plans, 3,000 links to online education information, and more than 200 question archived responses to educator's questions. Review this site at **www.eduref.org/Virtual/Lessons/index.shtml.**

Smithsonian Education is the education web site of the Smithsonian Museum in Washington, D.C. This list of science, technology, history, and cultural lessons offers high-quality, fully articulated plans and activities on a variety of unusual topics. Visit this unique collection at **www.smithsonianeducation.org/educators/index.html.**

Teachers Net offers their Lesson Plan Bank to all teachers in all content areas and grade levels. This web site encourages teachers to submit plans as well as browse an extensive database of curriculum ideas. There is even a lesson plan request board so teachers can communicate their unique curriculum needs to other teachers. **http://teachers.net/lessons/.**

English/Language Arts Lesson Plans and Standards

The **National Council of Teachers of English** web site provides standards for K–12 English and language arts curricula as well as lesson plans for all areas within the discipline. The Read/Write/Think link provides quality plans aligned to standards that integrate Internet resources into meaningful instruction. **www.ncte.org/.**

Math Lesson Plans and Standards

The **National Council for Teachers of Mathematics** offers their national standards for PreK through grade 12 at this site. E-Examples are provided for each standard to give teachers ideas for activities to meet each standard. The Illuminations link offers innovative math lesson plans for all grade levels aligned with standards. **http://standards.nctm.org/document/chapter3/index.htm.**

Science Lesson Plans and Standards

The **National Science Teachers Association** web site provides standards for teaching science at all grade levels. In addition, it offers a compendium of science educator web sites that covers science topics at every grade level, including numerous lesson plan sites. Visit the web site to become familiar with science standards and resources. **www.nsta.org/standards.**

Social Studies Lesson Plans and Standards

The **Library of Congress** offers powerful and innovative lesson plans that use the original resources stored in the library as their source. Lessons are organized by theme, topic, discipline, or era, with grade-level indicators for each lesson. Visit the Library of Congress for this resource at **http://memory.loc.gov/learn/lessons/index.html.**

The **National Council for the Social Studies** web site includes a list of standards and lesson plans aligned with those standards for use in the social studies curriculum. **www.socialstudies.org/standards/.**

interchapter 3

The DID Designer

Vowels Unit

STEP 1 Know the Learner

The class consists of kindergarten students. The class has eighteen students, ten girls and eight boys. There are seven Caucasians, five Hispanics, five African Americans, and one Asian American.

The learning styles of the students include seven visual learners, nine auditory learners, and two kinesthetic learners. The seven visual learners need materials to assist them in learning. The nine auditory learners need lessons to be discussed verbally as well as a quiet place to study. The two kinesthetic learners need hands on activities and an open space to learn.

The multiple intelligences of these students consist of musical, linguistic, spatial, intrapersonal, interpersonal, and logical.

The entry skills of this unit are very limited. Some students may know the letters of the alphabet, but overall students do not know what vowels are.

STEP 2 Articulate Objectives and Standards

The student will be able to differentiate vowels from consonants orally with 100 percent accuracy. (II 3, 5.1; SS 8.6)

The student will be able to identify letters that are vowels by creating a poster board with 100 percent accuracy. (II 3, 5.3; SS 8.7)

The student will be able to critique other student's vowel posters on a rubric with 100 percent accuracy. (II 3, 5.6; SS 8.6)

STEP 3 Establish the Learning Environment

The consonants on the alphabet chart that is posted in front of the room need to be covered, leaving only the vowel letters to be displayed. Also, the PowerPoint presentation needs to be saved onto each computer.

The computers all need headphones attached to them.

A flash card game will be placed at the manipulative center, a cassette will be placed at the listening center, a handout will be placed at the writing center, and books on vowels will be placed at the reading center.

Also, magnetic boards and cloth boards need to be placed at each group table with letter magnets and cloth letters.

Students will be encouraged to work together, with about four to five students per group, including a variety of multiple intelligences in each group. Within the groups, students will be encouraged to help their partners.

Students will be rewarded with stickers and smiley faces and by having a vowel celebration.

STEP 4 Identify Teaching and Learning Strategies

The consonants on the alphabet chart will be presented. The students will be asked to note that some letters of the alphabet are special. The students will read each vowel from the chart and the teacher will write each on the board as the students say it.

To review, as a class, students will be asked to recite the alphabet. The teacher will ask a student to read the letters that are written on the board. Students will be asked to think about how these letters are the same as each other but different from the rest of the alphabet. The teacher will discuss why it is important to know these special letters called vowels.

Teaching Strategies

- Ask a student to read the teaching strategies letters that are posted on the board. Then six students will be asked to come up to the board to write the vowels again. Students will be told how these letters are different from the rest of the letters. The importance of vowels in making words will be discussed. The class will read together the vowels that are displayed on the alphabet chart. Following that, students will write the six vowel letters in their journal.
- The teacher will show a vowel PowerPoint presentation to the class. After viewing the slide show, the students will again say all the vowels and a word that begins with each vowel.

SOURCE: Adapted from a unit developed by Elizabeth Polo, former Miami Dade College and Nova Southeastern University Education Major, currently a Dade County public school teacher.

Learning Strategies

- As a class, students will sing a vowel song. The song will be repeated multiple times. Then students will be divided into groups, and each group will come up to the front of the room to sing the song. As groups of students are singing the song, the remaining students will follow along with the vowels they wrote in their journals.
- Students will draw on a blank sheet of paper a vowel that is in their first or last name. For instance, John will draw the letter O on a paper as well as write his name in pencil, but color the vowel in green. The students will write their name on construction paper and color the vowel a different color or decorate it in some way to differentiate it from the consonants.
- As a class, we will read the section covering vowels in the language arts text. Following the reading, students will have time to play with the magnetic boards or cloth boards that are placed at each group table. Students will be encouraged to create words with vowels and help their partners to do so. The teacher will be visiting each group and asking students about their words and the different vowels used. Also, a worksheet will be given to the students to be done as part of their home learning weekly packet.
- Students will visit the different learning centers. Students will rotate among all the centers in intervals of ten minutes. After the students are done at each center, they will return to their desk to begin illustrating their poster.
- Students will work independently composing a vowel poster. The poster must illustrate all six vowels with pictures that begin with that vowel. Pictures can be drawn or cut out of magazines. The pictures must be labeled. When students are done making their poster, they will present it to the class. All posters will be hung in the classroom after presentations are completed.
- While the posters are being presented and displayed, students will fill out an easy rubric evaluating each other's work. Students will evaluate the presenter on categories such as speech, listing of all vowels, and pictures drawn with labels.

STEP 5 Identify and Select Support Technologies

Technologies and materials needed include:

Magnetic boards, cloth boards, flash cards, poster boards, art supplies, alphabet chart, books on vowels, CD player and talking books, rubric and worksheets, computer, LCD display, PowerPoint presentation.

STEP 6 Evaluate and Revise the Design

Students will be graded upon the outcome of the vowel in the name drawing, the home learning worksheet, and the vowel poster.

If more than three students score less than 100 percent on the vowel in the name drawing, then this assignment will be assigned as a home learning activity.

If more than three students score less than 100 percent on the home learning worksheet, the worksheet will be completed together in class.

If more than three students score less than 100 percent on the vowel poster, then a second poster will be assigned as a group activity.

Changes to the design will be made if two of four evaluations are lower than anticipated per the unit objectives.

The Lesson Planner

Vowel Unit Day One

STEP 1 Ready the Learner

Students will be asked to observe that the alphabet chart has only a few letters showing. Students will be asked to share why the vowels displayed may be different from the other letters.

STEP 2 Target Specific Objectives

The student will be able to differentiate vowels from consonants orally with 100 percent accuracy. (II 3, 5.1; SS 8.6)

STEP 3 Prepare the Lesson

Classroom Preparation

- The alphabet chart needs to display only the vowels. A handout will be shared with all students. Magnetic boards with magnetic letters and cloth boards with cloth letters need to be placed at each group table.

Lesson Preparation
Preorganizer

- Cover consonants on the alphabet chart and post each vowel on the board. Also, post words that begin with the vowel on the board.

Bridge to Prior Knowledge

- Recite the alphabet as a class. Then have one student read the letters posted on the board.

Introduce New Knowledge

- Ask students why there are only six letters posted on the board and why the rest of the alphabet chart is covered.
- The teacher will explain to students why these letters are vowels and how they are different from the rest of the letters.
- A PowerPoint presentation will be shown to the class. We will discuss the slide show and the students will practice writing vowels in their journals.

Reinforce Knowledge

- As a class, the students will sing a vowel song. The class will sing the song at least two times. Then a few students will lead the rest of the class singing the vowel song for the third time.

Provide Practice

- Students will use alphabet manipulatives and flash cards in groups at the class centers to find vowels and create words using vowels.

Technology/Media Used

- PowerPoint presentation
- Flash cards and alphabet manipulatives
- Magnetic boards with magnets and cloth board with cloth letters

Check for Success

- Review journal pages of vowels and observe students using manipulatives and flash cards to ensure that students can distinguish vowels and consonants.

Vowel Unit Day Two

STEP 1 Ready the Learner

As a brief review, students will be asked to write the vowels on a sheet of paper and recite them aloud together in class. Students will sing the vowel song practiced in the previous lesson.

STEP 2 Target Specific Objectives

The student will be able to identify letters that are vowels by creating a poster board with 100 percent accuracy. (II 3, 5.3; SS 8.7)

STEP 3 Prepare the Lesson

Classroom Preparation

- The alphabet chart in the classroom will have all letters uncovered.
- Art supplies and poster materials will be placed at each group table.

Lesson Preparation
Preorganizer

- Ask students to review the alphabet chart. Ask volunteers to come to the board to write one letter from the chart they think is a vowel.

Bridge to Prior Knowledge

- Recite the alphabet as a class. Ask students to identify which of the letters written on the board are in fact vowels. Ask students to think of a word that begins with each vowel.

Introduce New Knowledge

- Explain that the remaining letters of the alphabet are known as consonants.
- Write short words on the board and circle vowels. Write additional words on the board and ask students to come to the board and circle vowels and underline consonants.

Reinforce Knowledge

- Students will draw on a blank sheet of paper a vowel that is in their first or last name. For instance, John will draw the letter O on a paper as well as write his name in pencil, but color the vowel in green. The students will write their name on construction paper and color the vowel a different color or decorate it in some way to differentiate it from the consonants.

Provide Practice

- Students will be encouraged to create words with vowels and help their partners to do so. The teacher will be visiting each group and asking students about their words and the different vowels used.

Culminating Review

- Students will work independently composing a vowel poster. The poster must illustrate all six vowels with pictures that begin with that vowel. Pictures can be drawn or cut out of magazines. The pictures must be labeled. When students are done making their poster, they will present it to the class. All posters will be hung in the classroom after presentations are completed.

Technology/Media Used

- Art materials, poster board

Check for Success

- Student names will be checked for accuracy in identifying vowels. Vowel posters will be reviewed for accuracy.

Vowel Unit Day Three

STEP 1 Ready the Learner

Student characteristics remain constant. The vowel song will be sung in preparation for the final day of the unit.

STEP 2 Target Specific Objectives

The student will be able to critique students' vowel posters on a rubric with 100 percent accuracy.
(II 3, 5.3; SS 8.7)

STEP 3 Prepare the Lesson

Classroom Preparation

- Student vowel posters will be displayed around the classroom.
- Rubrics will be provided to all students with extras at group tables.

Lesson Preparation

Preorganizer

- Rubric will be reviewed. The criteria for a correct poster will be discussed.

Bridge to Prior Knowledge

- Students will be asked to recite the vowels. Students will then be asked to recite consonants. The class alphabet chart may be used in the recitation.

Introduce New Knowledge

- Steps in rubric assessment will be presented. The concept of fairness and accuracy in evaluation will be discussed.

Reinforce Knowledge

- The PowerPoint presentation will be shown to the class. The slide show will be discussed and since the song correlates with the presentation, it will be sung again.

Provide Practice

- A sample poster prepared by the teacher that includes errors will be shared with the class. Students will be asked to evaluate it to see if they correctly detect errors and fairly evaluate the poster. After students finish the assessment, the teacher will demonstrate appropriate application of the rubric by assessing the sample poster.

Culminating Review

- Posters on display in the classroom will be assessed by peers. Students will fill out the rubric and turn it in for a grade. The rubric will evaluate posters based on categories such as speech, listing of all vowels, and pictures drawn with labels.

Technology/Media Used

- Assessment rubrics

Check for Success

- Rubric evaluations of peer posters will be reviewed and should demonstrate understanding of vowels.

The Instructional Action Planner

Vowel Unit

TO-DO #1 Prepare for the Learners

_____Prepare PowerPoint.

_____Make copies of handouts and rubrics.

TO-DO #2 Ready the Classroom

_____Cover the consonants on the alphabet chart.

_____Set up materials at all centers.

_____Place magnetic boards with letters and cloth boards with cloth numbers at each group table.

TO-DO #3 Teaching and Learning Activities

_____Get poster boards and art supplies.

_____Test talking books, CD players, and headphones at listening center.

_____Secure flash cards and alphabet manipulatives for group tables.

_____Review and select pages from language arts text for practice.

_____Set up magnetic boards with magnetic letters and felt letters for cloth boards.

Activity Backup Plan
Vowel and consonant word game: Students can draw a vowel or consonant on a piece of paper, which will be taped to the front of their shirt. Students can then arrange themselves in words for reward points.

TO-DO #4 Personal Prompts

Talking Points

- Why are there vowels?
- Which letters are consonants?
- How many vowels are there?
- Name some words that begin with a vowel.

Don't Forget to:

- Monitor students at the different learning centers.
- Close all applications on the computer.
- Lock your computer.
- Uncover consonants on Day 3.

TO-DO #5 Support Technologies

Technology Checklist

_____Make sure the listening center equipment works.

_____Make sure the computer, display, and PowerPoint presentation work.

_____Make sure manipulatives, flash cards, and magnetic and cloth letters are full sets.

TO-DO #6 Feedback

_____Prepare and distribute rubrics for assessing poster presentation.

TO-DO #7 Follow-Up

_____Set up student computer with the PowerPoint presentation for continued practice and review.

PART TWO

Applying Technologies for Effective Instruction

Every classroom has its own personality, which is usually defined by a teacher's teaching style. Some have desks arranged in tidy rows; others have pods of desks arranged in circles. Some classrooms have an abundance of technology to help a teacher teach and students learn; others have only a few types of technology present.

Part Two examines the many kinds of technology available, how they work, and how they might best be used to help you teach and your students learn. Chapter 4 introduces the varied technologies available to address the needs of diverse learners. Chapters 5 through 7 explore the most prevalent classroom technology: the personal computer. According to the U.S. Census Bureau, in the 2004–2005 school year, report the total number of computers available to students had reached 14.2 million—one for every four students. This number has continued to grow. Although the distribution across classrooms nationwide varies, most educators want to see more computers, preferably connected to the Internet, in their classrooms. Chapter 5 explores the personal computer as a classroom tool. Chapter 6 examines how various computers and their components can support teaching and learning. Chapters 7 and 8 explore the wide variety of administrative and academic software tools available to help accomplish the many tasks involved in teaching and learning. Chapters 9 and 10 explore the Internet and the World Wide Web and their role in education. These chapters will give you a chance to take a closer look at all aspects of the personal computer and related digital technologies as educational tools and see why so many teachers want computers in their classroom.

Chapter 11 examines audio, visual, and video technologies. It explores the role of traditional visuals such as posters, bulletin boards, and models as well as computer software tools such as projected visuals, slides, and overhead transparencies. It further explores digital and analog video technologies and how motion media materials and equipment can aid in instruction.

Together, these chapters will help you build the knowledge base and skills you need to evaluate and select the most appropriate technology for your instructional design. Furthermore, these chapters will help you learn how to teach with and effectively implement the technologies you will find in schools.

To begin the exploration of the application of effective technology solutions in the classroom, it is useful to look at how two educators met their challenges with technology. Liz Brennan and Stacy Still found strategies to incorporate technology into their planning process in order to create a technology-rich learning environment for their students.

REAL STORIES

REAL TEACHERS

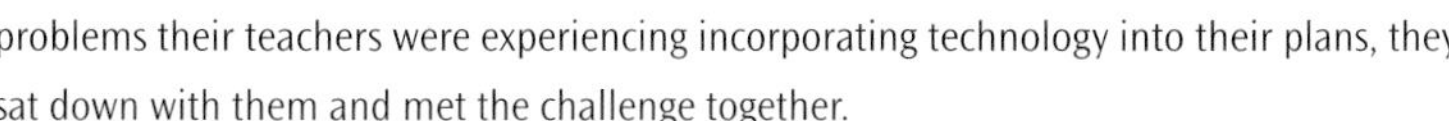

Liz Brennan

Stacy Still

Meet Liz Brennan and Stacy Still. To build an effective learning environment requires planning. While planning may not be as exciting as delivering the instruction, careful and systematic planning is what makes effective teaching and learning. When Liz Brennan and Stacy Still recognized the problems their teachers were experiencing incorporating technology into their plans, they sat down with them and met the challenge together.

University School of Nova Southeastern University is a campus-based, independent college preparatory day school located in Fort Lauderdale, Florida. I am Liz Brennan, Associate Head of the University School of Nova Southeastern University. I would estimate that at least 75 percent of the "work" I do each day involves curriculum design and development. Whenever we think of curriculum, we are also thinking planning; and, one cannot think planning without thinking learning. On a daily basis working with my faculty, I can see that issues with student learning can, many times, be connected to breakdowns in classroom curriculum design planning.

My name is Stacy Still. I am the Technology Facilitator at the Lower School. There are many aspects to my job as Technology Facilitator, but one of the most important functions is to assist faculty in the planning of lessons that tie technology into the learning process.

Our problem involves a condition where, despite the knowledge and skills for generic lesson planning, the teacher is unable to effectively or consistently "fit" appropriate uses of computer-based learning experiences into a previously developed lesson plan. In addition, either she may lack the personal technical skills to feel comfortable with available hardware or she lacks an understanding of software options available either within the school or via the Internet.

Liz: To get the most from a planning experience, Stacy often sits with an individual teacher, and together they plan the lesson in a collaborative mode. Stacy, with her expertise in technology, is able to guide the teacher and help her gain certain technical skills; the teacher, with her expertise in pedagogy, is able to assess the design of the plan as they study it together and make decisions as to how and where to use technology effectively. This empowers the teacher to determine if the technological ideas that Stacy suggests, or the ones that they find together, are appropriate for the lesson, connect to the outcome objectives, address various learning styles of their students, and match the students' current performance levels. During their collaborative planning process, teachers can practice the lesson with the selected technology to simulate how it will work in their classrooms. This pre-instructional step helps the teacher feel more comfortable and confident in the quality of the plan and in his or her use of technology.

Stacy: I worked with one of our teachers in planning a lesson. Through our discussion, the teacher determined that her plan was sound in most of the steps of the planning process. We identified and listed the areas of strength: clearly stated objectives, an appropriately established learning environment, and a well-targeted summative evaluation. However, given the large number of students for whom the lesson was intended, it was difficult for her not only to identify but to manage the learning styles and specific learning needs of all of these students. We decided to strengthen several areas: knowing the learner, identifying teaching and learning strategies, and identifying and selecting technologies to be used to enhance and extend the lesson to be meaningful to more students.

Our first planning collaboration was to go online and find instructional plans that effectively integrated technology. The first time, the teacher searched while I assisted and guided her through the general search to locate the most appropriate lesson plan sites. We started with a simple search using www.google.com. We found hundreds of sites that included well-planned technology-enhanced lesson plans. I suggested that we try to use a kid's search engine, such as www.yahooligans.com, sunsite.berkeley.edu/KidsClick!/, or www.ajkids.com to look for other resources and lesson plan sites that would be more limited or controlled by age level and content. She was able to incorporate both audio and video experiences from sites such as

www.rainforesteducation.com/FunNGames/canuseethem.htm
www.exploratorium.edu/frogs/rainforest/
www.christiananswers.net/kid/vidclips.html
http://schools.pinellas.k12.fl.us/educators/tec/templ1.htm

The next step was to determine how to incorporate these links and the other information into a PowerPoint presentation. Having me there as a guide enabled her to learn, in a hands-on mode, how to do these things, yet she was not "afraid" of the task or the technology. The final step in the plan then was to determine the best way to display this presentation. We decided to use a portable smart board to deliver the instruction and present the PowerPoint project.

This was a tremendous experience for both of us. The teacher gained confidence in herself, as a professional, and in her own ability to use the technology effectively, and I was able to see the lesson plan implemented and use its outcome as a reference later with other teachers.

For further information, you may contact the writers at the following:

Dr. Elizabeth C. Brennan's email:
brennan@nova.edu
phone: 954-262-4484
Stacy Still's email: **stacy@nova.edu**
phone: 954-262-4500

CHAPTER 4

Technology for Diverse Learners

Steve Wormowski/The Image Works

CHAPTER OVERVIEW

This chapter addresses these ISTE National Educational Technology Standards:
- NETS•T Standard 1
- NETS•T Standard 2
- NETS•S Standard 2

- **Planning and Using Technology to Meet the Needs of Diverse Learners**
- **Technology Solutions for Students with Special Needs**
- **Issues in Implementing Technology for Students with Special Needs**
- **Technology Solutions for Gifted Students**
- **Technology Solutions for Culturally and Linguistically Diverse Students**
- **Issues in Implementing Technology for Culturally and Linguistically Diverse Students**
- **Technology Solutions for All Learners**

In Part 1, you have considered how and why technology will play a pivotal role in your professional life, you have developed a foundation in learning theory, and you have been exposed to the considered steps of the planning process. Before you begin to explore the specific technologies you will be using and the technology implementation issues you will face, Chapter 4 asks you to consider how design and technology can combine to meet the unique and diverse needs of the learners you will find in your classroom.

As you already know, students are diverse in many ways, from ethnicity to culture to learning styles to the ways in which their various intelligences are dominant. However, some students not only vary in these ways but also have very unique and special needs. Students with special needs, whether students with disabilities, gifted students, or students who have cultural or language differences, require special attention from all of their teachers to achieve their personal potential. These students still vary in the many ways all students do, but layered on top of that level of diversity are the challenges associated with their particular needs. Technology can offer a very significant helping hand to teachers who must find ways to support these students.

This chapter will help you to explore the potential needs you might find among the students in your classroom and the technologies and resources that may assist you in designing instruction for them. The chapter will also review areas of diversity you are likely to find in your classroom and the issues associated with addressing unique student needs. The chapter concludes with a look at Universal Design for Learning, an initiative to ensure that all students have what they need to learn.

After this chapter the student will be able to:

- Describe diversity and develop lessons that accommodate diverse learners.
- Apply what they have learned to develop instruction that shows sensitivity to cultural and gender differences.
- Identify technology solutions for students with special needs, including the Culturally and Linguistically Diverse (CLD) and the gifted.
- Analyze and evaluate the technology solutions that are available to maximize their effectiveness for students with special needs.

Using Technology to Meet the Needs of Diverse Learners

You have learned about the role of technology as a support for and enhancement to your carefully planned instruction. You have also been introduced to the many ways in which students are diverse, including culture, ethnicity, socioeconomic level, learning styles, and multiple intelligences. All of these differences affect your instructional plan. But some students have a unique range of abilities that calls for additional instructional attention and creativity to meet their needs. It is a teacher's responsibility to try to find every possible way to reach and teach every student. Technology can play a special and effective role to support your efforts and address these students' needs.

PEARSON myeducationkit™

Go to the *Assignments and Activities* section of Chapter 4 in MyEducationKit and complete the video activity entitled *Technology Supports Diverse Learners.*

The National Council for Accreditation of Teacher Education (NCATE) has created standards that all schools of education must meet to prepare future educators. Standard 4a addresses the design, implementation, and evaluation of curriculum and experiences. It articulates future educators' required proficiencies related to diversity. As expressed in the standard:

- Candidates understand diversity, including English language learners (ELL) and students with exceptionalities.
- Candidates develop and teach lessons that incorporate diversity.
- Candidates connect instruction and services to students' experiences and cultures.
- Candidates demonstrate sensitivity to cultural and gender differences.
- Candidates incorporate multiple perspectives in their instruction.
- Candidates develop classroom/school climates that value diversity.

- Candidates understand teaching and learning styles and can adapt instruction.
- Candidates demonstrate dispositions valuing fairness and learning by all.

Future educators and teacher education programs thus have a mandate to prepare teachers to become aware of and to meet the needs of diverse learners. With this requirement in mind, it is essential that every educator become familiar with the technology solutions available to help them effectively meet this standard.

Technology Solutions for Students with Special Needs

The term *students with special needs* refers to both students with disabilities and those who are gifted.

The terms **students with special needs** and **students with exceptionalities** refer to both students who have disabilities that interfere with learning *and* students who are gifted and may need special instructional strategies to reach their potential. A disability may be an obvious condition, such as a physical disability that affects walking and motor coordination, or it could be something that cannot be readily seen, such as a learning disability that makes reading and writing difficult. Other disabilities include visual impairments, hearing impairments, attention deficits, and autism. Technology solutions can be effective in supporting this very diverse group of students.

Technology to Support Participation and Independence

Technology can help to remediate visual, auditory, and physical disabilities.

For students with disabilities, technology can offer an important avenue to increased independence and participation in classroom activities. It can provide access to the standard curriculum that might require additional support to address. It can also enable students who have disabilities that interfere with prerequisite skills, such as writing, to demonstrate their understanding of subject matter. Technology can provide a voice for students who cannot speak, physical assistance for those who cannot move, and alternative input modalities for those who cannot see or hear.

For students who are gifted, computers can provide access to information and stimulating resources at appropriately challenging levels. Although gifted students do not need support or remediation for minimal skills, they do need continual challenges to maintain interest and motivation. Typical curriculum objectives must be expanded upon, and greater depth and levels of critical thinking are required for gifted students to meet their personal potential. Technology offers teachers support to meet these challenges creatively.

Technology to Support Content Area Goals

Technology can also support diverse learners in specific content areas. Whether helping a student write, read, or organize abstract ideas, such technology offers students with special needs an assist in very targeted ways. Depending upon the unique needs of the learners, both hardware and software can be utilized to assist them in accomplishing their academic goals. Below, some of the most popular of these technologies are described and they are summarized in Table 4.1 on page 93.

Writing

Students with physical disabilities such as cerebral palsy and muscular dystrophy often find the task of handwriting very challenging. Many either cannot hold a pencil or lack the dexterity to manipulate one to write legibly or at a functional rate. Students with other disabilities, such as autism, Down syndrome, or learning disabilities, may lack fine motor coordination and may therefore suffer from dysgraphia, or illegible handwriting. Dysgraphia not only makes it difficult for students to share their final products with others, but the illegible handwriting makes it difficult or impossible for them to reread and edit their own work. Many students with learning disabilities and attention deficits can be overwhelmed by the entire process of writing: brainstorming, writing a first draft, editing, and publishing. To address these challenges, technology can play a key role.

A powerful solution offered by technology is the application of word-processing software. This software offers everyone, including students who cannot easily hold a pencil and those with poor fine motor coordination, the ability to create documents with clear, legible text. By using spell-checking and allowing the student to insert new text, delete unwanted text, and replace text through cut-and-paste commands, word-processing programs allow writers to improve the quality of their writing as well as sentence construction and idea development without the drudgery involved in recopying.

Word processing can help students who cannot easily hold a pencil to produce neat, legible documents.

Concept Mapping

Other, more specialized technology tools are available to support idea formation as well as each step of the writing process. Using **concept mapping software** during the brainstorming process helps to capture ideas and then allows students to easily manipulate them (Figure 4.1). Concept mapping provides structure and organization for the writing process and allows students to visually see how abstract ideas are interconnected.

Concept mapping software helps students to visually organize and relate abstract concepts.

Concept mapping software offers special features that further support students with disabilities. Students can brainstorm in either a diagram or outline mode, and with the click of a mouse, students who prefer to brainstorm in the diagram mode can transform their diagrams into an outline for further development.

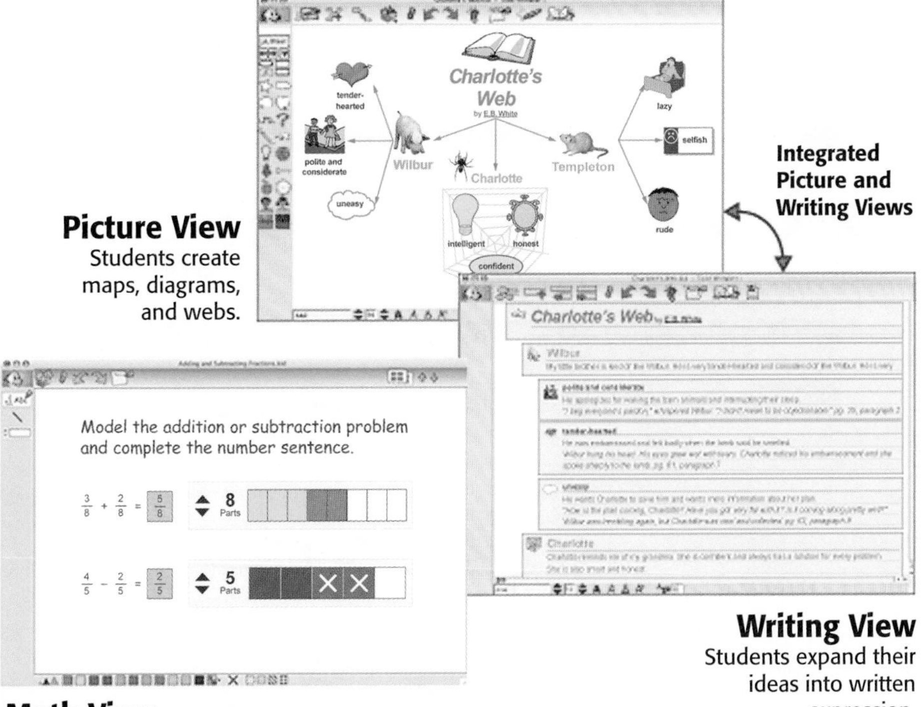

FIGURE 4.1

Concept Mapping Software

Word Prediction Software

Word prediction software makes educated guesses about the word being entered, and enables creation of custom dictionaries.

The composing process that is a challenge for many students with special needs can be supported through the use of **word prediction software.** Word prediction programs make an educated guess about the next word a student wants to type based on the first letter or letters the student enters; the guesses are then presented as a list of choices. A version of word prediction is now commonplace on cell phones to help with text messaging. Word prediction reduces the number of keystrokes needed to express a thought. Therefore, word prediction is a very helpful tool for students with physical disabilities who have difficulty typing and/or whose typing speed may be slow. It has also become a helpful writing tool for students with learning disabilities who have spelling problems. Word prediction programs such as *Co:Writer* (Don Johnston) (Figure 4.2) or *WordQ* (Quillsoft) can be set to "remember" the words a user typed earlier and will present these words first in the lists of guesses. For example, if the student's name is Katrice, any time she types a shift-K and the program infers that a noun may be needed, "Katrice" will appear as one of the choices in the list.

PEARSON myeducationkit™

Go to the *Assignments and Activities* section of Chapter 4 in MyEducationKit and complete the video activity entitled *Software for Diverse Learners.*

One of the most powerful features of word prediction programs is the ability to create **custom dictionaries.** Using custom dictionaries helps to predict vocabulary specific to a particular writing activity or subject. For example, if a student is writing a paper on dinosaurs, a custom dictionary can be set up that includes words such as Triassac, Early Cretaceous, Plateosaurus, Coelophysis, and Scutellosaurus. When a student types the letter S, the word "Scutellosaurus" is presented as a possible choice. Custom dictionaries can be extremely helpful for students with learning disabilities whose spelling mistakes make it difficult for standard spell-checkers to guess the intended word. Additionally, when a student using a word prediction software program moves the computer pointer over a choice in the predicted words list, the programs speaks the word aloud. Students who cannot visually recognize the correct spelling of a word can make their selection based on the way the word sounds.

FIGURE 4.2

Word Prediction Programs

Word prediction software reduces the number of keystrokes needed to express an idea.

Courtesy, Don Johnston, Incorporated

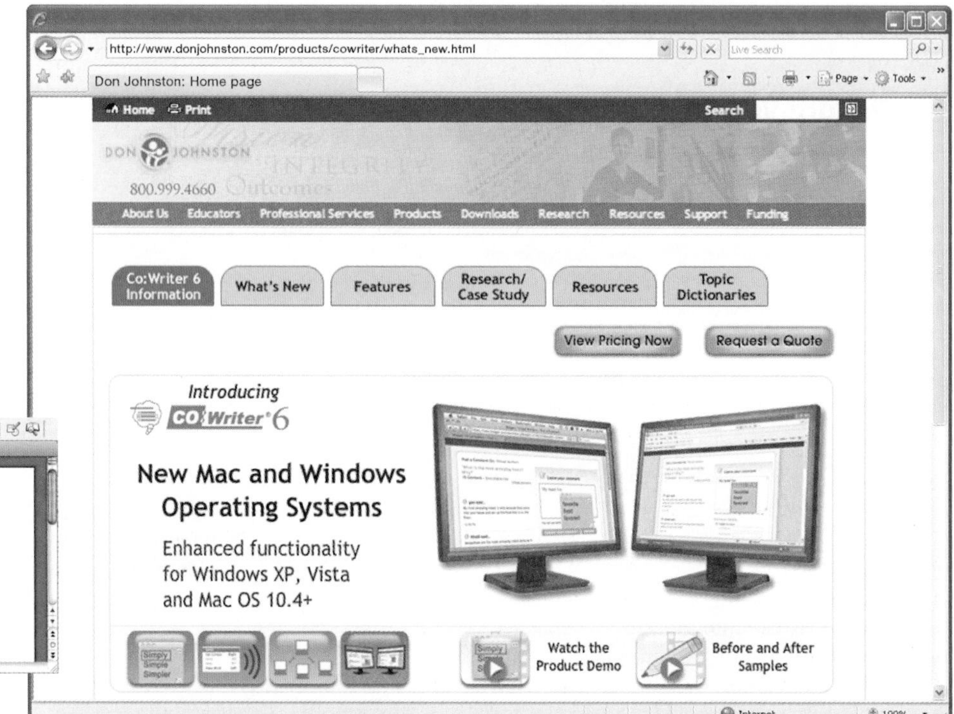

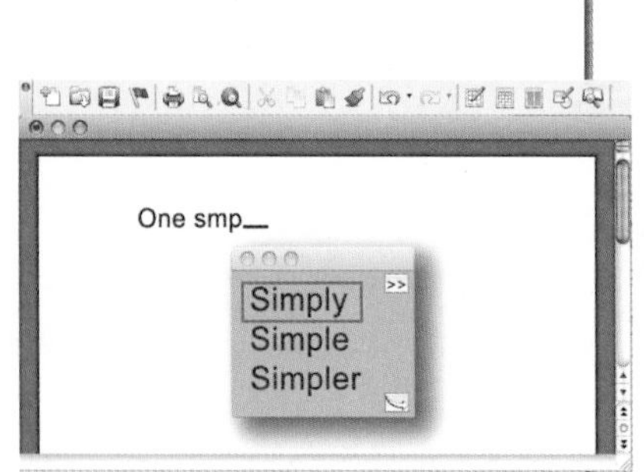

Text-to-Speech Software

Reviewing and editing one's work, which is so difficult for students who have poor reading skills, is made easier by the use of **text-to-speech programs** or **talking word-processing programs.** These programs read aloud whatever a student has written. There are options to hear word-by-word, sentence-by-sentence, or entire paragraphs or documents. Users can also adjust the speed of the reading and the quality of the voice. The auditory feedback provided by text-to-speech programs enables students to listen to what they have written and catch spelling and syntax errors they often overlook when visually proofreading their work (Wanderman, 2000).

Text-to-speech features read aloud whatever students have written to provide needed auditory feedback for some learners.

Talking Spell-Checkers

Some word-processing programs that offer text-to-speech features include additional support by featuring spell-checks that talk. **Talking spell-checkers** read aloud the misspelled word and every suggestion in the list of correctly spelled words. Students who cannot easily recognize the correctly spelled word can make their selection on the basis of how it sounds.

Although technology offers powerful tools that can improve writing skills of students with disabilities, the research conveys a consistent message: **assistive technology**, that is, hardware and software specifically designed to meet the needs of exceptional students, will succeed in helping students improve their writing skills *only if* it is paired with good teaching strategies. Simply providing the software will not lead to improvements in the writing skills of students with disabilities (MacArthur, 1996, 2000). Students need to receive three-pronged training: (1) instruction on the writing process, (2) training on specific technology tools, and (3) training on how to use these technology tools to enhance the writing process.

The term *assistive technology* refers to hardware devices and specially designed software created to meet the needs of students with exceptionalities.

In the CLASSROOM

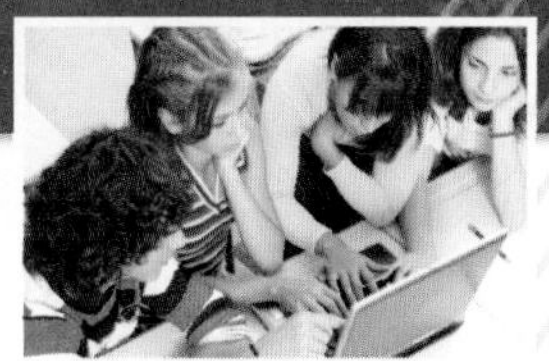

Assistive Technologies for Students with Special Needs

From reading disabilities to limited vision to speech impairment to developmental disabilities, assistive technology is the doorway to participation in classroom learning for students with special needs according to Lisa Wahl, a former director of the Center for Accessible Technology. In Contra Costa, California, a second-grade child with reading difficulties can hear a book read aloud with the help of headphones and a computer on which the child can select a text file for a book scanned into the computer. The teacher can select a software option that lets the child click on words the child doesn't know and hear how they are pronounced. The teacher can adjust the print size and font to best fit the child's needs.

At the Fremont Unified School District in California, fourteen students with varying disabilities—poor vision, wheelchair bound, physically or neurologically unable to speak, and developmentally delayed—lead their class in saying the Pledge of Allegiance with assistance from the DeltaTalker, "a device that speaks in response to commands sent by a head-mounted infrared pointer." The DeltaTalker also has keys that can be pressed by a single finger that will bring forth a spoken word such as *Hello*. The computers in the room sit on height-adjustable carts with adaptive keyboards. These keyboards have "a large, flat surface along with adjustable 'key' size, as well as trackballs, which are easier to use than a mouse for some users with motor difficulties."

Also in use is MathPad software, which helps students with fine motor disabilities to work through math problems because the digits and alignment have more clarity. The software provides feedback to indicate correct answers entered, and it will speak numbers as they are entered. The teacher can design math problems to meet each student's learning needs.

These technologies are just a few of the many assistive devices that make inclusion and participation in classrooms a reality for the special students of the twenty-first century.

Source: Wahl, L. (2008). *We all have special needs.* Retrieved February 27, 2009, from **http://www.edutopia.org/1045.**

Reading

When students who struggle with reading have alternative access to text-based materials, they can concentrate on understanding and learning rather than on decoding and processing.

Being able to read and understand textbooks and other required reading material is critical for academic success, especially as students progress from upper elementary to middle school, high school, and college. Once students leave elementary school, they are required to complete extensive amounts of reading on a daily basis—textbooks, works of literature, journal articles, reference materials—much of which may have readability levels well beyond the skills of many students with disabilities (Boyle et al., 2002). Slow readers and students with reading comprehension problems struggle to complete their reading assignments and will fall behind in their work if they cannot keep up. This is not only frustrating and stressful for the student, but it also interferes with learning the subject matter. Therefore, students with reading difficulties can utilize assistive technology to improve reading comprehension and increase reading independence.

Technology can support students who struggle with reading by providing alternative ways to access text-based materials. When students are provided with alternative access, they can concentrate on understanding and learning the content rather than on decoding and processing the text. The major types of alternative access to help with reading are recorded books, electronic text, and high interest–low level books.

Recorded Books

Recorded books are appropriate for students who can understand material at their grade level when they hear it, even though they may struggle with decoding and comprehending when they read it. When a person reads a book aloud and a recording is made, the resulting product is a recorded book. When listening to recorded books, students should follow along in a printed book to view the text. Recorded books are available both from nonprofit organizations, such as Recording for the Blind and Dyslexic, and from commercial companies. Materials obtained from commercial companies are produced for the general public and can be listened to on standard audio equipment such as CD players or MP3 players. Materials obtained from nonprofit organizations typically require a specialized device or special software.

High Interest–Low Level Books

High interest–low level books are appropriate for students who have not yet mastered the skills needed to read and understand material written at their grade-level. These alternatives offer age/grade-appropriate content presented at an easier reading level. To help with fluency, some computer-based books highlight the text as they read it aloud. The narration is digitized (recorded) speech, not synthesized (text-to-speech), so different characters speak differently, and the reading sounds more like a dramatization, which captivates students and involves them in the story. These books enable students who are reading on a second- or third-grade level to read a version of classics. Given this technology as a support, a student whose reading is far below grade level can still enjoy an assigned class story and participate in class activities.

Scan/Read Systems

Scan/read systems combine the use of a computer, a scanner, optical character recognition software, and speech output to read aloud any printed text.

Scan/read systems combine the use of a computer, a scanner, optical character recognition software, and speech output to read aloud any printed text while providing a visually enhanced display on a computer monitor. Users scan the printed pages to be read, and the print is converted into an electronic file, similar to a word-processing file. Scan/read programs then speak the words on the screen while highlighting the corresponding text. The highlighting helps readers to keep their eyes on a line of text, while the speech output provides ongoing auditory input.

TABLE 4.1 Summary of Technology Solutions for Special Needs Students

CONTENT/SKILLS AREA	SPECIAL NEED	TECHNOLOGY SOLUTIONS
ORGANIZING	Assist students with processing difficulties in organizing and relating concepts and instructional content	Outliners Concept-mapping software
WRITING	Assist students with coordination difficulties in creating clear, precise, and legible written communication	Word-processing software Word prediction software Text-to-speech software
READING	Assist sight-impaired or learning-disabled students in correctly understanding and processing written words	Recorded books Electronic texts Scan/read systems High interest–low level books
COMMUNICATION	Assist hearing-impaired students with correctly hearing and processing auditory information	Personal amplification systems Sound-field amplification systems Augmentative communication devices
COMPUTER USE: INPUT DEVICES	Assist physically impaired students with using a computer to input information for learning tasks	Accessibility options Sticky keys Mouse keys Keyboard labels Pointing devices Keyguards Onscreen keyboard Expanded keyboards Single switch
COMPUTER USE: OUTPUT DEVICES	Assist sight-impaired students with using computer output for learning tasks	Magnification software Screen readers

One obstacle when using scan/read technology is the time it takes to scan large amounts of text, such as a novel. Fortunately, a variety of Internet sites provide files of text that have already been converted into electronic format, commonly referred to as *e-text*. Most literature that is in the public domain, such as all of Shakespeare's plays, are available for free download and can be read aloud using a scan/read system.

Table 4.1 summarizes the various content and skill areas supported by the appropriate use of technology. Effective application of these by creative and skillful educators can go far in assisting students with special needs to achieve their academic goals.

Communication

To be successful in school, students must be able to communicate thoughts, feelings, and ideas. They must also be able to understand other people's communication attempts. For people with vision and auditory disabilities, technology offers an exciting range of solutions.

Go to the *Assignments and Activities* section of Chapter 4 in MyEducationKit and complete the video activity entitled *Assistive Technology for the Hearing Impaired.*

Assistive Listening Devices

Students who are hard of hearing often have difficulty following lectures and class discussions, particularly if the acoustics of the room are poor and/or if the teacher speaks softly, quickly, or unclearly (Do-It, 2004). Although a student's hearing aids may be adequate in one-on-one conversations, the poor acoustics of many classrooms lessen the hearing aids' effectiveness for understanding classroom conversations. Exacerbating the problem of poor acoustics is the need for teachers to speak while moving around their classrooms and to turn their backs to the students to write on a whiteboard. In addition to making it more difficult to hear, this also prevents students who utilize lip reading from seeing their teachers' faces. Similarly, when teachers look down while demonstrating a science experiment or other activity, students who reads lips can no longer interpret the information being presented.

Assistive listening devices (ALDs) can capture a desired sound, such as a teacher's voice, and amplify it for the student.

Assistive listening devices (ALDs) help to reduce the effect of poor acoustics in classrooms. They catch a desired sound, such as a teacher's voice, and amplify it for students with hearing difficulties. There are two major types of ALDs: personal amplification systems and sound-field amplification systems. In both types, the teacher wears a wireless microphone and small transmitter clipped to his or her clothing.

Amplification systems broadcast an auditory signal when the teacher speaks, to be received by personal or class systems.

With a **personal amplification system,** the student wears a small receiver and a sound output device, usually headphones, ear buds, or a direct connection to his or her hearing aid. When the teacher speaks, an auditory signal is broadcast and is received by the student. The student then hears the amplified teacher's voice transmitted to the personal output device. With a **sound-field amplification system,** the teacher's voice is broadcast through classroom loudspeakers. This kind of system is useful when more than one student can benefit from sound amplification. Sound-field systems are also beneficial for students who have attention deficit disorders. They can help the students to focus on the teacher's voice when distracting background noise is filtered out (Boswell, 2006).

Augmentative communication technology gives voice to those who cannot speak.

Many students who have physical disabilities such as cerebral palsy or neurological conditions such as autism are unable to speak. Have you ever had laryngitis or another illness that temporarily took away your ability to speak? Or have you ever been in a foreign country in which nobody understood your speech? If so, you have experienced the frustration and powerlessness of being voiceless. Bob Williams, a disability advocate who cannot speak because of cerebral palsy, expresses it this way: "The silence of speechlessness is never golden. We all need to communicate and connect with each other. . . . It is a basic human need, a basic human right" (2000, p. 248).

FIGURE 4.3

Augmentative devices help give voice to those who cannot speak.

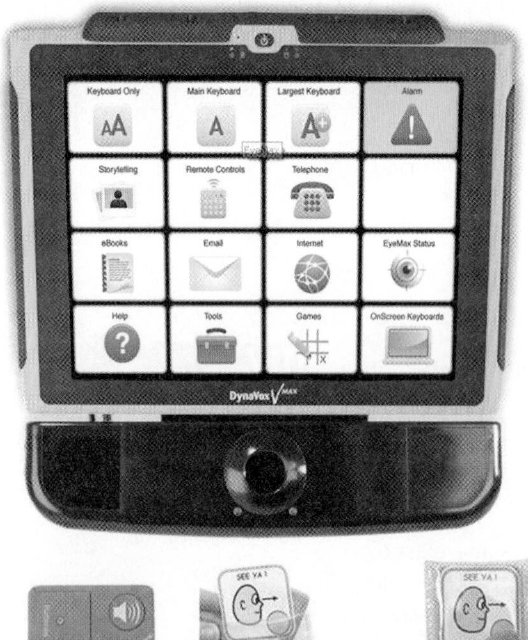

Top: Photo courtesy of DynaVox Mayer-Johnson, Pittsburgh, PA, www.dynavoxtech.com. Bottom left: Used courtesy of Augmentative Resources Inc., www.augresources.com. Bottom center: The Picture Communication Symbols © 1981-2014 by Mayer-Johnson, Inc., Used courtesy of Augmentative Resources Inc. Bottom right: Used courtesy of Augmentative Resources Inc., www.augresources.com.

One of the most powerful applications of computer technology has been the development of devices that give a voice to those who cannot speak (Figure 4.3). The term for this technology is **alternative and augmentative communication,** which is frequently referred to more simply as **augmentative communication.** Augmentative communication devices range from simple homemade picture boards to sophisticated computerized systems that can cost thousands of dollars. These communications devices use digitized speech and/or text-to-speech technology. The process of deciding which type of device will best serve a student is complicated. Typically, a speech/language pathologist, classroom teacher, parents, and the student must all be involved in the selection process. After a student has received an appropriate system, teachers have an important role to play: supporting the student's efforts to communicate.

Teachers who have a student using an augmentative communication device in their class need to learn how the student's system works so that the teacher can assist the student when needed. Even the fastest augmentative user will communicate at a much slower rate than speaking students; therefore, teachers need to provide ample time for augmentative communication users to complete their communication attempts. For example, before beginning a new topic of study that has specialized vocabulary such as characters' names or technical terms, teachers must convey this vocabulary to the speech/language therapist, who will add the custom vocabulary to the augmentative communication device so that the student will be able to participate in class discussions.

Technology to Support Computer Use

When methods use technology to help students with disabilities write, read, communicate, and learn academic skills, the first step is to ensure that students are able to use a computer. Many students with disabilities need to have adjustments made to standard computers. Others may need special hardware and/or software to be able to type. Many computer features offer the flexibility of adjusting aspects of the computer, from font to color to keyboard speed, to better suit the student's needs. Teachers need to become aware of these capabilities in order to implement their computer-rich instructional strategies.

Both Apple and Microsoft offer special features in their operating systems that enhance their usability by people with disabilities.

Most personal computer systems provide a variety of special features to enhance the usability of their products by people with disabilities. Accessibility features are available in the Apple Macintosh Universal Access options and the Windows Accessibility Options. For example, both offer screen magnification and a high-contrast setting for users with low vision. Both also offer **StickyKeys,** a feature that allows students to press keys sequentially to execute functions that typically require pressing the keys simultaneously. This simple feature enables students who type with only one finger or a head pointer to carry out essential commands such as Save (*Control* + *S*), Print (*Control* + *P*), or Copy (*Control* + C).

MouseKeys allows users to direct the mouse pointer and execute all mouse functions using the numeric keypad on the keyboard. Both the speed at which the mouse pointer travels and the acceleration speed are adjustable to meet individual needs. MouseKeys gives students who can use a keyboard but not a mouse the ability to direct the mouse pointer, click, double-click, and drag directly from the keyboard.

Assistive Input Devices

In addition to built-in usability options, specific hardware and software assistive technologies can help students with special needs input data into computers. Assistive input tools fall on a continuum from low-tech to high-tech. Low-tech adaptations use no electronic components and are usually inexpensive. Examples of low-tech devices include keyboard labels, pointing devices, and keyguards. **Keyboard labels** are self-adhesive and sized to fit on the computer keys. The labels are available with larger letters and higher contrast (e.g., white letters on a black background) and can be a simple solution for students who have difficulty distinguishing the letters, numbers, and symbols on a standard keyboard. Blank keyboard labels can be used to cover nonessential keys and can make the keyboard less confusing for students with cognitive deficits and/or autism.

Low-tech and high-tech assistive input helps students with mobility issues to input data correctly and issue computer commands.

Many students with physical disabilities cannot isolate a finger or use their hand to press a single key on the standard keyboard. **Pointing devices** help these students to use a computer. A pencil eraser affixed to the end of a dowel can be crafted into a pointing device to be held in a fist, in the mouth, or attached to a headband as a headstick. Students using these low-tech devices can then use StickyKeys and MouseKeys, mentioned above, for full computer access. Ideas and suggestions for both commercial and teacher-crafted assistive devices such as these are abundant and available on the Internet. Many web sites, such as ABLEDATA (Figure 4.4) offer specific information on devices that address the needs of the varying disabilities you may find in your classroom.

Keyguards are acrylic or metal covers with holes for each of the keys that are placed atop the computer keyboard. Keyguards increase typing accuracy because the holes allow only one key at a time to be pressed. Keyguards make it easier for students using a pointing device or those with poor fine motor control to target specific keys and to help keep unintended keystrokes from registering.

Modified keyboards and touch screens offer students with motor control issues easier command of the computer.

For students who cannot use a standard keyboard and mouse, even with low-tech adaptations, additional alternative input devices are available. Alternatives to a mouse include trackballs that have been adapted with a keyguard and separate buttons for double-click

FIGURE 4.4

Assistive Input Devices

Many web sites offer detailed information on the assistive devices that are available to support those with disabilities.

Courtesy of ABLEDATA. Used by permission.

as well as click and drag; adapted joysticks; touch screens; and mouse emulators that are controlled by one's head movement, known as head pointing systems. Additionally, students using a **head pointing system** for mouse emulation can word process and access other applications using an **onscreen keyboard.** The onscreen keyboard displays an image of a keyboard on the computer monitor and is operated either by clicking on a key or by simply placing the mouse pointer on a key for a designated period of time. Head pointing systems are an option for students who cannot use their hands for operating the mouse but are able to move their heads in small increments for precise positioning. Touch screens also offer input capabilities to those students with limited muscular control.

> Touch screens receive input by being touched at relevant points on the monitor screen.

Assistive Output Devices

A **touch screen** is a computer monitor screen that responds to human touch. Touch screen software usually displays a series of graphics or icons. Instead of using a mouse and pointer to select an icon or command, you touch the icon itself as it is displayed on the touch screen, and the computer responds. The screen is touch sensitive and the touch screen software interpolates your finger's location on the screen as a command to select the icon or option that is displayed on that spot. On computers equipped with a touch screen, a keyboard and/or mouse might not even be available.

Touch screens are quick and easy to use. If large amounts of data need to be entered or many choices need to be made from complex sets of options, touch screens are an inappropriate choice of input device. They work best with simple, straightforward displays. Touch screens are often used in information kiosks at hotels and airports and with medical or other complex equipment that requires quick setting changes. They can also be useful in the classroom for young children who are preliterate, cannot type, or have difficulty controlling a mouse owing to physical impairment.

Other alternatives to the standard keyboard include expanded keyboards, mini-keyboards, one-handed keyboards, and customizable keyboards. **Expanded keyboards** offer a larger surface area and larger keys than the standard keyboard. They are beneficial to students who lack fine motor control and might benefit from a large target area to execute an accurate keystroke. Often these are students whose hands are fisted because of cerebral palsy or other physical disability. **Mini-keyboards** are substantially smaller than the standard keyboard and are typically helpful for students whose motor impairments restrict the range of motion in their arms and wrists, making it difficult to reach all the keys on the standard keyboard. To use a mini-keyboard, a student must have good accuracy within a narrow range of motion. One-handed keyboard options are also available for those who have good finger dexterity but only with one hand.

Customizable keyboards can be configured to meet students' individual needs. That is, the keyboard can be programmed to enter specific text or to execute particular commands when keys are pressed. A single key could be programmed to enter an entire word, phrase, or sentence with one stroke. For example, the closing to a letter, space for a signature, the typed name, and the command to send the letter for printing could all be executed with a single keystroke.

Some students who have severe physical disabilities do not have enough motor control to use any of the common support methods mentioned above. However, if they can control a single movement, such as flexing a fist, turning a head to one side, or pressing a foot, they may be able to access a computer using a **single switch** with scanning. Scanning in this context refers to a selection method in which a highlighter moves from item to item in an onscreen array. The student watches the highlighter as it moves from item to item. When the highlighter is on the item that the student desires, the student activates the switch to select the item. The computer then performs as if it received conventional input (i.e., as if the keyboard or mouse was used). Onscreen arrays can be used to do anything a keyboard or mouse can do: access operating system functions, surf the Internet, and enter text into word-processing or other programs. Single switch scanning is an important access method because even though it is slow, it is often the *only* means of computer access available to individuals with severe physical disabilities.

For students who are blind or visually impaired, the two primary technology tools available to provide an alternative to a standard visual display are screen magnification software and screen readers. **Screen magnification software** magnifies the entire visual display—the desktop, menus, and documents within applications—and can benefit students who have limited vision. The degree of magnification can be adjusted depending

TECH TIPS for Teachers

Touch Screen for Special Needs Students

Touch screen monitors and related software that enable a traditional monitor to emulate a touch screen are powerful tools for students with disabilities. Touch screens may display graphics that the user can touch to enter commands and make software selections. Special software can display the image of a computer keyboard on the screen so that keys or commands can be pointed to and clicked on. Whether hardware- or software-based, touch screen technologies can improve the life of a student with disabilities.

The Alliance for Technology Access (**http://ataccess.org/**) is a network of resources that provides information and support services to children and adults with disabilities including information about assistive devices. Its web site includes many success stories. Two such stories demonstrate the power of touch screen technology.

United Cerebral Palsy of Idaho shared the story of Melissa. Melissa, a 4-year-old with cerebral palsy, had difficulty holding her head up and moving her arms. In her school's computer lab, a TouchWindow was installed so she could play math games. In addition to practicing math concepts, Melissa was able to strengthen her right arm by reaching out to touch the screen. She was also able to strengthen her neck as she worked to keep her head up to see the monitor and work with the software. This adaptive technology not only assisted in teaching skills, it helped improve the learner's muscle tone.

Technology Assistance for Special Consumers in Huntsville, Alabama, shared the story of Steven, who had a stroke at age 16 that left him a quadriplegic. He had partial paralysis of all extremities and was unable to speak. After the stroke, he could move only his head, but that was enough, with the help of a combination of assistive technologies that included a keyboard display on a screen. Steven learned to use a computer by scanning. Scanning is a system in which a keyboard is displayed on a screen with keys highlighted one after another. Simply by pressing a single switch button when the highlight appeared on the right key, Steven was able to communicate via computer. Today, having gained more movement in his arms, he can use a similar keyboard display that allows him to point to and click on the keys he desires with a glide pad.

SOURCE: Retrieved April 20, 2002, from **http://etacess.org/community/successes/successes.html**.

Go to the *Assignments and Activities* section of Chapter 4 in MyEducationKit and complete the video activity entitled *Adaptive Technology.*

Switches are an alternative input device for students who have extremely limited movement.

Screen magnification and screen readers are the two major options that provide an alternative to the standard visual display.

on students' needs. Screen magnification software also offers choices of enlarged cursors and pointers and high-contrast options such as white text on a black background.

Screen readers can support students who have no usable vision or who get fatigued from using screen magnification. Full-featured screen readers speak the contents of everything on the screen: menus, dialog boxes, toolbar buttons, and URLs, as well as text in web sites, word-processing documents, and other applications. Screen readers will also alert users to new windows opening and the presence of graphic images. Screen-reading software can enable students who are blind to do anything on computers that sighted students can do.

Issues in Implementing Technology for Students with Special Needs

Clearly, when appropriately used, technology can support both teachers and students in meeting diverse needs. However, implementation of such technology does give rise to several considerations. Examination of these issues is necessary to use technology solutions effectively.

The issues in technology implementation for students with special needs include determining which technology solution will be most effective, collaboration of technical support, and training.

The first key issue in technology implementation for students with special needs is determining which technology solution will be most effective. This is best done with input from both professionals and family members who are familiar with the student as well as input from the student. Classroom teachers, occupational therapists, physical therapists, speech language pathologists, and technology personnel all have expertise that can contribute to the development of effective technology solutions. It is essential that the technology solutions match the specific needs of individual students. Many online resources provide professionals and families with relevant information and potential solutions. Web sites such as the one sponsored by the National Council for Learning Disabilities offer extensive discussion on all aspects of disabilities, including potential technology support (Figure 4.5). The Techmatrix web site sponsored by the National Center for Technology Innovation (NCTI) and the Center for Implementing Technology in Education (CITEd) offer searchable educator resources. Explore these resources to become familiar with the challenges faced by students with special needs and the possible options to best address their needs.

The second key issue in technology implementation for students with special needs is training. Students need to be taught how to use the technology tools and then how to use the technology tools to accomplish whatever tasks have been identified. Teachers and other adults who work with the students need to learn at least the basics about the specific technology so that they can support the student in the classroom. Additionally, technical support staff need to become familiar with the assistive technology so that they can provide troubleshooting and support when needed.

The third key issue in technology implementation for students with special needs is the need for collaboration between assistive technology (AT) personnel and information technology (IT) personnel (Newton and Dell, 2009). They share the responsibility of providing appropriate technology and technical support to students with special needs. This may mean that not all computers in a school will be configured in exactly the same way. It may mean that a special software program will need to be installed on a classroom computer in the middle of a school year or a trial version of a program will need to be downloaded onto a school computer. AT and IT personnel need to work together to make sure students with special needs have access to and support for the tools they need to be successful in school.

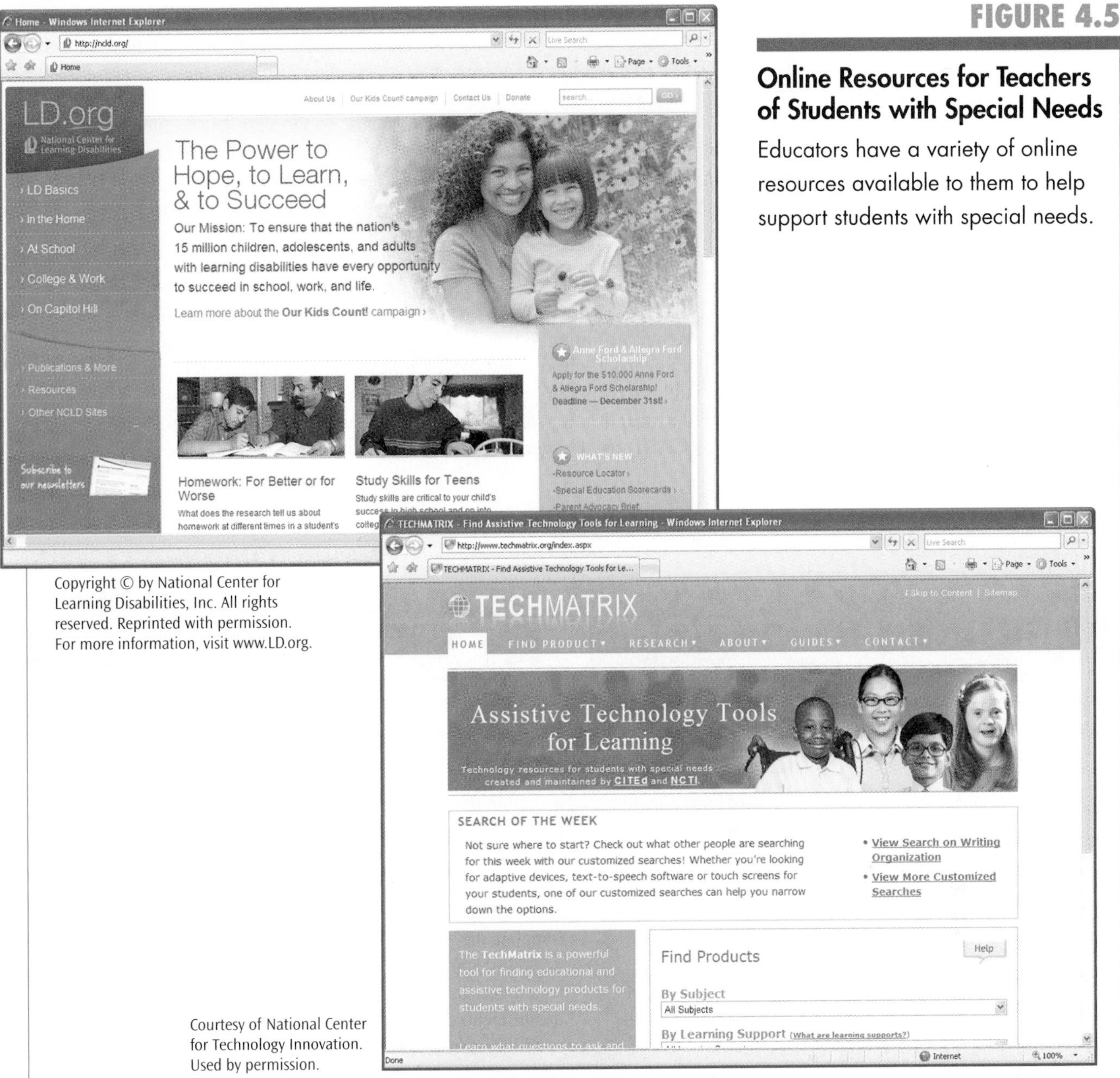

FIGURE 4.5

Online Resources for Teachers of Students with Special Needs

Educators have a variety of online resources available to them to help support students with special needs.

Technology Solutions for Gifted Students

Educational technology can also offer valuable support for meeting the instructional needs of students who are gifted. In addition to helping to meet the academic needs of these students, technology can serve their social and emotional needs as well. Computer technology can help gifted students remain engaged in the learning process even if they have already mastered the content being presented or master new concepts quickly when they are introduced. For example, Internet-based activities can provide access to innovative

Educational technology can help keep gifted students engaged, meet their academic needs, and address their social-emotional needs.

resources, such as professional experts, that can broaden and deepen the learning of gifted students. Students can research topics at their achievement level rather than their grade level and can present their findings in creative ways using multimedia technology tools such as digital stories. Using such technology tools, gifted students may create DVD-based presentations that include musical introductions, voice overlays, and special-effects displays of their digital photos to develop teaching tutorials for peers or for lower grades. Well-structured inquiry-based Internet projects give gifted students the opportunity to interact with their peers in cooperative learning activities while still providing them with appropriate levels of challenge. Additionally, Internet-based communications tools such as email, discussion boards, and video conferencing can connect gifted students with peers who have similar interests and abilities.

Gifted students, particularly those in multilevel classes, need **differentiated instruction** to address their unique need for challenge and engagement. As defined by the Center for Applied Special Technology (CAST), differentiated instruction is an approach that recognizes and targets instruction to the varying abilities found in the same classroom. Differentiated instruction is a key aspect of the broad approach to teaching and learning supported by CAST, the Universal Design for Learning. This approach suggests that all

In the CLASSROOM

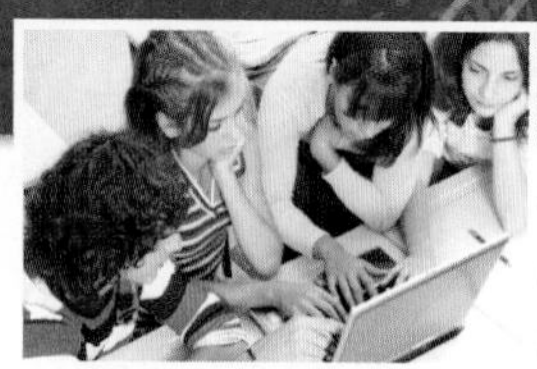

The "Also" Special Needs: The Talented and Gifted Students

All too frequently, the term *special needs* is used to refer to students with disabilities rather than including those with special abilities. The category of gifted and talented students as a special needs population is also recognized in districts such as that in Harlingen, Texas. There, talented and gifted students (TAGS) are enrolled in programs tailored to provide ample opportunity for these young people to develop to their full potential. As early as first grade, Harlingen begins special education for its gifted and talented students. Teachers are trained in the Gifted and Talented Program, which recognizes the critical importance of integrating technology into the curriculum with the Tech Training Curriculum and Instruction resource team. This team provides teacher instruction and leadership resources as implementation.

Taking into account that TAGS know they are "different," Jeryl Phillips, Special Education Resource–Assistive Technology of the Peel District School Board in Mississauga, Ontario, designed a special web quest for his students: "So, You're Gifted . . . A WebQuest of Self-Discovery for Enhanced Learners in Grades 6–8." The introduction states that "there are many types of gifted people" and presents a discussion of what it means to be gifted. The task is a performance-based assignment that will culminate in a presentation that conveys the individuality of each student in the class. The process leads the students through research and testing to ascertain their uniqueness and, once identified, to choose a quotation from a list that pertains to giftedness that they would like to have as their personal motto. The students are given a choice of formats for the presentations: oral, visual, media, or other as approved by the teacher. Ample resources and an evaluation rubric followed by the conclusion and the teacher pages complete the web quest.

Gail Hanninen, Director of Seabury School in Tacoma, Washington, recognized the need for her gifted students to recognize the differences in their cognitive-processing pathways and to design her lessons accordingly. Her approach works for gifted students who are considered "twice exceptional," meaning that they are gifted but have learning disabilities. For example, a gifted high school student named Joel had a significant learning disability related to reading and written language. He was exceptionally talented when it came to social skills and computers and video productions. Computer technology linked to video production made it possible for Joel to demonstrate his giftedness and convey his ability to think analytically and creatively despite his language difficulties.

Sources: Phillips, J. *So, You're gifted . . . A web quest of self-discovery for enhanced learners in grades 6–8.* Retrieved March 6, 2009, from **http://www.ldcsb.on.ca/schools/cfe/WebQuests/Gifted/index.htm.** Hanninen, G. E. (2008). *Focusing on our gifted youth.* Retrieved July 13, 2008, from **http://www.newhorizons.org/spneeds/gifted/hanninen3.htm.**

instruction should be designed so that all learners, regardless of their unique needs, have effective, quality access to education. Technology serves as a powerful tool to ensure universal access and to differentiate the teaching and learning process to meet the special needs of gifted students.

Technology Solutions for Culturally and Linguistically Diverse Students

English language learning (ELL) students (sometimes referred to as *limited English proficient* [LEP] *students*) are one of the most rapidly growing student populations in K–12 schools. Although most ELL students are from Spanish-speaking backgrounds, they also include students from diverse international heritages. For that reason, ELL students are more appropriately referred to as students who are *culturally and linguistically diverse (CLD)*.

Culturally and linguistically diverse (CLD) students include English language learning (ELL) students and students from diverse international heritages.

The advances in technology in the Information Age have opened up enormous opportunities to address the challenges these students may face. The Teachers of English to Speakers of Other Languages (TESOL) organization has developed goals and standards that guide teachers in developing their capacity to support all students in achieving the digital literacy that will help them to address their unique needs. These standards guide the preparation of prospective K–12 teachers and the ongoing professional development of in-service teachers to effectively evaluate and use technology as an instructional tool for teaching CLD students.

Educational technology is often underutilized for providing **comprehensible input** to CLD students. Comprehensible input is information in the second language (e.g., English) that the learner is better able to comprehend. Comprehensible input is designed to support understanding for students whose culture and language differ from that of the classroom context. Through the use of visuals, cooperative tasks, guarded vocabulary/language used during teaching, and hands-on activities, the teacher scaffolds content area concepts and vocabulary for CLD students as they learn the English language.

PEARSON myeducationkit™

Go to the *Assignments and Activities* section of Chapter 4 in MyEducationKit and complete the video activity entitled *Technology Supports Second Language Learners.*

Scaffolding is generally defined as providing support for learners by taking them from their individual baseline and moving them beyond this point. It is particularly important for CLD students. Their baseline includes another language and/or culture. Scaffolding to the English language is a critical component, and technology is a significant support for this process. For example, language software programs can incrementally increase language acquisition task difficulty, altering modes for practice and application in innovative ways, and providing immediate feedback for learning. The one-on-one attention and targeted practice that CLD students so often need are readily available via these technology tools that offer comprehensible input. Further, with the teacher's continual monitoring of students' content comprehension, the planned targeted use of technology assists in correctly aligning additional curricular interventions to a CLD student's specific needs. Table 4.2 summarizes such technology tools.

Additionally, for second language learners, an ongoing need is the development of vocabulary skills in English. In its comprehensive review and analysis of thirty years of reading research, the National Reading Panel (2000) described multimedia methods, such as graphic representations and hypertext, as significant contributions to teaching vocabulary. Exposures to vocabulary through multimedia software programs that are rich and contextualized offer teachers a valuable tool to integrate into the lesson. These programs may also include easily accessible ancillary materials and visuals that help to activate and build students' background knowledge.

Technology offers CLD students opportunities for scaffold learning and to practice vocabulary.

One of the most critical issues in addressing the special needs of CLD learners is teacher awareness and preparation. Many Internet resources are available for teachers to help them address the language diversity they may find in their classroom. For educators, one of the

TABLE 4.2 Technologies for Comprehensible Input

COMPREHENSIBLE INPUT	SOFTWARE-RELATED SUPPORT	HARDWARE SUPPORT
VISUALS	• Graphics creating • Graphics editing • Internet • Screencasting • Video • Visual representations (e.g., concept maps, flow charts)	• Computer/laptop • Digital camera • Interactive whiteboard • LCD projector • MP3 player • Response systems/clickers
GUARDED VOCABULARY	• Internet • Sound editing • Sound recording • Voice recognition • Voice synthesis • Word translation	• Computer/laptop • Digital audio recorder • Interactive whiteboard • MP3 player • Response systems/clickers
COOPERATIVE TASKS	• Internet • Simulations • Document processing • Online media	• Computer/laptop • Digital camera • Interactive whiteboard • LCD projector
HANDS-ON ACTIVITIES	• Internet • Graphics creating • Graphics editing • Document processing • Instructional games • Online media • Word processing	• Computer/laptop • Digital camera • Interactive whiteboard • Keyboard • Mouse • MP3 player • Response systems/clickers • Trackball

most useful resources is the National Clearing House for English Language Acquisition, sponsored by the Office of English Language Acquisition a part of the U.S. Department of Education (Figure 4.6). This site offers research and webinars (web-based seminars) on a variety of topics for teachers of CLD students.

> One of the most critical issues in addressing the special needs of CLD learners is awareness and preparation by those who will teach these students.

Teachers can also visit helpful web sites for lesson plan ideas, teaching resources, and research sponsored and maintained by organizations, universities, and even innovative teachers. You may wish to visit the many resources in MyEducationKit to examine these sites. Many of these sites also offer searchable resources for lesson ideas and teaching materials in any language. The Internet offers a wealth of resources for educators who are interested in meeting the unique needs of CLD students, regardless of their cultural background or language.

Issues in Implementing Technology for Culturally and Linguistically Diverse Students

To maximize technology's potential with CLD students, teachers must move beyond utilizing technology as a remedial tool and recognize its full potential in meeting CLD students' linguistic and academic needs. Remediation suggests that a CLD student needs additional instruction in content or cognitive process. This may not be the case for the CLD

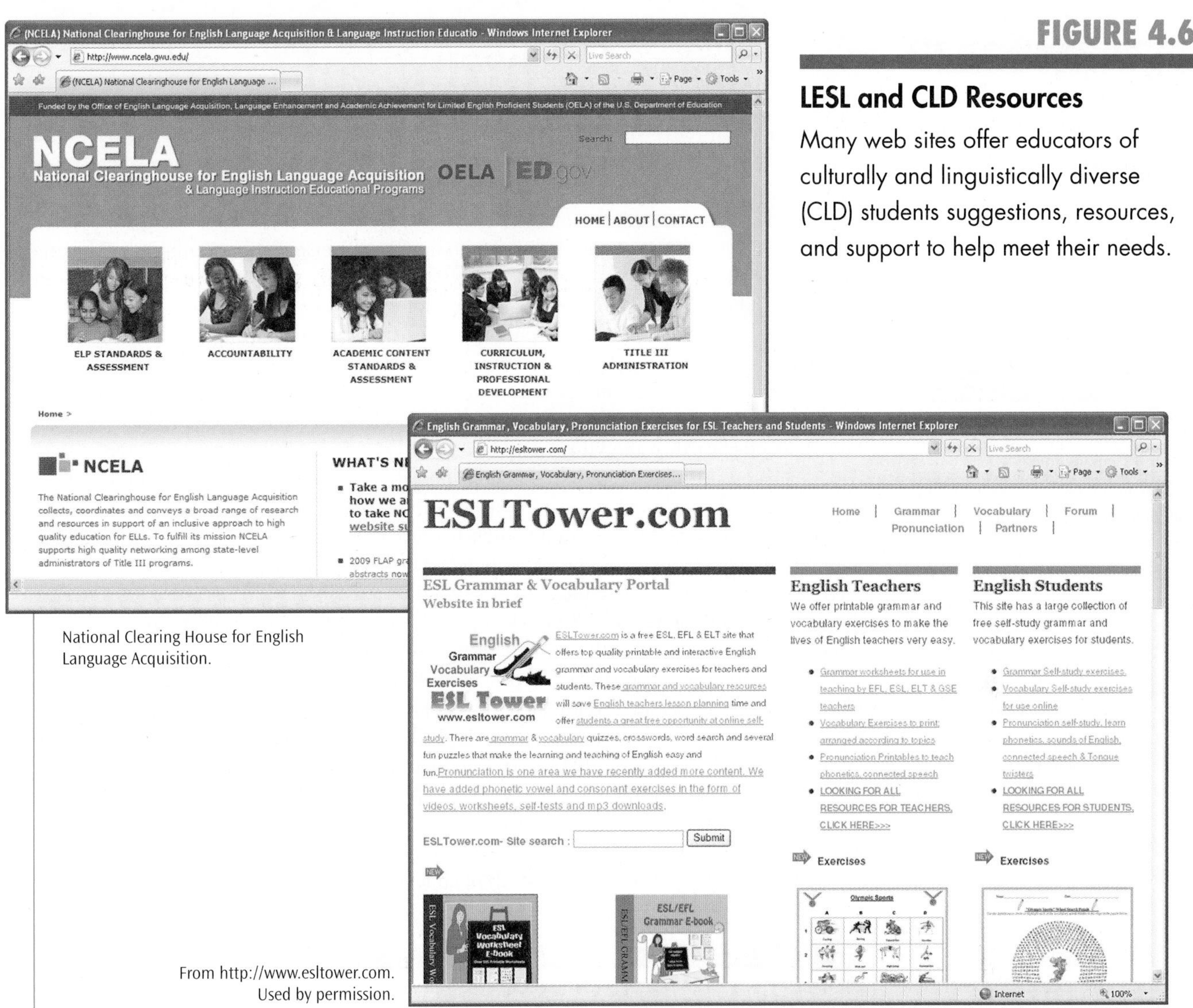

National Clearing House for English Language Acquisition.

From http://www.esltower.com. Used by permission.

FIGURE 4.6

LESL and CLD Resources

Many web sites offer educators of culturally and linguistically diverse (CLD) students suggestions, resources, and support to help meet their needs.

student who functions at grade level but is impeded by language. CLD students, especially those at low levels of English language proficiency, are all too often assigned an English language game or activity that is not cognitively appropriate or challenging. Instead, teachers should consider their stated objective and then assign activities that are of the technological and linguistic complexity appropriate to that objective.

Methodology for effectively employing technology to address the varied needs of CLD students is still being explored. Just as the needs of CLD students are diverse, so too are the many ways in which technology might be implemented to meet them. Educators must use creativity to infuse technology to meet the unique needs of their CLD students, particularly as the students successfully move from level to level in their second language proficiency. Yet technology alone is not sufficient to provide needed support. As is the case in meeting the needs of all learners, effective pedagogical practices for CLD students must be built on a solid foundation of theory and planning designed by creative technology-competent educators.

Technology Solutions for All Learners

PEARSON myeducationkit

Go to the *Assignments and Activities* section of Chapter 4 in MyEducationKit and complete the video activity entitled *Universal Design.*

Student diversity is a reality that teachers at all grade levels and in all content areas must address. Diversity is in every classroom, not just in special education or language classrooms. Awareness of the many ways students differ is the first necessary step in effectively meeting student needs. Many web sites are dedicated to helping educators prepare for the diversity they will need to address and maintain their vigilance in meeting the challenges of teaching to diversity. Respect for and dedication to meeting diverse needs, combined with careful planning that considers and addresses such diversity, are essential to meet your curriculum standards and content goals. Technology, creatively applied, is a powerful tool that can be utilized to address the needs of diverse learners and make the teaching and learning process more effective, efficient, and successful.

PEARSON myeducationkit

To check your comprehension of the content covered in this chapter, go to the MyEducationKit for your book and complete the *Study Plan* for Chapter 4.

As was mentioned earlier in this chapter, CAST has developed very specific guidelines for ensuring that educators address the diversity they will find in their classrooms. These guidelines, collectively called the **Universal Design for Learning** (UDL), offer educators a set of parameters for instructional design that consider what all students, regardless of the ways in which they are diverse, need to ensure learning success. Universal design principles were originally developed by architects and designers to ensure that access by individuals with disabilities to buildings and products is not restricted. These same principles have been applied to many other areas including education. The Universal Design for Instruction as defined by the University of Washington's DO-IT (Disabilities, Opportunities, Internetworking, and Technology) project, suggests that there are many ways in which all aspects of the education process can be more inclusive, from physical spaces to instruction (Burgstahler, 2008). CAST has refined this application and developed a framework "for using technology to maximize learning opportunities for every student" (Rose and Meyer, 2002, Preface). UDL principles are critical to consider to ensure that the instruction you create maximizes learning for all students regardless of their unique and diverse needs and therefore deserves a unique focus.

Universal Design for Learning (UDL) offers educators a set of parameters for instructional design that consider what all students need to ensure learning success.

Interchapter 4 offers an indepth review of Universal Design for Learning. While a focus for learners with special needs, an understanding of UDL principles will assist all educators in effectively meeting all the needs of all learners.

FIGURE 4.7

Resources for Diverse Learners

The U.S. Department of Education Institute of Education Sciences offers educators publications and resources to effectively support diverse learners.

Key Terms

alternative and augmentative communication, 94
assistive listening devices, 94
assistive technology, 91
augmentative communication, 94
comprehensible input, 101
concept mapping software, 89
custom dictionary, 90
customizable keyboard, 97
differentiated instruction, 100
expanded keyboard, 97
head pointing system, 96
high-interest–low-level books, 92
keyboard labels, 95
keyguards, 95
mini-keyboard, 97
MouseKeys, 95
onscreen keyboard, 96
personal amplification system, 94
pointing devices, 95
recorded books, 92
scan/read systems, 92
screen magnification software, 98
screen readers, 98
single switch, 97
sound-field amplification system, 94
StickyKeys, 95
students with exceptionalities, 88
students with special needs, 88
talking spell-checkers, 91
talking word-processing programs, 91
text-to-speech programs, 91
touch screen, 96
Universal Design for Learning, 104
word prediction software, 90

Student Activities

CHAPTER REVIEW

1. What are five different types of diversity? Why is it important that teachers understand the diversity of their students?
2. What are five significant contributions that effective technology tools can make to meeting the needs of students with disabilities?
3. How can word-processing software help a student who lacks dexterity or has trouble holding a pencil?
4. What is word predictive software? For whom can it be most helpful?
5. What are three ways in which students who struggle with reading can be supported by technology? How can each type of technology help these students?
6. Augmentative communication support for students who are unable to speak can range from very simple and inexpensive to complex and costly. Give two examples of augmentative communication devices.
7. Why is it important for a student with special needs to be able to use a computer?
8. Give five examples of assistive input devices, and briefly describe how each works.
9. How can technology help gifted and talented students?
10. Who are CLD students? Why does technology too often take a remediation approach when used to support these students? Why would this have negative consequences?

WHAT DO YOU THINK?

1. The concept of universal design suggests that all instructional activities should ensure equal access for all learners regardless of their unique needs. After reading Interchapter 4 and examining the evolution of universal design from architecture to learning, consider how you might include it in your classroom. Do you intend to adjust your instruction to include universal design principles when you teach? Explain why or why not.
2. Students with special needs include both students who have disabilities and those who are gifted. Technology can provide solutions to help meet their unique needs. However, schools typically have limited budgets for technology. Given that the needs of all students should be met, what do you think the best allocation of limited technology dollars should be to support these student needs? Give examples to support your views.
3. When technology is used to support culturally and linguistically diverse students, it is often remedial. Some students find themselves using technology that has been designed for younger learners simply because the vocabulary level matches their current level of language acquisition. This type of remediation via technology can be frustrating to use. Imagine yourself living in another country, trying to acquire the language, and being asked to learn via remedial software. What concerns would you have about this instructional approach? What other options might be found to avoid remediation when it is instructionally unnecessary?

LEARNING TOGETHER

1. Too often, teachers with culturally and linguistically diverse students in their classroom have little time to work with such students individually to help them to understand both instructions and content. One solution is to use technology to provide the additional support. In a group of three or four, research the ways in which technology can offer support for these learners. List of at least five technologies and methodologies that demonstrate how technology can address CLD student needs. Include the web sites you used in your research.
2. One of the issues teachers face when attempting to meet diverse students' needs is that teachers typically have only modest instruction in teaching students with special needs during the years in their teacher preparation program. Therefore, the primary means to prepare teachers to adequately address diversity is through post-degree teacher training. In a group of three or four peers, identify your group's specific professional needs if you were facing a diverse class. Research via the Internet to determine the kinds of training opportunities available and the organizations that offer such training. Summarize the list of your needs and the possible training options to address them.

TEACHING WITH TECHNOLOGY: INTEGRATION IDEAS WEB QUEST

As you become familiar with the many issues associated with teaching diverse learners and the technologies available to address their needs, it is useful to examine how other teachers are applying technology to support them. Let's take a look at some specific, innovative ways in which educators are addressing diversity via technology using the links that follow.

ACTIVITY: After you explore the links that interest you, select one aspect of diversity of significance to you. Complete a web search to discover at least three technology-rich ideas to address this need. Write a one-page summary of your web quest that includes (1) the link you used and the integration ideas and technologies you found, (2) how you might use technology to address this need, and (3) any organizational or support web sites that might offer you resources to use the technologies you found or that will help you to address the need you selected.

Integration Ideas: Integrating Technology into Language Arts

To improve literacy skills in a summer intervention program at the Schaumberg District 54 Extended School Year Program, special education students were assigned Don Johnston's interactive online novel, *Building Wings*, to read. The process involves reading the novel in class and carrying out follow-up activities online; the students were treated to hearing Johnston read the audio version. Activities in which the students took part were the Readers' Theater, Illustrators, and Compare/Contrast. For more information, visit **http://techlearning.com/article/8898**.

Integration Ideas: Integrating Technology into Science

Peggy Renfranz of Hyde Park High, a School to Career School, teaches students with multiple handicaps in an occupational skills program that meets Learning Standards for Access & Entry Skills for Biology and for Math. The program, GardenWorks, lets the students with severe disabilities learn Adaptive Daily Living (ADL) skills through building terraria, creating a windowside habitat and observatory, and raising and donating plants to landscape the school yard and to school fundraisers. The students search the Internet for gardening information and use digital cameras and software that assist them in using pictures as communication symbols, as well as PrintShop, Excel, PowerPoint, and Word. In recognition of their accomplishments, her students recently came in first in the school's Science Fair in the category of Teacher-Assisted Projects. To learn more, visit **http://bostonteachnet.org/renfranz/renfranz.htm.**

Integration Ideas: Integrating Technology into Mathematics

Kathy, a sixth-grade special education teacher, teaches data analysis and probability by means of spinners from both traditional, textbook, and digital (a computer connected to a projection plate) sources. She discusses with her students how spinners are used in games they play and how spinners affect the ease or difficulty of winning a game. In pairs, the students work problems from their math textbook to find how likely it is for a specific color to be selected on different spinners. Going to the computer, Kathy pulls up a digital spinner from the Shodor web site (**http://www.shodor.org/interactivate/activities/AdjustableSpinner/?version=1.3**) that shows theoretical and experimental probability, how sectors on a spinner can be changed as to number and color, and how the number of spins could also be changed. Integrating technology in this way is a feature of the UDL approach to teaching that can be read about in depth at the "What Is Universal Design for Learning?" web site at **http://www.cast.org/research/udl/index.html.** Learn more at **http://www.cast.org/teachingeverystudent/toolkits/.**

Integrating Technology for Teaching English Language Learners (ELL)

Barbara Gottschalk, an ELL teacher at Angus Elementary School in Sterling Heights, Michigan, uses drill-and-practice software from Pearson Education's *SuccessMaker* program. She noted that the module "Discover English" that is part of the program is a valuable assistive instrument for teaching English to her elementary school students. In response to criticism of drill-and-practice-based instruction, Ms. Gottschalk said that too often teachers don't take the time to learn how to use it properly to reap the full benefits of this mode of instruction, which is derived from behaviorist theory. She has found that the immediate feedback students receive on the work they do has helped her second-language students significantly. The computer program generates reports that are not only immediate but also informative in identifying areas of weakness in language acquisition skills. Not the least of the plus factors for the drill-and-practice software in the "Discover English" module is that it is computer-based, and students are highly motivated to engage in activities that allow them to use technology. For more ideas on how to use technology to assist ELL students, visit **http://www.edweek.org/dd/articles/2007/09/02ell.h01.html.**

interchapter 4

Universal Design for Diverse Learners

At the core of teaching is the effective and accurate transfer of appropriate knowledge to all students. Teaching is complex, particularly because the process typically requires that one person teach many students and because those students can be diverse in so many different ways. Teachers must adapt instruction so that all students in the classroom have equal opportunities to learn. One approach to achieving this is universal design. Adapted from outside of education, this approach offers a way to think about how we can best ensure effective, quality access to education for all learners. Awareness of universal design principles and how they apply to education can be indispensible in the creation of effective and meaningful lesson plans that address the needs of all learners.

What Is Universal Design?

Universal design (UD) has its roots in architectural design. The original intent of UD was to remove physical barriers so that people with disabilities would have the same ease of access to physical spaces that others take for granted. When first envisioned, UD addressed access to buildings. For example, UD suggested that buildings have no steps or have alternatives to them; that restrooms have wider doors, larger rooms, and more supportive fixtures; and that streets have curb cutouts. When this same concept of eliminating the barriers that made life easier or more fulfilling for those with disabilities was applied to other products and environments, innovations in meeting the needs of disabled citizens were launched. UD was soon applied to the design of products and information technology. For example, products were developed that were easier to use because of the addition of larger controls and easier-to-read markings. Kitchen cabinets were made with slide-out shelves. Packages became easier to grip or open. Even the "undo" command on your PC had its origins in UD, as do features such as screen magnification and screen readers.

UD has seven basic principles, as defined by the Center for Universal Design at North Carolina State University (1997). Each of these principles requires that the designer of a space, product, or environment take the principles into consideration to maximize access for all users, regardless of their abilities. The seven principles as stated by the Center are as follows:

- Equitable use—*The design is useful and marketable to people with diverse abilities.*
- Flexibility in use—*The design accommodates a wide range of individual preferences and abilities.*
- Simple and intuitive—*Use of the design is easy to understand, regardless of the user's experience, knowledge, language skills, or current concentration level.*
- Perceptible information—*The design communicates necessary information effectively to the user, regardless of ambient conditions or the user's sensory abilities.*
- Tolerance for error—*The design minimizes hazards and the adverse consequences of accidental or unintended actions.*
- Low physical effort—*The design can be used efficiently and comfortably and with a minimum of fatigue.*
- Size and space for approach and use—*Appropriate size and space is provided for approach, reach, manipulation, and use regardless of user's body size, posture, or mobility.*

Even though these principles originally applied to making barrier-free spaces, it was quickly recognized that they are broad enough to be applied to areas beyond their original focus. Improving access should be a goal for every area of human endeavor so that resources and experiences are available to the widest possible range of people. Applying these principles to circumstances beyond physical spaces and products improved access. Nowhere is this more true than in the field of education.

Universal Design in Education

Universal Design in Education (UDE) began to be applied approximately two decades ago. An outgrowth of the work of the Center for Universal Design at North Carolina State University, the UD principles were applied to ensure that schools too would use practices, materials, equipment, and physical environments that would support the widest spectrum of students. The intent was to ensure that all students have the opportunity for learning in a manner that supports their abilities and learning styles. The UDE concept suggests that all aspects of education should accommodate all students' needs as well as their potentials.

Technology is a key component of UDE to help students with disabilities get the same depth and breadth of learning experiences as do nondisabled students. Guidelines help computer makers and software companies create products that are usable by the widest audience address so that all students, regardless of their abilities, have equal access to technologies. Technology accessibility typically focused on output and display technologies, input and control devices, manipulations, documentation, and safety. As with the broader UD principles, technology accessibility has informed the development of effective products and environments that have the capacity to serve a wide audience with diverse needs. But like all implementation of technology in education, the critical component is not the technology itself, regardless of how accessible it is or how much more accessible it makes instruction. Equally important are teachers and their ability to plan meaningful learning experiences for all learners. Well-planned instruction that is mindful of the needs and abilities of all learners remains at the heart of UDE. The application of this approach to UDE has led to the development of the Universal Design for Learning.

The Universal Design for Learning

The Center for Applied Special Technology (CAST) has created a UD framework to use in considering the teaching and learning process. Universal Design for Learning (UDL) addresses curriculum and instructional strategies so that they are focused on supporting all learners. UDL suggests that instruction be offered in multiple formats and that it address the three primary systems that make up learning: "(a) recognition systems that identify patterns and objects, (b) strategic systems that tell us how to do things, and (c) affective systems that determine what is important and provide the motivation for learning" (Meyer and Rose, 2000). According to UDL, instruction should include a variety of multimedia experiences, tools, and strategies that are designed to target these systems. As CAST noted on its UDL web site (**http://www.cast.org/research/udl/ index.html**):

"Universal Design for Learning calls for . . .

- *Multiple means of representation,* to give learners various ways of acquiring information and knowledge,
- *Multiple means of action and expression,* to provide learners alternatives for demonstrating what they know,
- *Multiple means of engage* to tap into learners' interests, offer appropriate challenges, and increase motivation."

For educators who are dedicated to addressing the needs of diverse learners, UDL offers clear guidelines for the design of instruction so that all learners can experience success. These guidelines help teachers to avoid the one-size-fits-all approach to instruction. Instead, UDL emphasizes a broad-spectrum approach that includes diverse opportunities aimed at the diverse audience in every classroom. In today's schools as in today's society diversity is the norm, not the exception. Instruction must address this reality. UDL principles help teachers to stay mindful of diversity and adjust their instructional efforts to truly serve every student.

Universal Design for Learning Guidelines

I. Representation

Use multiple means of representation

1. Provide options for perception
- Options that customize the display of information
- Options that provide alternatives for auditory information
- Options that provide alternatives for visual information

2. Provide options for language and symbols
- Options that define vocabulary and symbols
- Options that clarify syntax and structure
- Options that promote cross-linguistic understanding
- Options that illustrate key concepts non-linguistically

3. Provide options for comprehension
- Options that provide or activate background knowledge
- Options that highlight critical features, big ideas, and relationships
- Options that guide information processing
- Options that support memory and transfer

II. Expression

Use multiple means of expression

4. Provide options for physical action
- Options in the mode of physical response
- Options in the means of navigation
- Options for accessing tools and assistive technologies

5. Provide options for expressive skills and fluency
- Options in the media for communication
- Options in the tools for composition and problem solving
- Options in the scaffolds for practice and performance

6. Provide options for executive functions
- Options that guide effective goal-setting
- Options that support planning and strategy development
- Options that facilitate managing information and resources
- Options that enhance capacity for monitoring progress

III. Engagement

Use multiple means of engagement

7. Provide options for recruiting interest
- Options that increase individual choice and autonomy
- Options that enhance relevance, value, and authenticity
- Options that reduce threats and distractions

8. Provide options for sustaining effort and persistence
- Options that heighten salience of goals and objectives
- Options that vary levels of challenge and support
- Options that foster collaboration and communication
- Options that increase mastery-oriented feedback

9. Provide options for self-regulation
- Options that guide personal goal-setting and expectations
- Options that scaffold coping skills and strategies
- Options that develop self-assessment and reflection

From http://www.udlcenter.org/aboutudl/udlguidelines

CHAPTER 5

Computers in the Learning Environment

Jose Luis Pelaez/Getty Images

CHAPTER OVERVIEW

This chapter addresses these ISTE National Educational Technology Standards:
- NETS•T Standard 2
- NETS•T Standard 3
- NETS•S Standard 2
- NETS•S Standard 6

Imagine that you enter a time machine and travel back fifty years. When you arrive, you decide to find out how things have changed from the past to the present. You select a few places to visit. Close by, you see a hospital and decide that it would be a good place to start. You go in and are amazed at the changes. There are beds, patients, doctors, and nurses; but you wonder what happened to all of the equipment you are so used to seeing in a hospital. Where are the many monitors that keep tabs on every patient's status? Where are the many diagnostic machines that pinpoint illness? Where are the constant audio messages paging one doctor or another? Where are the sophisticated life-support systems in the operating room? It is immediately clear that the medical technologies of the twenty-first century are as abundant as they are sophisticated when compared with those available fifty years ago.

Your time-travel investigation continues as you decide to visit a school. As you walk into the school of fifty years ago, you see teachers, students, and administrators in familiar classroom and office settings. When you peek into a classroom, you see a teacher at the front of the room, chalk in hand, writing on the board while lecturing on a topic. You see maps and charts on the walls and a globe and other models around the room. Sets of books are available on classroom bookshelves. The teacher may be preparing to show a movie. Students are sitting in rows of desks taking notes on what the teacher is saying. Sound familiar? Unlike medicine, a field in which technology has transformed the way doctors and other medical personnel work, education has changed relatively little, despite technological advances. With the exception of the addition of a DVD or VCR and monitor and perhaps a few personal computers in the typical classroom today, very little has really changed in the last fifty years. (Adapted from the metaphor described by Seymour Papert, 1992.)

Yet the same computer revolution that dramatically altered medicine will certainly alter education. There are many reasons why this has not occurred; one of the key reasons is that teachers simply don't know why and how to use much of the audio, video, and digital equipment that is available, even if it is accessible. Until recently, courses like the one you are taking in educational technology were not emphasized in teacher preparation. Now, with the investment schools are making in technology and the need to prepare students for life in the twenty-first century, teacher technology skills have become a critical element in teacher training. This chapter introduces you to computer technologies and their role in education and helps you build the skills you need to be an effective educational user of this technology.

This chapter will help prepare you to use personal computers in your classroom for administrative tasks, classroom management, and instruction. In Chapter 5 you will:

- Discover and identify the components of a computer system
- Examine the role of input devices and explore the most common types
- Explore the roles and most common types of output devices
- Investigate the relationship and functions of the central processing unit, memory, and storage
- Explore the roles and most common types of storage devices
- Relate the components and functions of a computer system to teaching and learning tasks

Computers, Teaching, and You

PEARSON myeducationkit™

Go to the *Assignments and Activities* section of Chapter 5 in MyEducationKit and complete the video activity entitled *Supporting Technology Use in Classrooms.*

You might be one of the many future or current educators wondering how you are going to use computers in your classroom. Perhaps you wonder whether their use will undermine your role as a teacher. Or, like many educators who are happy to use personal computers to create a test or an assignment, you might see their value in classroom management but wonder whether they are worth the expense and extra effort when it comes to teaching and learning.

Educators often feel a degree of concern when they are faced with the idea of using personal computer technology in their classrooms. This is not surprising because most teachers teach the way they were taught. They are comfortable using the tried-and-true strategies from which they learned. There is no doubt that these strategies continue to be valuable, but new technological tools make many enhancements to these strategies possible.

ISTE Standard

Learning about the computer technology available to teachers in the classroom will help you address **NETS•T STANDARD 3:**

MODEL DIGITAL-AGE WORK AND LEARNING Teachers exhibit knowledge, skills, and work processes representative of an innovative professional in a global and digital society.

To overcome any possible reluctance to use a computer, it is best to begin by becoming more familiar with computers. This process starts by developing an understanding of how computers work and how they can be used for administrative and academic tasks. During this process of familiarization, it is also important to develop hands-on skills with the hardware and software that educators frequently use. As teachers increase their knowledge, they also increase their comfort level so let's begin by getting to know what a computer is and how it works.

Computer Basics

Computers are simply machines, but unlike other technologies, they have no predetermined purpose. Instead, they are designed to be versatile, able to do a variety of tasks depending on the instructions they are given. Understanding how this unique digital technology works will help you to judge when a computer's capabilities will be useful in your classroom and how you can use computers to enhance your planned instruction. It will also help you to be able to recognize and correct minor computing problems and when you need to call for technical support.

A personal computer is a device that takes in data (input) from you, processes it according to your instructions, and then sends out the finished information product (output) to you. Because the quantity of data you input might be large and the size and complexity of the processing you want done can sometimes be great, computers have both short-term memory and long-term storage capabilities. These are used to help in completing the larger and more complex processing jobs you require. Computer **memory** is a temporary electronic storage space used by the computer to do short-term tasks or to complete a task that is too complex to do all at once. Longer-term **storage** is a more permanent electronic storage space in which the computer can store instructions and data for use at a later time. The use of a combination of temporary memory and long-term storage makes it possible for the computer to work on complex jobs a little at a time until the entire task is completed.

Computer memory is short-term storage, and storage devices offer long-term storage.

Together, these steps of taking in data, processing the data, storing it as necessary, and outputting the results to the end user make up the **computing cycle.** This computing cycle and the components of a computer system are diagrammed in Figure 5.1. Regardless of the complexity of the task the computer is asked to perform, this basic computing cycle is always the same. With an understanding of this basic operational framework, you can more easily understand the interrelationship of the various components of a computer system.

Programs are a computer's digital instructions.

The computing cycle takes place in and with the help of computer hardware and computer software. Computer **hardware** includes all of the computer components that are physical, touchable pieces of equipment. Together this collection of hardware is known as the **computer system.** Computer **software** is the term for **programs,** or sets of computer instructions, written in special computer languages that tell a computer how to accomplish a given task. You, as the end user of the hardware and software, really need to know relatively little about the details of how the computer components work together electronically or how a program is written. What you do need to know is which pieces of hardware and software you might need to accomplish the classroom management or instructional tasks you want done and how to use these computer components effectively for teaching and learning.

Go to the *Assignments and Activities* section of Chapter 5 in MyEducationKit and complete the web activity entitled *Teaching with Computers.*

What Educators Need to Know about Software

As incredible as computers are, they lack the ability to accomplish much of anything unless someone tells them precisely what to do and how to do it. When we turn the computer's power on, the collection of metal, plastic, chips, and wires can function only because someone first created a set of instructions to tell the computer how to start itself up. Without these instructions, it would be unable to function in any of the ways we have come to expect. These initial instructions, or Basic Input/Output System (BIOS), are stored inside the computer's

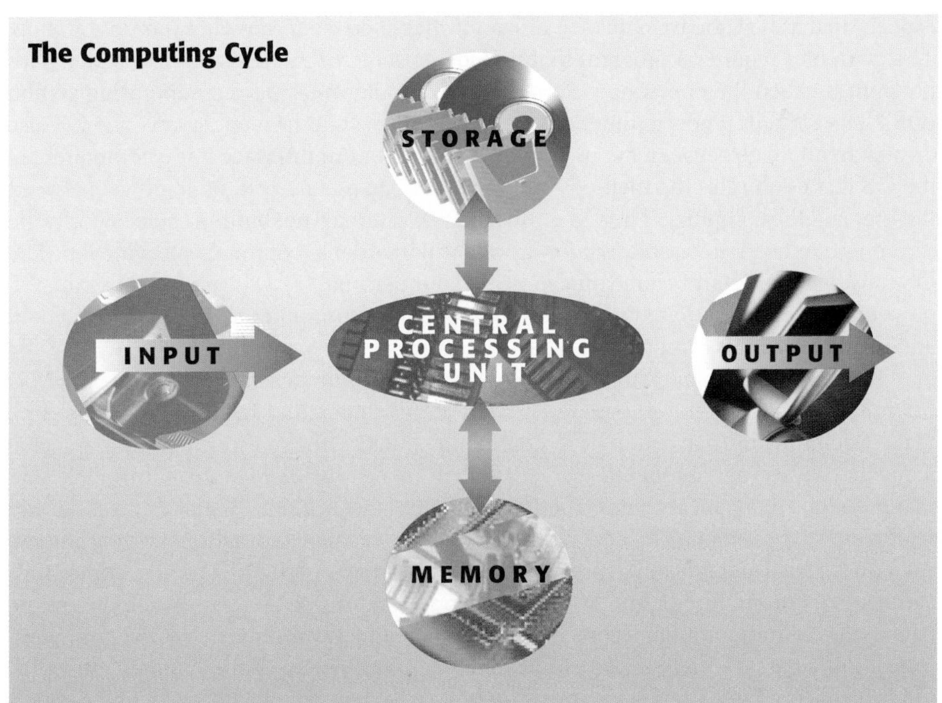

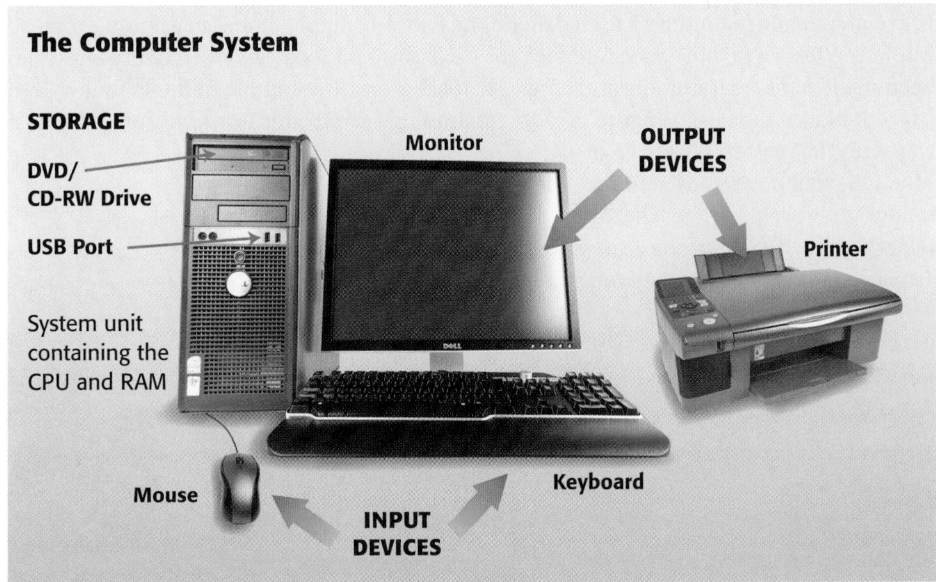

FIGURE 5.1

The Computer

All computer systems use the same computing cycle to operate. A computer system consists of the computer and all related peripheral hardware.

Photos courtesy of Mediablitzimages (UK) Limited/Alamy Image (computer); Peter Mlekuz/: Stockphoto (mouse); Jupiter Unlimited (printer)

hardware on special ROM **chips.** Chips are tiny silicon slices—often only ¼ to ½ inch square—that contain millions of electronic circuits. **ROM** chips are "read only memory" chips on which the BIOS program is stored, but no other data can be saved.

When you turn the power on, the computer reads the instructions stored in ROM that tell it how to start itself up and immediately begins to carry these instructions out. This is sometimes referred to as **booting up** the computer, a term that comes from the phrase "pulling oneself up by one's own bootstraps." It is in this very automated way that the system boots (starts) itself up and prepares to interact with you.

"Booting up" the computer means starting it.

The computer is now ready to operate, before it can begin to function like the computing device you have become familiar with, it must first be given instructions on how to operate. It must be told how to respond to and perform the many little interactive tasks you

The operating system (or OS) is the program that runs the computer and provides an interface.

expect, such as how to save data on a disk and what to do when you click a mouse button. The computer requires a program that provides specific instructions on how to act. This program is called the operating system. Every computer must have an **operating system (OS).** The OS tells it how to function and how to manage its own operation. The OS also creates an interface between the user and the computer. An **interface** is the component of the OS that establishes the methods of interaction (via menus, text, or graphics) between the user and the computer. The OS is thus the first external (not built-in) piece of software the computer needs to be able to know how to run in order to communicate with you. The OS must therefore start before you can begin your personal tasks. Learning to use the OS on your computer is a prerequisite skill for getting your computer to do the management and instructional tasks you need it to do.

Today's most popular operating systems are **Windows** for personal computers and Mac OS for the Apple Macintosh computer. Both of these operating systems use an interface that is a combination of typed-in (text) commands, choices from preset menus, and selected icons that appear on the opening screen, called the desktop. A **menu** is a listing of command options that appears across the top of the program window. Usually, after the user selects one of these menu choices, additional options will appear in a drop-down submenu. An **icon** is a small graphic that represents one of the system's options. Typically, **commands** can be issued in multiple ways: by typing a series of keystrokes, selecting a menu option, or clicking on the appropriate icon. There is no one right way to issue most OS commands; instead; there are a variety of ways to use the operating system. Both Windows and Mac OS present command options to users via windows, or boxed collections of icons and text. The user can then choose commands by clicking on an icon. This style of interaction between user and computer, which depends heavily on graphics and visuals instead of text, is referred to as a graphic user interface, or **GUI** (pronounced "gooey"). Every effort has been made to make it friendly and convenient for users. An example of the Windows and Mac interfaces appears in Figure 5.2. As a technology-using educator, you should make it a priority to master Windows or Mac OS, whichever is used in the school in which you teach. Although some OS basics are presented in this chapter, practicing with an OS is the only way to increase your comfort level and gain the skills you need.

From **www.apple.com/macosx.**

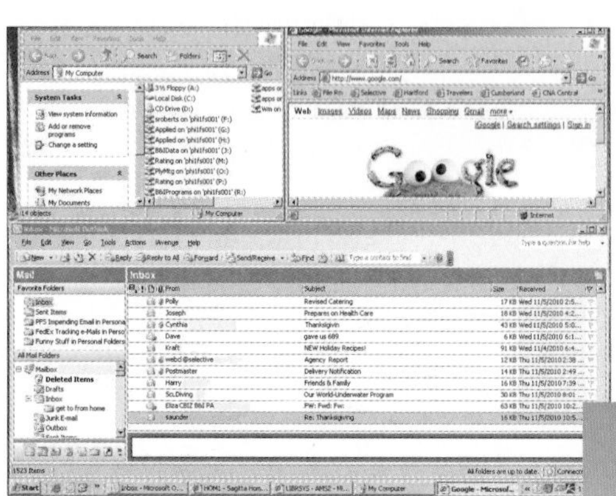

Microsoft Corporation. Microsoft product screen shot reprinted with permission from Microsoft Corporation.

FIGURE 5.2

GUI Interfaces

The Windows and Mac OS allow users to interact by pointing and clicking.

You can tell the machine what you want it to do by selecting a menu option, entering a text command, or clicking on an icon with an arrow that you control through manipulation of a mouse. A **mouse** is a pointing device that rolls about on your desk, usually on a special pad. It moves the pointing arrow on the computer screen in the same direction in which you move the mouse on your desk. Most people find the mouse very intuitive and are comfortable with it after only a little bit of use.

The OS controls and interacts with both the hardware components of the computer and any compatible software you choose to use. It also provides common ways for you to select options and to issue commands across a wide range of programs. You control the operating system through the menu or icon choices you make; they, in turn, control the rest of the computer's functions for you.

Once the OS is loaded and running, the computer is ready. However, it still needs one or more specific programs to enable it to perform the particular tasks you have in mind. The OS enables the computer to use software, but to understand how it must perform for you, the computer has to have instructions installed and running. These task-specific instructions are provided by an application program. An **application program** is a set of instructions that tell the computer how to complete a unique task such as word processing, database management, or drawing. Applications range from **utility programs** that improve or monitor computer operations to administrative applications (e.g., word-processing and gradebook programs) to academic applications (e.g., tutorials and electronic encyclopedias). Every application is a specific computer program written to accomplish a single task or a group of interrelated tasks. For example, if you want to use your computer to type up a test, you need a word-processing application. If you want to use an electronic spreadsheet to keep your gradebook, you need a spreadsheet application. The advantage of this versatility is that a single bundle of hardware—the personal computer system—can do many different jobs. The disadvantage is that you need as many pieces of application software as you have tasks to perform. Table 5.1 lists some of the most frequently used types of application software.

Different software applications are needed to do specific tasks.

TABLE 5.1 Popular Microcomputer Software

COMMON SOFTWARE	FUNCTION
OPERATING SYSTEM	The operating system provides the interface for the user and controls the computer operations.
WORD PROCESSING	Word processing gives the user an environment for entering text and other data and manipulating its format prior to printing it out.
ELECTRONIC SPREADSHEETS	Spreadsheets manipulate, format, and calculate numerical data and arrange them in a display called a worksheet.
DATABASE MANAGEMENT	Database software provides an environment in which large quantities of data can be entered, stored, manipulated, queried, and reported.
PRESENTATION SOFTWARE	Presentation software enables the user to create electronic slide shows with special effects, including sound and animation.
DESKTOP PUBLISHING	Publishing software combines word-processing capability with desktop layout capability for easy-to-use layout and design of complex publication formats.
GRAPHICS PROGRAMS	Graphics programs provide an environment in which the user can draw pictures, create diagrams, or manipulate digital photos for inclusion in other programs or to print out.
COMMUNICATIONS SOFTWARE	This category of software includes the software to connect a computer to one or more other computers via phone lines and the browsers that let users examine the sites on the World Wide Web.
UTILITIES	Utilities include all of the various types of software that help users maintain their computers in good working order.

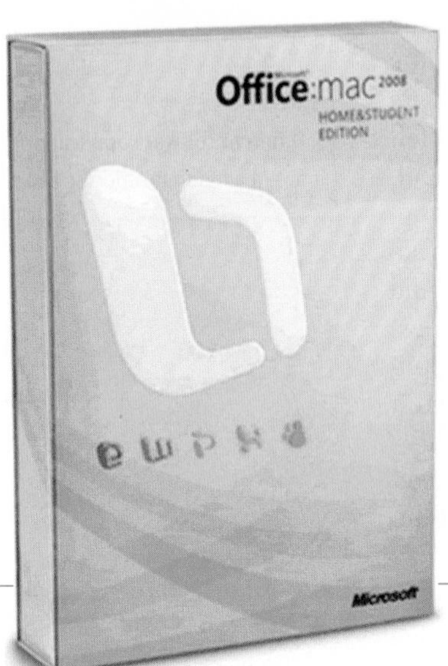

FIGURE 5.3

Software Specifications

All reputable software includes system requirements so you can determine whether it will work on your computer.

Programs included and system requirements for:

- Windows version Microsoft Office 2007

  and

- Mac version Microsoft Office 2008

	Windows	Mac
Processor	500 megahertz (MHz) or higher	G5 or PowerPC G4 500 MHz or faster
Memory	256 megabyte (MB) RAM or more	512 MB of RAM or more
Hard disk	1.5 gigabyte (GB) available hard disk space	1.5 GB available hard disk space
Drive	CD-ROM or DVD drive	DVD drive
Display	1024 x 768 or higher resolution	1024 x 768 or higher resolution
Operating system	Microsoft Windows XP with Service Pack (SP) 2 or later	Mac OS X version 10.4.9 or later
Programs	Word, Excel, PowerPoint, and OneNote	Word, Excel, PowerPoint, Entourage, and Messenger

Software manufacturers, aware of the need for multiple types of programs to perform common tasks, often bundle their most popular applications into a related collection (suite) of applications. One of the most popular suites available today is Microsoft's Office Suite, shown in Figure 5.3, which includes a word processor (Word), a spreadsheet (Excel), a database management system (Access), and a presentation package (PowerPoint). Together, the programs in this suite, like those in its competitor products, can enable you to accomplish almost any administrative task.

Integrated software combines popular programs into one.

Another approach, one that reduces the number of application programs needed, is to integrate the main features of a collection of popular applications into a single comprehensive application, called an **integrated software package.** Such a package has the capability to perform many, but not all, of the functions of the full-blown versions of the software. Microsoft Works and iWork for the Mac are examples of integrated software packages. They contain most of the same types of software as does the full suite, but each component piece is a little less powerful than its full-featured counterpart, including fewer features and capabilities.

Most integrated and/or bundled software products include the most popular types of applications—typically, word processing, a graphics program, a spreadsheet program, a database management program, a communications program, and a presentation program. An advantage of both bundled and integrated packages is that all parts of the software offered in this manner use similar commands and have a common "look and feel." This can make it easier to learn and use each of the applications. Also, an integrated package usually takes up less space on the computer's hard disk. A disadvantage of an integrated software package is that each of its components might not contain as many functions as similar software sold in separate application packages.

It should be remembered that every piece of software is written with specific hardware in mind. Typically, software specifications identify the minimum levels of hardware necessary to use a given piece of software. These details are included on the side of every commercial software box. It is important that you be sufficiently familiar with your hardware to be able to select appropriate software. Information about the technical aspects of hardware can be found in the documentation that accompanies the hardware when it is purchased. The hardware specifications required for determining whether software will run typically include the speed of the computer processor, the amount of available memory, the capability of the monitor, and the space required on the hard drive. You should take a moment to jot down the specifications of the machine on which you plan to install the software and have these specifications available whenever you shop for software.

Standard

ISTE

Learning about and using the software and hardware available to teachers for instruction will help you address
NETS•T STANDARD 2:

DESIGN AND DEVELOP DIGITAL-AGE LEARNING EXPERIENCES AND ASSESSMENTS Teachers design, develop, and evaluate authentic learning experiences and assessments incorporating contemporary tools and resources to maximize content learning in context and to develop the knowledge, skills, and attitudes identified in the NETS•S.

What Educators Need to Know about Hardware

Although it is not necessary to understand the intricacies of how hardware works at the level of its electronics, it is important to understand what different hardware components do. This baseline knowledge will help you to identify the components you need to get the job done in your classroom. The remainder of this chapter will introduce you to these components.

Input Devices

To make the computer look for, load, and run application software, you, the user, must first tell it to do so. To issue this type of command and to later add your personal data, you need some way to communicate your wishes to the computer. This is done through the use of an input device. An **input device** includes any computer peripheral that you might use to enter data into the computer. A peripheral is any device that can be connected to a computer. The keyboard and the mouse are the most often used types of input devices. Let's take a closer look at each of these devices to determine its respective role in accomplishing your tasks.

The keyboard and mouse are common input devices.

The typical computer **keyboard** is laid out much like the keys on a typewriter. However, the computer keyboard has several additional keys not typically found on a typewriter, which are used to control the computer or give software commands. Typing commands or data into the machine is usually referred to as *keyboarding*. Because of the prevalence of computer technology in schools and in society in general, many schools now require their students to have keyboarding competencies before they leave elementary school.

The other most prevalent input device is the mouse. The mouse is the most common type of pointing device, allowing the user to move the selection arrow on the screen. Pointing devices include any input device that enables users to point to and select the commands or icons they wish to use. The selection arrow is sometimes called a pointer. It is an icon shaped like an arrow. Other common types of pointing devices include a trackball, a joystick, a touch pad, and a pointing stick. As you can see in Figure 5.4, each

TECH TIPS for Teachers

Mouse buttons are typically set up for right-handed students, but this can be modified. If your students are left-handed, you can switch the button's function. All operating systems provide this option. In Windows, click on the Control Panel, found via the Start button, and select Mouse to change the mouse from a right-handed to a left-handed orientation. The Mac OS uses similar commands. Using the same Mouse menu, you can also make the pointer larger or enhance the visual representations of the mouse movement (pointer trails) for students who have sight impairments.

FIGURE 5.4

Input Devices: The Keyboard and Various Pointing Devices

A variety of input devices are available for inputting data or commands.

Photos courtesy of Logitech; bottom photo courtesy of Synaptics, Incorporated

The keyboard is configured like a typewriter keyboard with some additional keys. It is used primarily to enter data, but it also includes cursor keys to move the pointer.

A mouse is used to give commands, make selections, and move objects on a computer screen. It is used by moving it around on the desktop and clicking its buttons.

The trackball is a different style of mouse. It is used by rolling the ball on the top with your fingers to move the pointer on the screen. It too has buttons you can click or double click.

Often found on a laptop, a touch pad is a flat, pressure-sensitive panel. To move the pointer, you just press lightly and move your fingertip around on the surface of the panel. It too has buttons for clicking.

of these devices has a slightly different configuration, but all control the movement of the selection arrow, allow you to issue commands, and make it possible to move (drag and drop) items on the desktop.

Each of these devices also includes one, two, or, in some cases, several buttons. Once the pointing device is used to position the pointer arrow on the icon or menu item desired, the appropriate button is clicked to select the menu item or to execute an action represented by an icon. When a mouse has two or more buttons, the leftmost mouse button is typically preset by the software to work in a specific way, and those settings are fairly consistent across all pieces of software. The other one or more mouse buttons either control scrolling (moving up and down the screen) or are programmable by the software; that is, different types of software use those buttons in different ways, or you can assign special functions to them. You should read through the documentation that accompanies the software you want to use to see what convenient features may be available through the use of the buttons.

Although the keyboard and mouse are the two most often used input devices, there are several others. Each of these other input devices has unique properties that make it very useful in an innovative teaching and learning environment. These other input devices are more fully described in Chapter 6, "Digital Technologies in the Classroom." For now, it is sufficient that you understand the function of input devices in general and the mouse and keyboard in particular. This will serve as a basis for contrast with the hardware necessary at the other end of the computer cycle: output devices.

Output Devices

If input devices are used to put data into the computer, then **output devices** are the pieces of hardware that move information (data that have been processed) out of the computer. The two primary output devices for most computer systems are the monitor and the printer. The monitor displays information in **soft copy** (electronic form), and the printer turns that information into **hard copy** (printed form).

A **monitor** displays computer information on its screen. The screen works much like a digital television screen. **Resolution** refers to the clarity and crispness of the images on the monitor screen. Resolution can be measured by the number of pixels the screen displays. A **pixel,** or picture element, is a single colored dot on the monitor screen that, when combined with other pixels, forms an image. Resolution measurements are provided both vertically and horizontally (see Figure 5.5). You have probably seen this type of measurement indicated in relation to computers. A screen resolution may be 1280 x 1024, for example. This measurement means that the screen image is made up of 1280 vertical columns of pixels in each of 1024 horizontal lines of pixels. The higher the numbers, the more detailed but smaller the image becomes. Another measure of a monitor is screen size. Screen size refers to the number of inches measured diagonally across the screen. The common monitor sizes are 17", 19", 21", 22", and 24". Larger sizes are needed for exacting work such as digital graphics and computer-aided design. Widescreen LCD monitors allow the users to view two programs side by side.

Hard copy is printed output; soft copy is displayed on the monitor.

The resolution on most monitors is adjustable to accommodate different software. It is important to check the software's hardware specifications to ensure that the program's output can be displayed with the monitor you are using and to ensure you have your resolution set correctly.

FIGURE 5.5

Output Devices—Monitors

Different monitors and screens provide different levels of display.

A monitor's resolution is determined by the vertical number of pixels (picture elements) and the horizontal number of pixels. Monitors also vary in terms of the number of colors they can display. The greater the resolution and the number of colors, the more realistic and detailed the picture.

A monitor's screen size is measured diagonally in inches.

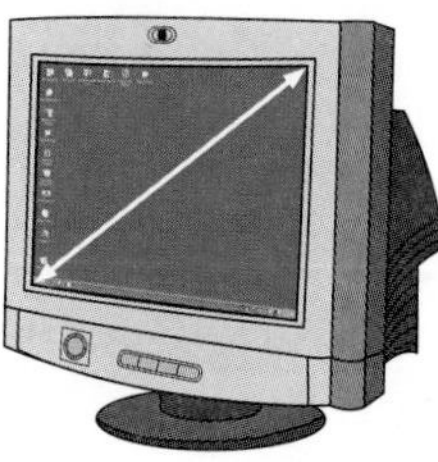

Flat-screen LCD monitors, like their bulkier CRT counterparts, vary in resolution and screen size. While they take up less desk space, they may be more easily damaged in a busy classroom.

The viewing screen on a notebook computer is really a high-resolution color liquid crystal display (LCD) screen. It is based on the same technology that is used in digital clocks and wristwatches, but much more sophisticated. This same technology is used for flat-screen monitors.

TECH TIPS for Teachers

You can create transparencies for an overhead projector on your printer. Using a variety of standard software packages, you can create a document that includes text, clip art, and photos to teach your target concept. Then you can print the document on special printer transparency film instead of paper. Once printed, it is ready to use on your overhead.

If you have an ink jet printer, you will need to use transparency film made especially for it. Ink jet printers work by squirting small droplets of ink onto the printing surface. Using an ink jet with standard transparency film will result in the ink running off and smearing. Ink jet transparency film has been specially prepared so that one side of the plastic has a rough, porous surface. Printing on the porous side of the film will allow the ink to adhere and dry. Ink jet printing of transparencies lets you create full-color transparencies for use in instruction.

If you have a laser printer, be sure to use laser transparency film instead. Laser printers transfer images by heating toner. Laser transparency film is thick enough to be unaffected by the heat needed to transfer the image. Any other type of film may at best buckle and at worst melt inside the printer. The limitation of laser-printed transparencies is that most laser printers print in black only.

To avoid costly mistakes and wasted transparency film, you should carefully read the transparency film boxes to be sure you are purchasing the appropriate material for your printer.

Now more popular than traditional CRT computer monitors is the **LCD** (liquid crystal display) screen that has been used on notebook (small portable) computers for years and has made the leap to the desktop. LCD screens have the advantage of being much thinner and lighter than CRT monitors, making them easier to position on a desk or in the classroom. LCD monitors also consume less energy. They are still somewhat more expensive than traditional monitors of the same screen size but may be worth the additional cost. Their prices have been dropping in recent years.

Monitors of all types display soft copy. Soft copy is volatile (temporary). It will disappear when power to the machine is cut off. To output the same data to a more permanent form, a printer is used. There are many types of printers, each with its own advantages. The most common types of printers and their respective advantages and disadvantages are summarized in Figure 5.6.

Like monitors, printers vary in their resolution. The higher the resolution, the crisper and clearer the text and graphics that are produced. With printers, resolution is measured in **dpi** (dots per inch). Like images on a monitor, printed text and graphics are really just a series of tiny dots, in this case printed on a page. The more dots there are in an inch of print, the crisper the text or graphic appears and the more intense its color seems.

If you make copies of a printout for your class, the greater the clarity of the original, the better the copies will look. For this reason, it is wise to make at least one original hard copy at the highest possible resolution. Most printers offer you the opportunity to print out in various modes, from draft to normal to high quality. Draft mode saves printer ink and usually prints more quickly. Normal is good for most documents. However, you should select high quality for your copier masters.

Printers not only produce their output on paper, they can also be used to produce their output on transparencies for use with an overhead projector. Specific types of transparency film are available for different types of printers. Many other specialty papers and other media are available for both ink jet and laser printers. Using your classroom printer and selected specialty output media, you can print T-shirt transfers, custom stickers, CD labels, magnets, glossy digital photos, and a variety of other unique printouts. To do so, you must buy the media appropriate to your printer, whether ink jet or laser. Specialty outputs can add interest and customized activities to any classroom.

The number and variety of output devices that can be added to a computer system offer many possibilities for innovative application to teaching and learning. These devices will be explored more fully in Chapter 6.

A variety of transparency film and specialty media are available for use with ink jet and laser printers.

Courtesy of Georgia-Pacific Corporation.

The System Unit

Each component of a computer system is assigned a different part of the total information-processing job. However, at the core of every computer is the system unit. It holds the computer's circuit board (motherboard) with the chips and

FIGURE 5.6

Output Devices—Printers and Their Print Resolutions

Printers vary in technology, speed, and quality of display.

Photos courtesy of Xerox Corporation (laser printer and multifunction device) and Lexmark International (ink-jet printer)

LASER PRINTER

This printer uses a laser beam, toner, and heat to transfer letters and graphics to paper, similar to copy machine technology. It offers the best resolution, fastest print speeds, and highest quality.

INK-JET PRINTERS

Ink-jet printers squirt a small puff of ink onto paper to create the image. They include both black and color ink. These usually inexpensive printers are slower than laser printers but offer good resolution.

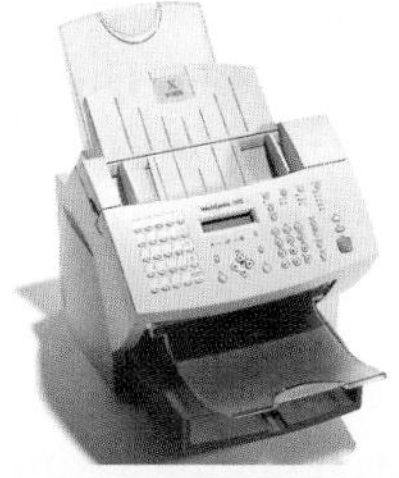

MULTIFUNCTION DEVICES

These combination fax/copier/printers (all-in-one devices) actually use ink-jet, thermal, or laser printing technology to print images from a fax, a computer, or another sheet of paper.

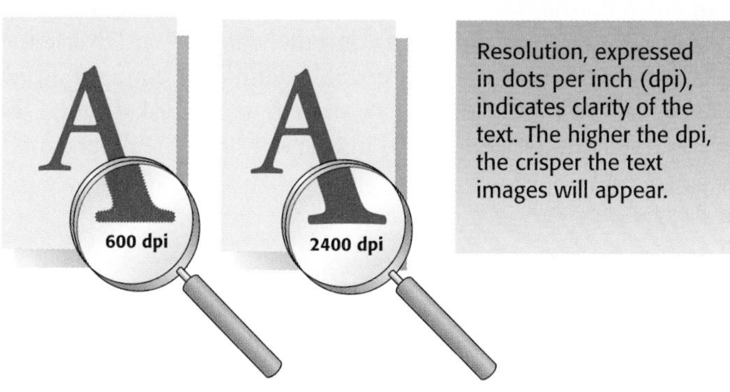

circuits that make processing on the computer possible. Input, output, and storage devices enable the movement of data into and out of the system unit. But within the system unit, it is the central processing unit, or **CPU**, a powerful microprocessor chip, that is responsible for controlling almost all operations of the computer and processing data as instructed by the user. All computer components are ultimately interconnected through and coordinated by the CPU. Within the CPU chip, calculations are performed; the flow of information among input, output, and memory is coordinated; and program instructions are transmitted at a speed measured in billionths of a second (nanoseconds). Current CPU chips, such as Intel's Pentium series, can carry out billions of instructions per second. Such speeds, typically measured in gigahertz (megahertz in older machines), are necessary, especially for complex software, to minimize the time the user has to wait for processing to complete. The faster the CPU, the more responsive the computer can be. For that reason, computer users want the fastest microprocessor chips with the highest number of gigahertz they can acquire.

When you issue a command to begin a computing task, the CPU must find the instructions for how to do what you want done and then accept the data you input to perform the processes on it that you have requested. The CPU typically seeks its instructions in one or more of the storage devices attached to the machine and in the instructions it received from you via an input device.

Once the CPU has located the appropriate set of instructions or program (such as a word processor), it will load the program into the portion of the computer's memory called random-access memory (RAM). **RAM** is the temporary memory space located on a set of chips that the CPU uses while it is carrying out its processing. The CPU reads the program

Courtesy of Intel Corporation

Microprocessor chips are the "brains" of a computer system.

from its permanent storage location (a disk) and then places a copy into RAM to make it readily accessible. The CPU then uses RAM to store the input you enter so that it can be processed in accordance with the program's instructions. When you are finished with your processing tasks, at your command, the CPU will save the processed data it has stored in RAM on a storage device so you can use the data again later. Because data in RAM are volatile, the data will be lost when power is lost. It is therefore critical to frequently give the Save command, which moves data in RAM to a more permanent location on a disk. When you complete your task and close the application, the CPU empties RAM of both program and data so that it is clear and available for your next task. Throughout every task, you ask the computer to complete, the CPU controls the job and automatically uses RAM as necessary to assist in getting your processing task done.

Storage

Because we generally do not want to have to reenter data every time we want to use the same data, we need to store the data in a more permanent location. Furthermore, we need to be able to store programs that we want available when we need to complete a specific type of job. Permanently storing data and programs is the function of the storage devices included in a computer system. Almost all computers have a hard disk drive to store programs and data. However, there are many possible additional configurations for storage devices in a computer. You may select any combination of a disk drives, CD drives, and a DVD drive. How a machine is configured in terms of storage is determined by your needs.

Hard Disks

Each type of storage device uses its own media. Figure 5.7 and Table 5.2 summarize and compare the most common types of disk storage media. Because of its large storage capacity, the **hard disk** drive is the most commonly used mass storage device for a computer. Inside the hard disk drive are a series of stacked metal platters (hard disks) on which data are stored. These disks comprise the storage area in which the operating system, applications programs, and most personal data files are stored.

The disks, or platters, built into the hard disk drive can hold **gigabytes,** or billions of bytes, of data, with some disks now capable of storing terabytes (trillions). A **byte** of data is roughly equal to one alphabetic (A) or numeric (1) character of information (see Table 5.3). Thus, a typical hard disk can hold billions of letters or numbers (alphanumeric characters) as stored data. In the physical world, the hard disk might be analogous to a roomful of very large multiple-drawer file cabinets. The surfaces of hard disks are so sensitive that ordinary airborne contaminants such as dust or a strand of hair can interrupt the flow of information if caught between the drive head and the disk itself. Hard disks are therefore usually encased in their own protective housing. Because they are typically permanently fixed inside the computer, internal hard disks are also sometimes called *fixed disks.*

Permanently fixing the hard disk inside the computer does not make it immune to problems. Problems can and do affect the data you store on a disk. Because any electronic or mechanical device can break or wear out, it is important to remember to **back up** your data, that is, make a duplicate or backup copy of your files. When a disk crashes (malfunctions), all of the information that was stored on that disk is often lost. If you suffer a hard or floppy disk crash, your data may be irretrievable

GSO Images/Getty Images

Today's hard disk drives offer storage space for billions of pages of text, millions of graphics, and thousands of audio and video clips.

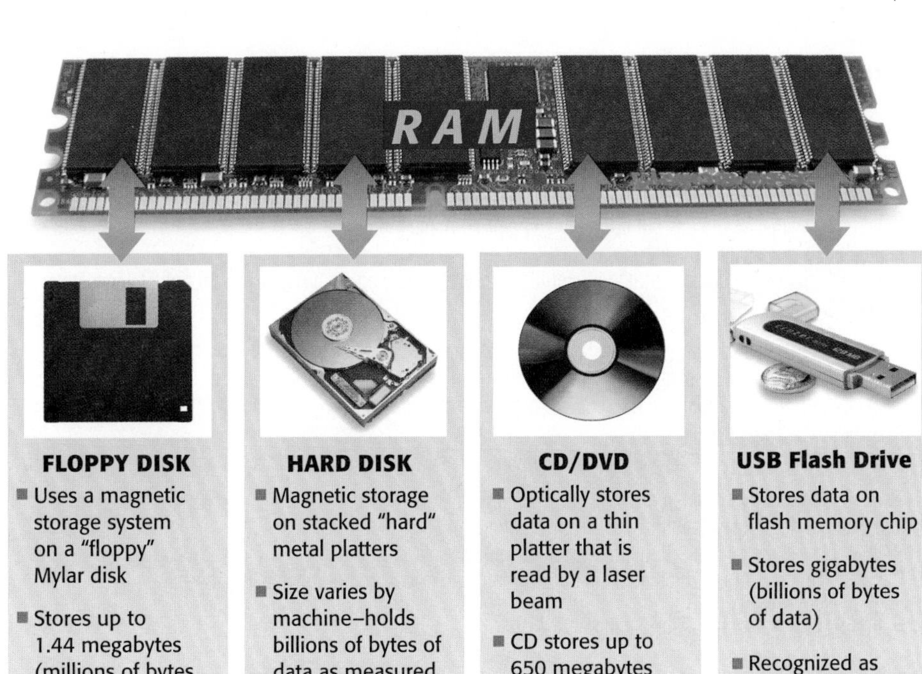

FIGURE 5.7

From Storage to Virtual Desktop

Data and programs are moved into RAM whenever the user needs to start an application or use information stored on one of the available storage devices. Once in RAM, the program or data are active and available to use.

Photos a, c © PhotoDisk/Getty Images; b, courtesy of Maxtor Corporation; d, courtesy of Kingston Technology.

unless you have a backup copy. For teachers with lesson plans, tests, activity sheets, and student grades stored on a hard drive, such a loss can be devastating. Backup files are often made on removable storage media (floppy disks, external hard drives, CDs, or DVDs) that can be stored away from the machine. It is not necessary to back up your application programs, because they can be reinstalled. However, it is a good idea to keep the original media and their documentation in a safe place and available for reinstallation if it becomes necessary.

Most of the time when you are working on the computer, you will be using the hard disk drive for storage. If you need to use more than one machine, perhaps one at home or in the faculty workroom as well as one in your classroom, you will need a way to move your data from one machine to the other. This is one of the reasons for the popularity of removable storage media.

Floppy Disks

Although **floppy disks** are an aging technology, many classrooms still have computers with floppy disk drives. The floppy disk drive is an electromechanical device that is usually mounted inside the computer. Like its bigger cousin, the hard drive, it is sensitive to many environmental factors. The standard floppy disk can contain 1.44 megabytes (millions of bytes) of data, compared to the many-gigabyte (billions of bytes) capacity of today's hard disks. However, the floppy disk's durability makes it a viable and inexpensive medium for use in schools with other computers.

The floppy disk stores 1.44 megabytes of information.

TABLE 5.2 Comparison of Storage Media

STORAGE MEDIA	CHARACTERISTICS
FLOPPY DISK	• Disk of magnetic Mylar in rigid plastic case (successor to original floppy, which was larger and would bend) • Must be formatted before use but normally come preformatted today • Estimated to last around 5 years • Previously the most popular format for user files but is all but obsolete because of very limited capacity of 1.44 megabytes
INTERNAL HARD DISK (or DRIVE)	• Thin stacks of encased magnetized metal disks inside almost all computers • Most common form of data storage for both software and user files • Capacity varies, but normally in hundreds of gigabytes (billions of bytes) and can be in terabytes (trillions of bytes) • As with floppies, magnetic data storage is estimated to last around 5 years
PORTABLE MEDIA	• Two most popular types: flash drives (static magnetic memory, roughly 2–4 inches long and ½ inch thick) and external hard drives (roughly the size of a paperback) • Both are self-contained and plug into a computer's USB port • Capacity can range from less than a gigabyte (older flash drives) to hundreds of gigabytes or a terabyte or more (external hard drives) • Both getting larger in capacity, smaller in size, and lower in cost
COMPACT DISCS (CD-ROM, CD-R, CD-RW)	• CDs, optical discs of plastic onto which microscopic pits are burned by laser and then read by laser in a CD or DVD drive • CD capacity is 650 megabytes • CD-ROM is "read only," typically used to transfer software to a computer or for music • CD-R can be recorded to. Additional data may be added, space allowing, but data cannot be modified • CD-RWs are rewritable, data can be changed or added to • Estimated to last up to 7 times as long as magnetic storage
DIGITAL VIDEO DISCS (DVD-ROM, DVD-R, DVD+RW, DVD-RW)	• DVDs, optical discs of plastic onto which microscopic pits are burned by laser and then read by laser in a DVD drive • DVD capacity can be up to 17 gigabytes (double side and double layer), but 4.7 gigabytes is the most common (single side/single layer) • DVD-ROM is read only. Movies come in this format • DVD-R can be recorded to. Additional data may be added, space allowing, but data cannot be modified • DVD-RW and DVD+RW are two competing formats. Both are rewritable and can record approximately 2 hours of high-quality video • Estimated to last up to 7 times as long as magnetic storage
ONLINE STORAGE	• A recent alternative to data storage on local hardware • Advantages are capacity and safety of offsite storage • Disadvantages are the need to be connected to the Internet to access data and uncertainty about the storage company's security and business viability • Usually a monthly or annual cost • Although increasing in popularity, the current primary use is for offsite backup of data

Floppy disks have proven their usefulness in classroom settings. Students who are creating their own personal files for an activity need a place to store them. If the files are saved on the hard disk drive, other students in the class can potentially have access to them. Furthermore, if you are teaching in a secondary school with a student load of more than 150 students per day, the available space on your hard drive is rapidly consumed. Instead, to ensure privacy and to save hard disk space, it is easier to give each student his or her own floppy disk(s) to use throughout the term or the project. Students can then be responsible for their own data for the duration of the project. At the end of the term or year, the disks can all be erased and reused by the next group of students. While the floppy disk remains an inexpensive and reliable media for student files, the **USB** flash drive is quickly gaining dominance.

TABLE 5.3 Relative Sizes of Stored Data

SIZE	CHARACTER EQUIVALENT	EXAMPLE
1 BYTE	1 alphanumeric character	The letter A or number 5
1 KILOBYTE	Approximately 1,000 characters	Slightly less than 1 page of typed, double-spaced text
1 MEGABYTE	Approximately 1 million characters	1,000 pages of typed, double-spaced text
1 GIGABYTE	Approximately 1 billion characters	1 million pages of typed, double-spaced text
1 TERABYTE	Approximately 1 trillion characters	1 billion pages of text

Storage Organization

Whether on a floppy or hard disk a CD or DVD, or a flash drive, the organizational units for storing data are known as files and folders, as illustrated in Figure 5.8. An electronic **file** is a collection of related data, usually a product of a single task. A file is typically created through the use of a single application program. An electronic **folder** is a digital organizer that you create to hold related files on a disk. In the physical world, a file would be equivalent to one or more printed sheets of information that resulted from the completion of a task. A folder, like its paper counterpart, the file folder, would be used to hold related documents (files).

Copying files onto portable media also allows you to transport them from one computer to another. Just copy the file to the medium and copy the data from it into the new computer. Of course, it is necessary that the application software that created the file also be available in the second computer. Copying a file copies the data only; it does not copy the application program that made and initially saved the file.

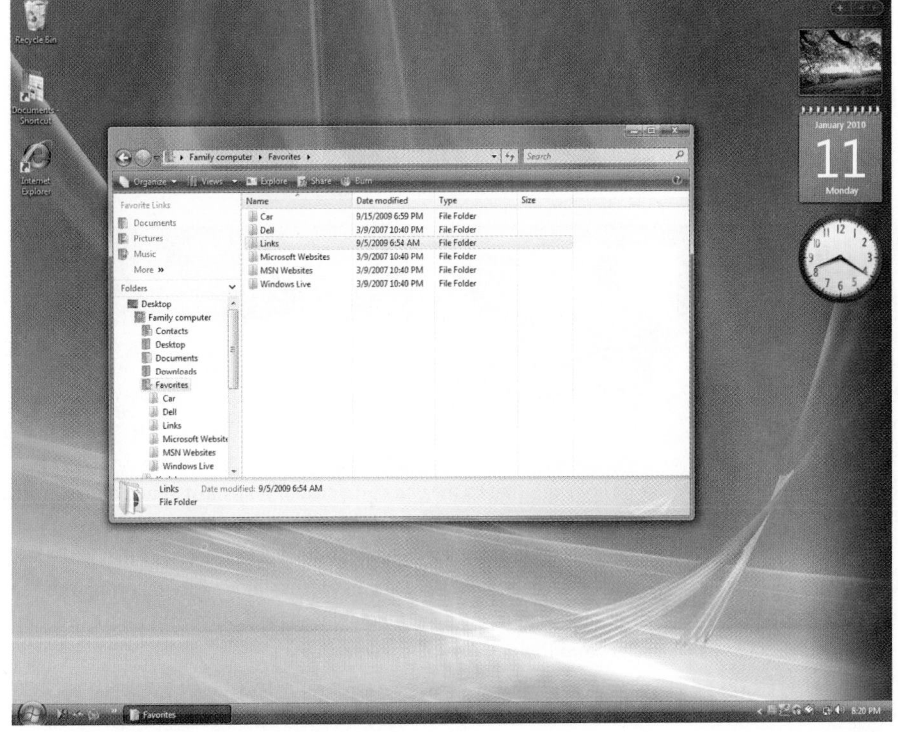

FIGURE 5.8

Windows Explorer and Its Organizational System

Windows organizes your data using a file and folder system. When a folder is expanded, in the left pane of Explorer you will see icons representing the contents of the folder.

Microsoft Windows Explorer® is a registered trademark of Microsoft Corporation.

Portable Hard Drive

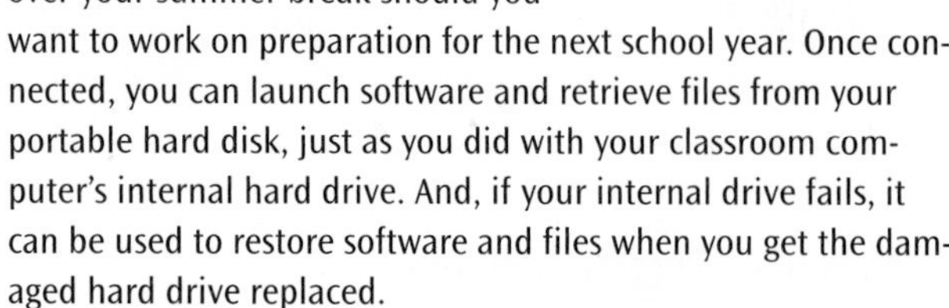

Backing up your files is an important task. However, large files or just many smaller files can quickly overwhelm the storage capacity of floppy disks and recordable CDs. Even with larger-capacity DVDs, while you may have enough space to back up your documents, you do not have enough space to back up your software. You would therefore not be able to use your DVD in place of your hard drive if it crashes. So how best can a teacher back up his or her computer system?

A portable external hard drive can be used to create a backup of your computer's internal hard drive. This backup includes all the software and files stored on your computer system. The portable unit typically plugs into the USB port of any machine and can move from computer to computer. You can even take your portable drive home over your summer break should you want to work on preparation for the next school year. Once connected, you can launch software and retrieve files from your portable hard disk, just as you did with your classroom computer's internal hard drive. And, if your internal drive fails, it can be used to restore software and files when you get the damaged hard drive replaced.

Portable drives are often packaged with software to make the backup process a simple one-click procedure. For under $100, this device offers busy teachers a very reasonable data "insurance policy."

Computer Viruses

Any storage media, but particularly floppy disks, can store and transmit a computer virus. A computer **virus** is a malicious program written specifically to disrupt computer operations and/or destroy data. Viruses are often transmitted from computer to computer by surreptitiously attaching themselves to normal files. When these carrier files are saved on a floppy disk and that disk is later used in a virus-free computer, the virus can be transmitted to the "healthy" computer's hard disk drive (Figure 5.9). Once there, it executes its damaging program either immediately or at a later time. If designed to do so, the virus may infect other floppy disks used in the once-healthy computer, thus further spreading the problem.

Viruses can be a challenge for computer-using teachers. Clearly, students' floppy disks and flash drives are effective for ensuring their file privacy and for keeping the classroom

In the CLASSROOM

There are many examples of how technology and computers are being used to effectively support learning. Many teachers have found that computers can make learning fun, flexible and effective.

Chris Gathers, a kindergarten teacher in Kansas, has found technology to be the biggest and most exciting change in her thirty-year career. Her classroom is equipped with Macs. Chris begins the year with Mouse Practice© to master "drag and click" skills. Then she moves on to the Broderbund program Kid Pix Studio Deluxe. It supports her goals for her students, enabling them to use their imaginations and creativity using the computer as a tool.

Some years, using the computer lab is a joy, and some years it's a headache, but Chris feels that it's very important to her students, and she uses the computer whenever she can.

Chris finds that by the end of the school year, most of her kindergarten students are familiar with the different creative tools she has given them to use. The foundation for creating multimedia projects at other grade levels has also been laid. Her students really enjoy experimenting with the computers and trying new things. They have gained confidence in themselves and their ability to use technology.

Source: Chris Gathers, www4Teachers, *Teacher Testimony, Chris Gathers teaches kindergarten in Fredonia, Kansas.* *© 2000, 2001 High Plains Regional Technology in Education Consortium.*

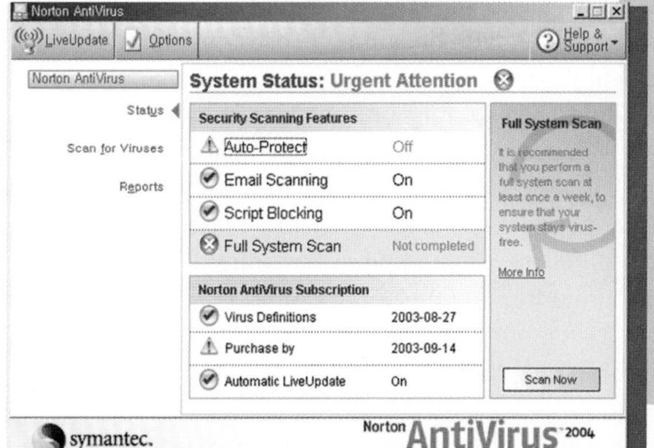

FIGURE 5.9

Computer Viruses

Schools need to be on the alert for computer viruses.

computer's hard disk space available. However, students often exchange games and information if they have home computers, or they may download infected files from the Internet. Once a virus infects a student's home machine, a disk or flash drive carried back and forth to school for a class assignment can result in that same virus infecting and destroying data on the classroom machine.

To protect the classroom computers, teachers and technology-support personnel often install **antivirus programs.** Antivirus programs detect and destroy computer viruses. They scan the hard drive, floppy disks, and email and warn if any possible virus is detected. Every classroom computer should have an antivirus program installed. It is also important to subscribe to continuous updates of the installed antivirus programs. Unfortunately, as fast as viruses are recognized and neutralized, new virus programs are written by malicious programmers and let loose on unsuspecting computer users. The typical classroom computer should therefore have its antivirus program updated at least weekly, preferably more often. A frequent update will ensure that the antivirus program has the latest list of new viruses and virus countermeasures.

Portable Media

Some hard disk drives are designed to be used as removable hard disks. This portable version of a hard disk offers the transportability and convenience of a floppy disk while providing much greater storage capacity and the durability of a firm, hard disk. Portable hard disks are external drives with storage capacities in the hundreds of gigabytes. They are typically plugged into the computer's USB port.

Portable hard disks have become very popular, now that many programs incorporate graphics, animation, and sound files. These types of **multimedia** files—files that include multiple types of media (text, graphics, sound, video, and animation)—are often too large to fit on a floppy disk. To transport them, a portable disk is ideal.

For the classroom, portable hard disks are especially useful. A single portable hard disk can serve as a backup medium for an entire class's individual personal files, or it can store all multimedia files related to a specific content area for easy access. Further, for older machines with smaller hard drives, the addition of a portable hard disk can make the computer more usable by increasing its storage capacity.

CD-ROMs

A **CD-ROM** (compact disc–read-only memory) is also removable. However, this is a read-only medium, so you can get information from it but you cannot store any information on a typical CD-ROM. Most computers today are equipped with a drive that will read CD-ROMs. Such a drive reads the information from CD-ROMs that contain programs, files, music, or other data.

Unlike magnetically recorded floppy and hard disks, CD-ROMs are recorded by a laser beam that burns pits into the tracks on the disc's surface. Then another laser reads those pits and the remaining flat surface of the disc as data. Because CD drives use light to record and read data, they are known as optical drives.

Approximately 650 megabytes of data (text, sound, graphics, animation, or video) can be stored on a single CD. This is equivalent to the storage capacity of approximately 400 floppy disks. Because of their storage capacity, CD-ROMs are used to store and transport large programs and graphic files that should not be altered. These programs are usually full-featured applications designed to be installed on your computer. Installing a program means moving essential components of a program from a transport medium to the hard drive so that it can be accessed and run whenever it is requested. CDs may also store self-contained multimedia programs that are too large to install on most computer systems, such as educational games.

Programs are designed to either install themselves on the hard drive or run from the CD drive. Installed software can take up sizable amounts of space on the hard drive. However, programs that are run from the hard drive are quicker to access and run. On the other hand, if the programs are left on the CD-ROM, you will keep your hard drive space available for other uses. However, you must keep the CD available in the drive at all times to use the program. For data files (usually graphics files and clip art libraries), you must keep the CD available in the drive until you are done with the files stored on it. Many teachers prefer to install programs to classroom hard drives even though they are large programs. Doing so allows the teacher to store the original CD in a safe place and avoids costly and inconvenient loss.

CD-Rs and CD-RWs

A **CD-R** (compact disc–recordable) is a unique type of CD on which you can record (write) data. You must have a CD-R drive, CD-R recording software, and blank CD-Rs to use for this process. Any data that you can create with any application (text, graphics, sound, video) can be stored permanently on a CD-R (see Figure 5.10). Once recorded, the data are not changeable. However, you may be able to add more data to the CD-R if there is sufficient space. The data become read-only. Once created, a CD-R can be read by any optical drive.

Because of their permanence and large storage capacity, CDs are particularly useful for archiving information (such as student portfolios) and storing teacher- or student-created multimedia files.

A **CD-RW** (compact disc–rewritable) takes the concept of reusable CDs one step further. These drives and the special discs that are designed for use in them allow users not only to record but also to change stored data. Because a CD-RW holds approximately the same amount of data as other CDs, it offers the same advantage of large storage capacity. However, its usefulness has been somewhat limited by the fact that the CD produced by a CD-RW drive might not be readable by the optical drives in older machines.

CD-RWs can be written on repeatedly.

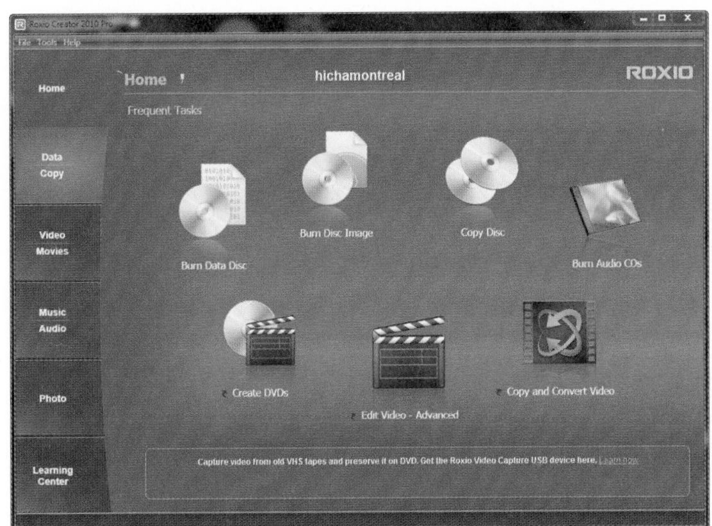

FIGURE 5.10

CD/DVD recording software such as Roxio's Creator helps you to select and organize the files you want burned on your recordable optical media.

DVDs

DVD-ROM (digital versatile discs) are another type of optical medium. A DVD drive can read both DVDs and CDs, thus allowing DVD-equipped computers to use older CD-ROM technology as well (a phenomenon called backwards compatibility). The advantage of a DVD is its ability to store considerably more data than a CD. Some DVDs can store data on both sides (unlike the one-sided CD) and on up to two layers per side. A DVD can store 4.7 gigabytes of data in the same physical space (one side, one layer), a great advantage compared to the 650 megabytes of data that can be stored on a CD-ROM. With the two sides, a two-layered DVD can store up to 17 gigabytes of data, enough to hold a full-length movie. (See Table 5.4.)

For education, DVDs hold the promise of a high-quality, fairly durable video medium. Unlike videotape, which can wear out or break relatively easily, with care, a DVD will last through years of classroom use without degrading—that is, losing any of its audio or video quality. Some DVDs even offer special options, such as displaying subtitles with the video or zooming in on an image.

Recordable DVD drives are the most common optical storage technology found on newer computers. This technology allows users to record data on a DVD just as you can record on a CD-R or CD-RW. This medium makes it possible to store and update large files, teacher- or student-made videos, audios, and computer-based multimedia data all on a single disc.

Recordable DVDs are currently available in several formats. It is important for teachers to be aware of the type of DVD used by their classroom computers so that they buy the appropriate type of DVD.

For a teacher interested in a recordable DVD, it is also important to first decide whether a recordable DVD is necessary for the storage task at hand. Recordable CDs are typically a more economical choice. If the extensive DVD storage capacity is not required, CDs may be a better option.

Regardless of the type of DVD player or recorder a computer is equipped with, one advantage of a DVD in a classroom computer is that it can take the place of a VCR and monitor. If the classroom is equipped with a projector capable of displaying computer images, then it can be used to display a DVD image as well. Using a computer display and the computer's DVD player, you can easily display a video recorded on DVD so that the entire class can view it. This type of configuration thus can serve two purposes and may make a VCR and monitor combination redundant.

TABLE 5.4 Optical Media Comparison

OPTICAL MEDIA	CHARACTERISTICS	CLASSROOM APPLICATION
CD-ROM	• Holds 650 megabytes of data • Read-only • Stores data or music	Used to deliver commercial software or music to end user
CD-R (CD-Recordable)	• Holds 650 megabytes of data • May be recorded on once by an optical drive (CD or DVD) that can record (burn) a CD • Once recorded, cannot be erased	• Most inexpensive recordable optical media that can be used to store teacher- or student-made files • Can be used to duplicate CDs
CD-RW (CD-Rewritable)	• Holds 650 megabytes of data • May be recorded and erased by an optical drive (CD or DVD) that can record (burn) and erase a CD	• More expensive recordable optical media for storage • Can be used to duplicate CDs • Most useful to store files that need updates
DVD (Digital Versatile Disc)	• Holds up to 4.7 gigabytes on one-layer, one-sided disc or 17 gigabytes on two layers for two-sided discs • Read only, cannot be recorded on or erased	• Used for video recordings
DVD±R (DVD-Recordable)	• Holds up to 4.7 gigabytes on one-layer, one sided disc or 17 gigabytes on two layers for two-sided discs • Can be recorded once (burned) with DVD drive that can record; cannot be erased • DVD-R drives can also burn CD-Rs	• Most inexpensive recordable DVD that can be used to store very large teacher- or student-made files • Can be used to duplicate DVDs
DVD±RW (DVD Rewritable)	• Holds up to 4.7 gigabytes on one-layer, one-sided disc or 17 gigabytes on two layers for two-sided discs • May be recorded and erased by a DVD drive that can record (burn) and erase a DVD • Can also burn CD-Rs and burn/erase CD-RWs	• Most flexible but expensive recordable DVD; can be used to store very large teacher- or student-made files • Can be used to duplicate DVDs • Most useful to store very large files that need updates

Networking Computers

A network connects a group of computers to a server to share resources and files.

One of the most cost-effective and powerful ways to configure school computer hardware is to **network** it. Networks offer schools a way to communicate information and share resources. Individual computers connected to a network are usually called network **workstations.** In a network, workstations and sharable peripherals (such as printers) are connected together to a single, more powerful computer called a server. A server provides services to all the machines on the network. A network's server contains the networking software that manages networkwide communication. The server includes one or more very large hard disk drives on which it stores the network management software, common files, and programs that the workstations can share. Together, the server, the workstations and peripherals, and the wiring that connects them constitute a network.

Networks are configured, or arranged, in many different ways to suit the facilities and the number of workstations that need to connect to that particular network. Configurations vary, but all networks have some common elements and terminology. Every workstation connects in some way to the server. This is accomplished through a special piece of equip-

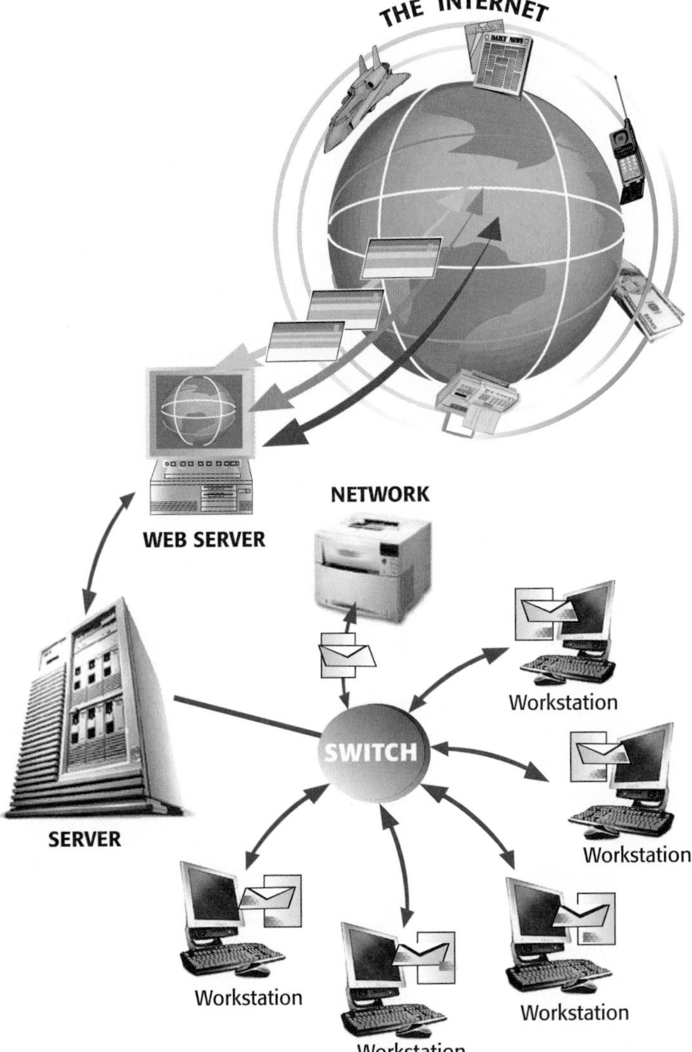

FIGURE 5.11

Networks make communication and resource sharing possible.

ment, called a **switch,** that offers a series of centralized connections. Any workstation or peripheral that is connected to the network becomes a **node** on the network, with all nodes ultimately connected back, through one or more switches, to their server. Individual workstations, peripherals, and switches are connected to the server through some type of wiring or, in some cases, through a wireless communication channel. This relationship is illustrated in Figure 5.11.

In a typical school, workstations and a **server** are usually wired together by using a type of cable similar to telephone wire. The wiring is strung from the server, often above ceilings, to each classroom, where a single network wire is provided for each computer in the room. Each network wire, in turn, connects to a network card that is installed in each computer to be able to connect to the network.

Often, when schools are retrofitted for a network, because of the cost of pulling network wire through existing ceilings and walls, only one or two drops are made to a classroom. In such cases, one connection is often designed to connect a teacher workstation to the school network. A second drop would provide for one other workstation to be connected for student use. Deciding how to use available network connections and arranging classroom space around them can be a challenge. As you learned in previous chapters, it is important to create a physical classroom environment that meets diverse learner needs. The addition of networked workstations can add further complexity to the classroom arrangement. You will need to look for the network connection point(s) in the classroom in which you will be teaching and plan your teaching and learning space accordingly.

One alternative to wiring schools and classrooms that is rapidly gaining popularity is wireless networking. In a **wireless network,** information is transmitted wirelessly rather than using hard wire connections. A wireless network may require that transmitter hubs be strategically placed in rooms and across the campus to receive and transmit data from computers. This approach to networking has several advantages for schools. First, wireless networking eliminates much of the retrofitting cost. Although some retrofitting may still be required, it is less work than what is necessary for wired networks. Second, a wireless network makes it easier to create a flexible learning environment that fully integrates networked resources. Classrooms no longer have to set up workstations according to where network connections are available. Additionally, with the use of notebook and handheld computers that are equipped for wireless networking, a classroom could conceivably have a bank of computers available for students to take to their desks for individual or group research. The downsides of wireless networks are the cost of the technology itself and some security issues typical of wireless networks. As the cost falls, however, and network technology improves, wireless networking may well become the strategy of choice for more schools.

Local area networks (LANs) serve local areas, and wide area networks (WANs) serve large areas.

Regardless of the networking technology selected, individual classrooms with multiple computers can be networked, computer labs can be networked, schools can be networked, and entire districts can share resources across a network. Smaller networks that connect machines in local areas, such as a classroom or school, are called **local area networks (LANs).** Networks that connect machines across a wide area, such as all of the schools in a district or all of the districts in a state, are called **wide area networks (WANs)**. The interconnectivity of the workstations on both types of networks and the potential for connecting these networks to each other are what make possible our modern-day ability to communicate instantly.

Using a School Network

Networks have promise as powerful teaching and learning tools, but to use networks for teaching and learning, some challenges must be addressed and overcome. Although it is usually not a teacher's responsibility to respond to these challenges, it is useful to understand how they affect this technology.

Many different sizes of files of information may be sent across a network. Large text files are measured in thousands of bytes or kilobytes. But other files, such as graphic, photo, video, and audio files, can be multiple megabytes (millions of bytes) of data each. To better understand the impact of file sizes in networking, imagine a network wire as a roadway. On that electronic roadway, some files are of a size analogous to subcompact cars, while others are more like tractor-trailer trucks. Furthermore, some types of wiring offer a roadway the size of an alley, while others offer a roadway the size of a ten-lane superhighway. The challenge for communication occurs when you try to fit a large "tractor-trailer truck" of data through an "alley"-sized network wire. It can be done, but the going is alarmingly slow. Servers manage such feats by breaking the data into small units, or **packets,** and sending them through one packet at a time. The network software then reassembles the data at the other end into their original form. This transmission process can take considerable time with large, complex files.

Bandwidth is the capacity and the speed of transmission of network connections.

In network terms, the carrying capacity (size of the roadway) of the transmission media for sending information is called its **bandwidth** (see Figure 5.12). The speed at which the network can transmit data is measured in the number of bits that can be sent per second. The larger the bandwidth and greater the speed of the transmission media, the faster the data flow across it, even if the data include large files. As a network-using educator, you need to be aware of the capabilities of the network you are going to use so that you can plan

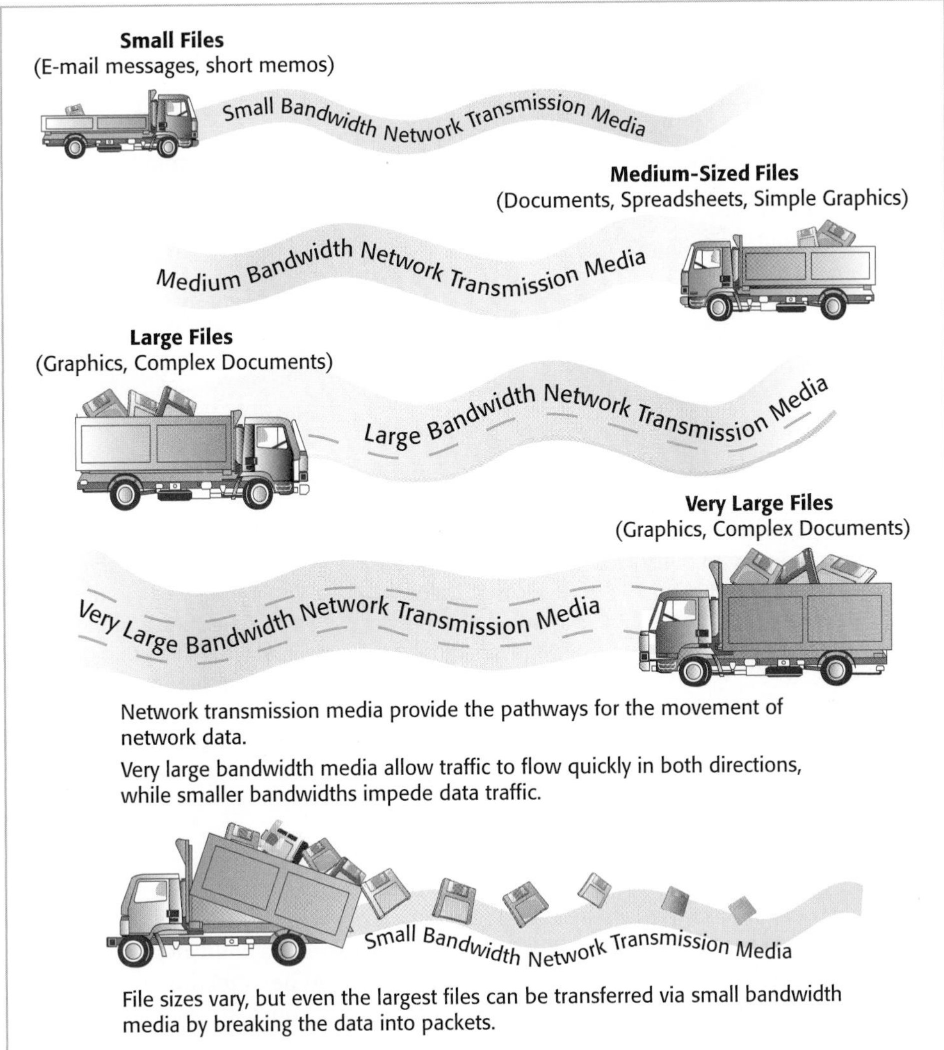

FIGURE 5.12

Bandwidth

Different transmission media offer different speed and capacity for data transmission, just as physical highways provide different capacities for automobile traffic.

appropriately. If you want to share the digital or scanned photographs your class took on their last field trip with a class at another school, you need to discover how long that process will take before you schedule it into a lesson. If you want to add audio components to a PowerPoint presentation for use in all sixth-grade classes via the network, you need to be aware of a potential delay caused by the transmission of large audio files. Although you, as an educator, do not need to be able to create a network, it is important to be a well-versed consumer with regard to the network you use.

Another challenge in using a network for teaching and learning is the question of data privacy and security. For educators, ensuring that students do their own work and that their efforts are private is essential. If networks allow users to share files and resources, how can a teacher ensure the security of each student's work? Furthermore, how can a teacher's files be securely segregated from student files? This challenge is addressed by the network software and the network support staff through the use of security measures inherent in the system. User security on a network is provided through a system of user names (also called log-in names) and **passwords.** Even though all of the computers in any given room may be physically capable of providing access to the network, such access is granted only when the network recognizes that a specific authorized user is at a computer.

Log-in names and passwords are features that help to ensure network security and user privacy.

FIGURE 5.13

Individual User Accounts on a Network

Every account includes a user profile that contains a log-in name, password, and the rights that individual user has to access files and move about the network.

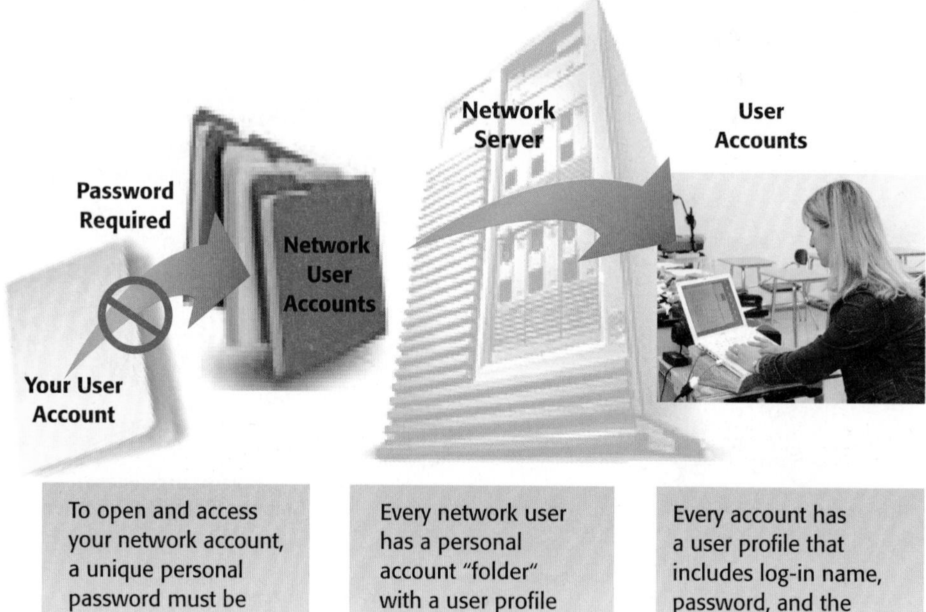

To open and access your network account, a unique personal password must be entered.

Every network user has a personal account "folder" with a user profile and storage space on a server hard disk drive.

Every account has a user profile that includes log-in name, password, and the rights that the individual user has to access files and move about the network.

Every network user is given access to some or all of the files and programs stored on the server's hard drive(s), as shown in Figure 5.13. This assigned ability to access specific files and resources is called the user's rights or privileges. When creating user accounts, the network administrator issues specific rights to every account, thus ensuring that no account has access to resources or files that are inappropriate for that user. Student network users therefore can access only files and resources for which they have been given rights. These restricted rights typically allow them only to use particular software and to access the files that they created themselves or that were created for them by their teacher. This system of user names, passwords, and assigned rights enables a high degree of security and privacy for most users. Of course, people with advanced computer skills can sometimes break through the security and hack into a network. But vigilant network administrators can implement and monitor various levels of roadblocks, called **firewalls,** to keep hackers out of their networks and keep your data safe.

> Firewalls prevent unauthorized access to data and files from outside the network.

Sharing and Communicating via a Network

Networks enable and support communication and the sharing of resources in many ways. Communications are enhanced through a variety of tools, including the most familiar of them: electronic mail (email). Hardware and software resources on the server and across the network can be shared via the coordination offered by the network software. For teachers looking to maximize their computing capabilities while minimizing costs, networks offer many advantages. These are summarized in Table 5.5 and are described in more detail in the following sections.

TABLE 5.5 Network Features and Applications

NETWORK FEATURE	USE	CLASSROOM APPLICATION
SHARED HARDWARE	Costly hardware can be shared by many workstations.	One printer, scanner, or other peripheral can be shared by all computers in the classroom.
SHARED SOFTWARE	Programs can reside on the server or be pushed to individual machines to save space, maintenance, and technical-support time.	Classroom software is simple and quick to install, upgrade, or maintain in a single process via the server.
DATA SHARING	Files and folders can be made accessible to all network users or can be tagged for use by specific users.	Class handouts and other content files can be made available to all or some students for copying or printing.
NETWORK TOOLS	Groupware offers common organizing tools and calendars across the network. Network monitoring and tracking methods ensure appropriate use of technology.	Class calendar and address book are simple to maintain and access from anywhere in school; teacher can monitor all students' activity while they are logged in to the network.
COMMUNICATIONS	Electronic mail provides all users the ability to communicate with each other or groups and to send attachment files along with messages.	Students can communicate with peers and their teacher; electronic pen pal (e-pal) projects can be initiated.

Shared Programs

Programs can be installed on the server and made available via the network to all workstations. This process can save the time and labor that would otherwise have been necessary to install identical programs on every computer. In such situations, the programs reside on the server's hard disk, and the workstations run the software from there through the network. This leaves the local workstation's drives available for file storage or for non-network software. Other network scenarios use workstation hard drives to store some or all elements of common network software. In such cases, the network can be used to "push" (copy) the software from the server to the workstations' hard drives to update or maintain it. In either scenario, sharing programs makes their update and maintenance easier and more efficient.

ISTE Standard

Learning about how teachers can use networking to support teaching and learning will help you address **NETS•T STANDARD 3:**

MODEL DIGITAL-AGE WORK AND LEARNING Teachers exhibit knowledge, skills, and work processes representative of an innovative professional in a global and digital society.

Another advantage of shared networked software resources is that such an arrangement may save software acquisition dollars as well as worker resources. Many software vendors provide discounts for network versions of software that can be used on all machines in a network. Such network **site licenses** allow the use of a program on any machine on the network at a defined site, usually at a substantial savings over the purchase of multiple copies of the same software for use on individual computers. When you work in a networked environment and you are considering acquisition of software that may benefit others at your school, you should explore the costs of a networked version of the program you desire. You may find that for close to the purchase price of a few individual copies, you can buy a site license for many computers at your school.

Site licenses offer discounts across a school.

A final advantage for sharing programs via a network relates to the support that all software eventually needs. With a network, when software upgrades become available, the support staff need only upgrade the software on the server to make the upgrade available to each workstation, rather than having to visit and upgrade every individual computer at a school. Similarly, if problems arise with any software, they are resolved at the more centralized server level, normally a much faster support process. For a busy teacher, waiting for a "house call" from the support staff to fix a problem with a single computer's unique software is likely to take longer than reporting to the network administrator a network problem that can be corrected simultaneously for all workstations via the server.

Although server-based software has these support advantages, there are some disadvantages. Because workstations rely on the server's software, should any problems occur with software on the server or with the server itself, all workstations will have the same problem. For that reason, many networks have redundant systems such as backup servers in place to ensure that there is no interruption of service. Other networks keep redundant backup disks of all server programs and data so that the administrator can quickly reinstall files and restore services if a problem occurs. Still other networks may store backup copies of critical software programs on the hard drives of the individual workstations as a redundancy. In a classroom that has integrated network resources into instruction, it is important to be aware of your network's backup system and to develop your own backup plan in case the network or a shared program is not accessible when you need it. Although such situations are rare, it is a good idea to anticipate them and discuss the options with the network administrator at your school.

Shared Data

File sharing is a major advantage of networks.

Using programs across a network is just one of the ways networked workstations can share resources. Of equal importance is the ability to share data and other files. Network servers are usually configured with ample storage that can be used in several different ways depending on the needs of the users of that network system. Typically, each user is given a small network storage area associated with his or her user name, on which he or she can store personal data. Such user storage areas are private to the extent that they can be accessed only by using both the user name and password of the individual user. The advantage of user storage areas on a network is that the user can go to any workstation, regardless of its location, and still be able to access the files in his or her user space stored on the server. For teachers, this can mean that they can access their class files from their networked classroom computer, from a workstation in a networked computer lab, or from a networked workstation in the faculty workroom. For students, this means that they can work on an interdisciplinary assignment while in the media center or in different subject-area classrooms. This ease of accessibility to files is a major advantage of user storage on a network server. A disadvantage may be the quantity of hard disk storage that the network server gives each user. Nevertheless, the relatively low cost of expanding disk storage space and the significant benefit of easy access usually make this option worth the investment.

Shared Administrative Tools

Most network software provides a series of **administrative tools** that are shared by all network users. Often called **groupware,** it usually provides, at minimum, a common calendar, address book, and facilities reservation list, as well as email. Using this type of shared tool, a busy educator who wishes to set up a meeting with other teachers on the network can have the server automatically poll all the teachers' electronic calendars to find a free common meeting time. If a teacher wishes to reserve a special classroom space for his or her class, the common facilities reservation list on the network can be automatically checked for open dates for that space. Although these time-saving tools vary with the network system installed, most network software provides abundant groupware options. You should explore your school's network to see which is available for your use.

Network software may also offer teachers a way to monitor activity on, and take control of, student workstations in the classroom or media center. This type of software allows the teacher to observe student progress by "tuning in" to an individual workstation and monitoring the activity on the screen. It also allows the teacher to take over one or more workstations to provide a demonstration or instruction. Finally, it allows the teacher to broadcast the images on any one workstation's monitor to all other workstations to share a student's

In the CLASSROOM

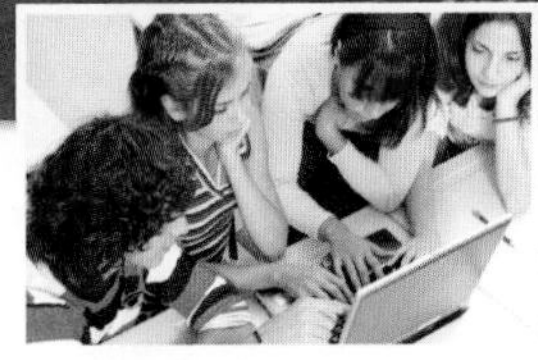

Networks in the Secondary Classroom

Coming up with the best of both worlds, the Frederick County Public Schools in Virginia have a school network, sometimes called an intranet, that has links to the Internet. Rod Carnill points out that the two "nets" complement each other. The intranet is especially helpful to teachers because students' work and identifiable photographs, special projects, and events at school can be shown without having to obtain permission in the form of releases. The intranet, he relates, "uses a collection of HTML files in a single folder on the school's web server" and is, at the same time, "a self-created portal for Internet use." The portal provides guided access to the Internet for students to use in completing research and other coursework and also permits in-house file sharing.

Progressive schools like Tampa Catholic High School in the Diocese of St. Petersburg, Tampa, Florida, have found many ways to make their schools' intranets perform services for the teachers and administrators alike. Kevin Yarnell, the technology director, wrote in *School Executive* of some of these methods that simplify and improve the overall operating infrastructure of the school. When scheduling tests, teachers can check to see what other testing is being done on the same day. Student data—birthdays, clubs, athletics, and honors—and other information can be stored in a database on the intranet. Announcements and even personal communications to and from school personnel can be posted. School records and reports can be archived in a database for that purpose. Student work, if electronic, can also be kept on the site. The limited access to the intranet makes it invaluable to schools, whether it is a small site affecting only one or a few classrooms or a large site that connects an entire school district, for many school-related communications are confidential legally and ethically.

Sources: Integration via a browser-based intranet. 2002. Retrieved June 11, 2003, from **www.nps.k12.va.us/infodiv/it/techconf/integbrw.htm;.**
K. Yarnell. 2002. Intranets: Repositories of school data. *School Executive* (September/October), 39 (1), 28.

work. Although often used in computer lab settings, this software can be very useful in classrooms and media centers with multiple student workstations.

Shared Hardware

Software sharing is not the only type of resource sharing made possible by a network. Hardware sharing is another advantage of school networking. In a classroom or media center that is configured only with stand-alone computers, each needs its own printer plugged in to be able to print. In a networked scenario, a single, usually higher-end printer can be used by all workstations in the vicinity. This can be done either by attaching a networkable printer as an independent network node or by attaching a printer to one of the workstations on the network. In either configuration, the printer hardware is then available to be shared by all local network workstations. Using this arrangement makes it possible to maximize the use of printer resources.

Networks enable sharing of hardware resources.

Educational Computing

Computers and networks are tools that can help you build the kind of learning environment you might once only have imagined. Using a computer, your students can publish their own class newsletter with digital images from their recent field trip. They can create interactive stories that their peers can explore. They can connect to online resources that place the world's knowledge base literally at their fingertips. Using a network, they can share data and resources across a school or district. But having such powerful tools available means

Buying a computer podcast.

Hardware Evaluation **Rubric**

HARDWARE:

DESCRIPTION:

VENDOR: **COST:**

NOTES ON USE:

Please rate the features below for each hardware component. Next to each of the items in the rubric, mark the box that best reflects your opinion.

EVALUATION CRITERIA

HARDWARE FEATURE	1 Poor	2 Below Average	3 Average	4 Above Average	5 Excellent
CPU	☐ Speed below school standard; insufficient to run class software	☐ Speed below standard but sufficient to run most class software	☐ Speed at standard; will support current class software	☐ Speed at or above standard; will support newer software	☐ Speed above standard; likely to support next-generation software
RAM	☐ Capacity below school standard; insufficient to run class software	☐ Capacity below school standard but sufficient to run most class software	☐ Capacity at standard; will support current class software	☐ Capacity at or above standard; will support newer software	☐ Capacity above standard; likely to support next-generation software
Input Devices	☐ Keyboard flimsy with limited features; mechanical mouse; no scroll wheel	☐ Keyboard flimsy but with some extra features; mechanical mouse with scroll wheel	☐ Keyboard includes features (wrist guard, etc.); optical mouse with scroll wheel	☐ Multimedia keyboard; optical mouse with scroll and programmable buttons	☐ Multimedia keyboard; laser mouse with scroll/tilt wheel and programmable buttons
Monitor	☐ Low resolution; slow scan rate minimum color depth; insufficient for newer software	☐ Low resolution; acceptable scan rate and color depth; may be insufficient for some software	☐ Resolution, scan rate, color depth meet school standards; will display most software	☐ Resolution, scan rate, color depth meet or exceed school standards; will display newer software	☐ Resolution, scan rate, color depth meet or exceed school standards; will display next-generation software
Hard Drive	☐ Capacity below school standard; insufficient to run class software	☐ Capacity below school standard but sufficient to run most class software	☐ Capacity at standard; will support current class software	☐ Capacity at or above standard; will support newer software	☐ Capacity above standard; likely to support next-generation software
Portable Media Drives	☐ No removable media drive; no expansion capacity	☐ Limited to 1 floppy disk drive; limited expansion capacity	☐ 1 or more floppy disk drives; expandable	☐ Floppy disk and 1 other removable media drive; expandable	☐ Multiple removable media drives; capacity to expand
Optical Drives	☐ No optical drive	☐ CD-ROM only	☐ 1 optical drive (CD-R or CD-RW)	☐ Multiple optical drives (CD-RW and CD-ROM)	☐ Multiple optical drives (CD-RW and DVD or DVD-R)
Sound System	☐ Minimal sound card; nonpowered speakers	☐ Minimal sound card; powered speakers	☐ Adequate sound card; powered speakers	☐ Upgraded sound card; amplified speakers	☐ Upgraded sound card; amplified speakers with woofer
Ports	☐ Minimal ports; no USB ports	☐ Adequate ports; 1 USB port	☐ All standard ports; 2–4 USB ports	☐ All standard ports; 4 or more USB ports	☐ All standard ports; 4 or more USB ports, front-accessible and/or Firewire
Warranty Support	☐ No warranty; no free phone support	☐ Less than 1-year warranty; no free phone support	☐ 1-year warranty; free phone support for less than 1 year	☐ 1-year warranty; free phone support for 1 year	☐ 1-year warranty; free phone support; on-site support

PEARSON myeducationkit™ Go to the *Rubrics* section of Chapter 5 in MyEducationKit to download the *Hardware Evaluation Rubric* for your use.

little if you don't know how to use them. Mastery of the computer basics presented in this chapter is an excellent first step.

As you increase your understanding of and skills with computers, you will find your own personal applications for this unique digital technology. Computers have changed our world as they've ushered in the Information Age. There is little doubt that they will ultimately have the same impact throughout education. Your own personal mastery of this revolutionary digital tool will serve both you and your students well. And as with all educational technologies, it is important to carefully evaluate computers before selecting them for your classroom. An evaluation rubric can be a powerful tool in reviewing and evaluating computer hardware.

Of course, digital technologies include more than just a computer system. As an outgrowth of computers, a true digital revolution has begun. Many of today's cameras use digital methods of capturing and storing images instead of film. Audiotapes and vinyl records have been replaced by CDs and DVDs, which are giving way to electronic formats such as MP3s. What does all this mean to educators?

As you will see in the next three chapters, it means that more and more tools are becoming available to help you individualize instruction, meet learner needs, and help you teach and manage your classroom. It means that a more diverse and robust learning environment can be constructed for your students. All you need to do to use current and emerging digital innovations is, first, be aware that they exist and, second, be willing to learn to use them. Increasing your digital awareness and helping you learn to use digital technologies are the purposes of the rest of this unit.

To check your comprehension of the content covered in this chapter, go to the MyEducationKit for your book and complete the *Study Plan* for Chapter 5.

Key Terms

administrative tools, 136
antivirus programs, 126
application program, 115
back up, 122
bandwidth, 132
booting up, 113
byte, 122
CD-R, 128
CD-ROM, 128
CD-RW, 128
chips, 113
commands, 114
computer system, 112
computing cycle, 112
CPU, 121
dpi, 120
DVD-ROM, 129
file, 125
firewall, 134
floppy disk, 123
folder, 125
gigabytes, 122
groupware, 136
GUI, 114
hard copy, 119
hard disk, 122
hardware, 112
icon, 114
input device, 117
integrated software package, 116
interface, 114
keyboard, 117
LCD, 120
local area network (LAN), 132
memory, 112
menu, 114
monitor, 119
mouse, 115
multimedia, 127
network, 130
node, 131
operating system (OS), 114
output devices, 119
packet, 132
password, 132
pixel, 119
programs, 112
RAM, 121
resolution, 119
ROM, 113
server, 131
site license, 135
soft copy, 119
software, 112
storage, 112
switch, 131
utility programs, 115
USB, 124
virus, 126
wide area network (WAN), 132
Windows, 114
wireless network, 132
workstation, 130

Student Activities

CHAPTER REVIEW

1. Describe each of the four major components of the computing cycle.
2. What is the difference between hardware and software? Give an example of each.
3. What is the difference between memory and storage in a computer system? Why are both necessary?
4. Describe the role of the operating system. How does it help you interact with a computer?
5. What are the three different classes of application software? What different types of tasks does each perform?
6. What is the CPU, and what is its role in the computer system?
7. Describe the difference between input and output devices. Give two examples of each.
8. What do you need to know about monitor resolution before purchasing a monitor? About printer resolution before buying a printer?
9. What is a computer virus and how is it transmitted? What can you do to protect your classroom?
10. How do the following storage devices differ: hard disk, floppy disk, flash drive, CD-ROM, CD-R, CD-RW, DVD, DVD±RW?
11. What is a network? What is the relationship between a server and workstations?
12. How are typical classrooms wired? What impact does this have on the learning environment?
13. How do bandwidth and transmission speed affect network communications?
14. Describe the techniques used in networking to protect the privacy of an individual's data and the security of the network.
15. Why is it advantageous for educators to share resources and programs on a network? What concerns are associated with program sharing?

WHAT DO YOU THINK?

1. Interview three of your fellow students to find out how they think computers affect their learning and the teaching they have been exposed to in their academic careers. On the basis of the interviews and your own views, what can you conclude about the role of computers in instruction?
2. Interview a network administrator to discover the issues he or she is most concerned with relating to network security. Be sure to ask what other issues are of concern with regard to helping users. Summarize the interview questions and responses. Explain how the network issues may affect the way in which you use this technology in your classroom.
3. Interview one of the technical support staff members at your school and ask what types of storage devices he or she would recommend in a computer system. Be sure to ask whether the person prefers CD-RW or DVD drives and ask what size permanent and portable hard drives he or she recommends and why. What can you conclude about how to configure a computer for your classroom?

LEARNING TOGETHER!

The following activities are designed for learning groups of two or three students.

1. Select three different computer systems and compare them using the hardware evaluation rubric. After discussing the options with your group, describe which system you would buy and explain why. Be prepared to share your preference and your reasons with the class.
2. Each member of your group should interview a teacher who uses a computer in his or her classroom. Ask the teacher how the computer is used for academic and for administrative tasks. Compare your interviews with those of the other members of your group and list the uses you discover.
3. Brainstorm how computers have changed society in general and education in particular. Identify and list all of the ways in which computers have had an impact. Then determine five ways in which they are likely to change society and education in the future. Be prepared to share your group's outcomes with your peers.

TEACHING WITH TECHNOLOGY: INTEGRATION IDEAS WEB QUEST

As you become familiar with the many technologies available for teachers' use in their classrooms, it is useful to examine how teachers are applying technology to support and enhance the learning process. Let's take a look at some specific, innovative ways in which educators are leveraging technology to teach using the links that follow.

ACTIVITY: After you explore the links that interest you, select a topic you are likely to teach for a subject you will teach at the grade level you prefer. Complete a web search to discover at least three new integration ideas. Write a one-page summary of your web quest that includes (1) the link you used and the integration ideas you found, (2) an idea of yours of how you might teach with technology for your selected content area, and (3) a description of the technologies you will need in your classroom to implement your own integration idea.

Integrating Technology into English/ Language Arts

Writing and Grammar Help

Purdue's **Online Writing Lab**, OWL, at **http://owl.english.purdue.edu/**, has earned a reputation for excellence in helping secondary and postsecondary students in reviewing and practicing grammar, citations, types of writing styles, and the writing process. This online lab offers an example of the seamless integration of technology and teaching writing skills. This is an excellent support resource for any writing assignment. **National Council of Teachers of English** sponsors ACE, the **Assembly on Computers in English.** This group offers a workshop at the annual NCTE conference and online. The workshop provides an online journal and recommended links and resources to integrate technology into language arts at **http://aceworkshop.org/.**

Integrating Technology into Math

Virtual Manipulatives

Using manipulatives to reinforce abstract math topics has become a common practice in math education. For teachers who do not have an abundance of manipulatives for their classrooms, another option is to put the classroom computer to work to present students with "virtual manipulatives." Not only are a large variety of manipulatives instantly available, their flexibility exceeds their real-world counterparts. To explore virtual manipulatives, visit **Educational Java Programs** at **www.arcytech.org/java/** or the **National Library of Virtual Manipulatives** at **http://nlvm.usu.edu/en/nav/vlibrary.html** and try the manipulatives available through this site.

Spreadsheets

Spreadsheet software can be used to organize data, test formulas, or graph information. Students can use an electronic spreadsheet to test their hypotheses and perform what-if analysis. **The National Council of Teachers of Mathematics** offers **Illuminations,** a series of lesson plans and activities that demonstrate a vision for math in schools. This resource at **http://illuminations.nctm.org/** offers unique lessons using spreadsheets as well as links to mathematics standards.

Integrating Technology into Science

Science Exhibits

At the **Exploratorium (www.exploratorium.edu/exhibits/f_exhibits.html)** your students can view and interact with an assortment of science exhibits for an in-class science field trip. Access the Exploratorium directly or link to it via the **Science Learning Network (www.sln.org/resources/index.html)** for other computer-based science resources.

Science Experiments

Bring science to your students so they can take it home with them at **http://pbskids.org/zoom/games/kitchenchemistry/, PBS's Kitchen Chemistry** web site. Virtual experiments are presented in an online kitchen, and their home counterparts are outlined for students to try. Kids get rewards for participating. Use this site to help students individually participate in science experiments, even in the most crowded classroom.

Integrating Technology into Social Studies

History Museum

Visit the **Constitution Center** at **www.constitutioncenter.org/timeline/** to explore an interactive multimedia timeline of our history. History topics come alive with images and audio of key events in U.S. history. This site also offers an interactive Constitution; Abraham Lincoln Crossroads, an online social studies game; and numerous other resources. Bring history to your classroom when you bring your students to this museum.

Government Resources

Go to the **National Archives** at **www.archives.gov/education/index.html,** where you can have your students print out and sign the Declaration of Independence, view the Emancipation Proclamation in Lincoln's own hand, or view an online photo album of the last century. Just one of many government resources available to teachers, this site brings historical documents into your classroom.

interchapter 5

Teachers' Buying Guide for Classroom Computers and Peripherals

Before selecting a personal computer system and peripherals for your classroom, complete the decision matrix below to help you determine whether the equipment is right for you.

Place checks in the columns that match your answers.

	COMPONENT	QUESTIONS TO ASK ABOUT THIS COMPONENT	YES	NO	N/A
Unit	CPU	Is the CPU chip a name brand? Is the chip speed faster than required by the majority of the software you want to use? Can the chip be upgraded if necessary?			
Unit	RAM	Does the amount of RAM exceed the requirements of the software you want to use? Can you add more RAM if needed?			
Unit	Bays	Is there room in the system unit to add more internal drives if you want to?			
Unit	Ports	Are there multiple USB ports available? Are some of the USB ports available on the front of the machine?			
Storage	Hard Drive	Is this drive the largest size possible for your budget?			
Storage	CD Drive(s)	Is a CD-RW drive included in this computer? Is the CD-RW drive high-speed (more than 40x)? Does CD recording software come installed? Is there more than one CD (or DVD) drive included to facilitate copying student CDs?			
Storage	Floppy Drive	Is a floppy disk drive included in this machine?			
Storage	DVD Drive	Is a DVD drive included? Is a DVD-recordable drive included?			
Storage	USB Drive	Does the drive provide sufficient storage space for your largest collection of files? Does the shape of the drive allow it to be easily plugged into accessible USB ports? Do any necessary software drivers come with the drive? Does the drive come with a lanyard or key chain?			
Output Devices	Monitor	Is the monitor resolution sufficient for your highest-output program? Is the monitor size appropriate to your viewing and space needs? Does the monitor have an adjustment control in front so it is easy to access?			
Output Devices	Printer	Is the page per minute (ppm) speed sufficient to print in a timely manner? If ink jet, is each color inkwell separate so colors can be replaced independently when they run out? If laser, is the cost of replacement toner cartridges reasonably within your budget?			

COMPONENT	QUESTIONS TO ASK ABOUT THIS COMPONENT	*Place checks in the columns that match your answers.* YES	NO	N/A
	Is the paper tray large enough so you don't have to continuously load paper? Can the printer print two sides automatically?			
Speakers	Is a headphone jack easily accessible? Are the speakers powered with a separate plug? Are the speakers and amplifier (if included) small enough for classroom space requirements?			
Digital Projector	Is the brightness (in lumens) sufficient so that it will display with classroom lights on? Is the bulb easily replaceable? Can the device display both video and digital data? Does it have built-in speakers? Does it have a remote control? Does it have sufficient adjustment controls (focus, align, zoom, etc.)? Are all necessary cables provided?			
Keyboard	Are the keys sufficiently tactile (not spongy to the touch)? Does the keyboard include a wrist rest? Are there additional easy-access multimedia keys or buttons? Does the keyboard have a built in USB hub?			
Mouse	Is the mouse an optical rather than a ball mouse? Is a scroll wheel included on the mouse? Is a mouse pad needed?			
Microphone	Is a microphone built in or included? Is its cord sufficiently long to be used comfortably? Is a holder provided to store the microphone when not in use?			
Scanner	Is the resolution sufficient for the type of scanning you want to do? Is the scanner software easy to use? Is the software OCR-capable? Will the scanner scan larger documents? Does the scanner have a feeder for multiple pages?			
Digital Camera	Is this camera's image quality (in megapixels) sufficient for the types of photos you wish to take and print? Is extra storage capacity available at a reasonable cost? Is the battery type rechargeable? Is a charger included? Can the camera zoom sufficiently for your needs? Is there an LCD display to preview pictures? Is there an easy-to-use download system to move images to your computer? Are the setting adjustments easy to use? Are a case and strap provided for easy carrying?			

Output Devices, *continued*

Input Devices

Make Your Decision!!

Add the number of checks in each column. The higher the number of *Yes* checks, the more likely the computer system is appropriate for your classroom.

TOTALS		
YES	NO	N/A

CHAPTER 6

Digital Technologies in the Classroom

Courtesy of InFocus

CHAPTER OVERVIEW

This chapter addresses these ISTE National Educational Technology Standards:

- •NETS•T Standard 1
- •NETS•T Standard 2
- •NETS•T Standard 3
- •NETS•S Standard 6

- **Digital Technologies in the Classroom**
- **Input Devices for Teaching and Learning**
- **Output Devices for Teaching and Learning**
- **Emerging Digital Technologies for the Classroom**
- **From Hardware to Software**

Computers have changed our world, both inside and outside the classroom. It is not just the computer itself, with all of its capabilities, that has caused this change. Indeed, the computer has proven itself to be just the forerunner of a much greater digital revolution. As a result of the advances in personal computers, many other digital devices have evolved. These devices can serve teaching and learning in dramatic and innovative ways.

Consider for a moment the process teachers once used to duplicate materials for their students. Have you ever heard the term *dittos* applied to teacher-prepared worksheets and wondered where this term comes from? Before personal computers were widely available, teachers had to go through a laborious process to prepare student worksheets. Two technologies were available: the spirit duplicator, which used blue-backed transfer paper to run a limited number of duplicate copies, and the dittograph machine, which used a waxed paper that was cut (like a stencil) by typewriter keys or by a special sharp stylus. The duplicator used an alcohol-based chemical to transfer the blue ink from the master to plain paper. The dittograph ran ink through the temporary stencil the teacher created and transferred that ink to paper. Both technologies were slow and very messy and could reproduce only a limited number of copies before the masters deteriorated. Also, teachers had to be very careful not to make mistakes. No "delete" keys were available on typewriters or when creating a master by hand! Mistakes were transferred along with correct content. And, of course, these types of technology could not change the size or style of the font, add graphics, or make transparencies.

With the first personal computer came the first word processor. This combination made it possible for teachers to see the finished product on the screen, edit, correct mistakes, adjust fonts, and even add graphics before transferring the document to paper. Furthermore, as printers became more sophisticated and cheaper, it became easy to print out high-quality transparencies and worksheets that incorporated color and graphics.

The computer was just the beginning. The digital tools that have resulted from it are even more amazing. The change from laborious duplication to quick word processing and printing is just one example of the digital revolution that personal computers began. Just as this necessary teaching task was simplified and enhanced by digital technologies, so too have countless more teaching and learning tasks been improved through the application of digital equipment.

This chapter will help you explore a number of digital technologies that have evolved out of the digital revolution led by the personal computer. In Chapter 6, you will explore:

- How digital input technologies can be used in teaching and learning
- How digital output technologies can be used in teaching and learning
- The issues and concerns associated with using these diverse technologies in the classroom
- Emerging digital technologies that may be useful to teachers and learners in the future

Digital Technologies in the Classroom

Once you have computer systems in the classroom, the possibilities for expanding their capabilities by the addition of digital peripherals are enormous. You can add input devices that let you scan leaves from your nature walks and load photos from your field trip; let students operate a computer by touching a display projected onto the classroom whiteboard; or let you dictate input via voice instead of a keyboard. Or you can add output devices that enable you to share what's on your monitor with the whole class; that can turn segments of a videotape into digital pictures; or that can read sections of the textbook to your auditory learners. Whatever your academic or administrative needs, you can usually find hardware and software to add to your computer to get the job done. The subsequent sections of this chapter will examine some of the more useful and innovative digital technologies for classroom use.

ISTE Standard

Learning about digital technologies for the classroom will help you address

NETS•T STANDARD 2:

DESIGN AND DEVELOP DIGITAL-AGE LEARNING EXPERIENCES AND ASSESSMENTS Teachers design, develop, and evaluate authentic learning experiences and assessments incorporating contemporary tools and resources to maximize content learning in context and to develop the knowledge, skills, and attitudes identified in the NETS•S.

FIGURE 6.2

Comparison of Digital Cameras and Their Features

Digital cameras are made by a number of manufacturers. Each type of digital camera has features that affect its price. Most have an LCD display that lets you preview your pictures as soon as you take them.

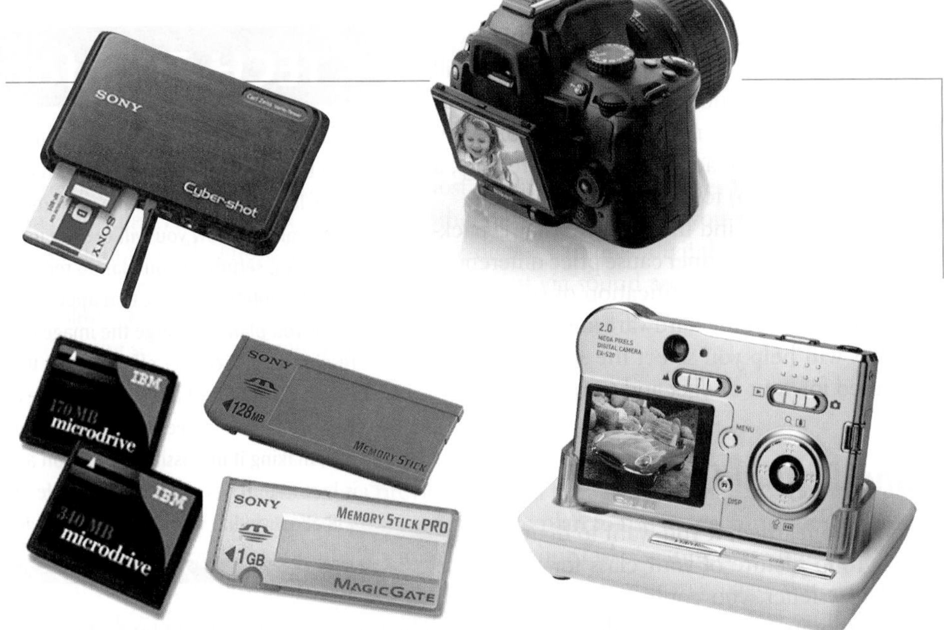

COMPARISON OF DIGITAL CAMERAS AND THEIR FEATURES

DIGITAL CAMERAS store photographs either on reusable storage cards, disks, or miniature hard drives.

- Storage cards come in various capacities and you can buy more than one if you need to be able to store large quantities of pictures. Photos can then be downloaded via cable or card reader to the computer for editing and printing.
- CD recordable disk storage uses mini compact disks for easy portability to the computer.
- Microdrives are miniature hard drives that store many gigabytes of high-resolution photos.

Sony Cyber-shot used by permission of Sony Electronics, Inc; Olympus with LCD used by permission of Olympus America, Inc.

Another storage media option for digital cameras is the Microdrive. This miniature hard disk drive is capable of storing multiple gigabytes of information. To use Microdrive storage, the camera must have been designed with a storage card slot that is compatible with this technology. This format is a bit slower than other formats.

Most of these formats have increased digital camera capacity to multiple gigabytes of storage space. Furthermore, the price of digital camera storage media has consistently fallen while capacities have increased. In selecting a digital camera, it is important to note the type of storage media the camera uses and the cost associated with it.

When the camera's storage media is full, the images can then be transferred to a computer for more permanent storage. This is done by connecting the camera to the computer with a special cable that comes bundled with the camera, by removing the media card and inserting it into a card reader, or by a camera cradle that connects to the computer. Some newer cameras are available with wireless link capability as well. Once copied to the computer's hard drive, the images can be enhanced with a photo-styling program or used in other software applications. Ultimately, digital photographs can be printed out on photographic or regular paper with a color printer. After transfer to the hard drive, the images can be deleted from the camera's memory so that space is again available for new pictures.

Digital cameras allow you to input photographic images directly without having to scan them, but the scanner may be a more versatile addition because it enables you to digitize text and printed graphics as well. Compared to traditional photographic equipment, digital cameras have many unique features. In addition to letting you directly manipulate the photos with computer software, digital cameras allow you to preview photos as you take them. Digital cameras are equipped with small LCD screens on the back that let you look at pictures you have taken before saving them or view the photos you have already taken and saved. This feature saves you the time and expense of taking film to a developer only to find that your photos did not turn out as you expected. It also allows you to use your available photo storage space wisely by deleting shots you don't like and retaking a photo whenever you choose.

When determining a camera's potential for high-resolution images, manufacturers specify how many megapixels the camera is capable of producing per image captured. A pixel (or picture element) is a single dot in the image captured by the camera. Millions of dots make up a single image. The higher the number of dots captured, the clearer the image will be. Thus, a digital camera's resolution is indicated by the number of megapixels (millions of dots) it can capture. The Tech Tip for Teachers feature summarizes the relationship of a camera's megapixels and the types and quality of images it can produce. When

TECH TIPS for Teachers

Selecting the right digital camera for your classroom is a challenge. One of the most significant features to consider is the possible image quality or resolution that you need. The megapixel number for a camera identifies how many millions of pixels (picture elements) the camera is capable of. The table below will give you an idea of how many megapixels you want to do the job.

Camera's Megapixels	Image Quality and Size
2–3 megapixels	Good, detailed screen images; excellent 4 × 6 and very good 5 × 7 prints; some cameras may produce reasonable 8 × 10 prints
4–5 megapixels	Equal to 35-mm photos; able to print high-quality 8 × 10 images
6 or more megapixels	Allow you to crop and blow up portions of photos without losing clarity; able to produce high-quality images greater than 8 × 10

In the CLASSROOM

Digital Cameras in Schools

Ideas for using digital cameras to enrich and enliven learning abound on the Brunswick, Maine, "Teacher to Teacher" handbook webpage. **Patti Irish,** seventh-grade science teacher, along with her students, is creating an online field guide for insects. They collect insects (live if possible), identify them, photograph them, and research their habitats and habits. With this information, they write a field guide that they publish online. Check it out at **http://www.brunswick.k12.me.us/lon/lonlinks/digicam/teacher/ home.html.**

Dorothy Small, technology integration specialist in MSAD#54 (Maine School Administrative District #54), points out how art teachers showcase student art by posting digital photos on the district's web site. **Matthew Charland** and **Mr. Chin,** both art teachers, use the District Wide Art Program web pages to share their students' work by keeping updated displays available online. You can see them at **http://www.msad54.org/.**

Liz Sheldon, K–5 teacher in Framingham, Massachusetts, has students present reports on books and/or famous people that include the students dressed in era appropriate character costume. Their image is captured and put into a KidPix slide show, and a voiceover tells who they are and why they are famous. Or they may document the steps of a science experiment in a slide show to share with other classes. In first grade, shapes are taught by using pictures taken of familiar objects around the school. The students then draw the shapes they saw in KidPix (using the pencil tool). Fifth graders took pictures during a field trip to an aquarium and placed them in a presentation. Each student was responsible for a picture and adding a brief description, which included new highlighted vocabulary words. Upon completion, the presentations are added as additional examples of digital cameras in the classroom on Ms. Sheldon's web page, at **www.framingham.k12.ma.us/k5.**

For students with special needs, **Katie Tyrrell** in Yarmouth, Maine, takes pictures of items around the room that a student with autism may want or need. The student can learn to communicate using symbol-size photos when the Mayer-Johnson symbols have not been successful.

Source: Dollof, K. *Teacher to teacher.* Retrieved August 13, 2006, from **http://www.brunswick.k12.me.us/lon/lonlinks/digicam/teacher/home.html.**

FIGURE 6.3

Webcams can be used to share digital still and video images via the Internet.

Courtesy of Logitech.

you request or purchase a digital camera for your classroom, its capacity for the type of image you want to create is likely to be your most important consideration.

Digital cameras vary in terms of many optional features as well. Some cameras record brief video with audio as well as still pictures. Although the digital video clip files are of relatively low resolution, if the ability to capture a brief video is important, the inclusion of this feature may be a buying consideration. Further, cameras vary in their ability to zoom or take close-ups. If close images of student work or of objects is a consideration, then zoom capabilities must be taken into account. These features and others, as well as a camera's megapixel capacity, are some of the reasons for the dramatic variation in the prices of digital cameras. For you as a teacher, it is best to first determine what you want to use the digital camera for and then select one within your school budget that gives you the capabilities you desire.

One other type of digital camera that is useful for the classroom is the webcam (Figure 6.3). This type of digital camera is usually mounted on top of the computer's monitor and connected via cable to a USB port. Some computers come with built-in webcams. It often has a built-in microphone as well as still and video capabilities. A webcam can be used to capture still and video images for communication via the Internet. It can be used for teleconferencing across the Internet, that is, conducting a live conference via the Internet that includes still images, video, and audio as well as text communication. Or it can be used simply for sharing still or video images via the Net. This adaptation of the digital camera has some of the same resolution parameters as a still camera, but because it is attached to the computer, it does not need to have independent storage capability.

As you can see, different types of digital cameras are available to classroom teachers. Applications of this technology in the classroom range from capturing a field trip to taking digital photos of children's work, to displaying work on classroom web sites, to customizing a class newsletter, to documenting a science experiment. The applications are as diverse as the talents and creativity of the teachers who use these versatile input devices.

FIGURE 6.4

With a digital tablet, the teacher can create complex images, emphasize points, or fully annotate graphics.

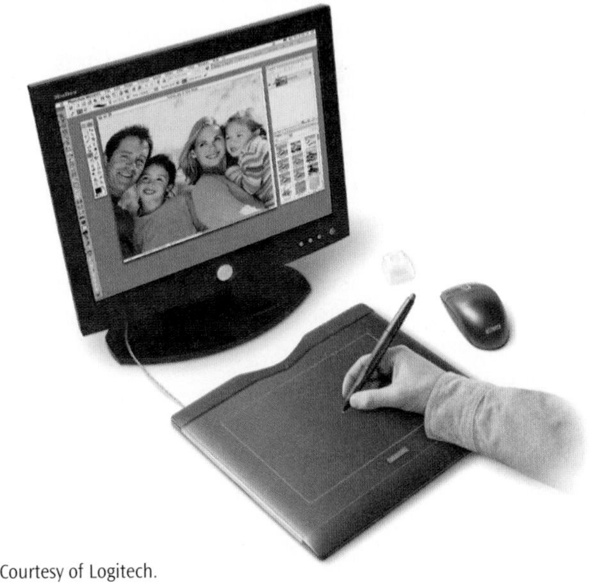

Courtesy of Logitech.

Graphics Tablets

A **graphics tablet** lets you use a stylus with an electronic pad to draw diagrams or create artwork. A stylus is a pen-shaped device that is designed to write or draw on the pressure-sensitive surface of a graphics tablet. Graphics tablets are also sometimes called **digitizers** or digital tablets, because they convert the lines sketched on the tablet into their digital equivalents on the screen (Figure 6.4).

Architects, designers, and artists are the most frequent users of graphics tablets, because the stylus gives them more precise control than a mouse or other pointing device can. However, digitizer technology can easily be adapted for educational use by teachers and learners. Using this type of tablet, teachers can place a word-processed or graphics document on the computer screen. With a digitizer, they can add comments to these images, mark them up, or add emphasis as they are displayed on the computer. For example, when reviewing material with a small group of students, a teacher might annotate and circle key features on a computer-generated map displayed on the classroom computer's display. In combination with appropriate software, the teacher can mark up the diagram using various colors, lines of various types, and predetermined shapes. The computer image with annotation can then be saved and printed out or used in another document.

Graphics tablets are useful for drawing or annotating displays.

Art students can use a more typical digitizer to draw original images, enhance computer-generated images or photographs, or annotate scanned images. Digitizers that are designed primarily for this type of art function usually offer color, brush, and other art command options on the tablet, making it easier for the artist to use these features. Such customized tablets are often designed to be compatible with specific art software. Once again, it is important to balance your potential uses to determine the type of equipment that will work best in your classroom. Once that decision has been made, it is important to remember to examine both software and hardware specifications to ensure compatibility.

HANDSON LEARNING

Multimedia helps to address the diverse learning styles of your students. Input and output devices let you create and use multimedia by capturing text, audio, still images, and video clips that might be just the added extra to help that unique student learn. Consider a topic you will be teaching at the grade level or in the content area of your choice. Using the available multimedia capture technology, including scanners, digital cameras, graphics tablets, and microphones, create images and audio and video elements that you feel could enhance a lesson on that topic. Share the multimedia elements with your peers and explain how you would use each in your lesson.

Using Microphones

Computers today, especially those found in schools, are typically multimedia machines. These types of machines are equipped with the hardware and software necessary to record and play back sound and show video clips as well as to display text and graphics. To play back the sound files and clips that come with multimedia software, computers are equipped with a set of small speakers. To record audio, they are also usually equipped with a microphone. Both speakers and microphone plug into ports located on the computer.

Through the microphone, music, sounds, and the spoken word can be input, digitized (turned into digital data), and stored. The digitized sound can then be saved and played back by using a sound program, or it can be included in a multimedia program. In the classroom, the teacher might record a brief comment, instruction, or sound effect to be included in a teacher-made computer tutorial, or a student might add recorded sounds to his or her presentation of a field trip experience. Digitized sound can also be edited and enhanced by using sound-editing software. Sounds can be clarified, have special effects added, or be speeded up or slowed down. The edited or enhanced versions of sound recordings can be a valuable part of a computer-based lesson.

With the use of a simple, inexpensive microphone, sound can be added to add impact to computer-based materials and help address the needs of auditory learners. It should be noted, however, that sound files tend to be large, requiring a lot of storage space. Programs are available to compress sound files for easier storage. These programs compress and convert audio into common formats such as MP3 or AAC. Classroom applications using sound without compression need to be saved on high-capacity storage media such as a hard drive, a removable hard drive, or a CD.

Go to the *Assignments and Activities* section of Chapter 6 in MyEducationKit and complete the web activity entitled *How Can Digital Sound Capabilities Help Learning?*

Using Pen Input Devices

Pen input devices use a stylus to input handwritten information, to select commands, and to make predetermined written symbols, called gestures, that represent computer commands. Pen input is typically used with a **personal digital assistant (PDA)** or a **tablet PC.** A PDA is a portable computing device that can recognize handwritten notes and translate them into a word-processed document through the use of the PDA's handwriting recognition software. These written-to-word-processed documents are usually transferred to a desktop computer for storage or further use. PDAs also typically offer simplified office management tools, such as a calendar and contacts, and some offer wireless connectivity

Personal digital assistants combine a handheld computer and organizer.

In the CLASSROOM

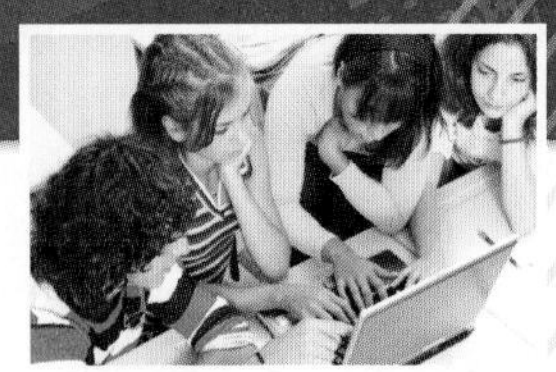

Tablet PCs in the Elementary Grades and Secondary Education

Saint Mary's School in Raleigh, North Carolina, has moved from classroom use of laptops to pen-based handheld computers for their 1:1 computing program. The flipped open screens on laptops had created barriers between teacher and students. With the laptop screens open, students were shielded from monitoring by the teacher. And there were many distracting temptations: email, blogging, nonacademic Internet surfing, YouTube, Facebook, MySpace, and the like. Even a teacher roaming around the room can, at best, keep an eye on only a limited number of screens. Some schools are going to tablets "to replace laptops altogether, sending the flip-up screen the way of the Dodo bird and the joystick," as reported in "Tablet PCs: The Write Approach."

Heather Sherer, third-grade teacher at San Onofre Elementary School in San Clemente, California, is cited in the article for integrating the tablets into her math classes "by giving students the option of working through problems on their tablets rather than paper." When the students complete the problems, they can email them to her. Not only does this strategy cut down on paper use, it also saves time by making it possible to grade the students work more quickly. Principal **Barbara Barnes** notes that the students have less clutter on their desks, giving them more space to work on assignments that do not lend themselves to computers. This elementary school is located near Camp Pendleton, a U.S. Marine base, and many of the students are children of military personnel who are frequently separated from their parents. The tablets are at the heart of the school's efforts to help the children keep in touch with their parents who are in faraway places.

Cris Branker, a second- and third-grade teacher at San Onofre, had her students write holiday poems on their tablets. When the poems were completed, the children stood and shared their poems aloud. Finally, with her students' help, she compiled the readings into a CD-ROM videography. Then she used military mail to send dozens of copies of the disk out to parents in time for Christmas.

David Schroeder, a high-school math teacher at Cabrillo High School in Lompoc, California, noted how tablet PCs helped him to teach math interactively. In comparison to subjects such as science, lack of interactivity is a longstanding problem math teachers face. He said, "The challenge with math classes is to get students to participate. My premise was that if I could get the students to practice more class material in front of me, in an environment where I could immediately respond to a larger number of students, then they would learn more." Schroeder found that the tablets accomplished this interactivity he sought and also "afforded students the opportunity to deconstruct and replay class material as they first received it, step by step."

Source: Milner, J. (2006, April). *Tablet PCs: The Write Approach.* Retrieved August 4, 2008, from **http://www.thejournal.com/the/printarticle/?id=18238.**

PEARSON **myeducationkit**™

Go to the *Assignments and Activities* section of Chapter 6 in MyEducationKit and complete the video activity entitled *Tablet Computers Facilitate Learning.*

to a network (see Figure 6.5 on page 153). Pocket-PC types of PDAs may also include scaled-down versions of familiar computer software such as a word processor or electronic spreadsheet.

Make PDA technology considerably larger and more powerful, and you have tablet PCs. A tablet PC is approximately the size of a traditional writing pad (although substantially thicker), and you use it much as you would paper. You write on the surface of the tablet with your stylus, and the software converts written text into a word-processing file or a drawing. You can also use the stylus as you would a mouse pointer, to give commands and make selections. The tablet is essentially an LCD screen mounted over a motherboard with a hard disk drive, making it portable, convenient, and relatively lightweight.

PDAs and tablet PCs can be very useful classroom management tools. They allow the teacher to make notes on lessons and activities, record and annotate student behavior, and track appointments. The data written into a PDA can be stored for later use, so the information can be easily transferred into computerized gradebooks, lesson plans, and student files. Essentially, PDAs are digital memo pads, the pages of which can be transferred to a computer disk for safekeeping and easy retrieval. In the case of pocket PCs, they can also serve as very portable "palmtop" computers with many of the same capabilities of a desktop computer.

FIGURE 6.5

Pen Input Devices Go to School

PDAs and tablet PCs are versatile pen devices in the classroom. Using a stylus, these computers can be used to take notes, organize data, create drawings, and, when connected to display devices, present information.

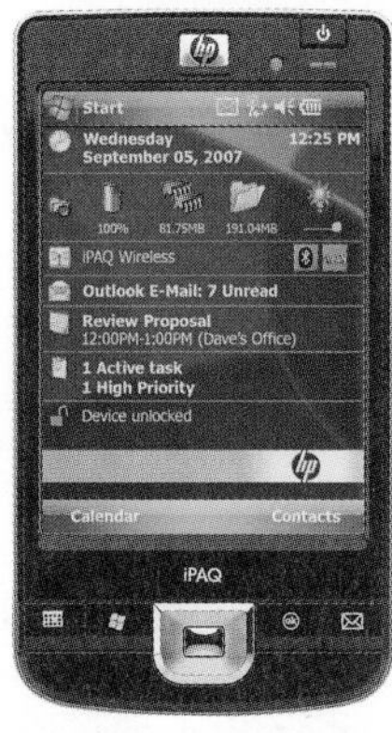

In the classroom, tablet PCs offer teachers and students some unique opportunities. Teachers can download students' word-processed essays and grade them via the tablet PC. The word-processed document is displayed on the tablet screen, and the teacher can add comments via the stylus. The graded document can be saved and returned to the student electronically for review. Connected to a classroom display device, the tablet PC can also be used for sharing digital images without the physical barrier of computer and monitor between teacher and class. And while displaying digital presentations via tablet PC, teachers can easily add annotations with the stylus to emphasize or annotate key points.

PEARSON myeducationkit™

Go to the *Assignments and Activities* section of Chapter 6 in MyEducationKit and complete the video activity entitled *Tablet Computers*.

The tablet PC presents distinct options for students as well. Students can take notes and organize them into clear word-processed documents without typing. They can easily integrate multimedia and web resources into their work and create documents for activities that include a full range of resources. They can also use the tablet PC to download and read the pages of electronic books and magazines, thereby bringing the library into the classroom.

Using Touch Screens

A **touch screen** is a computer monitor screen that responds to human touch. Instead of using a mouse pointer to select an icon or command, you touch the icon itself on the touch screen, and the computer responds. On computers equipped with a touch screen, a keyboard and/or mouse might not even be available.

Touch screens are quick and easy to use. However, if large amounts of data need to be entered or many choices need to be made from complex sets of options, touch screens may be an inappropriate choice of input device.

Magic Touch courtesy of KEYTEC, Inc.

Touch screens can be used in the classroom by prereaders or as an assistive device for students with special needs.

Touch screens receive input by being touched at relevant points on the monitor screen.

Touch screens work best with simple, straightforward displays. They can be useful in the classroom for children who are preliterate, cannot type, or have difficulty controlling a mouse owing to physical impairment. Touch screens are also often used in information kiosks at hotels and airports and with medical or other complex equipment that requires quick setting changes.

Electronic Whiteboards

Virtually every classroom is equipped with display surfaces on which teachers can write and illustrate concepts as they teach. Some classrooms may still have blackboards and chalk. Most now use whiteboards with erasable color markers. These media offer the advantage of spontaneous explanation during the teaching and learning process. Once these display surfaces are filled with explanations, to continue, the teacher must begin to erase what has been previously written. For students who were absent on a particular day, for students who were not able to copy the information down quickly enough, or for the teacher who would like to refer back to previously erased material, the blackboard or whiteboard offers no support.

Electronic whiteboards convert whiteboard images and text into computer files.

What if it were possible to write on a whiteboard and, just before erasing the information, print it or save it to a computer file? That is precisely what an **electronic whiteboard** can do. As you write on an electronic whiteboard, a built-in scanner records the drawings or text in the colors you are using. The recorded digital image is then displayed on a monitor. The recorded image can be saved, edited, or printed. The image can then be erased from the electronic whiteboard, and a new computer file can be opened to capture and record new images. Once saved, whiteboard information can be included in other documents or placed in an electronic archive for you or your students to access for review.

If desired, some whiteboards in different locations can be connected via the Internet so that the writing in one location can be shared at other locations at the same time. This can be especially useful in bringing a distant guest speaker into your class or in delivering instruction to a home-bound student.

Electronic whiteboard technology is available in different types, including whiteboards that are touch sensitive and rear-projection whiteboards. Each of these has its own features and advantages, although they are still somewhat expensive for the average classroom. A newer technology turns your own classroom whiteboard into its electronic counterpart (Figure 6.6). This type of whiteboard technology uses a projection unit that attaches to the corner of your traditional whiteboard and a series of electronic sleeves for your markers.

FIGURE 6.6

Stand-alone electronic whiteboards (left) and electronic conversion kits for a traditional whiteboard (right) allow you to work interactively with your classroom's displays and save or print for future reference.

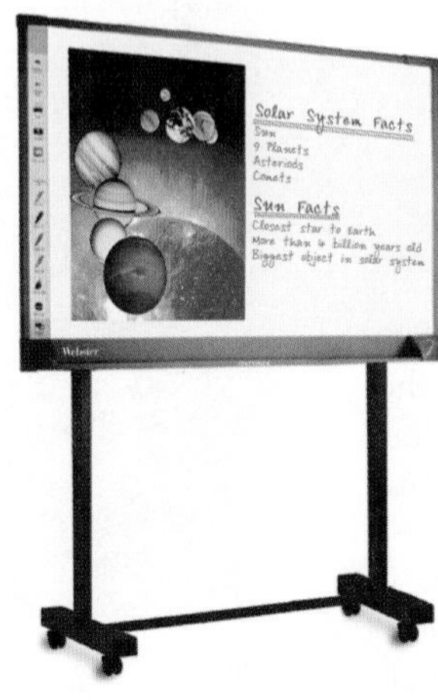

Courtesy of PolyVision

Courtesy of Luidia, Inc.

In the CLASSROOM

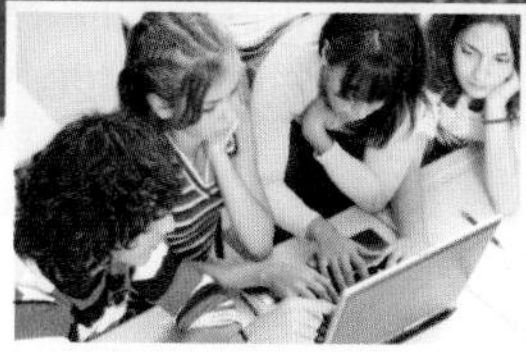

Interactive Whiteboards

Shasanna Francis's third-grade class at Rock Island Elementary School in Fort Lauderdale, Florida, used their interactive whiteboard to learn about President Barack Obama and his wife, Michelle. The information was displayed on a Promethean whiteboard. Students used an electronic pen to add important dates in the President's and First Lady's lives in a Venn diagram. They shared the session with Fox Trail Elementary School third-graders thirteen miles away. Cameras and microphones positioned in the two classrooms enabled the two classes to communicate with each other. Rock Island Principal James Griffith commented on how these lessons are more readily received by the young "Wii generation" learners.

In the next three to five years, all classrooms in Broward County will become digital, according to schools Superintendent James Notter. Noting that 60 percent of the students in schools such as Rock Island come from low-income families, Principal Griffith said that "the technology can expand students' worlds beyond their neighborhoods and expose them to people from different backgrounds—in classrooms across the country or across the Atlantic Ocean." Ms. Francis observed that "the whiteboards and software have changed education."

Cheryl Teaters, ninth-grade biology teacher at Gateway High School in Monroeville, Pennsylvania, conducts review quizzes for her ninth-grade honors class by projecting multiple-choice questions on the parts of the neuron on an interactive whiteboard. As the students select their answers via their wireless laptops, their responses are tallied on the board. When she found that fewer than 80 percent of the class had answered correctly, Ms. Teaters discerned where additional attention was needed. She also uses the Promethean Activboard as a virtual world in which she can "review the structure of nodes in the nervous system." She can show a diagram of the nodes, manipulate it for movement, enlarge it, and focus on specified sections, as well as annotate the diagram and store it with notations. The diagram can be saved as a PDF file to upload to the classroom web page, where it is available to students.

Sources: Bushouse, K. (2009, February 12). *Interactive technology in Broward schools expands world of learning: Software puts the universe at students' fingertips*. Retrieved February 21, 2009, from **http://pqasb.pqarchiver.com/sun_sentinel/access/1643924071.html?dids=1643924071:1643924071&FMT=ABS&FMTS=ABS:FT&date=Feb+12,+2009&author=Kathy+Bushouse&pub=South+Florida+Sun++Sentinel&edition=&startpage=B.1&desc=STUDENTS+AT+HOME+IN+DIGITAL+UNIVERSE+INTE.**

Rujumba, K. (2007, May 24). *Gateway High's 16 science classes part of pilot program to computerize teaching*. Retrieved May 25, 2007, from **http://www.post-gazette.com/pg/07144/788463-56.stm.**

Bluetooth Whiteboard Tablets

An adaptation of the digital tablet, this innovative device uses Bluetooth technology (the ability to wirelessly connect unlike devices) to connect multiple tablets to a computer and/or an electronic whiteboard. The teacher can use the tablet to freely move around the room while adding annotations to the whiteboard or computer display. The tablet can be used to control the computer or change from one image to another. Students can use their tablets from their desk to make real-time additions or comments on the teacher's presentation, fill in answers to questions displayed on the whiteboard, or create their own presentation to the class via the classroom whiteboard from the tablet at their desk. These classroom tablets use a stylus to issue commands, capture written comments, or make annotations to whatever is displayed to the class. When added to your classroom, digital presentations become entirely interactive, with both teacher and students able to operate the computer from anywhere in the room.

Photo courtesy of InterWrite SchoolPad and SchoolBoard

ISTE Standard

Learning about the input and output devices available to teachers in the classroom will help you address **NETS•T STANDARD 2:**

DESIGN AND DEVELOP DIGITAL-AGE LEARNING EXPERIENCES AND ASSESSMENTS Teachers design, develop, and evaluate authentic learning experiences and assessments incorporating contemporary tools and resources to maximize content learning in context and to develop the knowledge, skills, and attitudes identified in the NETS•S.

Once connected to your computer, the projection device captures anything written on the whiteboard with the marker in its sleeve and saves it as a digital file. This type of system can do most of the tasks of its more expensive dedicated electronic whiteboard counterpart but typically at much lower cost. Additionally, this system does not require any extra wall or floor space, since it uses your existing whiteboard. For these reasons, this input device is becoming a popular electronic whiteboard alternative for K–12 classrooms.

Output Devices for Teaching and Learning

Data Projection

One of the challenges of using a computer in a classroom is that the computer's monitor is too small to share with a large group. To meet this challenge, a variety of computer data projection units are available. **Data projection units** plug into the computer's monitor port and project the same information as the computer's monitor. Each type of data projection unit has unique features and capabilities (see Figure 6.7) with a corresponding difference in prices.

Data Projectors

Computer screen images can be projected using data projectors.

The **data projector** is a projection unit that combines an LCD display and a light source into a single, relatively lightweight box. As a result, data projectors are often referred to as LCD projectors. These units can typically project both images from a computer and video

FIGURE 6.7

Digital Display Technologies and Their Characteristics

Teachers have several options for displaying computer images.

LCD PROJECTOR

LCD projectors are compact LCD display units with their own built-in light source. The typically brighter picture, enabling displays that are clear even with room and outside light, and its compact, lightweight size are key features for the classroom.

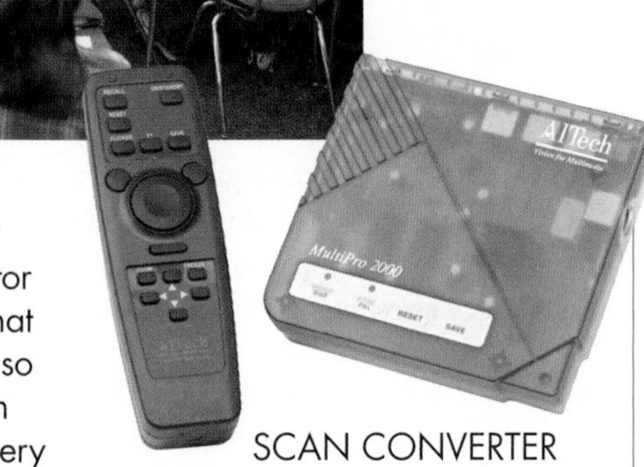

SCAN CONVERTER

Scan converters connect a computer and video monitor through a converter box that alters the computer signal so that it can be displayed on the video monitor. These very inexpensive devices are the most reasonable method for sharing and projecting computer images. The disadvantage is the reduced resolution when compared with a digital display.

from a video source in a display that is large enough and bright enough to be seen across a classroom. For the brightest, clearest, and best results, these images should be displayed on a projection screen. Projection to a wall will not offer the same level of clarity and brightness; projection to a whiteboard will often be difficult to view, owing to the high reflectivity and resultant glare of the whiteboard surface.

Different data projectors offer different levels of resolution and brightness (measured in lumens). As the resolution and brightness of data projectors increase, there is a corresponding increase in price. It is best to purchase a projector that exceeds the capabilities of your current computer in terms of resolution. In terms of brightness, it is best to select a projector with the maximum brightness your budget will allow. If you select a less costly projector that may be of insufficient brightness, you might find that you have to turn lights off in the classroom and/or cover the windows to be able to see the computer display clearly.

Other features that are typically available on data projectors include built-in speakers, multiple computer input capability, software storage capability, and remote control. Many projectors are designed to accept a variety of video inputs, making them an effective alternative to the large TV monitors so often seen in today's classrooms. Thus, the same projector that can display your computer image can also display a videotape, DVD, a TV program from the school's cable connection, or the images from your digital camera. When compared to large CRT monitors, a large-screen plasma or LCD monitor can be a cost-effective means for classroom display.

PEARSON myeducationkit™

To practice setting up and using a data projector in your class, go to the *Video Tutorials* section of Chapter 6 in MyEducationKit and select *Data Projector.*

Scan Converters

One of the most inexpensive methods for displaying a computer image to an entire class is to use a digital (computer signal) to analog (video signal) converter, or **scan converter.** This device converts a computer's digital image into one that can be displayed through analog (video) technology. To use it, one end of the converter's cable is plugged into the computer's monitor port and the other is plugged into the video input port on the back of a classroom television monitor; the computer image is then visible on the monitor.

Scan converters offer low-cost classroom digital displays.

These converters are well within the budget of most schools, making it an option to share computer displays in classrooms equipped with older televisions. The disadvantage of this type of display is in the quality and image size. Many television monitors are not designed with as high resolution as computer monitors. Although graphics may look acceptable, text may appear choppy and difficult to read. Additionally, even the largest television monitors can be difficult to see from the back of a large classroom. Thus, the details of the computer image may be lost to those unable to sit close to the classroom television monitor.

Speakers and Headphones

Computer systems today are sold with varying levels of sound capabilities. **Speakers** are now a common component. Some systems have built-in speakers; others have external speakers. Although sound is not critical for many administrative applications, such as word processing, it is an integral part of much of the academic software that is available today. To address multiple learning styles, most learning software is designed with a rich auditory component. To take advantage of this aspect of the software, an audio output device is necessary.

Speakers and headphones help meet the needs of auditory learners.

Just as is the case with home audio systems, computer speakers vary significantly in capability. Some are designed for a single user working on his or her home computer. These speakers, even at maximum volume, are often incapable of playing back sound at a level and clarity that would be useful for a small group of students. It is important to consider how audio-rich computer software will be used to determine what type of sound output hardware is necessary.

If there is a single computer in the classroom and it is used for a large-group display, good speakers are essential so that all students can hear as well as see the program. Of course, if the display unit used is multimedia capable, that is, it includes both visual and audio capability, additional speakers might not be necessary. If the computer display is through a

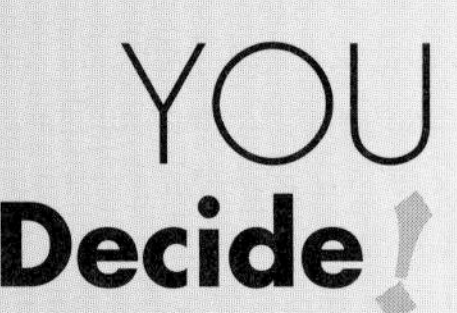

Every teacher needs to be able to communicate visually with the class during instruction. As you have learned, there are many technologies available to do so. But is it worth the time and trouble to invest in and use high-tech displays and whiteboards?

YES! Teachers need to use every possible tool available to meet student needs. Older technologies like a blackboard or whiteboard or an overhead projector may work, but they don't offer a teacher a way to use all of the possible resources. Also, these older technologies are very static and don't offer the excitement and interactivity of a digital display or electronic whiteboard. You may have to invest a bit of time to learn how to use them, but the effort can be well worth it for your students. Why use a teaching and learning support that is less effective when something better is available?

NO! New digital technologies are complicated and expensive. They take time to learn and use. They take up space in the classroom and may even break down in the middle of a lesson. Why go through all that trouble? Besides, it is the teacher who is the heart of every lesson. The support technologies are just there to help the teacher teach. Fancy new technologies don't guarantee that a lesson will be any better than one presented via a whiteboard and markers. We don't need all of this new equipment to teach. Students learn from teachers, not from technology.

Which view do you agree with? YOU DECIDE!

FIGURE 6.8

Headphones can allow students to hear computer audio output without disturbing others.

© Charles Gupton/CORBIS

multimedia-capable data projector, the projector itself contains sufficiently large speakers for all to hear. Alternatively, if you use a converter, the speakers in the television monitor will carry the audio component of the software.

If the instructional intent is to use academic software as learning support for one student at a time, speakers might not be the preferred type of audio output. When a single student is working with software to master a targeted skill, the audio component of the software can be distracting to those around him or her. In that case, instead of speakers as audio output, you might want to select headphones. **Headphones** allow individual students to listen to audio without disturbing others (Figure 6.8). Most computers include headphone ports and speaker ports. You might even be able to use headphones that are intended for other audio devices. Occasionally, a headphone plug may not fit into the jack (port) on the computer. It is, however, very possible that the headphones can still be used. Local electronics stores often stock a good selection of converter plugs. These are typically very inexpensive and easy to find.

Emerging Digital Technologies for the Classroom

At this point, you have learned much about computers and the peripheral digital technologies that you might use in your classroom. Computer technology, however, is rapidly advancing, and new digital equipment is constantly emerging. As these new technologies evolve and become part of our world, many will be adapted for use in teaching and learning. Let's examine some of the most fascinating types of hardware that are likely to be adapted for use in schools.

Wireless Devices

Wireless connections for computers and other digital equipment are quickly becoming as commonplace as cell phones. Today most cellular phones offer incoming voice calls, text messaging, and Internet access. Wireless hot spots through which you can access your e-mail and the Internet are widely available at many public places such as coffee shops, malls, airports, libraries, and hotels. Similar access at schools is not far behind.

Classroom wireless technologies can take several different forms. Classroom wireless often uses radio frequency (RF) technology to connect classroom workstations to a network server. Access points, or points at which connection is made to the wired backbone, are strategically placed throughout the school building. Adapters are used in workstations to connect to the access points. Since no wires tether computers to the wall, computers with adapters can be moved as needed, as long as they stay in range of an access point.

One of the fastest-growing wireless technologies is called **WiFi** (wireless fidelity). It too uses radio frequency to connect WiFi-enabled computers and other digital devices to networks at very fast speeds. Base stations serve as access points, and these can be placed anywhere, inside or outside of buildings. A WiFi-enabled building, campus, or other area allows individuals to access the local network and the Internet from anywhere in the area. Schools use WiFi to connect buildings, auditoriums, and outside areas. Some business districts even provide WiFi capability to shops, restaurants, offices, and even homes within the WiFi zone. This technology is likely to continue to grow and to expand wireless connectivity significantly. Indeed, some metropolitan areas are already attempting to create WiFi access across their entire cities. Purchasing WiFi-enabled mobile technologies may therefore be a good investment for the future.

For educators, **wireless devices** have the potential to solve several challenges. Wireless technologies allow you to eliminate the hard wire connection necessary in the wired classroom. Using a portable wireless computer, students can research an interesting insect they discover while they are still on a field trip rather than wait until the next day when they return to their classrooms. The teachable moment when students inquire and are ready to learn does not have to be postponed until wired connections are available. Furthermore, teachers can access online resources or their stored instructional files from anywhere they can access a wireless hot spot, in or out of the classroom. What you need to teach remains at your fingertips wherever you may be. The advent of wireless devices also means that computer-enhanced classrooms do not need to be physically arranged according to where network connections are available on walls. Instead, computers can be easily moved to locations that are best for student interaction and communication.

ISTE Standard

Learning about emerging technologies will help you address **NETS•T STANDARD 3:**

MODEL DIGITAL-AGE WORK AND LEARNING Teachers exhibit knowledge, skills, and work processes representative of an innovative professional in a global and digital society.

PEARSON **myeducationkit**

Go to the *Assignments and Activities* section of Chapter 6 in MyEducationKit and complete the video activity entitled *Teaching with Wireless Devices.*

Emerging hardware holds promise for teachers and learners.

COOL TOOLS

Clickers in the Classroom

Wireless response systems, also called clickers, can be used to get instantaneous feedback from your students. Students are provided a remote device (clicker) that is connected via infra red, radio-frequency, or WiFi technology to the teacher's workstation. A teacher can then ask for responses throughout the lesson, and students simply click a button to send their answer. Everyone's response is instantly received and tallied. Results can be displayed for everyone to see in the form of data or charts, or the teacher can simply view the responses privately on the teacher workstation to see whether everyone is following the lesson.

With instantaneous feedback available, a teacher can modify a lesson, add additional information or practice sets, or just use student opinion data as a jumping-off point for further discussion or research. And since the student responses are anonymous from the point of view of others in the classroom, even the shyest student feels free to respond and express his or her views. This emerging classroom technology may make raising hands and counting them a thing of the past.

Turning Technologies, LLC

Courtesy of Palmone, Inc.

PDAs let teachers move about the class while taking advantage of computer support.

Wireless communications and the emerging smaller and more powerful digital devices that are supported by this type of interaction are quickly evolving and coming into wide use. Wireless technology offers greater flexibility in terms of physical location and logistical arrangement. Creative educators will no doubt develop many innovative applications for wireless devices in teaching and learning.

Handhelds, Smartphones, and Mini-Laptops

Several years ago, PDAs (personal digital assistants) or **handhelds** appeared to have great promise, and sales were in the millions. They offered the capabilities of personal information management (calendar, phone list, notes, to-do list, address book, and the like). Some offered versions of the most popular types of software (word processing, spreadsheets, games, music recording and playback, and even email). While still in use, demand for them has waned as **smartphones,** such as the BlackBerry (from RIM), the Treo (from Palm, the originator of one of the most successful PADs), and the iPhone (from Apple), have soared in popularity. In late 2008, Google added its phone to the mix. Each of these smartphones has its own operating system. These new devices are essentially computers in your pocket, capable of performing many of the tasks previously the domain of desktop or laptop computers. The trend from handhelds to smartphones has altered this technology potential in schools. Since many schools do not allow live cell phones in class, smartphones as handheld computers have not integrated well into schools.

PEARSON myeducationkit™

To learn more about the technology of handheld computers and explore applications specific to education, go to the *Video Tutorials* section of Chapter 6 in MyEducationKit and select *Handheld Computing*.

A new option that has become available and is already having a large impact in schools is **mini-laptops** (sometimes called *netbooks*). These scaled-down computers are larger than PDAs and smartphones but smaller than laptop computers. The lower price and convenient size of these computers have found them an audience in education and among travelers. They typically have either no hard drive or a small solid-state version that is similar to the storage media found in flash drives but on a larger scale. Mini-laptops normally include wireless Internet capabilities. Many can use either the Windows or Linux operating systems. These reasonably priced, compact computers will most likely continue to find a place in schools. Given their convenience, the lack of some features provided by more expensive, larger laptops will continue to be a reasonable trade-off. A rather famous model of mini-laptop was launched by visionary MIT professor Nicholas Negroponte and his One Laptop Per Child (OLPC) foundation. OLPC has a goal of a $100 mini-laptop that could reach wide distribution, especially in impoverished schools in Africa and Asia. Mini-laptops have found their niche in education by offering a laptop with a very compact size and modest weight, making them extremely portable, and that niche continues to expand.

PEARSON myeducationkit™

Go to the *Assignments and Activities* section of Chapter 6 in MyEducationKit and complete the video activity entitled *Cooperative Learning with Handhelds.*

E-Books

Electronic books, also known as **e-books,** are electronic versions of books for PDA, portable computers, and e-book readers. A single device can store and display many digital books along with related instructional and reference materials. E-book software typically has the capacity to allow you to take digital notes on segments as you read them, and some can play sound and audio enhancements or read text aloud.

The educational applications for this emerging mobile technology are many. Rather than having multiple textbooks and notebooks, students and teachers will need only a single, lightweight device on which several texts can be stored. New versions of texts can be quickly and easily updated without the time and expense of printing new editions. The capacity to embed audio and visual enhancements in text makes it possible to address diverse learning styles from within the text itself. Note taking on text content is convenient and is done in digital form that allows it to be edited and reorganized for studying. The potential for this technology in education is clear and is likely to change the future of how we see and use books.

Voice-Activated Devices

PDAs have expanded input capabilities to include keyboard input or both keyboard and pen input. Voice technology is the next technology that will revolutionize how we input data into computers. Already available for assistive devices and for business and home computing, **voice technology** enables a computer to accept voice commands and dictation of data. As voice input technology improves, more and more digital devices will be adapted to accept voice commands. Already, cellular phones allow callers to simply speak the name of the person to be called, and the cell phone will dial the number.

As you learned in Chapter 4, voice activation makes it easier for learners who are physically disabled or who have limited keyboarding skills to fully use the capabilities of a computer. It enables teachers to start up and conduct an Internet search demonstration without having to leave a part of the classroom that needs their attention. Rather than having to return to the desk to issue commands via keyboard and mouse, the teacher can simply speak to the computer from across the room. This technology, too, has great potential for improving the convenience of using computers in the classroom.

Portable Storage

Portable data storage has been revolutionized by the **USB** flash drive. This drive, also called a key chain drive or jump drive, is small and lightweight enough to attach to a key chain. The USB drive is usually one to two inches long and weighs less than an ounce. It can store gigabytes of information or more than 100 CD-ROMs. The inner working of this drive is similar to that of a memory card, such as that found in digital cameras. Although the term *drive* is used, it is not an electromechanical device like a hard disk or floppy drive that records and plays back data from different types of disks. Instead, the USB drive plugs into a computer's USB port and is recognized as an external drive, albeit based on memory card technology. Data can be saved to the USB drive, and then the device is unplugged from the USB port. Later, the device can be plugged into a different computer's USB port, and that machine too will recognize it as an external drive. Thus, data are easily saved and transported on a large-capacity storage device that can fit on a key chain.

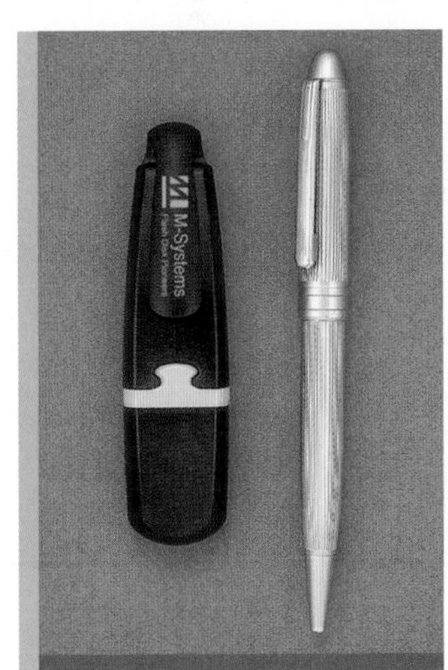

USB drives offer a way to make large files easy to move between computers equipped with a USB port.

For teachers and students, this inexpensive device can offer massive storage relatively inexpensively. Teachers using USB drives do not have to be concerned about finding the right disk or securing sensitive files. Data stored on the USB drive can be easily and safely carried with the teacher anywhere in the classroom, school, or even back and forth to home.

When selecting a USB drive, teachers should be aware of two possible issues. First, older machines may have few or no readily available USB ports, making the use of these devices problematic. Even if USB ports are available, they may be inconveniently located at the back of a computer in an awkward location. If that is the case, extension USB ports may be necessary to use this technology easily. Second, USB drives are changing as their popularity rises. Newer, faster 2.0-type USB drives, while backward compatible, will work much more slowly when used in 1.0 ports. The original USB 1.1 type may not offer the additional features and capacity you desire. However, USB drives are powerful portable storage devices that can serve a busy classroom teacher well.

Classroom Equipment Evaluation **Rubric**

EQUIPMENT:
DESCRIPTION:
VENDOR: COST:
NOTES ON USE:

Please rate the features below for each piece of hardware. Next to each of the items in the rubric, mark the box that best reflects your opinion.

EVALUATION CRITERIA

HARDWARE FEATURE	**1 Poor**	**2 Below Average**	**3 Average**	**4 Above Average**	**5 Excellent**
Ease of Setup	☐ No or minimal setup instructions; poor or missing summary list of hardware components	☐ Instructions poorly written and somewhat difficult to follow; minimal description of equipment components	☐ Instructions complete and adequately user-friendly; necessary equipment	☐ Clear and complete instructions; parts identified by letter or code to correspond to instructions	☐ Pictorial or video guide showing step-by-step assembly with clear, easy-to-follow instructions; equipment goes together easily and smoothly
Ease of Use	☐ Equipment complex and difficult for students to use alone; time consuming and complex for teachers	☐ Students can use with minimal support by teacher; teachers can use with some difficulty	☐ Students can use without support after initial orientation; teachers can use with minimal practice	☐ Students can use with brief orientation; teachers can use with little or no practice	☐ Students can use without orientation or supports; teachers can use with no practice
Space	☐ Space required may exceed maximum available	☐ Space required somewhat large, but available room could be adjusted to accommodate equipment	☐ Space required by equipment is appropriate to available space with current room configuration	☐ Space requirement is appropriate and equipment will fit comfortably in the room	☐ Space requirement is equal to or less than the space available; equipment adds to the look and usefulness of the room without crowding
Tutorials/ Training Available	☐ No tutorials packaged with equipment; no online or other training available	☐ Minimal tutorials packaged with equipment; few free or inexpensive optional tutorials or training available	☐ Brief tutorial provided on CD-ROM with equipment; some additional tutorials or training available at minimal cost	☐ CD and online tutorials readily available for free or minimal cost; some in-house training available for a reasonable fee	☐ CD and online tutorials and training materials available without charge; in-house training provided for free or minimal cost
Other Criteria (List your own topic and criteria)					

Go to the *Rubrics* section of Chapter 6 in MyEducationKit to download the *Classroom Equipment Evaluation Rubric* for your use.

From Hardware to Software

Software enables computers to support instructional and administrative tasks.

The abundant hardware resources explored in this chapter clearly show the potential for computer hardware's enhancement of the teaching and learning process. A broad range of administrative and academic **software** related to almost every aspect of education is also available for use in the classroom. Administrative software programs support almost every area of classroom administration, from helping you to track and average student grades to helping you create a class newsletter to helping you make custom, lesson-specific crossword puzzles. Academic software packages that help you teach range from a variety of multimedia encyclopedias to content-area drill-and-practice programs to software that provides a simulation that promotes discovery learning.

The next two chapters focus on the software resources available to you and explore how they might be effectively used to teach and to learn. As you begin considering these various tools, it is helpful to have a way to determine the usefulness of any particular piece of hardware. Clearly, not only do you need to be aware of many types of computer hardware and how each might be applied in your classroom, you also need to know how to evaluate them effectively. To assist you in determining the value of the hardware you are considering, a Classroom Equipment Evaluation Rubric is included on page 162. Similar evaluation tools are available in Chapter 7 for software evaluations.

PEARSON myeducationkit™

To check your comprehension of the content covered in this chapter, go to the MyEducationKit for your book and complete the *Study Plan* for Chapter 6.

Key Terms

data projection units, 156
data projector, 156
digital camera, 147
digitizers, 150
e-book, 160
electronic whiteboard, 154
flat-bed scanner, 146
graphics tablet, 150
handheld, 160
headphones, 158
mini-laptop, 160
OCR software, 146
personal digital assistant (PDA), 151
ports, 146
scan converter, 157
smartphone, 160
software, 162
speakers, 157
tablet PC, 151
touch screen, 153
voice technology, 161
WiFi, 159
wireless devices, 159

Student Activities

CHAPTER REVIEW

1. What is a scanner? How might it be used in the classroom?
2. How does a digital camera differ from a film camera? Which do you think would be better for you to use in teaching? Why?
3. How does a graphics tablet (digitizer) work? How might it be used to help you teach and your students learn?
4. For digitized sound to be used in your classroom, what computer input and output components must be available? Describe how you would use each to teach.
5. What is a mini-laptop? Tablet PC? How might you find each useful in your classroom?
6. How does an electronic whiteboard differ from other whiteboards? What is the advantage of using an electronic version?
7. Why are data projection units necessary in a classroom? Describe the different choices available for data projection. Which would you purchase and why?
8. Name some emerging technologies. How might they affect teaching and learning?
9. How do increasing computer power, decreasing size, and wireless communications make technology-enhanced classrooms more flexible?
10. What is a virtual environment? What potential does it hold for education?

WHAT DO YOU THINK?

1. After considering the various types of digital technologies presented in this chapter, what three pieces of equipment do you think you would most want for your future or current classroom? Explain why you selected these three and how you would use them for teaching and learning.
2. Some teachers believe that too much emphasis is placed on computers in the classroom. Considering the computer technology you have learned about in this chapter, do you agree or disagree? Defend your view.

LEARNING TOGETHER!

The following activities are designed for learning groups of two or three students.

1. Imagine that your grade-level team or department has been given a $20,000 grant for adding technology to your classrooms. How would you spend the money to best equip your classrooms for teaching and for learning? Include a budget showing how the money would be spent.
2. Visit a technology-rich classroom and interview the teacher about how he or she uses the technology in place. Compare your interviews with those of the other members of your group and develop your group's ideal classroom. Describe the technologies you would include and how you would plan to use them.
3. Select three different computer systems and compare them using the classroom equipment evaluation rubric on page 162. After discussing the options with your group, describe which system you would buy and explain why. Be prepared to share your preference and your reasons with the class.

TEACHING WITH TECHNOLOGY: INTEGRATION IDEAS WEB QUEST

As you become familiar with the many technologies available for teachers' use in their classrooms, it's useful to examine how teachers are applying digital technology to support and enhance the learning process. Let's take a look at some specific, innovative ways in which educators are leveraging technology to teach using the links that follow.

ACTIVITY: After you explore the links that interest you, select a technology you would like to use to teach. Complete a web search to discover at least three new integration ideas for the technologies of your choice. Write a one-page summary of your webquest that includes (1) the link you used and the integration ideas you found, (2) an idea of yours of how you might teach with these technologies for your selected content area or grade level, and (3) a description of the equipment you will need in your classroom to implement your own integration idea.

Integrating Digital Display Technologies in the Classroom

Electronic Whiteboards

The very useful education portal Education World offers information, links, and ideas for using the electronic whiteboard in the classroom. Review the article at **www.education-world.com/a_tech/tech/tech206.shtml.** This comprehensive resource even provides tips for selecting an electronic whiteboard and links to the vendors offering this technology.

Integrating Handheld Devices into the Classroom

Discover Handhelds

This site by Annette Lamb presents the basics of and ideas for using PDAs and other handheld devices in the classroom. Included on the site are links to videos, research, lessons, and information useful to classroom teachers. Explore the possibilities of handheld technology at **http://eduscapes.com/sessions/handhelds/.**

Integrating Other Digital Technologies into the Classroom

CameraScope

Visualization tools can help students observe events that are too small, too fast, or too slow to see otherwise. CameraScope is a free software product developed by the Thinking Spaces Tools Initiative for use with digital microscopes and digital cameras. In addition to capturing images, the software lets you collect and transfer data for analysis into an electronic spreadsheet. For more information and to download the beta version go to **http://teacherlink.org/tools/.**

Digital Tablet

The Wacom drawing tablet site presents K–12 lesson ideas for using a digital tablet in the classroom. Visit **www.wacom.com/education/** to view these innovative uses of this versatile device.

Images and Sound

Apple iPhoto, iMovie, and iTunes software can be used to bring social studies, math, language arts, and science to life. To examine innovative lesson plans using Apple's products visit the iLife web site at **http://ali.apple.com/ali_sites/ali/ilife.html.**

Integrating Digital Imaging Technologies in the Classroom

Explore the many ways in which teachers have used digital cameras in the classroom in many content areas. This site also provides links to rich graphic resources for teachers available via the Internet. Other links offer tutorials and free downloads for imaging software and digital cameras. Visit **http://techintegration.cciu.org/DigitalImages/index.html.**

Wireless Technologies in the Classroom

This web log explores the benefits and challenges of using WiFi in schools. Like most blogs, this resource provides numerous links that explore the technical, educational, and social issues related to using wireless networks in K–12 classrooms. Visit **http://www.wireless-weblog.com/50226711/wifiintheclassroom benefitsandchallenges.php.**

Classroom Clickers

This paper introduces and explores the use of classroom response systems (clickers). It provides a complete list of benefits and challenges to using this innovative and interactive technology in the classroom. Visit **http://apps.medialab.uwindsor.ca/ctl/downloads/clickerdwn/Resourcesandclicker%20ideas.pdf.**

Mini-Laptops Worldwide

This Intel web site demonstrates the impact of mini-laptops in classrooms all over the world. Explore the stories of teachers who have integrated these inexpensive yet powerful computers into instruction and the positive impact on their students. The site also offers information about the worldwide effort to bring computers to all children. Visit **http://www.classmatepc.com/technology-in-the-classroom/.**

interchapter 6

The Technology-Rich Classroom

What exactly would the ideal technology-rich classroom look like? Take a look in the table below at one teacher's description of the technology that she would like to have in a middle school classroom. Which of the technologies do you feel are must-have technologies for you? Which would you do without? Are there any that make little difference to you? Enter a checkmark next to each item to develop a profile of your ideal technology-rich classroom.

MY TECHNOLOGY-RICH CLASSROOM SPECIFICATIONS AND RATIONALE	Check which you prefer. MUST HAVE	DON'T NEED	NO PREFERENCE
TEACHER'S COMPUTER SYSTEM:			
3-gigahertz CPU: This is enough speed for editing video and graphics, and more than enough for common office tasks.	○	○	○
4-GB RAM: I'll need the RAM for multitasking and for graphics and video applications.	○	○	○
500-GB hard drive: I'll need a lot of space for multimedia applications, video, and pictures of my classroom activities.	○	○	○
DVD+/-RW drive: For reading and backup with any type of optical media, and to create my own instructional DVDs.	○	○	○
22" LCD monitor: Takes up less desk space, and I need that much viewable space for graphics and video editing programs, which tend to have cluttered interfaces.	○	○	○
Six or more USB 2.0 ports: Almost everything connects to USB ports these days. I'll need several of them or a USB hub to keep all my high-tech gear connected!	○	○	○
Upgraded speaker system: I'll need a relatively powerful speaker system so that when I'm using a CD-ROM or DVD for classroom instruction, all the students can hear clearly and without distortion.	○	○	○
Bluetooth connectivity: This new wireless standard for computers will be used for many of my high-tech devices.	○	○	○
Approximate cost: $900–$1,200			
5 STUDENT COMPUTER SYSTEMS			
3-gigahertz CPU: Going slower here probably wouldn't save me much money, so I wouldn't sacrifice the speed. It would be expensive to update later.	○	○	○
512-MB RAM: Additional RAM is inexpensive and easy to upgrade later; I'll wait until it looks as though I'll need more.	○	○	○
120-GB hard drive: Also easy and inexpensive to upgrade later. There are also some good reasonably priced external options that students could share when working on multimedia or video projects.	○	○	○
DVD+/-RW drive: This will make sure students can write to whatever media they bring in from home.	○	○	○
17" flat-panel monitor: Less expensive than 19" monitor. I'd go to a CRT before going to something smaller than 17" since so many programs require higher resolution than a 15" LCD can display.	○	○	○
Six or more USB 2.0 ports: Same as teacher station.	○	○	○
Headphones: This helps keep the noise down when students are working individually with multimedia applications.	○	○	○
Approximate cost: $600–$1,000 each			

MY TECHNOLOGY-RICH CLASSROOM SPECIFICATIONS AND RATIONALE	Check which you prefer. MUST HAVE	DON'T NEED	NO PREFERENCE
PRINTER			
Laser printer: I would probably go with an inexpensive laser printer that can connect to the network. This is *much* less expensive in the long run than an ink-jet printer, and the whole class can use just one printer. Approximate cost: $400	○	○	○
VIDEO/DATA PROJECTOR			
Ceiling mount LCD data projector: This is one of the most important parts of the whole package. It makes my teacher computer a teaching tool rather than administrative one. I can download and show free educational videos, show DVDs, demonstrate how to use software, or share a web site with the whole class. With a VCR attached, we can view TV or in-school broadcasts. I can also let students present their multimedia projects to the class. Approximate cost: $700	○	○	○
DIGITAL CAMERA			
Eight-megapixel camera: They're so inexpensive, I would want at least 8 megapixels to capture images of student projects, record short video clips, and to make great decorations with my students for the bulletin board. Make sure they're at least 5 megapixels for decent prints and to record video with sound if I don't also get a digital camcorder. Approximate cost: $150 each	○	○	○
SCANNER			
Combination scanner/copier/printer: Another inexpensive way to get student projects and drawings imported to make rich multimedia lessons. Also great for getting images from trips or books to display on my LCD projector. In a pinch, I can even use it to make a few copies or as a backup printer. Approximate cost: $150	○	○	○
HANDHELD TABLET			
Bluetooth Tablet: A wireless Bluetooth tablet would let me roam the entire classroom but give me all the functions of an interactive whiteboard. It's great being able to teach "from the board" when I'm in the back of the classroom! It's a whiteboard, remote control mouse, and graphics tablet all in one. Approximate cost: $500	○	○	○

CHAPTER 7

Administrative Software

Bob Daemmrich/The Image Works

CHAPTER OVERVIEW

This chapter addresses these ISTE National Educational Technology Standards:
- •NETS•T Standard 2
- •NETS•T Standard 3
- •NETS•T Standard 5
- •NETS•S Standard 3
- •NETS•S Standard 6

- **Understanding Software**
- **Evaluating and Using Productivity Software**
- **Evaluating and Using School and Classroom Management Software**
- **Software, Teaching, and Learning: A Practical Approach**

Imagine that your school district has decided to conduct a districtwide upgrade of technology in the coming year. As a result of this initiative, you have just been given five new computer systems for use in your classroom. The computer-support department tells you that the district will make a variety of administrative software packages available to you. Will you know how to use them? Will you know how to apply them to improve the teaching and learning environment in your classroom?

As you can see, the understanding of computer hardware that you gained from Chapters 5 and 6 is only half the challenge for a computer-using educator. You must be just as competent when it comes to understanding and selecting the software programs that will run on that hardware. This chapter will lead you through an exploration of administrative software and how its types of programs can assist you in your professional responsibilities, from managing your classroom to helping your students learn. It will also help you gain the skills you need to effectively evaluate and select the software that will help you do your job and benefit your students.

In Chapter 7, you will:

- Explore the differences between administrative and academic software
- Identify how various types of administrative software can help you be more effective and efficient in carrying out your professional responsibilities
- Examine how the major types of administrative software can be used to enhance the learning environment
- Explore key theoretical frameworks relating to the use of software in teaching and learning
- Investigate and use methods for reviewing and evaluating software so that your technology acquisitions will meet your needs

Understanding Software

The knowledge that you gained from the chapters relating to the use of computer hardware is the first step in a two-step process leading to the computer competencies an educator needs. The second step is to be able to identify, evaluate, and apply computer software to the direct and indirect tasks associated with teaching and learning.

Whether an educator needs to use software as a tool to create a letter to send home to parents or to turn a computer into a tireless student tutor, being able to select and use the best software package for the task is a valuable skill for every educator. The ability to evaluate software is especially valuable when you are selecting software specifically designed to assist educators. It is the educator's expertise in teaching and in learning that ensures that the programs acquired by a school address the specific, targeted competencies that have been articulated through the instructional design process. Educators must be sufficiently software literate to be able to recommend software that can help their students learn and then be able to serve as guides through the software acquisition and implementation process.

> Being able to select and use the best software package is a skill every educator needs.

Educational computer software can be divided into two major categories. The first category is **administrative software,** that is, software that assists an educator in accomplishing the administrative, professional, and management tasks associated with the profession. The second category is **academic software,** or software that assists both educators and learners in the teaching and learning process itself. Both types of software can be important tools for educators in helping them work efficiently and effectively as classroom managers and educational professionals. This chapter focuses on the use of administrative software for teacher productivity and for classroom application. Chapter 8 more fully explores academic software.

The vital role of software in education is consistent with the role of software in many other aspects of contemporary life. Few businesses could do without the use of software. Word processing has become as critical a skill as typing once was. Spreadsheets are essential for accounting, budgeting, and other financial tasks. The use of the Internet and its support software for information, sales, and communication is as commonplace as the use of a library or telephone. For teachers, the role of software is no less important for their administrative and academic tasks. Standards, today's measure for effectiveness in education,

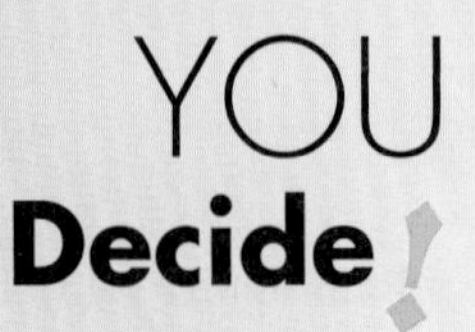

ISTE's NETS•T standards suggest that it is a teacher's responsibility to use technology to enhance his or her professional productivity. Administrative software is one of the primary tools to accomplish this standard. Most districts use and make available to teachers a suite of productivity tools including a word processor, spreadsheet, database, and presentation tool as well as communications tools such as an email program. Should teachers be required to be knowledgeable in each productivity tool in the suite available to them?

YES! As the NETS•T standard indicates, it is part of a teacher's professional responsibility to be productive and effective, not just in teaching tasks, but also in the administrative tasks expected of him or her. To be productive, you have to learn to use the tools the district provides. Whether you learn the software on your own time or take the in-service training classes the district provides, it is every teacher's job to be familiar with and use the tools available.

NO! A teacher's job is to teach. While everyone has to do administrative tasks, there is no reason these need to be done using technology. Teachers have barely enough time to get lessons together, grade papers, and do the extras the students need to help them learn. There just isn't time to learn other types of software packages that aren't directly related to teaching. Teachers can be just as productive using their own ways of handling administrative tasks. Technology shouldn't be a requirement.

Which view do you agree with? YOU DECIDE!

have even been developed to specifically address the use of software by educators. ISTE's NETS emphasize the importance of being able to use software appropriately for teaching, learning, and productivity.

Given the recognized importance of software in education, it becomes necessary for every educator to develop sufficient software literacy, that is, the ability to effectively identify and use appropriate software. To do so, you as an educator must be able to locate and review software options to select the software package that will accomplish the desired task. Then, you must be able to objectively evaluate the software to see whether it indeed fills your need. Resources for the acquisition of educational technology are typically very limited, and careful purchases will make those limited resources go much further. Once the software has been acquired, you might even need to install it on the hardware you have available to you. Finally, so that you and your students can get the most out of the software, you will need to become familiar with how it works. If this sounds like a somewhat time-consuming process, that is because software evaluation, acquisition, installation, and training are indeed extensive tasks. The up-front investment of time and energy in this process, however, will make the difference between the acquisition of valuable educational tools and the purchase of software that looked good on first inspection but ended up gathering dust in a storage closet.

> Administrative software includes productivity and classroom management support software.

To begin the exploration of software, we will first examine administrative software, the programs you might use in accomplishing tasks associated with your teaching and professional responsibilities as well as classroom management. Administrative software can be divided into two general software types (see Table 7.1). These are productivity software and school and/or classroom management software. **Productivity software** is typically generic business application software that educators can use and adapt for the administrative and professional tasks. Word processing, spreadsheet, and database management software are all examples of productivity software. In contrast, **classroom management software** is usually customized software written for educators to help them manage school and classroom tasks, including the creation and maintenance of seating charts, class rolls, student records, or school budgets.

All these administrative software tools help educators do their jobs more effectively and productively. Because a fairly significant time investment is involved in finding, installing,

TABLE 7.1 Administrative Software for Educators

SOFTWARE TYPE	ADMINISTRATIVE TASKS	PROFESSIONAL TASKS	TEACHING AND LEARNING TASKS
PRODUCTIVITY SOFTWARE Microsoft product shots reprinted with permission from Microsoft Corporation.	Assists educators in preparing memos, letters, reports, and budgets	Assists educators in tracking student information, computing grades, and preparing lesson plans and IEPs	Helps educators create student activity sheets, transparencies, grade reports, and parent letters
CLASSROOM MANAGEMENT SOFTWARE Used by permission of Edline, LLC.	FOR DISTRICTS AND SCHOOLS		
	Assists educators in reporting required student information	Assists educators in gathering data for student reports	Assists educators in gathering data for academic decision making
	FOR CLASSROOM		
	Helps educators prepare required reports	Assists educators in tracking and reporting grades; helps create seating charts, rolls, and other classroom tasks	Assists educators in analyzing grade and student data for better academic decision making

and learning software, you should be cautious in your selections. That is the reason software evaluation skills are so important for computer-using educators. This chapter includes evaluation rubrics to assist you in this critical process.

Administrative software can be purchased as an off-the-shelf commercial package or as a custom-made program, or it can be acquired as freeware or shareware. **Freeware** is software that is offered to users without charge; **shareware** is software that is offered to users for a small fee or for a limited time and is sometimes paid for on the honor system after you have had a chance to try it and determine whether it is useful to you. Freeware and shareware present a great temptation for educators on a very constricted budget. Even though many fine administrative software tools are offered as freeware or shareware, they too must be carefully evaluated. Low-cost or no-cost software still costs you the time and effort it takes to install and learn the software. When making software decisions, it is useful to complete a rubric like those included later in this chapter comparing products to determine the features and value of each program you plan to purchase. Rubrics help you to objectively determine the effectiveness of the software. Freeware and shareware can be found on many education sites on the Internet, often along with some reviews of the software's quality.

Freely distributed software can be either freeware or shareware.

Evaluating and Using Productivity Software

Much of an educator's time is consumed in completing the many administrative tasks necessary to prepare and maintain an effective learning environment and to meet the record-keeping demands of the typical school system. The office productivity software that has facilitated business operations can frequently serve educators equally well for their administrative tasks. Such software is typically designed for ease of use, with each application performing a

Go to the *Podcasts* section of Chapter 7 in MyEducationKit and click on *Selecting Software.*

Most productivity software packages include a word processor, electronic spreadsheet, database management system, and presentation software.

Standard

ISTE

Learning about productivity software for the classroom will help you address **NETS•T STANDARD 3:**

MODEL DIGITAL-AGE WORK AND LEARNING Teachers exhibit knowledge, skills, and work processes representative of an innovative professional in a global and digital society.

specific function for the user. Although created for different purposes, productivity software programs often have a similar look and feel so that it is easy to learn one type of software and then apply the same skills to learning another software package produced by the same company. At MyEducationKit, you may want to try the *Office Tools and Tips* Skill Builder activity to experience the format and skills associated with one of the most common types of productivity software groups, Microsoft Office.

The four major types of productivity software found in most business environments are word processors, electronic spreadsheets, database management systems, and presentation software. These can be purchased in individual packages or in application suites and are available for either a PC or Macintosh. Often, a school system will equip the administrative component of its operation with productivity software, which teachers can adapt to address educational tasks. The district will often purchase a **site license**, that is, a license that allows the use of a software package on multiple machines at locations within one organization. The acquisition by district or school computing departments of a site license for productivity software for administrative purposes can benefit the educational staff as well. Although individual educators may have little choice in what productivity software is available to them, with a bit of creativity that software can be applied to myriad teaching and professional tasks. Office productivity software, used in the classroom or other academic spaces such as the media center or faculty workroom, can be a great asset to busy educators. The computer-using educator's job is to learn to use the software and apply it to the many nonteaching tasks for which he or she is responsible. Let's look at the characteristics of the "big four" applications (word processing, spreadsheets, database management, and presentation software) that are included in office software suites and explore how educators can use each of them (see Table 7.2).

Word Processors

Word-processing software is the most commonly used computer application. Computers loaded with word-processing software have all but replaced typewriters for text-oriented tasks, although the typewriter still has a niche in the completion of noncomputerized forms. Today's word processors, however, are capable of doing far more than even the most advanced elec-

TABLE 7.2 Productivity Software Summary

SOFTWARE TYPE	APPLICATION TO ADMINISTRATIVE/PROFESSIONAL TASKS	APPLICATION TO TEACHING AND LEARNING TASKS
WORD PROCESSING	Prepare letters, memos, reports, flyers, rubrics, lesson plans, forms, and newsletters	Prepare transparencies, activity sheets, posters, study guides, and class notes; help students prepare stories, essays, and group reports; use in class to dynamically illustrate writing and outlining skills
SPREADSHEETS	Prepare budgets, numeric tables and summaries, and grade and attendance rosters; compute grades; prepare visuals (charts) of numeric data	Provide students with a method for tracking and analyzing data and creating charts from it; demonstrate what-if analyses visually; support student research such as tracking stock market data
DATABASE MANAGEMENT SYSTEMS	Organize and track student and other professional data; prepare inventories, mailing lists, and reports	Organize and provide easy access to lists of academic resources; provide support for students' tracking data; extract and report targeted summaries of content or resources to address student needs
PRESENTATION SOFTWARE	Create presentations for workshops, conferences, and meetings	Create class lecture support that features text, audio, and visual elements with special effects; produce transparency masters; create student worksheets to accompany class lectures

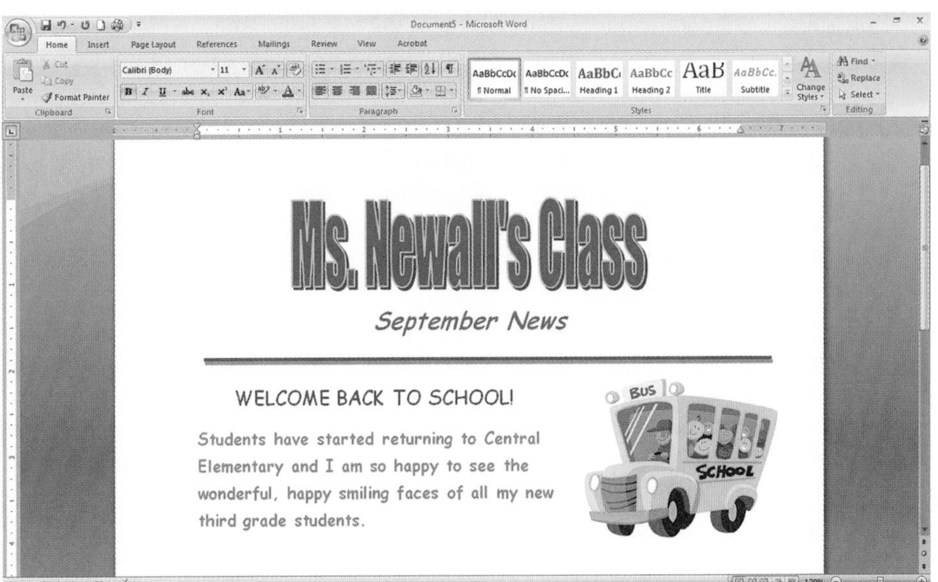

FIGURE 7.1

Word Processing in the Classroom

Word processors can create flyers and transparency masters in addition to text documents.

Microsoft product screen shot reprinted with permission from Microsoft Corporation. Microsoft Word® is a registered trademark of Microsoft Corporation.

tronic typewriter. In addition to creating, editing, and printing documents, these software packages are capable of desktop publishing, creating and editing graphics, and developing web pages. Combined with an inexpensive color ink jet printer, word-processing software packages are also powerful tools for creating full-color transparencies, classroom signs and posters, customized certificates and awards, and even personalized stickers and buttons (see Figure 7.1). Of course, they are also essential tools for creating tests, student worksheets, and memos.

Unlike typewriters, word-processing programs maintain large amounts of data in an electronic format until it is ready to print out. This allows educators to store and easily update or modify the many documents they use in the daily administrative tasks that are a part of every educator's job. Word processors also include a built-in capacity to check grammar and spelling and an interactive thesaurus, which make this software application a valuable tool for every educator.

Most word-processing packages share several significant and useful features. These can be broadly grouped in terms of the word-processing functions they enhance. These functions include document preparation and editing, desktop publishing, and archiving and printing.

At MyEducationKit, each of these functions is explored. As you try each of the word-processing exercises, you will experience and practice the unique and powerful functions built into one of today's most popular word processors, Microsoft Word.

Document Preparation and Editing

Document preparation is the most common use of word-processing software. Error correction, adjustments to the document's text, and experimentation with different fonts and formats can be completed before the document is printed in hard copy. Editing features may vary with the complexity of the word-processing software, but all word processors include the following key features. You will practice using many of them when you try the Word Skills Builder, *Bake Sale Flyer* activity accessible through MyEducationKit.

- *Insertion and Deletion of Text.* The cursor, or insertion point, that is displayed on the word-processing screen indicates the point at which text will be entered. As a document is created, the cursor stays at the end of the data and moves along as additional text is entered. By using the computer's mouse or arrow keys, the user can move the cursor backward or forward to any point in the body of the document.
- *Text Selection and Enhancement.* Once text has been entered, specific letters, words, paragraphs, lines, or whole pages can be selected. The word processor then is ready to

PEARSON myeducationkit™

To learn more about wording processing and Microsoft Word, go to the *Video Tutorials* section of Chapter 7 in MyEducationKit and select *MS Word for PC, Basics* and *MS Word for Mac, Basics.*

apply subsequent commands to that portion of the text only. You can change the type size or font used or add visual augmentation, making text bold, italic, or underlined.

- *Word Wrap and Formatting.* Word processors automatically wrap text down to the next line when a word reaches the end of the line. This feature is especially useful when you decide to insert additional text. Page formatting features allow you to change the look of the page, such as changing margins, adding headers and footers, or altering line spacing on all or part of the document. Such page changes may cause the text in any given line to move. Word wrap once again automatically adjusts the text and line length to accommodate such formatting changes.
- *Spelling and Grammar Tools.* The most popular of the common word-processing tools include built-in spell-checker, grammar checker, and thesaurus. The spell-checker will check spelling word by word against a built-in dictionary of thousands of words and suggest alternatives to words it does not recognize. This dictionary can be used as a thesaurus to provide both synonyms and antonyms of selected words. And the software can recognize proper grammar and sentence construction and suggest alternative grammar choices.
- *Copy, Cut, Paste, Drag, and Undo.* Editing functions in word processors provide the user with the ability to select letters, words, or blocks of text and then remove them from the document or move them to a different location within the document. The *copy* feature creates a duplicate version of the selected text, which can be *pasted* elsewhere. The *cut* feature removes a block of text from its original location permanently. The material can then be pasted into another location. Some word processors have combined a cut-and-paste function into a single feature called *drag and drop.* This feature allows you to select text and drop it anywhere else in the document. Finally, the *undo* feature provides a safety net against mistakes. It allows the user to back up and undo the last several actions.

Desktop Publishing

Most word processors include the ability to manipulate the look of a page. By using this feature, an attractive arrangement of graphics and text on a page can be created and manipulated with a few clicks of the mouse button. Although word processors can perform some desktop publishing tasks, they cannot perform the extensive adjustments to page displays that dedicated desktop publishing software can make. Listed below are some desktop publishing capabilities that are included in most word processors.

- *WYSIWYG Displays.* Word processors are able to display a document on the screen in a "what you see is what you get" (**WYSIWYG**) format. This feature allows the user to preview a document and see exactly what it will look like before it is printed.

Clip Art

Microsoft Word includes a large library of clip art images for use in illustrating documents for your students. But beyond the images that come with Word, you can tap into an expansive and ever-changing library online. Microsoft's online clip art and media web site at **http://office.microsoft.com/clipart** offers clip art, animation, and photos that you can download for free. It also provides templates for specialty documents such as banners and greeting cards for special occasions as well as tips on how to use and edit images. Teachers are always looking for the right image to illustrate the concept they are teaching or to communicate an idea. Word's clip art library offers thousands of useful images. Microsoft's clip art and media web site adds many thousands more.

- *Graphics and Clip Art.* Most word processors today include rudimentary graphics capabilities that allow you to add and position a drawing on a document page. The creation of a complex or custom graphic is typically done with dedicated graphics programs, but most word processors include a library of clip art (ready-made artwork) that can be inserted into a document to add interest to an all-text document.
- *Tables and Columns.* Text data can easily be arranged into multiple columns of data per page or into a table or grid. This gives the user the ability to organize data, with just a few clicks of the mouse, into a format that can display data more clearly than a narrative. Once the data are in table or column form, all of the typical text enhancements can be applied.
- *Autoformats.* Tables, columns, and documents can be formatted in many different ways. Borders can be added, titles can be enhanced, and graphics can be placed in any type of document. For users who do not have the time or experience to experiment with formats, many word processors include an autoformat feature. This feature lets you preview the look of various styles that can be applied to a document and then select the one you like best to use with your document. Once selected, the format is automatically applied to the entire document under construction.
- *Word Art.* A fairly recent addition to word processors' publishing features is the ability to create fancy, colorful titles. This word art feature offers you the ability to add color, shapes, and styles to a document's title or to make sections of your document stand out.

Today's word-processing software can create and edit documents, complete desktop publishing tasks, and develop web pages.

Archiving and Printing

When a document is complete, word processors provide the ability to save it in numerous file formats and to print it in black and white or color, depending on the available printers. Archiving or storing a document to a removable drive or hard disk stores the text you typed, along with all of its related formatting commands, in a single word-processor file.

The final feature shared by all word processors is the ability to print documents. One of the sets of word-processing codes saved with every document is information about the type of printer to be used to print the document out. Because many printers are available, the printer that is set up as the default printer for the word processor will be used automatically unless you instruct the program to do otherwise. Some formatting features may change when printer defaults change, thus unexpectedly changing the way your document looks. Of course, as you learned in Chapter 5, printers can just as easily output crisp laser copies as they can colorful transparencies, depending on the specific capabilities of the hardware.

Ready-Made Word-Processing Tools

Because word processors are such commonly used tools in education, educators have developed many documents, templates, and macros. **Templates** are documents that are preformatted for a specific use but contain no data. An example might be a meeting announcement flyer. To use it, you would open the template with your word processor to find a fully laid-out flyer. You would then only need to type in your organization's name and the date and time of your meeting. You can also create templates for your own future use.

TECH TIPS for Teachers

When you save a word document you are creating, the file will include the text you type in as well as formatting codes. Every word processor saves these unique codes within the file so that when you open the file at a later date, it looks exactly like the one you saved. However, these codes can become a problem when you open a document using word-processing software different from the program you originally used to create the document. When trying to open the file, you may find the document unreadable or containing many extraneous characters.

Microsoft Word includes a translator feature that will automatically translate document codes from most other word processors so that they may be opened by Word. However, not all word processors do. If you are unsure of the software that will be used to open a document you are creating in Word, it is a good idea to save the document in a more universal format. When saving the document, select Save As, and in the dialog box that appears, note that you can save a file as various types including text and rich text formats. These formats can be opened by any word-processing software and may therefore be the best choice for documents you create for use outside of your classroom.

In the CLASSROOM

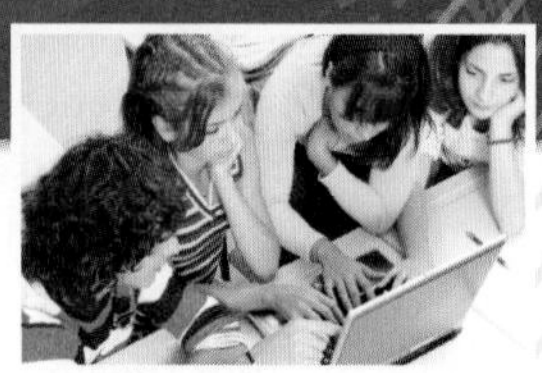

Word Processing in Middle School and High School

Jackie Saucier, sixth-grade social studies teacher at William J. Berry Elementary School in Heidelberg, Mississippi, introduces her students to Latin America by giving them a project-based lesson. The students research online the people, government, geography, natural resources, and manufactured products of our neighbors to the south. Then they use Microsoft Word to create a trifold travel brochure. To enhance the appeal and look of their brochures, they use Clip Art and Word Art, as well as Word's clip art gallery.

Students are guided by the travel brochure checklist that Saucier prepared that lists the brochure components. They also have instructions on how to use Word for their trifold brochure. The assignment accommodates all students' abilities and needs. Artistically gifted students can illustrate their brochures with pictures they make with Draw software or by drawing freehand. Students with disabilities can receive help from peer tutors in the use of the technologies. The Accessibility features of Microsoft's operating system are utilized as needed for special needs such as handwriting or speech recognition. The culminating activity for all students is sharing their travel brochures with the class with the option to present them using PowerPoint.

Lorrie Jackson, Director of Communications and Marketing at Lausanne Collegiate School in Memphis, Tennessee, collaborates with the classroom teachers to integrate technology into their lessons in this school. Jackson's "Biography Brainstorm: Using Word and the Web to Jumpstart Research" gets students started learning formal research skills, which will serve them throughout their secondary, post-secondary, and graduate education. After confirmation that students are familiar with Word's menu bar features and how to search on the Internet, the lesson begins. Many students today think graphically, so Word's drawing tools found under View>Toolbars>Drawing are used to help the students organize the biography.

The teacher asks the students to vote on which famous person they would like to meet. Once in Draw, the students create a circle in which they type the person's name. Next they decide on questions to ask the person and type the questions in small circles that they create on the Word document. With the line or arrow, they connect the question circles to the main circle. The students enjoy adding color, images, and even using shapes other than circles. Once they complete their questions, they are ready to begin the research process for the answers so they can write their assigned biographies.

Sources: Saucier, J. (2006). *Cruising Latin America.* Retrieved March 31, 2009, from **http://www.create.cett.msstate.edu/create/classroom/lplan.view.asp?articleID=40.** Jackson, L. (2006, February 28). *Biography brainstorm: Using Word and the Web to jumpstart research.* Retrieved March 31, 2009, from **http://www.education-world.com/a_tech/techlp/techlp052.shtml.**

You can also modify a template further if you want to. A word-processing **macro** is a prerecorded set of commands for your word processor that automates a complex task such as formatting output to fit on labels. Macros are stored in files that can be retrieved and activated with a few keystrokes. An example of a macro might be a file that automatically sets up the official school letterhead using the school's logo and name. Often, such predesigned templates and macros are freely shared among educators across the Internet.

A final tool built into most word processors is a **wizard.** A wizard is a mini-program that creates a customized template for you. It asks a series of questions about the format you desire for your document and then creates a custom template as you respond to each question. Wizards will help you create sophisticated documents without having to know how to issue complex formatting commands.

Word Processors in the Classroom

Templates, macros, and wizards can facilitate complex word-processing tasks.

Word processors are a great teaching tool as well as a productivity tool for busy educators. The same features that facilitate the creation of memos and tests can be creatively applied to teaching and learning. The application of these features to teaching and learning is summarized in Table 7.3. There are numerous examples of the creative ways in which teachers have applied the same word-processing software they use for productivity tasks to teaching

TABLE 7.3 Word Processing in Teaching and Learning

WORD PROCESSING FEATURE	APPLICATION TO ADMINISTRATIVE/PROFESSIONAL TASKS	APPLICATION TO TEACHING AND LEARNING TASKS
DOCUMENT PREPARATION	Provides capabilities to • Enter documents • Edit documents • Format documents • Correct grammar and spelling • Enhance with graphics • Print color and black and white	Allows students to • Create organized documents • Edit errors easily • Add graphics and enhanced text elements • Print draft copies for review and proofreading • Finalize, correct, and print final copies
DESKTOP PUBLISHING	Provides or lets you create formats for • Forms • Flyers • Invitations • Newsletters	Provides students with a tool for preparing • Creative presentation of text • Alternative report formats (newsletter, comics, minibooks) • Supports for oral reports
FORMATTING	Lets you adjust documents for • Professional appearance • Emphasis on key points • Consistency of appearance • Letterhead and memo styles	Students can • Experiment with formats for best presentation Teachers can • Create appealing documents for their students • Alter documents to meet specific learning needs
GRAMMAR CHECKING	Helps to ensure that documents are grammatically correct	Assists students in • Proofreading and correcting their work • Practicing the application of grammatical rules Assists teachers in • Demonstrating grammar corrections in real time • Helping students find and correct grammatical errors
SPELL-CHECKING	Helps to ensure that documents are free from spelling errors	Assists students in • Proofreading and correcting their work • Practicing correct spelling Assists teachers in • Demonstrating spelling corrections in real time • Helping students find and correct spelling errors
MAIL MERGE	Provides an easy way to make form letters personal	Can be used by teachers to individualize reports to students and letters to parents
TABLES	Provides tools to present information professionally, concisely, and clearly in an organized format	Assist students in • Organizing data • Presenting data clearly • Summarizing key data Assist teachers in • Creating clear summaries for study guides • Displaying organized data in support of presentation • Teaching interpretation of data
WEB FORMAT	Converts files from documents to web format so that they can be easily added to web sites	Allows students and teachers to create documents and save them in web format for display on a class web site without knowing any HTML
ARCHIVING	Provides an inexpensive and easy-to-access archive system for documents	• Saved teacher data files are easy to access and update to keep lessons current and available • Students can save files for later work or find and reprint lost hard copies • Archived files can easily be added to electronic portfolios

Go to the *Podcasts* section of Chapter 7 in MyEducationKit and click on *Administrative Tools.*

and learning as well. Teachers use word processors to make calendars, publish class books of poetry, create newsletters, prepare flyers, make class stationery, and even author classroom web sites. In the Classroom feature on page 176 features just a few innovative teacher-developed applications of this common productivity software.

Electronic Spreadsheets

Electronic spreadsheet software is to numeric data what word-processing software is to text. With an **electronic spreadsheet,** you can organize, input, edit, and chart data and produce accurate professional reports for any administrative task that deals extensively with numbers. Spreadsheet software not only allows you to organize numeric information but also has built-in mathematical and statistical formulas that can be applied to the data with just a few clicks of the mouse button. With a spreadsheet, budgets can be easily developed and modified, grades can be tracked and averaged, and class statistical information can be extracted. Furthermore, most spreadsheets include built-in graphing capabilities that can turn numeric data into colorful, three-dimensional charts that will visually illustrate numeric results.

One of the key advantages of electronic spreadsheets over their manual counterparts is in their accuracy. A second advantage is the fact that spreadsheets can be modified easily. Consider as an example the grade-level media budget pictured in Figure 7.2. If it had been done manually and the cost of printer cartridges turned out to be $10 instead of the budgeted $8, you would have to erase and recalculate a number of different entries on the spreadsheet. With an electronic spreadsheet, however, you would need to type in only the new value, and all the other entries associated with that value would be automatically recalculated. This time-saving feature makes electronic spreadsheets easier to use, less time consuming, and far more accurate than doing the calculations manually.

Spreadsheets manipulate numeric data and display it in tables and charts.

Several software vendors produce electronic spreadsheet programs. Some of these, such as Microsoft Excel, are powerful, business-oriented software packages that have numerous features. Others are for home or general consumer use, such as the spreadsheet component of Apple iWork or Microsoft Works. Regardless of the capabilities of any given spreadsheet package, they all have a full range of common features.

In MyEducationKit, there is material that demonstrates and provides you practice with Excel, one of the most common of all electronic spreadsheets. When you try the Excel Tutorial, you will have an opportunity to see firsthand how the features of this useful tool can be applied in your classroom for both administrative and academic tasks.

Spreadsheet Organization

To learn more about spreadsheets and Microsoft Excel, go to the *Video Tutorials* section of Chapter 7 in MyEducationKit and select *Excel for PC, Basics* and *Excel for Mac, Basics.*

Electronic spreadsheets, like their paper counterparts, organize data into vertical columns and horizontal rows. The user then types in alphabetic or numeric data in the appropriate locations. This organizational structure provides the framework for lining up and clearly labeling numeric information.

The intersections of spreadsheet rows and columns are called cells. It is in the nature and use of these cells that electronic spreadsheets have great advantage over their manual counterparts. Each cell of a spreadsheet can contain text, values, or a formula. This variety of cell content can be seen in Figure 7.2. The cells in column A all contain text labels, and the cells in column B all contain data representing budget amounts. The cells in columns C through E contain labels, values, subtotals, or totals. Column D's cells do not contain totals calculated by hand and then typed in. Instead, they contain instructions to the spreadsheet software directing it to perform a mathematical calculation—in this case, multiplying the data entered in columns B and C.

This independent data-handling capability of each spreadsheet cell makes it a quick and easy task to alter or correct the data entered. Furthermore, once a single cell's data have been changed, that change will be reflected in all cells that use those data for a calculation. Thus, if the budget amount for lined paper in Figure 7.2 is changed, the print media subtotal will also be changed, as will all other related totals. This automatic recal-

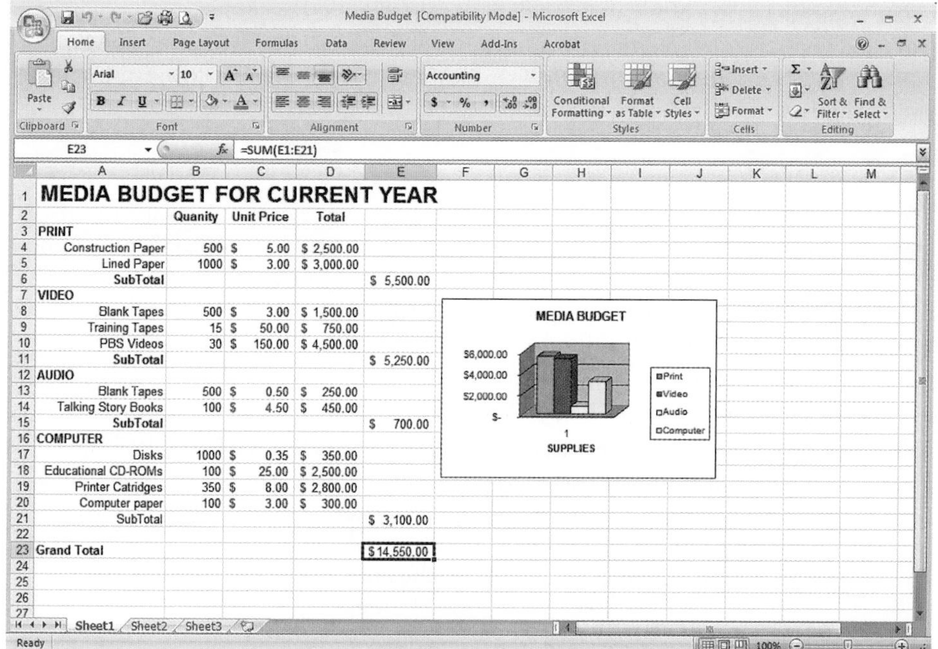

FIGURE 7.2

Electronic Spreadsheet Application

Spreadsheet software is a useful tool in maintaining school budgets.

Microsoft product screen shot reprinted with permission from Microsoft Corporation. Microsoft Excel® is a registered trademark of Microsoft Corporation.

culation feature is one of the key reasons why spreadsheets have become as popular a tool for handling numbers as word-processing software is for handling text.

Formulas and Functions

Formulas are used in a spreadsheet to indicate the types of calculations that should be performed to achieve a specific outcome. The cells that contain instructions that tell the software to perform specific mathematical activities may, in fact, contain detailed formulas that the user has typed in. In addition to user-entered formulas, most spreadsheets contain hundreds of stored, premade formulas that the user can easily place into a cell. These range from formulas appropriate to finance and statistics to those necessary for trigonometry. These built-in formulas make it particularly easy to perform complex mathematical tasks. You will practice using formulas and functions in the Excel tutorial activity, *Club Budget*, in MyEducationKit. Once you are comfortable with the software, you will find spreadsheets to be powerful and useful tools.

What-If Analysis

Perhaps the most intriguing feature of an electronic spreadsheet is its ability to perform **what-if analysis.** Because some cells contain the mathematical results of the data in other cells, changes to those data can be immediately reflected elsewhere. For example, a teacher who is using a spreadsheet to compute grades will have entered not only student grade data but also the formula needed to reflect how those grades will be averaged or weighted. So if a student wanted to know what his or her average would be if the score on the next test were 100 percent, the teacher could enter the hypothetical 100 percent into the spreadsheet, and the student could see the result in terms of a final grade computation. This is a what-if analysis; that is, what if the student gets a grade of 100 percent—how will that affect the outcome? This is a valuable tool to help students keep track of their own grades in a course.

Spreadsheets offer a what-if feature for decision making.

Charts and Graphs

Another useful feature of spreadsheet software is the ability to turn the data that have been entered into rows and columns into its graphic counterpart. The graphing (also called charting) function allows the user to create a graph in any number of formats from line

Spreadsheet graphing makes it easy to visualize data.

to bar to pie charts in color and three-dimensional shapes. For professional-looking displays and to assist visual learners, this spreadsheet tool is extremely useful. The *Student Measurement* Skills Builder activity in MyEducationKit will demonstrate the instructional power of this feature.

Templates and Macros

Like word-processing software, spreadsheet software makes use of templates and macros, allowing the user to create and reuse useful spreadsheet formats and commands. Spreadsheet templates and macros can also be found as shareware or freeware at numerous educational web sites. You can also create your own spreadsheet templates. Try the Excel tutorial activity *Grade Keeper*, in MyEducationKit to experience this feature.

Electronic Spreadsheets in the Classroom

Table 7.4 shows how many of a spreadsheet's key features can be used both administratively and in teaching and learning. Just as word-processing software can be repurposed for academic projects, so too can spreadsheet software. Whether a teacher uses a spreadsheet to track grades or a student uses a spreadsheet to collect and record data from an experiment, this software provides a wealth of possibilities to the creative teacher.

Database Management Software

Every educator's job includes the cumbersome tasks of organizing, maintaining, and retrieving many types of data. Whether it is a student's home phone number or a school district's targeted language arts objectives for the sixth grade, educators must be able to easily and quickly gain access to and extract the information they need. The productivity software that accomplishes this type of task is called database management software.

Database management software offers educators an easy-to-use system for creating customized records to contain data, retrieving targeted records, updating and editing the information in those records, and then organizing clear and accurate reports from the data (see Figure 7.3). Furthermore, database software allows you to sort all your data automatically at the touch of a key or to query the database for a match to any single word or phrase. Considering the amount of information an educator must deal with, database management software can save a busy teacher much time and energy.

Database management software can organize, sort, retrieve, and report data.

An electronic card catalog in a media center library is one example of a useful database management application in schools. Consider for a moment the complexity of cataloging or locating a book using a manual system. In manual cataloging, a book must be cross-referenced on at least three different index cards under title, author, and subject. All of these must be typed out and manually sorted and filed. To find the book, the card catalog user must look through drawers full of cards until just the right card is located. For both the media specialist and the library patron, the process can be laborious. With an electronic

FIGURE 7.3

Using a Database Management System for Student Data

Database management software helps teachers organize student information.

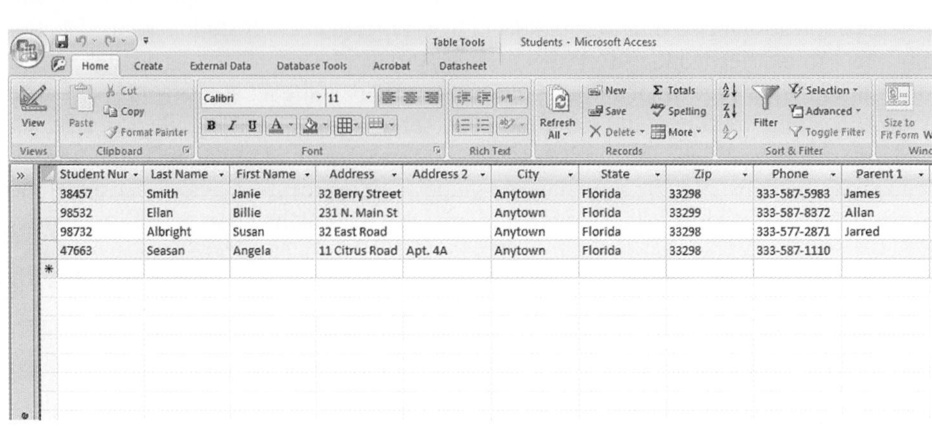

TABLE 7.4 Electronic Spreadsheets in Teaching and Learning

SPREADSHEET FEATURE	APPLICATION TO ADMINISTRATIVE/PROFESSIONAL TASKS	APPLICATION TO TEACHING AND LEARNING TASKS
SPREADSHEETS AND WORKBOOKS	Allow for the preparation and display of clearly organized numerical data on individual spreadsheets and in workbooks or related spreadsheets	Assist students in • Organizing numerical data • Creating and testing formulas • Formatting data to produce clear and concise reports Assist teachers in • Organizing and reporting numerical data • Creating customized gradebooks • Tracking student data • Presenting clear reports
AUTO FORMATTING	Provides premade formats to give a spreadsheet a distinct professional appearance	Teachers and students can create appealing, professional-looking spreadsheet reports
CHARTING	Provides easy-to-use tools for visual displays of numeric data	Provides students with • A tool for visual presentation in student reports • A tool to view saved data visually for better understanding • A way to visually explore alterations of the numeric data stored in the spreadsheet Provides teachers with • A tool for preparing visual reports of abstract mathematical relationships • A presentation tool to demonstrate numeric data visually
FORMULAS AND FUNCTIONS	Assist in preparing accurate calculations that will automatically adjust to changes in data	Help students • Create and test formulas • See changes in mathematical relationships as data changes Help teachers • Demonstrate mathematical concepts in action • Test and use appropriate grading formulas • Demonstrate to students how final grades are calculated
WHAT-IF ANALYSIS	Allows for the real-time demonstration of the impact of changes in data; e.g., budgeted amounts can be tested for different results	Assists students in • Seeing the impact of data changes on outcomes in mathematical scenarios • Testing relationships and outcomes by manipulating data Assists teachers in • Demonstrating changes and their impact on the results • Explaining how different test grades will affect a student's final grade
ARCHIVING	Provides an inexpensive and easy way to store and access worksheets for budgets and other numeric files	Saved data files are easy to access and update to keep records current; students using spreadsheets for math practice can retrieve as needed

In the CLASSROOM

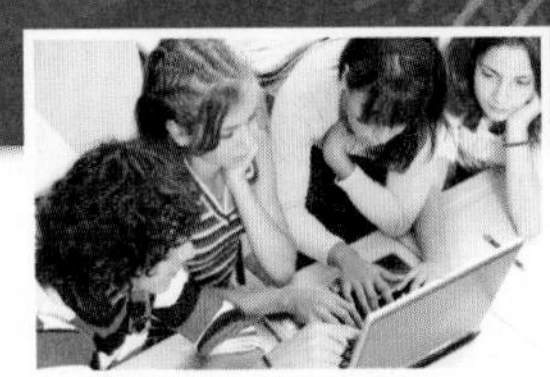

Spreadsheets

Kimberly Schaunaman, a South Dakota elementary school teacher, worked with her student teacher, Korrie Face of Northern State University in Aberdeen, South Dakota, to develop a lesson plan for teaching third- to fifth-graders about electromagnets that integrates spreadsheet and graphing software.

The students discover how electricity and magnetism together make electromagnetism and how it affects everyday life. They experimented with picking up paper clips with a spool of electrical wire, using various amounts of wire wound around a nail, and, alternatively, a pencil connected to a 6-volt battery, and they recorded the results. They create a bar graph with their data, using spreadsheet software to show the number of paper clips picked up each time the nail is rewrapped. Ms. Schaunaman and Ms. Face then explain the properties of electromagnetism that produced the results shown on the bar graph.

Donna Bartelli, a mathematics teacher at Valencia High School in Placentia, California, developed a way for middle-school students to solve a classic problem by using a spreadsheet. The problem, "A Thousand Lockers," states that the school has 1,000 shut and unlocked lockers and 1,000 students. Suppose:

1. The first student goes along the row and *opens every locker.*
2. The second student then goes along and *shuts every other locker*, beginning with the *second locker*.
3. The third student *changes the state* of every *third* locker, beginning with *number 3*. (If the locker is open, the student shuts it; if the locker is closed, the student opens it.)
4. The fourth student *changes the state* of every *fourth* locker, beginning with *number 4*.

Imagine that this continues until the 1,000 students have followed the pattern with the 1,000 lockers. At the end, which lockers will be open and which will be closed, and why? Ms. Bartelli presents the solution using a spreadsheet simulation. In just ten steps, she walks the students through the problem, beginning with opening a new spreadsheet file and naming it **lockers** and proceeding to the solution and the explanation as to why the answer turns out to be what the spreadsheet shows. To find out the answer if you don't already know, go to the second web site listed below.

Sources: Schaunaman, K., & Face, K. *Technology integrated lesson plans: Electromagnets*. Retrieved March 31, 2009, from **http://www.northern.edu/soe/ilp/schaunaman.html**.
Bartelli, D. *A thousand lockers: Locker problem activity*. Retrieved March 31, 2009, from **http://www.mathforum.org/alejandre/frisbie/locker.html**.

card catalog that is a dedicated database management system of the library collections, the process is much simplified.

All database management software contains key features to make the organization and manipulation of data easy. These features are summarized in Table 7.5. At MEL you will find activities that demonstrate and provide you practice with Access, Microsoft's popular and powerful database management software.

Database Organization

In database management systems, a field is the electronic storage location in which a specific type of data is stored. In our library example, a field might contain an author's last name in a Last Name field. A record is a collection of all related fields, such as a record that contains all the information about a specific book. A file is a collection of all related records, such as a file containing records representing all the books in a library. This organizational structure provides the library with the ability to organize and manipulate data at both the macro and micro levels and to easily update and accurately maintain the data.

In our library example, the media specialist can type the data representing a new acquisition in a new record in the media center's database file. The database software automatically stores the new record. From that point on, the user can access that new record according to the data stored in any of the information fields on the record. By typing in a key word or phrase, the user can retrieve the desired record from the database. This electronic process is a fast and accurate data input and retrieval system.

TABLE 7.5 Database Management Software in Teaching and Learning

DATABASE FEATURE	APPLICATION TO ADMINISTRATIVE/ PROFESSIONAL TASKS	APPLICATION TO TEACHING AND LEARNING TASKS
DATABASES	• Allow for the definition of customized database formats • Provide for inputting and storing large amounts of complex and/or cumbersome data	Assist students in • Thinking through and creating logical data organizations • Easily entering data for subsequent organization and reporting Assist teachers in • Creating customized data organization that suits their specific needs • Managing student and content data
FORMS	Provide a format for support staff and aides to input data	Teachers can create easy-to-use and familiar input screens for students to use
REPORTS	Professional-looking output created by tools and wizards	Assists students in • Presenting project data in a variety of attractive formats Assists teachers in • Customizing output for each student, class, or lesson
SORTING	Provides multiple levels of sorts to make data easy to comprehend Assists teachers in	Assists students in • Practicing alphabetizing skills • Thinking abstractly to determine appropriate sorts • Presenting data clearly • Presenting data to students in an easy-to-use format • Demonstrating critical-thinking and alphabetizing skills • Preparing logical reports
QUERIES	Provide for customized output through the selection of specific records based on predefined criteria	Assist students in • Practicing logical and critical-thinking skills • Finding and reporting targeted data • Identifying key criteria to look for Assist teachers in • Finding and working with only those records needed • Demonstrating concepts in equality and Boolean logic • Presenting real-time demonstrations of critical thinking
ARCHIVING	Provides an inexpensive and easy way to store and access data	Saved database files are easy means to use to • Query data • Access data • Update information • Sort data • Make reports

Sorting

Once entered, records can be sorted according to the data in any one or in multiple fields. Sorting arranges all records in a database into ascending or descending order based on the alphabetic or numeric characters stored in any field. In our library example, with this sort function, no matter how many additions or deletions to the library's collection of books may occur, the database of holdings is always in alphabetical order and ready to use. And because all the data are stored electronically and automatically sorted, a record cannot be as easily removed or misfiled as is possible in a manual system.

Querying

One of the most significant features of database management is the ability to find one single item of data from the potentially thousands of items in a database. When querying a database, the user instructs the software to look for and match targeted criteria. In our library example, to find a specific author's name, you would, in a query operation, instruct the software to look in the Last Name fields of all records to find that targeted last name. Once it is found, the software returns the record in which the matching name resides. Despite the size of the database, any single item of information can be quickly and easily accessed.

Reports

The query feature selects and displays data that match specific criteria.

Whether you need to print a written summary of all of the records in the database or only those resulting from a query, most database management software packages contain report formats that ensure a professional and polished look. Reports are essentially templates built into the software to create output that is attractive and easy to read. Although it is possible to print the entire database, including all fields of all records, if the database is large, this can result in an overwhelming and difficult-to-read quantity of data. Using a report instead allows you to use the results of a database query to report only those records you want and then to identify and display only the desired fields within the records. In our library example, we can easily query the database to find any new additions to the library and then create a New Acquisitions Report that includes only the most pertinent information about each book.

Database Management in the Classroom

Like word-processing and spreadsheet software, database management software, when creatively applied by educators, can be more than a productivity tool. It can become a creative teaching and learning tool when used to categorize, store, access, and retrieve large amounts of data or to demonstrate logic when creating a query.

Presentation Software

Whether for teacher-led presentations or student-led class reports, presentation software can help to organize and enhance the delivery of content. **Presentation software** includes programs that are designed to create digital support materials for oral presentations. From a software perspective, presentations are a prearranged group of electronic slides that present one idea after another. Completed presentations sequence and display these slides on a computer monitor, large-screen video monitor, or projection screen (see Figure 7.4). Presentations typically proceed through all slides in a linear sequence but the software has the capabilities needed for nonlinear, linked sequencing. These programs, originally designed for use in business as a sales and presentation tool, have been adapted by educators to assist the communication process.

Presentation software lets you create and show electronic slides to enhance a presentation.

Presentation software includes a wide range of capabilities in one typically very easy-to-use package. The most common features of presentation software are summarized here.

Multimedia Elements

The individual slides in a presentation slide show can contain a number of multimedia elements including text, graphics, animation, sound, and video clips. The software can thus create a presentation appealing to the variety of learning modalities found in a typical audience of learners.

To learn more about presentation software and Microsoft PowerPoint, go to the *Video Tutorials* section of Chapter 7 in MyEducationKit and select *PowerPoint for Mac, Basics* and *PowerPoint for PC, Basics.*

Templates

Although multimedia presentations of this complexity may seem difficult to create, most presentation software programs include a variety of slide templates with designer formats already created and ready to fill in. For busy teachers who use these templates, the design tasks are already done, and only the content needs to be added.

Hyperlinks

Many presentation software programs include hypermedia features that make them seem more like multimedia authoring software than presentation tools adapted from business. Such programs include hyperlink capability via buttons to hyperjump (move directly to a target slide) to out-of-sequence slides, to the Internet, or to other software. Adding a hyper-

FIGURE 7.4

Using Presentation Software

With presentation software, you can construct slides and view the results in a slide show presentation.

link to a word, image, or button is as simple as clicking on a toolbar button and typing in the slide number or Internet address you wish to jump to.

Animation

Many presentation software packages also come with built-in options for dramatic special effects that can be applied to the moment of transition between slides or to the way bulleted items appear on a slide. Such animation schemes add visual interest and excitement to the concepts presented in text on the screen. Sound effects may be included with animation to add auditory interest.

Printing

In addition to displaying the presentation itself, presentation software typically includes a variety of printing options. Once the presentation is created, a hard copy can be printed and copied for distribution to the viewers. A presentation can be printed out as an outline, as a speaker's note pages, or as customized audience handouts displaying anywhere from one to six slides per page. In addition, with a color printer and transparency film, each slide of the presentation can be printed out as a transparency for use on an overhead projector.

Display Options

In addition to a presenter-controlled display, presentation software provides alternative display options. A presentation can be set to display itself as a timed, self-playing slide show that will run without assistance by either the presenter or the viewer. This is a particularly useful feature to use for a self-guided display in a classroom center or in a library to guide students as they begin a group or individual task.

Presentation Software in the Classroom

One of the most successful applications of presentation software takes presentation preparation beyond helping an educator prepare an effective lecture. Presentation software is especially valuable when used by students to create support materials for their own presentations. The software can help students organize their thoughts into manageable and logical chunks as a result of the automatic limitation of information displayable on any given slide. Further, discrimination and critical thinking are applied as the students review the

FIGURE 7.8

Electronic portfolios provide an easy-to-use and efficient way to digitally record, store, organize, and display student work.

Source: From Oswego City School District web site, **www.oswego.org/staff/burger/portfolio.html.** Copyright © 2004 Julie C. Burger. Reprinted by permission of Julie Burger, Oswego City School District, Oswego, NY.

Source: Courtesy of Chalk & Wire Learning Assessment, Inc.

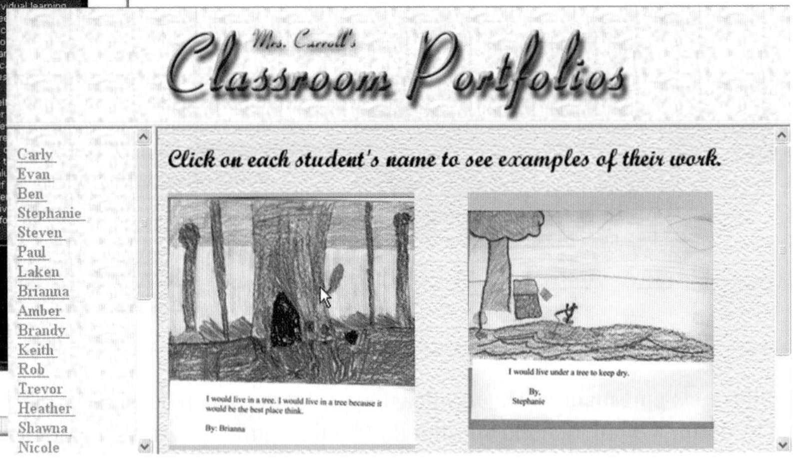

Source: From Oswego City School District web site, **www.oswego.org/staff/ccarroll/portfolio.** © 2004 Carol Carroll, Oswego City School District, Oswego, NY.

PEARSON myeducationkit™

Go to the *Assignments and Activities* section of Chapter 7 in MyEducationKit and complete the video activity entitled *Teachers Learning with Digital Portfolios.*

Copies of student work and its evaluation can then be organized according to the competencies it evidences. Over time, organizing and storing longitudinal records in this manner offers a cumulative view of student achievement over the course of an academic year or from year to year.

Observations

Portfolio assessment software often includes a way to record observations of student behaviors and notations on academic progress. Using either standard or teacher-defined commentary, observation entries offer teachers an opportunity to record student evaluations and comments related to them.

Multimedia Samples

Many portfolio assessment software packages include the ability to record images and audio and video samplings of student works. Audio-clip recordings of students reading standard passages or a sample of a student-created PowerPoint presentation offers multimedia evidence of current student progress.

Customization

Because every school district has its own standards and assessment guidelines, most portfolio assessment software is customizable to address specific standards and to assess student work using the district's criteria. Legends identifying standards and assessment methods are often definable by teachers so that their grading and assessment notes match the requirements of their school or district.

Hyperlinks

Some portfolio assessment software provides the capability of creating links that can be used to navigate the electronic portfolio of a student's work. Often related to standards, benchmarks, or competencies, these links offer an accurate and holistic picture of a student's achievement relative to target achievement. Hyperlinks also offer an intuitive and easy-to-use method for examining a portfolio's contents.

Electronic portfolio assessment software may be dedicated software designed specifically to create e-portfolios, online software, or multipurpose software adapted to creating portfolios.

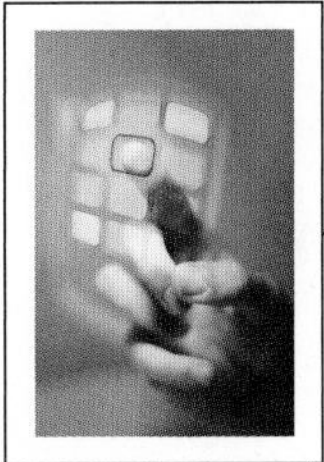

HANDS ON LEARNING

Electronic portfolios enable you to capture and present student work for a more authentic and holistic assessment of progress and achievement. Visit at least three electronic portfolio web sites, including an e-portfolio software vendor web site, a publication about electronic portfolios in the classroom, and a web site presenting samples of student portfolios in K–12 classrooms. After visiting the sites and becoming more familiar with the use of electronic portfolios, create an e-portfolio template using the administrative software of your choice. The template should be designed to assist you in presenting and sharing your future students' work. Be prepared to demonstrate and share your template with your peers.

Evaluating and Selecting Management Software

School or districtwide management software may be custom tailored to meet the needs of the district. Educators' interaction with this type of districtwide software may be limited to attending the necessary training sessions to ensure that they know how to use the software effectively. Classroom management software, however, requires careful review and evaluation on the part of the teachers who will be using it. Some classroom management systems are offered as freeware or shareware from the Internet or other software sources. Others may be inexpensive packages available to educators who are using a vendor's other software titles. Still others may be substantial and expensive comprehensive classroom management solutions. Although it is tempting to decide quickly to select freeware or shareware rather than the expensive software, there is a longer-term investment that must be considered. Whichever software is selected, educators must spend precious time learning to use it and entering data into it. In addition to this initial time investment, once student records are stored in a particular software format, the format may be difficult to change. If, after the initial selection of management software, an educator decides that the program does not have all of the desired components, changing to another software package may require reentering a great deal of data. Thus, even more time is invested. As with all software acquisitions, it is important to make a careful and thoughtful selection at the onset. The Classroom Management Software Evaluation Rubric will help you evaluate and choose the most appropriate classroom management software.

PEARSON **myeducationkit**™

For additional information about portfolios, go the MyEducationKit, select *Resources* and then *Preparing a Portfolio.*

Software, Teaching, and Learning: A Practical Approach

To end this discussion of administrative software, let us return to the hypothetical situation presented in the chapter preview. Imagine that your school district has decided to make a major technology initiative for the twenty-first century. As a result, you have just been given five new computer systems for use in your classroom. The computer support department tells you that you have a software budget with which you can augment the collection of

Classroom Management Software Evaluation **Rubric**

SOFTWARE:
DESCRIPTION:
VENDOR: COST:
NOTES ON USE:

To help you determine the value of a piece of classroom management software that you want to evaluate, please rate the features listed below. Next to each of the items in the rubric, check the box that best reflects your opinion.

EVALUATION CRITERIA

SOFTWARE FEATURE	1 Poor	2 Below Average	3 Average	4 Above Average	5 Excellent
Installation Instructions	☐ Minimal or missing installation instructions	☐ Instructions poorly written and somewhat difficult to follow	☐ Instructions fairly clear and complete	☐ Clear and user-friendly written instructions	☐ Step-by-step installation instructions appear when the CD is inserted
Site Licensing Provisions	☐ No licensing available	☐ Somewhat expensive and/or limited site licensing	☐ Site licensing available at reasonable cost	☐ Low licensing rates for educators	☐ Multiple educators may use without paying a fee
Technical Support	☐ No local or toll-free telephone support available	☐ No local support; phone support available for an hourly fee	☐ Local support and phone support available for modest fees	☐ Local tech help available for modest fee; no-charge phone support	☐ Local help and toll-free support readily available at no charge
Ease of Updates	☐ No provisions for updates	☐ Must purchase new versions; most data will transfer to new version	☐ Updates for less than cost of new versions; data transferrable	☐ Minimal fee for updates; data fully compatible	☐ Free updates available online; seamless transfer of data
Tutorials	☐ No tutorials provided	☐ Tutorials may be ordered for a fee	☐ Limited tutorial provided on CD or may be requested without charge	☐ Tutorials offered as an online option or on CD	☐ Extensive online and CD-based tutorials provided
Multiple Platforms	☐ Works on only one operating system	☐ Although purchased for one platform, versions for other platforms may be purchased	☐ Program will run on multiple operating systems; features may vary with platform	☐ May be used on multiple platforms; features similar although not identical	☐ May be used on multiple platforms with consistent features across platforms
Student Report Capabilities	☐ Can record and report out data only in form they were entered	☐ Reports can be modified so only the data are reported out	☐ Using templates, reports can be generated; minor modifications can be made	☐ Customizable reports and forms can be easily created and printed	☐ Data may be reported out in any format desired
Notation Capabilities	☐ No provision for notations	☐ Can attach brief notes on problems but can't add action taken at a later time	☐ Notes can be entered and added to later	☐ Data entry forms include provision for unlimited comments on the problem and the actions taken	☐ Call up record by name; click on problem type; appropriate report form appears automatically
Special Needs Report Capabilities	☐ No capability for notes or reports	☐ Notes limited to 10 words; may be reported out on templates provided	☐ Notes may be made up to 50 words and printed out; supplied templates may be modified by user	☐ Limit of 100 words; both templates and instructor-designed forms may be used for reports	☐ Unlimited notes may be made, and desired reports can be designed and printed out
Nonacademic Information Capabilities	☐ Cannot record or report any nonacademic data	☐ Limited provision to record and report nonacademic data in the same form they were entered	☐ Numerical and text data, up to 50 characters, can be entered and then selectively printed out	☐ Numerical and text data may be entered; multiple field sizes available; various templates for reporting	☐ Unlimited data entry capabilities; customizable reports can be printed as desired

Go to the *Rubrics* section of Chapter 7 in MyEducationKit to download the *Classroom Management Software Evaluation Rubric* for your use.

district productivity software from which you can choose. Will you know what to do? Will you know which types of software will best accomplish the tasks you need to do? Will you know what to select to improve your productivity and make the administrative tasks associated with your job easier? Perhaps now you are better able to tackle these questions.

Still, even armed with an understanding of the role of administrative software in teaching and learning, with so many types of software packages available, a busy teacher is faced with a significant demand of time and energy just to explore and decide on software for his or her classroom. Indeed, the tasks of researching, evaluating, and mastering the features of even the most appropriate software packages might seem daunting, but they are entirely necessary. Technology resources are limited in most school districts. Wise use of these limited funds is a skill every computer-using teacher must master. From the discussion of software on the preceding pages, it is clear that administrative software can facilitate a wide variety of teaching tasks in the classroom, in your school, and across the district. It is up to you to become adequately familiar with this type of software to make the time you devote to administrative tasks as productive as possible.

In the next chapter, you will explore the other major category of software used by educators: academic software. There you will learn about the wide variety of academic software possibilities that you can integrate into teaching and into learning. For computer-using teachers, knowledge of administrative and academic software packages and the hardware necessary to run them is the foundation for the effective use of computers in teaching and learning. You are well on your way toward establishing the firm foundation you will need when you teach.

PEARSON myeducationkit™

To check your comprehension of the content covered in this chapter, go to the MyEducationKit for your book and complete the *Study Plan* for Chapter 7.

Key Terms

academic software, 169
administrative software, 169
classroom management software, 170
database management software, 180
electronic spreadsheet, 178
freeware, 171
integrated productivity packages, 187
macro, 176
presentation software, 184
productivity software, 170
school and classroom management software, 189
shareware, 171
site license, 172
templates, 175
what-if analysis, 179
wizard, 176
word-processing software, 172
WYSIWYG, 174

Activities

Student

CHAPTER REVIEW

1. How do academic and administrative software differ?
2. What is productivity software? How can it be adapted to benefit teaching and learning? Give specific examples.
3. Name three types of software that might be included in classroom management support software. Describe an application for each.
4. What is desktop publishing? How does it differ from word processing? How is it the same?
5. What are the key features of word-processing software? How might you use each in completing administrative tasks?
6. What are the advantages and features of electronic spreadsheets? How do you see them as a benefit in an educational environment?
7. Define database management software and describe how you might use it to help you in your teaching responsibilities. How might you construct a learning assignment for your students that uses this productivity tool?
8. What is presentation software?
9. Describe the difference between an integrated productivity package and a productivity suite.
10. Why is it important to take the time to fully evaluate administrative software before buying it?

WHAT DO YOU THINK?

1. List the top ten things you think you need to know about administrative software to be an effective computer-using educator. Why is each of these things critical in your technology decision making?
2. For most productivity software, many see the ability to save data in electronic format as a significant advantage over hard copy. Do you agree that this characteristic of productivity software is of value in education? Explain why or why not.
3. There is some concern over the use of database software for private student records. How might using a database management system make it easier to violate the privacy of student information? Do you think the benefits of such systems outweigh the risks? Explain your position.
4. Some teachers think that it is too much trouble to learn the administrative software packages that might assist them in completing their required paperwork. Others believe that the benefits in productivity and editability of records outweigh the effort it takes to master the programs. What do you think?

LEARNING TOGETHER!

The following activities are designed for learning groups of three to five students.

1. Assume that you and your learning group make up the technology committee for your school. The committee has been assigned the task of deciding whether to upgrade or change the productivity software application suite your school has used over the past two years. Create a list of all of the issues that must be considered before making this decision. Then itemize the list and weigh each item in terms of its priority in importance to teaching and learning. Finally, describe the process you would go through to use the list and make your software decision.
2. Have each member of your learning group interview a teacher who uses any of the four major types of productivity software. Ask the teacher how he or she uses the software to help perform teacher management tasks and how he or she uses it to help children learn. Compare the interview responses with those of the other members of your group. Be prepared to share what you have learned with your peers.
3. You and your group members are team-teaching a science unit on climate to the grade level of your choice. Describe how you might integrate each of the four main types of productivity software into your unit. Create an instructional design, using the dynamic instructional design model you learned in Chapter 3, that articulates your unit.

TEACHING WITH TECHNOLOGY
INTEGRATION IDEAS WEB QUEST

As you become familiar with the administrative software that teachers use, it is useful to examine how teachers are applying this diverse group of software packages to support the many administrative tasks teachers are expected to complete as well as repurposing the software to support instruction. Let's take a look at some specific ways in which teachers are using administrative software.

ACTIVITY: Explore the links that you feel might be useful ways to use administrative software when you teach. Select the software package you feel would be of greatest interest to you and find two additional examples on the web showing how teachers can use this software in addressing administrative tasks or in support of instruction. Write a one-page summary of your web quest that includes (1) the links you used and the integration ideas you found and (2) an idea of your own of how you will utilize the software.

Integrating Database Software into Science

"The Wave of Spring" is a science lesson that guides students in creating a database that reports on their observations of when tulips bloom at locations around the world. This is a year-long project that involves students from Palo Alto, California, in communicating with fellow students in Europe and middle Tennessee. From these data, they track the arrival of spring around the world. Visit **www97.intel.com/en/ProjectDesign/UnitPlanIndex/WaveOfSpring.**

Integrating Presentation Software into Math

"The Stock Market" is a lesson plan that gives each group of students $1,000 to spend on the market but in a competitive setting. Each group competes with the other groups to determine who will gain the most from their investments. Whether they win by making the most money or lose, each group prepares a PowerPoint presentation to represent their buying and selling strategies. Go to **www.lessonplanspage.com/printables/PMathSSLACITheStockMarketGame6.htm.**

Integrating Word Processing into Social Studies

This lesson plan provided through the Microsoft Education web site has students discovering a Mayan village through a variety of research media, both online and offline. Students then prepare a word-processed report that analyzes, summarizes, and explains information they discover. Microsoft lesson plans provide all the resources needed to carry out the lesson, including downloadable directions that can be used or adapted. Visit **http://www.microsoft.com/education/lessonplans/mayanvillage.mspx.**

Using Productivity Software in the Classroom

Education World's Techtorials archive offers lessons and ideas for innovative uses for a variety of productivity software packages. Applications of software range from administrative uses, such as creating a gradebook with Excel or creating a blogging platform, to student uses, such as making trading cards with Word or using PowerPoint to create audio books. For more ideas, visit **http://www.educationworld.com/atech/archives/techtorials.shtml.**

interchapter 7

Administrative Software Summary

In addition to the traditional productivity software suites such as Microsoft Office, many dedicated administrative software packages have been created to help teachers manage their classrooms and districts manage their schools. Numerous web sites offer summaries and reviews of these software packages. The list of software below demonstrates the diversity and capability of some of the many unique types of administrative software you might find available in your classroom and in your school. This is just a small sample of the kinds of software you can find to help you with your administrative tasks. Many alternative software packages exist in each category of use, and it can therefore be difficult to decide which one to buy. When selecting administrative software, it is a good idea to use an evaluation tool such as the rubric presented in this chapter.

USE	NAME	VENDOR	DESCRIPTION
Assessment	Exam View	eInstruction	Exam View Assessment software helps teachers to administer and manage assessments easily. It offers a complete toolset to build comprehensive tests, administer them, and then analyze the results. This assessment software offers a variety of question formats, links to test banks, and administration both via hard copy and across a network; it even integrates student response clickers and scanners. Testing reports are comprehensive for detailed analysis of individual and class results.
Classroom Management	NetOp School	Cross Tec Corp.	NetOp School allows a teacher using a classroom network to broadcast his or her screen, multimedia files, or any student's screen to everyone on the network; it allows teachers to record and play back instructional screen sessions for later review, mark up or magnify a portion of the featured screen to highlight a lesson, monitor students as they work, restrict the use of applications and web sites, and interact with students as a group or one-on-one. The software gives teachers total management of their classroom network.
Curriculum Management	Curriculum Mapper	Collaborative Learning, Inc.	This software enables teachers and administrators to identify standards, analyze when standards are being addressed, and show exactly what is being covered and when. It also provides a venue for teacher collaboration and identification of resource needs and parental communication.

USE	NAME	VENDOR	DESCRIPTION
District Management	Active Classroom	C2T2 Educational Systems	This web-based system allows teachers to align with state standards and implement their lesson plans and deliver them to students online. Both parents and students have access to the lessons. Capabilities include developing lessons, uploading files, posting homework and calendars, corresponding with students and parents, managing grades, and creating forums for open discussion.
Grading	Easy Grade Pro	Orbis	This software lets teachers record all of their classes' work, create their own custom grading system, create seating and assignment charts, record attendance, print out reports in multiple formats, and import and export data to the school network. It also provides summaries of student results to help a teacher analyze lesson effectiveness.
School Management	Infosnap Online School Forms	Infosnap, Inc.	This software will change any school form to an online form and then enable the data entered to be exported to database management software for easy use.
Worksheet Creation	Essential Teacher Tools	Tom Snyder Productions	This multipurpose worksheet software helps teachers to create a variety of engaging student activities such as worksheets, puzzles, flash cards, and tests. A teacher enters the content once, and it can be used to create many types of worksheets.

CHAPTER 8

Academic Software

Shutterstock

CHAPTER OVERVIEW

This chapter addresses these ISTE National Educational Technology Standards:
- NETS•T Standard 1
- NETS•T Standard 2
- NETS•S Standard 1
- NETS•S Standard 6

- **Academic Software**
- **Software Repurposed for Education**
- **Software Designed for Education**
- **Academic Software in Teaching and Learning**

In Chapter 7, you explored the advantages of using administrative software as a tool to make you more productive as a teacher. This chapter presents the other category of software available to educators: academic software. Academic software enriches the teaching and learning process. Carefully selected by the teacher, academic software can significantly enhance a lesson and address the needs of learners.

As you learned in Chapter 3, when you design instruction, you must articulate your objectives carefully and then select the appropriate methods and media to support those objectives. Even in a one-computer classroom, the many types of academic software that are available to educators today offer a broad array of new and exciting media choices. You might decide to have students research a topic using a multimedia encyclopedia that appeals to a wide variety of learning styles. Or you might have cooperative learning groups experience discovery learning through a simulation on CD-ROM. Or you might simply give a child who needs additional practice with the content an opportunity for computer center time with math practice software that lets the child shoot down aliens bearing the correct answers to math problems on their ships. The choices are broad and appealing and can add visual, auditory, and kinesthetic interest to many lessons.

To be able to select the best academic software from the thousands of such packages, you need first to be aware of the choices available to you. In this chapter, you will explore the principal types of academic software and review a sampling of their application in the teaching and learning process.

In Chapter 8, you will:

- Explore the major categories of academic software and their application in teaching and learning
- Review a sampling of how academic software is used in different classrooms
- Investigate and use methods for reviewing and evaluating software so that your technology acquisitions will appropriately meet your needs

Academic Software

Academic software includes the wide variety of software packages that can be used to enrich the teaching and learning environment for both teachers and students. Academic software may include packages that help the teacher teach and those designed to help the learner acquire targeted competencies. A teacher needs to be aware of the many common categories of academic software to be able to select the best software to achieve his or her objectives. Table 8.1 lists the most common categories of academic software and their uses. Within each of these categories, there are literally hundreds of commercial, freeware, and shareware programs available to educators. As with administrative software, although the initial costs vary, the need to invest time in mastering, using, and supporting a software program does not. Educators need to be careful in selecting the software to which they commit themselves and their students.

In the remainder of this chapter, you will be introduced to and have the opportunity to explore fully the many types of academic software that will be available to you for use in your classroom. As you can see from the list in Table 8.1, the options are many. Taking the time now to explore what each type of academic software can do to help you teach and help your students learn will save you time, effort, and some of your classroom budget when you teach.

PEARSON myeducationkit

Go to the *Assignments and Activities* section of Chapter 8 in MyEducationKit and complete the video activity entitled *Technology Support for Teachers*.

Software Repurposed for Education

Productivity software has made business more efficient and aided educators in completing administrative tasks. Many other types of application software help individuals address their personal tasks. However, repurposed for academic tasks, these same software packages have significant potential for supporting teaching and learning. Presentation software can easily make simple yet effective flash cards or tutorials. Desktop publishing software can offer

TABLE 8.1 Academic Software Summary

SOFTWARE TYPE	APPLICATION TO TEACHING AND LEARNING
DESKTOP PUBLISHING 	Desktop publishing software enables teachers to create professional-looking newsletters, flyers, transparencies, and other printed media. Microsoft product shot reprinted with permission from Microsoft Corporation.
GRAPHICS 	Graphics software enables teachers and students to support teaching and learning through visuals created or enhanced electronically. Courtesy of Corel Corporation
REFERENCE 	Reference software, usually on CD-ROMs, includes visual- and sound-enhanced, hyperlinked electronic resources, such as dictionaries, encyclopedias, and atlases. Microsoft product shot reprinted with permission from Microsoft Corporation.
TUTORIALS AND DRILL-AND-PRACTICE 	Tutorials and drill-and-practice software give students one-on-one, usually interactive reviews of target concepts. Courtesy of Laureate Learning System, Inc.
EDUCATIONAL GAMES 	Games present content in a format that engages the learner while providing practice. Courtesy of Knowledge Adventure, Inc.
SIMULATIONS 	Simulations provide students an opportunity to interact with model environments that promote discovery learning. © 2006 Riverdeep Interactive Learning Limited

Continued

AUTHORING SYSTEMS 	Hypermedia and web authoring systems enable teachers to create their own hypermedia tutorials and web pages to support their curriculum.
SPECIAL NEEDS 	Software for students with special needs assists them in multiple ways, from reading screens to enlarging pointers, in order to help them function effectively in school. Courtesy of Dolphin Computer Access
INTEGRATED LEARNING SYSTEMS  SuccessMaker® ENTERPRISE	Combining classroom management tools with tutorial software designed to reinforce target objectives, ILS software provides an integrated package of resources. Microsoft product shot reprinted with permission from Microsoft Corporation

students a way to self-publish a story or report. Repurposing software for academic purposes offers the creative educator numerous opportunities to support teaching and learning using a wide variety of applications. Some of the most common of these are described below.

Desktop Publishing Software

Desktop publishing software produces professional-looking hard-copy output.

Originally written to make the work of manual layout and design in the publishing business easier, **desktop publishing software** has brought to the average computer-using educator the ability to create professional-looking printed or electronic pages. Sophisticated documents can be created that include text, graphics, digital pictures, stylized headlines, and professionally prepared design elements. These elements can then be arranged and manipulated on a page until the best possible page layout is achieved (see Figure 8.1).

At myeducationkit.com, you will find a tutorial for Microsoft Publisher where you can learn and practice the skills you need to effectively use the software to create handouts, fliers, and more.

Publishing software is a versatile tool for educators. With it, an educator can easily design and print

- Customized transparency masters to illustrate a critical concept
- Customized student worksheets with clip art or digital pictures
- Posters and signs for the classroom, media center, or school
- Class or school newsletters
- Customized booklets for reading, coloring, or reinforcing concepts
- Customized award certificates

Standard

Learning about academic software for the classroom will help you address

NETS•T STANDARD 1:

FACILITATE AND INSPIRE STUDENT LEARNING AND CREATIVITY Teachers use their knowledge of subject matter, teaching and learning, and technology to facilitate experiences that advance student learning, creativity, and innovation in both face-to-face and virtual environments.

FIGURE 8.1

An Example of Desktop Publishing Software

Microsoft Publisher is an easy-to-use DTP program that creates professional-looking publications.

Microsoft Publisher® is a registered trademark of Microsoft Corporation.

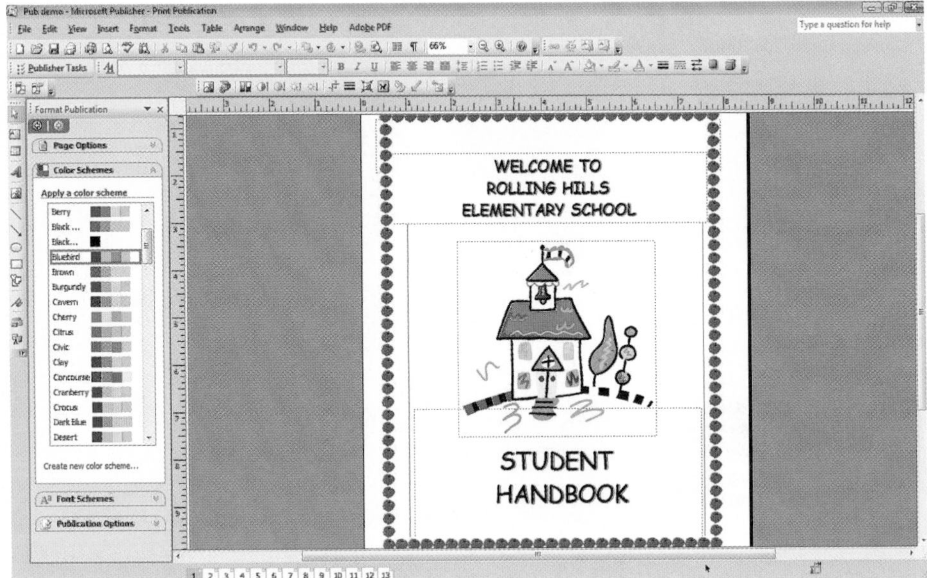

- Flash cards and sight-word cards
- Custom instructional packets for review of targeted competencies

In students' hands, desktop publishing software can be used to

- Create cards and letters to give to parents
- Produce hard-copy enhancements to group projects
- Write up a field trip report
- Make classroom or school banners
- Create homework calendars and assignment tracking sheets
- Lay out school yearbooks

Many popular desktop publishing software packages include a web site authoring component. With this feature, web pages can be laid out using the same tools and skills that it takes to create a print document. Then, with a built-in conversion component, the software automatically converts the elements of the laid-out page into one that can be viewed on the World Wide Web with any suitable browser. Thus, teachers or their students can very easily create and maintain a very sophisticated, attractive web site.

As you can see, desktop publishing software can be used to create a wide range of instructional materials, and neither teacher nor students need to be computer experts to create attractive and useful materials. To maximize effectiveness, materials created with desktop publishing software should follow some general design suggestions. Elements of effective visuals will be more extensively explored in Chapter 11, but for the purposes of desktop publishing, educators should stay mindful of the design principles demonstrated in Figure 8.2.

At myeducationkit.com, you will find hands-on Microsoft Publisher activities that demonstrate good visual design as well as the features of desktop publishing software. Try these activities to gain skill in using this useful educational software tool.

PEARSON myeducationkit™

To learn more about desktop publishing, go to the *Video Tutorials* section of Chapter 8 in MyEducationKit and select *Microsoft Publisher.*

Graphics Software

Digital visual images, whether drawings, photos, or graphs, are typically referred to as graphics. **Graphics software,** then, is the broad category of software that can be used to create, edit, or enhance digital images. Different types of graphics software perform different

FIGURE 8.2

Design Principles in Desktop Publishing

Whether publishing web pages or creating flyers, always follow the principles of good design. Contrast the balanced design of the web page on the left with the poor design of the flyer on the right. Which is more likely to effectively communicate information?

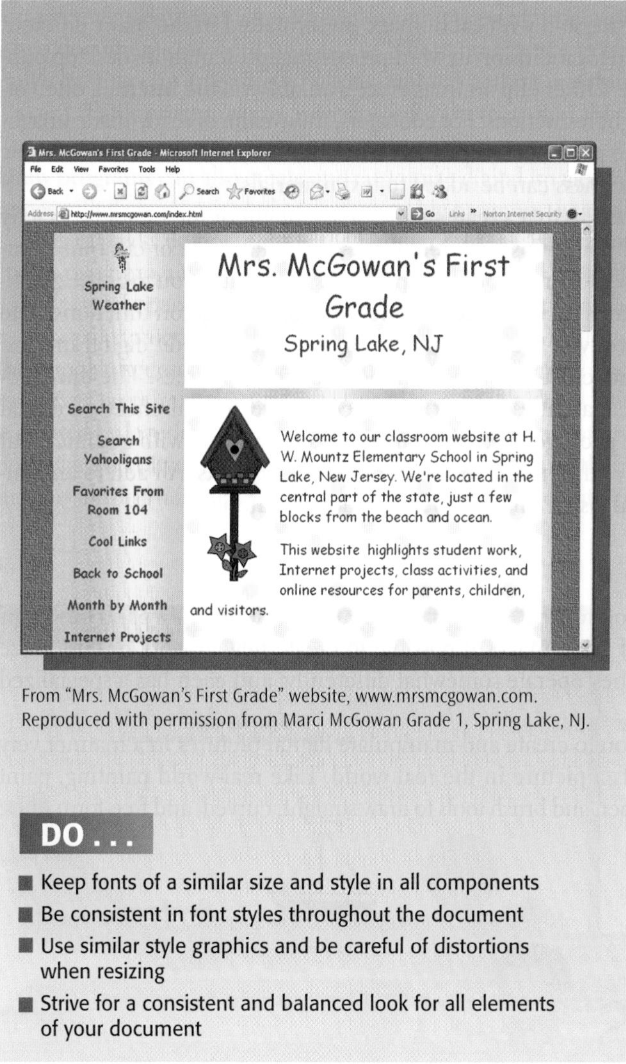

From "Mrs. McGowan's First Grade" website, www.mrsmcgowan.com. Reproduced with permission from Marci McGowan Grade 1, Spring Lake, NJ.

DO . . .

- Keep fonts of a similar size and style in all components
- Be consistent in font styles throughout the document
- Use similar style graphics and be careful of distortions when resizing
- Strive for a consistent and balanced look for all elements of your document

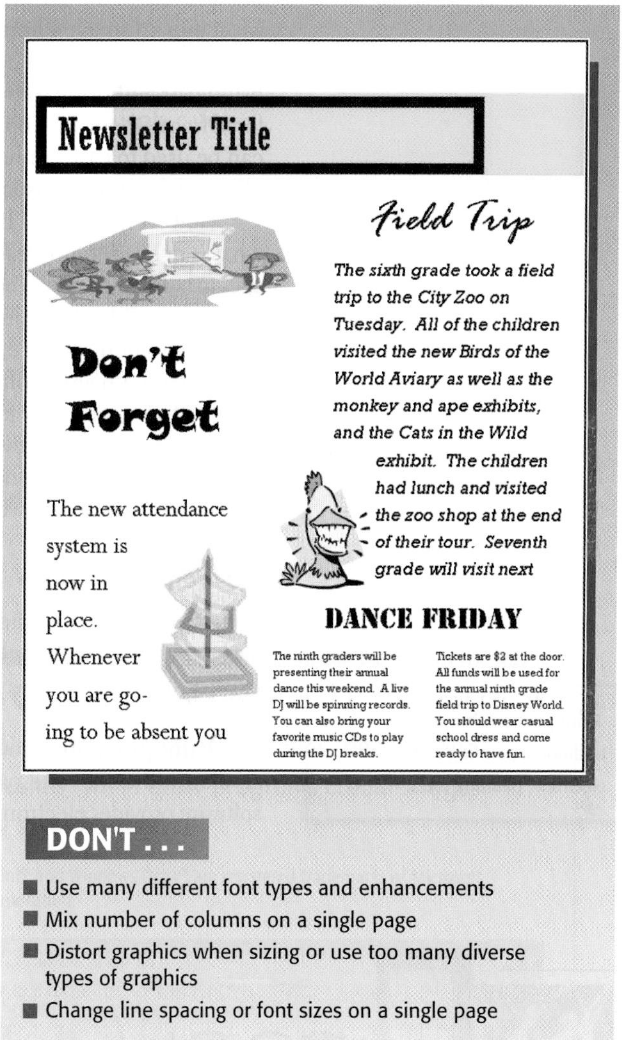

DON'T . . .

- Use many different font types and enhancements
- Mix number of columns on a single page
- Distort graphics when sizing or use too many diverse types of graphics
- Change line spacing or font sizes on a single page

functions and have different capabilities, as you will see next, but all can help you add digital visuals to clarify and enhance instruction.

Graphics software also includes packaged collections of prepared graphics that are usually organized into libraries of images. Such collections may include drawings, photos, and even animated graphics. The images included in these graphics libraries are organized so that you can easily preview the images, copy them, and then paste them into other applications. You may choose to paste them directly into a document you create with desktop publishing software, or you can paste them into other graphics software to further edit the images before using them. In either case, these collections offer a valuable alternative to creating visual images from scratch.

transparencies or graphic elements for presentation with a draw program even if they do not have extensive art skills. For those who are artists, paint programs provide the electronic means to create editable artwork for inclusion in materials. For students, drawing software provides limitless tools to create or edit just the right picture for their oral report, an electronic card to send to their parents, or a page for their class web site.

Further, both types of software are capable of editing existing clip art or graphics, although with different sets of tools. Using such software, teachers can enhance a digital image by highlighting targeted areas for emphasis or adding text annotation to a graphic's components. Students can create a collage of selected clip art to add interest and dimension to their work. Draw and paint programs can range widely in price and capabilities, but even the easiest and most inexpensive of these software packages can visually enhance all types of instructional materials.

Imaging Software

Imaging software generally refers to the family of software packages that are used with scanners to convert hard-copy images to digital images. Typically, scanners are bundled with imaging software that is compatible with their hardware. All imaging software is capable of converting a hard-copy page of text or graphics to a digital graphic (Figure 8.4). This graphic can then be treated like any other digital image. A photograph of a flower could be scanned with imaging software and saved as a digital graphic; it could then be opened in a drawing program so that arrows and text enhancements could be added to label the image. In this way you can add instructional elements to any image.

Some imaging software is capable of not only converting hard copy into graphic elements but also converting pages of text into pages of electronic text that can be manipulated by a word processor. Hard-copy versions of worksheets or tests can be digitized and saved as

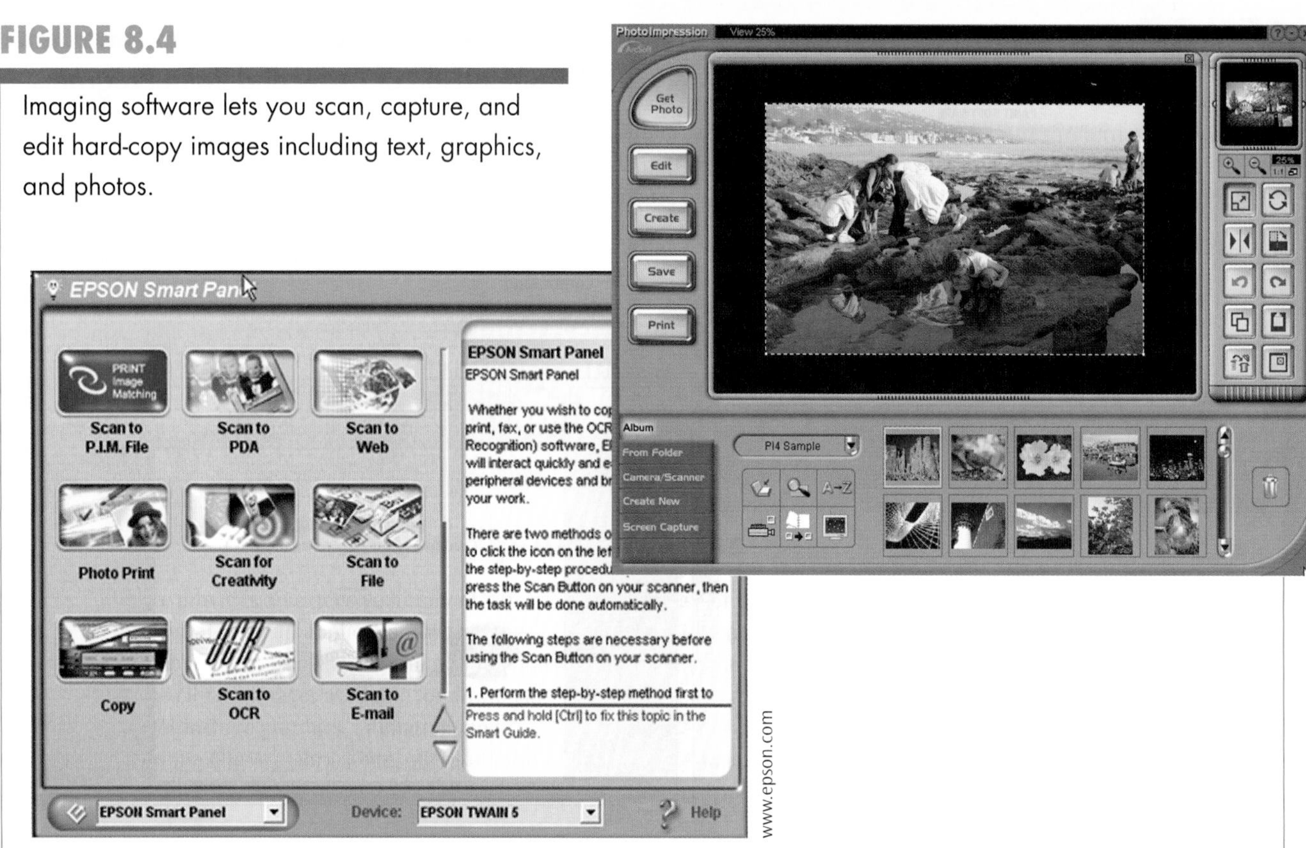

FIGURE 8.4

Imaging software lets you scan, capture, and edit hard-copy images including text, graphics, and photos.

word-processed documents. They can then be updated, edited, or entirely repurposed for other instructional activities. This feature found in some imaging software packages can add a valuable tool for busy educators while adding very little additional cost to the software.

Editing Software

Editing, the third category of graphics software that works with digital images, provides the tools to alter and enhance images. Whether the images are digital photographs, clip art, scanned images, or images you have created, **editing software** allows you to change the image.

Some draw and paint software packages include an import feature that allows you to bring in an image created or saved outside of that package. The image may be a digital photo, a scanned image, clip art, or even something saved from the Internet. Once imported, the software may then let you alter the image using the same tools that are available to alter images you create. The ability to import software for further editing is a useful feature to look for when selecting draw and paint software.

Imaging software more typically offers the capability of in-depth editing of digital images, whether acquired through scanning or digital photography. This type of imaging/editing software usually includes a variety of photo-styling and special effects software packages that range in price and capability from those used at home to the powerful packages that are used to create the dramatic digital special effects seen on television and in films. Many medium-priced programs allow you to edit images in unusual ways, ranging from blending one image into another to creating animations that can be included in presentation and multimedia files. These effects add significant interest and appeal but may require a substantial investment in time.

For educators, imaging and editing software adds an element of control over the quality of images produced by digital photography or via scanning. Photo-styling software can typically alter the lighting, contrast, color intensity, and cropping of a digital image (see Figure 8.5). Many can also add corrections to an image, such as correcting "red-eye" in

PEARSON **myeducationkit**™

To learn more about software tools and digital imaging, go to the *Video Tutorials* section of Chapter 8 in MyEducationKit and select *Digital Imaging*.

FIGURE 8.5

Using a Photo-Styling Program

Photo-styling software lets you edit, alter, enhance, or add special effects to digital or scanned images and photos.

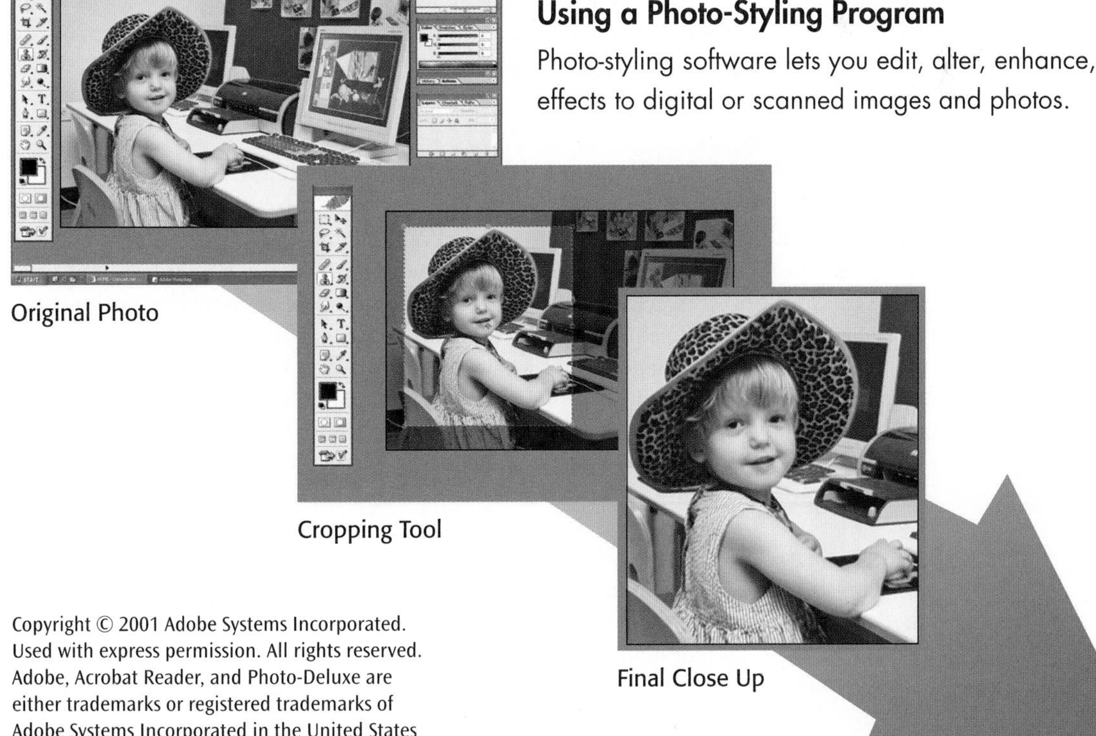

pictures of animals and people. Still others offer some special effects capabilities such as blurring parts of the image or making it into a mosaic display.

For those who need advanced special effects features to add artistic elements, special effects software packages are available that enable all types of enhancements, from morphing, in which one image appears to melt into another, to altering images to appear as if they were created through a variety of different camera lenses. These more advanced styling features are particularly dramatic in multimedia displays, as they add interest to the multisensory elements included in that type of presentation.

Reference Software

CD-ROM and online reference software hyperlinks multimedia data.

Reference software, digital versions of volumes of reference materials, can now be easily stored on a single compact disc or made available online. Using digital reference software, students can jump to any points of information. With a simple point and click on an interactive link, a student or teacher can follow an idea and questions that emerge from exploring that idea in whatever order he or she chooses. In addition, because it is just as simple to store digital images, sounds, and video as it is to store text, reference material that was once confined to text with only an occasional static illustration can become dazzling and informative multimedia information. The potential of these additional types of digital information for learners of different modalities is clear.

These types of digital enhancements, combined with the compact and easy-to-use storage media offered by CD-ROMs, have led to the creation of a variety of new educational reference software tools. These broad categories of CD-ROM-based reference programs and their applications are summarized in Table 8.2. Many of these tools are also available in online formats.

The wide variety of software manufacturers that produce digital reference leads to great variability in the features in any one piece of software. Some programs have extensive multimedia components; in others, text is dominant. Some include facilities for printing the text and graphics elements; others may not. Because of the variety in this type of software, it is important for educators to carefully review and evaluate the capabilities of this type of software before investing in it. The academic software evaluation rubric can be a valuable tool for effective software decision making. This rubric or one like it should be used before making any academic software purchases.

Authoring Systems

As you learned from Chapter 3, the first step in effective instruction is to analyze your learners carefully so that you can adjust instruction to their needs. Even when educators teach at the same grade level or the same course content, good instruction is bound to vary as the result of its responsiveness to the unique group of learners being addressed. For that reason, some educators are reluctant to use commercially produced instructional software simply because it does not fit well enough with their particular students or with their lesson plans and objectives. Software developers, mindful of these concerns, have developed a class of academic software that allows the educator to create custom computer-enhanced lessons of all sorts. This category of academic software is known collectively as **authoring systems.**

Authoring systems vary greatly in their interface format, their capabilities, the platform on which they run, and the hardware requirements necessary to run them. Some authoring systems produce multimedia tutorials that can be used only on the Web, while others run on stand-alone computers. Regardless of the authoring software chosen, they can do a very good job of helping a teacher create effective computer-based multimedia lessons. However, to further examine the usefulness of these programs, let's look at some examples of the levels of authoring systems available to better understand which might fit your potential needs.

TABLE 8.2 Reference Software Summary

SOFTWARE TYPE	FEATURES	APPLICATION TO TEACHING AND LEARNING TASKS
ENCYCLOPEDIAS 	• Easy-to-use hypermedia connections to browse cross-referenced items • Can include text, graphics, animation, and audio and video clips to support information • Some support note taking on content Courtesy of Dorling Kindersley	• Enables teacher and student research in all content areas • Interactive format promotes discovery learning • Presentation can help meet multiple learning styles
ATLASES 	• Hypermedia connections allow user to move between countries and features by pointing and clicking • Often includes satellite images from NASA to present topographical features • Can include text, graphics, animation, and audio and video clips to support information Courtesy of GSP, Ltd.	• Some support note taking on content • Enables teacher and student examination of global geography • Interactive format promotes discovery learning • Presentation can help meet multiple learning styles
GRAMMAR TOOLS 	• Can include a thesaurus and grammar checker • Provides suggestions for alternative words or grammatical structures from which the writer can choose Courtesy of Laser Publishing Group	• Provides students support for editing their work • Interactive format promotes discovery learning • Presentation can help meet multiple learning styles
DICTIONARIES 	• Provides quick search for target words • Can include text, graphics, animation, and audio and video clips to support definitions Courtesy of Merriam-Webster	• Provides students support for vocabulary • Interactive format promotes discovery learning • Presentation can help meet multiple learning styles

Hypermedia Authoring Systems

Hypermedia authoring tools are available in a variety of levels of sophistication. Most include all the components necessary to create full multimedia lessons. **Hypermedia software** is an adaptation of multimedia in that it not only uses multiple media, it also organizes information such that the student can make hyperjumps, that is, student-driven connections in either linear or nonlinear sequences, from and to different components of the instructional content. Hypermedia programming more closely resembles the way we think and learn than does linear programming.

Available for both Macintosh computers and PCs, hypermedia authoring systems let educators or their students create a series of screens or slides that can contain text, graphics, sound, animation, and/or short video clips. Together, these are ordered to create a file that will teach the lesson at hand. Teachers can then display the completed hypermedia lesson on a computer monitor, on a large-screen TV monitor, or via an LCD projector and projection screen. Students can also use the customized lesson individually or in small groups

Authoring systems allow teachers to create multimedia lessons to fully engage learners by addressing diverse learning styles through interactive experiences.

Harry Sieplinga

to review the content. Since the material is presented via multiple modalities and requires active participation, it is especially effective in reaching and engaging learners.

Some hypermedia authoring software suites are designed to create very sophisticated, commercial-grade lessons. More common software, such as Microsoft's PowerPoint, has included hypermedia authoring as a function of the software. Whether sophisticated or an added feature, this tool in the hands of a creative educator can provide students with very targeted and effective instruction.

Web Authoring Systems

Some authoring systems are designed specifically to create lessons for presentation online. This class of software, known as web authoring systems, can assist you in creating multimedia web pages that can be linked to other pages within the lesson or to support sites elsewhere on the web (Figure 8.6).

Web authoring software shares many of the tools and features of hypermedia authoring software. Programs designed for creating web-based displays generate hypermedia that is saved in a unique format called Hyper Text Markup Language (HTML). **HTML** is the computer language that has been agreed upon for use on the Internet's World Wide Web

FIGURE 8.6

Office templates facilitate the creation of a web site by offering predetermined design choices.

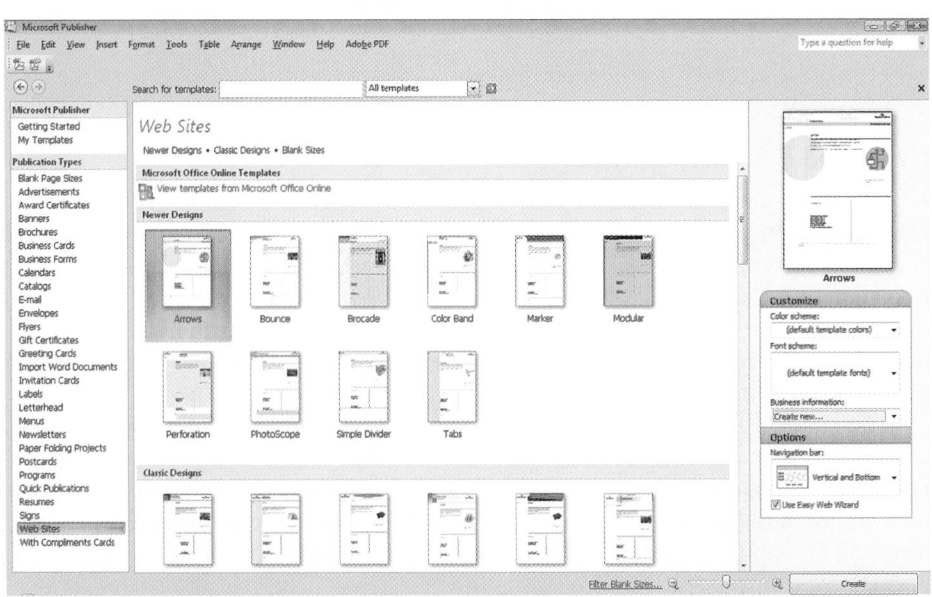

Microsoft product screenshot reprinted with permission of Microsoft Corporation.

sites. Internet browsers, that is, programs designed to translate HTML data into computer displays, are then used to view and navigate these types of hypermedia pages.

The demand for software to assist in the creation of web pages by educators and their students has created pressure on software vendors. For this reason, in addition to software that was specifically created to produce web pages, many software companies are adding an HTML conversion feature to their software. Most word processors include the ability to turn a word-processed page into an HTML page with just a click on the appropriate button or menu choice. However, the software that was originally designed to create web pages is typically much more sophisticated and full-featured than those that have simply added a conversion component.

Web authoring tools range from extremely sophisticated to relatively simple to use and from very expensive to free. Some Internet services that offer free web space to the public also provide free and easy-to-use web authoring tools. The web pages that can be developed with this wide variety of software vary just as significantly. High-end authoring packages are used to develop very sophisticated commercial web pages; freeware or shareware authoring packages can create very attractive personal home pages or whole web sites. Educators need to carefully review and evaluate their options before investing time in learning a web authoring tool and developing a web site.

Go to the *Assignments and Activities* section of Chapter 8 in MyEducationKit and complete the video activity entitled *Web Site Supports Learning*.

Using Authoring Systems

Regardless of the authoring tool selected, with training, both you and your students can use this software to create customized, targeted lessons. Teacher-made lessons allow you to create learning software that meets the specific lesson objectives identified in your instructional design. Such lessons can be used in large or small group presentations to present and demonstrate key content points. They can also be used with individual students for additional review and reinforcement of content or to study a missed lesson after an absence. Teacher-authored lessons can be specifically designed to present material consistent with identified student learning modalities and at content levels appropriate to those observed in any given class of students.

Teachers can use authoring tools to meet specific lesson objectives.

Software Designed for Education

Tutorials and Drill-and-Practice Software

Software designed to teach new content or reinforce a lesson can assist an educator in addressing learners' needs, particularly when time demands or the teacher–student ratio limits the teacher's ability to provide sufficient one-to-one interaction. This category of academic software can offer students opportunities to learn new content or provide additional practice to reinforce concepts already presented.

ISTE Standard

Learning about academic software for the classroom will help you address

NETS•T STANDARD 2:

DESIGN AND DEVELOP DIGITAL-AGE LEARNING EXPERIENCES AND ASSESSMENTS Teachers design, develop, and evaluate authentic learning experiences and assessments incorporating contemporary tools and resources to maximize content learning in context and to develop the knowledge, skills, and attitudes identified in the NETS•S.

Tutorials

Tutorial software presents new material, usually in a carefully orchestrated instructional sequence with frequent opportunities for practice and review. These software packages are self-contained lessons, often aligned with standards, and are designed and planned according to the principles of instructional design.

Tutorials may be primarily text or a combination of text and multimedia components, including graphics, animation, and audio and video clips. Some may have built-in classroom management components that track, record, and report individual student progress on each included lesson. All are interactive, in that the student must respond and interact for the tutorial to progress.

Tutorials can give the student control of the pace and, sometimes, the path of interaction.

Tutorials give the student control of the pace and often the path of instruction. Tutorials are limited by their inability to respond to students' questions or concerns outside their

Tutorial software presents and practices new concepts in a format that maintains learners' interest throughout the process.

Bill Aron/PhotoEdit

programming. Even the best-designed tutorial software may not be able to respond to the divergent thinking of many learners. For many users, tutorials seem limiting and potentially boring because of their rigidity in the presentation of topics. Still, a well-written tutorial that is programmed with multimedia components in the presentation of materials can be very useful for support or review of material or even as an additional strategy in the communication of content.

photos_alyson/Getty Images

Drill-and-practice software lets learners practice and review concepts as often and as long as they need to gain mastery.

Drill-and-Practice Software

Whereas tutorials may present new material, **drill-and-practice software** is designed to reinforce previously presented content. Drill-and-practice software is used to question learners on key content points, giving them the opportunity to practice their knowledge. This type of software provides instant feedback as to the correctness of a response. Some drill-and-practice software packages track correct answers and move the level of questioning to more complex content as the students' responses indicate increased mastery.

Drill-and-practice software, like tutorials, ranges from fairly simple text-based, flash-card-type software to complex and sophisticated multimedia software. Drill-and-practice software allows the student to control the pace of the interaction, but users typically cannot alter the path of the review until they have mastered each level. Unlike answering review questions or taking a pop quiz for content practice, using drill-and-practice software provides instant feedback, and it may respond with additional drills targeting diagnosed weaknesses.

Critics of this type of software refer to it as "drill-and-kill" software, expressing the notion that it can be a boring and passive learning experience. Indeed, some drill-and-practice software lacks quality and interest. Furthermore, if used for overly long periods of time or for too many review sessions, it does not stimulate learning or promote interest in the content practiced. However, well-constructed, multimedia-rich drill-and-practice software can provide valuable supplemental experiences and targeted feedback for learners. It can also provide excellent practice before formal evaluations and can be used as a diagnostic for teachers who are fine-tuning their classroom instruction. As with all software, it is critical that educators carefully evaluate the academic value of drill-and-practice software before acquiring it and using it in the classroom.

PEARSON myeducationkit™

Go to the *Assignments and Activities* section of Chapter 8 in MyEducationKit and complete the video activity entitled *Practicing Math and Social Studies Skills on the Computer*.

Educational Games

Educational games present and review instructional content in a game format. Content is repackaged so that it is furnished within the framework of a sequence of game rules and graphics (see Figure 8.7). Although educational games may present the same competencies that drill-and-practice or tutorial software presents, they are often better received by learners because the game component adds an element of interest and entertainment. Clearly, however, it is important to be sure the game elements do not overshadow the instructional elements.

Several broad categories of educational games are available to teachers who are interested in adding entertainment as an enhancement to the classroom, as shown in Table 8.3. Adventure games provide students the opportunity to solve mysteries and participate in educational adventures. An example of this type of game is the Carmen Sandiego adventure series. In this game series, students must have knowledge of a region or country to find the game's heroine. This educational game thus exercises social studies knowledge and critical-thinking skills while presenting the experience in an adventure game format.

A second category of educational games simulates traditional board or card games. These games typically require that the student respond with correct answers before advancing a game piece on a graphic of a board or playing a card in a virtual hand. This type of

FIGURE 8.7

Examples of Educational Game Software

Educational games present content in colorful and engaging formats.

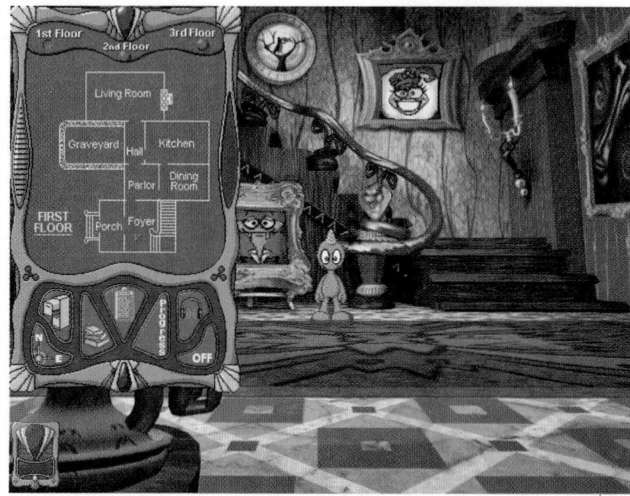

TABLE 8.3 Spotlight on Academic Games

TYPES OF GAMES	POTENTIAL BENEFITS	EXAMPLES OF GAMES	POTENTIAL CLASSROOM APPLICATIONS
ACTION	Exercises hand–eye coordination, reasoning, content practice	• Blaster series (Math, Reading, etc.) *Davidson* • Jump Start Series *Vivendi*	Content practice in a shoot-'em-up format
ADVENTURE	Promotes problem-solving skills through adventure scenarios and role playing	• Carmen Sandiego series *Broderbund* • Magic School Bus series *Scholastic*	Geography/social studies in mystery format Math, reading, science, and art skills
STRATEGY/SIMULATION	Exercises problem solving, decision making, critical thinking, and content	• SimCity *EA Games* • Biology Explorer *Riverdeep*	Civics/architecture/urban studies/social studies Anatomy, science
PUZZLES AND GAME CLASSIC	Reinforces and builds memory, logic, verbal, and planning skills	• Scrabble *Hasbro Interactive* • Zillions of Games *Zillions Development Corp.*	English and vocabulary review General knowledge

game superimposes content material on the traditional real-world game. Students must know how to play the traditional game to participate in the educational version.

Educational adaptations of television and popular video games can also add an element of "entertainment" to the classroom. Games that let students shoot down the right answer or race their virtual cars to the finish line by driving over the correct responses in the road are examples of video-game adaptations. Students enjoy the stimulating visuals and sound, practice eye–hand coordination, and review content simultaneously. Familiar and popular TV quiz shows have been adapted to software and can be used to review material preformatted into the software or added by the teacher. This category of educational games can add excitement and interest to content review.

Whether in the use of software games or a classroom game of hangman, gaming has been a widely accepted instructional strategy that has value in a classroom. As a reward for completing class assignments or as a replacement for other review strategies, playing educational games is a popular alternative for many educators. Clearly, it is important

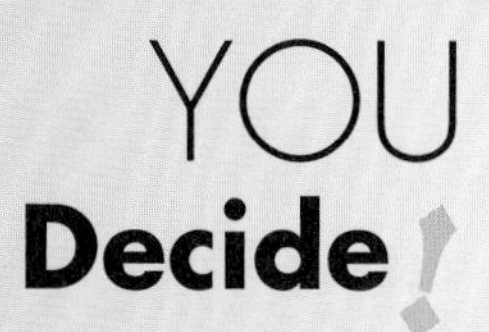

The role of educational games in the classroom is controversial. Some educators see value in the excitement and active learning a gaming environment presents. Others believe that the games detract from the implicit personal excitement and joy of learning. Still others object to educational games because they believe that students become too involved in the games themselves and lose focus on the content. Some believe that game experiences are unnecessarily cumbersome ways to review content. Do you think educational games are valid learning tools?

YES! Just because software is fun for the students doesn't mean that it isn't meaningful. Educational games require students to solve math problems, spell correctly, or answer content-oriented questions to advance and win the game. Students are therefore practicing the content while playing and are more motivated to do so than if they were doing yet another review worksheet. Educational games have a very valid place in the classroom to both motivate and review.

NO! Games may have some use as a reward for good classroom behavior for brief amounts of time, but that's about all. Nothing takes the place of direct teaching and good old-fashioned practice. Students need to learn to accept and find self-motivation for the work that they are required to do. Sugarcoating the work in a game format detracts from it and is a detriment to teaching students to get the job done. When they get into the workplace, they will be expected to learn without playing any games. Teachers are not doing them any favors including games in instruction.

Which view do you agree with? YOU DECIDE!

for you to carefully evaluate game activities in general and educational game software in particular for its suitability as a strategy to achieve your instructional objectives. Using the Academic Software Evaluation Rubric before incorporating educational game software into the classroom can help to ensure that classroom time is well spent.

Simulations let students take part in virtual experiences.

Simulations

Simulations are software packages that present the user with a model or situation in a computerized or virtual format. When using the software, learners interact with the simulation, and it responds to their actions. For example, flight simulator software mimics the conditions of flying various types of planes. As the user moves the mouse or press different keys assigned to represent speed, altitude, or various other aspects of the plane's conditions in its virtual sky, the screen displays a graphic of what one would see from the plane's cockpit. Conditions are thus simulated in response to user input.

In a more academic context, simulations are available that duplicate the conditions and appearance of a chemistry lab so that students can mix and heat virtual chemicals and see the results without having to deal with the real substances. Or students can dissect a virtual frog or examine parts of the human body and see how each individual component works. Social science simulations might allow students to make decisions for virtual civilizations and then watch their impact on the social order and on the individuals within that society.

Whereas tutorials and drill-and-practice software provide very structured content environments, simulations offer the student opportunities to interact with the content and to participate in discovery learning. Simulations can time-shift models by slowing processes down or by speeding up the impact of student-directed changes. They can also provide safe versions of what would be dangerous experiments in the real world.

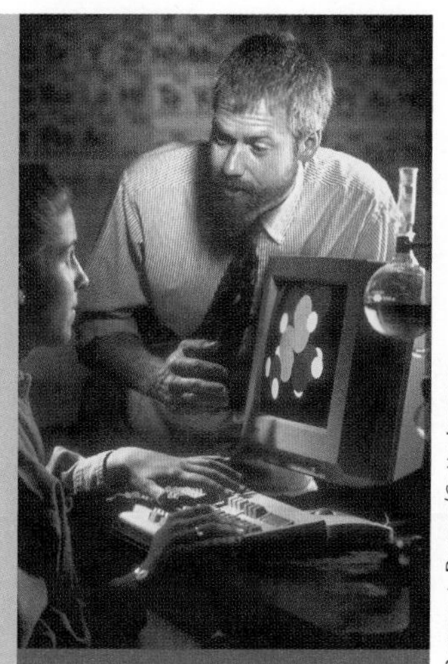

Barros + Barros/Getty Images

Simulations allow students to virtually manipulate models and situations safely in the classroom.

Academic Software Evaluation **Rubric**

SOFTWARE:

DESCRIPTION:

VENDOR: **COST:**

NOTES ON USE:

Please rate the features below for each piece of software. Next to each of the items in the rubric, check the box that best reflects your opinion.

EVALUATION CRITERIA

SOFTWARE FEATURE	1 Poor	2 Below Average	3 Average	4 Above Average	5 Excellent
Documentation	☐ Documentation is excessively technical and/or difficult to follow	☐ Documentation is generally understandable but not very user-friendly	☐ Documentation is easy to follow and understand; includes all necessary components	☐ Clear documentation that is logical and easy to follow	☐ Very clear, easy-to-read, logical, and complete documentation
Site License	☐ No licensing available	☐ Site licenses are available but limited or expensive options	☐ Site licensing available at reasonable cost	☐ Special, low site licensing pricing for education	☐ Educators may use for free without a site license
Installation	☐ Complex to install; poor installation instructions	☐ Installation somewhat difficult; instructions minimal	☐ Installation process typical; instructions fairly clear and complete	☐ Easy to install; clear, easy-to-understand instructions	☐ Self-installing; step-by-step installation included
Technical Support	☐ No toll-free telephone support available	☐ No local support; phone support available for an hourly fee	☐ Local support and phone support available for modest fee	☐ Local tech help available for modest fee; no-charge phone support	☐ Local help and toll-free support readily available at no charge
Help Features	☐ No online or text-based help available	☐ A Read-Me text file is included; no online help	☐ Both online and text help available on CD	☐ Online help is context-sensitive and provides clear assistance; text included	☐ Automatic online help available for every feature; supplementary text help included
Grade Level	☐ Not suitable for intended grade level	☐ Some features unsuitable for intended grade level	☐ Majority of features suitable for intended grade level	☐ Most features appropriate and suitable for intended grade level	☐ All features both suitable and appropriate for grade level
Standards	☐ Does not address target standards	☐ Few standards addressed; many ignored	☐ A majority of the standards are addressed	☐ Most of the desired standards are addressed	☐ All of the target standards and others are addressed
Active Learning	☐ Interaction is passive; no active learning encouraged	☐ Interaction mostly passive; a few active learning opportunities included	☐ Interaction offers average active learning opportunities; some activities too passive	☐ Good active interaction provided through a majority of the software	☐ Students are actively engaged during all components of software
Save Features	☐ Students cannot interrupt and save work	☐ Student work can be saved on an external disk, but it cannot be reused	☐ Students may save their work to continue working on it in the future	☐ Automatically saves the student's work when the program is closed	☐ Both automatically and manually, student's work can be saved and restarted at the same point later
Hardware Compatibility	☐ Works on relatively few available computers; requires additional hardware	☐ Works on several machines; requires upgrades to some available computers	☐ Will work on most machines with minimal or no hardware upgrades or additions	☐ Works on most available machines without hardware upgrades or additions	☐ Works on all machines available without hardware upgrades or additions
Cost	☐ High cost relative to features	☐ Somewhat expensive relative to features	☐ Average cost for features offered	☐ Reasonably priced with numerous features for the cost	☐ Special low pricing for educational users for abundant features

Total the score for each piece of software. Compare the scores. The piece of software with the highest score is your best choice.

Go to the *Rubrics* section of Chapter 8 in MyEducationKit to download the *Academic Software Evaluation Rubric* for your use.

Michael Newman/PhotoEdit

Special needs hardware and software assist physically challenged students and those with special needs to complete their academic tasks.

Special Needs Software

Educational software specifically designed to address the requirements of learners with special needs was more fully explored in Chapter 4. However, its importance as academic software merits an additional mention. The category of **special needs software** ranges from software that reads words or letters aloud as they are displayed on the screen and software that enlarges text on the screen to speech-synthesizing software, which converts spoken sounds and words into their graphic equivalent or into the text the sounds represent. Special needs software also includes prepared multimedia software that targets specific learning skills, such as listening skills, helps students with learning disabilities who require content presentation via additional modalities for accurate perceptual processing. Often, the assistive devices discussed in Chapter 6 are sold with customized special needs software that takes advantage of the full range of features incorporated into the device.

Integrated Learning Systems

Integrated learning systems (ILS) are online or hardware–software combinations of equipment and programs designed to assist students in learning targeted objectives. An ILS typically includes tutorial and drill-and-practice software aligned to standards as well as a comprehensive classroom management support system that records and can report on each student's progress after completion of every software lesson. Such systems address very detailed and specific objectives and can be used in whole or in part as reinforcement to an entire course or for a specific competency within a course (Figure 8.8). Often, ILS software is written to cover several consecutive grade levels and can therefore be easily adapted to address the different levels of skill found in the typical classroom.

ILS software includes both academic and administrative components.

Network-based integrated learning systems tend to be a more expensive solution to the need for technological support of instruction. They are often bundled with their own hardware as well as software and are typically set up in a centralized location that allows all grade levels in a school to share the technology. Because of the cost and the shared implementation of these systems, a typical ILS may be sold to a district as a complete solution to the need for computers in schools and may take the place of individual computers

FIGURE 8.8

Integrated learning systems, whether network based or online, correlate their products with each state's content area standards to ensure instruction is targeted to desired performance outcomes.

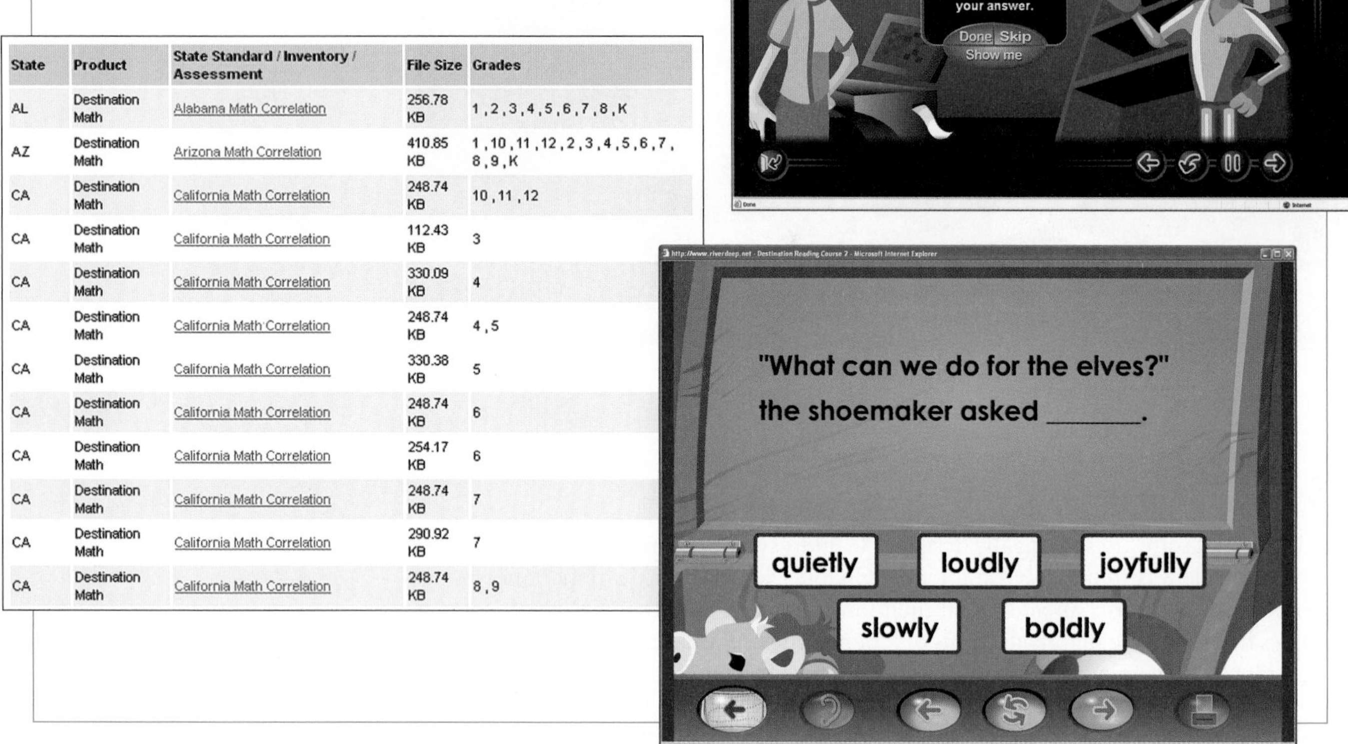

State	Product	State Standard / Inventory / Assessment	File Size	Grades
AL	Destination Math	Alabama Math Correlation	256.78 KB	1,2,3,4,5,6,7,8,K
AZ	Destination Math	Arizona Math Correlation	410.85 KB	1,10,11,12,2,3,4,5,6,7,8,9,K
CA	Destination Math	California Math Correlation	248.74 KB	10,11,12
CA	Destination Math	California Math Correlation	112.43 KB	3
CA	Destination Math	California Math Correlation	330.09 KB	4
CA	Destination Math	California Math Correlation	248.74 KB	4,5
CA	Destination Math	California Math Correlation	330.38 KB	5
CA	Destination Math	California Math Correlation	248.74 KB	6
CA	Destination Math	California Math Correlation	254.17 KB	6
CA	Destination Math	California Math Correlation	248.74 KB	7
CA	Destination Math	California Math Correlation	290.92 KB	7
CA	Destination Math	California Math Correlation	248.74 KB	8,9

in teachers' classrooms. This has led to some controversy over how computer dollars should be spent: by individual teachers addressing their students' needs or by a school district making decisions that try to address the needs of as many students as possible. Most schools and districts continue to have limited funding for the acquisition and implementation of computers, so this controversy is very likely to persist. Online subscriptions to ILS software are therefore fast becoming a preferred alternative.

Problem-Solving Software

Problem-solving software is written to help students acquire and practice problem-solving skills. Such skills include forming and testing a hypothesis; finding multiple-step strategies to solve problems such as math word problems; correctly applying theories, rules, and concepts to predict outcomes; and sequencing critical-thinking steps to come to targeted conclusions. Software of this type can be content oriented (such as math problem-solving software) or of a more general nature to help develop problem-solving skills that can be broadly applied and transferred to other areas.

Problem-solving software gives learners a platform on which they can learn by doing. Such software is designed to allow students to try to explain why a phenomenon occurs

LWA-JDC/Corbis

Students can use academic software to participate in problem-solving, critical-thinking, and creative experiences not otherwise available to them.

and then to run a series of tests to find out whether they are correct. Well-adapted to science experimentation, such software may let students develop an explanation of an aspect of the physical world, such as what friction is, and then test their concept to refine their assumptions. In math, the software may provide opportunities to test logical or mathematical relationships. The value for learners in using this type of software exceeds the content they experiment with. The greater value may be the refining of their ability to see and solve problems independently. The ability to transfer such problem-solving skills to other content and activities may well be the greatest benefit.

For teachers who are interested in developing their students' problem-solving skills, such software offers a way to enhance the learning experience via a constructivist approach and a multimedia environment. Students can extend their knowledge by extending hypotheses based on what they already know, and they can do so in an environment that offers audio, visual, and text components. Problem-solving software can add dimension and depth to content while letting students expand and refine their problem-solving skills. For many teachers, problem-solving software offers learning opportunities for their students that would be difficult to construct and present any other way.

Brainstorming/Concept-Mapping Tools

Brainstorming tools provide a digital environment in which the learner can develop ideas and concepts and then create connections between them. Some of these software packages are primarily text based, while others allow for the creation of visual concept maps. Such **concept-mapping software** generates digital "maps" of concepts that represent a visual depiction of the brainstorming process and the interrelationships between ideas. In the classroom, this tool can be used to capture a cooperative learning group's diverse ideas and turn them into a cohesive whole; help individual learners to grasp large, complex ideas by enabling them to visualize the ideas on a computer screen; or help the class as a whole to develop a joint overview of a new instructional topic that is about to be explored.

Concept-mapping tools allow students to visually organize ideas and then link them to one another to show relationships. Such maps give students an opportunity to visually represent prior knowledge and then extend that knowledge base by linking it to new

PEARSON myeducationkit™

To learn about one type of concept-mapping software, go to the *Video Tutorials* section of Chapter 8 in MyEducationKit and select *Inspiration*.

PEARSON myeducationkit™

Go to the *Assignments and Activities* section of Chapter 8 in MyEducationKit and complete the video activity entitled *Concept Mapping in a 1-2 Computer Classroom*.

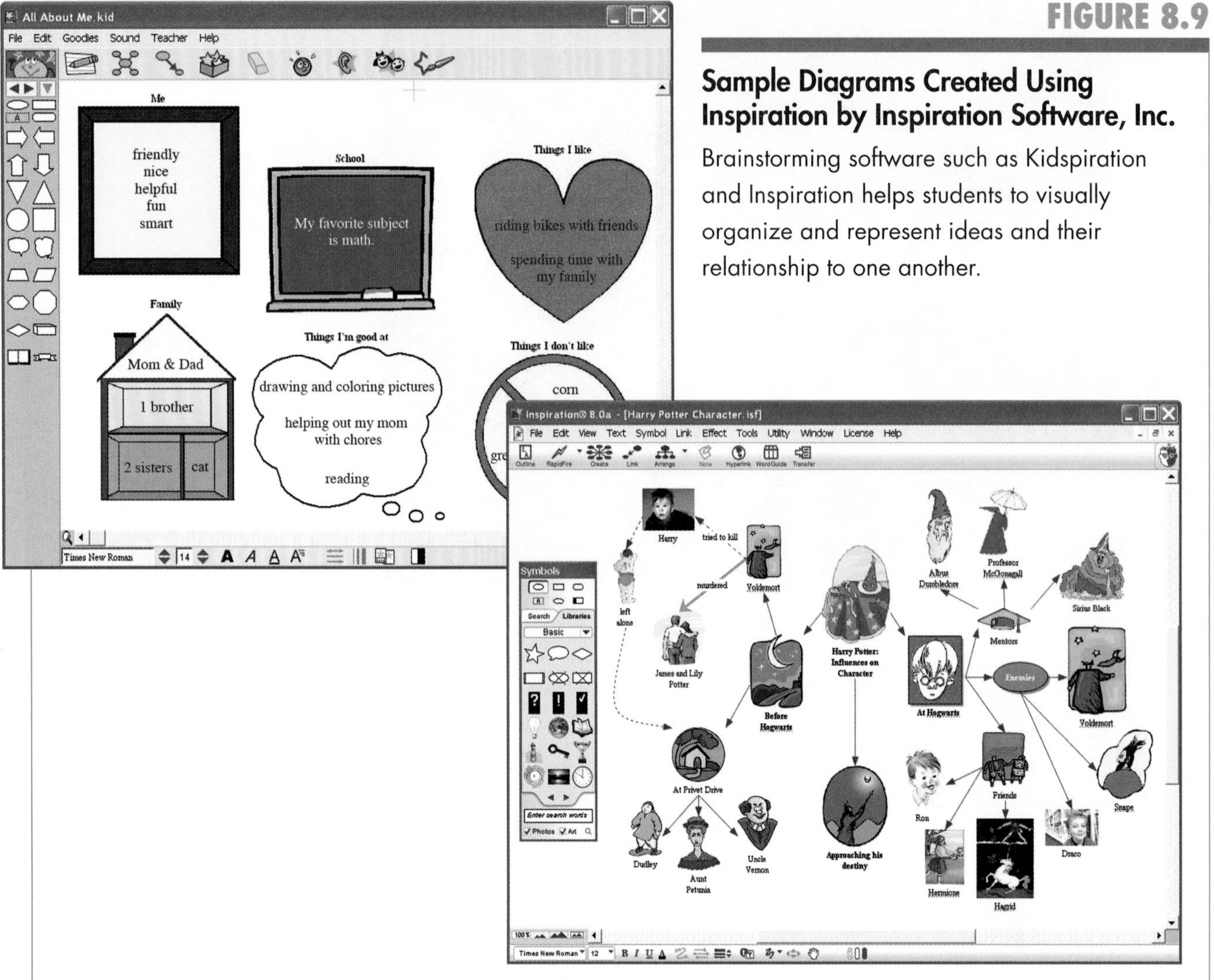

FIGURE 8.9

Sample Diagrams Created Using Inspiration by Inspiration Software, Inc.

Brainstorming software such as Kidspiration and Inspiration helps students to visually organize and represent ideas and their relationship to one another.

ideas. This constructivist approach offers students a chance to build and then test the connections between the ideas they have already assimilated and those they are just learning. As you can see in Figure 8.9, most concept maps (also called *mind maps*) are not highly structured but instead allow for a free-form summary of the relationships between ideas. This type of software tool offers individual learners and cooperative learning groups an opportunity to visually plan writing projects, see relationships between concepts they have learned, and brainstorm solutions in a highly visible and flexible format.

PEARSON **myeducationkit**™

To learn about another type of concept-mapping software, go to the *Video Tutorials* section of Chapter 8 in MyEducationKit and select *Kidspiration*.

To better understand this unique academic software tool, you may wish to experience it for yourself. The material at MyEducationKit includes a demonstration version of Inspiration software and its companion software, Kidspiration. You may install this demonstration version on your own computer and use it for thirty days to experience concept mapping. To better help you see the instructional possibilities of this software, you may want to complete both the Inspiration and Kidspiration Skills Builder activities included on your CD.

Concept-mapping software incorporates the principles of visual learning into a single, easy-to-use software package. It offers opportunities for students to clarify thinking, understand relationships, and identify their own misconceptions. With this unique software tool, students will be encouraged toward creative thinking and deeper understanding. It can also be a powerful instructional tool for teachers wishing to visually present complex or multi-dimensional content to their students.

Academic Databases

When seeking information for researching a school project or activity, most students turn to online sources. They typically use a search engine on the Internet such as Google. What they do not realize is the search engine's list of returned web sites may or may not be reliable and authentic sources. A much more direct approach to finding research information would be to use a subscription database. As you learned in Chapter 7, a database is an organized and searchable collection of related information. Different academic databases are dedicated to particular types of information so that when selecting the one focused on the information you seek, you are ensured that the results of your search efforts will be on target. Most of these databases can be accessed only with paid subscriptions. These subscriptions are typically paid for by the district or schools. Once a subscription is purchased, students are provided log-ins and passwords and can then use the databases as much as desired. Online subscription databases, if available at your school, offer a unique academic reference that may well be a better option than a more general Internet search.

Content-Specific Academic Software

Some academic software is entirely unique to the content area that it supports. This type of software cannot easily be classified into typical academic software categories. Teachers should be aware of the availability of these content-specific applications so that they can call on them when needed to support instruction. Following is a sampling of this type of software.

PEARSON

Go to the *Assignments and Activities* section of Chapter 8 in MyEducationKit and complete the video activity entitled *Software for Math Instruction*.

Math Software

Software programs written for math instruction are designed to support the instruction of abstract mathematical concepts and theory (Figure 8.10). This software includes software

FIGURE 8.10

Mathematics software helps students bring complex concepts to life and see how mathematics represents solutions.

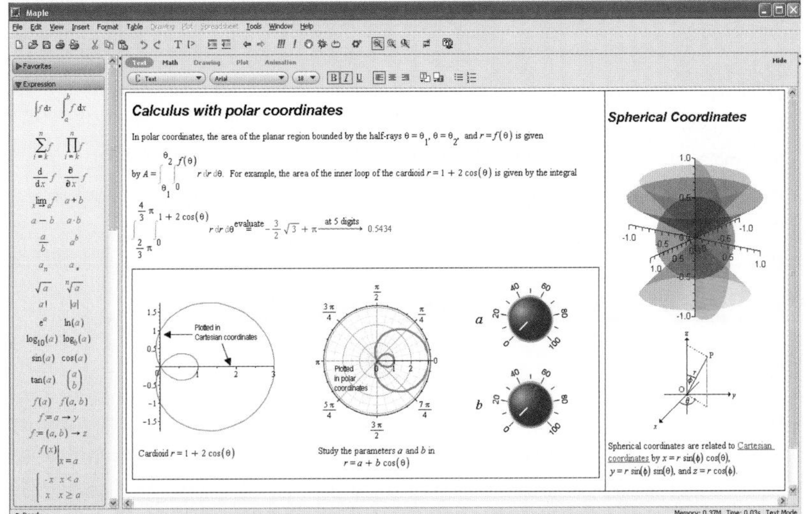

Maplesoft is a division of Waterloo Maple, Inc., Waterloo, Ontario. Used with permission.

TECH TIPS for Teachers

Imagine having millions of articles from magazines, newspapers, and scholarly journals available to you at your fingertips. Subscription databases provide just that. Offered through your school or public library, subscription databases are an ideal technological tool for teaching and learning. While they are primarily used for research, features of these databases can be integrated into classroom instruction to enhance learning. Because these sources are 100 percent reliable, they usually make a better choice than a Google search on the Internet for doing research. There are many subscription databases out there. Below are a few of the best and most useful for educators.

- SIRS databases are useful to students in upper elementary grades and higher for research projects. They are easy to navigate with user-friendly interfaces and provide overviews of hot topics such as global issues, health, scientific developments, and more. Students can read pro and con arguments on topical issues and access many additional resources such as maps, profiles of notable people, and suggested research topics, among others. SIRS provides information through newspaper and magazine articles, as well as government documents, graphics, and many other resources.
- Grolier Online includes access to multimedia encyclopedia databases loaded with features, as well as magazines, web sites, dictionaries, and interactive atlases. With the Grolier Multimedia Encyclopedia, for example, students can find up-to-date news stories from wire and press services, historical timelines, suggestions for research topics, educational quizzes and games, and more. A useful feature for educators is the Teachers' Guide for news stories, providing questions and activities that can make current news stories come to life in the classroom. It's easily navigable for students, and teachers will find practically limitless ideas for classroom instruction. Grolier provides separate interfaces customized for elementary students and for secondary school students, making this database appropriate for most grade levels.
- NewsBank provides access to news articles from hundreds of local and national newspapers. Students in middle school through college can search for articles concerning social issues, economics, health, environment, sports, science, and government, going back over thirty years. NewsBank also offers many special features for students and teachers: current event hot topics for research papers, which even includes search terms to help guide students in the research process; news stories with accompanying activities; quick links to special reports; and access to political, physical, and black-and-white maps. Some especially useful tools for educators are the Teacher/Librarian Resources. These include the Big6 Resource Center for teaching research skills, a NewsBank training and support center, and links to state-by-state educational standards.
- Academic Search Premier, geared for high school and college students, is a collection of general academic, general science, business, social science, humanities, and education periodical sources. Included are some popular magazine titles, such as *People* and *Newsweek,* as well as thousands of peer-reviewed professional journals. Students and teachers can create an account and sign in to Academic Search Premier's EbscoHost and create a web page related to a classroom topic; save articles, images, and videos to their folder; save links to searches; and create search or journal alerts to be notified by email when a topic of interest becomes available. These EbscoHost features give this database the potential to be an essential teaching and learning tool.
- Biography Resource Center, suitable for middle school through college, is a database that can help students find that much-needed biography when doing a research report. Students can just type key words into the search field and be presented with several encyclopedia biographical articles, thumbnail biographies, magazine articles, and links to web sites about the individual. As with all other databases, these articles can be printed or emailed to the student or teacher. Using the Biographical Facts Search feature, biographies can be searched for by occupation, nationality, ethnicity, gender, and more. Students will find that this database makes doing biographical research easy and efficient.

These databases, available to you and your students through your schools and public libraries, can help learners be successful in today's competitive, information-rich world. In teaching our students the critical-thinking skills necessary to locate and manage information independently through databases, we can help them become information literate and more likely to be successful researchers and lifelong learners.

Source: Contributed by Rita Mayer, MS, MLS, a former special education teacher and elementary school media specialist. She is currently a part-time reference librarian at Miami Dade College and can be reached at **rita.mayer@gmail.com.**

that displays virtual manipulatives that students can move, group, and arrange to visually see math operations. Other math software provides students with interactive graphing so that students can see the results of as well as solve algebraic formulas. Geometry software allows students to manipulate forms and examine their related mathematical theory. Dedicated mathematics software can also provide students in-depth, interactive exploration of statistical, trigonometric, and calculus concepts. This specialized group of software packages is available for every math discipline to introduce math concepts to any grade level.

Science

Software unique to the science classroom ranges from software to conduct a virtual dissection, to software that can be used with probes to measure science experiments accurately, to software that explores the stars (Figure 8.11). Almost any scientific topic has dedicated software that offers the student the opportunity for in-depth exploration of the topic. Virtual chemistry, biology, and physics labs can be created on the computer so that students can conduct experiments safely and effectively. Modeling software allows students to examine the galaxy while Geographic Information Systems (GIS) software can provide the information needed to study wetlands that need protection or analyze other map-based data to solve real-world science concerns. Simulation software allows students to run long-term experiments that would otherwise have taken years and see the results instantly. Dedicated science software can provide students with an opportunity to explore concepts, problem-solve, practice scientific inquiry, and conduct experiments. This software is available for every discipline within the sciences and targets all grade levels.

FIGURE 8.11

Science software offers students a chance to explore all areas of science from the microscopic to outer space without leaving the classroom.

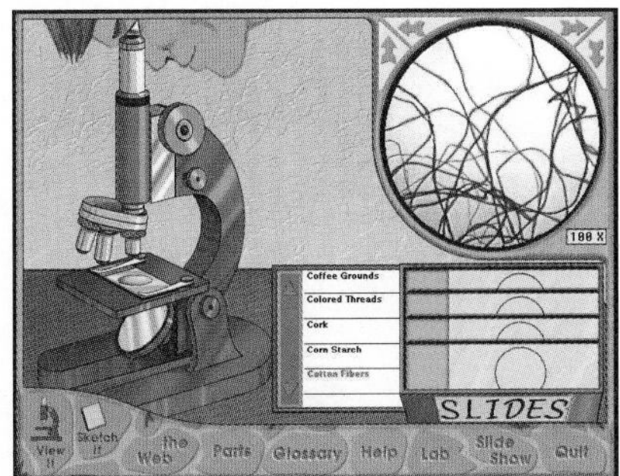

Social Studies

Software for the social studies ranges from software that creates timelines, to CDs of famous speeches, to software that provides multimedia reenactments and information of specific historical events or ages. Social studies software includes packages targeted to specific disciplines including geography, ecology, economics, history, political science, and sociology and is adjusted for all grade levels. Examples of social studies cross-disciplinary software include searchable collections of historical photos, essays, and music. In our changing political world, map software offers teachers and students the most accurate possible world atlas on CD. Software is available to create virtual dioramas of historical periods (Figure 8.12), experience and practice the decision-making process related to current events, and examine the implications of population on the earth's resources. Social science software is one of the most abundant of all content-specific resource areas.

FIGURE 8.12

Social studies software includes history and geography software that lets students visualize historical events and geographical features.

FIGURE 8.13

Language arts software helps students practice skills in spelling, reading, writing, and grammar using games, practice, and interactive activities.

Language Arts

In addition to the many tutorials and drill-and-practice software packages for language arts, there are a number of unique packages to practice language arts skills. Some packages help students move step by step through essay construction by presenting a series of screens to help them think logically through the essay. Others help students practice spelling lists by reading words to them and allowing them to type in the correct spelling (Figure 8.13). Still other language arts software helps students develop literacy skills by exploring meanings of sounds, passages, and story lines. Reading software presents auditory stories and provides activities that practice comprehension, phonics skills, and sequencing, while other language arts software packages teach and practice the specific skills inherent in business writing or journalistic writing. Whether introducing and pronouncing the letters of the alphabet or constructing complex essays, language arts software dedicated to introducing and practicing these skills is available for your classroom.

David Roth/Getty Images

Integrating academic software into instruction adds excitement and innovation to the teaching and learning process.

Academic Software in Teaching and Learning

As you consider the methods and media you choose to employ to achieve your instructional objectives and best address the needs of all learners, academic software can be a most valuable asset. There is indeed a wide variety of types of academic software and, within each type, hundreds of choices. With so large a selection from which to choose, it is clear that the amount of effort necessary to review, evaluate, and select academic software and integrate it into teaching and learning is indeed high. However, the benefits derived from that effort are even greater.

Whether there is only one computer in a classroom or many, carefully selected and integrated academic software can patiently and tirelessly reinforce concepts for learners who need review, offer opportunities for exploration and discovery for learners who need additional opportunity, or provide creative experiences for cooperative learning groups working together to develop a multimedia report to share with peers. The possibilities are as vast as the number of academic software packages available to enrich the learning experience. It is true that exploration of academic software appropriate for your classroom does take time and effort, but for computer-using teachers and their students, inclusion of these packages in the teaching and learning environment will increasingly become a necessary and exciting part of teaching and learning in the twenty-first century.

Key Terms

academic software, 201
authoring systems, 210
clip art, 206
concept-mapping software, 221
desktop publishing software, 203
draw programs, 207
drill-and-practice software, 214
editing software, 209
educational games, 215
graphics software, 204
HTML, 212
hypermedia software, 211
imaging software, 208
integrated learning systems (ILS), 219
paint programs, 206
problem-solving software, 220
reference software, 210
simulations, 217
special needs software, 219
tutorial software, 213

PEARSON myeducationkit™

To check your comprehension of the content covered in this chapter, go to the MyEducationKit for your book and complete the *Study Plan* for Chapter 8.

Student Activities

CHAPTER REVIEW

1. Describe the differences and applications of each type of graphics software that might be used in teaching and learning.
2. What is reference software? How has it changed the research process?
3. What is the difference between drill-and-practice software and tutorial software? When is it appropriate to use each in teaching and learning?
4. How do educational games and simulations differ?
5. What are authoring systems? How are they used for teaching and learning?
6. How is special needs software effective in meeting the unique needs of special education students? Give examples.
7. What is an integrated learning system? What controversies surround the implementation of such systems in schools?
8. What is problem-solving software? Contrast it with brainstorming tools. How does each promote critical-thinking skills?
9. What is content-specific software? Give examples.
10. Describe the process a teacher should follow when selecting academic software.

WHAT DO YOU THINK?

1. School budgets are typically limited in the amounts allocated for teachers to purchase materials and supplies for the classroom. With the additional expense of purchasing academic software packages, some teachers feel that even less money will be available for instructional basics. Do you think this may prove to be a problem as academic software continues to become a critical component in instruction? If so, how might it be resolved?
2. If an educator is given the time and training to author pedagogically sound multimedia teaching software for use in the classroom, how might this change his or her role in the classroom, if at all? Be specific in describing what might change, how it would change, and why; or explain why it would not change.
3. Some educators fear that academic software, especially game-oriented software, shifts the focus from the content to the delivery system. Do you think the entertainment aspect of academic software interferes with and detracts from the content? Why or why not? What are the benefits and disadvantages of using such software? What are the benefits and disadvantages of using more traditional instruction?

LEARNING TOGETHER!

1. With so many types of academic software available, it seems an overwhelming task to try to examine and evaluate enough software to make an informed decision about which packages to use. In a learning group of two or three participants, develop strategies for effectively selecting academic software for use in your classroom.
2. Assume that you are members of a grade or departmental team in a local school. Your grade or department has been given $2,000 to spend on educational software for this school year. Collect two to five educational software catalogs as sources and together decide how you plan to spend your funds. Be prepared to defend your decisions.
3. With your group, examine the objectives and contents of a unit of curriculum at the grade level you would like to teach. Consider how each type of academic software might be integrated to enhance the delivery of this unit. Which type of academic software packages would you use to achieve the objectives and how might you use them? Create a group consensus lesson plan using the software and strategies you have agreed on.

TEACHING WITH TECHNOLOGY: INTEGRATION IDEAS WEB QUEST

As you become familiar with the wide variety of academic software available to teachers, it is beneficial to explore software you may want to use in your classroom. In the links that follow, let's take a look at some examples of teachers using academic software.

ACTIVITY: Explore the links below and then search the Net for a software package for the grade level and content area you plan to teach. What academic software package can you find that you feel would be of greatest use to your students? Write a one-page summary of your web quest that includes (1) the links you explored and the integration ideas you found, (2) a detailed description of the software you selected and the computer specifications to run that software, and (3) an idea of your own of how you will utilize the software in your classroom.

Integrating Technology into Social Studies

"Africa Trail" is another one of the "Oregon Trail" series that follows the successful and ever-popular design of the original game-plus-learning formula of its predecessors. This CD takes students on a biking expedition across 12,000 miles of the African continent. As they travel, the team members learn about African history and culture, meet Africans and learn their customs, and encounter the topography of this huge and diverse land. As with the original version, decision-making skills and problem solving are called for. Visit **www.childrenssoftwareonline.com.**

Integrating Technology into Language Arts

"Reading for Meaning," a Tom Snyder Productions product, teaches the five main skills associated with reading for comprehension: main idea, inferences, sequence, compare and contrast, and cause and effect. A model lesson is included, along with literature-based lessons written for different levels of competency. This is a cartoon-animated software that introduces a "Kid Cam" for teaching each of the five skills. For the literature-based passages, omit the animated clips and allow students to both read and listen to passages from literary works to illustrate the five skills in authentic writing. Visit **www.tomsnyder.com.**

Integrating Technology into the Sciences

A comprehensive aid to teaching science is "PLATO Life Science." This software gives visual images of scientific concepts to enable students to use the audio-narrated multimedia content as a means of tying new concepts into prior knowledge. The program has seven units, each with a read-along text, glossary, a scientific calculator, and unit converter. For teachers, there are Teachlinks so they can add to the program's content and materials, a test bank, and objectives for each unit. Visit **www.plato.com.**

Integrating Technology into Math

"I Love Math" is a Dorling Kindersley (DK) publication that puts a positive spin on learning math skills. This software is designed as a time-travel adventure that engages children in learning measurement, basic geometry, problem solving, and fractions—all while taking part in six games that have animation and sound. An example of the creativity embedded in this program is the approach to teaching fractions: saving an underwater kingdom by laying pipes. Visit **www.kidsclick.com/descrip/ilove_math.htm.**

interchapter 8

Writing Grants to Fund Your Technology Purchases

There are never enough funds to purchase all the software and technology you would like to have for your classroom. Often, teachers will dip into their own pockets to supplement the limited software funds available in most schools. However, there is another option. Grant writing may sound ominous, but it is actually a straightforward process in which you state an innovative idea you have and your need for funds to carry it out. You must describe in detail your objectives, the idea, and how funds will be used. You create a budget to identify how much each of the items you need will cost. And you complete all forms required by the granting agency and your school. Since granting agencies often have a requirement to annually disburse all of their grant funds, the fact is that agencies are looking for innovative ideas to fund. A creative idea shaped into a well-written grant may be all that is needed to supplement your classroom technology.

Granting agencies may be public or private. Public agencies include such organizations as the U.S. Department of Education. Private agencies may be corporations such as Microsoft or foundations such as the George Lucas Foundation. Each type of agency has very specific requirements as to what they are willing to fund and the procedures for applying for the funds. Governmental agencies are often very rigorous in their requirements, while foundation requirements may range from requiring multipage forms to simple letters of request.

When an agency has monies available, it may publicize an RFP (Request for Proposals). These can be found in professional journals and on the Web. The RFP lets interested individuals know that monies are available, what they are for, and what process must be completed to apply. An example of a list of K–12 grants can be found at TechLearning's grant resources web site at **http://techlearning.com/resources/grants.jhtml.**

Agencies do not disburse funds to individuals but to institutions such as a school or your district. So while you may write the proposal for a grant, once it is accepted, the funds go to your institution and not to you. However, since you took the initiative to get the funds, you will typically be appointed the grant director or team leader and be responsible for spending the money, ensuring the terms of the grant are fulfilled, and reporting the grant outcomes when it is completed.

Grants are highly competitive. Depending on the grant, many applicants may be competing for the same funds. Simple need for technology is not the primary criteria. Instead, you must have a creative idea that is consistent with the objectives of the agency, and you have to be willing to make the effort to write the grant in accordance with the RFP criteria. While competition will be stiff, funds are ultimately awarded to someone. It could be you.

Following are some helpful hints for grant writing. Many web sites offer you more detailed advice, and the granting agency will provide you with everything you need to know for their particular grant, including, in some cases, an online or telephone support line to answer your questions. While it is an effort to write a grant, if you are funded it is well worth it for you and, most important, for your students.

Top Ten Helpful Hints for Grant Writing

1. Be sure your idea matches the granting agency's mission. You may have an innovative technology solution for teaching science, but if the agency grants are for ESL students only, you will not be funded.
2. Follow the RFP requirements exactly. There is no flexibility in grant writing. A ten-page limit means no more than ten pages exactly.
3. Be innovative and creative. Grants are most often awarded to fund a new idea or way to solve a teaching problem. They are not to supplement your day-to-day operating budget.
4. Build partnerships. Many granting agencies want to see partnerships between grade levels, schools, and community agencies. The more "bang for the buck" that you can demonstrate through partnerships, the greater your investment is worth.
5. Be sure you have a well-researched budget. You need to state how the money will be spent precisely and accurately. "Guesstimates" will not get you a grant.
6. Have a clear evaluation plan. If you state that you are adding this software to improve reading scores, you will need to explain how you will know that has happened. You need to state how you will assess whether the grant objectives were met.
7. Cite applicable research. If your idea has a basis in previous research, do your homework and mention the studies that support why you believe this will be a successful project.
8. Proofread your grant carefully. If you want an agency to fund you, make a good impression.
9. Let someone unrelated to your project review it. Your writing must clearly convey your project to someone unfamiliar with the idea. Have someone else review it for clarity.
10. Don't get discouraged. You may get several rejection letters, but you need only one acceptance letter from one agency to achieve your goal.

CHAPTER 9

The Internet and the World Wide Web

LOOK GmbH/Alamy

CHAPTER OVERVIEW

This chapter addresses these ISTE National Educational Technology Standards:
- •NETS•T Standard 2
- •NETS•T Standard 3
- •NETS•S Standard 2
- •NETS•S Standard 3
- •NETS•S Standard 5

- **The Internet: Connecting Networks to Networks across the Globe**
- **Connecting to the Internet**
- **Telecommunication Technologies**
- **Internet Tools and Services**
- **The World Wide Web**
- **Using the Internet and the Web in Teaching and Learning**

People are inherently social creatures. Being alone and without other human contact, although pleasant for a while, usually turns into a longing to interact. People like—perhaps need—to communicate with each other. It is logical, then, that computers, as tools in the hands of such social creatures, would also be made to interact. Enabling individual, stand-alone computers and their users to interact with each other is what computer networks are all about. Enabling networks and their users across the globe to interact is what the Internet is all about.

You have learned so far that the teaching and learning process is essentially one of communication. Networked computers are an efficient and effective communication tool. It is not surprising, therefore, that networking would prove to be a remarkable and useful educational resource to enable a new format for communication. Networking on its largest scale, across the Internet, empowers every teacher and learner who is able to connect to the network with expanded communication capabilities. The Internet makes it possible to seek, find, and communicate information that might otherwise have been impossibly out of reach. These tools make such communication as simple as pointing and clicking a mouse. The Internet makes it possible for teachers and learners to interact with each other globally to discover new perspectives and broaden personal horizons. It is no wonder that so many educators are awed by possibilities presented by Internet access in their classroom or the media center.

For educators, the Internet is an amazing instructional tool. The Internet offers the potential to add a dimension to instruction that was previously unimagined. In the hands of innovative educators, the Internet becomes a powerful digital tool that can help them build exciting new instructional environments.

This chapter explores the Internet, the World Wide Web, and the role of these powerful digital tools in teaching and learning. In Chapter 9, you will:

- Review the history and current structure of the Internet
- Explore the most frequently used Internet resources
- Survey the World Wide Web and its features

The Internet: Connecting Networks to Networks across the Globe

You learned in Chapter 5 of the value of connecting the stand-alone computers in your classroom to the resources available through a local network. What if you could connect those same stand-alone computers to the resources available on millions of networks across the globe? If those networks allowed you to connect to them and provided you with guest rights to all or some of their resources, you could access huge amounts of information! That is the scope of the international network of networks known collectively as the **Internet** or simply the Net (see Figure 9.1).

Millions of interconnected networks form the Internet.

The Internet is actually made up of millions of individual machines and networks that have agreed to connect, provide resources to each other, and share data. Initially, just a few select military and university networks connected, primarily for the purposes of research and national security. Since its early beginnings of just a handful of connected sites, however, the Internet has grown to an estimated 650 million host computers distributing information across the globe, and it is still growing! A common protocol called **TCP/IP** (transmission control protocol/Internet protocol) is used so that communications between these diverse computers can be understood. Internet users, whose numbers are, at the time of this writing, estimated to exceed 1.7 billion around the world and still growing each month, can connect, via their school or business networks or from home via modem to the computers within this vast network of networks. Any single computer can,

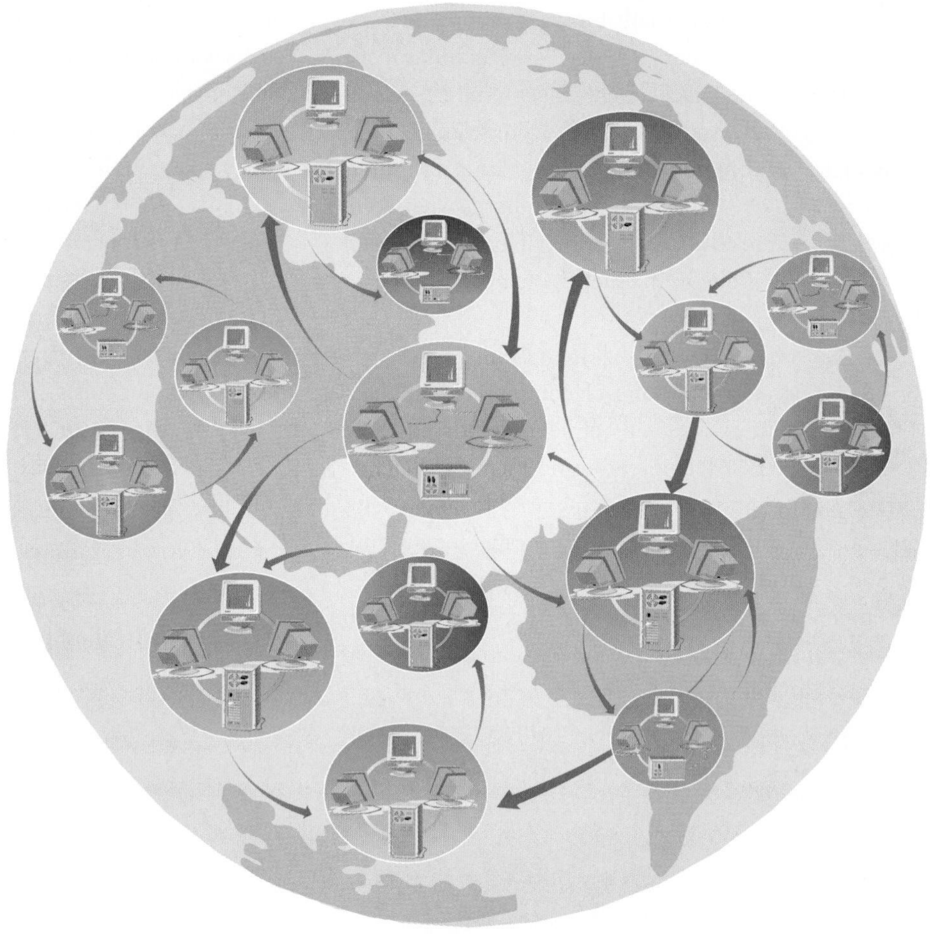

FIGURE 9.1

The Internet

The Internet is a global network of networks connecting hundreds of millions of users to each other and to worldwide resources.

by connecting to the Internet, access an almost unimaginable wealth of information. For educators, the potential to share our world's collective knowledge base with our students is staggering.

But how does such an immense array of information become manageable and usable for a busy teacher? Even if you can access the Internet, how can you put it to work to enhance teaching and learning? How can we empower our students to use the Internet for their own academic and personal growth? To answer these questions, educators must first become familiar with the Internet and the tools and applications available to make its content accessible and responsive to users.

Connecting to the Internet

To connect stand-alone computers in one location to the Internet, telecommunication technologies are necessary. **Telecommunication** is essentially electronic communication between computers over distance. Carrier lines (phone or cable) are used in lieu of network wiring to interconnect remote computers. Because computers work with digital signals, and telephone wires were originally designed to transmit only analog (voice) signals, some adaptation is necessary. Additional equipment must be used at both ends of the communication circuit—that is, to both the home computer and the network server—to make it possible for a telecommunication connection to take place.

Telecommunication Technologies

Modems

Computers send and receive digital signals. Telephone lines transmit analog signals. For a computer to use telephone lines to send information, it must alter, or modulate, its signals into a form that is transmittable by these carrier lines. The computer peripheral designed to MOdulate a computer's signal so that it can be transmitted across a carrier line and then to DEModulate a responding computer signal received via a carrier line is called a MODEM. **Modems** are essentially translating devices. They are necessary whether using telephone cable or satellite to carry a signal between a computer and the Internet. They translate computer output into a format that is transmittable across carriers and then translate signals received on these lines back into a format that the computer can understand, as illustrated in Figure 9.2.

Modems translate digital and analog signals back and forth.

Modems provide only the hardware solution that makes the communication possible. Telecommunications software is also necessary to give the hardware the instructions necessary to make the computer and modem work together to establish a telecommunications link. Typically, this software is packaged with the modem or provided by telecommunications services to which you subscribe.

Home-to-Network Connections

If a classroom workstation can connect to other computers relatively easily via the school network, is it also possible to connect a home computer with a modem to the school network and beyond? Can you connect to your school's network to check your email from your house after school or on weekends? The answer is yes but with some limitations.

If you have a home computer, modem, phone line, or cables and telecommunications software, your home computer can call your network's modem. If your network accepts incoming calls, it will respond and establish a link to your machine. Once a connection is established, the network software will ask that you enter your user name and password. When they are recognized as valid (or *authenticated*), you will be able to work with your network as you would when logging in from your classroom workstation.

Even so, you might find that the network responds sluggishly and that your requests take excessive amounts of time to fulfill. Network wiring usually has sufficient bandwidth and speed to accommodate workstation requests appropriately. However, other types of lines do not have broad bandwidth, nor are they fast, so transmissions may bog down, resulting in slow responses to user requests.

DSL lines offer faster transmission speeds.

Phone companies, aware of consumers' desire for better responses via phone lines, have made higher-speed digital phone lines available in many areas. **Digital subscriber**

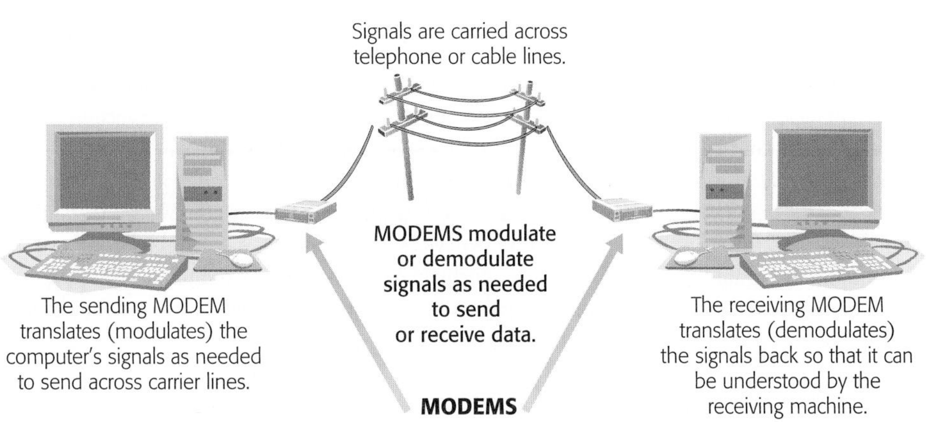

FIGURE 9.2

How Modems Work

Modems enable communication across carrier lines. Every modem can modulate or demodulate signals as needed to send or receive data.

lines (DSLs), a high-speed option for home users, provide speeds many times faster than a standard phone line. DSLs offer both voice and digital communications on a single line, thus eliminating the need for two phone lines at your home, one for voice and another for data.

Another type of high-speed connection uses cable television lines. Most cable TV companies offer digital access via the lines that have already been installed for television. With the addition of a specialized modem known as a **cable modem**, home users can get access speeds that are normally faster than those possible with DSL. Although not available in all areas of the country, this alternative is becoming a preferred option for home users.

A connectivity alternative that is becoming more widely available is wireless satellite access. Companies offering TV via satellite, such as Direct TV, also have the bandwidth and capability to offer access to networks that in turn connect to the Internet. Just as cable TV wiring provides faster transmission and greater capacity than phone lines, so too does the technology by which companies provide satellite television transmissions. Of course, to use this technology, you must first have the necessary dish to receive the transmission and subscribe to the service that sends the transmission via satellite.

WiFi, AirCards, Smartphones, and Handhelds

The explosive growth in popularity of the Internet and use of the World Wide Web in recent years have been matched by—or, more accurately have enabled—the faster and easier connections to it. In a few short years, we have progressed from slow hard-wired dial-up Internet connection to high-speed wireless DSL, cable, and satellite broadband connections. And we no longer connect just on our stationary desktop computers, but on a wide range of increasingly portable devices. Let's take a look at some of the tools you can use to get online almost anywhere you are.

As you have previously learned, WiFi enables computers and other devices to connect to the Internet wirelessly in homes, businesses, schools, airports, and even coffee shops among other places. Some entire cities have WiFi available to their residents. Hot spots are places where WiFi is available, often free, to users. WiFi can enable students in school to connect a laptop or other mobile device to the school's network. WiFi in a museum you visit for a field trip could enable you or your students to record and send a visual record of their experience to home or school computers. They can also use Google or another search engine to find information to answer questions about what they are seeing. WiFi can offer educators and students online access wherever learning needs to take place.

AirCards are cellular modems that enable you to make your laptop an independent connection to the Internet even when no WiFi is available. Anywhere there is cell phone coverage, you can connect to the Internet. AirCards require subscription as part of your cellular phone plan and are typically a bit slower than WiFi connections. However, if your AirCard is 3G capable and you are in a 3G coverage area, you can have a much faster connection, sometimes equaling WiFi speeds. Educators who are away from their classroom can use their AirCard to keep in contact with their school network, their students, or the educational resources they need.

Smartphones and other handheld devices, such as iPods, are including many of the functions of computers, and the ability to connect to WiFi is often one of them. Imagine the educational potential of being able to carry a connection to the Internet right in your pocket. With somewhat limited display capabilities, some smartphones use modified and simplified browsers, while others have full browser capabilities. Some of these devices even offer abbreviated versions of popular productivity packages. These handheld devices give teachers and students maximum mobility while still providing Internet access.

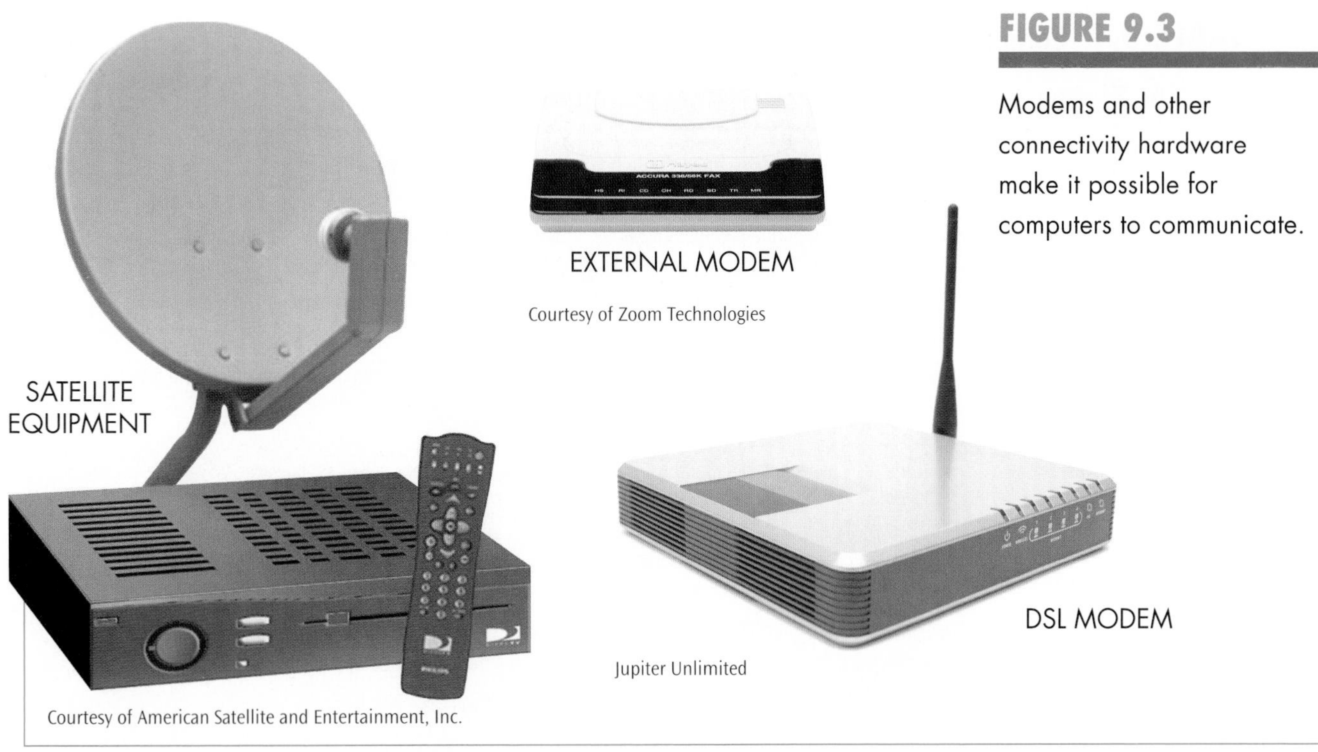

Courtesy of Zoom Technologies

Courtesy of American Satellite and Entertainment, Inc.

Jupiter Unlimited

FIGURE 9.3

Modems and other connectivity hardware make it possible for computers to communicate.

Internet Tools and Services

As the Internet has developed, a variety of tools and services have become available. Some are provided free to all Internet users. Others are offered as a part of a membership package when you subscribe to an Internet service. Still others are available for a subscription fee. To use the Internet effectively, it is important to be aware of the various types of tools and services available and how best to evaluate and select those you might want to use.

Internet Service Providers

The first step in using the Internet is accessing and connecting to it. If you are using your school network, the network itself has been connected to the Internet, and you can use that connection as an authorized network user. However, if you are connecting to the Internet from a home computer, you need first to connect your home computer to a service that is connected to the Internet to access the Net's resources. Special networks that have been created to provide home and business computers a way to connect to the Internet are called **Internet service providers,** or **ISPs.**

An ISP is necessary to connect to the Internet from a home computer.

ISPs are companies that provide home users with access to the Internet through their own network connections and communications software. Most ISPs charge a service fee (typically around $10 to $20 for phone and $30 to $50 for cable or DSL per month) for providing Internet access.

For the monthly ISP service fee, some large providers include a variety of services beyond simple access (see Table 9.1). Most offer email, and some offer extensive services such as news searches, entertainment, and technical support.

TABLE 9.1 Common Services Provided by Internet Service Providers

ISP SERVICE	EXPLANATION
INTERNET ACCESS	An ISP offers you a way to connect your home or classroom computer to the Internet through its Internet server.
COMMUNICATIONS PROGRAM	ISPs provide a customized communications program that works with your modem and connects to the ISP's network. It may connect via cable, DSL, or dial-up.
BROWSER	ISP software packages may include a browser (such as Safari or Microsoft Internet Explorer) to use on the Internet. Some ISPs (such as Google or America Online) offer customized browsers adapted for their service.
EMAIL	Most ISPs provide email services to users. However, the size of a user's mailbox may differ from ISP to ISP. Small electronic mailboxes may fill quickly, especially when receiving attachments, and cause your email to bounce back to the sender.
TECHNICAL SUPPORT	All ISPs provide technical support when you have problems on their networks; however, you may experience long telephone wait times. User satisfaction surveys may give you an idea of the level of support from an ISP.
CHAT ROOMS	Some ISPs provide chat programs as a part of their service packages. Chats may be public or private and may include only people within the ISP network, so investigating chat options of an ISP is important if this is a critical tool.
INSTANT MESSAGING	Instant messaging services allow you to create a one-to-one chat with Internet users outside the ISP network. Nonnetwork users may need to download and install the free ISP chat software to communicate with you.
DISCUSSIONS	Some ISPs provide conferencing software that allows you to create and moderate an ongoing discussion group via the ISP services.
PERSONAL WEB SPACE	Some ISPs offer web space, web tutorials, and web authoring tools as a part of their service. As with electronic mailboxes, web space size varies with ISP; so if you plan to create a robust web site, you will want to determine if the ISP offers sufficient space.
OTHER SERVICES	ISPs offer a variety of services, from online malls to custom search engines to personalized, responsive home pages. It is a good idea to investigate these services to determine if they will be useful for you.

Standard

Learning about Internet resources for your classroom will help you address

NETS•T STANDARD 2:

DESIGN AND DEVELOP DIGITAL-AGE LEARNING EXPERIENCES AND ASSESSMENTS Teachers design, develop, and evaluate authentic learning experiences and assessments incorporating contemporary tools and resources to maximize content learning in context and to develop the knowledge, skills, and attitudes identified in the NETS•S.

Email is the primary communications tool on networks and on the Internet.

Internet-Based Communications

In addition to accessing a worldwide bank of information, the Internet offers some remarkable communication tools. These tools can offer both **synchronous** (same-time) and **asynchronous** (time-shifted) **communications** over the Internet. Because of their ability to link students to other students in classrooms across the globe, most of these tools offer fascinating educational applications. By far the most popular asynchronous communication tool is electronic mail or email.

Communicating via Email

Email is the key communication tool provided in a networked environment. Email works similarly to post office boxes in the physical world. When a log-in name is assigned to a network user, that same log-in name is used to create an electronic mailbox. This is similar to assigning a post office box to an individual post office customer. Just as mail can be delivered to your post office box at any time, to be picked up by you at your convenience, so too can electronic mail be delivered to your electronic mailbox. Email addressed to your log-in name may be received by the server from one of the network users and then directed to your electronic mailbox, where it will be stored until you pick it up. Once you review your stored email, you can choose to delete it or save it, just as you might throw away or keep mail that has been delivered to your physical post office box. You may even decide to forward email to other network users or to leave it in your mailbox for later disposition. Figure 9.4 summarizes some of the key features most email systems provide.

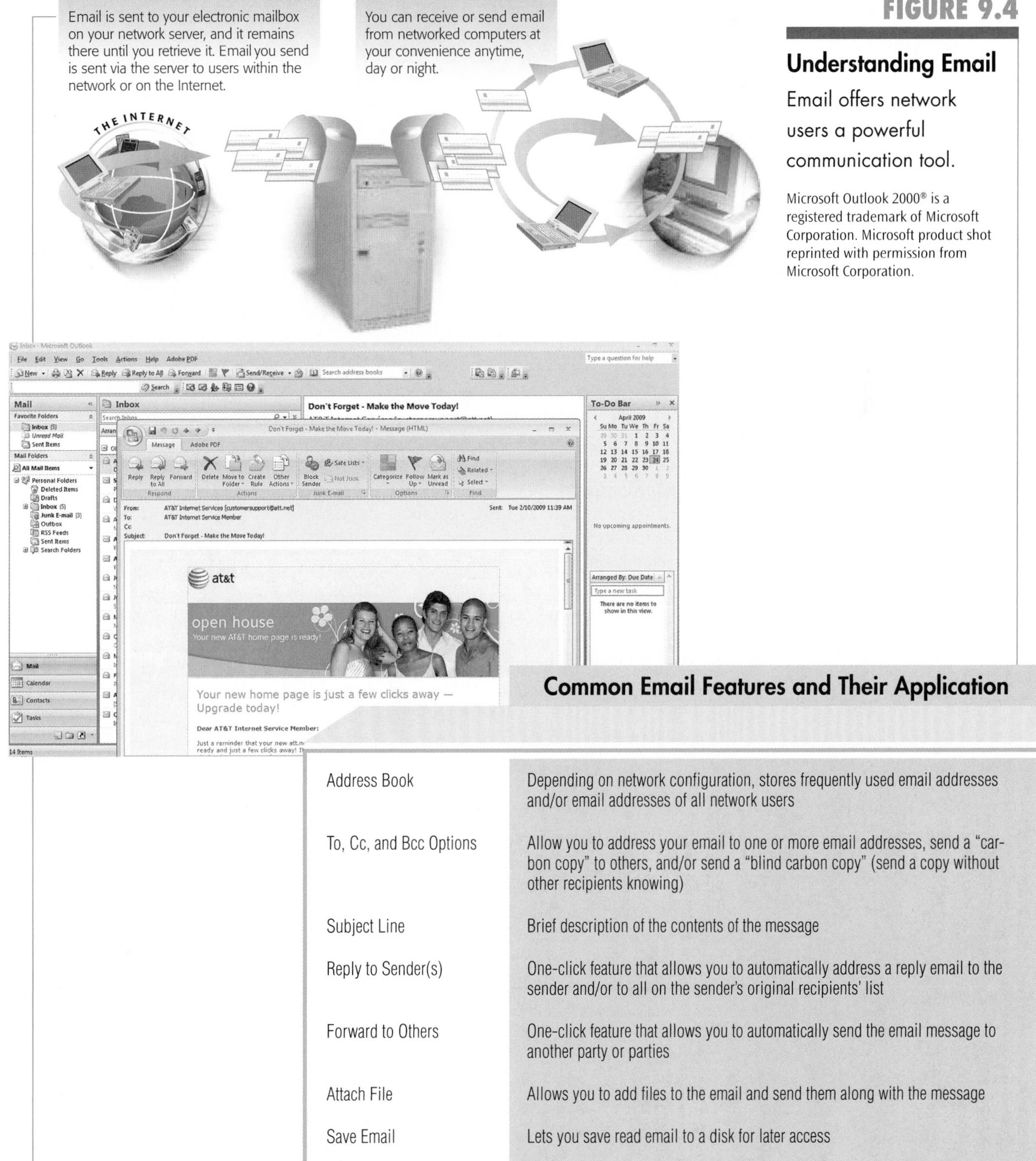

FIGURE 9.4

Understanding Email

Email offers network users a powerful communication tool.

Microsoft Outlook 2000® is a registered trademark of Microsoft Corporation. Microsoft product shot reprinted with permission from Microsoft Corporation.

Common Email Features and Their Application

Feature	Application
Address Book	Depending on network configuration, stores frequently used email addresses and/or email addresses of all network users
To, Cc, and Bcc Options	Allow you to address your email to one or more email addresses, send a "carbon copy" to others, and/or send a "blind carbon copy" (send a copy without other recipients knowing)
Subject Line	Brief description of the contents of the message
Reply to Sender(s)	One-click feature that allows you to automatically address a reply email to the sender and/or to all on the sender's original recipients' list
Forward to Others	One-click feature that allows you to automatically send the email message to another party or parties
Attach File	Allows you to add files to the email and send them along with the message
Save Email	Lets you save read email to a disk for later access
Print Email	Lets you print email you have received or sent

TABLE 9.2 Using Email in Teaching and Learning

APPLICATION	USE	BENEFITS
ASSIGNMENT TRANSMISSION	Assigned activities are emailed to teacher, may be corrected and emailed back for revision.	Activities remain soft copy until final revision; absent students can keep up with assignments; copies can be sent to parents.
CLASS DISCUSSIONS	Discussion question is asked by teacher and mailed to the discussion group list; responses are sent to all group members.	Responses can be thoughtful and delivered at students' own pace; allows shy students to respond; student responses are more carefully prepared when shared; responses can be tracked for review and grading.
ELECTRONIC KEYPALS	Students are assigned pals in other classes (at the same school or other schools in the district, state, or country) to communicate with for a given assignment.	Communication with others provides for social learning opportunities and multicultural exchange; information exchanged broadens data as compared to what individuals may have gathered; student responses are more carefully prepared when shared.
COMMUNICATION: Student–Student Student–Teacher Teacher–Parent	Students can email among group members to complete group activities; teacher and students can exchange information or ask questions outside of class; teacher and parent can communicate outside school hours about student progress.	Email participants can communicate privately or publicly with other concerned parties regarding student progress or with questions or concerns about classroom activities or homework.

Email operates like a virtual post office box.

Schoolwide and districtwide email offers exciting communication possibilities for students and teachers, some of which are shown in Table 9.2. Students can use email to become "keypals" or "e-buddies" with students in other classes within a school or with students at other schools within a district. Keypals can communicate socially or share written assignments for feedback. Older students can be "e-mentors" to younger students to help with grade-level transitions or to assist on specific activities. Opening the lines of communication among students makes many innovative activities possible. Because email is asynchronous communication, that is, communication that can occur at different times convenient to the participants, students' schedules do not impede communications.

Teacher use of email makes it possible to share ideas and lesson plans and to discuss concerns with colleagues across the school or district. Teachers often have very different schedules. If they do not have the same planning periods, it can be difficult to meet face to face with peers. Email provides an alternative way to interact with colleagues, share information, and get quick responses. Once accustomed to using email, few teachers are willing to give it up.

If the school server can receive email from outside the network, such as through the Internet, your email account can also provide you with a powerful opportunity to establish links to parents. Many parents work outside the home, and communicating with them during your work hours by phone may be difficult. Printed notices carried by students might or might not make it home to parents. Even so, if you provide your email address to parents and if they too have email accounts, you can establish a direct and personal communication link with them. This gives both you and your students' parents a convenient way to establish a partnership and open lines of communication for the benefit of the students in your charge. Email can be an important bridge to many homes.

With Internet email, each Internet user is given a log-in name and password. That same log-in name is thereafter used to designate the user's email account, including the email storage space assigned to that user. You can send and receive email via your ISP or school email account. Because Internet email can be sent to any email server available on any network that is attached to the Net, you need to add some information to your assigned email name to give it more specificity. For example, if your user name is bsmith and your ISP account is with a company called bignet.com, your email address would be

In the CLASSROOM

Chats and Email for Students, Parents, Teachers, and Administrators

Chats in School

Andrew Katz, Director of Technology and Academic Operations, and **Larry Patton,** Head of Middle School and Foreign Language Faculty, Poly Prep Country Day School, Brooklyn, New York, discussed the advantages of using the Internet to facilitate that all-important responsibility of teachers to communicate with parents. In "Online Parent-Teacher Conferences," they share the success their school has experienced by online sign-ups for parent-teacher conferences. The traditional sign-ups where the parent(s) came to the school the day of the conferences and signed in had built-in difficulties. The sign-up process was inconvenient and unwieldy. Parents had to walk the halls, fill in sign-up sheets on the doors of teachers' rooms, and then return for the conferences at their time slots. Parents with more than one child in the school had a particularly arduous task. If the conferences ran over the scheduled time, parents found themselves waiting in the halls and becoming increasingly frustrated. This could be a particularly awkward situation for those who had taken time off from work or come in on their lunch hours. Mr. Katz and Mr. Patton observed, "Due to these reasons, parents often entered the actual conferences visibly frustrated and harried, not conducive to establishing good parent-teacher rapport." For the lower grades with smaller populations, the parents could call ahead to schedule the once-a-year conferences, but for the upper grades with many more students, this procedure was impossible. Even in the lower grades, the time staff spent scheduling the conferences took the better part of two weeks. The solution: an online sign-up. Even though there were objections from within the school centered on the reliability of the technology involved and the reaction from parents, this resistance was diffused by the Head of School and two administrators. The program was offered with the responsibility for managing their conferences falling on the parents. Reminders were automatically emailed to the participants, and teachers' names appeared on a location map sent to the parents to expedite the check-in time and to facilitate finding one's way around the school. If parents did not have Internet access, they could call the school for a conference time. Parents were enthusiastic about the program and the ease of its implementation. Teachers were won over by the advantages of being able to plan ahead and organize materials for the conference as a result of having a two-week sign-up period that told them which parents would come in and the days and times they would arrive. Mr. Katz and Mr. Patton spoke for the administrators by saying the online system "worked wonders." These wonders resulted from the efficiency the new system provided to both parents and teachers. It was evidenced by a number of reports that the database-driven program produced, "such as teacher schedules and free slots, parent schedules, parents with duplicate time slots or teachers scheduled, and other helpful ones."

Kenai Peninsula students, Kenai, Alaska, along with other students from across Alaska, enjoyed a live interactive video downlink that connected them to the astronauts aboard the STS-116 space shuttle *Discovery* mission for a chat with the crew on December 21, 2006. The event took place at the Kenai Challenger Learning Center for the Kenai students and was accessible via GCI SchoolAccess for students in other locations even in isolated native ones. There are 52 Challenger Learning Centers for Space Education in an international network. An article in the *Boston Globe*, described the scene, "The seven astronauts sat two rows deep, smiling into the camera Thursday as welcoming cheers erupted in the Challenger Learning Center in Kenai where students posed questions to the crew during a live 10-minute interview. Students in several dozen other communities tuned in to watch the exchange on the crew's last full day in space." The pilot, Bill Oefelein, a former Alaskan, was asked by Matthew Morse, Kenai Middle School, what he liked best about space flight. Oefelein replied, "The views are spectacular. It's just incredible. In the first 20 minutes I was up here, I saw lights from cities, thunderstorms from above, and a beautiful sunrise." The Challenger Learning Center aims "to engage and inspire the next generation to pursue careers in science, technology, engineering, and math." Information about its ongoing programs can be found at **http://www.akchallenger.org** (2009, Summer).

Another Internet-based project supported by the Challenger Learning Center of Alaska was one in which students from the second grade in Kenai, Alaska, and ninth-grade students at Lahaye Middle School in Bordeaux, France, sent monthly emails and held seasonal videoconferences about climate change they observed in both places. The students presented their project online in a beautifully created PowerPoint that has slides giving photos of the two regions, an Abstract, an Introduction, a Data Summary, and a Hypothesis that change will be greater in Alaska than in France and that will be verified or rejected by studying temperature and phenomenological data. Materials and Methods, Discussion, Partners, and References/Bibliography are the slides which follow (2008).

Email in School

For teachers e-newsletters are a valuable source of current topics that arrive in daily emails for designing lessons that are relevant to the world in which the students function. Free online access is available to major American and worldwide newspapers such as for the *New York Times* at **https://select.nytimes.com/glogin?URI=https://select.nytimes.com/mem/email.html&OQ=_r...**

E-newsletters are available that can specifically target areas of interest and may be available daily, weekly, or monthly, depending upon the source. Education Week offers such service to educators

(continued)

In the CLASSROOM *(continued)*

and can be subscribed to at **http://www.edweek.org/info/about/newsletters.html.**

Challenger Learning Center of Alaska. Retrieved August 17, 2008, from **http://www.akchallenger.org.**

Katz, A., & Patton, L. (2007, June 1). Online parent-teacher conferences: Going online to end the parent-teacher conference logjam. Retrieved June 26, 2007, from **http://techlearning.com/shared/printableArticle.php?articleID=196604468.**

D'Oro, R. (2006, December 22). Alaska students link up with astronauts. Retrieved December 22, 2006, from **http://www.boston.com/news/science/articles/2006/12/22/ alaska_students_link_up_with_astronauts/.**

STS-116 astronauts to chat with Alaska students from space. Retrieved August 17, 2008, from **http://www.nasa.gov/centers/ames/news/releases/2006/06_98AR.html.**

bsmith@bignet.com. The @ symbol that connects your user name to the name of the web server on which your email account is located enables email that is addressed to you to travel to its intended location. Similarly, to send email to colleagues via the Internet, you will need to know their full email addresses.

Some people may confuse Internet email addresses with **uniform resource locators (URLs).** URLs are designations for specific locations on the World Wide Web. Email addresses designate individual users' electronic mailboxes on the Internet. Email addresses always consist of the user name, the @ symbol, and the location where the electronic mailbox is stored.

To read and send email, you will need email software, which is typically provided by your school network or ISP. Email software features typically include an address book to store frequently used email addresses and a location at the top of each email screen in which you can enter the email address of the person to whom you wish to send the email. Another area at the top of each email screen allows you to enter the email address of others to whom you wish to send a "carbon copy" of that email. Attachments, that is, separate files or even programs, can be attached to and sent along with the message. Most email programs also provide some sort of filing system that allows you to systematically store incoming and read messages that you have received and messages that you have sent (see Figure 9.4).

Discussions

Another asynchronous communications tool is the computer **discussion** (see Figure 9.5). Sometimes called a bulletin board, club, conference, or forum, this tool provides users with a way to communicate one-to-many. Just as you might post a message for anyone to read on a real-world bulletin board in a public area, so too can you post a message in an Internet discussion. Further, in a discussion, those reading your message can post either a public or private response. As various people post responses, and responses to responses, a "threaded" discussion evolves. Others accessing the discussion can follow the thread by reading through each original message and its responses.

Discussions offer electronic "threaded" conversations.

Discussions can be designated either public or private. Private discussions are created by emailing an invitation to participants and then setting up the discussion so that only invited members can read and respond. For teachers, discussions offer a way to open communication lines among students and educators. Teachers can interact with colleagues across the globe to share ideas. And their own students and students connected to the Internet anywhere in the world can join together to work collaboratively. Using a private discussion, students in your class can ask a question about the culture or community of students anywhere in the nation or world. Students from multiple locations can be invited to participate and respond, resulting in a lively cultural exchange. And because discussions provide asynchronous interaction, differing time zones or constraining classroom time schedules do not interfere. Students can check the messages posted whenever time allows.

Go to the *Assignments and Activities* section of Chapter 9 in MyEducationKit and complete the web activity entitled *Email in the Classroom.*

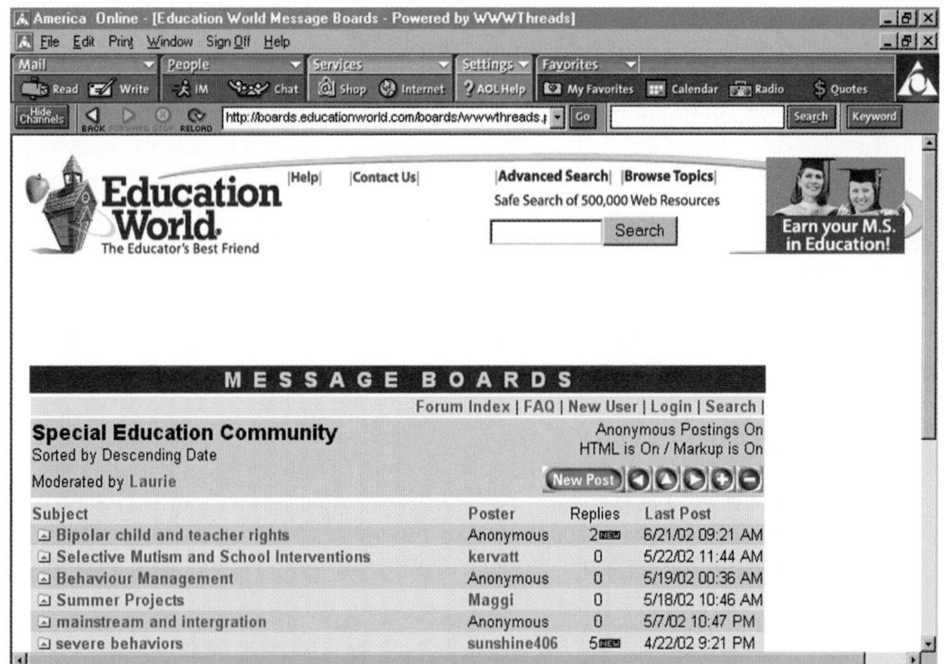

FIGURE 9.5

Online Teacher Discussions

Discussion software lets you view and participate in online conversations.

Mailing Lists

An electronic **mailing list** (sometimes known as a "listserv,") is another asynchronous communications tool. This tool automatically delivers email to those who subscribe to the list. Messages are sent to an umbrella email address of the list itself and appear in email inboxes of all subscribers; in format, they are like any other personal email message. Mailing lists can be set up so that all members can post a message that will be automatically mailed or so that only the list administrator can broadcast messages. When a list administrator monitors and broadcasts messages, the potential for junk mail is greatly reduced, and the value of the list for members is improved.

Many excellent educational lists are available for educators. Each offers teaching ideas, lesson plans, and/or links to Internet sites that are very useful. You should, however, check to see whether you are subscribing to a monitored list; even then, subscribe only to those that you find particularly useful. Subscribing to a lot of lists, especially unmonitored ones, can result in your getting many more pieces of email than you want to deal with.

TECH TIPS for Teachers

Unsubscribing from a Mailing List

When you have oversubscribed to mailing lists, you may find your email inbox inundated with mail. If you find yourself in this situation, you need to unsubscribe from some of the lists you are on. Since mailing lists are usually run by automated programs, sending an email asking to be taken off this list will usually not get your name removed. Instead, look at the bottom of one of the unwanted pieces of mail. Often directions and even a link will be provided to tell you how to have your email address removed from the mailing list. However, even if no directions are provided, most mailing list software will check the subject line of incoming email. If "unsubscribe" is found in that space, very often that will be enough of a command to the mailing list software to remove your name.

If the problem is severe enough to cause problems getting your desired mail, another option while you are waiting to be removed from the list is to identify the email from that list as spam. Spam is unwanted email, and most email programs provide a spam filter. With the spam filtering feature, you can identify email that you want to be blocked from entering your inbox. Blocked mail will be diverted to a spam folder, from which it can be deleted. While not a long-term solution, blocking mail from a mailing list may be a useful option in the short run.

Chats

So far we have discussed only asynchronous communication tools. These are especially useful because they can fit easily into a busy instructional schedule, but sometimes asynchronous

Electronic chats offer an opportunity for real-time interaction across the Internet.

tools simply are not the right tools for the activity you have planned. In some cases, it is important to the activity to provide real-time interaction. In that case, an Internet chat is a good option. A **chat** is a service offered by some ISPs and some Internet sites that set aside a space in which two or more Internet users can meet in real time. A virtual space, called a "chat room," is established, which participants can enter. Those in the chat room communicate by typing their messages and then sending them for public display in the chat room. Individuals thus respond to each other in real time in this Internet space. Internet chats require that both you and the other chat participants have the same chat software available. Chat software can be downloaded, but it is most often offered as a part of an ISP's services.

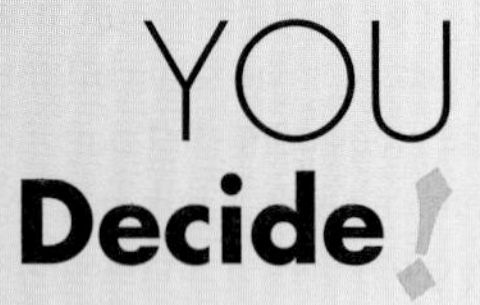

Go to the *Assignments and Activities* section of Chapter 9 in MyEducationKit and complete the video activity entitled *Online Connections.*

Public and private chat rooms can have multiple participants. Another form of chat, called **instant messaging (IM)**, is a one-to-one chat that can be started whenever another user is simultaneously online. With IM, you typically configure the software to notify you when specific individuals go online. Once you are notified that one of those people is online, you can IM that individual, that is, open a two-person temporary message room in which to communicate. Like a chat, the two parties communicate by typing messages back and forth. This more informal and spontaneous communication can offer teachers and students opportunities to communicate and interact with online peers in real time whenever they become available.

Like discussions, chats can be public or private. Public chats are very difficult to control and monitor for content and the use of profanity. They are therefore not particularly good tools for classroom use. However, private chats allow only designated individuals to participate. Using a private chat room, you can have your students exchange data for a common science project with experts in the field or with other classes participating in the project. You can also establish national and international dialog with colleagues across the globe. A chat room can be a powerful and useful tool, one that is often a free Internet resource. Of course, because chats are synchronous, all parties must be prepared to participate at a common time. This can take a bit more advance work than emailing or discussions, but if live interaction is desired, this can be an ideal tool.

YOU Decide!

Chats and instant messaging offer students a way to communicate with peers online. However, since the conversations are in real time, it is possible for interaction to become inappropriate before the teacher can intervene. Even with network monitoring software, it can be difficult for a teacher to oversee multiple live conversations and to ensure that nothing inappropriate is posted. Teachers must balance the risk of using synchronous chats with the value in encouraging online interaction. But is this tool worth it?

YES! Students can always say something inappropriate in a classroom. Just because the comments may be written rather than spoken, the risk of something inappropriate being expressed is no different. As long as the chat interaction is private and the general public does not have access, it is no different than the confined interaction of a classroom. It is definitely worth the effort to encourage student interaction, especially since that interaction could be with peers across the globe.

NO! Once an inappropriate comment is on the screen for all to see, it cannot be taken back. In a classroom a comment can be ignored or perhaps might have been heard by only a few students. In a chat room or on an instant message, everyone is sure to see everything everyone else says. Chats and similar live online communication are not worth the risk. It is better to use discussions that can be monitored and censored as needed before the damage is done.

Which view do you agree with? YOU DECIDE!

Videoconferencing

Zigy Kaluzny/Getty Images

Videoconferencing software lets you communicate via voice and visual images across a network.

If all types of files, from text to graphics to video and audio, can be transmitted over the Internet, then why not live voice and video images as well? That, too, is very doable using current Internet tools. **Videoconferencing** software allows users at either end of a synchronous connection not only to hear each other, but to see video images of each other as well. To add video to live conferencing on the Net, you can either use a built-in video camera or attach one to your computer. Thus, as you sit before the monitor looking at the screen, just by looking up and into the camera, you can make "eye contact" with the other participants in the video conference. Your image will display on their monitor, and theirs will display on your monitor.

In a classroom equipped with a multimedia computer, a webcam, videoconferencing software (such as the freeware program Skype), and Internet access, students can see, hear, and interact with their counterparts in similarly equipped classrooms around the world. Web sites such as the Global Schoolhouse (**www.globalschoolnet.org**) offer pages to help educators find and connect to other classrooms that are interested in videoconferencing. Students engaged in videoconferencing-based interaction can participate in real-time interactive learning experiences with their peers in classrooms anywhere in the world.

Classroom-based videoconferencing might look somewhat choppy, and there may be delays in transmission, but this system does add visual images to Internet-based communications. Of course, many dedicated videoconferencing systems are much more sophisticated and provide broadcast-quality images at higher costs. As Internet bandwidth and speed continue to increase, even classroom-based videoconferencing will be able to approach the quality we have all come to expect from video images.

Other Internet Services

The Internet provides a wide variety of other services that may be of interest to you as you expand your use of this network of networks. Each of the following services is described briefly so that you will be aware of its potential and possible uses (see also Table 9.3).

FTP

File transfer protocol (FTP) is the method used for transferring files among computers on the Internet. FTP programs are usually included in your Internet software. Typically, you are using this protocol whenever you download (bring files from the Net to your computer) or upload (send files from your computer to others via the Internet) a file, even if you are not aware that you have activated an FTP program.

File transfer protocol (FTP) programs transfer files across the Internet.

There are FTP sites on the Internet, many of which are maintained by the government or a university, that contain available text, graphic, sound, and video files for your use. Although some restricted sites require a password, many are "anonymous" sites that allow you open access. Some of these require that you type in "guest" or "anonymous" at the welcome screen. Such requirements are usually clearly written on the screen.

When you upload and download files to and from FTP sites—and, indeed, most Internet sites—such files are often sent in a compressed format. Compressed files, sometimes called zipped files, have been temporarily reduced in size so that they will transfer faster

TABLE 9.3 Internet Services for Educators

INTERNET SERVICE PROVIDERS (ISPs)	Companies that provide access to the Internet and various services for a monthly fee
ELECTRONIC MAIL (EMAIL)	Asynchronous one-to-one communications tool available to everyone on a network connected to the Internet
DISCUSSIONS	Internet-based electronic discussion groups that allow those interested to read or post comments on a topic
MAILING LISTS	Automated lists of subscribers interested in a topic; subscribers automatically receive a copy of emails sent to the list
CHAT ROOMS	Virtual spaces in which individuals can meet virtually to hold real-time conversations via text and sometimes voice
VIDEO-CONFERENCING	Live video with audio across the Internet that lets individuals communicate in real time by seeing and hearing each other speak
FILE TRANSFER PROTOCOL (FTP)	Program that uploads and downloads files; FTP sites provide libraries of downloadable freeware and shareware software and files
NEWSGROUPS	Discussion groups dedicated to a specific topic and open to anyone interested in that topic

and occupy less storage space on the FTP site. After they are downloaded to your computer, they must be decompressed to be usable. Some files automatically expand after being downloaded. Others require the appropriate **decompression program.** If a decompression program is needed for an FTP site's files, it too is usually available from the FTP site and should be the first thing you download. A variety of decompression programs are also available from the Internet.

FTP sites can offer a wealth of freeware and shareware. All you need to do is know that this resource exists, visit the FTP site, and download files that are of interest to you. On many FTP sites, the files are listed by name alone, although you may find them organized by category. To be sure that you are getting the type of file you want, you should note the file's extension, the three letters following the dot in the file name. Different extensions represent different types of files. Table 9.4 summarizes the most common extensions.

Newsgroups

Newsgroups offer a wide variety of Internet discussion groups on every possible subject of interest.

Using electronic conferencing, a large number of topic-oriented newsgroups are continuously running on the Internet. A **newsgroup** is a public conference dedicated to a specific topic. To participate in a newsgroup, you use a newsreader (see Figure 9.6), a program that is included with your Internet software, or Google Groups. The newsreader lets you read all the previously posted messages and follow the threads of the discussion. You can also post your own responses or start discussion of a new topic. Most newsgroups are open discussions on specific subject areas such as education, computers, news, politics, music, and many more. Newsgroup names often indicate their topic areas. For example, biz.jobs .computers would be a discussion group about computer employment in business, and ed .middle.science would be a discussion about teaching middle school science. A newsgroup with a name such as alt.education.disabled would be an "alternative" newsgroup for discussion of issues related to educating individuals with disabilities.

TABLE 9.4 File Types Available at FTP Sites

File extensions (the last three characters following the dot [.] in a file name) can help you determine the type of file you are dealing with. Common file extensions and their descriptions are summarized here.

EXTENSIONS	DESCRIPTION
.doc, .htm, .html, .txt	**Text files:** Word-processed files (.doc), files readable with a browser (.htm or .html), and those readable with any text reader
.bmp, .jpg, .pict, .dig, .eps, .png	**Graphics files:** Graphic data ranging from clip art to high-resolution photographs; most files are readable by better art and draw programs
.avi, .mov, .mpg	**Video files:** Motion video clip files that typically require software and adequate hardware for viewing; software is freeware on the web
.au, .wav	**Audio files:** Audio clips of music, speech, or sound effects; usually require hardware and software
.exe, .com, .bat	**Program files:** Files that are programs of some type, usually found on FTP sites in application categories (for example, utilities, word processors)
.z, .zip, .sit	**Decompression files:** Large files of any of the above types that have been compressed for faster upload and download; require a decompression program (usually freeware on the Web) to decompress them

The World Wide Web

People are often confused by the difference between the Internet and the **World Wide Web** (the Web). Actually, the Web is the most popular of the many services available on the Internet. It is not a separate network but *the Web* is not synonymous with *the Internet*.

In its early days, the Internet was not particularly easy to use. It was text-based, and commands to move about on or retrieve something from the Internet typically required very exact syntax. To use Internet resources, you had to know the precise sequence of commands and be able to use them in a very specific order. The complexity involved in using and navigating the Internet and the increasing demands by nontechnical users for access led to the creation of a user-friendly graphics interface in 1991. Tim Berners-Lee, working at the Eu-

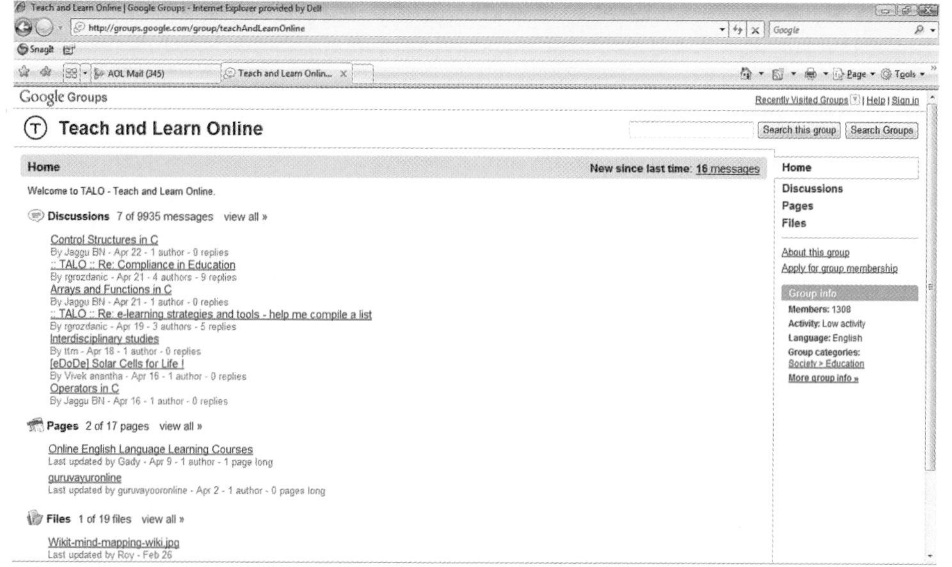

FIGURE 9.6

Reading a Usenet Group

Newsgroups let you participate in discussions about topics of interest to you.

ropean particle physics lab (CERN) in Geneva, Switzerland, wrote a program for use on the Internet that fundamentally changed how users and the Net interacted. His program allowed users to move between linked pages located on the Internet. Simply by clicking on a link, Internet surfers could jump from one document on the Net to another, without knowing a single complex command. These links, called **hyperlinks,** made Internet navigation as easy as pointing and clicking. The vast collection of hyperlink documents available on the Internet became known as the World Wide Web, W3, or simply the Web.

The World Wide Web is the user-friendly graphical side of the Internet that uses hyperlinks to move from one location to the next.

Web Sites: Linked Web Pages

A document that provides information and contains a series of hyperlinks to other resources is called a **web page,** and a collection of related web pages is called a **web site.** Web sites can contain multiple pages, and each page can contain text, graphics, animation, audio, and video data. Typically, web sites have a welcome or **home page** that provides basic information about the site and one or more connections to additional information pages. These connections, or links, are usually represented by colored and underlined words or **navigation button** graphics. Each of these is "hot-linked"; that is, it contains a hyperlink to another document at that web site or at another web site. Activating a link causes a jump to that connected page or web site. Almost all web pages contain links, thus allowing users to jump from that page to other web site pages, which may also contain links to still other sites. This method of Internet navigation is considerably easier than having to type a series of cryptic commands to move from one document to another. Indeed, the web and its easy navigation have changed the face of the Internet.

Web Browsers

Web browsers display HTML code as web pages.

A special program is necessary to translate the language with which a web page is written into an image on your screen. Web pages are written by using a language called **hypertext markup language (HTML).** Your web browser is actually a type of translation software that reads HTML and then displays it as the web page you are familiar with. Browser software also enables you to easily locate a web page by typing in its web address, move to and display the target web page graphically, and even move backward and forward between pages you have viewed. Figure 9.7 summarizes typical browser functions.

Locating Web Pages

Networks that are connected to the Internet usually have a dedicated server, called a web server, that stores web pages and responds to requests from web users. Each one of those web servers is given a very specific web address so that it can be located from among the millions of computers on the Internet. Web addresses can be easily recognized because they all start with a hypertext transfer protocol designation, written http://. This designation indicates that the document to be sought and transferred is using the web page protocol for transmission. A complete web address is written in a very specific format that can direct a browser to an exact location on a web server. This format is called a uniform resource locator (URL). URLs include precise components indicating a web location. At minimum they include the name of a type of web server on which the home page of the web site is found. A URL may also identify the specific directory, or folder and file name for the information you are looking for. Figure 9.8 summarizes the components of a URL to help you understand how it connects you precisely to a specific document.

URLs identify where a web page is located on the Net.

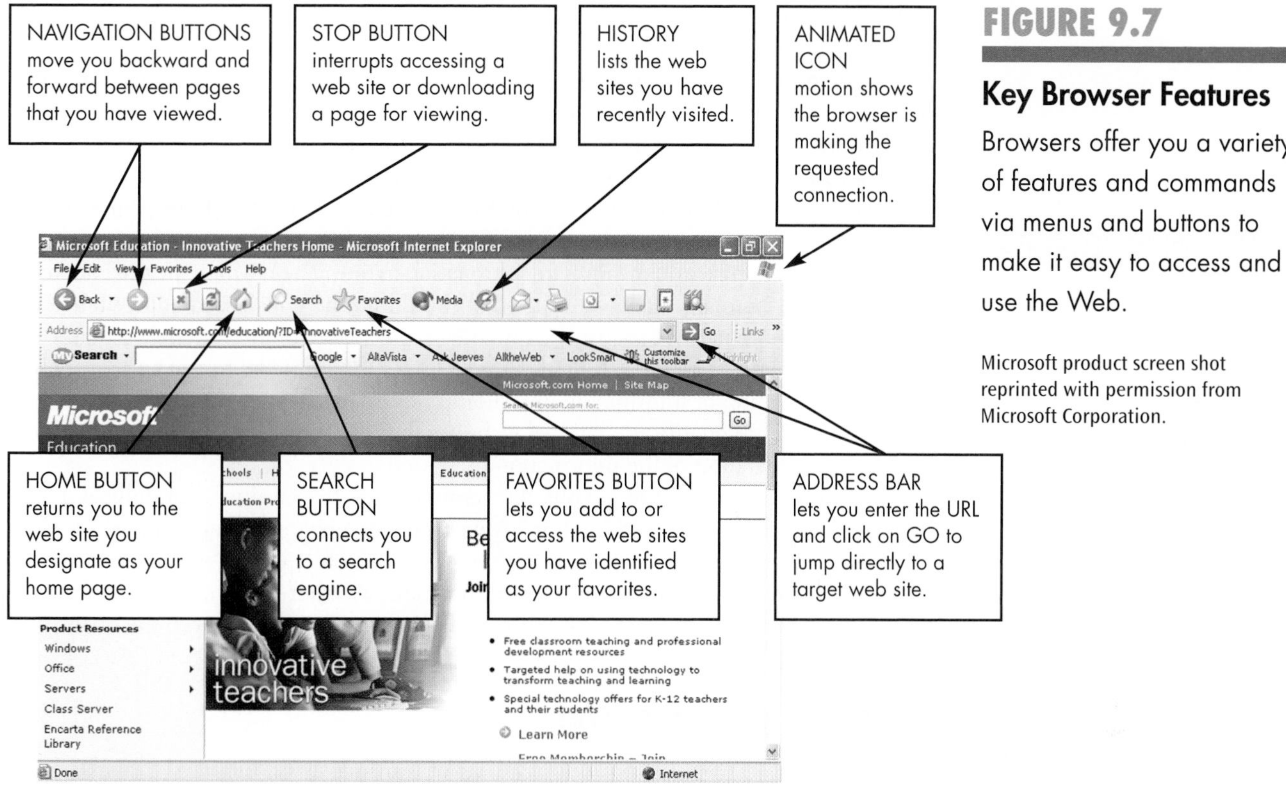

FIGURE 9.7

Key Browser Features

Browsers offer you a variety of features and commands via menus and buttons to make it easy to access and use the Web.

Microsoft product screen shot reprinted with permission from Microsoft Corporation.

Creating and Evaluating Web Sites

As you review various web sites, it might seem like a very complex task to create a web page. That is not necessarily the case. As you learned in Chapter 8, a wide variety of easy-to-use web page authoring software packages are available, many of which are provided as a component on common applications such as word-processing software. The fact that web page

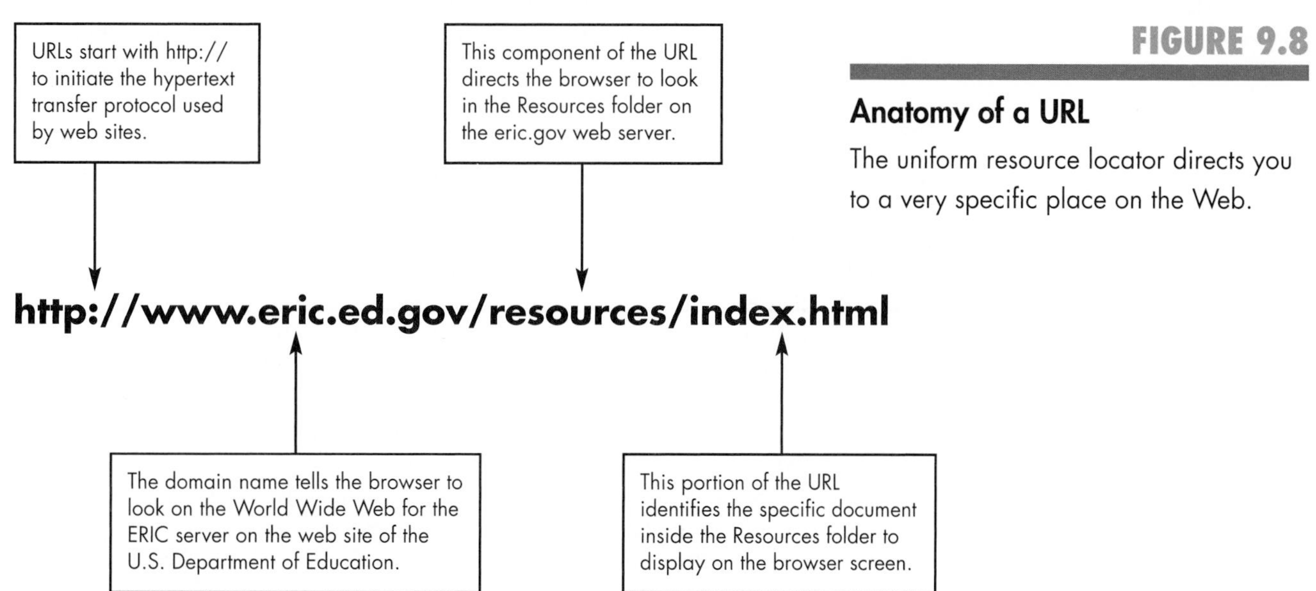

FIGURE 9.8

Anatomy of a URL

The uniform resource locator directs you to a very specific place on the Web.

authoring can easily be accomplished is evidenced by the many teacher- and student-made web pages on the web today.

However, not all web sites created by and for educators are well designed. Whether you are creating your own web site or you are reviewing another educational site for use in your classroom, it is important that you evaluate the site's quality.

A web site's design should be well organized and logical; the site should also be easy to navigate to find the information sought. Furthermore, and of critical importance for educational sites, the creator of a site should have the appropriate authority and expertise necessary to present correct and meaningful information in the area on which the site is focused. Unfortunately, there are many web sites that should not be considered authoritative but are too often assumed to be so just because they are available on the Internet. Equally important for educators and their students, educational sites should be free of any type of bias in their presentation of information and should not try to sell a product or their creators' views. Finally, high-quality educational web sites should clearly cite the sources that were used in the preparation of the information presented.

Before you use a web site in your classroom, be sure to examine it carefully and evaluate it using these criteria. Although many web sites are obviously inappropriate for classroom use, others may turn out to be so only after your careful evaluation. It is the teacher's responsibility to fully preview instructional materials, whether in print or on the web, before sharing them with students. The rubric will help you to evaluate web site quality.

ISTE Standard

Learning about Internet resources for your classroom will help you address

NETS•T STANDARD 3:

MODEL DIGITAL-AGE WORK AND LEARNING Teachers exhibit knowledge, skills, and work processes representative of an innovative professional in a global and digital society.

Multimedia on the Web

Because educators want to appeal to a variety of learning styles, the need to make a web page more than an "electronic textbook" is critical when using it for instructional support. Fortunately, web pages support the multimedia components that are so useful in addressing diverse learning styles. Creating multimedia features for use on an educational web site is not difficult. Web page authoring programs typically enable you to include multimedia files when creating your web pages. The main disadvantage to using multimedia on a site is that multimedia files can be quite large and therefore may take additional time to access and download. Furthermore, the user's browser may or may not include the program components that are needed to display multimedia. Some browsers may require an additional program, called a **plug-in,** to expand the browsers' capabilities in this area. Most plug-ins are offered free to those Internet users who wish to download them. This makes it possible for the users to easily upgrade their browser's capabilities via plug-ins so that they, too, can use web multimedia. Whenever you decide to use multimedia on a web page, you should also include the URL of the plug-in's web site. Adding this address to your web page makes it easy for those who wish to view your multimedia to upgrade their browsers if they need and want to.

Plug-ins add multimedia capabilities to browsers.

Graphics

Graphics files are the most frequent multimedia addition to web pages. The use of pictures and visual images can add significantly to the interest of a teaching page. To use graphics on the web, you need to be aware of the various types of graphic formats that are compatible for this purpose. Graphics may be created in these formats through the use of most of the popular draw or paint programs. It is simply a matter of creating the graphic and then saving it in the desired format. Art software provides the translation necessary to save from one format to another.

The most frequently used formats for web graphics are GIF and JPEG. **GIF** stands for graphic interchange format, a graphics format that is used primarily for clip art and line art. GIFs are best for images that have large areas of solid color, sharp edges, and no gradients. Animated GIFs are sequences of images that, displayed in quick succession, give the appearance of movement. No doubt you have seen these popular animations on web pages. Because they are essentially a sequence of GIFs, they too are relatively quick for a browser to

GIF and JPEG are common web graphics formats.

Web Site Evaluation **Rubric**

SITE NAME:

URL:

AREA/CONTENT OF SITE:

COMMENTS:

Using each of the criteria below, evaluate the usefulness of this web site for teaching and learning. For each dimension in the rubric, check the box that best reflects your opinion. Select web sites that score 4 or higher in the most dimensions.

	EVALUATION CRITERIA				
DIMENSION	**1** Poor	**2** Below Average	**3** Average	**4** Above Average	**5** Excellent
Design	☐ Poorly organized; contains obvious errors; loads slowly	☐ Organization somewhat confusing; some errors; loads slowly	☐ Organization acceptable; no obvious errors; loads adequately	☐ Good organization; no errors; loads quickly	☐ Excellent organization; clear and free of errors; loads quickly and completely
Navigability	☐ Difficult to find and follow site navigation links	☐ Navigation links visible but somewhat confusing	☐ Navigation links clear and readily available	☐ Navigation links clear and logical; site map included	☐ Navigation logical and clear; site map and search engine available
Authority	☐ Unclear who authored the site	☐ Author name and contact information included; but credentials lacking	☐ Author name, contact information, and some credential information included	☐ Author name, contact information, full credentials included	☐ Well-regarded author provides all necessary information; site is linked to by others
Bias	☐ Site attempts to persuade or sell views	☐ Site presents facts, but some bias is evident	☐ Site is mostly neutral; selling pages are segregated	☐ Site contains no attempts to sell or persuade	☐ Site presents multiple viewpoints with no bias
Citations	☐ No citations are evident	☐ Citations are included on some sources but not all	☐ All sources include brief citations, but site lacks bibliography	☐ All sources are properly cited with site bibliography	☐ All sources properly cited, full bibliography, with active links
Dates	☐ No dates evident	☐ Site contains creation date but no dates for update information	☐ Site contains both creation and dates for update information	☐ Site contains dates for creation and update information and some dates relating to data collection	☐ Site contains creation, update, and data collection dates for all key information
Content	☐ Data quality is questionable, and quantity is limited	☐ Data quality appears adequate, limited quantity	☐ Data are adequate in quality and quantity	☐ Data quality is established, and quantity is sufficient for coverage	☐ Data quality is unquestioned, and quantity provides excellent coverage
Links	☐ Few relevant working links included	☐ Adequate number of links, but many are no longer functional	☐ Sufficient number of links, and all are functional	☐ A good variety of useful, active links	☐ Active links to wide variety of excellent sites
Handicapped Access	☐ No options available for handicapped	☐ Some pages on site offer text-only option	☐ Site offers text-only option on all pages	☐ Site offers clear options for handicapped	☐ Site includes handicapped options on all pages and links to support software
Relevance	☐ Site does not meet instructional objectives	☐ Site meets some aspects of instructional objectives	☐ Instructional objectives are adequately met	☐ Site exceeds most objectives' requirements	☐ Site exceeds all instructional objectives

PEARSON myeducationkit™ Go to the *Rubrics* section of Chapter 9 in MyEducationKit to download the *Web Site Evaluation Rubric* for your use.

download and display. **JPEG** (pronounced "jay-peg") stands for Joint Photographic Expert Group, the agreed-upon standard for photographic images. JPEG graphics are used for high-quality images. This much higher-resolution image is needed to accurately reproduce scanned photos; however, JPEG files are typically large and require more time to display.

PEARSON myeducationkit™

Go to the *Assignments and Activities* section of Chapter 9 in MyEducationKit and complete the video activity entitled *Virtual Reality*.

When displaying graphics, browsers typically load and display text first and then begin the graphics transfers. The graphics often appear to the user as partial or blurred images that gradually resolve into clear, complete, full-color images. The smaller the file and simpler the format, the faster a graphic becomes viewable.

The Web contains millions of images that are available for you to use. Many of them are copyright free; that is, you can use them without having to pay the owner to use the image. Chapter 13 will help you better understand copyright and its impact on you as a teacher. However, at this point, it is sufficient to be aware that copyrighted images cannot be used or reproduced without the permission of their owners. For most educators who create web sites or use images from web sites, this is not a problem, because so many free resources are available.

Audio

Audio on a web site can add another multimedia dimension in using the web for teaching and learning. Audio files that are stored in WAV format require that you first download an entire file before playing it. Because such audio files can be quite large, long delays result from incorporating audio into web pages using these formats.

> To play audio files from the Web, you may need player software.

A more sophisticated audio technology for the web, called **streaming audio,** sends audio in a continuous stream or flow. Streaming audio players such as the ones shown in Figure 9.9 allow you to listen to the audio as it is received by your browser. There may be some short delays, but for the most part, you are able to listen as you download. Live In-

FIGURE 9.9

Software for Playing Streaming Audio and Video

Media players (plug-ins) such as iTunes and Windows Media Player make listening to and viewing streaming video and audio possible.

iTunes courtesy of Apple, Inc.

Windows Media Player® is a registered trademark of Microsoft Corporation. Microsoft product screen shot reprinted with permission from Microsoft Corporation.

ternet concerts and Internet radio stations use this technology. Some popular players for this type of audio include RealOne Player, Windows Media Player, Winamp, and Apple's iTunes and QuickTime. If you decide to listen to an audio clip that is in the one of the formats supported by these players, you may first need to download the plug-in to enhance your browser (see Figure 9.9).

Video

Just as audio clips can be added to a web site, so too can video clips be included. Video clips are typically short because they take considerable amounts of time to transfer. **Streaming video** has improved that situation by allowing the user to view the video clip as it is downloaded. With sites such as YouTube, video online is a growing potential resource for the classroom. For educators, being able to access and show video clips from around the world with just a click of a mouse button offers many exciting educational opportunities. Current and emerging web-based video resources will be explored in detail in Chapter 11.

Virtual Reality

Virtual reality (VR) provides a three-dimensional graphic environment that can be accessed on the Web. A VR world is one that is rendered in three dimensions and allows the user to manipulate and explore that three-dimensional environment. When you visit a VR world museum, for example, you can move down hallways, turn corners, and go up stairs to see the museum's displays. You can even manipulate objects of interest by coming close to them, picking them up with your mouse button, and turning them around to get a view of all sides. The promise of VR worlds for education is enormous. Imagine the possibilities of a student being able to enter a VR world at the molecular level and move electrons around to alter elements or being able to take a field trip to see the inside of the pyramids from a computer connected to the Web. Clearly, firsthand experiences are the best, but for experiences that are too far away or impossible to attain, the use of VR holds great potential.

> Virtual reality lets viewers become participants in virtual environments.

PEARSON myeducationkit™

Go to the *Assignments and Activities* section of Chapter 9 in MyEducationKit and complete the video activity entitled *Is Virtual Reality Really Worth the Visit?*

Search Engines

If an educator is interested in using any of the web resources described so far in this chapter, how can they be located from among the millions of web sites out there? The Web does not contain a central index or directory. Remember that it is, at its core, thousands of independent, interconnected networks and servers with no one single organization running it. With data spread so widely and no central index, the only way to find very specific data on the Web is to use a tool that searches the Web for you. This tool is called a search engine.

Search engines are programs that are designed to find web sites and pages based on key words that you enter. The key word can be a single word, a phrase, or a series of words. The search engine matches the search word against databases of web sites and their respective key words. When a match occurs, the search engine provides you with hyperlinks to the page or site related to the search term. These matches, sometimes called hits, provide you with a direct connection to relevant web pages.

Search engines use different techniques to generate their databases. Some store and read key words that web site authors provide when they register the site. Others use automated web robot programs, sometimes called spiders, to search for new sites. Because thousands of new web sites are

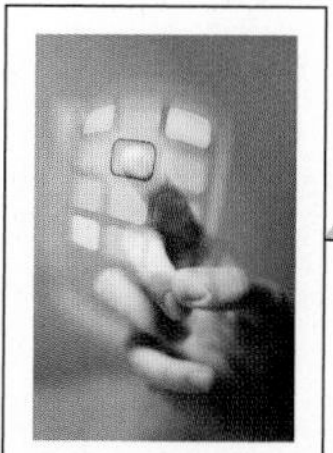

HANDSON LEARNING

Use a search engine to find an educational electronic discussion group and a mailing list for teachers. Join both. Monitor the discussions posted and post at least one comment of your own. Read the emails distributed through the mailing list. After using each for a week, respond to the following questions:

- What are the advantages and disadvantages of using each type of Internet communications tool?
- What type of information was shared on each?
- Would you recommend these tools to new teachers? Why or why not?

being added to the web daily and different engines use different techniques to build their databases, it is very possible for searches using different search engines to have very different results. You will need to experiment with different search engines to determine which ones seem to bring you the hits that are closest to what you are looking for.

When using a search engine, it is important to structure your request for information so that you do not get an unmanageable number of hits. If you were to request an engine to search on the word *education,* millions of hits would be returned to you, making it essentially impossible for you to find the few that pertain to the specific topic within education you are looking for. Although there may be some variation in the techniques used by any given search engine, all provide methods to narrow the search, typically using terms such as AND, OR, or NOT and quotation marks to control the scope of the search. By carefully constructing your search request, you will be able to get very precise results. You should always review the search instructions provided at a search engine site before using that search engine. Each engine differs somewhat, and a brief review will help you optimize your searches and may save you considerable time.

Portals

Various web sites, particularly those that began primarily as search engines, have begun to offer more and more services. Such sites, which include an assortment of services such as a search engine, news, email, discussions, electronic shopping, and chat rooms, are called portals. A **portal** is a doorway to the Internet and its many resources. The portal provides you with access and services that facilitate your use of the Internet. Creators of sites that have become portals hope that you will set your browser to open to their sites and then proceed with your Internet activity from there. To support their services, portals sell space on their sites to advertisers that are interested in marketing to you. Some of the most popular portals include Google, Yahoo!, and Excite. Portals such as Education World are dedicated to educational topics and services. Exploring portals may well be worth the expenditure of a busy educator's time.

The Internet is a powerful learning tool that offers access to the world's knowledge base to learners trained to use it.

Bill Aron/PhotoEdit

Using the Internet and the Web in Teaching and Learning

The Internet has, without doubt, great potential in teaching and learning. You have learned throughout this chapter of its many tools and services, as well as some of their innovative applications to teaching and learning. This global interconnection of thousands of networks has changed the way we communicate, much as the printing press revolutionized communication hundreds of years ago. We are all just beginning to grasp the social implications of this revolution as we have moved from the Industrial to the Information Age.

In Chapter 10, we will further explore how the World Wide Web can be used in teaching and learning. We will also review some of the key issues relating to the use of the Internet about which a prudent teacher should be aware. The Internet itself and the manner in which it is used by some offer potential for abuse. Educators who use the Internet in their classrooms must be aware of these issues and see to it that their own implementation of the Internet in teaching and learning is consistent with our highest professional standards and our responsibilities to our most important charges: our students.

PEARSON myeducationkit

Go to the *Assignments and Activities* section of Chapter 9 in MyEducationKit and complete the video activity entitled *Discovering Online Resources*.

PEARSON myeducationkit

To check your comprehension of the content covered in this chapter, go to the MyEducationKit for your book and complete the *Study Plan* for Chapter 9.

Key Terms

asynchronous communications, 238
cable modem, 236
chat, 244
decompression program, 246
digital subscriber line (DSL), 235
discussion, 242
email, 238
file transfer protocol (FTP), 245
GIF, 250
home page, 248
hyperlinks, 248
hypertext markup language (HTML), 248
instant messaging (IM), 244
Internet service providers (ISPs), 237
Internet, 233
JPEG, 252
mailing list, 243
modem, 235
navigation button, 248
newsgroup, 246
plug-in, 250
portal, 254
search engine, 253
streaming audio, 252
streaming video, 253
synchronous communications, 238
TCP/IP, 233
telecommunication, 234
uniform resource locator (URL), 242
videoconferencing, 245
virtual reality (VR), 253
web page, 248
web site, 248
World Wide Web, 247

Student Activities

CHAPTER REVIEW

1. What is telecommunication? What hardware and software are necessary to make it possible?
2. What is the Internet? What value does it hold for educators?
3. What is an ISP? Why is an ISP necessary for access to the Internet?
4. What is the difference between asynchronous and synchronous communication? Name and describe the Internet communication tools that fall into each category.
5. What is a web site? What role does a browser play when you are working on the Web?
6. What is HTML? Does a teacher need to know HTML to have a class web site? Why or why not?
7. What is a URL and how is it used? Why is a URL important when using the Web?
8. What are streaming audio and streaming video? How have they altered the use of audio and video on the Internet?
9. What is a search engine? How do search engines help you find specific information on the Internet?
10. What is a portal? How can it be useful for busy teachers?

WHAT DO YOU THINK?

1. The Internet offers an almost overwhelming wealth of information and is growing daily. It is becoming clear that it will be increasingly difficult to fully define a content area or discipline without incorporating this resource's expanding knowledge base. This may radically change the skills children will need for lifelong learning. How has the Internet changed our concept of information? What computer and Internet skills do you think children should learn so that they will be prepared for life in the Information Age?
2. Internet communication tools open broad new opportunities for interaction among students across the globe. Of the communication tools you have learned about, which do you think holds the most promise? How might you use this type of tool when you teach?
3. The Internet is a public communication area that many believe is protected by the First Amendment. Others believe that the contents of the Internet ought to be moderated and the public protected from inappropriate content. What is your view on this controversial issue?

LEARNING TOGETHER!

These activities are best done in groups of three to five.

1. Each group member should interview at least three teachers who use the Internet in instruction. Be sure to ask the objectives of the Internet-based activity used in their teaching and precisely how it is carried out. Share interview findings with your peers and together develop an Internet Best Practices summary that details the best Internet activities you discovered. Be prepared to share your best practices with other groups in your class.
2. Create a private chat or conference using one of the Internet portals. Use the communication tool you have created to develop a top ten list of ways you might use this tool in a classroom.
3. Assume that all members of your group have decided to connect to the Internet from home. Each member should select one of the available ISPs in your area and research the features and services it provides and the costs for providing those services. Share your findings and select the best way for you to connect to the Internet from the choices your group has researched.

TEACHING WITH TECHNOLOGY: INTEGRATION IDEAS WEB QUEST

The Internet has changed education, just as it has changed society. An unprecedented amount of information is now available in every classroom. Consider the following ideas for integrating the Internet and the World Wide Web into different content areas. These will help to give you ideas of some of the innovative ways to integrate this powerful technology into your classroom.

ACTIVITY: Explore the links below and then search the Net for three additional innovative ways the Internet is being used in the grade level or content area you plan to teach. Write a one-page summary of your web quest that includes (1) the links you explored and the ideas you found, (2) an annotation for each link briefly describing the idea presented, and (3) an idea of your own of how you will utilize the Internet in your classroom.

Integrating Technology into Social Studies

"An Online History of the United States" is a program organized by chapters. The program has a narrative base expanded by links to Internet resources. These resources encompass an amount of content that is suitable as a replacement for textbooks or as an enhancement to them. A lesson plan for the Age of Imperialism is representative of lessons for the other chapters. It includes Objectives, Setting the Context, Online History, Enrichment Activities, Unit Wrap-Up, and a Unit Test. The objectives target all levels of Bloom's taxonomy. The topics under "Setting the Context" review material already presented and tie it into the topics to be addressed in the chapter. "Enrichment Activities" are suitable for gifted and talented students who are placed in the regular or advanced placement classrooms. Check this out at **www.smplanet.com/imperialism/teacher.html.**

Integrating Technology into Language Arts

For writing instruction, ePals is a tool students can use as part of their English class curricula to correspond online, telling each other about their culture. As observed by Tim Discipio, ePals' cofounder, "Teachers say literacy is improving among students because when a child sends a message to another student, they spend a lot of time crafting it, wanting it to be right." This Internet tool, which brings communication to life and encourages a wide assortment of language arts skills, can be found at **www.epals.com.**

Integrating Technology into the Sciences

Following the lessons found in the NASA CORE (Central Operation of Research for Educators) site and the official NASA site, teachers can use "How Big Are We?" to tackle in the classroom a recognizably difficult scientific problem: finding a number that expresses the size of the universe. The NASA site has a search engine that brings up data to help students estimate numerically not only the size of the universe but also the number of stars in galaxies and the average mass of a star. The Procedure with Activities shows students how to design a rubric for assessment of their work. Extensions of this lesson can be found at "Astronomy Village," NASA's Classroom of the Future. The NASA sites are updated monthly. Science Standards and NETS Performance Indicators are given. Learn more at **http://education.nasa.gov/edprograms/core/home/index.html.** and **www.nasa.gov.**

Integration Ideas: Integrating Technology into Math

The National Council of Teachers of Mathematics (NCTM) web site, *Illuminations*, offers many activities and lesson plans for teachers at all grade levels. Whether you are a secondary advanced mathematics teacher or an elementary teacher supporting instruction in fractions, this web site provides high-quality activities and examples. Whether you need an activity to fill out a lesson and to apply the concept or skill under study, illuminations offers robust resources for teachers and students. From formal activities to games, this instructional web site dedicated to help teach math can provide you with interactive, entertaining lesson support. To investigate the activities and lessons on this site, go to **http://illuminations.nctm.org.**

interchapter 9

The Internet and Education

The Internet offers educators a storehouse of targeted information to help them teach, help their students learn, and grow as a professional. Educational web sites, web portals, and online databases provide teachers with the ideas, tools, and research they need to answer essentially every professional question they might pose. This annotated summary of some of the most popular of these educational Internet resources offers you a sampling of the extensive educational resources on the Internet. Since the Internet is dynamic and changes continually, go to the Web Links section of MyEducationKit for Chapter 9 for the most current list of educational Internet resources.

Teaching and Classroom Resources

The Gateway to Educational Materials (GEM)

This web site is the result of a consortium effort with organization and individual memberships. At GEM, you will find Gateway access to high-quality instructional resources and tools available on the Web. Go to **www.thegateway.org** to learn more.

Education World

Education World is a portal for educators. You will find information and links on everything an educator might be interested in, from professional development to lesson plans, at **www.educationworld.com.**

Kathy Schrock's Guide for Educators

This extensive web site offers ideas, links, and resources to expand and enhance curriculum and to augment professional growth. It offers lessons, ideas, and practical tools for your classroom at **http://school.discovery.com/schrockguide/.**

EduHound

This site offers a directory of educational links for K–12 educators, students, and parents. In addition to excellent resources, the site offers a mailing list service for a free weekly newsletter, EduHound Weekly, at **www.eduhound.com.**

Learning Page

The Learning Page web site provides teachers with a wide variety of professionally produced instructional materials that can be downloaded and printed for use in your classroom. Find it at **www.learningpage.com.**

Apple Learning Interchange

Apple offers this online resource for educators to collaborate and share ideas and materials. Educator-created lessons and activities are available for various content areas, grade levels, and target technologies. There are also special collections from content providers such as the Smithsonian. Many of these resources are rich with multimedia, including movies, images, and podcasts. Check this robust collection out at **http://edcommunity.apple.com/ali/.**

Federal Resources for Educational Excellence (FREE)

Developed by a working group in 1997, this site makes hundreds of federally supported teaching and learning resources easier to find. Go to **www.free.ed.gov** to learn more.

Sites for Teachers

A free compendium of links, this web site offers teachers a collection of sites that contain teacher's resource and educational material ranked by popularity at **www.sitesforteachers.com/.**

Blue Web'N

This web site offers an online library of outstanding Internet sites categorized by subject, grade level, and instructional format at **www.kn.pacbell.com/wired/bluewebn/.**

Scholastic

This portal for educators, students, and parents offers instructional resources, productivity and communication tools, and links. Featuring K–12 online interactive activities, this site is an engaging tool in the classroom. It can be found at **www.scholastic.com/.**

The Teachers Corner

A web site for primary and elementary teachers, this site offers lesson plans, thematic units, links, tips, and educational news for teachers at **www.theteacherscorner.net/.**

Professional Resources

Education Resources Information Center (ERIC)

Sponsored by the Institute of Education Sciences (IES) of the U.S. Department of Education, ERIC is the world's premier database of journal and nonjournal education literature. ERIC provides a public web site for searching nearly 1.2 million citations going back to 1966 and, with contributor permission, accessing more than 110,000 full-text materials at no charge. Find it at **www.eric.ed.gov.**

The Educator's Reference Desk

This web site, developed and maintained by the Information Institute of Syracuse, offers teachers' resource guides, thousands of lesson plans, links to online education information, and an extensive archive of responses to AskERIC questions at **www.eduref.org/.**

Education Index

This web site offers teachers, parents, and learners resources and links on a wide variety of subjects organized by topic and lifestage. It also provides a virtual "coffee shop" where individuals can meet and discuss educational concerns at **www.educationindex.com.**

Tapped In

This web site brings educators together both locally and worldwide to cultivate a community that supports each teacher as a professional. The web site also provides educators professional support through peer networks supported by the Tapped In community. Check it out at **http://tappedin.org/tappedin/.**

CHAPTER 10

Using the Web for Teaching and Learning

Bob Daemmrich/The Image Works

CHAPTER OVERVIEW

This chapter addresses these ISTE National Educational Technology Standards:

- NETS•T Standard 1
- NETS•T Standard 2
- NETS•T Standard 3
- NETS•S Standard 2
- NETS•S Standard 3
- NETS•S Standard 4

Now that you have learned about network basics, the Internet, and a sampling of the services available on the Net, it is time to explore more fully its application to teaching and learning. Using the Internet, as it was configured in its earliest years, would have been a somewhat daunting task for most teachers. With complex text-based commands and no user-friendly screen displays, the early Internet challenged its most experienced users. Today much of the Net has evolved into the easy-to-use graphic format known as the World Wide Web. This more intuitive Internet with its simple point-and-click interface and convenient links has become a powerful tool in the hands of teachers and learners. This chapter examines the World Wide Web and the resources it makes available to teachers and learners. It explores the components of an instructional web site and reviews what such a web site should include if you decide to use or create one when you teach. The chapter concludes with a review of the steps necessary to incorporate web-based instruction in your classroom.

In Chapter 10, you will:

- Explore sample classroom management and academic tools available on the web
- Examine instructional support web sites and the resources they provide to you and your students
- Investigate how to use the web to enhance communication and instruction
- Explore the steps necessary to create a classroom web site and make it available on the web

Educational Resources on the Web

Just as the Internet and the World Wide Web have had a dramatic impact on society, so too have they had an impact on education. Schools no longer have to be isolated without access to information and resources. Instead, the world's knowledge base can be placed at the fingertips of every learner. Communications, once limited to paper, pen, and post, are now instantaneous and international, opening new horizons for the development of learning communities. Crossing national boundaries and creating global connections, the Internet has joined the peoples of the world as no other technological revolution has. But harnessing this powerful resource and implementing it in the classroom require a knowledgeable teacher. With so vast and uncensored an information reserve and communications tool, the teacher's academic leadership has become critical to ensure that the Internet is used appropriately and wisely. For this reason, it is necessary for teachers to become familiar with the Internet, its academic resources, and the issues associated with implementing them in the classroom. Helping you to gain this familiarity is the goal of this chapter.

On the web, a number of broad categories of resources are available for teaching and learning. These resources range from online professional publications and organizations to blogs to videoconferencing to podcasts and every imaginable capability in between. To use these resources, you must first be aware of them and then have some idea of their potential application to teaching and learning. Below, you will find an introduction to a wide variety of resources available today.

PEARSON myeducationkit™

Go to the *Assignments and Activities* section of Chapter 10 in MyEducationKit and complete the video activity entitled *Promoting Innovative Thinking and Collaboration through WebQuests.*

Standard

ISTE

Learning about professional resources on the web will help you address

NETS•T STANDARD 5:

ENGAGE IN PROFESSIONAL GROWTH AND LEADERSHIP

Teachers continuously improve their professional practice, model lifelong learning, and exhibit leadership in their school and professional community by promoting and demonstrating the effective use of digital tools and resources.

Online Publications

Many educational journals are now online and available via the Internet (see Figure 10.1). Most of these **online publications** include current and archived articles of interest to educators. Most also have local site-based search engines that allow you to type in key words to look for on the site. Electronic publications also typically offer a page of related links that may prove useful in your quest for information.

Once found, electronic articles can be saved or printed for your use. Many articles that you can view on the web have been converted from their original word-processed format to HTML. Your browser displays the documents you select (click on), and your browser

FIGURE 10.1

Popular Online Publications

These publications are not rank-ordered, because their usefulness depends on the reader's purpose. The annotations list only a few of the features offered.

techLEARNING **www.techlearning.com** *(Technology & Learning* magazine*)*
Anecdotal classroom applications supplied by teachers in the "What Works" section are creative and practical. Contributors' email addresses are given for questions and commentary.

AERA **www.aera.net** *(Educational Researcher)*
ER Online from the American Educational Research Association is a downloadable publication of articles primarily on statistical research.

ASCD **www.ascd.org**
The Association for Supervision and Curriculum Development site includes *Educational Leadership* and the *Journal of Curriculum and Supervision. Bulletins*, updates, book reviews, and software evaluations, as well as other ASCD publications, are built into this site. Articles must be purchased.

T.H.E. Journal Online **www.thejournal.com**
Technological Horizons in Education's online version of *T.H.E. Journal* has product features, Internet information, conference listings, and suggestions.

Learning and Leading with Technology **www.iste.org/LL**
The International Society for Technology in Education provides *Learning and Leading with Technology* online with articles on issues and ideas encompassing all levels of instruction and all content areas.

FNO **www.fno.org**
From Now On: The Educational Technology Journal is a multipurpose site with editorials by Jamie McKenzie, assessment techniques, curriculum notes, grants information, and Internet policies.

JILR **www.aace.org/pubs/jilr**
The *Journal of Interactive Learning Research* is a scholarly site noted for research findings on interactive learning environments focused on technology-based instruction.

Scholastic—Teachers **www.teacher.scholastic.com**
Standards-designed, thematic lesson plans and reproducibles, web projects, research reports, and online activities from *Instructor* magazine are available here.

JIME **www-jime.open.ac.uk**
The *Journal of Interactive Media in Education* is an online professional journal with screen and multiple-screen interfaces of articles on the latest technological developments in education.

With Acrobat Reader, your PDF files will look just like the original printed page.

interprets their HTML code and displays them on your screen. The articles can then be saved or printed from the screen using your browser's Save or Print function.

Other web sites may offer their articles as **PDF files,** which are files that have been saved in Adobe Acrobat format. Acrobat is a conversion software package that lets the user

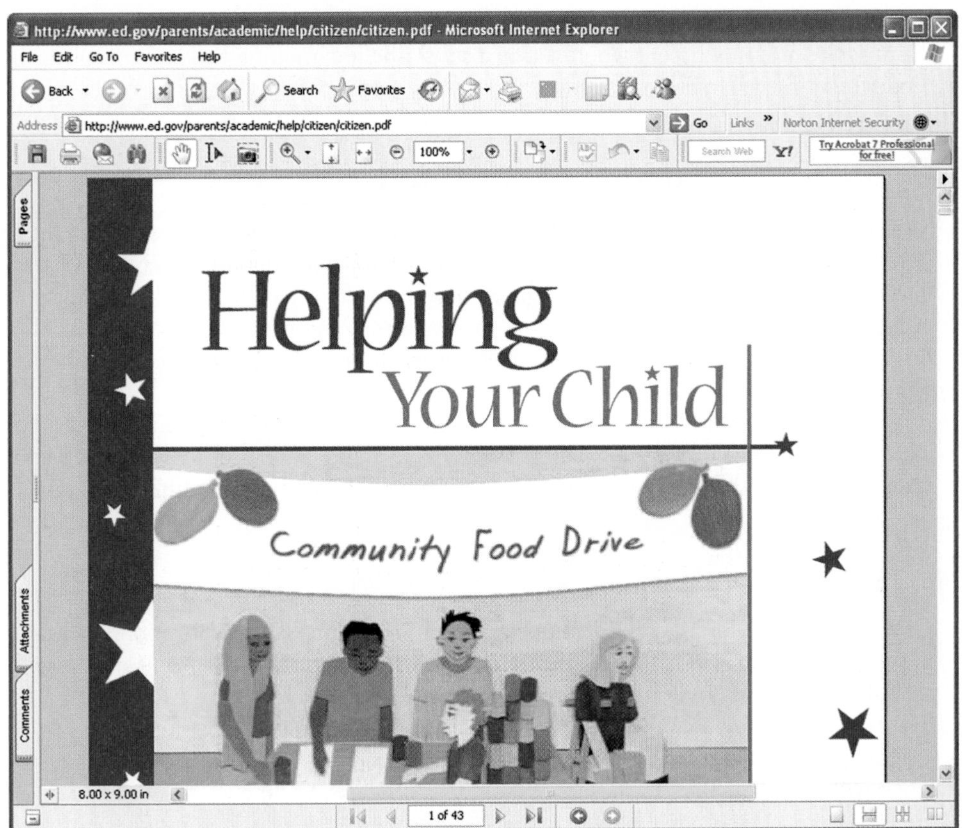

FIGURE 10.2

Adobe Reader

With Adobe Reader, Acrobat-created files display pages just the way they look in hard copy publications.

save a publication exactly as it looked on the printed page, including custom layouts, photos, and other graphics. PDF files are frequently used to share published information, since they maintain the formatting and detail that are lost when presented in HTML. To read an Acrobat file, you need Adobe Reader, a free download available from the Adobe web site. Usually, publication web sites that use Adobe Acrobat include a link to enable you to connect directly to Adobe's download page. Once you have downloaded and installed Reader, you are ready to use files saved in PDF. All you will need to do is click on the files of interest to you, and your browser and Reader will then take over the process. The files will be downloaded, and Reader will be launched to display the fully formatted document (see Figure 10.2). You can then read an exact reproduction of the original published article and even print it out.

Whether you read and print via your browser or via Adobe Reader, be aware that many journals copyright the information presented on their web pages. You should check the specific copyright policies for the e-publications you use. Further discussion of copyright is presented later in this chapter and in Chapter 13.

Some online publications offer a service that will automatically send email to you regarding upcoming highlights or news in brief. Most send weekly or monthly updates and may include special offers. Such emails often come with embedded links to the full-text articles they summarize. This type of service is an easy and convenient way to keep up with the latest news from e-publications of interest to you. Publication mailing lists can be valuable aids, but subscribe only to those in which you have sincere interest. Subscribing to too many of these services can easily result in a great number of email messages. On some school and ISP servers, you might not have unlimited space to handle all of your email. Mailing list messages may inadvertently fill up your mailbox, causing your personal email to bounce back to the sender. Typically, should you need to discontinue receiving email from a mailing list, you need only respond with an email message that includes "unsubscribe" in either the subject line or body of the email. Details on how to unsubscribe are usually sent when you first subscribe to a mailing list, and most lists include them in every mailing list email sent.

PEARSON myeducationkit™

Go to the *Assignments and Activities* section of Chapter 10 in MyEducationKit and complete the web activity entitled *Educational Technology Organizations.*

Online Professional Organizations

Most major professional organizations now have a web presence. Teachers' unions, professional associations, content area groups, technology groups, and many others have web sites that range from modest to robust. Organization web sites typically provide calendars of events, current and archived publications, online stores, and news about issues critical to that organization. Some even include conferences, chats, and live audio or video Internet broadcasts featuring key people in the field.

Professional organizations offer a wide variety of services keyed to their missions. For educators, such organization web sites can offer a central repository of relevant and useful resources related to the organizational focus as well as links to other pertinent web sites.

Wikis

Originally created for fast collaboration and communication via the web among programmers, a **wiki** site is a web site in which content is written collaboratively so that anyone with a computer and Internet access can edit and add to the information provided. A wiki results in a free and dynamic collection of information that anyone can alter.

PEARSON myeducationkit™

To learn how to create a Wiki, go to the *Video Tutorials* section of Chapter 10 in MyEducationKit and select *Wikis*.

One of the largest wikis, the Wikipedia, is published by the Wikimedia Foundation, along with its sister wiki web sites; Wikitionary, Wikibooks, Wikinews, and Wikiquote are among the most popular. Wikipedia is not a forum for personal opinion but is instead a collaboratively developed encyclopedia of information. Wikipedia articles offer links, cross-references, and citations contributed by those interested in that topic (Figure 10.3). Although vandalism (misinformation and deliberate deletions) may occur, the many individuals interested in maintaining wiki integrity typically correct such problems quickly. Vandals are banned from future contributions, thus weeding out disruptive elements. The potential vandalism and inadvertent misinformation that is the disadvantage of a wiki is balanced by the unique opportunity to offer and maintain very up-to-date topical information in this collaborative community.

FIGURE 10.3

Wikipedia

Wikis offer collaborative tools that can be contributed to and edited by participants.

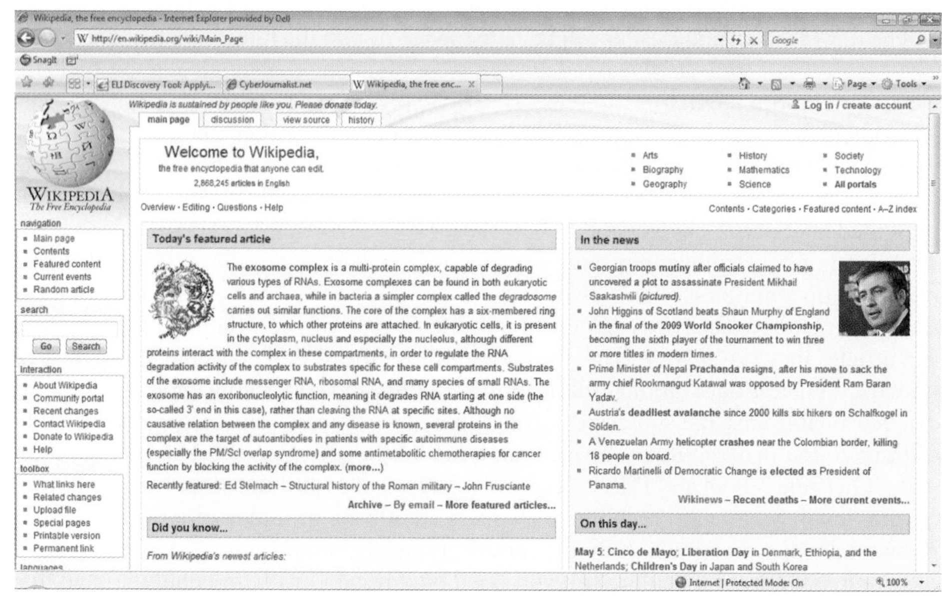

Screen capture "Home Page" from Wikipedia, en.wikipedia.org/wiki/Main_Page. Copyright © 2000, 2001, 2002 Free Software Foundation, Inc., 51 Franklin Street, Fifth Floor, Boston, MA 02110-1301 USA. Everyone is permitted to copy and distribute verbatim copies of this license document, but changing it is not allowed.

In the CLASSROOM

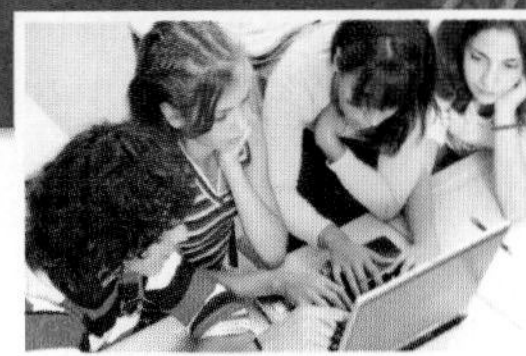

Using Wikis across the Curriculum

In an article in *Digital Directions,* "Wiki Wisdom: Lessons for Educators," Michelle R. Davis discussed the positive contributions wikis can make when used as an instructional tool, citing actual classroom applications. **William Bishop,** a Spanish teacher at Haleyville High School in Haleyville, Alabama, uses wikis to enrich the study of *Dia de los Muertos* (the Day of the Dead) by having his classes create and edit reports on it and post them as wiki entries. This is in addition to topics dealing with the Galapagos Islands and profiles of twenty-one Spanish-speaking countries. To maintain the integrity of the wiki entries, Mr. Bishop cautions, "The main thing is to have a strong acceptable-use policy. Make sure that it's in effect and you talk to the students about it."

Vicki Davis, computer science teacher and information director at Westwood Schools in Camilla, Georgia, notes that using wikis makes it possible for teachers to have total participation from all students. Adam Frey, cofounder of San Francisco–based Wikispaces, assures teachers that "while wikis track every editing change made to them and keep a history of what those changes are, some students have tried to game the system by making small alterations (such as adding a period) to make it seem as if they've been working hard on a project. Wikis do have the ability, however, to allow a teacher to sift through the changes to see the quality of what a particular student contributed." An award-winning wiki that Davis created had her students using wikis as they studied Thomas L. Friedman's best-seller *The World Is Flat*. Her students in Georgia linked up with students in Bangladesh to create wikis with information they collected and presented "on globalization and outsourcing, virtual communication, and how the Internet changed the world."

Leah Harrison, a fourth-grade teacher at College Park Elementary in Greendale, Wisconsin, lets her students use wikis in studying zoo animals. Rather than the traditional written report, they will use a wiki to "contribute information on their species in the form of notes, photos and text. Back-and-forth discussion is hosted on a different area of the wiki site. There are so many possibilities, and it allows the kids to do some of the amazing ideas they have, like videoing themselves reporting on an endangered species."

Chris O'Neal, contributor to *Edutopia,* in "Wiki, Don't Lose That Number: The World of Wiki," shares what he calls "low-level ideas to help you get your feet wet if you're new to the world of wikis." He suggests: "Have your students use a wiki space to plan the details of a field trip to make it as educationally fulfilling as possible. Writing a grant? Throw out a brainstorming page for the school to help edit. Let students manage an Earth Day project—tasks, goals, responsibilities, and so on. Be sure to alert the community so anyone can join in. Collaborate on an international unit, or even a spring e-pal exchange using a themed wiki." The article is followed by blogs from many teachers telling how they use wikis in their classes.

Lorrie Jackson, Director of Communications and Marketing at Lausanne Collegiate School in Memphis, Tennessee, wrote "Working With Wikis," a techtorial for teachers who have not used wikis. It is a step-by-step lesson on how to set up and use wikis, amply illustrated to simplify following the tutorial.

Davis, M. R. (2007, September 12). *Wiki wisdom: Lessons for educators.* Retrieved September 13, 2007, from **http://www.edweek.org/dd/articles/2007/09/12/02wiki.h01.html.**

Richards, E. (2008, August 4). *Teachers take on wiki technology at media conference.* Retrieved August 8, 2008, from **http://www.isonline.com/story/index.aspx?id=779634.**

O'Neal, C. (2007, April 4). *Wiki, don't lose that number: The world of wiki.* Retrieved August 17, 2008, from **http://www.edutopia.org/wiki-dont-lose-number.**

Jackson, L. (2006, March 21). *Working with wikis.* Retrieved August 18, 2008, from **http://www.education-world.com/a_tech/techtorial/techtorial098.shtml.**

In education, wikis can provide a space for brainstorming and collaborative writing. They can offer an online, easily accessible area for debates, group projects, and shared resources. A teacher can have students author and edit articles on assigned topics or provide space for the creation of a collaborative booklet on a topic of interest. Using MediaWiki (**www.mediawiki.org**), a free public-use software for servers with which to create wiki spaces, schools can create private or public wiki web sites for use in the classroom.

Weblogs

Weblogs, or **blogs,** are virtual online spaces that support the posting of personal commentary on the web. Blogs provide primarily one-way communication, but with the inclusion of comments and links, blogs become powerful interactive writing tools. Bloggers post their ideas, and others respond to these ideas, either in comments to the posting or in other blogs with a link back to the original posting. Bloggers can add links in their own commentaries to connect to other web resources or "backtrack" to other blogs. Since weblogs are powered by software that allows the writer and the audience to engage in an online communication cycle via the web, blogs have unique educational applications.

PEARSON **myeducationkit**™

To learn how to create a blog, go to the *Video Tutorials* section of Chapter 10 in MyEducationKit and select *Blogging with Wordpress* and *Blogging with Blogger*.

Unlike a structured discussion group, a blog provides each individual with his or her own web space in which to post personal views and comments on any topic rather than to comment within the confines of a discussion group topic. Whether entered daily or less frequently, blog postings can be read by anyone wishing to view them and can be responded to instantaneously. If the blogging software supports it, blog postings can be responded to with comments added to the original posting. Or an individual can post comments about various other blogs on his or her own blog site. The effect is a lively group discussion, with readers able to jump from blog to blog via connecting links to see what others have to say. In much the same way that our attention turns from one person to another in a classroom discussion as each expresses a view, blog readers can jump from one online blog to another to read comments in a posting thread. With these capabilities, educational blogging sites (edblogs) have evolved that have given online space to students from elementary age through college (see Figure 10.4). Edblogs have been used successfully to give students an opportunity to publicly post daily journal entries; to comment on peer postings; to collaborate on a group project even if participants are a world apart; to research what other bloggers have said on a topic; and to connect to resources they have found. Educational blogs have provided a unique forum for the expression of ideas and for the thoughtful consideration of other viewpoints. In the hands of a skillful technology-using educator, this tool can empower students to write and communicate and teachers to facilitate that expression. With an estimated 70 million weblogs of all sorts on the Web at this writing and approximately 175,000 new ones each day, this easy publish-to-the-web phenomenon is becoming as common as the home page.

FIGURE 10.4

Blogs support personal commentary, sharing, and reader reactions via the web.

Courtesy, Howard J. Martin, Austin Independent School District. Used by permission.

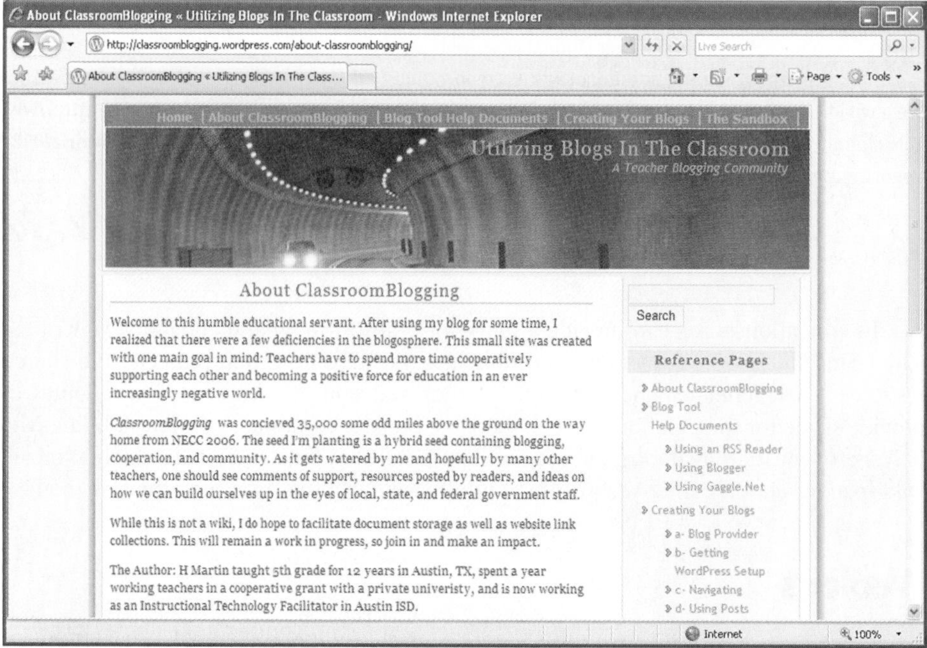

In the CLASSROOM

Using Blogs in English and Health Classrooms

Carey Applegate, a high school English teacher at Lowpoint–Washburn High School in Washburn, Illinois, incorporated blogging into a lesson on utopian literature, "Blogtopia: Blogging about Your Own Utopia." Students are given a chance to "design their own utopian society, publishing the explanation of their ideal world on a blog." They are to establish an infrastructure for their Utopia that covers a name for the community; a Declaration of Independence, in which they give the rationale for forming the society; a motto and seal; an animal to symbolize the society; at least ten rules the society will follow, with the justification for each rule; the type of government; a persuasive letter to friends to convince them to join the society; three journal entries describing daily life in the society; an itinerary for how a typical day will be spent; and an advertisement to publicize the community.

The first part of the instructional plan introduces the students to blogging and photo-hosting sites by tying the assignment to the class's study of utopian literature. The Blogtopia rubric is disseminated and discussed, after which brainstorming sessions are held. The next session is an orientation to blogging, followed by blogging work sessions. Once the group blogs have been created, the students visit and give constructive feedback to each other. After receiving the feedback, the students write a reflection about their own blogs. Resources available to the teacher on the site include the Blogtopia Assignment (10 components required for the ideal society), Blogtopia Rubric, Examples for the United States, The Bare Bones Guide to HTML, Bloggers' FAQ: Student Blogging, from the Electronic Freedom Foundation, Blog and Photo Hosting Sites, Persuasion Map, Letter Generator, and ReadWrite Think Notetaker.

In this ReadWriteThink lesson plan, the "From Theory to Practice" section states, "Literature often means nothing to students when it's not grounded in a context that matters to them. By providing teenagers with the chance to express their understanding of the literature using technology that is exciting and engaging, the literature becomes more significant to their lives and the writing that they do becomes something other than just another assignment."

Bridget Anderson of the Bank Street College of Education and **Catherine Hutchings** of The New York Times Learning Network include a blogging activity in the lesson plan they designed for secondary education health classes, "Welcome, Teens! The Doctor Will See You Now: Examining How Doctors Can Best Address Teens' Health Issues." The activity has students find and read blogs dealing with teen health and evaluate them for practicality and accuracy. The students then answer questions about how these blogs might be used "to educate teenagers about sensitive topics? How confident can you be that the information you read on a blog is accurate? Compare the blog to other online resources. Choose your favorite health blog and write a submission to it."

Traci Garner contributed to the National Council of Teachers of English (NCTE) Inbox Blog 10 tips for helping students to become good bloggers. She wrote, "You have a blog set up. You know how to work the blogging software. But how do you write an entry that gets read? Here are ten tips that make a blog entry grab readers." If you go to the web address and look for the tags "blogs" and "Internet writing," you will find her tips posted on October 21, 2008.

Applegate, C. F. (2008, March 6). *Blogtopia: Blogging about your own utopia.* Retrieved May 6, 2009, from Blogtopia Assignment: **http://www.readwritethink.org/lesson_images/lesson942/Assignment.pdf,** Blogtopia About Your Own Utopia: **http://www.readwritethink.org/lessons/ lesson_view.asp?id=942,** and Blogtopia Rubric: **http://www.readwritethink.org/lesson_images/lesson942/Rubric.pdf.**

Anderson, B., & Hutchings, C. (2007, April 23). *Welcome, teens! The doctor will see you now: Examining how doctors can best address teens' health issues.* Retrieved May 6, 2009, from **http://www.nytimes.com/learning/teachers/featured_articles/20070424tuesday.html.**

Garner, T. (2008, October 21). *Tips on a good blog entry.* Retrieved May 6, 2009, from **http://ncteinbox.blogspot.com/search?q=tips+on+a+good+blog+entry.**

RSS Feeds

Often found on blog sites, **RSS** (which stands for "Really Simple Syndication" or, alternatively, "Rich Site Summary") **feeds** refer to news or other topical updates that are continuously and automatically renewed via the web. RSS feeds provide a constant stream of headlines and links to help you stay abreast of topics that are of interest to you or that are relevant to the blog site on which they are displayed.

Feed readers, also called *news aggregators,* collect and display the feeds you select to receive to keep you updated without having to visit and peruse those individual sites of interest. Some of the most popular online feed readers are MyYahoo and Google Reader, both available to subscribers through these popular portals. When bloggers create their blog site, they often select feeds that they feel would be pertinent to their viewers. Readers are installed on their site for you to use. Other feed readers can be downloaded to your desktop. These computer-based readers, however, have the limitation of being available only from the specific computer on which they have been installed.

Feeds are primarily a headline, a brief text summary, and a link to additional information. For educators, RSS feeds can keep you informed of relevant updates on a content area you are teaching, professional postings on the topics of your choice, training and conference opportunities, and popular articles related to education as they are posted on the web. RSS feeds can also be used on a classroom web site or class blog to keep your students informed about relevant news articles and updates related to content under study. If you create your own blog, an RSS feed can be used to update information about your class on your school or class web site to keep students aware of upcoming class or school activities, classroom events, and even homework that is coming due.

> **ISTE Standard**
>
> *Learning about professional resources on the web will help you address*
>
> **NETS•T STANDARD 3:**
>
> **MODEL DIGITAL-AGE WORK AND LEARNING** Teachers exhibit knowledge, skills, and work processes representative of an innovative professional in a global and digital society.

RSS feeds and feed readers offer busy teachers and students an opportunity to preselect areas of interest and stay abreast in these areas without having to visit favorite web sites to check for updates. And rather than subscribing to mailing lists, which can make email inboxes overflow, feeds can offer an easy way to receive headline-style updates that can be followed up when time allows. Feed reader lists, either predetermined by teachers or created by a student research group, help students to filter and manage the sometimes overwhelming information available on the web.

Governmental Sites

The U.S. Department of Education and most state departments of education have comprehensive web sites with abundant resources for educators (see Figure 10.5). The U.S. Department of Education site (**www.ed.gov**) includes information about current education news, national standards, programs, grants, research, links to other federal agencies, and a wide variety of publications and reports available by mail or download. State department of education web sites offer similar services, but their emphasis is on educational issues within a given state.

FIGURE 10.5

Government Web Sites

Government education sites present critical and current educational resources.

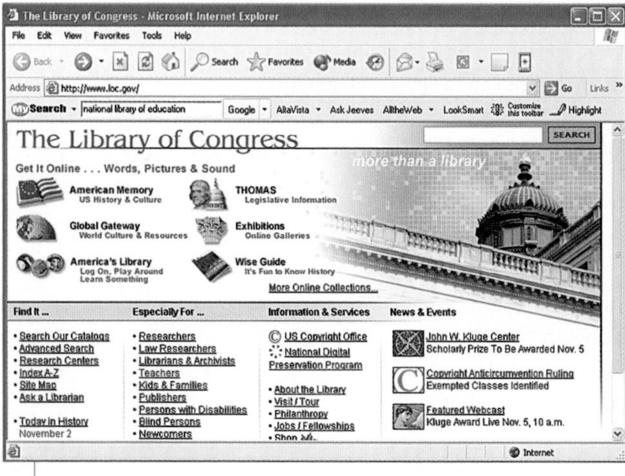

U.S. Department of Education. Microsoft Internet Explorer® is a registered trademark of Microsoft Corporation.

U.S. Library of Congress. Microsoft Internet Explorer® is a registered trademark of Microsoft Corporation.

The U.S. Department of Education web site also provides some of the most useful and comprehensive education links available, including access to **ERIC,** the Educational Resources Information Center. ERIC is the world's largest database of education information, with more than one million abstracts of documents and journal articles, many available through the Internet.

Education Portals

A number of portals include an area focused on education. Educational resources found at portals may include teachers' guides to the Internet, lesson plans, Net events, audio and video clips, web hosting opportunities, clip art libraries, educational games, information about schools and colleges, and a variety of instructional resources accessible by grade level and content area. Each portal offers differing services, so it is valuable to investigate what specific educational resources each offers. All portals and most web sites provide you with a wide variety of current links to other resources on the Net.

Portals can provide lesson plans and other resources.

Favorite Links

Some of the best online resources are discovered through links from one site to another. Web sites often link to other sites that have a focus consistent with the content of their own site. Some sites are a collection of links created for the sole purpose of providing connections to those seeking information on a given topic. When you find a useful web site, it is a good idea to check its links page and explore related sites.

Use "bookmarks" or "favorites" to store your favorite URLs.

But given that there are so many links and so many useful sites, how can a busy teacher possibly remember where they are? Browsers have a built-in function that assists you in creating your own collection of URLs called **bookmarks** or **favorites.** Bookmarking or adding to your favorites list allows you to store web site URLs that are of interest to you. When you decide to revisit a web site you have stored, you need only click on its name in your list, and the browser will immediately connect you to that site. Web sites can be added to or deleted from your list as you require. The use of bookmarks or favorites makes it easy to store and access the useful links that you discover as you search the Internet for valuable resources.

PEARSON myeducationkit™

To learn how to save your favorite web sites, go to the *Video Tutorials* section of Chapter 10 in MyEducationKit and select *Social Bookmarking*.

Classroom Management Tools

Classroom management tools on the web include downloadable or online tools that assist you in the tasks required for your classroom. Several sites offer software that creates online or paper tests and, if they are online, grades them for you and sends you the results. These **test generators** can create tests by randomly selecting questions within their databases of questions, or you can select the questions to be included. Some allow you to add your own questions to the database. Others let you create multimedia tests. Many textbooks (including this one) have added these types of resources to their faculty web sites.

Other Internet-based management tools include formal and informal diagnostic tests to assess learning preferences, tools that generate class rolls with seating charts, and **electronic gradebooks** that let you store and easily average student grades. Many of these tools can be used online or downloaded to your machine. If they are used

TECH TIPS for Teachers

Managing Your Favorite Links

Over time, you will save the URLs for numerous web sites. These links can be organized into folders for easy access. To save a favorite web site in Windows Internet Explorer, click on Favorites on the toolbar and then click Add. To create a folder, click on Organize in the Favorites window. The pop-up window will allow you to add and name a new folder. Once a folder is created, you can drag and drop your favorite links into it for easy access.

Folders and links within the folders are saved in a file on your hard drive or network space and can be backed up (saved on a jump drive, floppy disk, or other external device). It is a good idea to back up your favorites. It takes a significant amount of time and effort to collect links, and you will not want to lose them. To back up Internet Explorer favorites in Windows, go to My Computer, click on the C: Drive and then select a folder called Documents and Settings. Within that folder you will find a folder with either your name on it or the default name, Main User. Double click to open that folder and you will see a file called Favorites. Copy that file to your external storage device to back up your favorites.

online, some security and privacy issues may be involved. Student information is private and must be closely guarded. Making information accessible by using a nonsecure online resource may be an issue. A later section of this chapter will deal more fully with your responsibilities in this regard.

Academic Tools

There is an abundance of Internet tools that support instruction. Many of these can be either used online or downloaded to your computer as freeware or shareware. Some of the most popular **academic tools** include worksheet generators of many types that help you make interesting student activity sheets. These tools help you create content-specific crossword puzzles, word searches, cryptograms, math exercises, and multimedia flash cards. Most of these tools allow you to input the key content and then generate the activity sheet of your choice, which can then be either printed or saved to a file. These creative and time-saving tools help you add interest and variety to your instructional plan.

Explore online lesson plans when developing your lesson ideas.

One of the most useful academic resources available on the Internet is lesson plans. Some lesson plan sites offer subject-specific plans, others offer lesson plans submitted by colleagues across the nation, and still others offer lesson plans tied to national or state standards. In addition to sites dedicated to lesson plans, links on many educational sites offer lesson plans related to the content of that site. A related resource is lesson plan software programs that generate lesson plans for you and even relate them to specific standards. The abundance of lesson plan sites and tools, from those sponsored by the U.S. Department of Education to those supported by individual teachers, is one of the most remarkable educational Internet resources available to busy educators. Browsing through these many lesson plans can offer you valuable ideas for use in your classroom.

Go to the *Assignments and Activities* section of Chapter 10 in MyEducationKit and complete the web activity entitled *Lesson Planning Ideas*.

Reference tools and resources, including dictionaries in all languages, thesauri, grammar and spelling tools, and world atlases, are also available on the Internet. These reference tools also include translation references that translate from one language to another, specialty dictionaries and glossaries that relate to specific professions or hobbies, and other vocabulary aids to provide you with a wealth of information about acronyms, anagrams, and homonyms. These reference tools bring the reference section of a large library to every classroom via the Internet.

CD-ROM-based multimedia encyclopedias are common in school media centers. It is often too costly, however, to buy one encyclopedia for each classroom or to buy the network hardware and site licensing that allow sharing. An alternative is to access these same tools on the Internet. Many of the most popular multimedia encyclopedias and research resources are available on the Internet. These tools work similarly to those on CD-ROM, including the ability to download and save or print entries.

ISTE Standard

Learning about Internet resources for your classroom will help you address

NETS•T STANDARD 2:

DESIGN AND DEVELOP DIGITAL-AGE LEARNING EXPERIENCES AND ASSESSMENTS Teachers design, develop, and evaluate authentic learning experiences and assessments incorporating contemporary tools and resources to maximize content learning in context and to develop the knowledge, skills, and attitudes identified in the NETS•S.

In addition to the more formal academic tools and resources mentioned thus far, the Internet provides teachers with a storehouse of innovation and great teaching ideas at every grade level and for every content area. Teachers from around the globe contribute to a variety of web site ideas that have worked well in their own classrooms. Each site then categorizes and files these innovations to make them accessible via the site's search engines. Such sites are continually being updated and contributed to by creative educators. These sites are a storehouse of best practices that can be easily accessed with a few clicks and a few keystrokes.

Web-Enhanced Instruction

Whether you choose to use the Internet in your classroom daily or only occasionally, the web can enhance the learning environment. The ways to integrate the Internet into instruction, particularly via your own web site, are limited only by your own imagination. This section will explore a few of the possibilities.

Google Earth

In addition to searching, Google offers many other resources of significance to educators. One of the most innovative is Google Earth (**http://earth.google.com**). Google Earth offers teachers and students a three-dimensional view of the earth as it would appear from space. The software lets you appear to fly anywhere on the earth to see maps, buildings, terrain, and even inside the depths of the ocean. Using satellite imagery and the superimposition of digital imagery, Google Earth gives the impression of viewing the globe from space and allows you to zoom in on most places to a relatively high-resolution building-level view. Google has also added resources that provide historical views of the earth, weather, global awareness areas, international border maps, street maps, recent photographs of an ever-increasing number of streets and highways, and one of its newest additions, Google Sky, the view from the earth using images from the Hubble space telescope. This powerful tool brings together the capabilities of digital imaging and the web to provide views of the earth and the universe that will capture the interest of any learner.

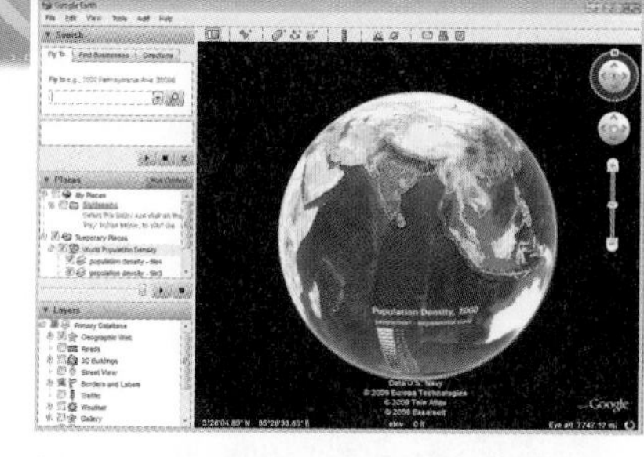

Data U. S. Navy, 2009 Europa Technologies, 2009 Tele Atlas, 2009 Basarsoft, © Google™ Earth.

Enhancing Classroom Communication

As you have learned throughout this text, it is important to address your students' individual needs and learning styles. Typically, a teacher will communicate instructional content and activities by telling students about them. However, for students who are primarily visual learners, this communication method can be difficult to follow. Web sites can help to support and enhance communication. For teacher-to-student communication, a classroom web site can contain daily, weekly, or unit assignments and thorough directions on how to complete them. It can also answer anticipated student questions on a linked **FAQ** (frequently asked questions) page. It can contain information about grading or tips for working on an assignment as well as links to relevant related pages such as the school's honesty or computer use policies. Finally, it can use web-based multimedia with voice, animation, or motion video to present key points in formats that address multiple learning preferences. This type of web page adds reinforcing dimensions to teacher-to-student communications as well as reiteration of key instructions.

A web site for your class can be a valuable tool for learning as well as communicating.

Student-to-teacher and student-to-student communication can be enhanced via a web site as well. Whether the student is in class but too shy to voice his or her questions or the student is at home and struggling with an assignment, email or an electronic chat can provide an opportunity for direct, private, and meaningful communication. Additionally, for students who can't seem to carry hard copy successfully from one location to another, attaching homework to an email message can be a very effective tool for ensuring that work is turned in on time. Electronic conferencing can also support and enhance communications if the teacher moderates posted public questions on activities or content. Using these web tools enhances student-to-teacher communications.

PEARSON myeducationkit™

Go to the *Assignments and Activities* section of Chapter 10 in MyEducationKit and complete the video activity entitled *Technology for All*.

For student-to-student communication, email, chats, weblogs, or electronic conferencing can encourage communication and build teamwork and communication skills. An activity in which students email the draft of a written assignment to each other for editing before completing the final version provides an opportunity for students to exercise proofreading and grammar skills. A group project that requires participation in a chat or conference helps students to develop communication skills while building technology

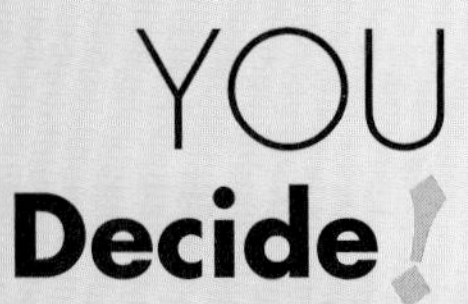

The Internet and, in particular, the easy-to-navigate World Wide Web are potentially powerful teaching and learning tools. But not all educators embrace and use this resource in their classrooms. Regardless of how ubiquitous the Internet and Web have become in our society, many teachers have been slow to integrate them into their lessons. However, since schools are indeed a reflection of and extension of the society they serve, many educators feel the full integration of the web and its resources are a mandate for all educators. Do you agree?

YES! Today computers and the Internet are as common as telephones. These technology skills are now life skills. Teachers need to help their students learn what they need to know to be successful adults, and that includes using the Internet. When we incorporate the web into classroom activities, we are not taking time away from required curriculum; instead, we are teaching our students that the Internet is a tool for them to complete their tasks at hand. Students need these skills and mastery of these tools to succeed. Our job is to give them an opportunity to learn how to use them, and when we integrate Internet skills, we don't even lose any curriculum time.

NO! Everyone is placing too much emphasis on computers and on the Internet. Students need to know the traditional ways to research and discover the information they need for their activities. What happens when the power goes off? Students need to appreciate books, journals, and the printed word. Traditional resources are more accurate anyway. Much of the information on the web is not authenticated and can mislead students. Our kids will learn about computers and the web at home and with their friends. We don't need to be taking academic time away from more important curriculum.

Which view on learning theories do you agree with? YOU DECIDE!

skills. For shy students who would otherwise be reluctant to contribute verbally in class, this opportunity for thoughtful communication at a pace that is comfortable for them may open new avenues of communication and build confidence in their own interaction skills.

Linking Your Students to Their World

E-Pals

Use the web to form a global learning community.

Student-to-student communication within a classroom, grade level, or school is just the beginning of what the Internet has to offer to your students. One of the most imaginative ways of utilizing your classroom web site as a communication tool is to connect your classroom to others across the globe, thereby building a **global learning community** for your students. *Keypals*, *e-pals*, and *cyberpals* are some of the terms used to refer to the other people with whom your students may correspond. Whatever term you prefer, the idea is to use Internet-based communications to extend interaction beyond the walls of your classroom or school.

Keypal assignments can help students practice communication skills while enhancing cultural awareness. Whole web sites are dedicated to establishing this type of learning community. Some provide teachers' guides, keypal lesson plans and projects, opportunities to request and make connections with global members, world maps, and even translation services. Communicating with keypals can be an invaluable personal growth experience as well as a directed learning activity.

However you decide to develop Internet-based links between your own students and their peers across the globe, the cultural awareness, communication skills, and content area enrichment that the Web makes possible can be a significant enhancement to classroom instruction.

Go to the *Assignments and Activities* section of Chapter 10 in MyEducationKit and complete the video activity entitled *Social Learning*.

The Web 2.0

The term **Web 2.0** refers to the second generation of the web, which emphasizes communication, collaboration, and sharing. The initial implementation of the World Wide Web can be considered the foundation for this next generation of the web. It focused on reading, whereas Web 2.0 has expanded its focus to include both reading and writing. The capacities of the next evolution of this powerful and pervasive technology have had significant impact on the resources being developed for the web and how they are used. Wikis, blogs, and RSS feeds are all part of the new "read-write web." One of the most revolutionary impacts of this new interactive web is the development of social networking.

PEARSON myeducationkit™

To learn more about social networking, go to the *Video Tutorials* section of Chapter 10 in MyEducationKit and select *Social Networking*.

Online social networking is the process of creating online communities through a series of web applications that promote communication, connections, and the sharing of information among participants in a social network. Taking communication beyond email and other Net-based software, social networking sites facilitate linking people with similar interests; provide them with easy-to-use resources for communication once linked; and then enable them to share information about themselves, their interests, and their activities. Social networking sites have thus created communities, both large and small, in which individuals can interact and build relationships. One report (Nielson, 2009) concludes that social networks are now the fourth most popular use of the Internet, ahead of personal email.

Some of the most popular U.S.-based social networking web sites include MySpace, Facebook, Twitter, and LinkedIn, with many other sites offering users similar capabilities. Approximately 200 million Internet users visited MySpace and Facebook alone each year (Nielson, 2009). There are also many sites emanating from other countries that are even larger than popular U.S. sites in terms of numbers of participants. Clearly, this social interaction phenomenon is growing and is changing the way in which people interact.

Facebook is now the leader among U.S.-based social networking sites with MySpace second in terms of users. Both of these sites allow participants to post and share information about themselves and make that information available to others who wish to become "friends." Friends thus create an online social network the participants of which can communicate, collaborate, and share in whatever common interest brought them together. LinkedIn is a similar service, but it focuses primarily on creating and maintaining contacts in business. Twitter is a somewhat different way to social network. It is essentially a microblog, an opportunity to post frequent short messages (tweets) relating what the participant is doing that can be read by those friends or "followers" who are interested. The social network created via Twitter informs participants of the events, views, or experiences of those they follow.

ISTE Standard

Learning about web resources that connect you and your students to the world will help you address

NETS•T STANDARD 3:

MODEL DIGITAL-AGE WORK AND LEARNING Teachers exhibit knowledge, skills, and work processes representative of an innovative professional in a global and digital society.

Social networking provides both interesting opportunities and serious concerns for teachers. It is likely that many of your students are familiar with and using these services, as perhaps you are as well. Given the potential for building community and positive interaction, social networking offers new and exciting ways to connect students within a class or in classrooms around the world in order to collaborate and learn together.

However, the use of social networking and unsupervised sharing, particularly among younger students who perhaps lack adequate judgment, have great potential for harm. Schools and technology-using educators therefore have the obligation to inform and protect students, just as they do with regard to other student safety issues. To do so, you too must be aware of both the positive and negative attributes of these powerful web tools so that you can model and teach their effective and safe use. Interchapter 10 provides you an overview of the most popular tools and options for their application in the classroom.

Building Bridges to Parents and the Community

Bring parents into the classroom through the Internet.

Parents and teachers share the goal of helping students meet their personal potential. By working together in partnership, you and your students' parents have the best chance of helping the children. Undeniably, life circumstances often make communications difficult. Many

PEARSON **myeducationkit**™

Go to the *Assignments and Activities* section of Chapter 10 in MyEducationKit and complete the web activity entitled *Web Uses for Classrooms*.

parents work outside the home and are available to teachers only after school hours. Time-shifted (asynchronous) interaction can help to open lines of communication that might otherwise not be possible. The web offers many opportunities for such communications.

By posting classroom rules, schedules, and homework on a web page, a teacher can directly communicate expectations to the parents of all students in a class. By using communications tools, including email, chat, and conferencing, a means for private and public dialog can be established. When you are seeking parent volunteers for classroom activities, posting such requests on a web site makes more partnerships and support possible.

Equally important, the ability to inform parents in a timely manner about student progress is a particularly powerful Internet-based communications tool. If you post grades via a secured web site, parents can track how students are doing and even monitor their attendance. Such daily or weekly feedback to parents gives them a chance to join you in resolving performance issues before they permanently affect a student's grades. This creates a powerful home–school partnership to support learners and keep them on the right track.

PEARSON **myeducationkit**™

Go to the *Assignments and Activities* section of Chapter 10 in MyEducationKit and complete the web activity entitled *Digital Storytelling*.

Linking your classroom to the greater community is another potential opportunity provided through the Internet. Community involvement can mean partnerships that enhance your learning environment through community members' participation as mentors or guest

FIGURE 10.6

Elements of an Effective Classroom Web Site

Classroom web sites let teachers reflect their own style while communicating information and instructional content and while providing links to other web resources.

Microsoft product screen shot reprinted with permission from Microsoft Corporation.

SITE PAGES

Classroom Connection page shares classroom information and current day's activities.

Homework Hotline page lets students and parents know what is required for homework this week.

Class Calendar tracks important due dates and holidays for students and parents.

News2View shares newsworthy events and class and student news.

Link-O-Rama offers students and parents links related to study units and school information.

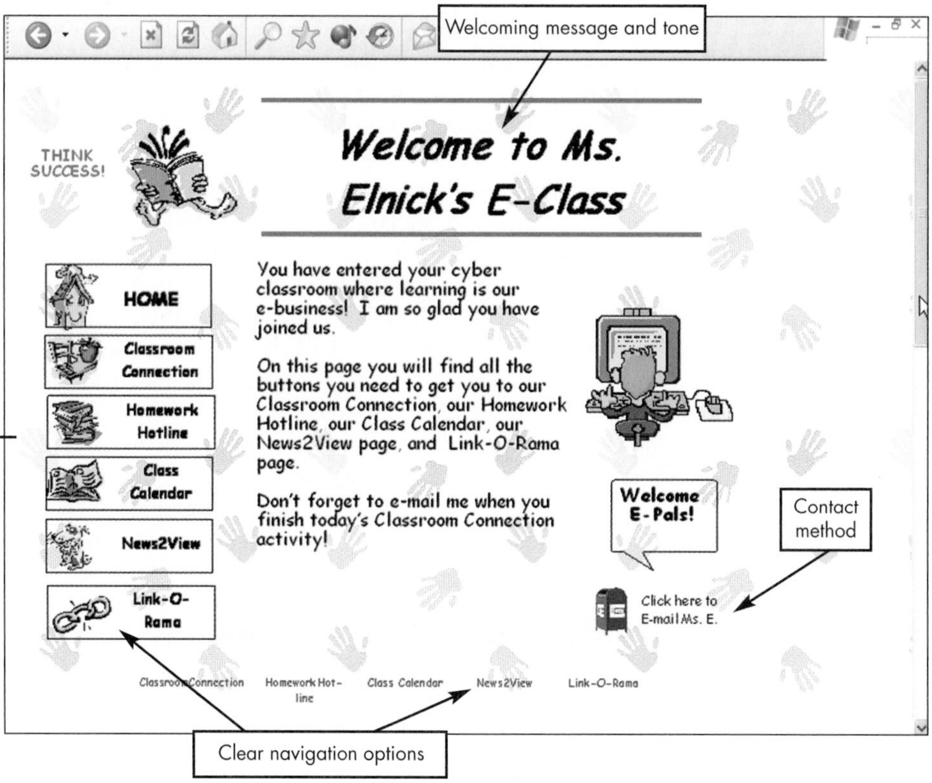

Welcoming message and tone

THINK SUCCESS!

Welcome to Ms. Elnick's E-Class

HOME

Classroom Connection

Homework Hotline

Class Calendar

News2View

Link-O-Rama

You have entered your cyber classroom where learning is our e-business! I am so glad you have joined us.

On this page you will find all the buttons you need to get you to our Classroom Connection, our Homework Hotline, our Class Calendar, our News2View page, and Link-O-Rama page.

Don't forget to e-mail me when you finish today's Classroom Connection activity!

Welcome E-Pals!

Contact method

Click here to E-mail Ms. E.

Classroom Connection Homework Hot-line Class Calendar News2View Link-O-Rama

Clear navigation options

speakers or through community contributions to class projects. Your students might become the hub of a virtual community learning center that links generations in dialog and support. Senior citizens might share oral history with your students, or your students might mentor younger peers on a project. Parents, community members, and students can join together to explore and share views on issues of significance to the local community. In whatever way you choose to provide communications opportunities to parents and the community, the bridges you create can only enhance the learning environment you provide for your students and open doors to their world.

Class Web Sites

Today, many teachers have created their own classroom web sites so that the Internet resources and communication tools they select are readily available. A classroom web site can offer class information as well as links to such resources and tools (see Figure 10.6). Just as every teacher has his or her own teaching style, a classroom web site offers a teacher the opportunity to customize what his or her students will do and see on the web via a unique virtual classroom space.

While a teacher might feel that creating a web site is too difficult, as you learned in Chapter 8, **web authoring tools** are available to make the job easy to do. The next section will review these authoring tools and help you to decide which is best for you.

PEARSON myeducationkit™

Go to the *Podcasts* section of Chapter 10 in MyEducationKit and complete the video activity entitled *Classroom Websites*.

Web Authoring Tools

So many web authoring tools are available today that you no longer need a working knowledge of HTML to create a web site. All you need is a well-planned idea for a site and some basic computer skills. Given the variety of tools available, which one you choose to use depends on your skill level and your expectations for the final product.

Authoring tools make creating your own web site something you can do.

Word Processors

One of the easiest ways to create a web page is to use a word processor with which you are already familiar. Word processors let you create files as you would any other file, laying them out with graphics and text, but then you can save them in HTML format for uploading to the web (Figure 10.7). This technique is reasonably simple to use, but creates only very basic types of web pages.

The advantage of using the word-processing software with which you may already be familiar could be canceled out by its inflexibility. You might want more sophisticated layout capabilities or more features than the web component of a word processor can provide. The best way to decide is to try word-processing web authoring. Materials accessible at **www.myeducationkit.com** include a tutorial that gives you hands-on experience with Microsoft Word's web authoring capabilities. If Word is insufficient for your needs, there are alternative software packages to consider.

Desktop Publishing Software

As you learned in earlier chapters, desktop publishing software gives you much greater design control than is possible with a word processor. Just as desktop publishing allows you to manipulate a printed page more easily, so too can the desktop publisher that is equipped with web production components give you more flexibility in manipulating a web site's page layouts. The more sophisticated desktop publishing programs include web wizards and templates allowing you to quickly create very dramatic web pages

FIGURE 10.7

Using Microsoft Word for Web Authoring Capabilities

MS Word makes creating a web site an easy process.

Microsoft Word is a registered trademark of Microsoft Corporation.

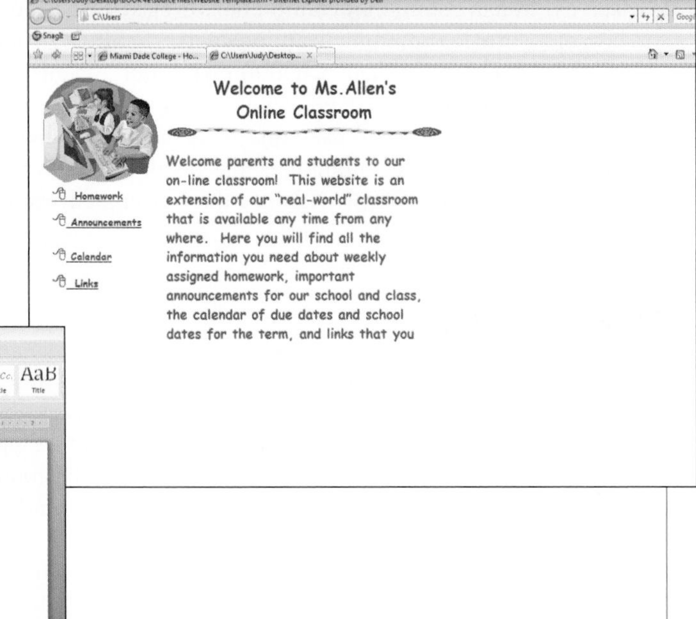

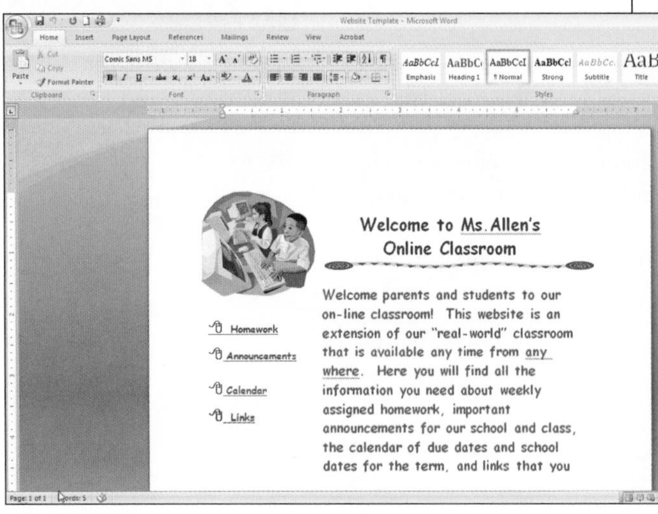

(see Figure 10.8). **Templates** are predefined formats, and **wizards** are interactive tools that use and help you customize these templates to your needs. Because publishing software allows more flexibility and design features, the web pages produced by it are typically a bit more sophisticated. Although this type of software will not allow you to include all of the bells and whistles you see on many commercial web sites, it will help you to create a very attractive, automatically linked web site.

PEARSON **myeducationkit**™

To learn more about creating your own web page, go to the *Video Tutorials* section of Chapter 10 in MyEducationKit and select *Microsoft Publisher*.

Accessible at **www.myeducationkit.com** is a hands-on activity using Microsoft Publisher. Publisher will help you to build a colorful and powerful web site using familiar and easy-to-use tools. It can then be easily saved in HTML format and uploaded to the Web.

Dedicated Web Development Software

PEARSON **myeducationkit**™

To learn more about available web development software, go to the *Video Tutorials* section of Chapter 10 in MyEducationKit and select *Adobe DreamWeaver*.

For those who are interested in developing a more sophisticated site, web development software programs are readily available (see Figure 10.9). These programs range from fairly easy to very complex, depending on the sophistication you are trying to achieve in the finished web site. Some will provide you with very advanced graphics and multimedia tools to add your own special effects to your site. You will have to decide what level of sophistication you want to achieve in your site and decide for yourself how much time and how many resources you are willing to invest. Although dedicated web authoring tools are easy to use once you have mastered the skills, they are typically not as easy as using a web component of an alternative software package with which you are already familiar.

Web authoring tools can help you create web pages.

A dedicated web authoring tool may also be available through the ISP or portal that you use. These resources allocate web space for their customers' web pages. Typically, those that do also provide a web creation tool. Usually, such tools do not have a great number of options, but they will allow you to create a web page with relative ease. Different web

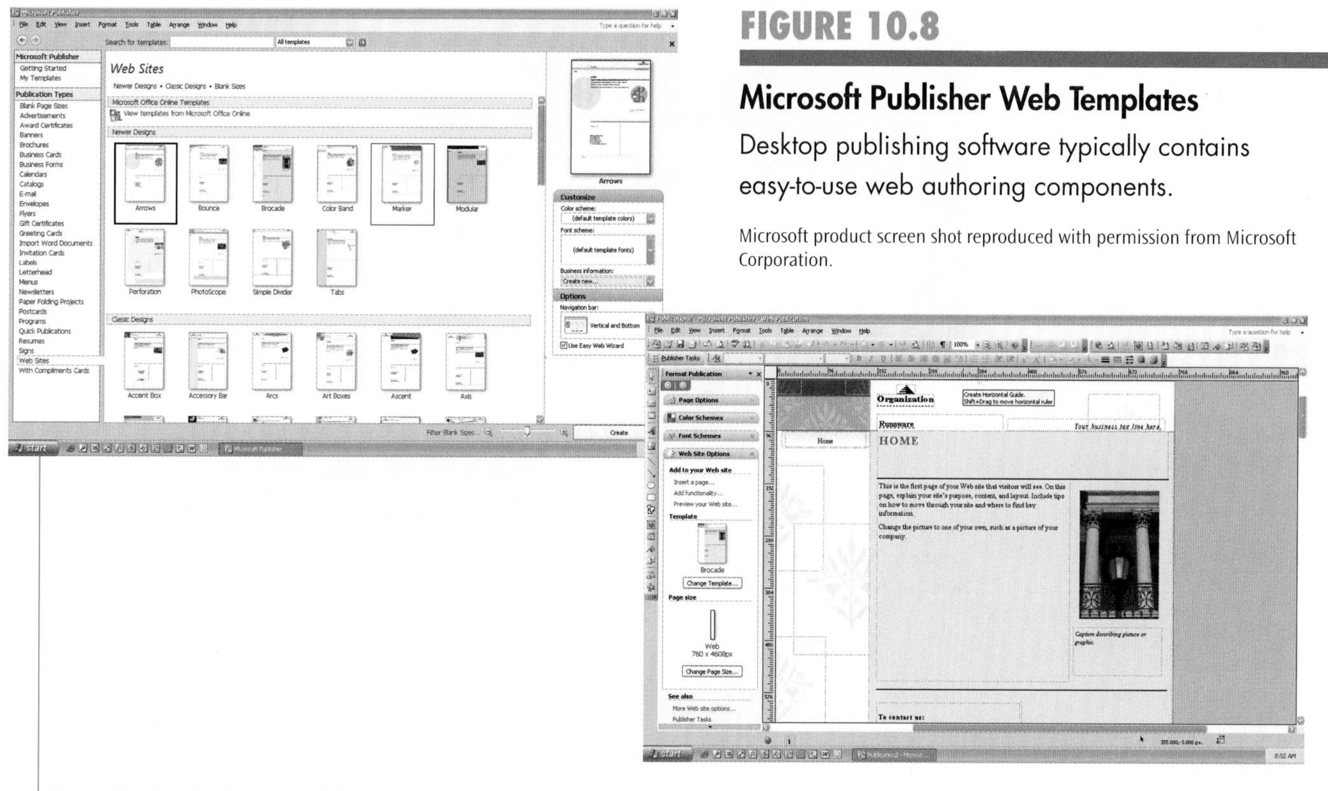

FIGURE 10.8

Microsoft Publisher Web Templates

Desktop publishing software typically contains easy-to-use web authoring components.

Microsoft product screen shot reproduced with permission from Microsoft Corporation.

resources provide different levels of service, so it is important to shop around if you decide to use them. Remember that most ISPs and portals that provide you with web space will also let you upload a site you have created using your own software of choice. They usually do not require you to use their specific tools.

Moving Your Site to the Internet

Adding Your Site to the School or District Site

Once you have completed your web site authoring, how do you move your site to the Internet? Your web site is actually a series of HTML and multimedia files stored on your hard drive. To put these files up on the web, you will need to move them to a web server.

Many schools and districts now provide space on their web servers for teachers' classroom web sites. In this case, to add your site to the school's or district's server, you will need to give all of the related web site files to the webmaster for your school. A webmaster's job is to create and maintain a site and to integrate new elements. Your school or district webmaster will take your classroom web site files and integrate them appropriately into the school or district site.

It is important to keep in mind that many webmasters have additional jobs as technical support staff or have their hands full maintaining complex institutional web sites. In either case, it may take a bit of time to see your web site come up on the web, a problem that may repeat itself every time you want to update the site. If you want to alter the site daily or weekly,

FIGURE 10.9

Web Development Software

Web development software gives you the potential to add every level of sophistication to your site.

FIGURE 10.10

Web Site Hosting

A web hosting service allows you to upload your web site to its web server to make it accessible on the Web. Many hosts offer free space for educational websites.

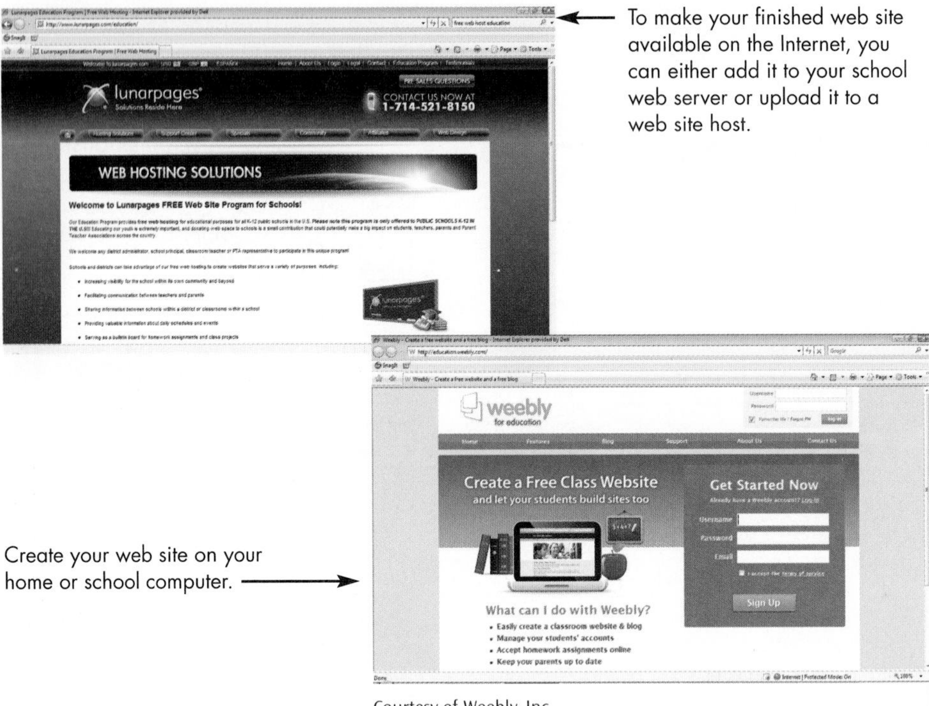

you will need to discuss your intention with the webmaster so that he or she can assign you the network rights to do so.

Uploading to a Web Host

Free or inexpensive **web hosting** is a service offered by a number of ISPs, web sites, and portals (see Figure 10.10). To use this type of service, you need only **upload** your pages to the host, usually via an **FTP** program. The service will take care of creating the web access for you. Links to very detailed instructions on how to upload files are usually displayed prominently on the service's web development page.

Hosting services allow you a given number of megabytes of space on the service's web server; some services offer an unlimited amount of space. In exchange, those who visit your site may be asked to fill in some personal information to "join" the service in order to access your page. At the very least, they will be exposed to ads on the service's home page as they navigate to your page. Other hosting services may add a banner ad to the top of your page or require you to allow pop-up ads. This is how services can offer to host your site for free or a reduced cost.

You should carefully investigate sites that offer these services, including reading the fine print in the online agreements. Because you will be asking your students to use the site, if the advertisements on a service's home page or the elements added to your home page seem inappropriate or too overbearing for young visitors, you might decide that it is best not to use that service. You need to make your best professional judgment about the value of a free or inexpensive web hosting service and the nonmonetary costs it entails. Your first responsibility is to ensure that your students are not exposed to excessive or inappropriate advertising within the requirements of your course. Before you use a free web hosting service, be sure to check with your school or district policies and procedures.

Uploading to Academic Web Services

A final type of web hosting service is one that is incorporated within broader academic services. Some private and publicly funded web sites offer schools and teachers a variety of free educational services, including web hosting. These services refrain from advertising on your web pages and strictly control advertising on their broader sites. They are designed to provide an appropriate Internet environment for your students and your site. The only disadvantage to this type of site is that it often provides only a relatively small amount of storage space, which may make it inadequate for larger web sites.

Internet Issues and Concerns

PEARSON myeducationkit™

Go to the *Assignments and Activities* section of Chapter 10 in MyEducationKit and complete the web activity entitled *Teaching about Online Safety*.

With any resource that is used in the learning environment, professional judgment must be used in determining the appropriateness of the resource and ensuring that the resource is used within the ethical and legal parameters of the profession. Using the Internet in your teaching and learning environment is no different. A number of significant concerns are frequently voiced relating to the use of the Internet in schools. Three of these issues—acceptable use, privacy, and filtering—are introduced in this section. An expanded discussion of these issues can be found in Chapter 13.

Acceptable Use

Like any technology, the Internet can be abused. In a school setting, it is therefore necessary to identify and enforce the acceptable use of a school's network and Internet access. This is usually done through a district's or school's acceptable-use policy (AUP). This policy articulates the ways in which the Internet can be used by students. Typically, parents are asked to confirm their understanding of the policy and the consequences for violating it through a signature acknowledgment. Teachers who use the Internet and who provide links to resources via their own class web sites should be familiar with the AUP that governs their students' use of the Internet.

Privacy

When sharing your students' work or including their images or names on a web site, a teacher must be sure to carefully guard a child's privacy. To include any student's information or work, it is best to first have the parent's or guardian's permission. Further, no specific details about the child should be divulged, including his or her name. People who might harm children might use a class web site as a way to target them. The problem has become so significant that districts and schools typically have developed very specific policies regarding the content of a class web site. It is up to each teacher to be sure his or her site is consistent with district and school guidelines.

Filtering

As you know, the Internet is not owned or controlled by any agency. Therefore, the Internet includes web sites and information that are inappropriate for children. A school has a responsibility to limit access to such web sites, just as a parent would limit access at home. Schools use filtering software that checks the content of a site before allowing it to be displayed. Students are denied access to sites with inappropriate materials. Claims of freedom of speech are sometimes invoked when filtering software is used. Such controversy is more fully addressed in Chapter 13, but most people would agree that it is appropriate to keep children safe from harmful Internet content just as they are kept safe from other harm while at school.

Academic Web Site Evaluation **Rubric**

DEVELOPER'S NAME:

URL:

AREA/CONTENT OF SITE:

PURPOSE:

Using each of the criteria below, evaluate the usefulness of this web site for teaching and learning. For each dimension in the rubric, check the box that best reflects your opinion. Select web sites that score 4 or higher in most of the dimensions.

EVALUATION CRITERIA

DIMENSION	1 Poor	2 Below Average	3 Average	4 Above Average	5 Excellent
Goal	☐ Goal of this web site unclear and confusing	☐ Conflicting themes make site's goal uncertain	☐ Goal is clear, but site contains some unrelated or distracting elements	☐ Clear purpose and goal; some elements seem unnecessary	☐ Goal and purpose of site clear with no distracting elements
User Friendliness	☐ Unwelcoming to users	☐ Does not evoke a welcoming message	☐ Welcomes visitors but does not appear friendly	☐ Welcoming and appears friendly	☐ Exciting, welcoming, and very user-friendly
Design	☐ Poorly organized; contains obvious errors; loads slowly; difficult to read	☐ Organization somewhat confusing; some errors; loads slowly	☐ Organization acceptable; no obvious errors; loads adequately; easy to read	☐ Good organization; no errors; loads quickly; easy to read	☐ Excellent organization; free of errors; loads quickly and clearly; all elements easy to read
Navigability	☐ Difficult to find and follow site navigation links	☐ Navigation links visible but somewhat confusing	☐ Navigation links clear and readily available	☐ Navigation links clear and logical; site map included	☐ Navigation logical and clear; site map and search engine available
Authority	☐ Unclear who the teacher is and what class the site relates to	☐ Teacher name and contact included, but sufficient class information lacking	☐ Teacher name, contact information, and some class information included	☐ Teacher name, contact information, full class information included	☐ Teacher provides all necessary information to student, parent, and community visitors
Dates	☐ No dates evident	☐ Site contains some dates	☐ Site contains both creation and update information but no dates related to class activities	☐ Site contains creation and update information and some dates relating to class activities	☐ Site contains dates for creation, update, and all class activities
Content	☐ Content limited and lacks relevance to students and parents	☐ Content appears relevant, but quantity limited in student needs	☐ Content is adequate in relevance and quantity to meet student needs	☐ Content is relevant and quantity is sufficient for student needs	☐ Content is on target and provides excellent coverage to meet student needs
Links	☐ Few relevant working links	☐ Adequate number of links, but many no longer functional	☐ Sufficient number of links, all functional	☐ A good variety of useful, active links	☐ Links offer connection to a wide variety of excellent sites
Handicapped Access	☐ No options available for handicapped	☐ Some pages on site offer text-only	☐ Site offers text-only on all pages	☐ Site offers clear options for handicapped	☐ Site includes handicapped options on all pages and links to support software

PEARSON myeducationkit™ Go to the *Rubrics* section of Chapter 10 in MyEducationKit to download the *Academic Web Site Evaluation Rubric* for your use.

Using the Web in Teaching and Learning: Final Thoughts

As anyone knows who has used the Internet, there can be little doubt that it holds enormous potential for education. But without the thoughtful integration of its marvelous resources into instruction by trained and knowledgeable teachers, learners will miss the potential of the Internet. As with all technology tools, it is not the tool itself that enhances teaching and learning, it is how the tool is used by the creative professional educator who is wielding it. The web is a marvel of limitless resources. But your students need you, their teacher, to help make the web truly meaningful in their attempt to achieve their academic potential. Just as you master your content area before you teach it, so too must you master Internet skills before you can use them effectively. This chapter, along with Chapter 9, has attempted to give you a foundation for this mastery. We hope that the potential of the Internet has been made abundantly clear and your enthusiasm for using this technology amply kindled.

To check your comprehension of the content covered in this chapter, go to the MyEducationKit for your book and complete the *Study Plan* for Chapter 10.

Key Terms

academic tools, 270
blogs, 265
bookmarks, 269
classroom management tools, 269
electronic gradebooks, 269
ERIC, 269
FAQ, 271
favorites, 269
FTP, 278
global learning community, 272
online publications, 261
PDF files, 262
RSS feeds, 267
templates, 276
test generators, 269
upload, 278
Web 2.0, 273
web authoring tools, 275
web hosting, 278
wiki, 264
wizards, 276

Student Activities

CHAPTER REVIEW

1. What online resources are available to assist educators in researching areas of interest? Describe each.
2. What is a PDF file? What advantage does it offer over files in HTML format?
3. What is a weblog? How might it be used for teaching and learning?
4. How are government educational sites of value in terms of resources? How do they differ from commercial and organizational sites?
5. What types of classroom management and academic tools are available via the Internet? Briefly explain how each tool might help you in your classroom.
6. How can a classroom web site improve communications with students, parents, and community?
7. What are web authoring tools? What types are available to educators?
8. How are new web sites added to the Web? What resources do teachers have to do so?
9. What is an acceptable use policy? What impact does it have on the use of the Web in the classroom?
10. Contrast the issues of privacy and filtering when using the Web in the classroom. What are the responsibilities of a teacher in each of these areas?

WHAT DO YOU THINK?

1. Your class has created a useful and interesting web site, but your school's technical-support staff is very overworked, so you might have to wait until the next grading period to have the site put on the web server. You decide to use a free web hosting service instead. What issues will you need to face in using a free web hosting service? How can you control unacceptable banner ads or pop-up ads that may be added to your site?
2. You have installed a filter on your stand-alone classroom computer that is connected to the Internet. You block all sites that you think might be pornographic, and then you decide to block all sites that may include what you feel might be communist propaganda. Some people would consider this a violation of your students' First Amendment rights. Do you think so? Why or why not?
3. You decide that you want to create an electronic learning community for your students this semester. You would like to be sure they can converse with other students in the district, the state, and even around the globe. You have decided that you want to center the community on a multicultural theme in which they compare holiday customs and celebrations. How will you go about creating such a community? What kinds of activities will you include?

LEARNING TOGETHER!

These activities are best done in groups of three to five:

1. Search the Internet for outstanding educational sites. Each group member should find at least five sites. Prepare an annotated list of your group's top ten finds. Word-process your list, and distribute it to all members of your class. You are also invited to send it to one of this textbook's authors so that it may be considered for inclusion on the web site that accompanies this text.
2. Assume that you are a grade-level team that has been asked by your school to create a grade-level web site. Storyboard the web site you want to create. You should provide enough detail so that the text to be included and the types of graphics are evident.
3. Each group member should observe a classroom in which the Internet is used. Interview the teacher to discover the successes and experiences he or she has had using the Internet in teaching and learning. Compare the information gathered through observations and interviews. Word-process a summary of your discoveries. You are also invited to email your paper to one of the text authors for inclusion on the text web site.

TEACHING WITH TECHNOLOGY: INTEGRATION IDEAS WEB QUEST

The web offers educators profound Information Age tools. Teachers in the twenty-first century will need to master them to make educational delivery meaningful to the children of this generation. Consider the following ideas for integrating the web. These are just a quick look at how some educators are using the web in teaching and learning.

ACTIVITY: Explore the links below and the web resources you have learned about in this chapter. Select the one resource of most interest to you, and then search the Net for three innovative ways in which the resource you selected is being used in the grade level or content area you plan to teach. Write a one-page summary of your web quest that includes (1) the web resource you selected and why you chose it above all others, (2) the links you explored and the ideas you found with an annotation for each link briefly describing the idea presented, and (3) an idea of your own about how you will utilize your favorite web resource in your classroom.

Integration Ideas: Integrating the Web into Math

Mission Possible: Solving Word Problems in Algebra is a web quest that Rod Chandler and Becky Van Wanzeele designed to familiarize students with the approaches they will need to know to be able to solve algebraic word problems. The Introduction alerts the students to an investigation they will take part in to overcome "one of the most challenging aspects of Algebra, the dreaded word problem." The Task calls forth memories of *Mission Impossible* as it relates to the students their mission. They work in teams and assume the role of expert teachers who will conduct research on certain types of word problems by going to the Internet, their textbook, and their parents. The results of their research will be presented to the class in the "debriefing." The secrets to decoding algebraic word problems will be recorded in a "mission notebook" that will be compiled from the presentations given by their "fellow agents"—the other students. Copies with the examples presented are to be provided to "every special agent (entire class)." If you wish to join this possible mission, go to Chandler, R., & Van Wanzeele, B. *Mission possible: Solving word problems in algebra* at **http://education.iupui.edu/webquests/math/index.htm.**

Integration Ideas: Integrating the Web into Language Arts

Glogster is a Web 2.0 educational tool that lets students create online interactive posters that include video, text, audio, and more. Students can collaborate, publish, and share their creations with the class through a Glogster class account managed by the teacher. Jared Nichols, a language arts teacher at Grand Centre High School in Cold Lake, Alberta, uses a variety of Web 2.0 tools, including Glogster. Jared used this tool to showcase student poems, research poets, and ultimately make an online visual poster in Glogster to share their own work and the work of the poet they researched. For more information about Jared's visual Glogster pages and about the other ways in which he is using Web 2.0 tools in the classroom, visit his blog at **http://2pointohteaching.blogspot.com/.** To find out more about Glogster, visit **http://www.glogster.com/edu/.**

Integration Ideas: Integrating the Web into the Sciences

Sixth-grade students accept the challenge to be heroes and to find out why dinosaurs became extinct in the science web quest *Dinosaurs: How Did They Become Extinct?*, created by Suzanne Eoff. After an introduction to the mystery surrounding the disappearance of the dinosaurs, the pages are populated by animated dinosaurs of different types and sizes. The student's task is "to be heroes and figure out what happened to the dinosaurs so that we can prevent such a huge catastrophic event from happening in the future." Addressed as paleontologists, the students are told to board the time machine for a trip that will take them back 60 million years and then to research the web for theories that scientists have come up with to explain the extinction. To make the journey back in time, go to Eoff, S. *Dinosaurs: How did they become extinct* at **http://www.montana.edu/webquest/science/grades6t012/eoff.**

Integration Ideas: Integrating the Web into the Social Studies

Twitter is a microblog that allows 140-character entries (tweets) to be made and distributed to followers. Imagine the possibilities if a significant event in history could unfold for your students one tweet at a time made by one of the participants in that event. The web site TwHistory does exactly that. It is an all-volunteer site that uses Twitter to inform followers of the events of history through the people who lived and experienced them. Instead of reading about a month-long campaign in a few hours, you experience it over the course of a month, in small, 140 character 'Tweets.'" This experimental application of Twitter to social studies is looking for additional volunteers. To participate or read more about TwHistory, visit **http://www.twhistory.com/.**

10 *inter*chapter

The Web 2.0

Social Networking

As you have learned, online social networks are virtual communities that evolve from the use of free and widely available online software that enables communications and connections. Most social network resources are primarily personal, but some focus on bringing social networking tools to education. Below, you will find a summary of some of the dominant social networks on the web today, including those used in education.

myspace® a place for friends

Brad Greenspan, Chris DeWolfe, Josh Berman, and Tom Anderson saw the potential of the early social networking site Friendster, to which they all belonged. In 2003, they launched their rendition of a social networking site. Called MySpace, the site offered participants the ability to post and share anything they wanted, including music, graphics, video, and text, and the option to include in profiles whatever the owner chose. Targeted at teens and young adults, MySpace quickly became a media-sharing site as well as a community-building site. Young musicians and artists used MySpace to showcase and advertise their work.

MySpace offers the common social networking features, which include a profile page, blog, chat, instant messaging, and a series of applications that are available to expand one's personal network of "friends." Other features include feeds to keep friends abreast of what the participant is doing, news that allows voting by friends, classifieds, and even karaoke and MySpace TV. MySpace emphasizes the sharing of media and an open profile, making it a useful site for undiscovered artists to share and market their talents.

In part because of its open format, MySpace has had some privacy issues. MySpace has been troubled by computer viruses and spyware launched via participants' profiles. MySpace has also had spam (unwanted email) and phishing (redirection to a suspect web site) schemes affect participants. At one point, videos on users' profile pages were harvested and made public. MySpace has also had issues with stalking and child predators, since the process of becoming a "friend" is open to all unless restricted by the owner of the profile. In response, MySpace has taken numerous steps to correct these security concerns.

facebook

Facebook was founded in 2004 by Mark Zukerberg while he was a student at Harvard. Initially run as a hobby project, Zukerberg quickly found that the network had jumped the campus of Harvard and spread across the nation to become the first student-based social network. Originally open only to students at registered schools, Facebook is now open to everyone. In early 2009, it became the number one social network in terms of the number of users.

Facebook offers participants an ever-growing number of features. In addition to sharing profile information, links, and photos, the "Wall" is one of its most popular features. It lets users post text, image, and even video messages to share with those in one's personal network of others identified as "friends." News feeds offer friends the option to feed personal news and entries to each other. Another popular feature is the "poke," which allows one friend to quickly get the virtual attention of another. Many applications are available in Facebook, from games to communications tools. Gifts, for example, lets you send small images to a friend as a gift for a modest fee, with a portion of that fee going to a favorite charity. Other applications let you share your Netflix queue or build your family tree, all to help you share and increase relationships with online friends.

Like all social network sites, Facebook participants need to be aware of privacy issues. Information posted can be used by others to your detriment if you are not careful to use Facebook security features to guard it. Unlike some social networking sites, Facebook does allow users to create settings that will restrict viewing and sharing of profile information with only those people you identify as friends. However, it is the participant's responsibility to activate appropriate settings.

twitter

In 2006, Evan Williams, Biz Stone, and Jack Dorsey started Twitter, a company focused on the microblog for social networking. Twitter is part social network and part blog in its capacity to share brief entries (Tweets) with a network of interested followers. Twitter also has the capacity to interface with SMS (Small Messaging Service), usually referred to as text messaging, so that Tweets arrive on a follower's cell phone. Participants can be either individuals or groups and organizations (e.g., CNN) using the service to keep followers abreast of the latest news or events.

A Tweet can contain only 140 characters of text, including links, so reading Tweets is essentially like perusing headlines. For more in-depth information, the Tweeter needs to direct followers to a blog or web site via Tweet links. To facilitate linking and avoid using character space, long URLs are abbreviated by Twitter into "tiny URLs," or coded versions of link's address. Applications are available to track Twitters through a desktop application, email, or instant messaging as well as via the Twitter web site and SMS. New applications are constantly being written to enhance Twitter's functions and accessibility. For example, Twittervision integrates Twitter and Google maps to show followers not only the Tweet but where the Tweeter user is located.

Twitter has had application beyond social networking. During emergencies, Twitter has been used to send updates on the crisis. And it has been a source for citizen journalism, the collection and broadcast of newsworthy events by everyday citizens. For example, when a US Airways plane landed in the Hudson, one participant on a rescue ferry took a picture of the downed plane and sent it as a Tweet to TweetPic.com, a Twitter photo-sharing web site, making it the first image of the accident. Although still in its infancy, Twitter is fast becoming ubiquitous, with its uses just being explored.

Social Networking in Schools

Most public social networking sites are just that—public and social. Such sites have somewhat limited use in the classroom, although some educators using these sites have set up education social groups of educator friends to share in professional conversations. However, for a school or classroom, the challenge is to focus the power of building community more directly on teaching and learning. Some early educational adopters of social networking are indeed finding direct use for this powerful web and social tool. Teachers have students follow the tweets related to news events or topics under study. Class projects include exploring the Facebook pages of significant political figures. However, at issue are the safety and privacy of children using these networks. In fact, as a result of these concerns, many districts prohibit the use of social networking. Still, social networks have students writing and reading, composing, listening, and sharing as no single class assignment can. How, then, will creative computer-using educators harness the power of social networks to enhance teaching and learning?

One answer may be in making social networks private and thereby safer. Currently, children using public social networks are at risk of encouraging the violation of their own privacy by exposing too much information about themselves or posting inappropriate images. With potential predators on networks as well, child safety is a critical concern. Cyberbullying on unmoderated social networks is also an issue. To use social networking effectively and safely in education, it is important to create a safe social network that is limited to the school audience and controlled by the school.

Online software is being developed to create such a restricted social networking place. Learning Landscape for Schools (LL4Schools) is one example of this type of software. LL4Schools is online customizable social networking software that schools can use. It restricts public use yet offers many of the tools found in public social networks that have applications to education. LL4Schools includes key community-building features including blogs, profiles, and feeds that are necessary to build online communities. However, participants are restricted to those submitted by the school using the software, thereby keeping students safe from outsiders.

Building community and encouraging social interaction have always been key components of schooling. Children and adolescents need a safe and protected opportunity to interact and grow personally through relationships. Online social networking—and, indeed, Web 2.0 of which it is a part—is the twenty-first century outgrowth of the human need to socialize. Creative educators have found and will continue to find new tools and methods for using these technological innovations in their classrooms. While privacy and other issues remain, educators focused on both child safety and innovative application of the web will no doubt find ways to bring the positive power of building communities through online social networking fully into the classroom.

CHAPTER 11

Audiovisual Technologies

Will Hart/PhotoEdit

CHAPTER OVERVIEW

This chapter addresses these ISTE National Educational Technology Standards:
- •NETS•T Standard 1
- •NETS•T Standard 2
- •NETS•S Standard 2

In the preceding chapters, you learned much about the computer technologies you are likely to find in instructional environments. However, if you were to visit any classroom today to examine the technologies in place, you would also find other technologies used on a daily basis. In Chapter 1, we defined educational technology in its broadest sense, that is, any technology that is used to support or enhance teaching and learning. To fully acquaint you with the types of technologies you are most likely to find in the schools you work in, it is important to become familiar with all of the types of technologies you are likely to encounter. This chapter will help you to explore some of the noncomputer technologies you will find.

Before the digital age, technologies that supported teaching and learning were often called audiovisual, or AV, media. Such technologies typically included overhead projectors, slide projectors, filmstrip projectors, movie projectors, tape recorders, and televisions. Today, as you have seen in this text, digital technologies have added significantly to the instructional tools educators have available to them.

This chapter will introduce you to audio and visual media of all types, from the more traditional visual, audio, and video technologies to their leading-edge digital counterparts. It will help you to explore how each of these traditional and digital technologies can be used to address learning styles to support the instructional event and to help you plan how to integrate these technologies into your classroom. You will then be ready to explore how they have been used to change the face of education in many areas and the issues these changes have generated.

In Chapter 11, you will:

- Examine the relationship and educational application of traditional and digital audio, visual, and video media
- Investigate the use of audio and video media in support of teaching and learning
- Review the application of visual media in support of teaching and learning
- Explore the use of projected and nonprojected visual media
- Examine the role of the Internet in providing audio, visual, and video support for teaching and learning

Audiovisual Technologies

Teachers know instinctively that the more interactive and multisensory they make their teaching, the more likely it is that learning will occur. Common sense and instructional experiences have taught us that a lesson delivered through lecture alone is less engaging than a lesson delivered with both audio and visual support. Few people would disagree that giving a talk about native birds in North America becomes more meaningful when combined with presentation of the recordings of songs of such birds and either beautifully colored still images or motion images. During an instructional event, adding the appropriate audio and visual components can engage more of the learner's senses and help to build multiple cognitive connections to the content presented.

To be able to use all of the available technological tools at hand, educators need to be familiar with the full range of tools that will support the learner's efforts to make meaningful contact with, and build mastery of, the content presented. Audio and visual tools of all types, whether traditional technologies or those that have emerged from the digital age, can be valuable in supporting the teaching and learning process. For this reason, it is important for those who work with learners to be aware of the types of audio and visual technologies available and their application in teaching and learning.

In the first half of the twentieth century, education was enhanced through the introduction of sound and video technologies. The record player, tape recorder, and movie projector all came into being, became a part of society, and ultimately were introduced into the classroom. These traditional technologies have not disappeared, although many have evolved in form. Movie projectors have given way to VCRs and then DVD players;

ISTE Standard

Learning about audiovisual resources for your classroom will help you address

NETS•T STANDARD 2:

DESIGN AND DEVELOP DIGITAL-AGE LEARNING EXPERIENCES AND ASSESSMENTS Teachers design, develop, and evaluate authentic learning experiences and assessments incorporating contemporary tools and resources to maximize content learning in context and to develop the knowledge, skills, and attitudes identified in the NETS•S.

TABLE 11.1 Audio and Video Technology Overview

FUNCTION	TRADITIONAL AV TECHNOLOGIES	DIGITAL AND OTHER EMERGING TECHNOLOGIES
DISPLAY INDIVIDUAL STATIC IMAGES OR PHOTOS	Overhead projector, slide projector, bulletin board, posters	Document camera, computer display, clip art, photo galleries on CD or the Internet
DISPLAY MOVING IMAGES	Film projector, VCR	Computer display, DVD player, computer CD-ROM, Internet video
PLAY BACK MUSIC OR SPEECH	Tape recorder, record player	CD player, MP3 player, iPod, DVD player, Internet audio
PLAY TV PROGRAMS	CRT TV monitor	LCD or plasma monitor, computer display, Internet webcast
RESEARCH SUPPORT	Books	Multimedia CD-ROMs, e-books, Internet searches

reel-to-reel tape recorders have been replaced by cassette recorders, CD players, and now iPods and MP3 players; and the record players that were designed to play sound stored on vinyl platters have also been superseded by these formats. Although the storage and playback technology has changed, the intent remains constant. Audio and visual technologies help you teach and your students learn.

In essence, audio and visual enhancements to text and the spoken word are just as important in the digital age as they were in the twentieth century. As technology advances, the format of audio and visual media may change, but their significance to teaching and learning will not. Given that many schools have many functional traditional audiovisual technologies still in service, it is important for educators to be aware of the potential of these traditional technologies. Digital versions of AV technologies will no doubt continue to replace more traditional media, but as long as these older technologies are still in use, they continue to support creative educators. And the instructional effort spent to use these more traditional technologies will easily transfer when they are eventually replaced by emerging technologies. The key to integrating both traditional and emerging technologies into teaching and learning is, as with all educational technology, not a question of their technical format but instead a question of the educator's creativity and familiarity with instructional design. Awareness of all the types of audio, visual, and digital technological tools available to you will give you more choices when you design instruction. See Table 11.1 for an overview of these technologies.

Traditional and digital AV technologies can help support diverse instructional designs while addressing different learning styles.

Audio in Teaching and Learning

Every teacher uses auditory delivery to teach students; the source of the audio is most typically the teacher's voice. Whether the teacher is verbally introducing a concept briefly to third graders or lecturing on a complex theory to college students, audio is a dominant delivery system in every educational environment. As you no doubt know from your own learning experiences, sometimes teacher-based audio is very effective, and sometimes it is not.

It is in such instances that audio technology can help. Capturing auditory information, storing it, and playing it back can be a very useful tool to support learning. A student can listen to a presentation multiple times at the pace necessary for full comprehension. For students who have difficulty listening effectively, being able to manage the pace of audio communication may be enough to turn a frustrating learning scenario into one that students are able to master. Audio technologies offer educators the tools needed to be able to support learners in this manner.

Recorded verbal information lets students control the pace at which they listen.

Traditional Audio Media

Although becoming less common, **audiocassettes** have been an economical, durable, and easy-to-use magnetic medium. Cassette tape players are still used in schools; they are inexpensive additions to the learning environment. Cassette players are compact and simple to operate for even the youngest learners. For small-group instruction, creating and playing back an audiotape can enhance active learning. When coupled with earphones, cassette players can make a valuable addition as a classroom aid for individualized learning and review (see Table 11.2).

One of the most popular uses of audiotapes is the **talking book.** Whether for primary students who are learning to read or high school students who enjoy the dramatization of a play, recorded readings of books, plays, or short stories can add an auditory dimension to such texts. Students can either read along with a talking book or listen and respond to questions as the audio book or story progresses.

Another popular use of audiotapes is the creation or acquisition of multimedia kits. Whether made by the teacher or commercially produced, **multimedia kits** usually include visual elements (texts and graphics) and supplemental audio

TECH TIPS for Teachers

Audio is a critical part of instruction, but using it effectively requires an understanding of the listening process. Listening is a two-part activity that involves the physiological process of hearing and the cognitive process of comprehending what is heard. Effective audio instruction requires that clear audio stimulation be available to be heard. Hearing content must then be followed by the opportunity to make cognitive connections to previously learned content or personal memories. For some learners, this two-step process requires practice. Teachers who wish to use audio technologies for instruction may find it necessary to assist learners in acquiring, improving, and applying hearing and listening skills. Focused listening activities are a method to that end.

Focused listening activities include listening games or activities delivered via technology. As clear, audible signals are provided via the teacher's technology of choice, interactive instructional experiences involving those signals will give students a chance to process what has been heard. Techniques for focused listening include listening games that allow students to respond to questions about what has just been heard; activity sheets combined with audio that students can control in terms of pace and repeated playback; reflective activities that allow students to listen to, process, and reflect on audio content from the web; and group listening to stored audio with built-in pause points for discussion. All of these technology-enhanced focused listening activities and others that you may develop help students to hear and listen effectively, a skill that will serve them well throughout their academic and personal lives.

TABLE 11.2 Components of a Listening Center

EQUIPMENT	PURPOSE	EQUIPMENT	PURPOSE
CASSETTE RECORDER AND PLAYER AND CD PLAYER 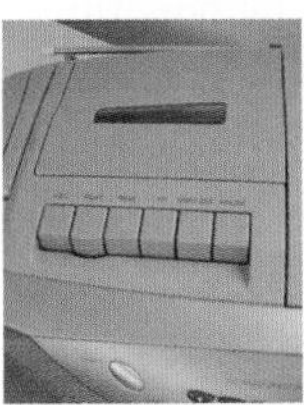	Play back student-made, teacher-made, and commercially prepared audiotapes; record student reports, stories, read-aloud practice; record lesson instructions and reviews	PRERECORDED AND BLANK CASSETTES AND CDS 	Cassettes and CDs available alone, with texts, and in multimedia kits provide tutorials, music, talking books, and lessons Variable-length, reusable blank cassettes and CD-Rs have a wide variety of student and teacher uses
EARPHONES 	Provide private listening; may require splitting device to plug in multiple sets of earphones	TABLE AND CHAIRS 	Table for listening center equipment; comfortable chairs contribute to a relaxed, nurturing learning environment

Listening centers with talking books help learners improve both listening and reading skills.

Ed Kashi/Corbis

PEARSON myeducationkit

Go to the *Assignments and Activities* section of Chapter 11 in MyEducationKit and complete the video activity entitled *Using Learning Centers*.

enhancements on cassette tape. Such kits also usually include student activity sheets and suggested lesson plans. Although they may also include motion video or even real objects, text, graphics, and audiotapes are common.

Talking books are a great way for students to practice their listening skills.

An additional effective classroom application of audiotapes is their use for oral history and oral journal assignments. **Oral histories** are typically interviews captured on audiotape related to a single significant event. Students might interview parents or grandparents and ask questions related to their memories of a specific historical event, such as the first moon landing. Or they might ask interview questions about a significant local event, such as a hurricane or the dedication of an important local monument. Interviews building an oral history of a significant event that have been captured on audiotape can be edited into a single audio collage of interviews. The edited oral history tape can be duplicated and distributed to all participants, creating an irreplaceable treasure that captures the voice and emotion of those who participated in history.

Oral histories and journals reinforce communication and listening skills.

Likewise, **oral journals** provide learners with the opportunity to make unrestricted observations and reflections on their own experiences. Whether making oral notes of their observations during a field trip or reflecting on a classroom experience, oral journals give learners the chance to capture their own voices and emotions while giving them the opportunity to practice and listen to their own oral communication skills. Oral journals can later be listened to, reflected on, and synthesized by individual learners or shared with groups or the entire class.

As technology evolves and digital audio gains ground, cassette tapes will continue to fade as an audio option. At the moment, however, many schools still have abundant tape resources. Applied creatively, cassette tapes can continue to provide auditory enhancement, teach listening skills, and reinforce content.

Digital Audio Media

Optical Media

Optical digital media are rapidly replacing analog audiotapes.

The more traditional analog storage media (audiotapes) have given way to their digital counterparts, the most common of which is the **compact disc (CD)**. CDs and DVDs have some distinct advantages over audiotapes. These advantages include clarity, storage format, and information access.

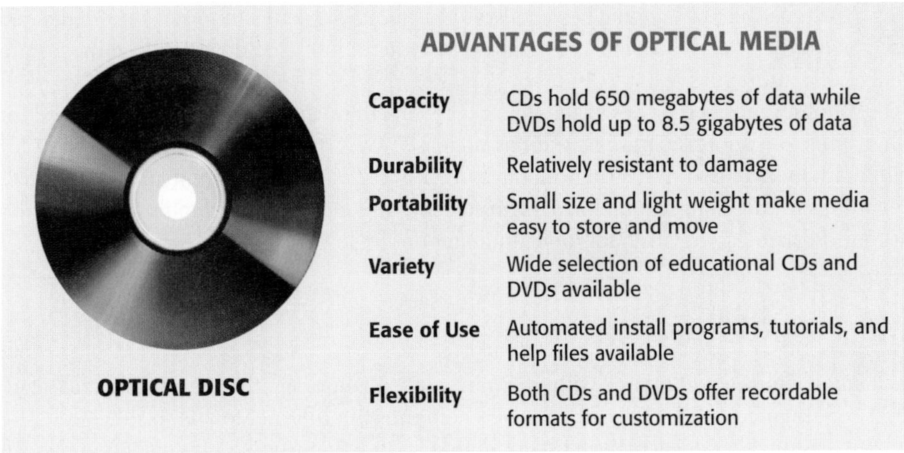

FIGURE 11.1

Optical Media for Teaching and Learning

CDs offer unique advantages in teaching and learning.

Digitized sound is sound recorded in distinct bits of data rather than analog waves. This results in a much crisper, clearer audio recording. Furthermore, because CDs and DVDs are highly durable media, the sounds recorded on them do not deteriorate with frequent use. Unlike magnetic tapes, which can become stretched or distorted, CDs maintain their shape and thus their clarity over time.

Additionally, CDs, with their capacity of approximately 75 minutes of audio, offer a capacity roughly equal to that of cassette tapes. Furthermore their digital storage format provides for random access of the data stored on them, which means you can directly go to and play any segment on a CD. Tapes use a process called *sequential access;* that is, you must move through the taped information in the sequence in which it was stored to reach the content you want. CDs save the time and effort necessary to sort through the entire sequence of stored data. This ability to access randomly is a useful advantage during instruction. Figure 11.1 summarizes the advantages of using CDs.

Internet Audio

Once digitized, audio can also be delivered through the Internet. The Internet lets you find and download very specific audio clips for use in your classroom. Using **Internet audio,** you can download and store only what you need rather than having to buy a full CD that may have only a few portions that are useful as supplements to your lesson. The increasing availability of Internet audio has resulted in its becoming the dominant audio technology in today's classrooms.

To use Internet audio, it is necessary to be aware of its various formats and the hardware and/or software necessary for its playback. The two most common formats of audio files available on the Internet are WAV files and MP3 files. **WAV files** are the digital version of analog audio. This means that a sound or music clip has been converted directly into its digital counterpart. WAV files maintain the quality of the original sound but often result in very large digital files. A CD-quality recording in WAV format would take up approximately 2 to 3 megabytes of space for every minute of sound recording. Obviously, a long song or story would take an enormous amount of time to upload or download and a substantial amount of disk space for storage. For this reason, WAV files found on the Internet are often short. As a result of the size of audio files and the need for faster download times, a newer audio file format has been developed and is widely used on the Internet. This format is called **MP3,** which stands for Motion Picture Experts Group, audio layer 3.

> Audio recordings on the Internet are usually stored as WAV or MP3 files.

MP3 is an audio compression technology that provides high-quality sound in a fraction of the space required for the same clip in older audio file formats. This compression significantly reduces upload and download times as well as necessary storage space. To play MP3 files, you must have MP3 playback software installed on your computer or a dedicated MP3 player device. MP3 player programs are available for free download online, as are many MP3 audio files.

Although most MP3 files available on the web are music audio, MP3 can be used for other kinds of sound recordings, such as podcasts. WAV files, once the staple format for digital audio files used in instruction, have been superseded by the compact MP3 format. Regardless of the digital audio format you select to use, educational applications are similar to those associated with traditional audio technologies.

Internet Radio

Internet radio brings live broadcasts from around the world into the classroom.

Using digital formats combined with streaming audio technology, the Internet offers a broadcast service called **Internet radio.** Internet radio uses the Internet to offer online radio stations consisting of a wide variety of programming including music, sports, science, and local, national, and world news. Live and recorded programming from around the world can enhance language, social studies, science, and current events curricula. Typically, Internet radio sites offer a brief text summary with graphics in conjunction with the audio broadcast (Figure 11.2). For educators who wish to expand their students' horizons, access to up-to-the-minute international radio broadcasts is just a mouse click away. And because visual, text, and audio information may be provided, different learning styles are addressed simultaneously. Whether used with a data projection unit for a whole class activity or with a single computer for an individual or small-group project, Internet radio broadcasts offer fascinating possibilities to creative teachers.

Digital Media Players

Windows Media Player, Winamp, RealNetworks' RealPlayer, and Apple iTunes are digital media players, all of which are available free on the Internet. These software players can collect audio and video data in a special storage location called a buffer and then begin playing back the sound and images as soon as enough is collected. They continue to play while collecting the multimedia data so that, once started, the stream is not interrupted.

All of these players manage streaming audio from the Internet. Streaming audio is usually compressed so that unessential components such as very high and very low sounds are omitted. This makes the file smaller and faster to transmit across the Internet. Each streaming audio player has a slightly different compression scheme with some players offering advantages across different bandwidths. Generally, however, these players all provide excellent playback of WAV and MP3 files for most classrooms.

Some of the unique features provided with media players include the ability to play back digital audio and video from the Internet, from CDs, or from DVDs. Some players also have copying capabilities, the ability to organize files into playlists for easy playback, and the ability to change "skins." Skins are the alternative player interfaces that can change how the player looks and which features are accessed via convenient on-screen controls.

To download these popular media players go to these web sites:

- For Windows Media Player go to **www.microsoft.com**
- For iTunes go to **www.apple.com**
- For RealPlayer go to **www.real.com**
- For Winamp, go to **www.winamp.com**

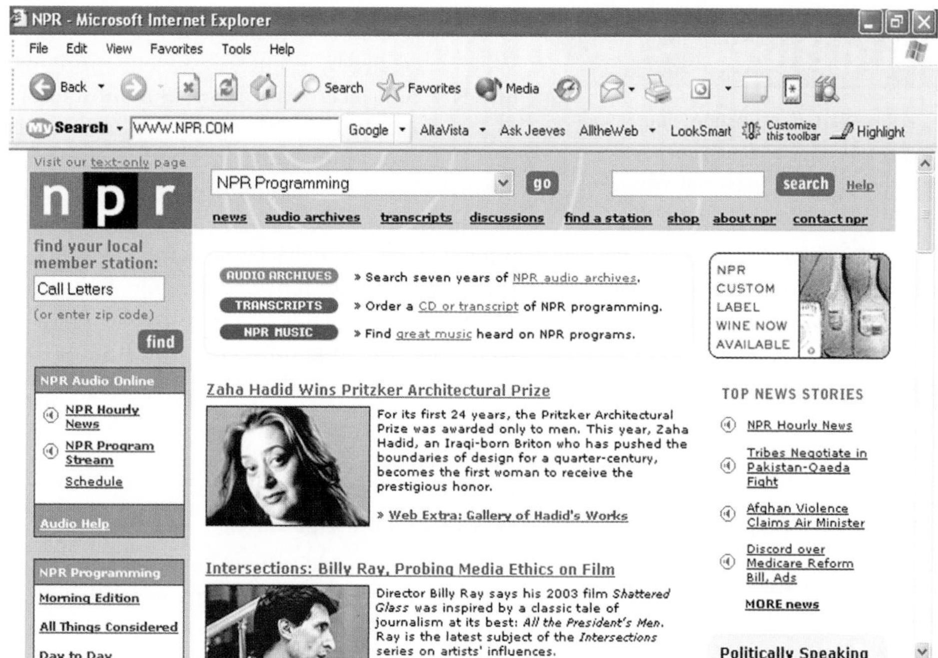

FIGURE 11.2

Internet radio broadcasts like those provided by National Public Radio can offer audio resources on a wide variety of instructional content.

Courtesy of NPR.

Visual Technologies in Teaching and Learning

Including audio in teaching and learning makes the instruction richer. However, for most learners, audio alone will not be sufficient to communicate content. For most learners, visuals are a necessity.

Whenever you visit an effective instructional environment, the most noticeable elements are the many eye-catching educational displays. Visual support for content can be seen throughout the teaching and learning space. Whether through posters, student work on bulletin boards, models, or dioramas, the content is articulated, clarified, and enhanced visually. Learning style research, brain-based instruction, and common sense support the use of visuals in instruction. The question that remains for educators is how to determine and select the most effective and appropriate visual technologies for the content under study.

> **ISTE Standard**
>
> *Learning about Internet audio resources for your classroom will help you address*
>
> **NETS•T STANDARD 1:**
>
> **FACILITATE AND INSPIRE STUDENT LEARNING AND CREATIVITY** Teachers use their knowledge of subject matter, teaching and learning, and technology to facilitate experiences that advance student learning, creativity, and innovation in both face-to-face and virtual environments.

Nonprojected Visuals in Teaching and Learning

The most common type of visuals found in today's classrooms are nonprojected visuals. These visual supports do not require projection for display and include real objects, models, exhibits, printed materials, graphics, and photographs. Although these visuals might not be high-tech, they may well be the best choice to support the content under study. Table 11.3 summarizes several popular nonprojected visuals and examples of how they can be used in the teaching and learning process.

TECH TIPS for Teachers

Educators would agree that visuals are a critical part of instruction, but visuals required a good design to be effective. Good visual design encourages and supports visual learning and does not confuse the instructional message with unnecessary or conflicting elements. To ensure effective visual design, follow these principles:

- *Relevance:* Be sure all components contribute and enhance the message.
- *Consistency:* Be sure elements are in harmony visually to send a clear single message.
- *Proportion:* Be sure the relative size of all elements is consistent with their importance to the message.
- *Unity:* Be sure all elements work together to communicate the message and focus attention.

Following these visual design parameters in creating or selecting visuals will result in visuals that encourage your students' visual literacy—their ability to correctly interpret visual images. Teaching these visual design concepts to your students will help them to create their own visuals that support and communicate the concepts they have learned.

The examples below demonstrate the difference between good and poor visual designs.

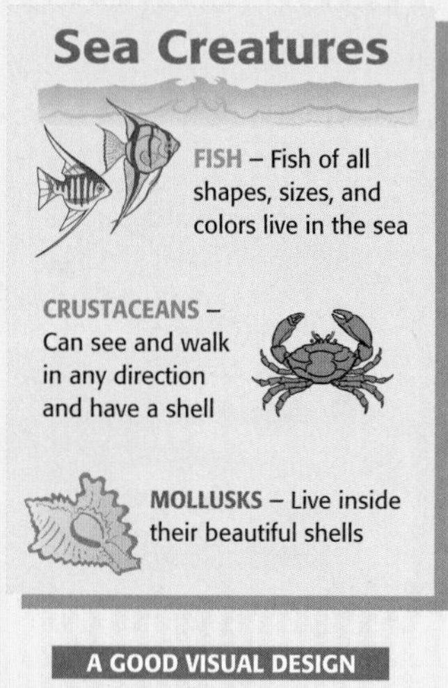

A GOOD VISUAL DESIGN

- Balanced design
- Legible text
- Minimal letter styles and sizes
- Appealing colors
- Provides unity and direction
- Consistent and cohesive
- Relevant images

A POOR VISUAL DESIGN

- Design lacks balance
- Text style difficult to read
- Too many letter styles
- Minimal color appeal
- Lacks unity and direction
- Inconsistent look
- Images disconnected

Print Materials

Whether created by teachers or students, **print materials** remain a centerpiece visual in most learning spaces. Individual print materials may include books and worksheets; group-oriented printed visuals may include posters and charts. Teacher-made, student-made, or commercially printed visuals, though a staple in most classrooms, vary in quality. Awareness and application of the criteria for high-quality visuals will assist you in selecting and creating print visuals for use in your classroom.

Display Technologies for Nonprojected Visuals

Once nonprojected visuals have been selected, the next step is to choose the appropriate display technology. To display print or graphic visuals, most classrooms offer a variety of display surfaces. The most common is the bulletin board. **Bulletin boards** offer a flexible surface that provides an easy-to-change venue for a variety of print and graphic elements. Other surfaces for nonprojected visual display that are often found in classrooms include flip charts, magnetic boards, felt boards, and chalkboards or whiteboards. Availability varies by school and grade level, but familiarity with each will serve you well as you decide how best to share nonprojected visuals with your students. Table 11.4 summarizes the nonprojected display technologies available in most classrooms.

Projected Visuals in Teaching and Learning

Visuals that require projection to be seen are a critical component of many classrooms. This type of visual and the technology that supports it require, in addition to the visual itself, special equipment and a projection screen for classroom display. As a rule, the visual is enlarged from its original format so that all students can see it. Because the visual and the technology necessary to project it cannot be separated, each will be considered with its projection technologies in the following sections.

Overhead projectors are common useful projection technologies.

Overhead Projectors

A long-standing visual display workhorse for the classroom is the **overhead projector.** It remains a frequently found tool in many schools. Visuals are created on thin sheets of clear

TABLE 11.3 Nonprojected Visuals and Their Application

NONPROJECTED VISUAL	DESCRIPTION	EXAMPLES	APPLICATIONS
REAL OBJECTS	Any real-world object that can be safely brought into the classroom	Rocks, stamps, fish, ants, plants, eggs, leaves	Scientific experiments, history projects, geology units, solar graphics, weather studies
MODELS	Scaled-down or full-size three-dimensional representations of concepts or real objects	Globes; scale models; gear box circuit kits; timing devices; teaching clocks; teaching torsos; ear, eye, and nose models; hands-on heart models; solar system simulators	Teach and reinforce basic geographic locations; design and structure of bridges, boats, skyscrapers; human anatomy; astronomy
EXHIBITS	Dioramas (classroom displays depicting a scene) or other collection of objects	Historical or geographical dioramas, artifact collections, book displays, dinosaur mountain display,interactive dinosaur sound station, student craft projects	Show historical, geographic, or other wide-view, three-dimensional landscapes; showcase books to be read for a class or new publications; teach animal sounds through touching electronic soundspots on a vinyl playmat; feature traveling artifact collections from local museums
GRAPHICS AND PHOTOGRAPHS	Pictorial image of graphic art or photos displayed in actual size or blown up to show detail	Drawings, cartoons, diagrams, photographs, graphic organizers, graphing mats, graphs, Venn diagrams, glyphs	Student drawings to illustrate stories read, holidays, portraits; relevant cartoons to add humor to an assignment; photos students take of field trips, their vacations, their families and friends; graphic organizers to help students visualize and organize schoolwork; graphing mats, graphs, Venn diagrams, and glyphs to teach concepts that connect math to other subjects

TABLE 11.4 Display Technologies for Nonprojected Visuals

DISPLAY TECHNOLOGY	DESCRIPTION	APPLICATION
FLIP CHART	Large pads displayed on an easel; some with sticky note–style adhesive	Used to capture text or graphics during a presentation or discussion that can be saved on the pad or torn off and displayed in the classroom
MAGNETIC BOARD	Small metal surface on which to arrange and adhere objects with small magnets attached	Inexpensive and easy-to-use display for young learners to practice organizing and manipulating objects
FELT BOARD	Small cloth surface on which to arrange and adhere colorful cloth letters of objects	Like magnetic boards, inexpensive and easy to use display for young learners to practice organizing and manipulating objects
CHALKBOARD	Black or green boards that can be written upon with white or colored chalk and easily erased	Used by teachers or students for impromptu text or graphics in support of concepts under discussion
WHITEBOARD	Slick white surface boards formulated for multicolor dry-erase markers; some with magnetic backing for display	Quickly replacing chalkboards, also used by teachers or students for impromptu text or graphics in support of concepts under discussion and may support paper displayed with magnets

TECH TIPS for Teachers

Printing Transparencies

When creating your own transparencies on a computer, you can either print them in black and white or color on an ink jet printer or in black on a laser printer. However, before you print, you should be sure you are using the correct type of transparency film. Ink jet printers use a film that is porous on one side and slick on the other. The transparency must be placed in the ink jet printer so that the droplets of ink that are shot out through the jets fall on the porous side of the film. Using the wrong side of the transparency film will result in a runny and smeared transparency that will not dry. In contrast, laser printers create images by melting toner onto the surface of the media. Because heat is involved, a thicker, more heat-resistant acetate must be used. Laser printer film is slick on both sides because melted toner, not ink, is used to create the image. You should avoid using ink jet film in laser printers as the film may buckle or melt under the heat of the laser printing process, leaving a mess of melted plastic inside the printer.

When adding handwritten text or notes to your transparency, it is a good idea to cover your printed transparency with a blank one on which to write. You can use a transparency mount to hold both in position so that neither will slip while you write. This "overlay" method allows you to continually make notes on and erase them without damaging your printed transparency or wearing it out.

acetate, typically called **transparencies.** A powerful lamp inside the overhead projector shines through the transparency and then through a series of mirrors and lenses so that the visual is magnified and focused onto a projection screen.

Visuals for overhead projection can be created by using black or color inks and can be hand drawn, printed via computer and printer, or photocopied from a printed page. To draw on a transparency, special transparency markers must be used, or the ink will blotch and smear. Such markers can be either permanent or washable. Computer-generated transparencies offer more professional-looking, permanent visuals.

Commercial overhead transparencies are also very popular options for use in the classroom. These visuals are created and sold in booklets or sets and are sometimes offered as supplements to a textbook. The obvious advantage of commercial transparencies is that they are high-quality, ready-to-use visuals designed for overhead projection. A disadvantage may be that they do not fully target the instructional concepts you have selected to present.

Overhead projectors and the transparencies that they project offer some unique advantages in the classroom. Perhaps the most important is that they allow the teacher to maintain eye contact with learners during group instruction. Instead of having to turn to write on a whiteboard, using an overhead projector allows you to face the classroom while creating impromptu visual images. Another advantage is the longevity of the visual images. Transparencies also allow you to build a concept; this can be done by adding successive transparency layers,

FIGURE 11.3

Elements of a Good Transparency

Guidelines for creating effective transparencies include limiting content, including graphics, and maintaining eye appeal through color and contrast.

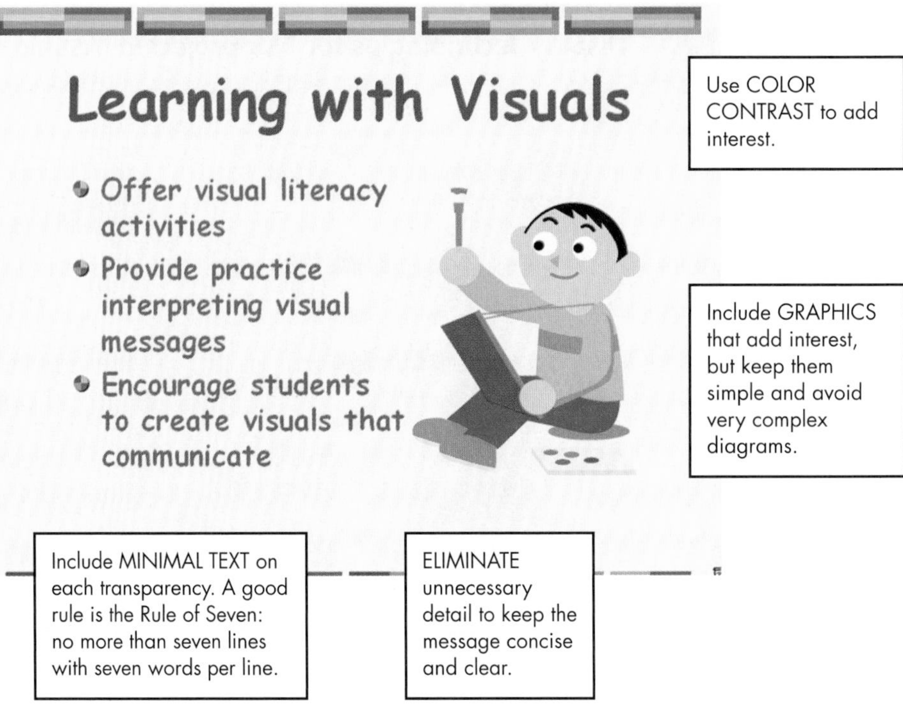

called overlays. Each overlay contains a bit of additional information that, when placed on top of the previous display, creates a more complex and detailed visual.

Transparencies offer an easy-to-create and easy-to-use option for educators. You should apply the same visual design principles when creating transparencies as you would when creating any other visual. Figure 11.3 offers some additional useful hints for effectively creating and using this visual technology.

Transparencies should be created following standard visual design guidelines.

Digital Projectors

With the advent of digital imaging, **digital projectors** have taken a firm hold in schools. As you learned in Chapter 6, these computer output devices project digital images onto a projection screen, large monitor, or whiteboard so that they can be shared with a large group. (Features of digital projectors, as well as overhead projectors, are summarized in Figure 11.4.) Images can be captured with a digital still camera, with a digital video camera, from an analog videotape using a video capture card, from the Internet, or even from an electronic whiteboard.

Regardless of the method used for capturing digital images, the use of digital projectors in education will no doubt continue to expand. As teachers become more familiar with the technology, the cost comes down, and schools increase their acquisition of digital imaging hardware and software, teaching and learning will continue to be visually enhanced through their application. Digital images are already being creatively applied and incorporated into innovative instruction. Digital projectors are becoming more powerful and full-featured as their cost continues to drop. More and more educators are discovering and using this versatile technology for sharing visual images with learners.

Document Cameras

A projection device that combines the applications of several other types of visual projectors into one has begun to gain popularity. The **document camera** is actually a video camera, mounted on a stand, that captures and projects an image of whatever is placed on the stand's document table. The camera, pointed down toward the document table, captures a live video image of the document or object placed on its table and plays that image back

FIGURE 11.4

Comparing Display Technologies

Various types of displays can be found in schools.

DIGITAL PROJECTOR

Courtesy of 3M

Features

- Attached to a computer, projector displays real-time computer images
- Displays software or Internet activities for large group
- Varies from inexpensive to costly along with the quality of the display and the features available

DOCUMENT CAMERA

Features

- Displays real-time still images
- Displays real-time 3-D objects
- Shows photographic slides
- Shows transparencies
- Captures video images

Courtesy of Barco

OVERHEAD PROJECTOR

Features

- Versatile and inexpensive
- Displays commercial or teacher-made transparencies against a screen, classroom wall, or whiteboard
- In combination with computer-generated images and a color printer, transparencies can be created that specifically target instructional objectives

Courtesy of 3M

YOU Decide!

Projection tools such as a digital projector or a document camera can offer teachers a unique way to share images in a large group setting. Document cameras help teachers display visuals or a text page without first having to create a transparency from them. Further, document cameras let students see live images of a science experiment or a hands-on demonstration. Digital projectors allow teachers to share any digital image from a photograph, to a map, to a live demonstration of research on the web. These technologies enrich teacher presentations and demonstrations so that they are as exciting as they are engaging. They are well worth the time and dollar investment when adding them to the classroom. Do you agree?

YES! For too long, teachers have used the board or, at best, the overhead projector as visual aids to their instruction. These older technologies, while useful at times, don't have the same impact on students. And the images from the board or overhead transparency can be difficult to read and can't be used for real-time demonstrations. But add a digital display device or use a document camera, and the content becomes exciting, interactive, and engaging. Both teachers and students can use these devices to share ideas, make reports, demonstrate projects, or for discovery learning. These devices make the difference between limited and boring presentations and those that keep everyone interested.

NO! Too much emphasis on audiovisual support misses the point of teaching. Good teachers make content interesting by the way they present it and by the types of activities they have their students do. It really doesn't matter whether the teacher uses the blackboard, overhead projector, or document camera as support. The real core of great instruction is the instruction. Besides, those technologies are complex, hard to learn, and expensive. It is better to pay for other things needed in the school and in the classroom rather than invest in presentation equipment that doesn't really contribute to effective teaching or student learning.

Which view do you agree with? YOU DECIDE!

through a video monitor or an LCD display. By using both top and back lighting on the table and the video camera's zoom features, overhead transparencies, slides, documents, and three-dimensional objects can all be projected for a large group.

This technology offers some practical projection advantages. Science experiments, demonstrations of small real objects, and procedural presentations can be easily shared. As the teacher proceeds with a live demonstration on the document camera table, the zoom feature built into the camera can be used to share minute detail with all students simultaneously. A teacher no longer needs to have students crowd around a demonstration to share it or walk around the classroom to show small objects. The document camera's live video makes sharing simple and readily viewable by all.

Video in Teaching and Learning

Video technologies have undergone a dramatic evolution from early silent movies to today's compressed video over the Internet. During each stage of this evolution, educators have used the most current video technology in support of teaching and learning. As each new video technology replaced the last, equipment and video media were also slowly replaced in schools. Still, because funds for technology and media are always in short supply, you may find some older video technologies still available and still useful in educational settings (Figure 11.5).

Deciding how best to incorporate motion video in teaching and learning can be a challenge for educators. Too often, watching motion video is an inactive, even boring

FIGURE 11.5

Video technologies have evolved, but many older technologies can still be found in schools.

Anthony Meshkinyar/Getty Images

Courtesy of Sony Electronics, Inc.

Courtesy of Panasonic

experience for the learner. The medium tends to be passive and therefore can be unengaging. Because the experience is too often limited to viewing without participation, focus is easily lost. This is the challenge of motion video.

Early movies and then television were the first major forms of motion video to affect classrooms significantly. Following these, a new method for capturing video, videotape (initially reel-to-reel, later on a cassette, and now on DVD), changed the way video was recorded and played back. Easy-to-use and compact video cameras that stored images on videocassettes opened new opportunities to capture sound and motion. Although many older video technologies can be found in schools, most have given way to digital video technologies that have emerged more recently.

PEARSON **myeducationkit**™

Go to the *Assignments and Activities* section of Chapter 11 in MyEducationKit and complete the web activity entitled *Video and the Web*.

Like older types of video, digital video technologies record and play back data, but the format in which the data are recorded also allows for full manipulation and editing. The recorded videos offer easier manipulation of images and sound, just as a word-processing document can be manipulated in terms of text. This capability opens up even more possibilities for the use of motion video in teaching and learning. Still, both traditional and digital video offer teachers a powerful tool in the classroom.

Traditional Video Technologies

Broadcast Video

Terrestrial and satellite connections make broadcast TV possible.

Broadcast video is what is commonly thought of as television. Television images can be broadcast using **terrestrial** (land-based) equipment, or, for longer distances, a combination configuration of both terrestrial and satellite equipment is required. In **satellite transmission,** signals are sent to a satellite (**uplinked**) and then sent back down (**downlinked**) to a terrestrial system at another location on the globe (see Figure 11.6). The positioning of a string of such satellites around the globe allows television transmissions to be bounced by means of a series of uplinks and downlinks to positions anywhere on the earth.

Broadcast video can be in either a commercial format such as the programming broadcast by the major networks (such as ABC, NBC, and CBS) or an educational format such as programming on the **Public Broadcasting Service (PBS)** or a local learning channel. Public television, created by an act of Congress expressly to provide high-quality educational programs,

FIGURE 11.6

Television Uplinks and Downlinks

Television signals can be globally transmitted using terrestrial and satellite links. Signals are bounced across the globe via a system of satellites in geosynchronous orbit and dishes located strategically around the globe.

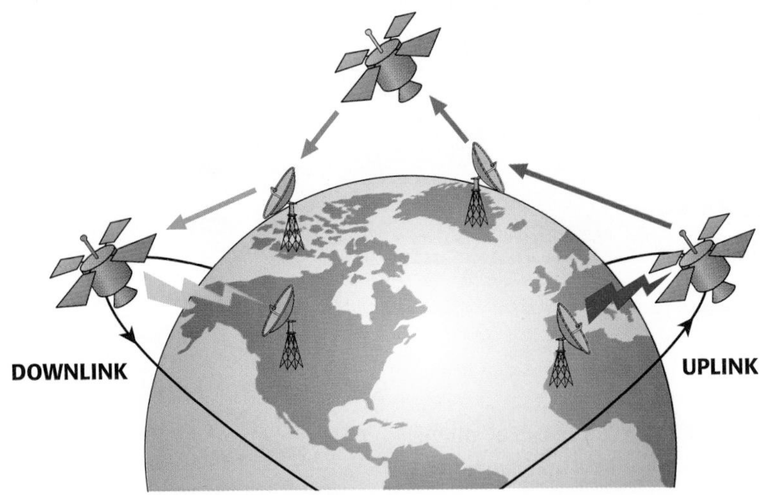

includes at its core the **Corporation for Public Broadcasting (CPB).** The CPB manages the acquisition and production of educational programming, and PBS disseminates the programming through local TV channels. Local learning channels, sometimes referred to as **instructional television (ITV),** use broadcast airwaves to distribute a wide array of instructional programs throughout a school district that can also be viewed by anyone who tunes in to that channel.

For educators, broadcast video can offer high-impact, high-quality video production that can dramatically demonstrate content. In particular, the educational programming offered by local PBS stations can add meaningful video support to instruction. News commentaries, documentaries, docudramas, plays, musical productions, and educational programs are typically available on public television stations. However, because broadcast video is synchronous (real-time) in delivery, it is often difficult to use in a classroom setting. The time a program is broadcast might be inconsistent with scheduled lessons unless video recording technology is used to capture it for more convenient playback.

Narrowcast Video

The alternative to broadcast video is a video transmission format that targets educational audiences. This type of video transmission is sometimes referred to as **narrowcast video.** Types of narrowcast transmissions are summarized in Figure 11.7.

Video within a school is typically distributed to all classrooms by using a **closed-circuit TV (CCTV)** system. A CCTV system is a network of television monitors connected by coaxial cables running throughout a school building that can distribute television signals to all the connected classrooms. Thus, once an ITV transmission is received at one central point in a school, it can be distributed via CCTV to all connected classrooms within the school. As with other forms of broadcast TV, there may be some difficulty arranging instruction around transmission times. However, programming can be recorded and distributed through CCTV or videocassette distribution for later replay in classrooms.

The school's CCTV system is also often used for other narrowcast transmissions. In-school TV production classes typically create video programs of daily announcements and school information. These in-school "morning shows" use the CCTV system to reach all classrooms.

Cablecast Video

The same coaxial cables that connect classrooms can also transmit cable television stations; this is often called **cablecast video.** Many cable companies, as a component of doing business in an area, offer schools cable connections. Schools that are hooked to their local cable TV company can use their classroom television monitors to tune in to cable channels just as you use your home television to tune in to cable channels there. The types of programming that are available to schools through their local cable companies range from standard commercial and educational television to premium stations supplied free to schools by the cable companies. Arrangements vary widely with each local area, but if cablecast video is available at your school, you would do well to explore the instructional possibilities it presents. Many high-quality cable stations, including the Cable News Network (CNN) and the Discovery

Channel, offer instructional programming that can enhance your instruction.

Recorded Video Technologies

To overcome the scheduling problems inherent in broadcast, narrowcast, and cablecast systems in schools, recorded video has become the traditional video format of choice. Although quickly being superseded by digital recording equipment, **videocassette recorders (VCRs)** have been widely used in schools to record video. VCRs use a magnetic **VHS format tape** for recording moving images. VHS tapes are relatively inexpensive and are still a staple of many school media centers. Prerecorded tapes of movies can be purchased or rented, or you can tape a broadcast television program for later viewing.

Videocassette recorders and monitors are usually either permanently assigned to the classroom or available on a rolling cart for checkout through the school media center. Large monitors can make it easy for a large class to view the videotape. If a larger image is desired, the VCR can be connected to a digital projector to project the image onto a large screen or light-colored wall. Although aging, this video technology can usually be counted on as a useful support for your instruction. It is often wise to begin the school year by visiting the media center to review the video library and to preview any tape you might choose so that you can carefully plan for its use in the curriculum.

FIGURE 11.7

Narrowcast Systems

Narrowcast systems provide video to local areas.

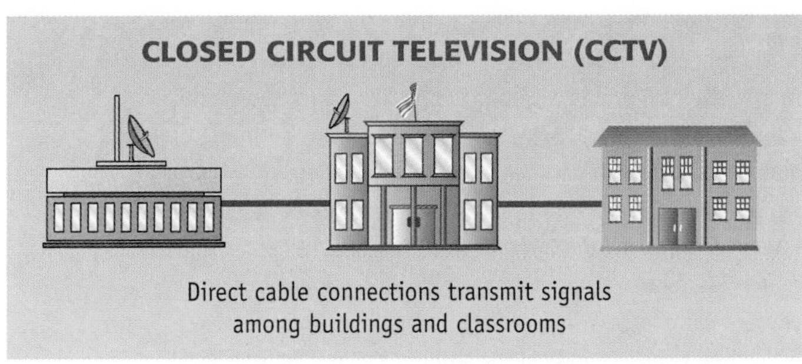

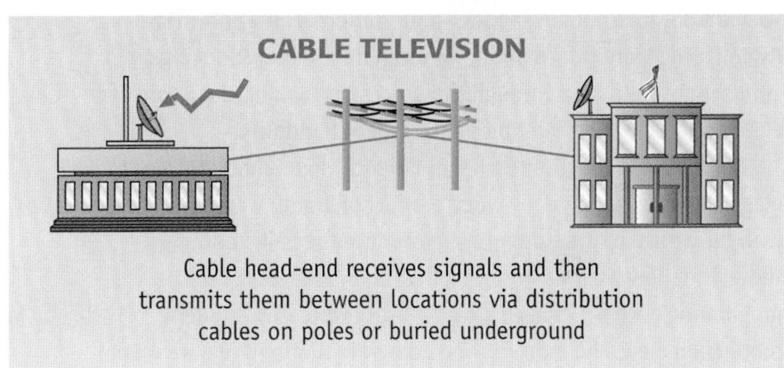

Your local school media center is usually your handiest source for videos.

Digital Video Technologies

Video images are easily captured and stored in a digital format by using a variety of digital video technologies. This format offers both high-quality images and limitless editing possibilities. Video saved in a digital format, like other digital data, can be changed, edited, displayed, shared, or sent from one computer to another. Regardless of the technology used to capture and record it (including the conversion of analog video to digital), digital video technologies offer a powerful teaching and learning resource that you can customize to support a specific lesson or to meet unique student needs.

PEARSON myeducationkit

Go to the *Assignments and Activities* section of Chapter 11 in MyEducationKit and complete the video activity entitled *Student Created Video Supports Science Teaching and Learning*.

Traditional video captures and plays back images and sound at approximately thirty frames per second. At this speed, the captured video looks just like real-time motion. To turn this true-to-life image into a digital form, each frame must be converted to its digital counterpart. The sequence of digitized frames, called a digital video clip, results in a very large file. In fact, a three-minute high-quality digital video clip can require as much as a gigabyte of storage space.

Because of the large file sizes resulting from digitized video, video **compression technologies** were developed. Video compression is often used to enable transmission of digital video across the Internet. Compression software and hardware work by capturing the initial video image in full but then ignoring the nonchanging components of the image. Rather than redigitizing and storing every bit of every image, subsequent frames store only those bits that have changed since the last frame (see Figure 11.8). Thus, the total storage requirements for the video clip are reduced.

Several popular compression formats are used for digital video. Each format requires software that can decompress and play back the compressed file, but the software is readily available. Playback software either is included with the operating system of the computer or

Go to the *Podcasts* section of Chapter 11 in MyEducationKit and click on *Cool Tools*.

In the CLASSROOM

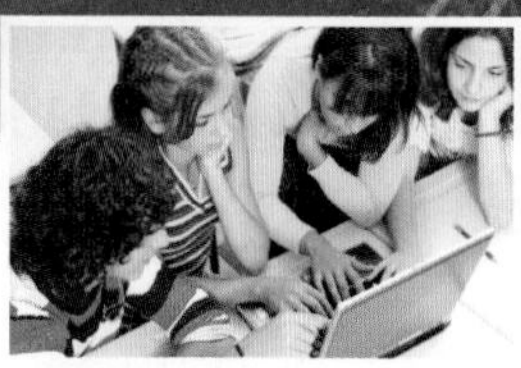

Video Production and Videos

Michelle Bourgeois, a fourth-grade teacher and tech coordinator, shared digital videos made by first- and second-graders in a Teacher's Guide to Making Student Movies page on Scholastic .com. "Lights, Camera, Action!" shows that even the youngest elementary students can make educational videos. Ms. Bourgeois wrote, "With the advent of inexpensive video-editing tools such as iMovie and MovieMaker, digital video has become accessible in many classrooms. Students can create professional-looking video content complete with voiceovers, transitions and text effects." To prove her assertion, look at the student movies "Matter: Gas," "David Goes to School," "Shapes," and "Clifford's First Snow Day." By going to "More Information," you can find four sections that will guide you step by step through the process of making classroom videos and providing examples and student handouts.

Bill Walsh, an English teacher at Billerica High School in Billerica, Massachusetts, has his daily video production under way at 5:45 A.M. with the arrival of the students who produce the daily morning TV show. The show will not air for another hour and a half, but the preparations and setup have already begun with a two-student production crew. The morning news program has to have a weather update, and Dave, the high school's weatherman, is the next to arrive on the scene. Part of Dave's job is to videotape radar weather maps using a VCR connected to a computer in the library. He draws the warm and cold weather fronts with magic markers on a big U.S. map before going to the keyboard to enter his forecast for the day. Getting closer to airtime, other students arrive and contribute news and announcements of interest to the high school. The anchor and camera people are in place, and as the 7:15 bell rings, Melissa looks into the lens and greets 1,500 students with a smile and "Good morning, Billerica High." The fifteen-minute program, which took an hour and a half to prepare, admirably emulates network and cable morning news programs. Mr. Walsh observed that learning video production is important, but even more so is "learning responsibility, how to take pride in their efforts, and to work together."

Bourgeois, M. (2009). *Lights, camera, action*. Retrieved March 12, 2009, from **http://content.scholastic.com/browse/article.jsp?id=6758.**

Walsh, B. (2007). *Student-produced morning news*. Retrieved July 12, 2008, from **http://www.medialit.org/reading_room/article372.html.**

AVI, MPEG, and MOV digital compression formats are among the most widely used formats today.

is available for download from the Internet. The most popular digital video compression formats are Audio Video Interleaved (**AVI**), Motion Picture Experts Group (**MPEG**), and QuickTime (**MOV**). Table 11.5 lists the advantages of each.

As compression technologies continue to advance, the large size of digital video files will become less and less significant. Each year, digital video technologies improve dramatically in their capacity and usability. Becoming familiar with the current digital video technologies is just a beginning.

FIGURE 11.8

How Digital Video Compression Works

Digital video compression reduces overwhelming video file sizes.

A *reference frame* is captured video that contains background and foreground images.

Subsequent frames omit the static, nonchanging background and include only the parts of the foreground that are moving.

Video compression (smaller digital video files) is achieved because all parts of every video image are recorded only in the reference frame. Thereafter, only changed images are saved resulting in significantly less video data saved for subsequent frames. The result...compressed video files.

TABLE 11.5 Digital Video Compression Formats

FORMAT	DESCRIPTION	ADVANTAGES
AVI	Audio Video Interleaved	Lower resolution, smaller video files; good for animation
MPEG	Motion Pictures Experts Group	Reduces video files up to 95 percent yet retains near television quality
MOV	QuickTime	Apple Computer's nonbroadcast-quality format; easy to use and create

DVDs

Although CDs offer excellent storage capacity, given the current sizes of compressed video files, even CDs cannot store a full movie. To remedy this storage limitation, a new storage technology was developed. The **digital video disc (DVD)** (see Figure 11.9) can store 4.7 gigabytes of data on a standard disk and up to 10.5 gigabytes per side of a dual-layer DVD. This means that hours of full-motion, high-resolution video and sound can be stored in a durable and compact format. Furthermore, once stored, all of the data are directly accessible and easy to manipulate for display. Teachers can then quickly access any segment of clear, high-quality video, frame by frame or in clips. In the classroom, a digital video image can be instantly accessed, replayed, and discussed as a part of a lesson.

DVDs offer large storage capacity.

Additionally, DVD recorders offer the opportunity to record video digitally and save to a DVD for playback. This allows teachers expanded opportunity to capture video sequences for use in subsequent lessons. DVD recorders and playback units are quickly becoming the preferred video equipment for the classroom.

FIGURE 11.9

Digital Video Discs for Teaching and Learning

Video discs offer advantages over videotape. DVDs can store video that can be directly accessed at any point in the video. Desired frames can then be played back as motion video or frame by frame.

George B. Diebold/Corbis

Digital Video Cameras

The most common option for creating digital video is to record it using a digital video camera (DV camcorder). **Digital video cameras,** like digital still cameras, capture and store the target images in a digital format that can then be downloaded to a personal computer (Figure 11.10). The resultant digital video files can then be manipulated, edited, and enhanced using **digital video editing** software.

The flexibility of digital video recording and editing has caused digital video cameras to largely replace tape camcorders. The many features included in even modest digital video cameras exceed the capabilities of previous camcorders, and their instant playback makes them popular favorites. These features can include the ability to record digital images to mini DV tape for later transfer to a computer or for playback on a television; real-time editing and built-in special effects that can be recorded while taking the video; compatibility with popular digital video editing software; and the ability to record digital audio and still digital pictures as well as video. The compact size and ease of use have made DV cameras the preferred choice, particularly as classroom tools in the hands of children.

Digital Video Editing

Just as you need word-processing software to edit a word-processed document, you need digital video software to edit video files.

FIGURE 11.10

Apple computers equipped with iMovie and iDVD software make a digital video camera in the classroom a powerful and simple-to-use tool for instruction.

David Young-Wolff/PhotoEdit

School TV production studios such as those that record the school's morning news might have specialized hardware for video editing. However, with the increased computing power of newer computers and the advent of desktop editing software, digital video editing is no longer confined to studios. For typical classroom or home use, video editing software that will run on a personal computer can easily be installed on the typical multimedia-capable computers that are available today. Such software allows you to select, edit, and manipulate digital video clips, add text, and even add special effects (Figure 11.11). Although not as powerful and capable as dedicated video editing hardware, this software can do a more than adequate job in customizing digital video to meet your needs. For a teacher who is interested in creating and using digital video for teaching and learning, it can be a powerful software tool.

Compressed Video Teleconferencing Systems

All of the digital video explored thus far has been for use in a single classroom. It would seem possible to easily transmit digitized video from one classroom to the next, just as you might send a text file to be shared between classes. But for full-motion, broadcast-quality video, there are currently some challenges. When you consider the size of compressed video and compare it to the bandwidth that is typically available for educational use, it is clear that transmission of compressed video has some specific requirements. For this reason, schools and districts that require the capability to transmit high-quality compressed video often invest in dedicated **compressed video teleconferencing systems.**

> Compressed video teleconferencing systems make live interactive video possible.

Perhaps you have seen digital video displays that seemed choppy or fuzzy or had delayed movement. With a dedicated compressed video system, digitized video can be transmitted with image and sound almost as clear as broadcast video. These systems also allow you to record and display using traditional video technology.

Schools that are equipped with teleconferencing systems can bring live, fully interactive instruction from one location to the next or have distant guest speakers visit the classroom without having to travel (see Figure 11.12). The only requirement is to have the appropriate equipment at both locations. Such systems are particularly useful for distance learning, the subject of Chapter 12.

iMovie courtesy of Apple, Inc.

FIGURE 11.11

Digital video editing software such as iMovie lets you and your students create videos, while recording software like iDVD lets you store them in a convenient DVD format.

iDVD courtesy of Apple, Inc.

Internet Video

Digital video on the Internet has taken multiple forms. As compression software reduces file sizes, bandwidth increases, and computers become more powerful, new formats will continue to be developed. Already, a number of Internet video formats offer great promise to education.

Internet Broadcasts

Many web sites are offering live **Internet broadcasts** of events and performances. These broadcasts use **streaming video** technology that compresses and plays digital video as it is being received. Streaming video requires that a player be installed on your computer. Such video players are typically available free for download on the Internet. Web sites that are sponsoring an event may add links to their sites that allow viewers to see and hear what the live audience sees. Others broadcast on the site alone, keeping the entire audience virtual. Internet broadcasts can range from musical events to scientific events and from pop entertainment talk shows to interviews with scientists. The capability of sharing events and interviews without having to purchase costly television time has made Internet broadcasting an exciting opportunity for education.

Streaming video makes motion video over the Internet practical.

Live Cams

An interesting application of Internet communication is the use of **live cams** (cameras) connected to the Internet. Live cams are cameras that are connected to a computer, which in turn is connected to the Internet. A live cam shares a digitized video image of whatever it is pointed at. For example, EarthCam (**www.earthcam.com**) is a gateway to a wide variety of live cams, such as the Penguin Cam at New York City's Central Park Zoo and the

FIGURE 11.12

A Compressed Video Teleconferencing System

Compressed video systems create real-time digital communication networks.

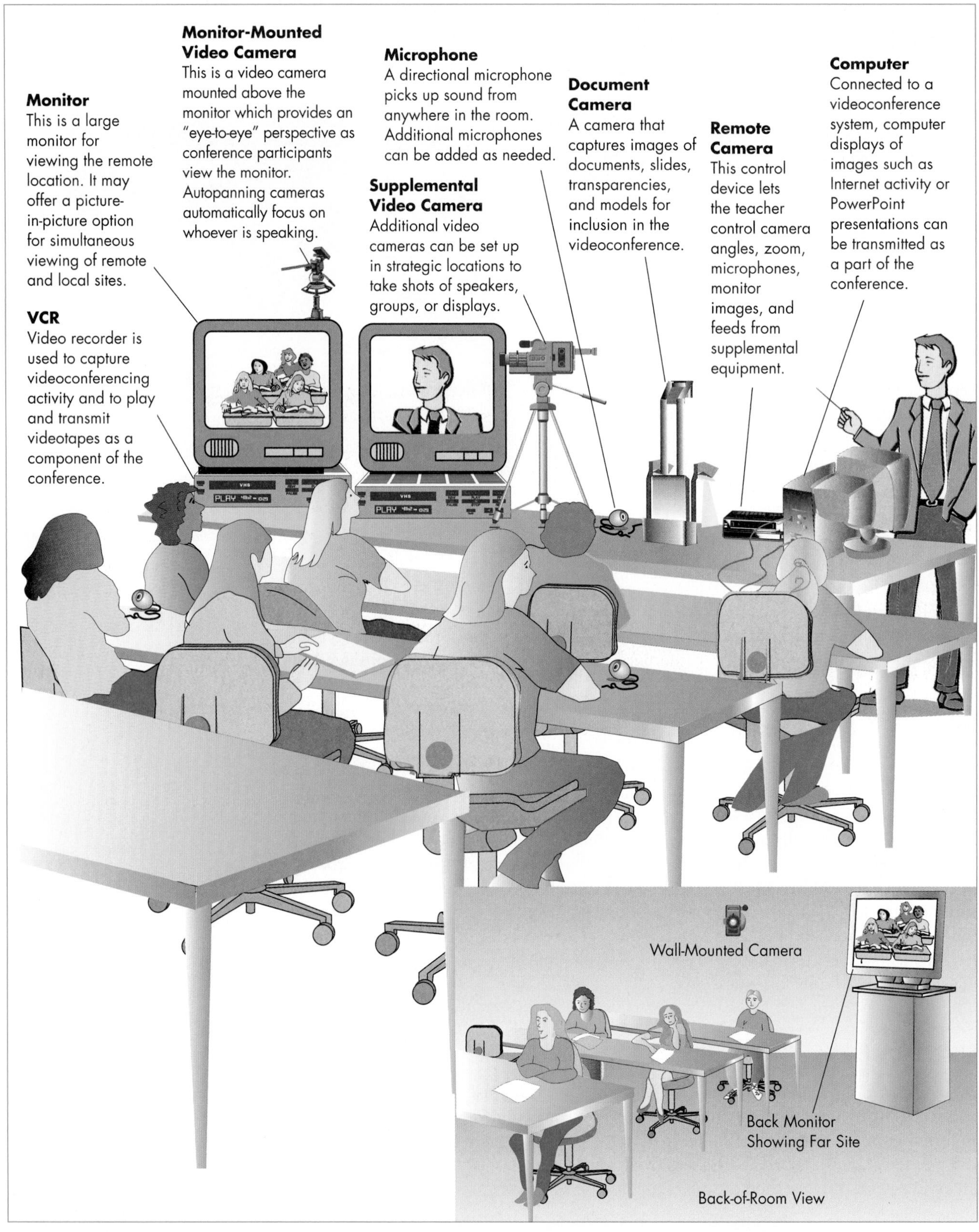

FIGURE 11.13

Live cams offer live streaming video feeds over the Internet so that students can view animals, science experiments, and locations from around the world.

Courtesy of Earth Cam, Inc.

American Museum of Natural History's Butterfly Cam (Figure 11.13). By connecting to sites such as these, you can see live video images of whatever is in range of the camera. Because the camera is connected to an online computer, you can view the digital video feed by accessing the web site sharing the camera's images. You and your students can monitor the live behavior of wildlife, an extraordinary virtual field trip experience made possible by this technology.

Live cams are available for viewing many geographic regions, the weather around the globe, animal habitats on land and in the sea, international museums and historical sites, and even other classrooms globally. The opportunities are limited only by places a camera can be carried and by Internet connectivity. Live cam sites have increased rapidly and will no doubt continue to do so. The educational possibilities for this technology will increase with their proliferation into fascinating educational locations.

Internet Meetings

Compressed video has produced another range of opportunities for educators and their students. **Internet meetings** are Internet-based "face-to-face" conversations with people around the world. With the addition of a monitor-top or classroom video camera and video compression software, individuals or groups can use the Internet to connect to each other and communicate live. As you learned in Chapter 9, several worldwide educational projects use meetings across the Internet to engage in collaborative projects. Compressed video transmitted across the Internet makes it possible for students around the world to work together and share educational experiences.

A recent addition to Internet meetings is the development of dedicated Internet meeting software such as Skype and Microsoft's NetMeeting (Figure 11.14). This type of software adds more capabilities to better simulate in-person meetings. For example, such software might add a virtual whiteboard that lets all Internet meeting participants collaborate in real time on a document or graphic, file exchange, and a chat feature that lets them share notes that they key in as they meet. With the expansion of the capabilities of Internet meetings software and the increased bandwidth capacities in the future, net meetings are likely to become a logical alternative for collaboration.

For educators, such Internet meeting software can let classes around the globe meet together in a single virtual classroom to share ideas, experience instruction, and communicate with each other. For teachers who are willing to work with colleagues globally to set up and implement worldwide instructional experiences, Internet meetings can offer students a chance to see and interact with their peers around the world.

FIGURE 11.14

Internet meeting software like Microsoft's NetMeeting lets you and your students communicate live with other classrooms anywhere in the world.

Microsoft NetMeeting® is a registered trademark of Microsoft Corporation.

YouTube

An Internet meeting connects multiple sites together for a meeting or class over the Net.

One of the most popular Internet video resources is **YouTube.** YouTube, which was started in 2005 to make it easier for Internet users to share videos, has fast become the dominant video resource on the Net. Initially meant for user-generated videos, YouTube now includes movie, television, and music clips as well. In a recent agreement with some movie houses, full-length movies will be added to YouTube offerings as well. While most of YouTube's content is still uploaded by users, news organizations such as CBS, the BBC, and CNN are also using YouTube to distribute content. Owned by Google since 2006, YouTube has become as ubiquitous a web presence as has Google itself.

Although educators may find much of YouTube's content irrelevant or even objectionable for the classroom, it has the potential for being a powerful video source. YouTube's terms of service prohibit inappropriate and copyright-protected video, but uploads of such video do occur. Not all video can be screened, and given the volume of video uploaded, despite monitoring by consumers and YouTube's video review teams, some inappropriate video does get posted. In fact, YouTube has been sued for violation of copyright and has been banned from some schools because of inappropriate or offensive content. Still, this video service is clearly a component of Internet culture and cannot be ignored. It continues to be one of the fastest-growing web sites in Internet history, with 100 million video views per day and 65,000 new videos uploaded each day.

In the 2008 presidential election, YouTube demonstrated its role in citizen journalism, the ability of the average citizen to report on and express views related to current events. Commentary and video on the party nominees and the presidential candidates demonstrated the potential of this Internet resource as a forum for expression for any citizen who can use a computer. In fact, YouTube was awarded the prestigious Peabody Award in 2008 for its role as a "Speaker's Corner" that embodies and promotes democracy.

Like all Internet resources, YouTube has both potential and peril for creative technology-using educators. It offers fresh and current video on any number of topics and from any number of reliable sources, but it does require careful review, selection, and monitoring. Still, it is a resource with which students are very likely to be familiar, and if the district and school permit its use, its educational potential should not be overlooked.

Using Motion Video in Teaching and Learning

Slow-motion and time-lapse videos provide unique perspectives.

Whether you use traditional or digital video technology to support teaching and learning, the key to using motion video in instruction is to fully engage the learner in the sensory experience that motion video offers. Once you have established your instructional design and created your lesson plans, if motion video is the support technology of choice, you should carefully consider this specific medium and how it will be implemented to maximize its effectiveness. Your preview, evaluation, and appropriate implementation will help you to engage your learners in this potentially powerful technology.

Using Video Media

Video offers some exceptional qualities that make it particularly useful in education. Video can appear to alter both time and space as it captures events. Video captured in real time can be played back in slow motion so that the eye can see events that occurred too fast to register through normal vision. Speeding up video playback (**time-lapse video**) may equally alter time for educational purposes. What might have taken days to occur can be viewed in the space of a few minutes. A time-lapse video of a seedling emerging from its shell and breaking through the soil into sunlight can offer students a science lesson that is not possible in the real world.

Of course, video has the potential to shift the viewers' location as well as the time frame they experience. Video travelogues, documentaries, and docudramas can seem to take viewers from the classroom to the location they are viewing. Furthermore, regardless of the location, the viewing angle is always excellent and completely safe. Such location shifting is one of the key assets provided by videos in instruction.

To be sure, not all videos are of the same quality. Some offer breathtaking, well-narrated views of events, whereas others display little more than "talking heads." For this reason, before you use a video in support of your instructional design, it is critical that you preview and evaluate it. Any video that is used in support of your lesson plan should be thoroughly previewed and evaluated to be sure it is appropriate to the content and of the quality necessary to engage the learners.

Creating Videos for Teaching and Learning

PEARSON myeducationkit™

Go to the *Assignments and Activities* section of Chapter 11 in MyEducationKit and complete the video activity entitled *Video Production*.

You may prefer to create your own instructional videos to precisely support the lesson you are teaching. Such teacher- or student-made videos may be necessary if appropriate support video is not commercially available or if a lesson calls for students to capture images and record them themselves.

Today's camcorders, whether traditional or digital in format, offer a relatively easy-to-use technology even for those who have never used a video camera before. In fact, creating a video is more complex in the planning stages than in the recording stage. Video production requires careful consideration of the images and sounds that will be captured.

Once you have planned your video's content, you are ready to record. One note of caution should be sounded with reference to student- and teacher-made videos. Some parents prefer not to have their child videotaped. Some believe that it is a violation of their child's privacy, or they may have justifiable concerns about when and how their child's picture will be distributed. Whenever a student's image is to be captured on videotape, permission must be obtained from the student's parent or guardian before taping. When you decide to begin a video production project that contains images of students, it is best to precede it with a notification to parents of what the project entails and how the video images will be displayed. Additionally, many districts require that you obtain written permission from the parents of all the children who are participating in the taping (whether they appear in the video or not) to authorize your creating a videotape that includes the child. Taking the time to research your school's or district's requirements on videotaping students and completing the necessary paperwork before taping are vital first steps whenever you plan classroom video productions that will include your students' images.

Parental permission is required before including children in videos.

Implementing Video in Instruction

Because video tends to be a passive experience and we know that the more engaged the learner is, the more effective learning will be, it is important to take steps to ensure that viewing the video will be a compelling experience. To begin, even though you might have previewed it, the video should be tested in the environment in which it will be shown. Sound volume and quality should be tested, seating should be arranged appropriately, and lighting should be adjusted as needed to avoid a washed-out image. Addressing these initial environmental variables before students arrive will reduce potential disruptions and distractions once the instructional event has begun.

The next, and perhaps most important, challenge is to fully involve the learner. It is a good idea to prepare your students for viewing by reviewing the concepts the video presents and discussing the objectives of the video and the key ideas it will present. Then, even though you have prepared your learners, it might be necessary to keep them engaged throughout the video screening. To create a more active video viewing experience, it is a good idea to provide a **video study guide.** Such a study guide may accompany commercial videos or could be created by you as you preview the video. For younger children or those with special needs,

A well-designed video study guide helps to engage the learner.

Video Evaluation **Rubric**

VIDEO TITLE:

DESCRIPTION:

SUBJECT AREA APPLICABILITY:

LENGTH: **COST:** **VENDOR:**

COMMENTS:

Using each of the following criteria, evaluate the effectiveness of the video for teaching and learning. For each dimension in the rubric, check the box that best reflects your opinion. Select videos that score 4 or higher in the most dimensions.

EVALUATION CRITERIA

DIMENSION	1 Poor	2 Below Average	3 Average	4 Above Average	5 Excellent
Relevance to Curriculum	☐ Video does not address significant aspects of the curriculum; addresses few targeted objectives	☐ Video includes both relevant and irrelevant elements; minimum objectives are met	☐ Some video elements add to and clarify the curriculum concepts; others are extraneous; some objectives addressed	☐ Most video elements add to and clarify key curriculum concepts and address targeted objectives	☐ All aspects of the video significantly add to and/or clarify key curriculum concepts; meets objectives
Currency and Accuracy	☐ Video is not current and has a significant number of factual inaccuracies	☐ Video is somewhat current in images and content; mostly accurate	☐ Video is current and accurate overall; but there is sufficient dated content to be distracting	☐ Video is mostly current and accurate; occasional images are dated, and some facts are less than accurate	☐ Video includes current images and presents accurate content
Engagement	☐ Video components do not provide sufficient interest and variety to engage the learner	☐ Video includes a number of elements that are likely to negatively affect the learner's attention	☐ Some video elements are interesting, while others are lacking; somewhat motivating and engaging	☐ Most elements of the video are interesting and motivating; some elements may not keep the learner's interest	☐ Video is interesting and provides motivation; fully engages the learner's attention
Support Materials	☐ No additional support materials are available with this video	☐ Few additional materials are available; those included are of average quality and provide limited support	☐ Some additional materials are available; quality of additional materials is good; some target key objectives	☐ Key materials of good quality are available to accompany the video; most are of high quality and target objectives	☐ Ample additional materials are of high quality, are easy to use, and target key objectives
Technical Quality	☐ Video has poor video and audio quality overall; production values are minimal	☐ The video is of moderate technical quality, ranging from poor elements to average production elements	☐ Aspects of the video range from average to good quality in terms of production	☐ Most aspects of the video are well done in terms of audio and video production	☐ All aspects of the video are excellent in terms of production quality

PEARSON myeducationkit™ Go to the *Rubrics* section of Chapter 11 in MyEducationKit to download the *Video Evaluation Rubric* for your use.

you might even choose to pause the video periodically to give learners time to respond orally or in writing. Video study guides can add significantly to the learning experience by helping to build connections to prior knowledge, focusing attention, and reinforcing learning.

Other methods for engaging the learners are to structure a discussion group after the video or at key stopping points during the video, to have students complete a kinesthetic project based on the video, or to create a sequel to the video they just watched. The possibilities are limited only by your own creativity. The key is to develop, as a component of video-enhanced instruction, some way to fully engage the learners in the concepts being presented by the video they are viewing.

The potential of video as an instructional tool is great, but it requires a commitment to responsible use. As an educator, you are responsible for ensuring that the motion video you display is as appropriate for your students as it is in direct support of your lesson. Motion video can have significant emotional as well as factual content. As an adult, as you view a video, you are able to react to content and discriminate facts from emotion because of your maturity and experience. Your learners might not be able to do this. Some video may include content that is emotionally powerful or that offers ideas that may be in conflict with the student's personal beliefs. Your responsibility when screening videos includes anticipating potential student reactions to the emotional content of a video as well as to its instructional content.

A final consideration in using videos in instruction relates to the issues of fair use of copyrighted materials. Copyright issues are fully explored in Chapter 13. Suffice it to say at this point that in using audio, visual, print, and video resources, it is critical that educators respect and adhere to copyright law. However, the law does include some options for educational use of copyrighted materials. These "fair use guidelines" offer educators detailed instructions for the legal use of copyrighted materials in the classroom. Interchapter 13 provides an in-depth look at these guidelines. It is every educators responsibility to follow them. This is particularly important for video. Commercial video, like other media, is typically copyrighted and therefore limited in how it may be used. As an educator, you must both model appropriate legal behavior for your students and conform to the copyright law your district expects you to observe.

TECH TIPS for Teachers

Video can enhance and enrich instruction when used appropriately. However, when used as an add-on to instruction without full integration, video can also result in passive and bored learners. To make video an effective and successful tool, follow the video tech tips below.

1. Use the potential of the medium:
   - Capture motion to bring instruction to life.
   - Use motion to add movement to the instructional sequence.
2. Use video to control time:
   - Be sure video images allow enough review time.
   - Record sequences that are long enough to communicate the message.
   - Use slow motion and time lapse to alter time.
3. Add special effects and text:
   - Add effects to emphasize the message.
   - Add text elements to clarify key points.

PEARSON myeducationkit™

To check your comprehension of the content covered in this chapter, go to the MyEducationKit for your book and complete the *Study Plan* for Chapter 11.

Key Terms

audiocassette, 289
AVI, 302
broadcast video, 299
bulletin board, 294
cablecast video, 300
closed-circuit TV (CCTV), 290
compact disc (CD), 304
compressed video teleconference systems, 304
compression technologies, 301
Corporation for Public Broadcasting (CPB), 300
digital projector, 296
digital video disc (DVD), 303
digital video cameras, 303
digital video editing, 303
document camera, 297
downlinked, 299
instructional television (ITV), 300
Internet audio, 291
Internet broadcasts, 305
Internet meetings, 307
Internet radio, 292
live cams, 305
MOV, 302
MPEG, 302
MP3, 291
multimedia kit, 289
narrowcast video, 300
oral history, 290
oral journal, 290
overhead projector, 294
print material, 294
Public Broadcasting Service (PBS), 299
satellite transmission, 299
streaming video, 305
talking book, 289
terrestrial, 299
time-lapse video, 308
transparencies, 296
uplinked, 299
VHS format tape, 301
video study guide, 309
videocassette recorders (VCRs), 301
WAV files, 291
YouTube, 308

Student Activities

CHAPTER REVIEW

1. Compare the four types of video found in schools.
2. What are the advantages and disadvantages of each of the following audio technologies in teaching and learning: Audiocassettes? Broadcast audio? Optical media? Internet audio?
3. Name and describe three types of nonprojected media. Explain how each is important in teaching and learning.
4. Name the four most common technologies for nonprojected media display. How do they differ?
5. What are projected visuals? When compared to nonprojected visuals, when are they most appropriate in the classroom?
6. What is a digital projector? How is it used? How might a document camera be used with a digital projector to enhance learning in the classroom?
7. How has recorded video improved video's usefulness to education? Name and describe the media used to record video.
8. What is a compressed video system? How can it assist in communications across a school district?
9. Contrast Internet broadcasts, live cams, and Net meetings. How can each of these Internet-based video technologies be used in teaching and learning?
10. Why is it important to preview and evaluate videos? What tools should you use to be sure a video is communicating the intended message to your students?

WHAT DO YOU THINK?

1. There is much discussion today about the role of computers in the classroom, often to the point at which this technology overshadows all other instructional technologies. What do you believe is the appropriate balance among the various technologies you have learned about thus far? Will digital technologies and computers indeed replace all others? What will your classroom be like twenty years from now in terms of the technologies you will be using?
2. Imagine that you have moved into a new classroom, and no audio or visual technology or media have yet been ordered. You have been asked to prepare a wish list of your audio and visual needs to submit to the media center. What will you order? Justify your requests by explaining how you would use each technology or medium in instruction.
3. Visual literacy and audio delivery are inherent components of instruction. What can you do to help build skills in visual literacy and in effective listening in the grade or content area in which you teach or wish to teach?
4. Student-made videos are an effective and interactive teaching and learning tool. However, there is concern over student privacy when the images of students are included on tape. Research this issue and talk to a local teacher or administrator to gain a better understanding of the issue. Then describe the key concerns and how a teacher might best address them when filming students.
5. The great advantage of video in teaching and learning is its ability to represent a shift in time and space. Explain what this means and how you might use it in teaching a unit of your choice.

LEARNING TOGETHER!

These activities are best done in groups of three to five.

1. Visit the media center of a local school and ask the media specialist to show you the audio and visual technologies that are available. Compare your media inventory and applications list with those of the other members of your group. Be prepared to share your list with other groups.
2. Listening centers are popular individual and group activity centers in classrooms today. As a group, design a listening center for the grade level you would prefer to teach. Describe the technologies and media you would include.
3. Each group member should locate five Internet live cams that could be useful for educators and create an annotated list of them. Summarize your lists, eliminate duplicates, and prepare a "Top Ten" live cam resource list to share with the class.

TEACHING WITH TECHNOLOGY: INTEGRATION IDEAS WEB QUEST

Traditional and digital visuals, audio, and video offered via the web empower educators to provide instruction in every student's dominant learning style. Whether powerful historical photographs, MP3s of famous speeches, or video clips of current events, web-based audio and visuals add depth to instruction.

ACTIVITY: Explore the following links to discover some of the ways in which educators are using audiovisual resources in their classrooms. Select the resource of most interest to you, and then search the Net for resources that would further support the instructional methodology you explored. Find three resources, and prepare a web quest summary that includes (1) each link and its URL, (2) a summary of the type of audio and/or visual resources found there, (3) explanation of how each link could offer educators support for instruction, and (4) all appropriate warnings or concerns associated with using that resource in the classroom

Integration Ideas: Integrating Audiovisual Technologies into Social Studies

"Amercian Rhetoric: Top 100 Speeches" is described as giving social studies teachers "a chance to make history come alive for their students." This web site is an audio database with full text of these speeches, which cover great oratory from as early as Clarence Darrow and William Jennings Bryan up to the present day. The audio is MP3 Stream and Real Audio Stream. The site's URL is **www.americanrhetoric.com/top100speechesall.html** and is is updated regularly (2006, June 30).

American rhetoric: Top 100 speeches. **www.techlearning.com/shared/printableArticle.jhtml?articleID=21100263.**

Integration Ideas: Integrating Audiovisual Technologies into Language Arts

Teaching point of view in high school English classes via making a novel into a movie is the creative approach that Patty Blome designed for her San Diego, California, classroom. With the help of either iMovie or Windows Movie Maker, the students select a novel and create video chapters. Each student in a production team is involved in storyboarding, writing, or choosing dialog from the novel to use; selecting sites as settings; and reviewing versions of the video segment for editing. Parents are invited to the screening, or upon completion of the film, "a novel-to-film film festival" is held. In evaluating the project, the teacher will discover how much students have learned about how point of view affects storytelling. A questionnaire seeking to find out how students' points of view of sections of the novel varied or coincided with those of their classmates is used as a means of judging the depth of comprehension the students have attained. To find how you and your students can become movie producers, click on **http://www.2.scholastic.com/browse/lessonplan.isp?id=1196&print=1.**

Integration Ideas: Integrating Audiovisual Technologies into the Sciences

One of the best sources for incorporating audiovisual technologies into curriculum design can be found at scientific governmental sites such as that of NASA. Principal Deanna Kowal of Jim Bridger Middle School in Las Vegas, Nevada, provided a prelude to a live video session with the International Space Station. They had a two-way video connection that, for twenty minutes, allowed seventeen students to talk to astronauts Mike Fincke and Sandra Magnus as they orbited in space. One of the highlights of the video for the students was the astronauts, when not on the microphone, showing off their antigravity somersaults. Astronaut Sandra Magnus told the students, "This is the part of our job that we really enjoy. It's always great to talk with students, and you guys had really great questions." To read more about this exciting event in the lives of the middle-schoolers, go to Cappello, C. **http://www.lasvegassun.com/news/2009/jan/10/north-las-vegas-students-link-astronauts.**

Integration Ideas: Integrating Audiovisual Technologies into Math

Watching VideoStream or listening the RealAudio Interview of the Rovers on Mars while learning calculus is definitely twenty-first century. Steve Crandall, mathematics and physical science teacher at Park City High School, Park City, Utah, uses Sprint and Opportunity, the Mars rovers, for mathematics lessons, as well as objectives for science lessons. The students listen to the RealAudio and watch the VideoStream from the Online NewsHour, January 26, 2004. In Lesson One, two overall questions are asked regarding the transmission times. Then they answer "Online Investigation Questions."

Crandall, S. rovers on Mars. **www.pbs.org./newshour/extra/teachers/lessonplans/science/marsrover_4-15.html.**

interchapter 11

Audio Visual Media Timeline

1902
First educational films exhibited; early films adapted from newsreels

1905–1920
The first school museums established for distribution of portable museum exhibits, stereographs, slides, films, study prints, charts, and other instructional materials

1908
Publication of *Visual Education,* describing how to teach with and use lantern slides and spectrographs

1911
Thomas Edison produced the first historical film to be shown in a classroom, called *The Minute Men*

1912
Early portable 16mm film projectors available

1914–1923
Formation of professional organizations and publication of professional journals for visual educators; bureaus of visual instruction established in metropolitan school districts

1919
Society for Visual Education formed to produce films specifically for school use

1920–1930
Introduction of audio capability to create audiovisual aids, including radio and sound films

1928
Eastman Teaching Pictures formed, ultimately creating 250 silent educational films

1929
Electrical Research Products, a subsidiary of Western Electric, added sound to educational films

1930s
Federal government produced educational films

1933
American Council on Education began the Motion Picture Project to study the use of instructional films

1941–1946
Audiovisual instruction adapted for wide use by the U.S. military

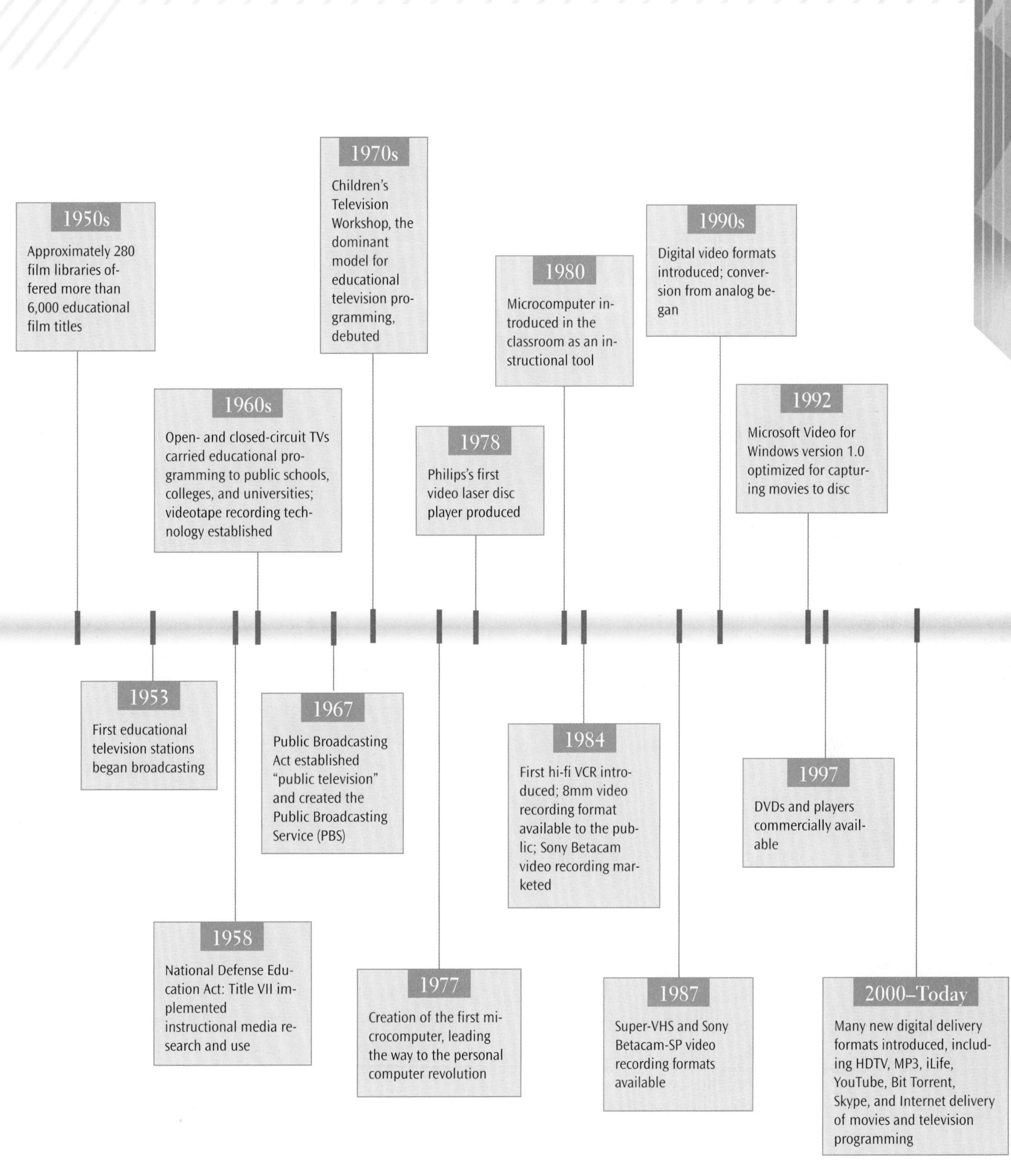
1950s
Approximately 280 film libraries offered more than 6,000 educational film titles
1953
First educational television stations began broadcasting
1958
National Defense Education Act: Title VII implemented instructional media research and use
1960s
Open- and closed-circuit TVs carried educational programming to public schools, colleges, and universities; videotape recording technology established
1967
Public Broadcasting Act established "public television" and created the Public Broadcasting Service (PBS)
1970s
Children's Television Workshop, the dominant model for educational television programming, debuted
1977
Creation of the first microcomputer, leading the way to the personal computer revolution
1978
Philips's first video laser disc player produced
1980
Microcomputer introduced in the classroom as an instructional tool
1984
First hi-fi VCR introduced; 8mm video recording format available to the public; Sony Betacam video recording marketed
1987
Super-VHS and Sony Betacam-SP video recording formats available
1990s
Digital video formats introduced; conversion from analog began
1992
Microsoft Video for Windows version 1.0 optimized for capturing movies to disc
1997
DVDs and players commercially available
2000–Today
Many new digital delivery formats introduced, including HDTV, MP3, iLife, YouTube, Bit Torrent, Skype, and Internet delivery of movies and television programming

PART THREE

Technology in Schools: Changing Teaching and Learning

Thus far, you have explored the teaching and learning process, examined how effective instruction can be designed and planned, and investigated the many technologies that can be used in support of instruction. Now it is time to take a look at how technology is changing education in today's schools and in the schools of the future.

We begin by looking at how technology helps creative teachers reinvent their classrooms. Just as you go into your classroom each year and arrange it to provide the best possible space for teaching and learning, so too you will use technology to create new spaces, even virtual ones, in which teaching and learning can occur. Some of these technology-enhanced instructional environments make it possible for the teacher and student to be at a physical distance from each other yet still allow for the teaching and learning process to occur. This type of instruction is often called *distance education* or *distance delivery of education*. These environments add a new dimension to the more traditional teaching and learning methodologies and are sometimes referred to as *the alternative delivery of instruction*.

This part begins with an exploration of both distance and alternative learning and how they are implemented in today's schools. Chapter 12 will help you understand the transformations in delivery that creative application of technology in education makes possible. Chapter 13 will take you further into the transformation we are experiencing as technology is implemented in schools. You will explore the process through which technology is implemented and inquire into the social, ethical, and legal issues associated with the implementation of technology. Finally, Chapter 14 will investigate emerging technology and how it will further transform the schools in which you will be teaching.

The three chapters in Part Three will help you to see the important role technology will play as our schools continue to evolve to better serve our society. As educators, we will continue to have the goal of helping our students prepare for the world in which they will work and live. That world, rich in technology and altered integrally by its existence, will make for a fascinating and exciting learning environment.

REAL STORIES

REAL TEACHERS

Darlene Haught

Meet Darlene Haught. Delivering curriculum from a distance, whether synchronously via two-way audio/video television, or online asynchronously via the Internet, requires innovative strategies that not only grab the attention of the students but also allow the students to break through the barriers to communication. Let's see how Darlene Haught handled this problem.

My name is Darlene Haught. I am the Dean of Distance Learning Technologies, and I work closely with the North Carolina School of Science and Mathematics (NCSSM) staff and faculty, as well as with those around the state, to coordinate the development and delivery of instructional programs that serve its outreach mission. NCSSM is located in Durham, North Carolina. It has a dual mission to provide a rigorous education to the 615 students who residentially attend the school, and equally important is its mandated mission to provide educational opportunities to students and educators throughout the state.

North Carolina is a state of 119 school districts, 42 percent of which are in rural settings. Getting upper-level curriculum to much of the state is a critical need. NCSSM created a Distance Learning Department to meet its mission and address this need. Since 1995, this department has provided curriculum via interactive videoconferencing (IVC), and more recently it is developing and delivering online curriculum. The need for this to be highly interactive and engaging is critical in the K–12 environment.

Being the major provider of IVC K–12 curriculum statewide, we have much experience in using multimedia and cutting-edge technologies to bridge the distance to the students, get and retain their attention, and foster their active participation. Additionally, with the emergence of asynchronous delivery, we frequently use these technologies to make our online courses equally engaging and interactive.

The NCSSM distance learning staff works closely with the instructional staff to use audiovisual technology effectively. In distance learning, this means more than simply pointing a video camera at a "talking head."

Our computer graphics illustrators will take a concept described by the instructor and develop a custom graphic image or animation to support or illustrate it. Other graphics support includes web graphics and HTML authoring that enhance instructors' web sites and courses. Diagrams, charts, maps, scanned images, and logos are developed frequently for printed materials to support courses, professional development workshops, and the like.

A high-end nonlinear video editing system gives us the capability to produce video segments and demonstrations for instructors to use. Instructors can prepare and present a host of videos, such as sophisticated science experiments, field observations, or mathematical problem solving. The capability to produce streaming media from video supports online courses; in addition, we stream and archive all IVC classes for students to access for review outside of class.

Four studios serve as the IVC distance learning instructor's "classroom." A computer is the hub providing access to the Internet and the school's network, as well as to specialized and application software. Classroom management software, such as Blackboard or Moodle, is used to electronically convey and collect assignments and communicate with students. A graphics tablet connected to the computer allows the teacher to write and draw diagrams with an "electronic" blackboard on the TV screen, just as if it were a blackboard on a classroom wall. The "flexcam," a small color video camera mounted on a jointed flexible arm, allows an instructor to show images from a textbook, zoom in on a science demonstration, or display three-dimensional objects for the class. Students can use one to show homework or work out a problem visually for the rest of the class. One tool most enjoyed by students is the chromakey. This is the same technology that is used by TV stations when they put the weatherman in front of a map. This visual technology uses a "green screen" onto which an image is overlaid and then combined with the image of the instructor.

The studio managers are encouraged to employ audio and visual techniques in the broadcast. For example, when slides are being displayed to the class, the studio manager will create a picture-in-picture, with the instructor's image in the corner of the screen. Maintaining visual contact with the teacher as much as possible facilitates keeping the student engaged. "POTS"—plain old telephone service—bridges communication among technical staff and privately between instructor and student. The fax machine is used to transmit tests or quizzes and assignments.

Calculators and CBL technology that are commonplace in high school math and science courses are not unique to distance learning, either. Data from the calculator's LCD display can be transmitted via IVC through a TI Presenter that connects directly to the calculator. CBLs are used to collect data through different types of probes with sensors. These are used most effectively in science and math distance learning classes.

In my job as the dean of this department, I encourage my staff to explore and implement new technologies that support our efforts. Distance learning protocols are changing, as well as the technologies associated with it. As we continue to move into more asynchronous online learning, we will continue to explore innovative and effective ways to use visual and audio technologies to keep the learner engaged in the learning process.

For more information and a virtual tour, please visit the distance learning web site at www.dlt.ncssm.edu. Please contact the writer at haught@ncssm.edu; phone: 919-416-2877.

CHAPTER 12

Distance Education: Using Technology to Redefine the Classroom

Joe Don Buckner/AP Images

CHAPTER OVERVIEW

This chapter addresses these ISTE National Educational Technology Standards:
- NETS•T Standard 1
- NETS•T Standard 2
- NETS•T Standard 5
- NETS•S Standard 2
- NETS•S Standard 5

- **Redefining the Classroom through Distance Education**
- **Distance Education: A Brief History**
- **Designing Instruction for Distance Delivery**
- **Support Technologies for Distance Teaching and Learning**
- **Issues in Implementing Distance and Alternative Delivery Systems**
- **Reinventing the Classroom: The Future of Distance and Alternative Delivery**

In your educational technology course, you have learned much about teaching and learning, designing instruction, and selecting the appropriate technologies to support instructional events—but all from the point of view of using technology to enhance what some refer to as *traditional modes of instruction*. As educators across the nation expand the use of technology in teaching and learning, it is becoming evident that technology might well end up doing more than just enhancing instruction; it might prove to be a serious force in changing the nature and form of instruction.

Consider for a moment how one technology—the cell phone—has changed the nature of personal and business communication. Being out of touch with family or business has become a thing of the past. The need for pay phones has been so significantly reduced that they are a rare sight. Just think for a moment of the scene in one of our nation's major airports. Banks of pay phones once lined the walls in gate areas. Now passengers use their own cell phones to make local and long-distance calls. In this scene, we can see for ourselves the decline of one technology and the rise of another.

Like this cellular technology, educational technologies are essentially communication tools. As you have learned, teaching is, at its core, communication. It may therefore be reasonable to anticipate that advances in educational technologies will fundamentally alter the way in which we communicate educationally, just as such advances have already fundamentally changed personal and business communications. Some people say that we are at the threshold of just such a change. So far, the predominant mode of educational communication has been the traditional classroom format, that is, a teacher and a given number of students working together in a predefined instructional space. But we are beginning to see technology broaden this concept. Indeed, implementation of current and emerging technologies may well redefine the classroom itself.

Such changes are already occurring. You have no doubt noticed an abundance of college courses offered as *distance education* courses. Such courses may be delivered online or through various combinations of digital and other distance-delivery technologies. But have you ever explored exactly what these courses entail? Have you considered their implications in changing the way teaching and learning are defined? Have you thought about how these new delivery systems might affect you and your students? These considerations are the topic of this chapter. And although distance education implementations are at the moment more frequently found in higher education, the instructional innovations reflected by these new delivery systems are already having far-reaching repercussions throughout all levels of education. It is important to be aware of their potential impact on you, on your students, and on your professional career.

In Chapter 12, you will:

- Explore distance and other technology-enhanced instructional delivery systems
- Examine the relationship and educational implications of traditional and alternative delivery systems
- Review the role various technologies play in the alternative delivery of instruction
- Explore the application of and issues associated with alternative delivery systems in teaching and learning
- Examine the role of the Internet in alternative delivery
- Explore ways to evaluate distance and alternative delivery systems

Redefining the Classroom through Distance Education

Most people would agree that technology has had a significant impact on our society and our schools. Regardless of whether any given teacher makes use of technology in the classroom, because technology is changing our world, its impact is felt in all social institutions, including schools. Some of the most dramatic changes enabled by technology are the options for alternative delivery of instruction that have been created through the adaptation of

Technology enables us to move information instead of people.

Standard

ISTE

Learning about distance learning resources for your classroom will help you address

NETS•T STANDARD 2:

DESIGN AND DEVELOP DIGITAL-AGE LEARNING EXPERIENCES AND ASSESSMENTS Teachers design, develop, and evaluate authentic learning experiences and assessments incorporating contemporary tools and resources to maximize content learning in context and to develop the knowledge, skills, and attitudes identified in the NETS•S.

In distance education, the teacher and student may be working in different locations and/or at different times.

communications technologies to education. Businesses are already using communications technologies to conduct virtual meetings and to hold virtual training sessions for employees who are spread out across the nation or the world. Many schools and institutions of higher education have adopted this idea of moving information rather than people and have applied it to the delivery of instruction. Such technology-enhanced delivery approaches are typically referred to as **distance education.**

Distance education can be broadly defined as the delivery of instruction to students who are separated from their teacher by time and/or location. The teacher may be located at a school site, but the student may be "attending" the class at home, using technology to bridge the gap. Or both teacher and student may be at either the same or different locations but available to work on the course only at differing hours. Once again, technology serves as a bridge across this time gap. In such cases, instructional events and interactions occur just as they do in traditional settings, but their form may be radically different from that found in the traditional classroom. Consider the following possibilities.

If you were taking a college course in a distance education format, you probably wouldn't see your teacher on a regular basis, as you would if you were taking a class that met every Monday evening. From an instructional viewpoint, how could teaching and learning occur? For example, you might have a critical question that arose while you were reviewing your text or related assignment. How would you get clarification? How is a student's interaction with an instructor and among peers possible in such a situation?

In a distance education scenario, technology is the key to providing a format for academic communication and exchange. For example, a student might choose to email a question from his or her home computer to the teacher, asking for clarification or explanation. The student and the teacher are at different locations; the student is at home, and the instructor is at school or at home. Or a student might choose to email a question at night when doing an assignment. The instructor might not respond to that question until the next morning. Thus, student and instructor are separated by time as well as distance. The student is engaged in the learning process at night, and the teacher is engaged in the teaching process in the morning. Still, with the help of technology, the student is able to communicate with the instructor and the instructor with the student. An instructional event has occurred. The student has asked a question, and the teacher has clarified and expanded on the content. Without the two parties being in the same location or even working in the same time frame, teaching and learning have occurred. This type of nontraditional interaction is at the core of distance education (see Figure 12.1).

Distance education was originally developed to deliver instruction to students in remote rural locations. For many years, distance education was accomplished primarily via correspondence courses or by sending an instructor out to remote locations to deliver instruction to groups of students. With the advent of technologies that make instructional delivery possible in ways never envisioned in previous years, distance education has come to have a much broader meaning. In fact, some educators have sought to broaden the term itself to better represent these new delivery systems. Thus, you will find terminology such as *distributed learning* or *virtual classrooms* used interchangeably with *distance education.* Regardless of the terminology, the idea behind them all is the delivery of instruction in nontraditional ways via technologies. Although the original term, *distance education,* remains dominant, it might not fully reflect the multitude of innovations and systems that make it possible for teachers and students to connect instructionally. Still, for consistency and clarity, we will use this terminology throughout this chapter but ask you to think of it in its broadest possible meaning.

Distance education is likely to have a direct impact on you on at least two significant professional levels. First, because teacher licensing requires continual renewal, you may participate as a student in a distance-delivered course to remain current professionally, to pursue an advanced degree, or to renew your professional credentials. Distance delivery of instruction to educators means that you are no longer bound by the colleges in your immediate vicinity. Through distance delivery, you have the opportunity to enroll in courses offered by any organization or institution in the nation—or indeed the world. This gives

FIGURE 12.1

Distance Education Technologies Enable Communication

Distance education uses technology to connect teacher and learner across time and space.

you timely access to the latest developments in the field and provides you with the widest possible professional development options.

The second impact of distance education is more subtle, though perhaps more significant. Distance-delivery systems, especially those that emphasize delivery by the Internet, have become both more refined and more robust. Advances in communication technologies and increases in available bandwidth are driving these continual improvements in distance-delivery systems. The instructional potential offered by these systems has, in turn, caused a rethinking of the nature of instruction. Which elements of the physical instructional environment must truly be fixed? Which ones can simply be redefined by using technology? Must a teacher and student be in the same physical space for teaching and learning to occur? The answers to these types of academic questions will ultimately affect every classroom. Instruction is already being redefined in many higher education environments, and this trend is now becoming evident in state and local school systems as well (Figure 12.2).

PEARSON myeducationkit™

Go to the *Assignments and Activities* section of Chapter 12 in MyEducationKit and complete the video activity entitled *Benefits of Virtual School.*

A number of states have created highly successful virtual high school programs that offer high school credit courses statewide. These programs expand the instructional opportunities for high school students across the state. Students are no longer limited to the courses that can be offered at the local high school they are assigned to attend. In some districts that have implemented distance education, low-enrollment courses that

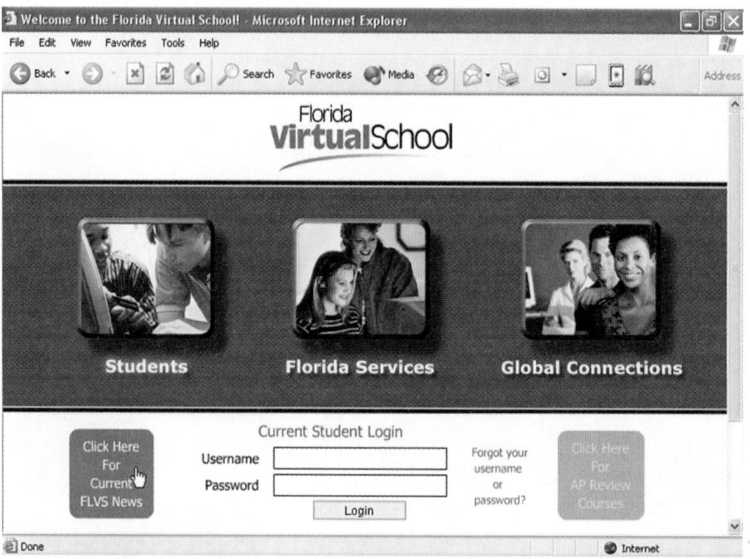

FIGURE 12.2

Many states have added online schools to their school systems to supplement those in traditional school districts.

would not be offered in a single school may be offered by means of a distance-delivery system that can combine students from multiple schools into a single districtwide virtual classroom. Or instruction that is not otherwise available at a school, owing to a shortage of qualified teachers in a given content area, may be offered by a districtwide master teacher to all district schools through distance delivery. These innovative programs expand the concept of the traditional classroom. Such delivery models are likely to be just a forerunner of more dramatic changes to come. As a technologically literate professional educator, you need to have an awareness of distance education and its potential application for you and your students.

Distance Education: A Brief History

> Distance learning has moved from correspondence courses to a rich, immediate, interactive environment.

As we noted earlier, the earliest distance-delivery systems were **correspondence courses,** consisting of books and assignments delivered to students via the postal system. As students did their readings and then completed assignments, they would mail their work back to the teacher. Tests were often given by local proctors, who mailed the completed exams to the teacher. Teaching was confined to the selection of books and the development of written learning activities. Learning was independent, with no interaction with peers and little interaction with the teacher. Of course, a student could mail a question to the instructor, but the time delay between question and response was critical, making meaningful exchange difficult.

As various other technologies were developed, they were added to enrich the correspondence course format (see Figure 12.3). The development of radio, and later television, resulted in instructional programming delivered via these two technologies. Distance students could listen to or watch a program featuring their teacher offering them direct instruction through audio and/or video. Distance students were also able to contact their instructor personally via telephone technology to ask a question or clarify content. Although these technologies did much to improve teacher-to-student communication when compared to a course delivered by the postal system, they did relatively little to enable student-to-student communication. Learners who were engaged in a distance course still missed the student discussion and interaction that can lead to a broadening of ideas. Learning still took place in relative isolation.

FIGURE 12.3

Distance Education Timeline

Distance education has evolved from correspondence courses to live interactive instruction supported by compressed video.

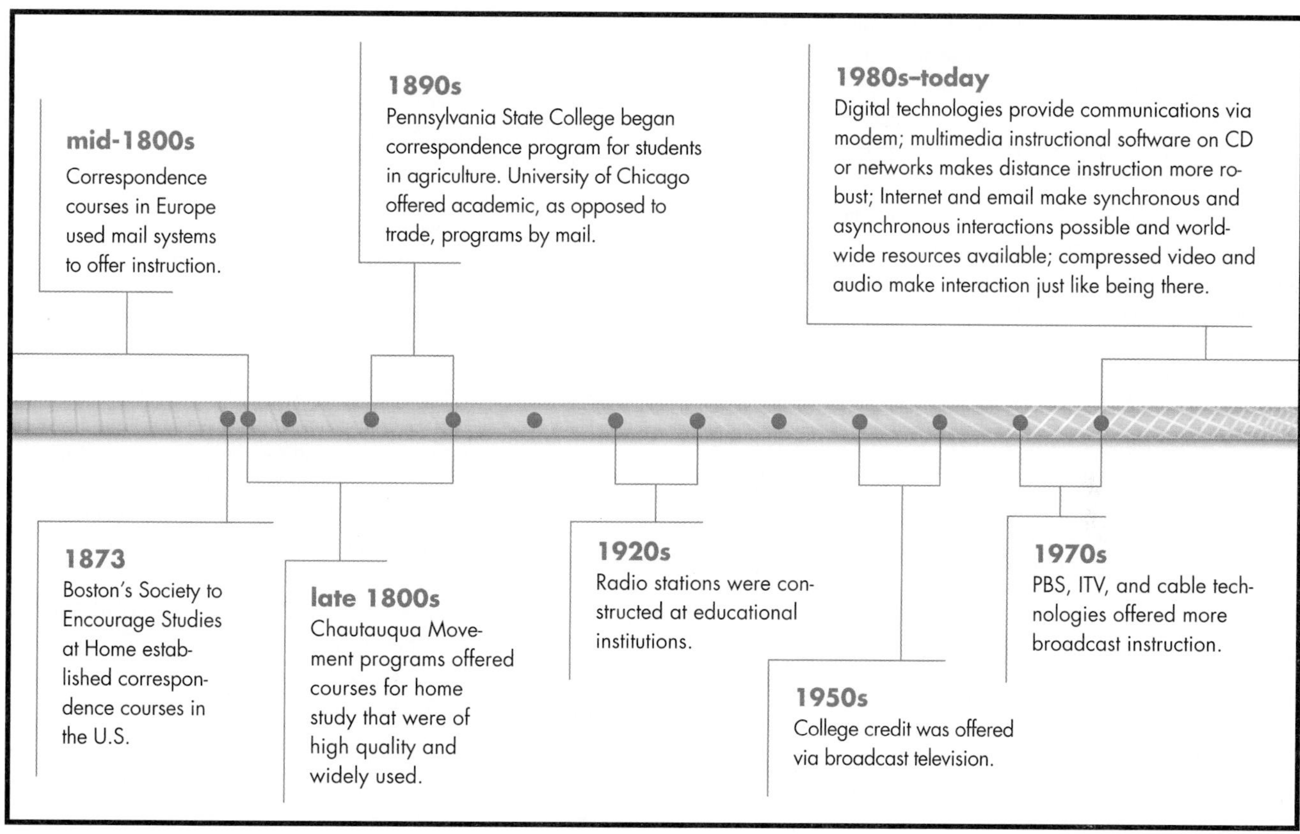

As other technologies emerged, a solution to learner isolation became possible. Phone bridges, a sophisticated telephone conferencing system, allowed a large group of students to dial in together and connect with each other and their teacher. Students could then interact and discuss content via the phone. Then, with the advent of the personal computer and later the Internet, live and time-delayed communication via modem became possible. Today, with the addition of streaming audio and video and telecommunications via the Internet to distance-delivery technologies, live video and audio interaction between teacher and student or among students is a viable alternative.

Each of the technologies mentioned above will be discussed in more detail later in this chapter, but it is clear that the nature of distance education is changing and is coming to emulate more closely the interaction that occurs in the traditional classroom. The impact of distance delivery may therefore have significant repercussions in education and may eventually blur the line between traditional and distance education. This potential for educational evolution offers fascinating academic possibilities, not only for distance education but also for education in traditional settings. Such alternatives to current delivery formats warrant further exploration.

In the CLASSROOM

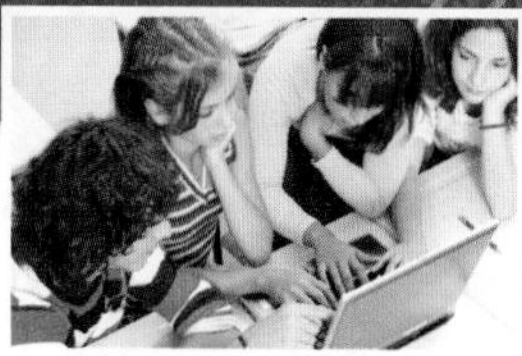

The Virtual Classroom

Virtual schools for K–12 students offer learning opportunities that are unavailable in traditional school settings. **Florida Virtual School (FLVS)** was started "so that students in rural and high-minority districts could have access to the same level of courses as students in other districts," according to Susie Meserve, in an article on the *School CIO: Strategies for K–12 Technology Leaders* web site.

At FLVS, Florida-certified teachers who teach the courses work with curriculum specialists and advanced programmers to maintain the integrity of the course content and to adapt it to delivery through a medium different from the traditional face-to-face classroom. Katerina Williams, a tenth-grader in Haines City, Florida, was able to take all of her college prep courses except trigonometry at the FLVS. Christina Wood, in the article "Highschool.com: The Virtual Classroom Redefines Education," notes that many students who take online classes do so "to obtain access to classes not available at their local school, gain a competitive edge when preparing for college, or accommodate a jammed schedule. A few, though, are so convinced of the efficacy of online instruction that they've abandoned traditional schools altogether."

Another group of students who benefit from online learning are those in special circumstances who need access to instruction from home. There are also students who live in areas that are growing rapidly, such as the Clark County School District in Las Vegas, Nevada, where the Virtual High School gives students an option to avoid the overcrowded schools in the metropolitan centers. At the Illinois Virtual High School, students from socioeconomically deprived neighborhoods can receive instruction from highly qualified teachers, who are difficult to find and retain in impoverished schools. Furthermore, students who live in geographically remote or sparsely populated parts of a state can benefit greatly from online courses.

Linda Pittenger, director of the Division of Virtual Learning in Kentucky, observed that in the online instructional venue, students reveal diverse gifts and talents that often go unnoticed in a traditional classroom because of the opportunity to freely express themselves online. The closer relationships that can be built between students and teachers can also occur among students from distant points on the globe. The Dalat International School in Penang, Malaysia, is in a partnership with the FLVS. Principal Karl Steinkamp says, "It allows our students to interact and take classes with kids in the U.S. and all over the world. It also give students in the U.S. a larger worldview."

In North Carolina, students such as Kylee Patterson in Laurinburg, North Carolina, graduated from Scotland High School of Math, Science, and Technology already having completed a year of college by taking courses through the North Carolina Virtual Public School program, which is open to public middle and high school students. Phone Keosouma, a dropout student from West Montgomery High School in Troy, North Carolina, took online courses to make up the credits he lacked, took some online college-credit courses, and graduated on time with the rest of his class.

The virtual schools, a venue of education that was once looked at skeptically or as something that might someday have potential, are well entrenched today and serving the diverse needs of many thousands of students. Find out more by visiting these sites:

Meserve, S. (2007). *Running a virtual school.* Retrieved January 20, 2007, from **http://www.schoolcio.com/shared/printableArticle.php?articleID=193401746.**

Wood, C. (2005, March 23). *Highschool.com: The virtual classroom redefines education.* Retrieved August 16, 2007, from **http://www.edutopia.org/node/1270/print.**

Robinson, N. (2008, August 7). *NC online students can graduate early, or catch up.* Retrieved August 9, 2008, from **http://www.districtadministration.com/newssummary.aspx?news=yes&postid=50544.**

PEARSON **myeducationkit**

Go to the *Assignments and Activities* section of Chapter 12 in MyEducationKit and complete the web activity entitled *Distance Education in K–12.*

Designing Instruction for Distance Delivery

You have already learned about the importance of a well-conceived design and a carefully planned lesson to ensure the quality of your instruction. In a distance-delivery environment, planning is even more crucial. Unlike the traditional classroom, in which the teacher is present and can make adjustments to the teaching and learning process while it is being carried out, distance delivery requires that all aspects of the process be fully established before the teacher and learners engage in it. The distance education curriculum and fully articulated activities are typically prepared well in advance of the instructional event. Distance educators must anticipate learner responses and prepare a curriculum that answers questions and concerns before they are asked. Once the curriculum has been disseminated to students working in different locations or in different time frames, it can be difficult to make and disburse changes to it for other than Internet-based courses. For these reasons, every aspect of instructional planning is a critical component of distance delivery.

Detailed advance planning is even more critical in distance learning than in traditional teaching.

Beyond the Lesson Plan

The instructional design process, when applied to distance education, requires a strategic approach. The design must respond to both the instruction itself and the benefits and/or impediments of the distance-delivery technologies that will be used. Often, district or school distance education programs begin by determining which technologies are available or will be acquired to deliver instruction across spatial or temporal barriers. This may be a less-than-ideal, though necessary, approach. A better scenario would be identical to the process used for traditional instruction; that is, start with the instructional design and then determine which distance-delivery technologies are necessary and appropriate to support instruction. Unfortunately, because of the significant cost of distance-delivery technologies and their integral role in the process, a district might have little choice but to begin by determining which existing technologies can be repurposed for distance education. These determinations will not define the instructional event, but they do determine the parameters. When preparing an instructional design for distance education, you must implement the design process with full awareness of the technologies that will be made available to you for delivery. Your design itself may suggest changes to the planned delivery technologies that will be necessary to ensure effective delivery and meaningful interaction.

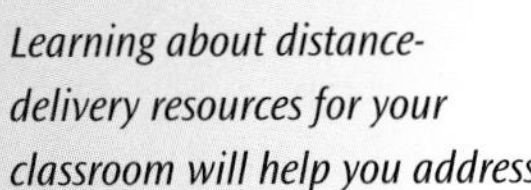

Learning about distance-delivery resources for your classroom will help you address

NETS•T STANDARD 1:

FACILITATE AND INSPIRE STUDENT LEARNING AND CREATIVITY Teachers use their knowledge of subject matter, teaching and learning, and technology to facilitate experiences that advance student learning, creativity, and innovation in both face-to-face and virtual environments.

The steps of the DID process you have already learned do not change in distance education. In fact, they become even more fundamental when you are conceptualizing instruction that will be difficult to alter once it has begun. The environment in which your design will be implemented is likely to be very different from the traditional classroom and therefore must be fully considered and adapted in the initial design. Because distance education teachers are not in frequent face-to-face contact with their students, impromptu changes in the instructional plan are typically not practical. Developing a fully articulated design is the only way to create an instructional sequence that is precise enough to flow unerringly without having to be frequently changed and adjusted.

Although instructional design for distance education takes on a strategic and situational perspective, the most significant change to the instructional planning process occurs in the lesson plan phase. Table 12.1 illustrates the relationship between the steps in a traditional lesson plan and those same steps as integrated into a distance education curriculum.

Preparing Students

Because students must work through their lessons without benefit of the immediate presence of the teacher, they must first be prepared for the differences this type of experience will present. From the earliest grades, student behavior and expectations are shaped so that the students will be comfortable in a traditional classroom, but few learners have been similarly prepared to work in a distance environment. Therefore, in addition to preparing the learners for the content, you must prepare them to work differently than they would in a traditional classroom. Typically, that means that you must prepare them to work much more independently. This, then, is the next major consideration in designing instruction for alternative delivery.

TABLE 12.1 Comparing Traditional and Distance Lesson Planning

OPTICAL MEDIA	TRADITIONAL CLASS	DISTANCE LEARNING CLASS
STEP 1: READY THE LEARNER.	*In your classroom, you would* • Ask questions to determine whether content needs to be reviewed • Review content as needed	*In your distance education materials, you should* • Prepare a pretest so students can self-assess whether they have the necessary previous content • Make review materials available
STEP 2: TARGET SPECIFIC OBJECTIVES.	*In your classroom, you would* • Select the target objective for the lesson • Prepare your students by explaining what they will be able to do as a result of the lesson • Respond to your students' questions about the lesson	*In your distance education materials, you should* • Post the target objective in a location students will notice • Explain the objective in detail, since there may be a time delay should students have a question • Articulate how questions should be asked and will be responded to
STEP 3: PREPARE THE LESSON.	*In your classroom, you would* • Decide how your classroom needs to be arranged for this particular lesson • Write notes for yourself as to how you will accomplish each step of the pedagogical cycle • Select and set up the materials, media, and technologies needed and decide how will they be used by you and your students • Decide upon assessments for the lesson and select materials and means for implementation	*In your distance education materials, you should* • Create content modules so that students have manageable materials to work with • For each module, sequence each step of the pedagogical cycle and provide a detailed explanation to the student as to how to proceed through each step • Prepare all materials with detailed instructions for their use and include them in the students' modules • Arrange for all media to be made available to students • Arrange for technologies to be available to students who do not have access • Provide students with detailed procedures for accessing and using media and technologies • Prepare assessments well in advance • Make arrangements for proctoring, and communicate procedures for assessments to students

In the traditional classroom, students listen to directions or instruction and then proceed to complete assigned work. If they have a question, they need only raise a hand, and their teacher responds to them. In a distance education environment, the process is different. Students working in this type of environment need to be trained to find the information they need from their materials and to use the systems in place to get answers to unresolved questions. This is a more independent learning format than the one that is typical of a traditional classroom.

Many distance education programs use a combination of screening and orienting students to prepare them to be successful in a distance education environment (Figure 12.4). Screening students, that is, determining whether or not their learning styles and study habits are consistent with the distance education format, is a frequently used first step. Each distance education program uses specific technologies and methods to deliver instruction. Matching students who have the potential to work well with these methods can increase learner success and decrease frustration. A second commonly used step is to prepare students for the distance education environment by providing a very specific orientation to and training in the methods and technologies they will be expected to work with. This step helps students become as comfortable with the experiences and tools of the distance teaching and learning environment as they would be if they were participating in a traditional environment. One or both of these preparatory steps will assist learners in maximizing their potential for success.

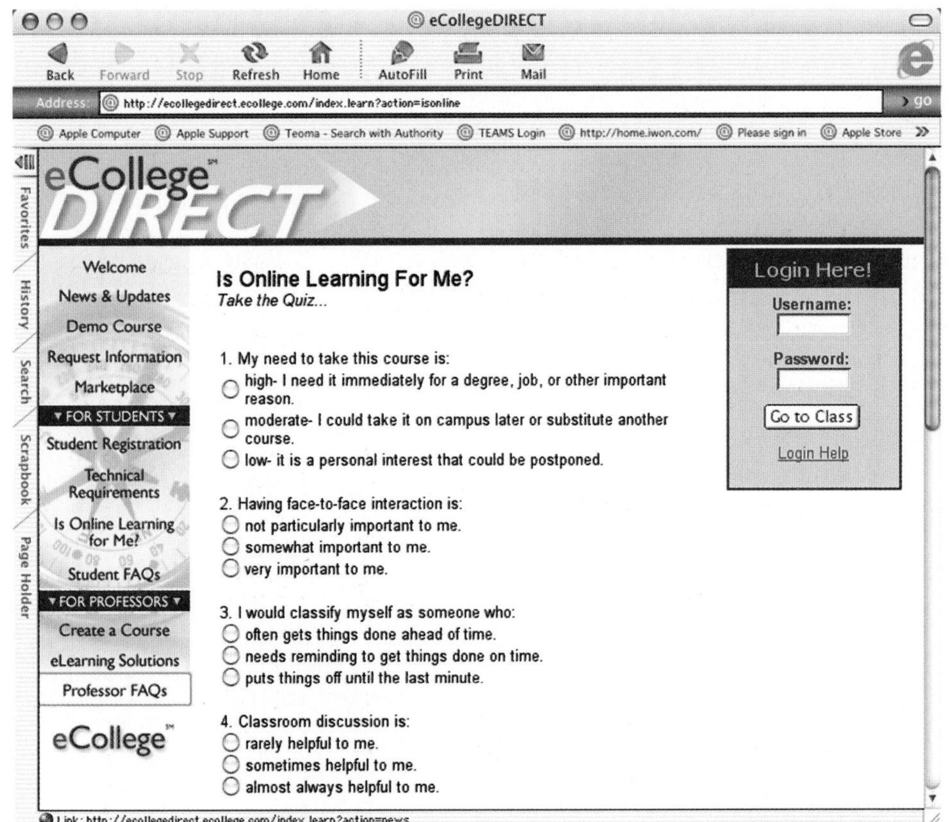

FIGURE 12.4

In an effort to ensure student readiness for distance education, many programs ask students to complete online self-assessments.

Planning Ahead for Murphy's Law

Murphy's Law says that anything that can go wrong will go wrong. Admittedly, Murphy's Law is an excessively pessimistic viewpoint. It does, nevertheless, offer those engaged in distance education an important warning. In traditional environments, the teacher is present to respond to any difficulties that arise. If you are planning to show a video and the DVD player does not work, you adjust your lesson to adapt to the circumstance with relatively little effort. But if you are teaching a distance education class to students located in neighboring schools and the communications equipment does not work, how can the lesson go on? What provision have you made for this eventuality?

Because distance delivery is heavily dependent on events and technologies outside of the teacher's immediate control, it is important to anticipate possible points of failure and to have a contingency plan. In the case of technology problems, having a redundant delivery technology available as a **backup system** can resolve crises caused by technology glitches. For example, scheduling a chat is a way to provide a backup communication system if the primary teleconferencing system fails. Planning potential solutions for possible technological problems and communicating such backup systems with students reduces the potential for interrupted instruction. Not all failures, however, are technological. Students might not get materials on time, or books might not be available. Such events as these and other nontechnical ones are unavoidable; yet you can still plan for how such possibilities will be handled. You might want to give a fellow teacher or the students a phone number they can call or an email address where they can send mail should such problems occur. How the event will be handled will be determined by the various circumstances of the school or distance education program. But anticipating that such events may happen and articulating appropriate responses are key responsibilities

Like teachers, students must be prepared to function in a distance learning environment.

TABLE 12.2 Contingency Planning for Distance Delivery

PROBLEM	SOLUTIONS
STUDENT SELECTION Is a distance education format right for the student?	Provide self-assessments of readiness for distance learning; offer online counseling and advising.
INTERACTIVITY Will interaction between student and teacher and among students be sufficient?	Establish technology and procedures for regularly scheduled electronic and/or telephone connections; train teachers to respond to students with alacrity, thoroughness, and compassion; schedule group interaction, such as group problem solving, study sessions, and online discussions; ensure that feedback is consistently and positively reinforced.
STUDENT SUPPORT AND SERVICES Will students have available the academic advising and mentoring, as well as the on-site technological assistance, that they need?	Tutors, academic advisers, and technology paraprofessionals must be provided to allow the student to focus on the product, not the process; support staff should be available to help both synchronously and asynchronously with advising and non-subject-area matters, such as stress, time management, and study skills.
ALIENATION AND ISOLATION Will social contact be sufficient?	Provide online discussions and chats, email, digitized photos, videoconferencing, and collaborative assignments to overcome isolation.
TECHNOLOGY SKILLS Will skills be sufficient to carry out the technological processes?	Prerequisite and in-progress technology training must be available; on-screen help, telephone access to technical experts, and hard-copy how-to manuals need to be easy to use.
DESIGN OF INSTRUCTIONAL MATERIALS Will the materials work at a distance?	Offer training sessions for teachers to help them modify materials to accommodate the delivery differences needed; include technology training and integration techniques as well as methods for interactively engaging students at a distance.

for the teacher planning for distance delivery. Table 12.2 lists some areas to consider in such planning.

Providing Feedback

One of the greatest challenges in teaching at a distance is how to provide **feedback** to your students. In the traditional classroom, you use body language and comments as well as written feedback to provide your students with an idea of how well they are mastering the content. In a distance environment, the technology you use often determines the types of feedback formats that are available to you. If you use a speakerphone in a classroom, you can ask questions and give voice feedback to individuals or groups. If you use the Internet, email feedback may be appropriate. Regardless of the feedback mechanism you use, it is critical to plan for adequate and frequent feedback within the instructional design itself. Just as with any instruction, students need confirmation that their understanding of concepts is correct. Continual feedback, in any form, is no less valuable in distance instruction. For those who teach in a distance environment, determining how and when to provide feedback can be a challenge met through creative teaching.

Evaluating Progress

Evaluation in distance learning can be achieved through alternative methods.

Evaluation of students in a distance education course is one of the key issues for distance educators. How can students be fairly and accurately evaluated if they are not in a traditional testing situation? The answer to these justifiable concerns involves a creative and flexible approach to assessment. One of the most common approaches is to provide performance assessment alternatives that can be used in addition to testing. Such alternatives may be group projects conducted in Internet chat rooms, individual research projects with PowerPoint presentations that can be shared via computer, or even oral reports given by telephone. Distance educators must carefully consider the intended objectives and then creatively develop assessment alternatives that take advantage of the technologies in place. Such assessments may challenge students to demonstrate competencies even more effectively than those commonly found in traditional classrooms.

Even so, traditional tests have a place in distance delivery. Proctored examinations remain appropriate and expected as a part of a class taught via distance education. How the proctoring takes place may vary, however. In classes that are set up with a single teacher, with facilitators at each receiving site, proctored testing is easily accomplished. The facilitators take responsibility for the testing environment, proctor the tests, and then collect and return them to the teacher for grading. Even at sites without facilitators, proctors can be arranged for and tests can be given in secure environments, such as media centers or administrative offices. The combination of performance assessment and testing can ultimately provide as valid an assessment of student progress in a distance instructional environment as is available in a traditional instructional environment.

PEARSON myeducationkit™

Go to the *Assignments and Activities* section of Chapter 12 in MyEducationKit and complete the video activity entitled *Collaborative Research via the Web.*

Support Technologies for Distance Teaching and Learning

Once the initial planning issues have been considered, just as in traditional instructional design, the next step is to examine the supporting technologies that are available or that need to be acquired to implement the instructional design. In distance education, such technologies fall into two broad categories, technologies that support synchronous distance education and those that support asynchronous distance education. **Synchronous** distance education is instruction that occurs at the same time, although typically not in the same place. In a web-based class, synchronous distance education might require that all students log onto a class chat room at the same time, although the locations from which they are working may vary. Synchronous technologies, then, are those that allow students to participate in the same time frame but in different locations. Table 12.3 lists synchronous and asynchronous technologies that can be used in distance education.

Synchronous instruction and learning occur at the same time.

In contrast, **asynchronous** distance education is time shifted; that is, teacher and students can participate at differing times from the same or different locations. An example of an asynchronous distance education class is one that is conducted via the Internet. In such a course, materials may be available on a web site, with students and teachers interacting by email or class conference. Students and teacher may be located at the same school, at different schools, or even at home, but they have the option of interacting at different times.

Asynchronous learning occurs at times when the instructor is not personally present.

The nature of the distance education program that a district or school chooses to implement will depend on whether the distance-delivery approach will be synchronous, asynchronous, or a combination of the two. Logic arguments for and against each approach can be made. Synchronous delivery most closely emulates traditional instruction and is the easiest for teachers and students to adjust to. However, synchronous approaches do not offer flexible time frames, a lack that can cause significant resource and scheduling problems. Asynchronous delivery is more flexible, making it easier to allocate and schedule resources while also making instruction more convenient and accessible for learners. Asynchronous instruction is more complex to plan for and requires new teaching and learning formats that may require some accommodation for both teacher and learners. Still, both formats have their place in distance- and alternative delivery programs. Which format is best can be answered only in response to the diverse needs of the learners, the district's needs, and the content to be delivered. Whichever approach is chosen, several specific technologies can be enlisted to support instruction.

TABLE 12.3 Delivery Technologies Summary

SYNCHRONOUS TECHNOLOGIES		ASYNCHRONOUS TECHNOLOGIES	
PHONE TECHNOLOGIES		VOICE MAIL/FAX	
BROADCAST VIDEO		CDS AND DVDS	
BROADCAST AUDIO	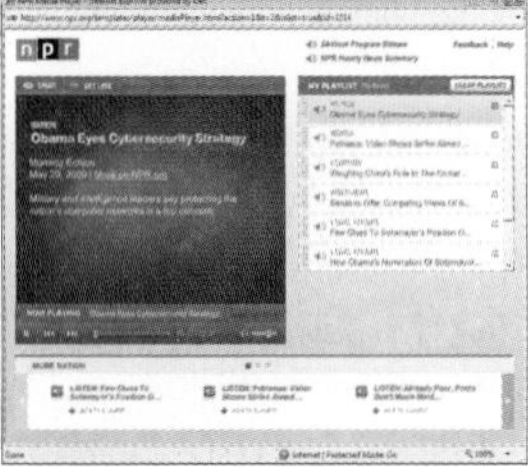		
INTERNET CHAT	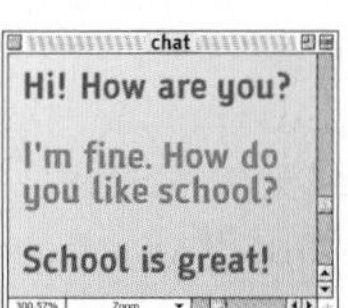	INTERNET CONFERENCING	
VIDEOCONFERENCING		EMAIL	
NET MEETING		PRINT MATERIALS	

Support Technologies for Synchronous Instruction

You are already familiar with a variety of technologies that can be used to support synchronous instruction. Some, like the telephone, are relatively low-tech, while others, such as Internet-based compressed videoconferencing, are emerging high-tech options. The variety of technologies that can be adapted by creative educators to assist in communicating synchronously cover the full range of technological options. The key to selecting technologies for this purpose is to look for those technologies that provide same-time communication formats and explore them for their adaptability to distance education.

Telephone Technologies

The **telephone,** whether local or Internet based, and telephone conferencing are among the staple technologies for synchronous delivery. Whether as a primary medium or a backup technology, the phone call offers an easy-to-use, inexpensive, and readily accessible method of communication. Like all synchronous technologies, phone calls require that all parties participate in the same time frame. Phone exchanges, whether direct instruction or questions and answers, can be one-to-one or, through conferencing, group communication.

The most basic type of conference system is the use of a **speakerphone** that allows participants to communicate using a single, specially equipped phone. Speakerphones offer a simple, though potentially unwieldy, conferencing system. Speakerphones are equipped with an omnidirectional microphone that is designed to pick up voices from anywhere in the room. They also have a speaker that is powerful enough to be heard across a room. Although this makes for a very easy-to-use and economical system, the microphones and speakers embedded in the phone might not accurately reflect voices on the other end of the line or in a larger room. Extended use of a speakerphone can be frustrating when critical content is being communicated. Furthermore, the phones pick up all sound, not just intended discussion, and extraneous room noise can be irritating.

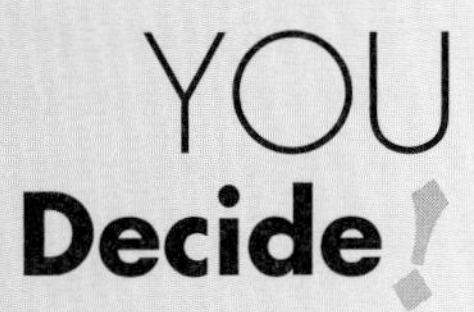

The value of distance education for college students is clear. Students often prefer or need the flexibility of classes offered any time and anywhere in order to fit their education into their busy lives. However, the use of this format in K–12 is more controversial given the nature of the less independent and self directed student found in public schools. Even so, K–12 distance programs offer students in small or rural high schools a chance to participate in classes they could not be offered any other way. And, for homebound students or those missing just one or two credits in order to graduate with their class, distance delivered programs answer a pressing need. Should every state make a distance education alternative available for public school students?

YES! Students and their families need flexibility and options. School choice should involve all options, including a distance education option. For students who need that last credit with no way to take a course in the time frame they have left, a distance education course can make the difference as to whether they graduate. And with new support technologies that make teacher and peer-to-peer interaction available, it is almost like being in a classroom. Good planning makes a distance delivered course just as effective as a face-to-face course. Why not offer this option?

NO! Students in K–12 are not capable enough learners to manage the type of independent experience upon which distance education is based. Especially in younger grades, distance education simply does not work. Students need the social learning experiences provided by interactions in the classroom. Students also need a teacher's direct supervision and guidance as they work through their learning activities. Distance education may be a convenience for college students but it has no place in public schools.

Which view do you agree with? YOU DECIDE!

A second audio option is the **conference call.** Conference calling via local or Internet-based phone service typically allows three to eight participants to connect together. This type of conferencing is excellent for small-group instruction or discussion. Because all participants are speaking into their own telephone handsets, the clarity of exchange is better than that with a speakerphone. Extraneous noise is also easily filtered out. Finally, because all participants use their own phones, unlike the use of a speakerphone, which must be located in a single central place, every member of the conference can conceivably be calling from a different location. This technology bridges the location gap for every participant. Diversity of location can, however, be a disadvantage. Gathering together for a speakerphone conference offers opportunities for social learning that conference calling does not.

A final and more sophisticated telephone-based method for synchronous interaction is the use of a **phone bridge.** This equipment, which is usually installed at the district level or subscribed to from phone service companies, provides the capabilities for large-group instruction via telephone. This technology allows from two to fifty callers to call a single central number and join in a conference call. The moderator or teacher has to establish ground rules so that two or more participants don't try to talk at the same time. Each speaker is also asked to identify himself or herself each time that person has something to say. The technology bridges all callers together and lets each caller join or leave the conference without affecting the conference itself. It is possible to arrange for a toll-free number as the bridge number, thus solving the problem of long-distance charges for participants.

Each of these phone-based technologies adapts a common medium to distance education. Although such solutions are clever, the real challenge in using such technologies is in the design of effective instruction that takes advantage of the technology's strengths and overcomes its weaknesses. Like all instruction, effective phone-based instruction is the result of innovative teachers being aware of this technology and able to adapt it to their purposes.

Videoconferencing

Videoconferencing over the Internet can make distance learning come alive.

You have already learned about the ability to communicate via computer using a compressed **videoconferencing** system. Compressed videoconferencing systems can be configured as individual systems on home or office PCs or as a classroom system. An individual system, as you will recall from previous chapters, uses the computer's speakers, a micro-

Videoconferencing systems help to create interactive classrooms across a school district or a state.

Syracuse Newspapers/Dick Blume/Image Works

phone, and a webcam for communication. Software enables the digital pictures and audio to be sent via modem to one or more similarly equipped machines on the Internet. Videoconferencing systems allow individual users to connect in a virtual meeting and exchange text, graphics, sound, and visual images. This combination of hardware and software is easily adapted for instruction at a distance. Teacher and learners connect to the Internet, create their virtual space using their meeting software, and communicate just as they would face-to-face.

This type of videoconferencing system offers individuals with the required hardware and software an excellent opportunity to participate fully in instruction. Students can be at diverse locations with the only parameter for participation being that they all go online at the same time. Students can interact in a virtual face-to-face instructional event with their teacher and/or with their peers. However, for students whose learning is augmented through social interaction, this technology might not offer sufficient social contact. Unless small groups meet informally—virtually or in person—outside of the instructional time, social interaction and the broadening of learning that often results may be lacking.

Another option for configuring compressed video for distance education is to connect compressed video classrooms across a district. In this application of compressed video, the personal equipment is scaled up to create an interactive classroom that can be connected by high-speed phone service to similarly equipped classrooms at other locations. Typically, such classrooms include one or more large monitors positioned so that all participants can see them; multiple microphones in strategic locations across the room to pick up individual and multiple voices; video cameras mounted on the monitors or in positions that allow for "eye-to-eye" contact when participants are looking at the monitors; supplementary video cameras for special shots; and the hardware and software to enable communication.

TECH TIPS for Teachers

Using videoconferencing to teach can be a rewarding and exciting experience. Like any instruction, it does take careful planning and some practice with the equipment, but as you and your students become used to the environment, the technology "disappears," and you become comfortable with your expanded classroom. When teaching or participating in a videoconference, it is important to become aware of how the equipment changes some aspects of the instructional environment. Some general guidelines include the following.

The Room
If you are teaching via video conferencing, be sure that you can see all seats in the room and that any permanent camera angle is focused, so that the students are at the center of the image.

Your Appearance
Be aware of the colors and patterns of the clothes you are wearing. Keep colors neutral or muted, and avoid checks, as they tend to "swim" on camera. Keep jewelry simple, and avoid anything that jingles, as the noise will be amplified by the microphones.

Visual Displays
A whiteboard can be difficult to see at remote sites. Shadows appear that blur the written content. Use PowerPoint or display prepared and previewed notes via a document camera. Black print on pastel paper displays best. When adding handwritten notes, be sure to use a thick pen, as regular ballpoint does not display well.

Audio
Instruct the students to use the mute button on microphones until they are ready to speak. The microphones are sensitive, and a tapping pencil or too much paper movement can be distracting. Pause frequently to avoid speaking over each other, as there is a few-second delay.

Other Movement
Movement can be exaggerated by the camera, so avoid nervous tics and keep body movements minimal. Rocking in a chair or tapping a foot can become a major distraction.

Adapted from Penn State's Etiquette and Tips for Successful Video Conferencing. Retrieved August 22, 2006, at **www.hbg.psu.edu/iit/mw2/etiquette.htm.**

The compressed video classroom most closely emulates the traditional classroom for both teachers and learners. Because students gather in each of the classrooms that are connected by compressed video, the potential for social learning is returned to the instructional environment in this configuration. Moreover, facilitators are often hired for the distant sites, so the teacher (located at the near site) has either team teachers or aides to help meet student needs. This allows for greater flexibility and more responsiveness at each far site. For most who have participated in this type of compressed video classroom, the technology quickly seems to disappear as participants become engaged in the instructional process. The fact that most participants are comfortable in the familiar surroundings of a classroom likely contributes to their ease in using this type of distance education technology.

Internet Chats

Using chats, students and the teacher can key messages to each other online in real time.

Another technology that is used for synchronous distance delivery is the **Internet chat.** Chat programs allow multiple Internet users to log on to and communicate within the same virtual space. This technology allows the teacher to conduct live interactive sessions or groups of students to communicate in real time with each other. Chats offer a way to hold an instructional session or a small-group discussion regardless of the participants' locations. Even though all must enter the chat room at the same time, distance barriers become irrelevant. For a large, physically spread-out school district or for a school that hires a distant expert teacher, this delivery technology provides a very effective solution to the need for interaction.

Chats can offer some marked advantages. Many who use chats for instructional interaction find that the quality of the exchange is quite high. Perhaps because participants have more time to consider and respond to questions or comments, the interaction is often more thoughtful than in the classroom. Also, unlike a classroom in which shy students may never raise their hands and contribute, chats allow the teacher to call on every student; in this way, everyone interacts. In addition, seeing that chat technology typically allows participants time to key in, reread, and correct their responses before sharing them, the delay gives reticent students a greater comfort level when participating. Figure 12.5 presents a segment of a class chat.

Internet Classroom Sites

A final communication technology that can be used to create a virtual classroom is Internet-based meeting space. Whether in the form of software created primarily for business use (for example, Microsoft NetMeeting) or an educational site (such as Blackboard), this technology offers a variety of tools for both synchronous and asynchronous exchange (Figure 12.6). Teachers can conduct a class via the Internet in which they can engage in a group discussion in real time, show a PowerPoint presentation, or share an electronic work

FIGURE 12.5

Class Discussion via an Online Chat

Online instructional chats offer students and teacher exchanges similar to those that would occur in a traditional classroom.

CHATROOM MSB01	
MSB:>	Ok, class, let's see who can answer the next question. What were some of the social conditions that changed after the Civil War? *Becky, can you think of one?-o-*
BSMITH:>	Slavery was stopped.-o-
MSB:>	*Good, Becky. That is correct. Did that change the way former slaves lived? Alan, can you answer that one?-o-*
ACHAMPS:>	I'm not sure, but I don't think it made a whole lotta difference since people who were slaves didn't have anything and being free didn't give them anything but freedom. Heck, they didn't know how to not be slaves!-o-
MSB:>	*Right, Alan. It was hard for the former slaves to adjust to their new status since they had no opportunity to learn the skills they needed to function as full citizens. And, of course, the situation in the South was desperate for everyone from former plantation owners to city dwellers to former slaves. It was a very difficult time. Does anyone know what a "carpetbagger" was and what these folks did in the South after the war? Gina, do you want to take a stab at this one?-o-*
GVERRICIO:>	Sorry, Ms. B. you got me. I know they were from the North, but I don't know what they did.-o-
MSB:>	*Well, that was a good start, Gina, they were indeed from the North. Tom, can you share any type of activity a carpetbagger might have been engaged in?-o-*

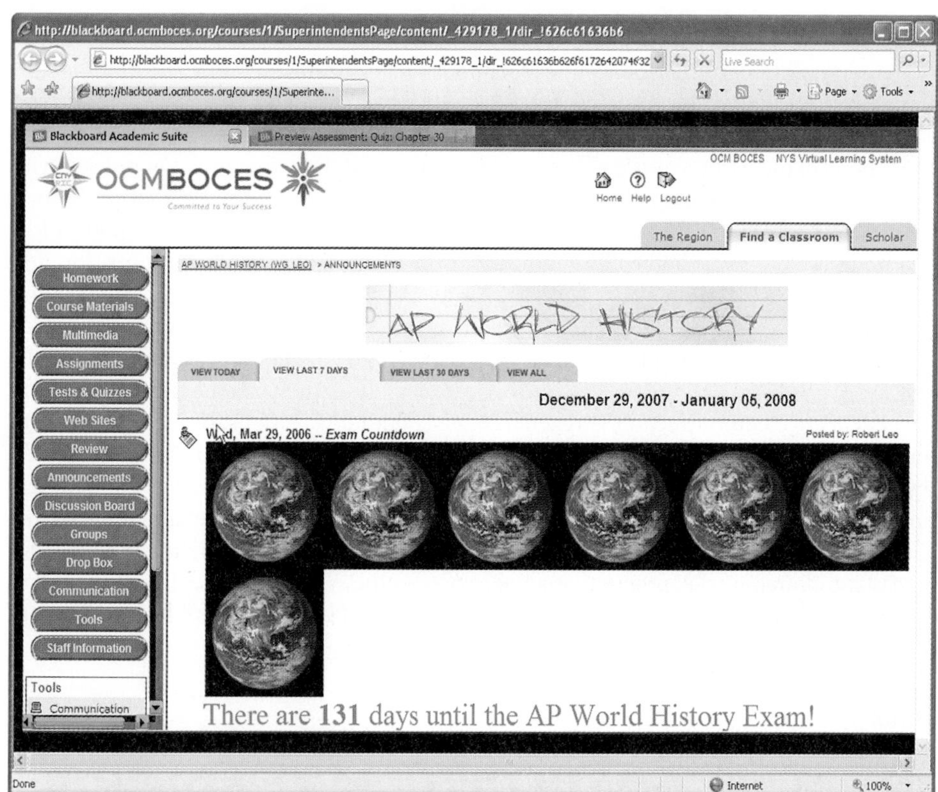

FIGURE 12.6

Students and teachers can participate in virtual classrooms with software such as Blackboard.

Allyn & Bacon, Inc. A Division of Pearson Education.

space. Together, these technologies, in the hands of a creative teacher, can offer a very solid learning environment.

Many sites offer authoring tools with which teachers can create and present site-based lessons. Such tools range from fill-in-the-blank virtual classroom authoring to test generators to syllabus makers. Different sites and meeting programs offer different capabilities. Some charge a school system a per-student fee to host a virtual classroom; others give the school system the software to run on its own network servers. In either case, preparing a distance education class using any of these resources requires a substantial up-front investment in a teacher's time and creativity. To be sure the investment is well spent, it is important to try and to compare these sites or programs and their tools before committing to using them.

Support Technologies for Asynchronous Instruction

Asynchronous (time-shifted) instruction is also supported by a wide variety of analog and digital technologies. Because the term *asynchronous* suggests that teacher and students need not be connected at the same time, even the most basic classroom technologies can be considered a part of this category. Printed materials, televised broadcasts on educational channels, DVD-based instruction, CDs, and podcasts are all potentially asynchronous delivery technologies. Teacher and students do not need to be in contact at the same time or in the same place for instruction to occur. However, in using these types of technologies, interaction is typically one-way. The teacher delivers instructional content with these technologies, but there is little or no opportunity for teacher-to-student or peer-to-peer interaction. In view of the fact that most teachers build interactive experiences into their instruction, it is important for distance educators to identify and repurpose available technologies to support asynchronous interaction as well as delivery.

Phone Technologies

Voice mail can transform a telephone into an asynchronous instructional tool.

The phone is ordinarily a synchronous technology, but when you add voice mail service, you also add asynchronous capability. Because these technologies allow teachers and students to leave each other **voice mail** messages, voice communication becomes possible even when none of the participants communicates via phone at the same time. For districts with more sophisticated voice mail systems, it is possible to create a virtual verbal space for a class. A voice mailbox can be created in which a teacher can request oral responses to a question. Students can then call in to the mailbox and leave their verbal answers for their teacher to listen to later. Oral responses are crucial for a foreign language class, for example, and voice mail technology can make it possible to give them asynchronously.

Another common telephone technology that can be adapted for asynchronous delivery is the **fax.** For instantaneous delivery of text or graphics, the fax machine provides simple yet effective communication. Teachers can fax questions, visuals, or replies to student inquiries directly to the students. Students can fax back responses, assignments, or questions. This common technology offers an instant and reasonably inexpensive communication tool yet does not require that sender and receiver be working in the same time frame. Even if you do not have a dedicated fax machine, most computer operating systems offer at least a rudimentary fax program as an accessory to the system. Thus, whoever has a PC and a modem available typically also has fax capability. This simple tool has great potential for communication in the hands of a creative teacher.

Email

Email messages are a private and thoughtful form of communication.

The most significant digital asynchronous technology to support distance delivery is **email.** Just as email has changed the nature of the way many individuals, businesses, and organizations communicate, so too has it revolutionized asynchronous instructional communication. This commonplace yet powerful tool makes possible easy yet thoughtful communications between teacher and student and among students. Unlike a voice mail message, email messages can include attachments. These attachments can include animated graphics, audio, and compressed video clips. Messages can be very brief or long, formal or informal. Because the sender has time to carefully compose a message and proofread it before sending, email messages tend to be a more thoughtful form of communication than speech. Finally, email messages can be composed, sent, and read whenever it is most convenient for the individuals involved. Email's attributes, harnessed together in support of the distance teaching and learning process, create a powerful and elegant tool for interactivity.

Email can be used to communicate one-to-one or one-to-many. A distance education teacher can communicate privately with each student or can choose to send a group email message to all, via a group mailing option or a formal mailing list. Students can respond to progress inquiries or content questions, or they can ask further questions. Additionally, because teachers can establish email processes and procedures, email interaction can be offered in private (email) or public (mailing list) formats. When private email is available to students, many feel more comfortable asking questions or requesting clarification without fear of their concerns and questions being seen as "dumb." Mailing lists, on the other hand, offer an email format in which questions and concerns can be automatically sent to all participants. Both public and private email offer channels that support the diversity of communication that might be found in a traditional classroom.

In an email-supported discussion, student participation tends to be greater than in the traditional classroom setting.

But email also offers an advantage over the typical interaction in a traditional classroom. The teacher's ability to address every student individually via email tends to increase participation. In an email-supported discussion on a topic of concern, a teacher can require that all students participate and respond via email. In this scenario, unlike the classroom, shy and thoughtful students are not overwhelmed by the enthusiastic responses of their more outgoing peers. There is also time for everyone to respond. The pressure to be the first student who has a hand up disappears. Students have enough time to respond within the framework of their own learning characteristics. Email can, in these ways, provide equity of response opportunities for all students and can fully engage everyone in an academic discussion.

Electronic Discussions

Electronic discussions, or electronic forums, offer a platform for one-to-many communications. These virtual bulletin boards let individuals post messages for all participants to read. Others can then post responses, resulting in a threaded discussion. For distance education, a class electronic discussion is usually moderated by the teacher, with all students participating at a convenient time and from any location that offers access to the local network or the Internet. The teacher might post a question or an announcement and ask all students to respond. Students then post their responses or ask additional questions. All students can read all responses and can even save them or print them out. This formalized electronic discussion provides an opportunity for thoughtful interaction and the potential for complete note taking because all discussion can be captured and reviewed.

Students can also use electronic discussions to support distance cooperative learning groups and study groups. With one student acting as moderator, a small group of students can meet asynchronously in an electronic discussion to work on a task or share content. Students can thus assemble at a time that is convenient to each of them and from any location and still participate in class activities. Electronic discussions make it possible for students to interact on group projects even if they are located in different schools across a district or are homebound. This tool makes it possible for the distance teacher to engage students in social learning as well as with the content.

Online Classroom

Many asynchronous technologies and even some synchronous technologies can be combined together in a class **web site** hosted on a school or district network or an Internet hosting service. The class web site can offer a distance student a single virtual place to go, at any time and from any place, to find all of the resources and tools needed to participate in a class. For district distance education classes, the class web site can offer an easy-to-access repository of all materials, a place where all students from any location can interact, and an efficacious communication tool for the teacher. Even if students meet synchronously via compressed video, a supporting class web site can become an important resource that will help to meet both anticipated and unanticipated needs.

In an electronic conference, questions, answers, and announcements can be posted for all to read.

An alternative to traditional class web sites is the use of a learning management system (LMS). An LMS is a bundled resource tool that schools purchase and use to create fully integrated online classrooms. A typical LMS offers a way to present and organize subject or course materials, testing capabilities, gradebooks, and a series of communications resources, including chats, discussions, and a closed email system. Schools license the LMS, and creative teachers use it to put some or all of their instruction online.

There are a number of advantages to using an LMS instead of a series of classroom web sites. One advantage is that all courses created to work through the LMS are similar in look and feel. Once students learn the system for one subject area, they can easily use the system for any other subject that uses the system. Furthermore, the LMS offer teachers many tools for assessment and grading that a typical classroom web site would not. Finally, the closed communications system offers greater privacy and a reduction in extraneous comments, since only the students who are enrolled in the course can access it.

Both an online classroom web site and a full-featured LMS system offer students an opportunity to access instruction any time and any place. They also offer teachers an opportunity to create innovative Internet-based lessons for students whether in their classrooms or at a distance.

Providing Interactivity via Distance Support Technologies

Both synchronous and asynchronous technologies support distance delivery not only by providing a channel for transmission of content, but also by providing a platform for interactivity. Unlike early distance education programs, in which instruction emanated from the teacher and learners remained essentially passive, today's technology-enhanced distance programs provide many opportunities for student-to-teacher and peer-to-peer interaction. Just as in the traditional classroom, the distance virtual learning environment can offer a variety of communication methods to meet learners' needs and preferences. A master teacher in a school district can present content to students across multiple schools or to those who are homebound by video, voice, or data. Then that same distance educator can have students engage in group activities that are not restricted by their particular location. Last, because school schedules may differ across a district, asynchronous technologies can offer a solution to scheduling problems. With these new tools at a teacher's disposal, it is no wonder that distance education programs are expanding at an amazing rate. Given its potential to emulate classroom experiences fairly accurately, distance education's early promises may soon be realized.

ISTE Standard

Learning about distance and alternative delivery systems will help you address

NETS•T STANDARD 5:

ENGAGE IN PROFESSIONAL GROWTH AND LEADERSHIP
Teachers continuously improve their professional practice, model lifelong learning, and exhibit leadership in their school and professional community by promoting and demonstrating the effective use of digital tools and resources.

Issues in Implementing Distance and Alternative Delivery Systems

Teacher and Student Readiness

Distance learning systems require that teachers and students be ready to work within a new environment. There are two key aspects to their necessary **readiness:** readiness to accept new roles and readiness to work with new technologies. First, teachers and students must be prepared for new roles. In distance learning, teachers become guides and architects of complex learning environments. Less time is spent in direct instruction, and more time is spent in creating a rich instructional environment and then guiding students through it. Students become less passive and more responsible learners. They must be ready to think through options rather than passively follow instructions. They must take more responsibility for their learning. These new roles may require some very specific orientation and training for both teacher and students for them to be ready to work in the new environments of these delivery systems.

A second type of readiness relates to being prepared to use the technologies selected to support these new environments. Both teachers and students may be expected to frequently use technologies they do not know or have not yet become comfortable with. When learners are expected to take more responsibility in these delivery formats, it can be frustrating if the technologies they need to use turn out to be a barrier to their tasks. When a teacher creates instruction to be delivered by a particular technology, it is essential for that teacher to fully understand the technology's capabilities and limitations. Teachers and students may need to participate in very specific training sessions before being able to fully use a distance or alternative learning environment.

Distance education participants may need additional training.

Preparation and Classroom Management Time

Teachers who use distance and alternative learning techniques might find themselves surprised by an increase in the demands on their time. Distance learning and alternative learning often require a greater allocation of available planning time because the learning environment must be carefully mapped out in advance of its implementation. Further-

PEARSON myeducationkit

Go to the *Assignments and Activities* section of Chapter 12 in MyEducationKit and complete the video activity entitled *Approaches to Online Learning.*

more, because distance education methods can sharply increase interactivity and because every student may now respond, teachers might find the number of responses overwhelming. Planning for instruction and responding to students will require that you carefully think through your time management strategies. Few would disagree that comprehensive planning and full interaction are both highly desirable, but for many teachers, finding adequate time to do both may be a problem. Districts that are interested in supporting distance and alternative instruction need to consider the requirements inherent in these alternative instructional systems and make adequate arrangements to meet them.

Technical Support

In implementing distance and alternative delivery systems that are supported by technology, it is critical to be sure that adequate **technical support** is in place. If instruction is dependent on a class web site and the district web server hosting that site goes down, how will instruction continue? If a class interacts by compressed video, what happens if one of the components does not function? Although technical problems are often unavoidable, adequate and readily available technicians, backup systems, and clear direction as to how to proceed if systems fail are critical for success. Too often, support personnel and related support costs are not fully considered in determining whether or not to engage in distance- or alternative delivery systems. Even if technical support is not the central consideration, nevertheless it is one of the critical components for successful implementation.

Sufficient technical support is necessary for distance education to operate smoothly.

Instructional Support

Learners in traditional classrooms have a variety of **instructional supports** readily available. In addition to the teacher being present for clarification and questions, a media center offering a wide variety of resources is also typically present. Some schools may also provide tutoring programs for students who need additional help. Together, these resources provide a comprehensive instructional support system for students. However, in a distance environment, some of these supports may be missing. In a cross-district distance course, the local media centers might not have the resources available to supplement and support the instruction. It may also be too costly to replicate resources at all participating schools. How, then, can distance learning students access the resources they need? If the students need extra help, where can they find the tutoring support they need? These questions must be addressed in determining how distance education systems will be implemented. Solutions may be as new and divergent as the programs they support. Such solutions may include providing tutor telephone hotlines and homework help chat rooms. Whatever the solutions that are finally chosen, it is important to address the issue of academic support as a critical component of a distance education program before that program is implemented.

Copyright

As you have learned, respecting copyright is a critical issue for teachers. The use of copyrighted materials in distance learning and on the Internet brought concerns over fair use in the digital age to the forefront. In 1998, Congress asked the U.S. Copyright Office to address the issue. The Technology Education and Copyright Harmonization (TEACH) Act was introduced in the legislature in 2001 as a result of the report produced by the Copyright Office. With the passage of the TEACH Act in 2002, many guidelines related to fair use for distance education were clarified, yet many issues still remain. For example, the TEACH Act conditions for the use of copyrighted materials are somewhat complex and often more restrictive than the fair use guidelines operating in traditional face-to-face classrooms. Further, restrictions under the TEACH Act limit the circumstances for use, which may in turn have an impact on the broader copyright policies adopted by the institution offering the distance education program.

Clearly, copyright will remain an issue for all teachers but particularly those teaching in a distance environment. However, as distance education becomes even more commonplace and instructional needs become more evident, policy decisions and law will no doubt evolve to better address these concerns. Indeed, the TEACH Act is likely to be just the first step in the resolution of copyright issues in distance education.

Reinventing the Classroom: The Future of Distance and Alternative Delivery

Technology is changing our society, and that changing society is putting new demands upon our schools. In response, our schools are changing. One aspect of the change is our perception of a classroom. Must the teaching and learning environment be a physical space? Can we offer effective instruction and help our students engage in meaningful learning without time and location constraints?

Whatever your views and experiences at this point, it is clear that many schools are currently attempting to create and implement high-quality distance programs. The number of schools, organizations, and even businesses that offer instruction at a distance increases each year. You may be asked to participate in such programs during your professional career. To adequately address such a possibility, your awareness of the methods and technologies that are currently being used and that may be used in the future to reinvent classrooms is a good start (Figure 12.7). How will classrooms evolve as the Information Age unfolds? That is difficult to predict with any precision. What is clear is that both traditional and nontraditional classrooms will evolve and may be completely reinvented to better address our changing world. Eventually, perhaps, there will be no distinctions among traditional education, alternative education, and distance education. Perhaps, instead, they will all be facets of the same complex and diverse educational system, offering options to meet every learner's unique situation and needs. As the future of instructional delivery unfolds, you can be sure that your classroom will be affected. Learning about and preparing for such potential change may be your best strategy for successfully changing with it.

PEARSON myeducationkit™

To check your comprehension of the content covered in this chapter, go to the MyEducationKit for your book and complete the *Study Plan* for Chapter 12.

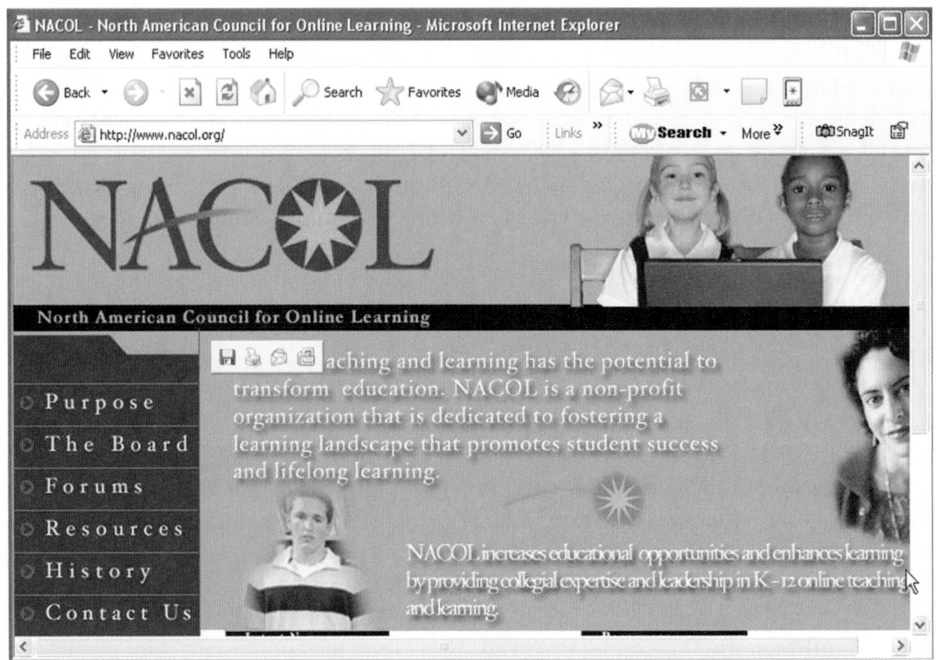

FIGURE 12.7

Distance learning organizations are helping to define standards, promote quality, and support dialog among distance educators.

North American Council for Online Learning.

Key Terms

asynchronous, 329
backup system, 327
conference call, 331
correspondence courses, 322
distance education, 320
electronic discussion, 337
email, 336
evaluation, 328
fax, 336
feedback, 328
instructional supports, 339
Internet chat, 334
phone bridge, 332
readiness, 338
speakerphone, 331
synchronous, 329
technical support, 339
telephone, 331
videoconferencing, 332
voice mail, 336
web site, 337

Activities

Student

CHAPTER REVIEW

1. What is distance education? How does it overcome temporal and spatial barriers?
2. Describe the two major impacts of distance education on K—12 teachers.
3. What early technologies enhanced distance education via correspondence? What impact did these have on student isolation?
4. What are alternative learning systems? How might they enhance traditional education?
5. Why is planning even more critical for distance delivery than for traditional instruction? How does planning differ between traditional and distance delivery?
6. Why is giving feedback a challenge in distance environments? How can this challenge be met?
7. What issues surround student evaluation in a distance environment? How might they be resolved?
8. What is the difference between synchronous and asynchronous delivery? What technologies support synchronous delivery? What technologies support asynchronous delivery?
9. How do synchronous and asynchronous technologies support interaction?
10. What types of support are critical to the success of distance education? Why?

WHAT DO YOU THINK?

1. There has been much discussion about whether distance education can provide students with instruction that is equal in quality to what they have received from traditional education. Do you think an equivalent experience is possible via distance delivery? Why or why not?
2. Distance learning and alternative learning require a significant use of technology to support instructional delivery. How does the inclusion of the technology affect the instructional experience for better and for worse?
3. One of the primary issues associated with implementation of distance education revolves around the teacher's ability to adequately and appropriately evaluate student progress and competencies. Do you believe that this is an issue? Why or why not?
4. Synchronous and asynchronous delivery both enhance and potentially impede instruction in different ways. What are your key issues and concerns related to each of these systems?
5. What role do you think distance education will play in education as the Information Age unfolds and technologies improve? What advantages and disadvantages for teachers and students do you foresee?

LEARNING TOGETHER!

These activities are best done in groups of three to five.

1. Research and examine your state's initiatives in distance education at the K–12 and postsecondary levels. On the basis of your research, prepare a summary of the programs that are available or under way and the pros and cons of each.
2. Each group member should locate and create an annotated list of three web sites offering access to technologies appropriate for distance or alternative delivery. Compare your finds and select your top five sites. Summarize these to share with your class.
3. Imagine that your group has been asked to develop a districtwide unit about your local ecology. You have decided to teach it by using distance delivery. Describe how you will deliver your unit across your district via synchronous and asynchronous systems.

TEACHING WITH TECHNOLOGY: INTEGRATION IDEAS WEB QUEST

Distance education and web-based alternative delivery of instruction have changed the nature of the classroom. Using these powerful tools, teachers can design instruction to enhance their traditional classroom or to create virtual classrooms that can reach students any time and any place. The impact of distance delivery has just begun to make itself felt.

ACTIVITY: Explore the links below to discover how teachers are using distance delivery and its tools to teach their content. Select the content area of most interest to you, and then search the Net for additional examples of innovative distance delivery. Find three examples, and prepare a web quest summary that includes (1) the content area being taught through distance delivery and the associated URL, (2) a summary of the distance delivery methods being used, and (3) a critique of the methods when compared to the options presented in this chapter.

Integrating Distance Education into Social Studies

Angie's Electronic Classroom is the creation of Angie Simms, the history/social science studio teacher for TEAMS Distance Learning of the Los Angeles County Office of Education's Center for Distance and Online Learning. The social science module is designed for grades 4–7 and includes these programs: Natural Events: Then and Now, Student as Historian, Student as Media Evaluator, California, Here I Come!, and Angie's TV Programs. Within each category, web pages of guided activities are available for the students. When the distance learner clicks on the Natural Events page, an entertaining page engages the learner. The "Powerful Natural Forces" page is decorated with the cartoon-like images of Jake the Quake, Jud the Flood, Myer the Fire, and Lind the Wind. The task is for the students to select one of the events that they believe has characteristics similar to their own personalities. A "Parents" page is provided with helpful links for parents to access to aid their children as they work on the guided activities. The visually attention-getting format of the electronic classroom and its interactivity is personalized to the student through individual responses and opportunities for reflection. The TEAMS online lesson design is a convincing example of how an online classroom can be presented in a student-friendly configuration that can hold its own with face-to-face instruction. To see what good design can do to make distance learning pedagogically sound, go to *Angie's Electronic Classroom* at **http://teams.lacoe.edu/documentation/classrooms/angie/angie.html.**

Integrating Distance Education into Math

Pat Laster teaches math at Arkansas Virtual High School (AVHS). She has integrated distance learning into the curriculum by following the Arkansas Frameworks. The framework is derived from the mission that AVHS sees as a means to reach students "who need assistance in completing coursework that is difficult to receive due to factors such as schedule conflicts, homebound due to extenuating circumstances, and other factors that might impede a student's progress through grades 9–12." "Weekly Routine" pages clearly direct the students about how the class will be taught online. Suggestions for being organized, as they undertake distance learning activities, are also provided. Each day's routine is described in detail, with information on when and how each activity is to be done. There follows step-by-step directions for "Accessing Lesson Plans/Handouts/Worksheets for the Following Week," are offered. Ms. Laster's lesson plans are available on a weekly schedule with daily entries and are presented in the AVHS tabular form of Date, Facilitators, Handouts, Class Activities, and Practice & Application. To view the way in which math classes are integrated into a distance learning format, go to **http://arkansashigh.k12.ar.us.**

interchapter 12

Alternative Delivery Systems

You have already learned how distance education was originally developed to deliver instruction across distances. But what if the same instructional designs, pedagogical methods, and technologies that make it possible to deliver across distance were adapted for the traditional classroom? How might these adaptations evolve into innovative classroom methodologies and alternatives? How might they affect instruction inside and outside of the classroom? How would they alter the traditional instructional delivery that is found in most classrooms? The answers to these questions are beginning to emerge as the influence of distance education techniques and technology expands.

Many educators who have taken or taught a course via distance education have found that they could adapt the innovative methods used for distance education to enrich and enhance their traditional teaching. Hybrid instructional delivery systems that use the best of both traditional and distance instruction are being adapted for and implemented in both types of programs. These alternative delivery systems, offered on a college campus, at a school, or across a district, may offer the first glimpse of how teaching and learning will ultimately change under the pressures of our current technological social evolution.

Using Distance Education Methods to Enhance Traditional Classrooms

Bob Daemmrich/PhotoEdit

Many of the techniques and support technologies that were originally introduced for distance education have proved to be useful in traditional classrooms. These alternative learning delivery options, when added to traditional delivery, offer more dynamic and diverse teaching and learning opportunities. Synchronous and asynchronous technologies and methods can add a new and distinctive teaching and learning dimension to classroom instruction when implemented by creative teachers. Adapting distance education lessons to the traditional classroom creates an alternative learning format that offers teachers and learners interesting and productive new tools. These can make instruction more engaging and can better meet learners' individual needs.

Using Distance Education Tools for Alternative Learning

Although the typical use of textbooks for independent reading assignments is asynchronous, most classrooms are by definition synchronous. Most synchronous technologies and methods that are used in a distance education classroom would therefore be redundant in the traditional classroom. But when you begin to use asynchronous techniques from distance education in your classroom, you may find surprising results. The table lists alternative learning strategies that can be used in traditional classrooms. These techniques are discussed in the following sections in the context of how they might enhance different aspects of the teaching and learning process.

Individualizing Instruction

The first application of asynchronous tools is in the area of individualized instruction. Traditional classrooms are designed to provide group instruction and to supplement that instruction with individual activities. Because children do not all learn in the same way or at the same pace, group instruction might not be as effective as intended. Distance education programs require an individualized approach because groups might or might not actually meet. Some of the techniques that are used for individualizing distance education can become important tools for traditional teachers who are seeking a supplement to group instruction. Posting classroom announcements and reminders on an electronic conference can provide students with an additional resource to refer to when questions arise. Emailing class assignment calendars to parents can open lines of communication. Creating a class web site that houses content, activities, and review exercises can offer students an opportunity to revisit classroom instruction at the time and pace that works best for them. These methods and support technologies can supplement classroom group instruction and further individualize it to better meet student needs.

Promoting Interaction

The traditional classroom's large-group format might not be conducive to providing equal opportunity for interaction. In our often overcrowded classrooms and for students who are naturally reserved, this format is not optimal. The same distance education strategies that make it possible for all students to interact in the virtual classroom can also provide the opportunity for all students to interact in a traditional classroom. An electronic conference on an important aspect of content can offer an opportunity for every student to express a view, or it can provide a place for a group's consensus opinion to be posted. Email can provide a way for students to ask private questions of their teacher or to submit homework even when they are absent. Voice mail can give parents a way to communicate with their child's teacher without having to play telephone tag. All of these communication technologies, when implemented by creative teachers, provide new avenues for interactivity between and among the teacher, students, and their parents.

Enhancing Independent Learning

The final area in which distance methodologies and tools can enhance and provide alternatives for traditional classrooms is in their emphasis on independent learning. In traditional classroom processes, students are often expected to rigorously follow specific instructions. This approach facilitates the smooth functioning of a large group, but it tends to make individuals dependent. The obvious message of this type of instruction is to act only in accordance with specific instructions. The implicit message may be to not act if instructions are not specifically given—that is, to be passive in a new situation. This promotes dependency when, in fact, we actually want our learners to be self-initiating and responsible for their own learning. Because the distance environment cannot, by its very nature, provide continual instruction and redirection, its strategies must rely on a more independent and responsible approach to learning. The parameters of the virtual instructional environment thus foster independence. Using some distance education techniques as a supplement to traditional delivery can have the same effect. Placing student activities on a web page rather than handing out copies in class requires students to seek out the work they need. Emailing a class calendar of due dates or adding it to your web site helps students take responsibility for paying attention to the posted due dates. Making copies of your PowerPoint lecture available electronically offers students the chance to be responsible for content missed due to absence. These strategies, while integral to a distance education class, can become powerful tools in helping students gain independence in traditional classes as well.

Distance Education Tools for Alternative Learning in Traditional Classes

ALTERNATIVE LEARNING STRATEGY	APPLICATION IN THE TRADITIONAL SETTING
ONLINE LECTURES Make PowerPoint lecture or lecture notes available on network or web site.	• Provides opportunities for self-paced review of class lectures • Provides access to missed lectures for absent students • Offers review opportunities before exams
COURSE CALENDARS Post announcements and calendar on class web site or school network.	• Makes due dates available outside of class • Provides access to announcements and dates for parents • Allows for easy updating over weekends and vacations
ONLINE ACTIVITIES Post activities on class web site or school network.	• Makes activities accessible outside of class • Allows for making corrections or adjustments to activities • Provides students an opportunity to explore coming activities to better budget time

ONLINE INTERACTIVITY
Conduct online conferences and chats; offer one-to-one interaction via email.
	• Conferences and chats provide opportunities outside of class to
	  • share concerns and exchange ideas
	  • work on group activities
	  • form study groups
	  • review materials prior to tests
	• Email provides for
	  • private teacher-to-student interaction after class hours
	  • student-to-student exchange of ideas
	  • clarification of content or procedures after class hours

WEB-BASED ASSESSMENTS Offer online practice tests.	• Provides opportunities to practice content outside of class hours • Provides readiness feedback before exams

CHAPTER 13

Issues in Implementing Technology in Schools

Tim Shaffer/Microsoft/AP Images

CHAPTER OVERVIEW

This chapter addresses these ISTE National Educational Technology Standards:
- •NETS•T Standard 4
- •NETS•S Standard 5

You have learned much about the many types of technologies that are available for teachers and their students. You have also learned about the theories related to teaching and learning and the process of designing effective instruction. As a result of the competencies you have gained so far in this course, you have already taken the first significant steps in using educational technology effectively in your classroom. But understanding the broader process inherent in implementing technology in schools and in districts requires that you expand your technological perspective even further. Indeed, the process of acquiring and implementing educational technologies in a school has its own set of challenges, both academic and administrative, of which you must become aware. Once a teacher has decided which technologies would be best for use in the classroom, these greater implementation issues can directly affect those initial decisions. Implementation issues, the concerns that arise in working through the details of acquiring and setting up a school's technology, may even alter the choices that have already been made. The implementation concerns that arise can be so significant that they can even change the direction and nature of a school's technology initiative. Will the preferred technology work with other types of technologies already in place? Must a school or district ensure that the technology decision making be strategic, that is, made within a larger school planning framework? Are there any legal, social, or ethical issues to attend to in implementing a technology initiative? Questions like these must be answered to ensure a successful technology initiative and implementation. These broad implementation issues and concerns are the focus of this chapter.

As a teacher, you might think that such concerns have little to do with you. That is not the case. You will find that teachers have a unique and significant role in addressing many of the issues associated with implementing technology in schools. You might be asked to serve on the technology strategic planning team, you might serve as the chair of your grade-level technology committee, or you might want to become your school's technology coordinator. Regardless of the role you choose, you will find that you will be more prepared to understand and successfully address technology implementation issues after you have fully examined them.

In Chapter 13, you will:

- Examine legal, ethical, and social issues that arise when a school implements technology
- Examine the ways in which these issues are likely to affect teachers and their students

Planning for and Implementing Technology

Because of the cost and complexity of acquiring and implementing the many educational technologies you have explored in this text, districts and schools typically begin the process with the creation of a formal technology plan. The technology plan is strategic in nature. This means that before any technology decisions are made, "big picture" planning occurs. Such planning is called **strategic planning** because it takes into account long-range goals as well as short-term objectives. Because a strategic plan will ultimately affect those inside an organization and those interacting with the organization, planning facilitators often create a plan through a formal group process that includes representatives of all concerned parties. Representatives from all groups that will be affected by the plan are selected and actively participate together in the strategic planning process. These individuals, called stakeholders, bring to the table their distinct sets of interests and perspectives. By including all stakeholders, the final strategic plan is more likely to fully address everyone's needs and is more likely to be accepted because everyone has equal ownership of the development process. The strategic planning process typically has several distinct steps, each of which contributes toward focusing the stakeholders and the district or school they represent in a single, clearly articulated direction.

Once technology is planned for and implementation has begun, many issues and concerns beyond those that are technical arise. A variety of legal, social, and ethical issues

Go to the *Assignments and Activities* section of Chapter 13 in MyEducationKit and complete the web activity entitled *Academic Tools Online.*

result from the use of technologies in schools. Teachers must be aware of these issues to ensure that they create a climate in their classroom that fosters respect for ethics, fairness, and the law as they relate to the implementation of technology. These issues are the subjects of the next section of this chapter.

Legal Issues in the Digital Age

Implementation of technology, whether in the classroom, school, or district, involves a number of legal issues (see Figure 13.1). Some of these issues, such as copyright violations, were of concern in education before the advent of technology. Technology implementation and the ease of accessing and incorporating digital data, including copyrighted text, graphics, video, and audio, exacerbated the problem. Other issues, such as the inequity of access to technology, sometimes called the **digital divide,** have arisen as a result of technology. Another set of issues involves ethical questions. Each of these issues affects how technology is ultimately implemented at all levels of an educational institution, from the classroom to the entire district. As a professional, you are responsible for becoming aware of these implementation issues and acting in accordance with professional ethics.

Copyright and Fair Use

Copyright protects the rights of the owner of intellectual property.

You have already been introduced to many of the issues related to **copyright.** In the Interchapter following this chapter, you will discover that although materials protected by the copyright laws should generally not be used without the owner's permission, there are some occasions when such use is allowed. **Fair use** guidelines describe circumstances under which a teacher can use copyrighted materials in face-to-face instruction. The TEACH Act offers similar guidelines for the use of copyrighted materials in distance learning. Perhaps the easiest way for educators to use such materials is to ask themselves four basic questions related to the use of a copyrighted work. These questions, summarized in Table 13.1, are focused on the instructional intent of the use and the potential impact on the owner of the work. Asking yourself these questions before using copyrighted materials in your classroom will help you to avoid copyright infringement, an illegal act. As copyright law evolves in the Digital Age, new guidelines will emerge. The use of multimedia clips and information from the Internet has developed into an entirely new and complex area of the law. Regardless of the ultimate rulings by legislators or courts, it will continue to be an educator's professional and legal responsibility to stay aware of changes to the law and to model its application in his or her classroom. Interchapter 13 offers an indepth review of teachers and their responsibilities with regard to copyrights. Understanding these responsibilities is critical for every educator.

FIGURE 13.1

Issues in the Digital Age

The Digital Age has enhanced education while giving rise to significant issues.

- Copyright and fair use
- Privacy
- Acceptable use
- Software piracy

- The digital divide
- Cyber bullying
- Online interaction

- Freedom of speech
- Privacy
- Academic dishonesty

TABLE 13.1 Fair Use Guidelines Self-Test

When concerned about whether or not to use copyrighted materials, answer this self-test to help you decide.

FAIR USE CONSIDERATION	ASK YOURSELF
PURPOSE AND CHARACTER OF USE	What is the intended use? • Are you using it for educational purposes? • Is the use noncommercial in nature?
NATURE OF THE COPYRIGHTED WORK	What type of work is it? • Is the work primarily factual in nature? • Does the work contain relatively little creative or imaginative substance?
AMOUNT AND SUSTAINABILITY OF THE PORTION USED	How much of the work do you intend to use?
EFFECT OF THE USE ON THE WORK'S MARKETABILITY	What impact does this kind of use have on the market for the work? • Would the use substitute for purchasing the original? • Would the use negatively affect the market potential of the original?

If your intended classroom use of copyrighted materials falls within fair use, then observe the following guidelines:

- Use the work only in face-to-face teaching. For distance learning, follow the guidelines in the TEACH Act.
- Limit copied materials to small amounts of the copyrighted work.
- Avoid making unnecessary copies.
- Be sure to include copyright notice and to attribute the work.
- Limit use to a single class and only one year. You need permission to use the work repeatedly.

For more detailed information, see Circular 21, "Reproduction of Copyrighted Works by Educators and Librarians," and other related materials at **www.loc.gov/copyright.**

Privacy

Every child in your charge, like every citizen in the United States, has a right to **privacy.** For minors, their parents must give permission to share any information about them to which you might be privy as a result of your position as their teacher. Technology has made the sharing of information simple and convenient. Nevertheless, this same convenience can lead to inadvertent or intentional abuse. The right to privacy is one of the most significant issues in the Digital Age, both in society and in education.

Violations of privacy when using technology can take many forms. One of the most significant relates to online privacy. Internet sites that serve children have not been reluctant to gather and share personal information about these children, including their names, addresses, phone numbers, and photographs and even information about their families, all without asking parents' permission to gather the information or to share it. At one time, this was often done simply by asking children to complete a form to gain access to a tempting game or entertainment site. However, the problem became serious enough to lead to a congressional investigation that ultimately resulted in the passage of the Children's Online Privacy Protection Act (COPPA) in October 1998 and the Children's Internet Protection Act (CIPA) in 2000. Given the climate of concern and the passage of these laws, how might the laws affect you as you protect your students' privacy?

Protecting student privacy in the Digital Age is a critical technology implementation issue.

Although the legal landscape around the Internet is continually changing, as a prudent teacher, you need to be aware of the steps you should take to protect your students' privacy. For example, if you want to show a picture of your class or a sample of your students' work on your web site, you need to be sure that you are acting within the stated policies and procedures of your school and district. Typically, schools and districts require that you get written permission from a child's parent or guardian before you post anything regarding that child that would otherwise have been private. When a child turns in work to you, there is usually an assumption that only you will read it. Although it is customary to hang children's work in a classroom, that is different in scope from posting work on the Internet. You typically do not have the right to share a child's work publicly without parental permission. Most important, above and beyond the legal issue, indicating on the Internet that a child is in a particular class at a particular school and perhaps even including that child's name can jeopardize that child's safety. Unsavory individuals can use such information to stalk a child or target the child for crime. Your primary responsibility, above all else, is to protect the safety of the children in your charge. Inadvertently exposing a child to risk by posting information about him or her on the Internet is a violation of your prime responsibility. A prudent teacher will become fully aware of the school and district policies related to posting students' names, pictures, or work on the Internet. The school and/or district policy will guide you in determining how student images or work can be used, as well as when and how parental permissions must be obtained.

Another area of concern is the collection of information about students at web sites they might visit. COPPA addressed this issue as well. Beginning April 21, 2000, operators of web sites directed at children under 13 had to conform to a series of rules and regulations regarding the request for and handling of personal information about their child visitors. One of the most significant regulations in this rigorous component of COPPA requires that these web site operators obtain verifiable parental permission before collecting personal data from children. Given that children may visit such sites in the course of a school day, what is the teacher's responsibility relative to such permission? COPPA allows teachers to act on behalf of parents during online school activities but does not require them to do so. However, district or school acceptable use policies may interpret this requirement differently. Each teacher should be fully aware of the school or district's acceptable use policy and act in accordance with it.

The Children's Internet Protection Act (CIPA) took protection one step further. This law required that libraries in schools and for public use establish and enforce policies to protect children. Primarily, this law required the use of filters and blocks to prohibit any Internet images that are harmful to minors. The law also required schools to monitor students' activity while they are on the Net. Schools and libraries that are not implementing such protections would become ineligible for federal funding for Internet access. Together, COPPA and CIPA mandated specific measures to protect children who use the Internet. School district and teacher responsibilities became clear with this legislation. As protectors of the children in our charge, we must take steps to protect them and their privacy or find ourselves legally liable.

Many web sites are available to help parents and teachers understand the issues related to protection of children while they use the Internet. One of the most comprehensive is provided by the Cen-

TECH TIPS for Teachers

Protecting Privacy

Just as you wouldn't post students' grades on your classroom door or tack letters to individual parents about student performance on your bulletin board, so too you must protect privacy in the Digital Age. Review this checklist for ways in which you can protect your students' privacy:

- Don't place confidential data or commentary on any unsecured electronic equipment.
- Guard your log-in names and passwords.
- Secure storage devices (floppies, CD-RWs, and USB drives) in places where they are not obtainable by people unauthorized to view their contents.
- Don't leave hard copy of assessments, evaluations, and reports of student behavior and achievement on printer trays in common areas.
- Once used, file privileged information, whether on storage devices or on hard copy, in secured spaces or, if no longer needed, shred it (preferably with a crosscut shredder).
- Follow school district policies and procedures in place to guard students' privacy.
- Guard photographs of students as well as text.
- Become aware of classroom and district software that offers parents access to their children's progress by password in read-only format.

FIGURE 13.2

Safety on the Internet

Web sites for children sponsored by the Federal Trade Commission or by children's advocacy groups offer current and relevant information on how to be safe on the Internet.

ter for Missing and Exploited Children. NetSmart offers parents, educators, law enforcement officials, and children pertinent information related to staying safe on the Net (Figure 13.2). This and many other web sites are available to help you understand the issues related to children's Internet privacy and your related professional responsibilities. Just as it is a requirement for you to become aware of and comply with your school district's acceptable use policy, it is a professional expectation for you to protect your students while they use the Internet. Exploring such sites will help you to do so.

Privacy when students are not online must also be protected. Software that allows you to manage grades and personal data relating to your students must be protected so that no others can gain access to information about them. If the school is networked, such grading software is installed on the network with specific rights for each account. That means that your account, as a teacher, has associated with it the rights to see and use software and data about all of your students. Student accounts have rights that may allow them to see only their own work. To protect student privacy, then, it is important for you to protect your own log-in and password because they allow access to private student data. Irresponsible sharing of your network account can result in a serious violation of a student's privacy. Even inattentiveness might be damaging. Leaving your computer logged into the network when you are not using it can make the areas you are privy to available to others. On stand-alone machines that are available for student use, it is best to be sure that no files that may be considered private are stored on a drive that is available for all to use. It is your responsibility to guard the privacy of your students whether you are using the Internet, a network, or a public-access machine in your classroom.

ADA Compliance

Another area of legal concern is the requirement to address the implications of the Americans with Disabilities Act (ADA), in particular Section 508, the section of the law that specifically addresses electronic and information technology. Schools and other governmental agencies must ensure that information presented electronically is as accessible to people with disabilities as to those without. This mandate, when implemented, requires that schools pay particular attention to the way in which digital information is presented via the Internet. For example, to comply with Section 508, a web site presented by a school or district should, among many requirements, caption multimedia presentations, offer text alternatives for nontext images, avoid using color as the designator for navigation, and provide verbal time-out warnings for pages that might expire unless users act. These are just a few of the guidelines to ensure that school web sites meet the needs of those with disabilities.

The need to make the web accessible for Section 508 compliance and to meet the needs of the general population using the web is so significant that the World Wide Web Consortium (W3C) implemented an accessibility initiative. According to this initiative, "Web accessibility means that people with disabilities can perceive, understand, navigate, and interact with the Web, and that they can contribute to the Web. Web accessibility also benefits others, including older people with changing abilities due to aging. Web accessibility encompasses all disabilities that affect access to the Web, including visual, auditory, physical, speech, cognitive, and neurological disabilities" (W3C, 2005). The W3C standards offer schools and districts clear recommendations to ensure that Section 508 is addressed and this legal responsibility is addressed.

Acceptable Use

Teachers must take steps to ensure students' acceptable use of technology.

Once technology is made available to students, it is the obligation of educators to ensure that the technology is used appropriately. Just as teachers oversee how students utilize textbooks and other media, they have a responsibility, to the extent possible, to ensure that access to and use of technology are consistent with the appropriate academic behaviors expected in the classroom. Just as educators would not allow questionable or inappropriate printed materials into the classroom, so too must they ensure that such materials available via technology be kept out of the classroom. The issues surrounding the use of technology in a manner that protects students from inappropriate behaviors and information are together referred to as **acceptable use** issues.

Go to the *Assignments and Activities* section of Chapter 13 in MyEducationKit and complete the video activity entitled *Supporting Technology Use in Classrooms.*

The most frequently voiced concern involving the acceptable use of technology relates to the Internet. The Internet contains salacious and inappropriate materials that do not belong in the classroom. You can do little to change the nature of the Internet, but a prudent teacher can help to ensure that the Internet is used appropriately in the classroom. Although your actions might not be able to guarantee that your students will never access an inappropriate web site, you can take every step possible to protect them.

The first important action you should take is to be sure that your students understand what constitutes appropriate use. Just as you might begin the school year explaining your expectations of classroom behavior, so too should you explain your expectations of how the Internet should be used in your classroom. Often, this is done through a **code of ethics** for computer use, a set of written expectations and definitions of what is considered appropriate or acceptable use. Codes of ethics should be signed by both students and their parents or guardians to ensure that they too are aware of these expectations. Signed codes should be stored for the duration of the school year. You should check with your school or district for its code of ethics or acceptable use policy (AUP). Most districts have established formal acceptable use policies, and schools within those districts are expected to follow them. After you check the details of the policy, it is wise to duplicate it and be sure to have your students and their parents sign it before your students are given Internet access or Internet assignments. If no such formal code has been established in your school or district, you should discuss these concerns with your school administrator. You might also want to review examples of various codes of ethics to determine what you might expect.

Many networked school systems have implemented **filtering software,** that is, software that filters out unacceptable Internet sites so students cannot access them (see Figure 13.3). Although not always successful in catching unacceptable sites, such filters

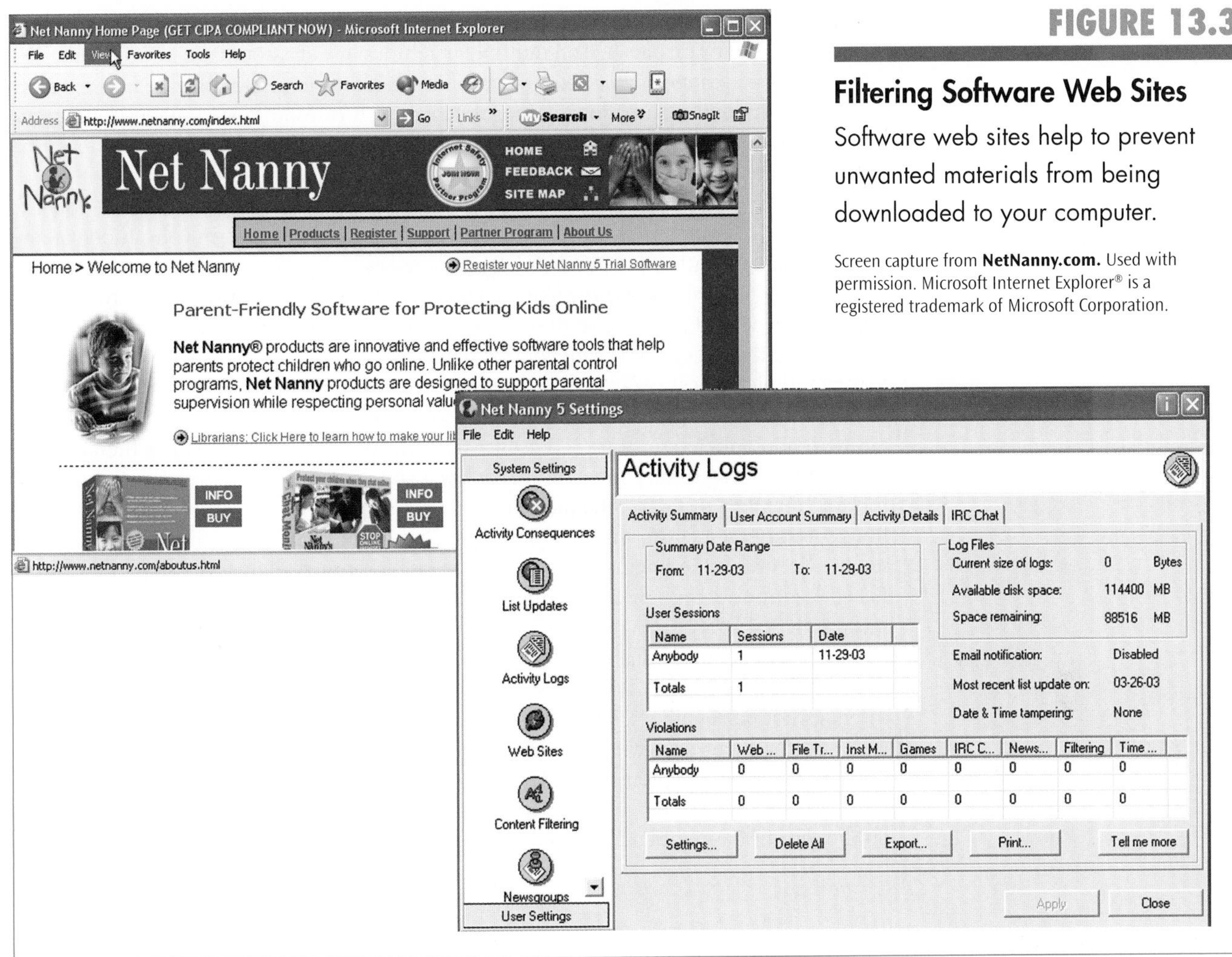

FIGURE 13.3

Filtering Software Web Sites

Software web sites help to prevent unwanted materials from being downloaded to your computer.

Screen capture from **NetNanny.com.** Used with permission. Microsoft Internet Explorer® is a registered trademark of Microsoft Corporation.

do improve the chances of intervening if a child accidentally or deliberately attempts to access an inappropriate site.

Typically, filtering software will not allow access to off-limit sites, and many packages also gather the names of the users who are attempting to access such sites. Because users might innocently mis-key a URL or click on a link that inadvertently brings them to an unacceptable site, network administrators typically take minimal action, if any, for an occasional attempted access. However, if a user repeatedly and purposefully tries to access inappropriate sites using a school network, the administrator does typically track such activity and records it. For students and teachers alike, such activity is grounds for disciplinary action.

Software Piracy

Copying software to share with others or installing software on multiple machines when only one copy was purchased is software **piracy.** It is a violation of copyright laws to make and distribute copies of software or to install illegal copies of software on the machines in your classroom. Just as it is a violation to make copies of a music CD or a movie on videotape, it is illegal to copy and distribute software packages. The owners of the software have invested considerable resources in creating the software, and they have the right to sell and distribute their creation. Just because you purchased one copy does not mean that you have the right to make and use multiple copies.

Software piracy violates the laws and must be discouraged through instruction and the teacher's demonstration of adherence to copyright laws.

Teachers who pirate software by making duplicate copies of a software package or by installing one software package on multiple machines in a classroom are in violation of the copyright laws. Teachers who know of and allow students to pirate software in their classrooms are condoning and allowing illegal activities. It is important to model appropriate behavior and ethical conduct and to proactively discourage software piracy whenever it is noticed. When a student offers you a copy of the new software he or she just got from a friend, you have a chance to model the correct behavior by refusing to accept it. You also have a teachable moment in which you have the opportunity to inform your student about copyright and his or her potential violation of the law.

Network administrators are charged with ensuring that all software on a network is appropriately licensed (the legal right to use the software). Every software package on a network must either be custom-made for that network or have a site license (a purchased right to use multiple copies) associated with it. Some network administrators also monitor all software that has been installed on the hard drives of any machine that is on the network to ensure that no pirated software is present on or attached to the network. It is therefore important for teachers to keep the software packages and documentation for any nonnetworked software that they install on the machines in a classroom. The network administrator who finds software on a classroom machine typically has the right and responsibility to ask to see the license. If the documentation and license are not available, the school or district network administrator may be required to erase any software that the teacher cannot prove was purchased.

Your school and/or district is likely to have very specific policies that address software piracy. A prudent teacher should research and become aware of such policies so that he or she does not personally violate them or allow students to violate them. Remember, like violating copyright laws with respect to multimedia, violating copyright with respect to software is also a violation of the law, which may result in you, your school, and your district being sued by the copyright holder. It is your responsibility as a professional and a public servant to uphold and support the laws relating to copyright.

Social Issues in the Digital Age

The Digital Age has brought up a number of new issues that have more to do with society in general than with education specifically. These societal concerns are nevertheless reflected in schools and relevant to them. Equity and accessibility of technology are the most pressing and critical of these issues. Inequities in access to technology can result in some children leaping ahead in technological skills and knowledge through their readily available technological resources and others falling behind because of their lack of access to technology. This gap between digital haves and have-nots is often referred to as the digital divide.

> The digital divide is the separation between those who have access to technology and those who do not.

For households in which parents can afford a home computer and modem, computers and Internet access are often present and readily available for the children in the home to use. A recent report by the National Telecommunications and Information Administration, *A Nation Online, Entering the Broadband Age* (2004), indicates that approximately 49 percent of households earning less than $35,000 have Internet access, while 72 percent of households earning more than $50,000 have access. This level of accessibility gives children in wealthier households a head start in gaining computer skills and in developing the cognitive skills necessary to use hardware and software and to explore the Internet. For households that cannot afford a home computer, the child's use is limited to school time or perhaps time that is available through the local library. This type of relatively limited access may well cause such children to fall behind in the skills they need to use computers and the Internet in school. Other factors may also limit access. Not all schools and libraries are equally equipped with computers and Internet connections. The ones

TABLE 13.2 The Digital Divide: U.S. Households with Internet or Broadband Access, October, 2003

The digital divide separates technological haves and have-nots.

TOTAL POPULATION	INTERNET USERS (PERCENT)	LIVES IN A BROADBAND HOUSEHOLD (PERCENT)
GENDER	58.7	22.8
Male	58.2	23.9
Female	59.2	21.8
RACE/ ETHNICITY		
White	65.1	25.7
White Alone	65.1	25.7
Black	45.6	14.2
Black Alone	45.2	13.9
Asian Amer. & Pac. Isl.	63.1	34.2
Asian Amer. & Pac. Isl. Alone	63.0	34.7
Hispanic (of any race)	37.2	12.6
EMPLOYMENT STATUS		
Employed /e	70.7	26.0
Not Employed (unemployed or NLF)	42.8	16.1
FAMILY INCOME		
Less than $15,000	31.2	7.5
$15,000–$24,999	38.0	9.3
$25,000–$34,999	48.9	13.4
$35,000–$49,999	62.1	19.0
$50,000–$74,999	71.8	27.9
$75,000 & above	82.9	45.4

SOURCE: NTIA and ESA, U.S. Department of Commerce, using U.S. Bureau of the Census Current Population Survey supplements.

with less technology are often in poorer areas, causing limited access for people who cannot afford computers at home.

The digital divide does not occur along socioeconomic lines alone. Research in *A Nation Online: Entering the Broadband Age* shows that the divide also occurs along ethnic, gender, disability, and education lines. Despite the increased presence of technology in our society, minorities and people with disabilities still have less access than others (see Table 13.2).

Furthermore, 69 percent of people with college degrees use the Internet, whereas Internet use is limited to only 15 percent of those whose education stopped before completing high school. Finally, gender differences exist as well. Although the numbers of men and women using the Internet are approximately equal, fewer women have computer-related degrees or work in computer-related fields. This reflects the continued math/science gender gap that has been present in schools for decades. This gap has now transferred to technology. According to many studies, boys are more encouraged to engage in technology-related activities than girls are, which may ultimately lead to the gender difference within the digital divide.

The digital divide cannot help affecting technology literacy at every level of education. Awareness of the gap in access and the possible inequities along ethnic, economic, gender, disability, and education lines can help teachers to become sensitive to their students' needs. Once aware that the digital divide does indeed exist, a teacher can choose to design technology and other content-area lessons to help bridge technological inequities. You might also decide to research and share information about community resources that provide access for those who do not have computers at home. You might decide to advocate in your school and your community for more and equitable opportunities for all of your students. The issue of the digital divide is so pressing and pervasive that many others are taking steps to close the gap as well.

The e-rate has enabled schools and libraries to connect to the information superhighway.

To make technology broadly available to all citizens, the Federal Commerce Commission has established an education rate (**e-rate**), a discounted cost for telecommunications service for community access centers (such as schools and libraries). The e-rate has enabled schools and libraries to connect to the Internet at a significantly accelerated pace. Private foundations, such as the Bill and Melinda Gates Foundation, have donated computers to libraries in rural areas to help make technology more available to all. Schools across the nation are piloting programs that provide notebook computers to students to help equalize access. These and many similar initiatives are working in combination to help bridge the digital divide and ensure that all citizens have equal access to the tools of our Digital Age.

Cyberbullying

With so many children interacting via the Internet, the bullying that has historically happened on the playground has entered cyberspace. The National Crime Prevention Council (NCPC) defines the phenomenon known as **cyberbullying** as an incident "when the Internet, cell phones or other devices are used to send or post text or images intended to hurt or embarrass another person" (2009). The spreading of lies, rumors, or insults targeting a person for the purpose of intimidation as well as posting personal information about a person on a web site can do serious harm to the victim. In fact, some children pressured by cyberbullies have sought to harm themselves rather than enduring the online hate. The problem is widespread. The NCPC in its online publication to help curtail cyberbullying, *Stop Cyberbullying Before It Starts*, indicates that 43 percent of teens have been victims of cyberbullying in the previous year, and these numbers are rising (Figure 13.4).

Although educators cannot monitor student interactions on the Internet while students are not in school, they can take steps to prevent and mitigate the harm caused by cyberbullying. Districts and schools can address cyberbullying in their AUPs, and the NCPC recommends that schools have students sign Internet safety pledges promising they will not cyberbully. This would help to raise awareness of the issue with both parents and the children. Teachers can educate their students about what cyberbullying is and how best to deal with incidents they either notice or are victims of. They can also help educate parents about the issue and suggest home Internet policies to protect the children. While cyberbullying is no more likely to be entirely eliminated in cyberspace than on the playground, educators can and should take action to ensure that students are as protected as possible.

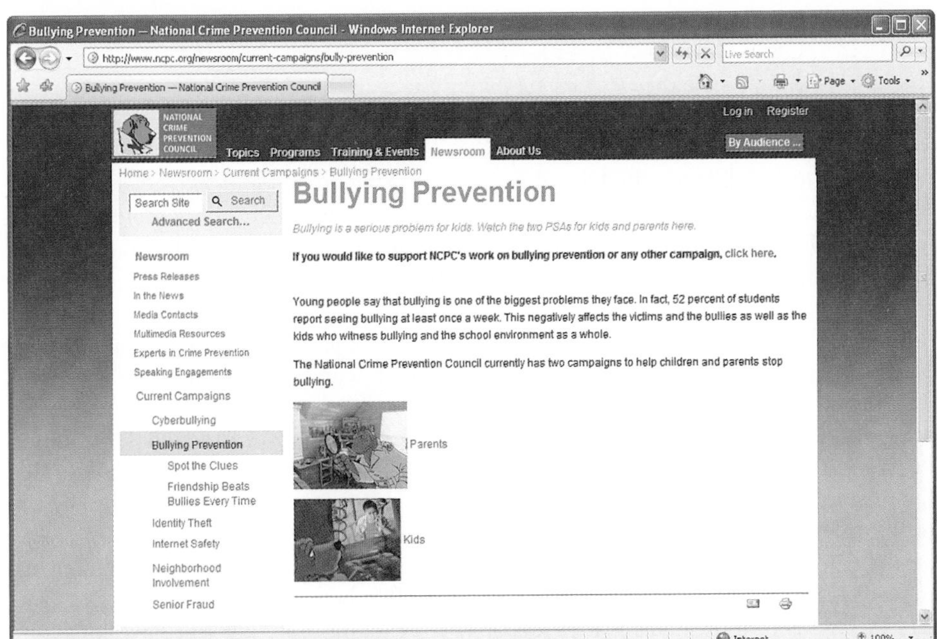

FIGURE 13.4

Cyberbullying

Prevention of cyberbullying is a critical responsibility for technology-using educators. Many web sites offer suggestions and lesson plans to support teachers and their students in the effort to stop bullying.

National Crime Prevention Council.

Online Social Interaction

As you have learned, Web 2.0 has offered computer users a vast opportunity to interact socially via the Internet. This powerful potential of the web helps to reduce isolation and encourage cultural tolerance for those who use its resources. However, for young children and teens who are not mature in their understanding or ability to interact appropriately, the online social interaction in which they engage can raise serious concerns. Children and young adults all too often do not consider the potential repercussions of their cyberspace social interactions. Images, words, and information posted on social networking web sites may never truly go away and may be viewed by relatives, peers, and later even potential employers.

A prime example of this issue is the recent phenomenon known as *sexting*. Teens attempting to get the attention and interest of members of the opposite sex have engaged in sending text messages that include nude images of themselves. Not only is this interaction inappropriate and ultimately damaging when such images are made public, the behavior also has legal implication. It is illegal to view and proliferate sexual images of underage children, even if done by children. Such activities are considered participating in child pornography, and even teenagers have been charged with this felony as a result. Unfortunately, the activity is widespread. In the National Campaign to Prevent Teen and Unplanned Pregnancy publication *Sex and Tech: The Results from a Survey of Young Adults* (2008), it was noted that 20 percent of the teens surveyed admitted to posting nude or seminude images of themselves online or in text messages, while 39 percent admitted to sending sexually suggestive messages. These unfortunate adolescent indiscretions can have a lifelong impact.

For educators, helping children and teens to become aware of the potential problems arising from inappropriate activities while social networking is fast becoming a critical part of Information Age socialization. Whether for the protection of young children from predators or the protection of teens from engaging in acts harmful to themselves, educating children and teens is the one of the most effective solutions to this social issue. Just as teachers encourage appropriate and positive social interactions in their classrooms, so too should they teach and encourage appropriate and positive social interaction while in cyberspace.

Ethical Issues in the Digital Age

Freedom of Speech

In addition to social issues, the Digital Age has also engendered ethical concerns. One of the most significant of these is **freedom of speech** and the Internet. The content on the Internet is not regulated and, as a result, does contain materials that are objectionable and inappropriate for children. However, an issue that arises whenever regulation of Internet content is discussed is the constitutional right to free speech. The Internet is essentially a forum for sharing information and opinions. Some of the information and opinions expressed are grounded in scientific fact and academic research. Others are simply personal viewpoints that may be offensive to some. The question then arises whether society should censor some views expressed on the Internet and whether the government has the authority to do so. Is the right to express a viewpoint digitally as protected by the Constitution as the right to free speech is? Is it the responsibility of an ISP or portal to monitor the content of the information and opinions expressed on the web sites, conferences, and emails available from its service? When do the actions of a few cross over into the legal domains that address fraud, libel, and hate crimes? The conflict between freedom on the Internet and the rights of individuals is a serious and far-reaching one that will have long-term ramifications for our society.

Free speech and privacy are two of the critical ethical issues related to Internet use.

While this controversy continues to rage, it remains a school's responsibility to control access on its network to areas of the Internet that are inappropriate for an academic setting. Through monitoring and filtering software and through teacher observation, schools can make a reasonable effort to curb access to objectionable materials. Ultimately, society will decide whether objectionable materials are within the realm protected by free speech. Until then, teachers need to be aware of their professional responsibilities to guarantee students' "digital safety" while using technology.

Privacy

A second ethical issue arising in the Digital Age relates to privacy versus control and monitoring. Individual rights and privacy are significant values in our society. In using any network or the Internet, it is technologically possible to monitor what an individual is doing and which sites he or she is visiting while connected. The controversy arises as to the rights of any agency, whether governmental or commercial, to closely monitor and record an individual's personal information or online activities. Is that not a violation of privacy? Should the government be allowed to monitor people who engage in illegal or dangerous activities? Who is responsible if activities are not monitored and someone gets hurt?

These complex social questions and the legal issues associated with them are evolving as the Digital Age unfolds. For educators, however, the situation is a bit less murky. In schools, the primary responsibility is the safety of the students. Because schools and their technologies are public entities, usually with clearly defined acceptable use policies, monitoring of activities is both appropriate and expected. Students and public employees alike agree to use the school facilities to engage only in appropriate activities. It is typically understood that monitoring to ensure appropriate use and the safety of students will be done. Network administrators can monitor activity, and software can track what is said and what is sent by network users. Personal activities on the Internet, though monitored, are thus no more curtailed than they would be in the classroom.

Academic Dishonesty

The ease of manipulating and sharing digital data has led to numerous problems relating to **academic dishonesty.** Some web sites offer "services" to students so that they can hire someone to write papers for them. Others let students post assignments they have

In the CLASSROOM

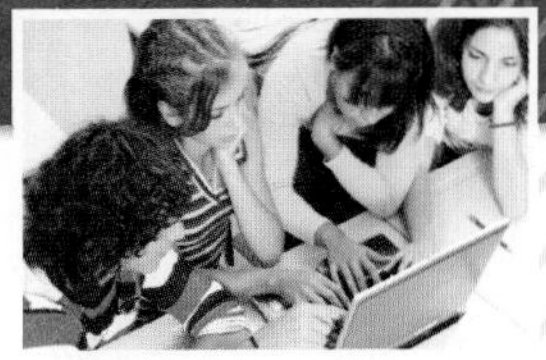

Preventing Plagiarism

Suggestions from educators who deal with possible plagiarized writing highlight the importance of preventing students from engaging in the unlawful act of passing someone else's work off as their own or of citing sources improperly. Such prevention is preferable to having to deal with an accomplished act of plagiarism and its consequences. Using online companies such as Turnitin.com has become a major strategy that schools at all levels are using to detect plagiarism. Teachers feel confident that students who know that their school will submit their papers to Turnitin.com are much less likely to commit plagiarism. ABC News reported on how Nels Johnson, a senior AP English teacher at San Mateo Union High School, has incorporated the services of Turnitin.com in his classes. Students submit their essays to Turnitin before they are handed over to Mr. Johnson. Students are informed about the capability the company has to compare their papers with millions of other student papers it has acquired from ones submitted by students for checks as required by their teachers, as well as the vast amount of proprietary content that is on file. Knowing that their teachers will receive a report on each paper submitted that shows the percentage of words that matched other documents serves as a strong deterrent to students who may be tempted to take the easy way out, as they perceive it, and submit writing that is not their own.

Other preventive measures include discouraging plagiarism by letting students know that teachers are aware of the most infamous sites that sell papers, such as Cheathouse, Perfect Essays, Direct Essays, and Monster Papers. These sites not only sell papers to students but also sell the names of students who have purchased papers from them to teachers. Teachers can also assign open-ended topics for writing that call for students to think creatively as well as critically in their writing rather than asking them to analyze and evaluate topics that have already been written on to the point of exhaustion. Teachers can also assign organizational formats that professional writers rarely use. If the students are lifting content from published works, the plagiarism is obvious. Another strategy teachers suggest is to have students research outside of class but bring notes to class for in-class writing of a draft to be turned in before leaving the classroom, which will be used for later comparison with the out-of-class product. Although there is no foolproof way to prevent all attempts at plagiarism, a computer-using educator can find useful tools to help monitor and minimize the problem.

Sze, K. (2009, March 16). *Software helps schools fight plagiarism*. Retrieved May 30, 2009, from **http://abclocal.go.com/kgo/story?section=news/education&id=6712085&pt=print.**

written or retrieve assignments written by others. Even web sites that do not intend to encourage dishonesty may support it as students copy and paste information from such sites into their assignments without giving the true authors credit. Cheating and plagiarizing are clearly not products of the Digital Age, but technology has made them easier to do and harder to detect.

To address potential digital dishonesty, teachers and schools should have clearly stated and enforced policies to deal with digital academic dishonesty just as they do for dishonesty of the more traditional sort. If academic dishonesty is widespread, a school can even install, or use online, **antiplagiarism software** that compares student's work with well-known authors' work and with work posted on the web (Figure 13.5). Whether the approach is to enforce policy or to monitor student work via software, it is a teacher's responsibility to ensure, to the extent possible, that checks are in place to promote and enforce academic honesty.

Resources for Teachers

The legal, ethical, and social issues presented in this chapter are far-reaching and critically important. But a teacher is not alone in addressing and dealing with these issues. Typically, a school has a media specialist and/or a technology specialist available to assist teachers in

FIGURE 13.5

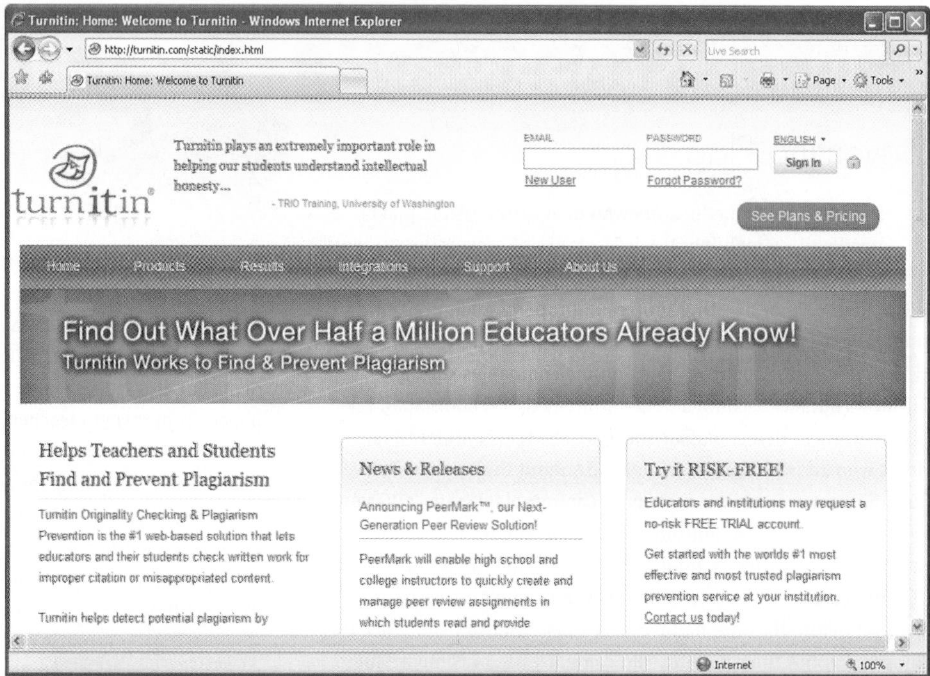

Software and web sites are available to educators to help reduce plagiarism.

PEARSON myeducationkit™

Go to the *Assignments and Activities* section of Chapter 13 in MyEducationKit and complete the web activity entitled *Discovering Online Resources.*

addressing these issues. Both media and technology specialists have typically undergone special training sessions or have taken in-depth courses dealing with the issues related to technology implementation. A prudent teacher, when faced with questions regarding technology and its use in the classroom, would be wise first to contact the school media specialist, technology coordinator, or a school administrator for guidance. You will likely be surprised at the wealth of information and enthusiastic support you will be given.

A Teacher's Role in Technology Implementation

Teachers have a critical role in the implementation of technology in schools. In the planning process, they are key stakeholders. They are advocates for the acquisition of appropriate and useful technology for their students as well as for themselves. Their voices must be heard to ensure that the technology that is purchased and implemented is used widely and effectively. But teachers have an even more critical role in dealing with the legal, ethical, and social issues associated with the implementation of technology in schools and classrooms.

Teachers must be aware of the issues in technology implementation so that they can be proactive in addressing these issues from their own professional standpoint and on behalf of their students. Teachers must understand the social implications of technology to ensure equity in access as well as to help their students protect themselves when using technology resources. Teachers must understand the legal issues associated with technology to ensure that they protect themselves and their schools from litigation and to model the best possible behavior for their students. And teachers must address ethical issues related to technology just as they must address ethical concerns in every aspect of their profession. The Information Age challenges educators not only to stay current in the skills necessary to use the technologies in place in schools, but also to stay aware of the implications of using the technologies.

Further, as technologies continue to evolve, teachers need to keep abreast of their evolution and the issues associated with them. Just as the concerns related to social networking were unheard of five years ago, so too are the concerns of tomorrow's technologies unrecognizable today. To that end, the final chapter of this text will introduce you to the new technologies that are emerging now and those that are evolving. Today's educators will need to be prepared for what is on the technological horizon in order to not only be able to utilize these upcoming tools but also to be prepared to deal with the issues they will raise. Tomorrow's technology-rich classroom will include much that is not yet within our technological frame of reference but there are trends and indicators. Chapter 14 will introduce you to them.

PEARSON myeducationkit™

To check your comprehension of the content covered in this chapter, go to the MyEducationKit for your book and complete the *Study Plan* for Chapter 13.

Key Terms

academic dishonesty, 358
acceptable use, 352
antiplagiarism software, 359
code of ethics, 352
copyright, 348
cyberbullying, 356
digital divide, 348
e-rate, 356
fair use, 348
filtering software, 352
freedom of speech, 358
piracy, 353
privacy, 349
strategic planning, 347

has enabled users to exercise while playing various games (golf, tennis, bowling, etc.), and the Wii can even be used for physical rehabilitation. The virtual environment enabled by Nintendo's Wii is being embraced by other video game makers and will continue to expand into new environments that incorporate physical activity and offer educational potential.

For education, improvements to online and systems-based VR offer the potential for interactive sensory experiences in learning scenarios constructed to teach. This technology also offers the possibility of altering virtual instructional environments to present and respond to unique differences in learners. Although advanced VR technology is on the horizon, its applications hold amazing promise for teaching and learning. For implementation of technology now, it is important simply to stay aware of the current VR resources and the emergence of VR environments and to explore how they might be used in teaching and learning.

Artificial Intelligence

Artificial intelligence programs provide intelligent assistants to help with computing tasks.

Artificial intelligence (**AI**) refers to programs that work similarly to the way the human brain works. In AI circles, software that learns and adjusts its responses on the basis of previous interactions is called a **neural network. Fuzzy logic software** is an AI program that resembles human decision making. **Expert systems** are AI programs that offer suggestions and advice on the basis of a database of expertise. Some AI systems use **intelligent agents** that are called on to help with specific tasks. Intelligent agents may ask questions, monitor work to determine patterns of action, and perform requested tasks. All of these types of AI programs are in existence now but have not yet evolved sufficiently to become significant tools in current teaching and learning environments.

Yet when applied to education, AI has the potential to improve and adapt software to a student's individual learning patterns and needs. An agent might be created for each individual student that would automatically customize learning software and instructional experiences in a manner that is responsive to the learner's learning style and needs. For education, AI holds the promise of programs that could become virtual teacher aides.

ISTE Standard

Learning about collaboration tools will help you address **NETS•T STANDARD 5:**

ENGAGE IN PROFESSIONAL GROWTH AND LEADERSHIP
Teachers continuously improve their professional practice, model lifelong learning, and exhibit leadership in their school and professional community by promoting and demonstrating the effective use of digital tools and resources.

Communications, Collaboration, and the Semantic Web

The web has provided a platform for unrestricted communication and collaboration for every purpose, including all things academic. Collaboration, once the domain of complex telecommunication systems, no longer calls for expensive equipment and specialized expertise to make it accessible in the classroom. The newest tools for collaborative work are small, flexible, and free and require no installation. Students can simply open their web browsers, and they are then able to edit group documents, hold online meetings, swap information and data, and collaborate in any number of ways without ever leaving their desks or their homes. One such example is WEbook, a web site that offers the opportunity to collaborate and publish online (Figure 14.2). WEbook offers everyone a chance to write, collaborate, review, and even publish. This literary version of a social network, when applied to schools, gives young writers a previously impossible opportunity to be heard. Many such collaboration tools are already widely available but not yet used in most schools. Future classrooms will evolve into district, state, national, and even international collaborative workplaces where peer-to-peer interaction outside of the classroom is commonplace. But collaborative tools are only the beginning in the classroom of tomorrow.

Data mashups involve applications that combine data sources to provide a new view of previously diverse information. The process of personalizing information retrieval may result in the personal web.

A new trend emerging on the web includes custom applications in which combinations of data from different sources are "mashed up" into a single tool. These **data mashups** are tools that can combine data from different sources to give the user new ways to look at and interact with the information available at these sources. An example of this conver-

FIGURE 14.2

Collaborative Work

Collaborative web sites such as WeBook offer students the opportunity to write, review, and publish individually or with peers.

Reprinted by permission of Webook.

gence would be using Google Earth with topographic information from another source to depict and zoom into land features for geography instruction. "Mashing up" the data from these two sources create a new online tool for instruction. The availability of large amounts of data from so many diverse sources makes such convergence useful and will transform the way we understand and represent information. In fact, many predict the emergence of the **personal web,** a World Wide Web that is focused on the presentation of information unique to and as needed by each individual. Such a personal view of the online world would use current and emerging data tools to gather and create a personal online environment that addresses personal, professional, and learning needs. Consider the implications of personal webs for education. Learners could create academic personal webs to support their unique learning styles and academic needs. The potential of this emerging technology for personalizing the instructional environment is enormous.

The kind of knowledge and understanding that emerge from large groups of people gathering, discussing, and collaborating on issues is referred to as **collective intelligence.** Data mashups are just one tool to facilitate this approach. A good example of the application of collective intelligence efforts is Wikipedia. As you know, wikis are the result of numerous online contributions and tweaking, ultimately resulting in very current and accurate information on every conceivable topic. Already under way are new collective intelligence applications and projects. Flickr, for example, offers users the opportunity to post images to be shared publicly or privately. Flickr Maps takes geocoded digital photographs and presents a global display of photographs based on map locations. This mashed-up collective effort offers opportunities for users from around the globe to post images so that others can view places that they might visit. The Massachusetts Institute of Technology climate change project is developing a tool called a Climate Collaboratorium that will allow experts and citizens alike to collectively consider and debate possible solutions to problems posed by climate change. Such a tool would allow minds from across the globe to automatically gather and mash up data, share ideas, and brainstorm solutions. The resulting collective intelligence may well make the difference in determining the right course of action for climate issues. Imagine how such tools, when applied to educational projects in and outside of the classroom, could engage students and make content meaningful.

> The vision of the semantic web is one in which a question can be asked of a search engine, which will provide simple and direct response after searching many sources.

One final emerging technology to make using the vast data resources of the Net accessible and available for personal and collaborative use is the **semantic web.** As first advanced by Sir Tim Berners-Lee, the creator of the World Wide Web, the concept offered a view of the web as a place where difficult problems could be solved via technology's ability to process and connect vast and diverse bits of information that would take people many years to interrelate. On the currently theoretical semantic web, you could pose a complex question, and the underlying applications would search all data, filter and connect pieces of information, and present an appropriate and intelligent answer. Current semantic applications have begun to offer more complex and sensitive search engines that allow you to ask a complex question rather than just search for key words. For example, a question posed to the semantic search engine True Knowledge (**www.trueknowledge.com**) such as "What is the highest mountain?" causes the web site to interpret the question and then seek out the answer from all online resources. The response would then be presented as the single answer, Mount Everest, without any extraneous matches to explore. This early version of an intelligent semantic search makes finding information on the web much simpler and more direct. The educational application is clear. Students and teachers alike could have any conceivable question answered without having to search through many web sites to find the right response.

Clearly, the evolving and emerging applications on the web will make it possible for educators to collaborate professionally and offer their students engaging interactive and collaborative learning opportunities. But perhaps one of the most fascinating aspects of these innovations is that they are very quickly being untethered from the classroom and even from schools themselves via the fast-expanding mobility technologies that are becoming more widely available each day. Mobile computing technologies promise to make learning any time, anywhere a reality for everyone.

Expanded Mobility

Increased mobile computing capabilities include increased and faster access to content, which is also becoming ever more portable. New and improved web-enabled cell phones such as the Apple iPhone, Google G1, and Pilot Pre, as well as a variety of netbooks offer Internet users the freedom to access the information they need and their personal resources from anywhere. And electronic book readers such as the Amazon Kindle make it easy to obtain and carry vast amounts of text and graphics in one small package. Movies, books, email, and more are already available on these relatively inexpensive lightweight, portable platforms, and the selection is growing exponentially. More mobile capabilities, including faster Net access, improved multimedia, GPS mapping, and thousands of mobile applications, make mobile computing an undeniable wave in the Digital Age. In fact, some observers suggest that a new web is emerging, known as **Web 3.0** (Mossberg, 2009); at its core will be the arrival and full implementation of the mobile handheld computer.

For education, the implications are significant. Teaching and learning in a fully mobile computing environment will mean that resources are at the fingertips of both teachers and students at any time and from anywhere. The brick-and-mortar classroom will not bound learning in any way. Educators will be able to embrace technology-rich computing from any place and create a meaningful and interactive instructional environment anywhere. The opportunities for teaching and for learning will be essentially limitless.

Grid Computing and Cloud Computing

Communication via networking, whether local or across the Internet, has begun a new phase that some people suggest may be as significant as the creation of the Internet itself. You will recall that the Internet began as a few networks experimentally connected together for research purposes. In a similar vein, some experimental networks, the purpose of which is to maximize computing power, are now being connected together. These computers are joined together on a "grid" to share resources and to communicate data so that the available computing power is a factor of the number of computers on the grid. The more computers are

Grid computing refers to connecting many computers at diverse locations to work together on a single complex task.

connected to the grid, the more CPU power is available for the targeted task. One of the first major breakthroughs using grid computing has been the SETI@home project. In this experiment, individuals volunteer their personal computers' idle computing power to help to analyze radio telescope data for the SETI (Search for Extraterrestrial Intelligence) project. This popular and continuously growing grid uses the idle computing power of approximately 900,000 personal computers, resulting in the fastest dedicated computer in the world (Newport, 2005).

Grid computing standards and tools are being refined, and more and more scientific computer grids are being created. Considering the cost and limited time available for the use of supercomputers, grid computing offers a viable alternative. For education, this may someday mean that everyday educators can have access to data and power previously reserved to only the most advanced research universities. Further, the power needed for intensive and complex multimedia instruction may become readily available to all despite any potential limitations of the computers located in any one classroom. The availability of seamless and powerful computing resources on every computer connected to the grid may revolutionize educational computing. For our society, grid computing may become a ubiquitous virtual master computer available on demand to anyone requiring its use. Indeed, it may well be the next evolution in worldwide computing and communications.

Today, on a smaller scale, the basic operating principle of the grid, resource sharing, is already in place in the form of **peer-to-peer networking.** This type of networking differs from the more conventional networking structure in several significant ways. In a traditional network, we typically store the files we want to share on a network server's hard drive, which in turn is made accessible to others on the network or the Internet. We must go through the server to reach one another. Peer-to-peer networking offers another communication alternative. Instead of connecting through a server, in this networking structure, computers connect together directly. Each "peer" computer in the network then makes a portion of its hard drive public or shares its drives. This "public" drive acts like a type of virtual mini server in that it allows others to use the resources we store there and gives us space to store resources we borrow from others. The need for specific services that offer server space and function and to which we must pay a fee is eliminated.

Peer-to-peer networks connect multiple computers to form a network for the purpose of sharing files.

Such a technology has been used extensively on the Internet to share music (MP3) files. Unfortunately, many of the files made available through this type of peer-to-peer network have been offered in a way that violates copyright laws. Many of the MP3 files stored on this type of private-public network were created by turning copyrighted musical CDs into digital files shared with other peers in the network without compensation to the artists and record companies that owned the music. As you know, this type of violation of copyright law is illegal. As a result, many of the music sites using this type of technology have been forced to shut down or modify their operations to comply with the laws.

Although some people have chosen to use peer-to-peer networking in an unethical and illegal manner, the core technology of sharing resources and data directly between computers has great potential for education. Whether ultimately adapted to become a worldwide computing grid or simply used to share resources on a smaller scale, this new communications technology holds great promise for teachers and their students. Using a similar peer-to-peer structure, learning communities working on an international science project could share data easily. Teachers who are interested in teaching a common subject could share their lesson plans and research without the need of an education portal. For educators, this quiet, ongoing evolution in networking may indeed offer every teacher in every classroom all of the resources necessary to help students learn.

While grid computing joins together many small and dispersed computing resources and applies them to a single task, another emerging networking environment takes distributed networked computing power and disburses it on a per-use basis to many small tasks. Such a networked environment is called **cloud computing** or simply *the cloud.*

Cloud computing is a networked environment made up of multiple computers, often in different locations, that offers small slices of computing resources on demand to many users.

FIGURE 14.3

Cloud Computing

MobileMe is one example of cloud computing that allows users to access data and resources from any computer connected to the Internet.

Courtesy of Apple Computer.

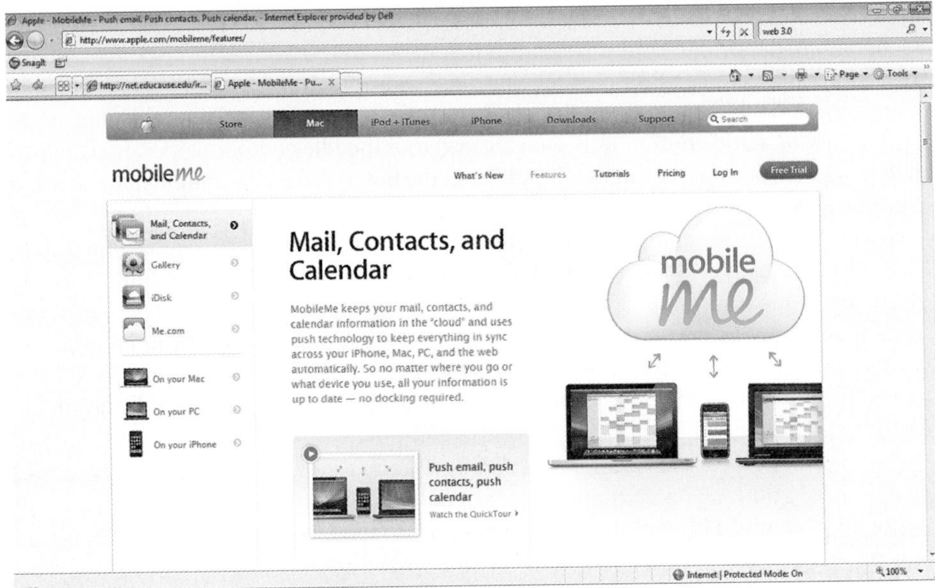

In a cloud, many local or nonlocal computers are linked together, and members of that cloud network use a small slice of the available computing resources to perform their own specific tasks. Cloud applications might be individual tasks that do not require the massive computing capabilities of the networks. Such applications might include image editing, word processing, social networking, data storage, and media creation. A primary example of such a cloud that many people use but few are aware of is Amazon. Amazon has an array of computers harnessed together to create its proprietary cloud, known as the Elastic Compute Cloud (EC2), which Amazon can also lease for many purposes. Other clouds include the Apple version that powers MobileMe, the application that synchronizes information stored on a user's multiple computers from phones to laptops to desktops (Figure 14.3).

For education, cloud computing offers a way to make applications easily and readily available from one source that requires only one point of maintenance and support. Users of the cloud's resources do not care where their applications are housed or even where data are stored, as long as they are available when needed. Resources on the cloud are available from any computer, so it would no longer be necessary to return to your classroom to find a file or print a worksheet. And having the latest computer in your classroom would no longer be necessary to run the software you desire. Any shared computer anywhere with the power to connect to the cloud would give you the capabilities you need. Wherever you had access to the cloud, you would have access to the cloud's applications and your personal resources. Combine this potential with that of increased mobile computing, and the educational opportunities are boundless. The trend toward cloud computing that is emerging today is very likely to change the way in which districts and schools make computing available to teachers and students.

Interactive Displays

Interactive multitouch displays integrate touch technology with geomapping and gesture recognition to make maps come alive for kinesthetic students.

During the 2008 presidential elections, news organizations used interactive hardware to display voting maps and examine the possible allocation of electoral college votes. Operated through a unique interactive touch screen technology, newscasters were able to select, zoom in, and change views with the movement of their hand or touch of a finger. This technology, featuring interactive displays and multitouch technology, has

Courtesy of TouchTable, Inc. Used by permission.

Touchable displays make interacting with maps and geoimages a kinesthetic experience.

also been used by government to display and deploy armed forces and using satellite imagery and geomapping capabilities, to examine the terrain of any location in the world. Using advance touch screen and gesture recognition technology combined with multimedia displays, interactive display hardware offers a new level of human–computer interaction.

The emergence of interactive displays opens many possibilities for education. Clearly, this technology combined with geomapping makes teaching and learning in various areas of the social studies a true kinesthetic experience. For science, interactive multitouch displays make it possible to manipulate the real world in ways that were previously only conceptualized. Still too pricey for most K–12 schools, this emerging technology holds great promise as its cost declines.

Static Displays

Flexible and wearable displays expand the possible ways in which we can view and interact with the data output from our computers.

Another area of emerging technologies that holds significance for education is in display devices. Flat-panel LCD monitors are primitive in comparison to displays currently under development. The new prototypes use flexible plastic film that can be rolled up or laid flat on a desktop to display computer data. Though still in the prototype stage, two of these technologies bear mentioning.

Flexible organic light-emitting devices (**FOLEDs**) are computer displays on flexible plastic that have the potential to be made small enough to roll up into a pen or large enough to be used as a wall-size mural (Figure 14.4) and will be able to be bent or folded without harm. These capabilities give them the potential to expand beyond the limits of current monitors and ultimately to become wearable computer displays, folded electronic newspapers, or displays that can be embedded in other devices, such as car windshields. These devices also offer better viewing, are less expensive to make, and are less power-hungry than LCD screens, in addition to being flexible. For the classroom, paper-size FOLEDs may become portable monitors that can be opened and laid flat on a student's desk or moved easily about the classroom and the school while staying connected to a CPU via wireless technology. Wall-size FOLEDs could potentially replace costly projection devices. Educational uses and applications for this emerging display technology have only begun to be projected. Clearly, as this technology evolves, edu-

FIGURE 14.4

Flexible display and electronic ink prototypes have the potential to change the way we display and interact with computer data in the classroom.

Courtesy of LG Display

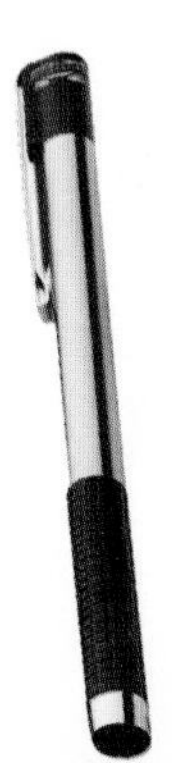

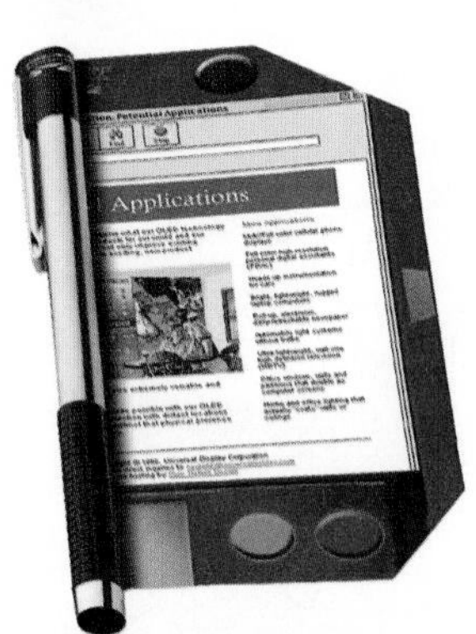

Microsoft product shot reprinted with permission from Microsoft Corporation.

Courtesy of Philips

cators will embrace its flexibility and potential to unclutter the technology-rich learning space.

A second, related display is **electronic paper.** Electronic paper is a sheet of transparent film containing millions of black-and-white beads of ink. When a current is applied, the beads rotate, showing either their black or white side, thus creating an image on the film. The image can remain or be repeatedly refreshed with new data, depending on the current applied. The data can be text, graphics, or even video. Both writable and erasable, a single sheet of electronic paper is capable of displaying an electronic newspaper or the pages of a multimedia textbook. With information stored on a chip or other portable device and a sheet of electronic paper powered by a battery, an entire library could be carried and viewed anywhere. Although thus far they have been marketed primarily as refreshable displays in stores, newer prototypes of electronic paper hold the promise of changing how and when the printed page might be used in the classroom. With the potential of providing all of a student's class textbooks while at the same time making the contents of the entire school library available to the student via a single sheet of electronic paper, the possibilities for the application of this technology to education are almost limitless.

Wearable Computers

An emerging technology that is still in its infancy is wearable computers. The future vision for such devices includes computing power built into clothing or devices small enough to pin to clothing or hang around the neck (Figure 14.5). Such devices would offer users enhanced information about the environment, reminders, and data on demand that might be useful within the context of activities. In education, wearable computers are being introduced for special simulation projects. One such project, sponsored by the Massachusetts Institute of Technology, has students study the spread of viruses by having them interact while wearing small computers that can communicate both data and a hypothetical virus. Thus, interacting students can simulate how viruses are spread within a healthy system. While wearable computers so small that they can be integrated into clothing are not yet possible, early applications of the concept include advanced displays built into helmets for use in the military and, in education, miniaturized computers used to assist special needs students. This earliest phase of this emerging technology may seem like science fiction now; but with the rate of current advancements in computing, wearable computers may well be reality before the next generation of teachers retires from service.

Convergence

Convergence refers to the blending of technologies into a single multipurpose technology. Such a technology would include the functions of television, radio, cell phone, music and multimedia player, GPS, email, and computer blended into a single pocket device. Convergence of many of these technologies is happening now. Cell phones such as the iPhone and Palm can send and receive email, have multimedia capabilities, and offer thousands of applications. This trend is likely to continue until the lines between all these technologies have blurred to the point of invisibility.

Converging technologies are blending into a single multipurpose technology.

For schools, convergence will mean being able to pull limited resources away from acquiring many types of technologies and to focus instead on buying more of the multipurpose convergent technologies for teachers and learners. It will also mean less time and fewer resources spent training to use diverse equipment and more time for mastering the skills necessary to make the most of convergent equipment. As technologies continue to converge, educational planning and implementation are likely to become less complex and more coordinated in scope and purpose.

Tsugufumi Matsumoto/AP Images

FIGURE 14.5

Wearable Computers

Wearable computers in every shape, size, and format make computing mobility a reality.

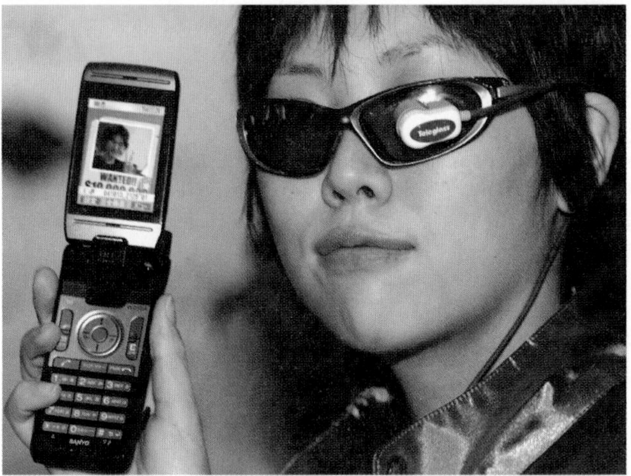

Katsumi Kasahora/AP Images

Emerging Issues: The Changing Face of Instruction in the Digital Age

With so much technological change occurring so rapidly, the future look and feel of technology are difficult to predict. Clearly, some emerging trends, such as those we have discussed, are evident, but others have yet to become apparent even to the most astute observer. In fact, the only thing that is constant about technology is that it is in a constant state of change. How do all of these changes affect education in planning for technology today, and how are they likely to affect education in looking ahead?

Computers as Appliances

As you learned earlier in this chapter, the digital divide does exist; but as a result of many initiatives, it is most likely closing. Eventually, the computer, regardless of the shape into which it evolves, will be as commonplace in households as the television or the telephone is today. It is already becoming an essential appliance that this and future generations will not be able to imagine living without. As this change occurs, schools will no longer be able to lag behind societal change. Classrooms will no longer be acceptable if they include primarily the instructional tools of fifty years ago. Instead, societal pressure will ultimately force change and demand that schools reflect the realities of today's Digital Age.

In the emerging Digital Age schools, e-readers will be as common as backpacks, with every student responsible for bringing his or her own to every class. Table PCs or their future equivalent may well replace books and paper and pencil. Students might simply download the required e-text, complete their work on their digital devices using voice or handwriting recognition software, and then send the work to their teacher's email account.

In a scenario in which computers are as commonplace and indispensable as the whiteboard, students will need training in how to use future technologies for academic pursuits. Teachers will need to learn how to design lessons using such tools. Privacy and security issues will continue to challenge the technical staff as these new technologies proliferate. Schools and districts will need to determine appropriate policies and add or train staff to support both technologies and procedures.

In such an environment, instruction will be able to be highly individualized as teachers will be able to download intelligent agents to guide students through lessons developed to meet their particular learning needs. Entire schools and tutoring services may be accessible via VR environments such as Second Life. Assessment and evaluation of student progress will be able to be gathered electronically and shared appropriately to determine performance. The teaching and learning process will be able to be customized and then evaluated for effectiveness. When the application of educational technology reaches the societal saturation point of the cell phone, teachers will have the ultimate teaching tool at their fingertips.

Computer Literacy

Each year, more and more children become computer literate in the elementary grades. Indeed, the NETS for Students (see Appendix A) already identify levels of technology literacy expected today. For people who have already completed school, lifelong learning opportunities via higher education and community schools will make it possible for more and more adults to achieve **computer literacy.** As the Digital Age unfolds, using a computer will become as essential a skill as reading.

Computer literacy will be as essential a skill as reading.

For educators, this change will mean that it will no longer be necessary to spend time or resources catching up students who missed learning about computers in their public elementary school years. In years to come, teachers will be able to expect computer literacy just as they expect students to read and write. This will make it easier for teachers to more easily integrate computer-enhanced instruction into the instructional design of their courses. At the same time, it will challenge teachers to maintain and improve their own levels of educational technology literacy to effectively use these powerful tools.

Teachers will have become computer literate either through preservice training or, eventually, through their own K–12 school experience. Expanded educational technology and computer literacy will allow courses like this one and in-service workshops to focus on integration skills rather than introductory skills. With teachers working at higher levels of technology integration competencies, the quality of technology-enhanced teaching and learning will no doubt improve.

Decentralizing Instruction

Perhaps the greatest change that may occur will not be in the equipment or the skill level of those who use technology. The most significant change may well be in the nature of instruction itself. As you have learned, distance delivery and alternative delivery already have the potential to redefine instruction. Classrooms that are now set within the framework of a given time and located in a particular place may expand to include virtual communities of learners located anywhere in the world. Virtual learning communities and environments may take students anywhere they wish to learn and at any time they wish to learn. Master teachers may join together from anywhere in the world to team-teach in their particular areas of expertise. Powerful communities of learners may assemble anytime, anyplace, and engage learners from anywhere.

Under such altered circumstances, will schools as we know them today survive? The answer is most likely yes, although schools must be prepared to fully evolve into institutions that prepare children for lives that will be lived in the Digital Age. Classrooms may ultimately look quite different from their twentieth-century counterparts, but they will no doubt provide enriched learning environments where children can share and grow into their potential. Schools may no longer be so isolated from one another. Like stand-alone computers that are networked together and become more powerful because of it, the term *school* may come to refer to a network of educational opportunities, both physical and virtual, for learners. And teachers, like their classrooms, will need to change to embrace the Digital Age and use its resources to help students learn.

The definition of schools may change as the Digital Age unfolds.

PEARSON myeducationkit™

To check your comprehension of the content covered in this chapter, go to the MyEducationKit for your book and complete the *Study Plan* for Chapter 14.

AP Images

Computers in the classroom will continue to be a ubiquitous tool for both teachers and learners.

The Changing Role of the Teacher

Some people believe that with so many coming changes, teachers will become obsolete. That is not the case. The technologies of the Digital Age can support instruction, but teachers will continue to have the central role in designing it, just as they do today. Of course, a Digital Age instructional design with so much capacity for individualization might look quite different from contemporary curriculum, but the educator behind it will never be obsolete.

Teachers may find themselves in a new, more challenging role. Rather than directing instruction in a single classroom setting, teachers will facilitate learning by creating optimal instructional experiences and then assisting their students through these. Furthermore, the same technology that supports worldwide student interaction will support professional interaction among educators. Teachers will not be isolated in their classrooms but will instead become part of a collegial network that is focused on high-quality educational practices. With the help of virtual teaching communities and with the ever-expanding resources available through technology, students will be better served than was ever before thought possible.

Your role in teaching will most likely change over the course of your professional career. Technology will play a large role in instigating changes in both our society in general and education in particular. Knowledge of educational technology will enable you to anticipate and adjust to the changes to come in this Digital Age. It will also help you to become an educational professional who is empowered by extraordinary technological tools that you can harness to help your students succeed. The tools are there for you, and your students are waiting. You need only pick up the tools and use them to build the powerful, technology-rich learning environments your students need and deserve.

Teachers will never be obsolete, although their roles may alter.

Key Terms

artificial intelligence (AI), 374
cloud computing, 377
collective intelligence, 375
computer literacy, 383
convergence, 381
data mashups, 374
electronic paper, 381
expert systems, 374
FOLED, 379
fuzzy logic software, 374
intelligent agents, 374
neural network, 374
peer-to-peer networking, 377
personal web, 375
semantic web, 375
virtual environments, 371
Web 3.0, 376
WiMax, 370
wireless networking, 369

Student Activities

CHAPTER REVIEW

1. What is the difference between WiFi and WiMax? How might each affect schools?
2. How might virtual environments enhance teaching and learning?
3. How could virtual technologies such as Second Life and the interactive experience possible with Wii alter teaching and learning?
4. What is artificial intelligence? How might intelligent agents assist teachers and learners?
5. What expanding and/or emerging technologies will affect the way in which people collaborate? Give an example of how one such technology might be used in a classroom experience.
6. What is the personal web? How does it differ from the World Wide Web that we know today?
7. How might the semantic web change the way in which people find answers to their questions?
8. How do grid computing and cloud computing differ? What impact might they have on education?
9. What display devices are emerging that may have significant impact on the classroom? Briefly describe each.
10. What is computing mobility? Describe the convergence it has begun. How will it change education?

WHAT DO YOU THINK?

1. As emerging technologies continue to affect education, there is little question that the role of the teacher will change. Imagine yourself teaching a class in the technological future. How do you think your role would be different from the typical teacher's role today?
2. The web is changing, becoming more responsive, more collaborative, and more personal in addressing the needs of the user. This will in turn change how teachers will use the web as they continue to try to ensure that individualized instruction that addresses the unique needs of the learner remains at the forefront. How do you think the emerging web will alter how you might use this resource in your classroom? Give at least three concrete examples. Be prepared to share your views and your examples with your peers.
3. Of the emerging technology trends presented in the chapter or those you discovered through your research on the Web, which emerging technology or trend do you think will have the most significant impact on education? Be prepared to share your views with your peers.

LEARNING TOGETHER!

These activities are best done in groups of three to five.

1. Determining how educational technology will evolve and emerge is a difficult task. In a group of peers, each person should select one technology futurist and research that person's views on the changes he or she expects to happen in the next five years. Summarize your findings by creating a future timeline that includes the key technologies they believe will emerge. Be prepared to share your timeline with the class, along with an example of how each of the emerging technologies you identified might affect education.
2. Educators must be prepared to learn about and integrate the technologies that are evolving and emerging into their classrooms. Ask each member of your group to interview a teacher or administrator at the grade level he or she plans to teach. Ask the interviewee what he or she is doing to stay abreast of the technologies available today. Follow up with a description of some of the emerging technologies mentioned in this chapter, and ask how he or she might learn to use them and incorporate them into his or her own classroom. Compare your interviews, and be prepared to share them with the class.
3. There are many technological trends that promise to have great impact in education. Ask each member of the group to select the one technology of greatest interest to him or her. After researching your technology of choice, as a group determine what the classroom of tomorrow would look like if it included the technologies you found. How would instruction differ as a result of integrating these technologies? Summarize the key features of your futuristic classroom, and be prepare to explain the technologies and their use with the class.

TEACHING WITH TECHNOLOGY: INTEGRATION IDEAS WEB QUEST

As you consider the trends associated with evolving and emerging educational technologies that are becoming or soon to become available for teachers' use in their classrooms, it is useful to examine how those trends are likely to affect education. Let's take a look at some specific, innovative ways in which educators are using the evolving technology available to them to teach their content.

ACTIVITY: Explore the links below that interest you, and then select an evolving or emerging educational technology you have learned about in this chapter or that you have discovered during your research on the Net. Complete a web search to discover how this technology could be used in at least three content areas you might want to teach. Write a one-page summary of your web quest that includes (1) a description of the technology you research and the link you found most helpful in learning about it, (2) a description of the ways you found online as to how this technology might be implemented including the links you used to find these implementation ideas, and (3) an idea of your own about how you might teach with the technology you selected in your own classroom.

Integrating Emerging Technology into Social Studies

Recognizing the increasing economic impracticability of taking students on traditional field trips, teachers such as Scott Mandel of Pacoma Middle School in Los Angeles, California, are making virtual field trips with little or no expense incurred to destinations that were never possible for the traditional field trip. Mr. Mandel took his ancient civilizations class on a virtual field trip to the British Museum, where the students viewed and interacted with exhibitions that featured Egyptian mummies and ancient treasures, by accessing the Museum's web galleries and taking part in video tours. The students were even able to play a 2,000-year-old game that once was enjoyed by children in North Africa. Mr. Mandel observed that virtual field trips are not limited to museums but encompass distant geographic locations, simulated space travel, and scientific experiments conducted in laboratories worldwide. Learn more at **http://www.edweek.org//ew/articles/2009/02/11/21virtualtrip.h28.html+destination=http://www.edweek.org/ew/articles/2009/02/11/21virtualtrip.h28html+levelid=2100.**

Integrating Emerging Technology into the Elementary Classroom

Robotics is not a new technology in the classroom, but the emergence of minirobots is enticing teachers to introduce innovative robotic strategies into their lessons in the elementary schools. Stella De Michele, an elementary school teacher with no experience using robots in the classroom, found the Bee-Bot, a large, programmable bee that responds to commands to move forward, backward, make turns, start, and delete by having buttons on its back pushed, to be a fascinating teaching tool in her second-grade classroom. She placed the Bee-Bot on a classroom windowsill and asked the children why this unusual bee was there. The children speculated widely before introducing themselves to the bee and giving it a nickname, Maya. They were allowed to explore how Maya would move when the buttons were pushed. Learning that occurred as the children continued to experiment with Maya encompassed decision making to determine what to do to make Maya move as they wanted her to and how to adjust the button-pushing if she didn't. The concept of measure was the next educational topic taught when the children figured out how far Maya had gone when she had been moving for a while. They used conventional tools such as a ruler to find how far Maya traveled at each step. How this information stimulated children to think became apparent when a child suggested different arithmetic operations: adding the length of one step to previous steps and multiplying how many steps were taken times the space covered by just one step. Other skills that the children learned with the help of Maya, the Bee-Bot, were how to count and think logically, how to solve topological problems, how to learn through solving problems, and how to learn with inquiry-based teaching strategies. Check out this fascinating experience at **http://monicareggiani.net/Simpar2008/TeachingWithRobotics/MicheleDemoSiega.pdf.**

Integrating Emerging Technology into Language Arts

Kindergartners in Melanie Coffett's class at Highland Elementary School in Rifle, Colorado, enjoy learning while using ten iPods that hold Success for All materials, the school's reading program. Sixth-grade gifted and talented students helped Ms. Coffett with the preparation of the iPods by loading them to deliver instruction in letter recognition and letter sounds. The sixth-graders took part in a full term's training and preparation program that found them using the program GarageBand to create the podcasts. Videos and iMovie were also used to further the visual appeal of the podcasts. The kindergartners can create their own recordings. The children can replay the recordings as often as necessary to achieve fluency. With the addition of headphones available to the children, distracting external sounds can be eliminated. All the equipment is available to the kindergarten class to check out and take home for extended learning. Find out more at **http://www.citizentelegram.com/article/20093019/NEWS/903189968+parentprofile=search.**

Integrating Emerging Technology into Mathematics

Julie Hudson, a professor at Vanderbilt University in Nashville, Tennessee, addressed the problem of long, nonproductive hours that students spend riding on school buses, especially students who live in remote rural areas, by launching in 2007 a mobile virtual classroom program, the Aspirnaut Initiative. It turns school buses into learning environments. The STEM subjects—science, technology, engineering, and mathematics—are taught through this medium. The students are given laptop computers, iPods, and headphones that tune out distracting sounds made by students on the bus who are not in the program. The Aspirnauts, as they are called, use this technology to carry out coursework delivered as distance education on their laptops and iPods while they make the long trips to and from school on school buses. Working in conjunction with professors of math and science at Vanderbilt, the students meet face to face with these professionals through weekend and summer visits to the campus. For more information about this program, go to **http://www.arkansasnews.com/archive/2008/09/28/News/348094.html.**

Integrating Emerging Technology into Literature

Retired english teacher Jerome Burg created **GoogleLitTrips.Com,** which allows students to explore the world's great literature as characters traveling through the places where the stories occurred. With the 3D capability of Google Earth, teachers can see the locale and even manipulate it visually. Seeing these locations through the eyes of the characters adds a dimension to the literary experience that was impossible before the existence of this software. Mr. Burg notes in his blog that letters from teachers indicate that students develop a deeper understanding of the plight of the characters as they explore the physical space in which their difficulties take place. For more information about integrating Google Earth into the classroom, visit the Google Teacher Academy at **http://www.google.com/educators/gta.html.**

interchapter 14

NETS•T Self-Assessment

Teachers are expected to meet the NETS•T standards. During this educational technology course, you have learned much to help you to meet them. It is useful to take the time to self-assess and determine your levels relative to the standards and consider what you can do to meet them if you have not already done so.

Use the rating scale below to determine your achievement level. If you score less than a 3 on any standard, note in the space provided what components of the standards you feel you have not met and what strategies you will employ to achieve full competency.

1—No parts met *2—Some parts met* *3—All parts minimally met* *4—All parts met* *5—All parts met with competence*

STANDARD	RATING	MISSING COMPONENTS/ STRATEGIES TO ACHIEVE THIS PERFORMANCE STANDARD
1. Facilitate and Inspire Student Learning and Creativity Teachers use their knowledge of subject matter, teaching and learning, and technology to facilitate experiences that advance student learning, creativity, and innovation in both face-to-face and virtual environments. Teachers:		
a. promote, support, and model creative and innovative thinking and inventiveness		
b. engage students in exploring real-world issues and solving authentic problems using digital tools and resources		
c. promote student reflection using collaborative tools to reveal and clarify students' conceptual understanding and thinking, planning, and creative processes		
d. model collaborative knowledge construction by engaging in learning with students, colleagues, and others in face-to-face and virtual environments		
2. Design and Develop Digital-Age Learning Experiences and Assessments Teachers design, develop, and evaluate authentic learning experiences and assessments incorporating contemporary tools and resources to maximize content learning in context and to develop the knowledge, skills, and attitudes identified in the NETS•S. Teachers:		
a. design or adapt relevant learning experiences that incorporate digital tools and resources to promote student learning and creativity		
b. develop technology-enriched learning environments that enable all students to pursue their individual curiosities and become active participants in setting their own educational goals, managing their own learning, and assessing their own progress		
c. customize and personalize learning activities to address students' diverse learning styles, working strategies, and abilities using digital tools and resources		
d. provide students with multiple and varied formative and summative assessments aligned with content and technology standards and use resulting data to inform learning and teaching		
3. Model Digital-Age Work and Learning Teachers exhibit knowledge, skills, and work processes representative of an innovative professional in a global and digital society. Teachers:		
a. demonstrate fluency in technology systems and the transfer of current knowledge to new technologies and situations		
b. collaborate with students, peers, parents, and community members using digital tools and resources to support student success and innovation		

1—No parts met *2—Some parts met* *3—All parts minimally met* *4—All parts met* *5—All parts met with competence*

STANDARD	RATING	MISSING COMPONENTS/ STRATEGIES TO ACHIEVE THIS PERFORMANCE STANDARD
c. communicate relevant information and ideas effectively to students, parents, and peers using a variety of Digital Age media and formats		
d. model and facilitate effective use of current and emerging digital tools to locate, analyze, evaluate, and use information resources to support research and learning		
4. Promote and Model Digital Citizenship and Responsibility Teachers understand local and global societal issues and responsibilities in an evolving digital culture and exhibit legal and ethical behavior in their professional practices. Teachers:		
a. advocate, model, and teach safe, legal, and ethical use of digital information and technology, including respect for copyright, intellectual property, and the appropriate documentation of sources		
b. address the diverse needs of all learners by using learner-centered strategies and providing equitable access to appropriate digital tools and resources		
c. promote and model digital etiquette and responsible social interactions related to the use of technology and information		
d. develop and model cultural understanding and global awareness by engaging with colleagues and students of other cultures using Digital Age communication and collaboration tools		
5. Engage in Professional Growth and Leadership Teachers continuously improve their professional practice, model lifelong learning, and exhibit leadership in their school and professional community by promoting and demonstrating the effective use of digital tools and resources. Teachers:		
a. participate in local and global learning communities to explore creative applications of technology to improve student learning		
b. exhibit leadership by demonstrating a vision of technology infusion, participating in shared decision making and community building, and developing the leadership and technology skills of others		
c. evaluate and reflect on current research and professional practice on a regular basis to make effective use of existing and emerging digital tools and resources in support of student learning		
d. contribute to the effectiveness, vitality, and self-renewal of the teaching profession and of their school and community		

GLOSSARY

academic dishonesty Cheating and/or plagiarizing in academic work that may be facilitated by the ease of copying and pasting information from web sites or multimedia.

academic software Software designed to assist and support both educators and learners in teaching and learning.

academic tools On a computer network, academic software that provides the teacher with tools to help in the instructional process; for example, the ability to monitor student activities on each networked computer, including the ability to take control of individual computers to demonstrate a process.

acceptable use The school or district policies to help ensure that school technology made available to students is used appropriately and for academic purposes.

Acrobat Reader A free application available online that enables reading files saved in PDF.

action plan The plan listing the specific action steps that describe how each of the plan's strategies will be accomplished.

ADA (Americans with Disabilities Act) Legislation Section 508 addresses electronic and information technology. Schools must ensure that information presented electronically is accessible to people with disabilities.

administrative software Software that assists educators in accomplishing the administrative, professional, and management tasks associated with their profession.

administrative software/tools Software programs that are shared by all network users and usually provide, at a minimum, a common calendar, address book, and facilities reservation list. Also called groupware.

administrators Members of the teaching profession who maintain the day-to-day organizational, curricular, resource, and financial management of schools and other educational institutions.

Adobe Acrobat An application that creates and saves files in PDF format so they can be later read using Acrobat Reader, a free application available online, to display them.

alternative and augmentive communication Devices that give voice to students who cannot speak. They range from simple and inexpensive to complex and very costly.

antiplagiarism software Software that compares a student's work with well-known authors' work and with work posted on the web to detect plagiarism.

antivirus program Programs that detect and disable or destroy computer viruses.

application program A set of instructions that tell a computer how to complete a unique task such as word processing, database management, or drawing.

archiving The ability to save a file for later use.

artificial intelligence (AI) Programs that work in manners that are similar to the way the human brain works, allowing computers to adapt and respond beyond their initial programming.

assistive listening devices (ALDs) Devices that support students with hearing difficulty to clearly hear their teachers and classroom discussions.

assistive technology Hardware and software that is designed or can be used to support the needs of exceptional students.

Association for Educational Communications and Technology (AECT) A professional association of thousands of educators and others whose activities are directed toward improving instruction through technology.

asynchronous A method of instructional or information delivery that is time shifted; that is, teacher and students can participate at differing times from the same or different locations. Another example is email or voice mail; you send it now, the recipient accesses it later at his or her convenience.

asynchronous communications Online tools or communications methods that do not require real-time interaction; examples are email, electronic bulletin boards, and voice mail.

attention Focusing on a specific object or thought sufficiently to become fully aware of it.

audiocassette An economical, durable, and easy-to-use magnetic tape medium that lets you record, and re-record, voice, music, or other sounds.

augmentive communication (see alternative and augmentive communication)

authoring system A category of software that allows the educator to easily create custom computer-enhanced lessons of all types, including multimedia lessons and web-based lessons.

AUP (see acceptable use)

AVI (Audio Video Interleaved) A popular digital video format that offers low resolution and smaller file sizes compared to other formats; good for animation.

back up To create a duplicate copy on another storage medium for use in case the original copy is lost.

backup system A system of redundant processes and technologies that provide for continuity of instructional delivery even when problems occur in the primary delivery system.

bandwidth The carrying capacity (size of the "roadway") of electronic transmission media for sending and receiving information, which translates to the speed at which the network can transmit data.

behaviorists Those who view all behavior as a response to external stimuli; they believe that the learner acquires behaviors, skills, and knowledge in response to the rewards, punishments, or withheld responses associated with them.

blogs Virtual online spaces that support posting of personal commentary that can be shared with others. They are primarily one-way communications, but can offer readers the ability to respond and comment or even post links to their own blog or another place.

Bluetooth A wireless technology used to connect over short distances used mostly to connect cell phones to hands-free devices like headphones.

Bloom's taxonomy A method for categorizing differences in thinking skills; it includes six levels of cognition ranging from recall of knowledge to evaluation of knowledge.

bookmarks A function that is built into Internet browsers which allows the user to create a collection of URL favorites. Once a web site is stored, it can be revisited later by simply locating it on the list of favorites and clicking on it.

Boolean logic A type of logic that uses operators, such as AND, OR, or NOT, to limit or expand the scope of a search such as one would do on the Internet using a search engine.

booting up The process of powering on a computer during which it reads the instructions stored in ROM to tell it how to start itself up.

broadcast audio Audio that is transmitted and received via radio and the Internet.

broadcast video Video that is broadcast via terrestrial equipment or by a combination of terrestrial and satellite equipment. Commonly thought of as television, signals can be received over the air, through cable or phone lines, or over the Internet.

bulletin board A surface usually made of cork that provides a flexible, easy-to-change display area for a variety of print and graphic elements.

byte Eight bits (on-off pulses) of data, roughly equal to one alphabetic (A) or numeric (1) character of information.

cable modem A type of modem that provides high-speed connections for digital access via cable lines that are also used for cable television. Users can get speeds up to 100 to 1,000 times faster than a standard modem on a telephone line, or 3 to 4 times faster than DSL. However there are variables that impact speed, and speed between the faster options may not be noticed by the average user.

cablecast video Video that is transmitted by a cable company via coaxial cable to remote locations.

camcorder A compact video device that includes a camera and recorder; used to record sound and images that can be played back by devices such as a VCR.

CAST (Center for Applied Special Technology) Organization that has designed specific guidelines for ensuring that educators address the diversity they will find in their classrooms.

CD (compact disc, also CD-ROM) An optical media that stores digital data via tiny holes burned into the disc surface with a laser.

CD-R (compact disc-recordable) A type of compact disc on which the user can record (write) data. Once recorded, the data cannot be changed. Each disc is capable of storing approximately 600 megabytes of data (text, sound, graphics, animation, or video).

CD-ROM (compact disc, read-only memory) An optical storage device on which data are stored and read via optical technology. CD-ROMs are written on when created, can be read many times, but the original data cannot be changed.

CD-RW (compact disc–rewritable) A type of compact disc that allows the user to record many times and to change the data stored on the CD. Each disc is capable of storing approximately 600 megabytes of data (text, sound, graphics, animation, and/or video).

chat A network or online service that sets aside a virtual space in which two or more users can meet in real time by typing their messages and then sending them for display in the chat room.

Children's Online Privacy Protection Act (see COPPA)

Children's Internet Protection Act (see CIPA)

chip A small square of highly refined silicon on which miniaturized electronic circuits have been embedded. Chips can be designed to serve many different purposes, from memory to CPU chips, such as Intel's Pentium IV microprocessor.

Children's Internet Protection Act (CIPA) Goes a step further than the COPPA legislation and requires that libraries in schools and for public use establish and enforce policies to protect children.

classroom management support software Off-the-shelf or customized software written for educators to help them manage school and classroom tasks, including the creation and maintenance of seating charts, class rolls, student records, and school budgets.

classroom management tools Downloadable or online tools such as test generators, diagnostic tests, and class roll generators that assist you in the tasks required for your classroom.

clip art A term from the days of manual page layout but now refers to collections of prepared artwork in digital/electronic form that can be inserted into electronic documents.

closed-circuit TV (CCTV) A network of television monitors connected via coaxial cables running throughout a school building that can distribute television signals to all the connected classrooms.

cloud computing (see grid computing)

code of ethics For computer use, it's a set of written expectations and definitions of what is considered appropriate or acceptable use that is published by a school or district.

codec A compression/decompression algorithm that is used to digitize and compress video and audio signals for transmission and to reverse the process on reception.

cognitive style How one thinks. Each person has his or her own unique tendencies and preferences when it comes to cognition (thinking).

cognitivists Those who focus on learning as a mental operation that begins when information enters through the senses, undergoes mental manipulation, is stored, and finally used.

collective intelligence The vast knowledge and understanding that emerge from large groups of people gathering, discussing, and collaborating on issues.

command An instruction that the user gives the computer or a program for the next operation to be performed.

communications cycle The interchange of information between two or more individuals, such as the teacher and a student. In the cycle, information is encoded by the sender and decoded by the receiver, with various filters affecting the clarity of the message.

comprehensible input Input in the second language of students (English) that students may be better able to understand. Technology is often underutilized for providing comprehensible input.

compressed video classroom/teleconferencing system An integrated system that includes a video camera and microphone with a codec to compress the signals to transmit them over ISDN phone lines for two-way video and audio communication.

compression technologies Software and hardware that make video files smaller by capturing the initial video image in full but then ignoring the nonchanging components of the image in transmitting the images.

computer literacy The basic skills and knowledge necessary to ensure that individuals can effectively use computers.

computer system The combination of input devices, central processing unit, memory, output devices, and storage devices.

computer-assisted instruction (CAI) A term that was originally applied to drill-and-practice software but is now more broadly used to describe any software that uses the computer to tutor or review content and provide a platform for reasoning with reference to content.

computer-managed instruction (CMI) Software that instructs as well as manages instructional lessons; in addition to reviewing content, it keeps track of student progress with reference to the material.

computing cycle A processing cycle that includes the steps of taking data in, processing them, storing them as necessary, and outputting the finished information to the user.

concept mapping software Software that generates visual, digital "maps" of concepts that depict the outcome of the brainstorming process and the interrelationships between ideas.

conference call A telephone call placed via personal phone services or the school phone system that allows up to eight locations to connect together to support small-group instruction or discussion.

constructivists Those who believe that knowledge is a constructed element resulting from the learning process and that knowledge is unique to the individual who constructs it.

contrast The communication power of a visual as determined by the arrangement and balance of the elements.

convergence The blending of diverse digital technologies into a single multipurpose technology such as a cell phone that can also access the Internet and provide the functions of a handheld computer.

COPPA (Children's Online Privacy Protection Act) Legislation established in 1998 that sets forth rules and restrictions to protect the online privacy of children under the age of 13. Website operators must have a privacy policy that includes minimum standards, and seek verifiable permission of parents for children using the web site.

copyright A form of intellectual property that gives the creator exclusive rights for a period of time. It's also the laws that protect the interests of those who create works, whether text, music, artwork, software, or any other creative product.

Corporation for Public Broadcasting (CPB) A public corporation that manages the acquisition and production of educational programming while PBS (Public Broadcasting System) disseminates the programming via local TV channels.

correspondence course The earliest distance-delivery system, consisting of books and assignments delivered to students via the postal system.

CPU (central processing unit) The "brain" of a computer, incorporated into a single microprocessor chip. Within it, calculations are performed; the flow of information between input, output, and memory is coordinated; and program instructions are transmitted.

custom dictionaries A powerful feature of word prediction software, they can help predict vocabulary specific to a particular writing activity or subject.

customizable keyboard Assistive device, a keyboard that can be configured to individual student's needs.

cyberbullying An incident when the Internet, cell phones, or other device is used to send or post text or images intended to hurt or embarrass another person.

data mashup Data are combined from different sources into a single tool giving users new ways to look at and interact with the available information.

data projection unit A device that combines an LCD unit and a light source, and plugs into a computer to display the computer image in an enlarged format for group viewing.

database management software (DBMS) A software system that can be used to easily and quickly record, organize, access, and extract information electronically from stored data.

decision matrix A chart containing choices to help the individual determine which choice is the one that she or he believes is best.

decompression program Utility software that decompresses files that have been compressed (or zipped) to make them smaller and easier to transmit; once decompressed they can be used.

Design-Plan-Act! (D-P-A) system A comprehensive three-part system that is designed to help maximize the quality of teaching plans. The D-P-A system includes three planning processes: designing the instruction, articulating specific lesson plans, and developing an instructional action plan.

desktop publishing (DTP) software Software that cannot only perform typical word-processing tasks, but also makes extensive and precise adjustments to page displays, such as creating an attractive layout of graphics and text on a page.

differentiated instruction An approach for gifted students that recognizes and targets instruction to the varying abilities found in the same classroom.

digital camera A camera that takes pictures and stores them as digital files rather than photographs on film. Photos are stored in the camera on a memory card or on a disk and can be transferred to a computer for processing or display.

digital divide A descriptive term referring to the gap between those who have ready access to and knowledge of digital technologies and those who do not.

digital media players Major ones are iTunes and QuickTime (Apple), WMP Windows Media Player (Microsoft), RealPlayer (RealNetworks), and VLC (originally developed by Èecole Centrale Paris).

digital projector A computer output device that projects digital images to display onto a projection screen, large monitor, or whiteboard to share with a large group.

digital subscriber line (DSL) A special phone line that provides speeds up to 25 times faster than those possible with a standard phone line. Both voice and digital communications can be provided on a single line, thus eliminating the need to subscribe to two phone lines.

digital video disc (see DVD)

digital video Video signals that are recorded as discrete numerical values that represent the video images.

digital video camera A video camera that captures and stores the video in a digital format that can then be directly manipulated by using a personal computer with digital video editing software.

digital video editing Integrated hardware and software that allow the user to edit images and audio frame by frame.

digitizer An electronic device that converts lines drawn on a special tablet into digital data that can be manipulated on a computer. Sometimes called a graphics tablet.

discussion An asynchronous Internet tool that allows users to communicate with other students or educators in a forum or bulletin board format. Discussions link individuals across geographic boundaries, and provide users with the flexibility of participating in the discussion at a time that is convenient for each individual. For educational purposes, the teacher typically moderates them, with opportunities for everyone to ask questions and post responses.

distance education The delivery of instruction to students who are separated from their teacher by time and/or location.

diverse learners There are many ways students are diverse including culture, ethnic, socioeconomic level, learning styles, and multiple intelligences.

document camera A video camera mounted on a stand that takes and projects an image of whatever is placed on the stand's document table.

downlink A data link by which signals are transmitted from a satellite to a terrestrial system on the ground.

dpi (dots per inch) A measure of resolution in printers and some other output devices.

draw programs Software that provides tools to create digital images; this software is known as object-oriented or vector graphic programs because the graphics are created by layering objects on top of one another.

drill-and-practice software Software that is designed to reinforce previously presented content using a behaviorist format that offers rewards following successful completion of routine exercises.

DVD or DVD-ROM (digital video disc) A laser disc that is similar to a CD-ROM but is designed to hold significantly more information than a CD. Some DVDs can store data on both sides of the disc (unlike the one-sided CD-ROM) and on multiple layers per side. DVDs are also available as DVD-R (recordable) and DVD-RW (rewritable).

dynamic instructional design (DID) model An instructional design model that includes these six phases: know the learners, articulate your objectives, establish the learning environment, identify teaching and learning strategies, identify and select support technologies, and evaluate and revise the design.

e-book (electronic book) A computing device designed to download books from the Internet, and store and display electronic versions of them. These devices usually include multimedia features as well as the ability to enhance or expand on linked text within the book.

editing software Software that provides the user with capabilities to alter, enhance, or add special effects to digital images.

educational games Software that presents and reviews instructional content in a game format.

educational technology Any technology used by educators in support of the teaching and learning process.

educational technology literacy The ability to employ technology to enrich teaching and to enhance student learning; because technology is perpetually changing, it is important that literacy skills be continually updated.

electronic discussions (or electronic forums) Virtual bulletin boards that offer a platform for one-to-many communications.

electronic gradebooks Grading tools that can be used online or downloaded that enable a teacher to store and easily average students' grades.

electronic mail (see email)

electronic paper A sheet of paper with millions of beads of black and white ink. An image is made when an electronic current is applied causing the beads to rotate.

electronic spreadsheet Software that enables the user to organize, input, edit, chart, and produce accurate professional analysis and reports for tasks that deal primarily with numbers.

electronic whiteboards A combination of computer technology with a whiteboard display. They offer a variety of capabilities, many not only displaying information, but also capturing the information written on them as a computer file. A digital projector can project the image on the computer screen onto the board, where it can become a large touch screen to which the computer will respond.

email Electronic messages sent from one computer to another across the many networks attached to the Internet. It's asynchronous communications unless it's done as instant messaging. Messages can include extended attachments enhancing the original message with animated graphics, audio, and compressed video clips in addition to text.

environmental factors Aspects of the learning environment that are external to the learner or teacher, but have an effect on the learning process; physical environmental factors, such as the room temperature, external noise or lighting, can create obstacles for student–teacher communication.

e-rate Also called the Education Rate, a discounted cost for telecommunications service for community access centers (schools, libraries, etc.).

ERIC A national information system that is supported by the U.S. Department of Education, the U.S. Office of Educational Research and Improvement, and the National Library of Education; the world's largest database of education information, with more than one million abstracts of documents and journal articles, many available through the Internet.

evaluation The final component of strategic planning in which the participants plan the processes that will be used to determine whether the plan has been successfully carried out. It is also a method of assessing a student's achievement of stated objectives. In a distance environment, it may include alternative assessments and proctored testing.

expanded keyboards Assistive devices that offer a larger surface area and larger keys than a standard keyboard supporting students who lack fine motor skills.

expert systems Artificial intelligence programs that offer suggestions and advice based on a database of expertise.

fair use A section of the copyright law that identifies the criteria under which you may be allowed to copy another's creative work. Guidelines that describe circumstances under which a teacher can use copyrighted material in face-to-face classroom instruction.

FAQ Abbreviation for the "frequently asked questions" that many web sites include to anticipate the questions that users will have.

Facebook A very popular social networking site that allows participants to post information about themselves and make it available with others who become "friends."

favorites A collection of URLs that have been saved by using a function of the browser, allowing the user to return to a desired web page quickly without having to retype its URL; also known as bookmarks.

fax technology With a combination scanner, modem, and printer that translates hard copy into digital signals, it sends them across communications channels, and then prints them when received by another fax machine. Fax technology is useful for communication of materials in a distance education environment.

feedback Providing another person with information on how well a task was performed or how successful an experience was in order to help improve future performance.

feedback loops Provisions within the instructional design plan to collect evaluative information for two main purposes: The information is used by the learners to see how they are doing so that they can change their approach, and the data are used so that immediate changes can be made to improve the plan.

file A collection of related data, usually a product of a single task that is saved on a storage device.

file transfer protocol (FTP) The application protocol that is used to facilitate the transferring of files between computers on the Internet.

filtering software Software that filters out and blocks unacceptable Internet sites so that students cannot access them.

firewall A combination of software and hardware that provides various levels of security measures designed to keep unauthorized users and computer hackers out of networks and to keep data private and safe.

flat-bed scanner A scanner with a flat glass plate on which the original is placed (allowing the user to scan a page from a book); a cover can then be placed over the back of the original to block ambient light during the scan process.

flip chart A large pad of paper usually mounted on an easel.

floppy disk A nonvolatile, portable magnetic storage device. The standard floppy disk can contain 1.44 megabytes (millions of bytes) of data. They are becoming increasingly rare due to small storage capacity.

focused listening Giving one's full attention to an auditory stimulus.

FOLEDs (flexible organic light-emitting devices) Computer displays on flexible plastic.

folder A digital organizer that is created by the user to hold related files on a disk; may also be known as a directory in non-Windows operating systems.

formative feedback Feedback that ensures a way to facilitate the continuous flow of information as a system is implemented so that corrections and adjustments can be made while the process unfolds.

freedom of speech The ethical issue that may arise when Internet content is regulated such that it may restrict the constitutionally guaranteed right to free speech.

freeware Software that is offered to users without charge.

FTP (file transfer protocol) A protocol used on the Internet for uploading and downloading files.

fuzzy logic software Artificial intelligence software that functions in a manner that resembles human decision making.

GIF (Graphic Interchange Format) A graphics format that is used primarily for color images, clip art, line art, and gray-scale images.

gigabyte Approximately one billion bytes of data or characters of data.

global learning community A community of learners built through the use of communication tools on a classroom web site to connect one classroom to others across the globe.

Google A company that offers Internet search, email, online mapping, social networking, and video sharing. Google has become so popular its name is often used as a verb referring to doing an Internet search, "I'll Google it."

graphic A pictorial image, such as a drawing, cartoon, or diagram that can represent and clarify concepts and relationships.

graphics software Software that enables the user to create, edit, or enhance digital images. It can also include packaged collections of prepared graphics called clip art usually organized into libraries.

graphics tablet An electronic device that converts lines sketched on a special tablet into their digital equivalent on the screen. Sometimes called a digitizer.

grid or cloud computing Similar in concept to the SETI (Search for Extraterrestrial Intelligence) project, computers will join together online to maximize power and share resources and data.

groupware Administrative software tools that are shared by all network users and usually include, at a minimum, a common calendar, address book, and facilities reservation list.

GUI (graphical user interface) Pronounced "gooey," the method of interaction in which the user enters commands or makes selections by using a device such as a mouse or trackball to point to and click on icons displayed on the monitor.

handheld computer (also personal digital assistant [PDA]) Palm-size computer that offers a scaled-down version of PC operating system and applications programs. Most are also Internet capable and offer wireless connectivity to networks.

handshaking The process that occurs when one computer calls another computer and the second computer answers the call and responds with a high-pitched sound known as a carrier signal.

hard copy The printed version of material generated by a computer. It is the most common output of a computer other than what appears on the monitor screen.

hard disk (drive) A disk or platter(s) on which data, operating systems, applications programs, and most personal files are stored. Most hard disks hold gigabytes, or billions of bytes, of data, although some can now hold terabytes, trillions of bytes. They are often housed inside the computer.

hardware Computer hardware includes all of the computer components that are physical, touchable pieces of equipment.

hardware and software specifications Certain minimum requirements from software applications for the program to be able to run on a computer. Includes a specific operating system, and version thereof, processor, memory, hard disk space available, and display type.

HDTV (high definition television) Digital broadcasting of television in higher resolution than traditional television. Can also refer to TVs capable of receiving HD broadcasts.

head pointing systems Assistive devices that can emulate a mouse's movement and are used in conjunction with an onscreen keyboard.

headphones Miniature speakers that are placed directly over the ears. They allow individual students to listen to audio without disturbing others.

hearing The physical process that includes the correct receiving of clear, audible sounds.

high interest, low lever books These are appropriate for students who have not yet mastered the skills to read and understand material written at their grade level.

home page On a web site, a welcome page that orients the visitor to the site and provides a connection to additional information pages.

hub A series of centralized connections for workstations or peripherals so that they can be connected to the network.

hyper text markup language (HTML) The agreed-upon computer language for use on the Internet's World Wide Web sites. Web browsers use this formatting language to determine how the information presented on web pages will look.

hyperlink A graphic or segment of text on a web page that contains instructions to link to another web page or a different web site.

hypermedia software Multimedia software that not only uses multiple media but also organizes information and allows "hyperlinks," in linear or nonlinear sequences, to quickly move to and from different components of the instructional content.

icon A small graphic image that represents one of a GUI's system options that a user can select.

illustration software Software used to create and manipulate digital images, comprised of paint programs and drawing programs.

imaging software Software that creates a digital version of an image from a hard-copy source.

input device A computer peripheral that the user can use to enter data into a computer.

instant messaging (IM) A type of chat software that allows two users to spontaneously open a private two-person chat room when both are online.

instructional action plan (IAP) A template in which the teacher is prompted to list lesson requirements and to detail what he or she will need for successful implementation.

instructional design model A plan of instruction that results in a complete and precise blueprint of what should happen and how to arrange the key critical components necessary to designing effective instruction.

instructional event A learning experience that has been designed by a teacher from specific learning objectives to outcomes with the use of appropriate media to enhance the learner's achievement of the objective.

instructional support Systems to support learners, such as a teacher being present for clarification and questions or a media center or tutoring program for students who need additional help. Because such systems are often absent in distance education, alternative support systems are required in their place.

instructional television (ITV) Local learning channels that use broadcast airwaves to distribute video signals of instructional programs throughout a school and/or district.

Integrated Services Digital Network (ISDN) High-speed digital phone lines that can provide speeds up to 5 times that of regular analog phone lines and can offer both voice and digital communications on a single line.

integrated software package A collection of the main features of popular applications integrated into a single comprehensive application. An example is Microsoft's Microsoft Works or Apple's iWork.

intelligence The inherent capability of a learner to understand and learn.

intelligence quotient (IQ) A quantitative measurement of the inherited capability of the learner to understand and learn. A commonly used measure is the Stanford-Binet, which is typically given to students several times during their academic careers.

intelligent agents Subprograms used by artificial intelligence systems to help with specific tasks such as asking questions, monitoring work to determine patterns of action, and performing requested tasks.

interactive displays Large screen displays that use advanced touch screen and gesture recognition technology.

interface The component of an operating system that establishes the methods of interaction (via menus, text, and/or graphics) between the user and the machine.

International Society for Technology in Education (ISTE) A nonprofit professional organization dedicated to promoting appropriate uses of information technology to support and improve teaching and learning.

Internet An electronic communications network of networks that connects millions of computers and organizational computer facilities around the world with a standardized means of communication called Internet protocols (IPs).

Internet audio Audio, usually digitized as a WAV or MP3 file that is delivered to the user over the Internet.

Internet broadcast The broadcasting of live events and performances over the Internet, using streaming video technology that compresses digital video and plays it back while it is being received.

Internet chat A synchronous communication in which two or more people online at the same time communicate, typically via typed messages in a virtual space.

Internet Explorer (or Windows Internet Explorer) The name of the web browser provided by Microsoft with the Windows operating system. Often referred to simply as IE, it was formerly named Microsoft Internet Explorer, or MSIE.

Internet meeting An Internet-based "face-to-face" conversation with people around the world via compressed video.

Internet radio Online radio stations consisting of a wide variety of programming, including music, sports, science, and local, national, and world news broadcast over the Internet.

Internet service provider (ISP) A company that provides home and business computers with a way to temporarily connect to the Internet usually for a fee, usually monthly.

Internet video Online video consisting of a wide variety of programming, including music, sports, science, and local, national, and world news broadcast over the Internet. Can be live or prerecorded, professional (network television) or amateur (YouTube).

JPEG (Joint Photographic Experts Group) The agreed-upon standard for high-resolution images; pronounced "jay-peg."

keyboard The primary input device for a computer. A typical computer keyboard is laid out much like the keys on the typewriter but with several additional keys that are used to control the computer or give software commands.

keyboard labels A low-tech assistive device that is self-adhesive and can be added to a regular keyboard. They can give keys larger letters and higher contrast, and blank labels can simplify a keyboard by covering nonessential keys.

keyguards Low-tech assistive devices that are acrylic or metal covers with holes for each key that are placed on a keyboard. They increase typing accuracy by allowing only one key at a time to be pressed.

keypal Students who use email to communicate socially or to share assignments using computers.

kilobyte Approximately 1,000 bytes or 1,000 characters of data.

LAN (see local area network)

LCD (liquid crystal display) A display screen made of two sheets of a flexible polarizing material with a layer of liquid crystal solution between the two.

learning environment The instructional climate in which the student is expected to learn. It includes all aspects of the environment from the physical to the nonphysical.

learning management system (LMS) A bundled resource tool that schools purchase to create fully integrated online classrooms.

learning strategies The way in which instruction is presented to the learner determines how the learner can process the information. Providing for active learning activities is an example of the use of an effective learning strategy.

learning style Those conditions under which an individual best learns. The most common learning style theory identifies three primary modalities for learning: auditory, visual, and kinesthetic.

lesson plan/planner/planning A detailed guide to creating a daily or weekly lesson plan. It is the pragmatic product of the instructional design process.

lifelong learner/learning The willingness to sustain intellectual curiosity across the life cycle.

link A connection to another point on the web, either on the same document, on a different page of the site, or on another web site altogether.

liquid crystal display (LCD) projection A clear display screen with liquid crystals that can be activated by an electrical current to form letters, numbers, and visual images. The panel is connected to the computer and placed on an overhead projector so that the projector's light shines through the panel's glass and projects the computer image onto a screen.

listening Being able to hear and comprehend auditory stimuli involving several steps: (1) actually hearing the auditory stimulus, (2) the brain turning that stimulus into neural pulses and processing them, and (3) making the appropriate cognitive connections to relate this new information to memories of real events or previously learned content.

live cam A digital video camera that is connected to a computer, which in turn is connected to the Internet so that the digital images from the camera can be seen by those connecting to the live cam web site. Can range from a serious purpose like traffic cams to lighthearted ones, like a goldfish bowl or puppy cam.

local area network (LAN) Small networks that connect computers in local areas, such as a classroom or school.

Mac OS The operating system used on Apple computers that tells the computer how to work. It interfaces with the user primarily as a graphical user interface but also includes typed-in (text) commands, choices from preset menus, and icons.

macro A prerecorded set of commands that automate a complex task for a word processing, spreadsheet or other program to simplify a task such as formatting output to fit on labels.

magnetic board A metal display surface on which visual elements with magnets attached to them can be arranged to illustrate instructional content.

mailing list An electronic list of email addresses for individuals and/or companies that is equivalent to a printed phone list. Email can be sent electronically to everyone on the mailing list at once with one command.

media Aids to teaching that assist a teacher during instruction. They range from printed materials to audiovisual equipment to computers.

media specialists Librarians who assist in finding information beyond the library, especially information that is available electronically or on the Internet. Media specialists are often responsible for training teachers and students in how to use technology as a tool to locate information.

megabyte One million bytes or 1,000,000 characters of data.

memory A series of RAM chips that provide temporary, volatile electronic storage that is used by the CPU to store short-term data.

menu A listing of command options. In the Windows and Mac operating systems, command menus appear across the top of open windows.

method(s) A technique or strategy of teaching, such as lecture, demonstration, or discussion.

microphone An audio input device than can enable the spoken word, music, and other sounds to be saved as digital files that can be played back or used in other ways.

mini-keyboards Assistive device, a keyboard that is smaller than a regular one. It is helpful to students with a good accuracy, but a restricted range of motion.

mini laptops (netbooks) Scaled and usually stripped down laptops larger than PDAs but smaller than laptop computers. They have found a niche with students and travelers.

modem A device that enables computers to send and receive information. It MOdulates a computer's signal so that it can be transmitted across a phone line or cable to a similar device that DEModulates the signal.

monitor The primary output device of a computer, displaying computer information on its screen.

mouse A pointing input device that connects to a computer by wire or wirelessly. It moves the cursor on the computer screen in the same direction that the user moves the mouse. Originally all had a ball that rolled and moved the cursor as the user moved the mouse. Today there are many variations: trackball, laser, joystick, pointing sticks, pens, and touchpads, to name a few, as well as a number of assistive devices.

MouseKeys Allows users to direct the mouse point and execute all mouse functions using the numeric keypad on the keyboard.

MOV The file type of one of the most popular digital video formats; it is known as QuickTime, and the file type is abbreviated as MOV for "movie."

MP3 (Moving Picture Experts Group Audio Layer 3) An audio compression technology that provides high-quality sound in one twelfth of the space that the same sound would take in previous formats of audio files.

MPEG (Moving Picture Experts Group) A popular digital video format that reduces the size of video files up to 95 percent yet retains near-television quality.

multimedia Multiple types of media that are combined into an integrated whole that presents instructional content. Although not only digital media may be included, the term is often used to refer to a computer-based format that combines text, graphics, audio, and even video into a single, coherent, digital presentation.

multimedia kit An instructional kit that includes multiple media to present content; a kit may include visual elements (texts and graphics), cassette tapes, student activity sheets, suggested lesson plans, motion video, and even real objects.

multimedia software Software that uses multiple types of technology that typically addresses different learning modalities.

MySpace A very popular social networking site that allows participants to post information about themselves and make it available with others who become "friends."

narrowcast video Video transmission that is targeted to a small (narrow) audience, particularly schools.

National Board for Professional Teaching Standards (NBPTS) A nonprofit, nongovernmental agency governed by a sixty-three-member board of directors, the majority of whom are classroom teachers.

national certification A set of standards developed by the National Board for Professional Teaching Standards (NBPTS) for the purpose of improving teaching and learning. The NBPTS awards certification to teachers who can demonstrate that they have achieved high standards for what they know and do as teachers.

National Council for Learning Disabilities An organization that offers helpful information on all aspects of disabilities, including technology support.

National Education Association The largest professional organization and largest labor union in the United States. It represents public school teachers and other support personnel, faculty and staffers at colleges and universities, retired educators, and college students preparing to become teachers.

navigation button A hot link that connects to other locations on the same or a different web site; usually colored or underlined words or graphics. When the cursor passes over one it turns the cursor arrow into a pointing hand, indicating it can be clicked on.

NCATE (National Council for the Accreditation of Teacher Education) An official body for accrediting teacher education programs. NCATE has adopted their own NETS Standards requiring teacher education programs to include courses or experiences to develop understanding of the use of technology.

netbooks (mini laptops) Scaled and usually stripped down laptops larger than PDAs but smaller than laptop computers. They have found a niche with students and travelers.

NETS (National Education Technology Standards) Developed by the ISTE to create a series of national standards used to facilitate the use of educational technology by students, teachers, and educators to promote school improvement in the United States.

NETS•A (National Education Technology Standards for Administrators) Requires administrators to enact effective school leadership for comprehensive and appropriate use of technology. These standards evolved from the Technology Standards for School Administrators (TSSA), a foundational document of the ISTE stressing administrators' obligation to use their leadership positions to promote technological literacy.

NETS•S (National Education Technology Standards for Students) Requires students to be proficient in using technological knowledge, to use technology in a responsible way, and to utilize technology as a tool to increase problem solving, creativity, and productivity.

NETS•T (National Education Technology Standards for Teachers) Requires teachers to use technology to plan and design learning environments and experiences, increase assessment capabilities, more effectively design curriculum, and increase productivity.

network A collection of computers and peripherals that are connected together so that they can communicate information and share resources.

network modem A modem that is connected to a network server, allowing computers that are connected by the network to share a single Internet connection.

neural network Artificial intelligence software that learns and adjusts responses on the basis of previous interactions.

neuron A nerve cell that consists of three major components—the cell body, the axon, and the dendrites—and is part of a vast neural network.

newsgroup An electronic public discussion or conference, dedicated to a specific topic, that is continuously running on the Internet. It may be hosted privately on one server, or it may be hosted on many servers in a decentralized fashion.

No Child Left Behind (NCLB) Act A federal law to improve U.S. primary and secondary schools through increased standards of accountability as well as flexibility of school choice. The major provisions of the act focus on outcome-based measurements of student progress, as well as measuring teacher quality.

node Any workstation or peripheral that is connected to a network. All nodes are ultimately connected back, through one or more hubs, to a server.

OCR (optical character recognition) software Software that recognizes printed characters when they are scanned and then converts them into an electronic word-processing document.

online publications Online, electronic versions of material that would traditionally be produced in hard copy, although some publications today are produced only online. Also known as e-publications or e-pubs, these resources typically include current and archived articles of interest to educators.

onscreen keyboard (see head pointing system)

operating system (OS) A program that tells the computer how to function and how to manage its own operation.

optical media Digital storage formats that are rapidly replacing traditional analog (audio and videotape) media include primarily CDs and DVDs.

oral history Historical commentary that is made up of a series of interviews captured on audiotape.

oral journal The use of audio technology to record observations, reflect on personal experiences, or practice and listen to one's own oral communication skills.

output device The pieces of hardware that move information (data that have been processed or accessed) out of the computer.

overhead projector A projector that uses a powerful lamp and a series of mirrors and lenses to shine through a transparent acetate sheet (i.e., a transparency) so that the images on the transparency can be seen by all. Sheets may be clear or colored.

packet Data that are broken into small units and sent through a network one unit or packet at a time.

paint programs Software that uses an electronic pen, brush, and other tools to create and manipulate digital pictures in a manner very similar to the way in which one paints a picture in the real world.

palmtop computer A palm-sized, handheld computer that merges the digital organizer and the computer into a single powerful but small computing device. Today, they are being supplanted by smartphones.

password A combination of letters and/or numerals users must enter along with their ID/log-in name as a second level of security.

PDA (see personal digital assistant)

PDF files Files that have been saved in Adobe Acrobat format so that the document appears exactly as it would look as a printed page, including layouts, photos, and other graphics; these files require the use of Acrobat Reader, a free application available online, to display them.

pedagogical cycle A sequence of specific methods that promote and support effective instruction.

pedagogy The actual function of teaching or what teachers do when implementing their craft to assist their students' learning.

peer-to-peer networking A network configuration that allows users to share files, not by uploading them to a central site, but instead by making files available on their machine, which in turn is accessible to others on the network.

performance objectives Objectives that specify what the learner will be able to do when the instructional event concludes.

PAN (personal area network) A network used for connecting devices over a short distance such as a hands-free device for a cell phone.

personal amplification system A device worn by a student that receives the teacher's auditory signal, can be earbuds or a direct connection to a hearing aid.

personal digital assistant (PDA) A handheld computer that may vary in capabilities from simply functioning as a personal organizer to running scaled-down versions of productivity software.

personal filter Personal characteristic of the learner/receiver that can impact the communication process by shaping how the individual processes objective messages. Individual characteristics, such as personal values, cultural heritage, and belief systems, that can have the effect of distortion or misinterpretation of communication.

personal web A predicted World Wide Web of the future that would focus on presenting information to an individual that would be uniquely valuable and needed by him or her.

perspective The way in which people look at things and interpret them; different people can look at the same thing and see it in their own unique ways.

phone bridge Communications technology that allows multiple users to call in to a central phone number to participate in a phone conference.

photograph A pictorial image captured via camera, film, and a photochemical development process.

piracy Illegally copying software to use when it was not legally purchased or installing software on multiple machines when only one copy was purchased.

pixel The smallest unit of information in an image. Each pixel represents a portion of the image in a specific color. The term pixel stands for "picture element."

plagiarism The act of passing someone else's work off as one's own or of citing sources improperly.

plug-in A program that may be downloaded from the Internet, usually free, to expand a browser's capabilities, for example, to allow multimedia to be displayed.

pointing devices Assistive devices that help students who have difficulty isolating a finger or using their hands to hit a single key.

port A connection on a computer into which peripheral devices can be plugged. Today, they are most commonly USB ports.

portable media Usually refers to hard disks not contained within a computer that are attached via a USB port and cable and can easily be disconnected and locked away or taken to another location. Also refers to USB flash (jump) drives.

portfolio assessment software A type of performance assessment that enables teachers to assess competencies on the basis of a collection of work rather than test scores.

portal A site on the Internet that offers one or an assortment of services, such as a search engine, news, email, conferencing, electronic shopping, and chat rooms.

preorganizer An early warning system to let the learners know what knowledge they are responsible for acquiring.

presentation software Software that includes programs designed to create digital support materials for oral presentations.

print material Hard-copy printed pages that are in many different forms and may include books and worksheets as well as posters and charts.

print server A dedicated computer that provides printing services to all local network workstations by attaching the printer to one of the workstations on the network or by directly connecting the printer to the network.

privacy An ethical issue that can arise when an individual's right to privacy conflicts with the actions of any agency, whether governmental or commercial, to monitor and record an individual's personal information or online activities.

problem-solving software Programs that involve the learner by focusing on creative problem-solving situations rather than on routine drill-and-practice skills.

productivity software Generic business application software that educators can use and adapt for the administrative and professional tasks they must address. Four main types are: word processing, electronic spreadsheets, database management, and presentation software.

program A set of computer instructions, written in a special computer language, that tells a computer how to accomplish a given task.

programmed instruction An instructional system in which material is presented in a series of small steps. Each step requires active learner response, to which there is immediate feedback to the learner as to the correctness of the response.

psychological factors The unique individual psychological differences that define and affect the reception of a communicated message.

Public Broadcasting System (PBS) Created by an act of Congress, it's comprised of a nationwide system of nonprofit public stations that disseminate high-quality educational programs, especially to schools but also to the general public.

public files Public storage areas on a network where files can be stored and read by all users; the files can be read-only, or they may be designated as read/write.

RAM (random-access memory) The chips that make up a computer's temporary memory area. This area empties when the application is closed and fills again when the user opens a new application, or when the computer is powered off.

readiness In distance and alternative learning, the capacity of teachers and students to work within the new environments; includes readiness to accept new roles and readiness to work with new technologies.

recorded books Can assist students who can understand material at their grade level when they hear it, but have difficulty with decoding and comprehending when they read it.

reference software Digital versions of volumes of reference materials recorded in a linear fashion on a CD that contains an interface that provides hyperlinks to quickly access any of the information recorded on the CD.

removable hard disk A hard drive that can be removed from the computer. It can either be mounted in the computer or plugged into the computer and run as an additional, external drive.

resolution The clarity and crispness of the image on the monitor screen or printer output. Pixels are the measure of resolution in monitors; printer resolution is measured in dpi (dots per inch).

resource sharing A network function that allows programs that are installed on the network server to be available to all workstations.

retrofit To prepare and remodel existing facilities to accommodate computer networks.

ROM (read-only memory) A chip created to hold a stored program such as the BIOS (Basic Input/Output System) that provides instructions to the computer as to how to start itself up. ROM chips are read but are typically not written on.

router Connecting devices used to direct (route) network communications along the correct pathways to and from the appropriate network.

RSS feeds Often found on blog sites, it stands for "really simple syndication" or "rich site summary." They are continuously updated feeds of news or other information that users can sign up for.

Safari The name of the web browser provided by Apple with the Mac OS (operating system).

satellite transmission Signals transmitted to a satellite (uplinked) and then sent back down (downlinked) to a terrestrial communication system at another location on the globe; the satellites are in orbits that allow signals to be bounced via uplinks and downlinks to positions anywhere on the globe.

scaffolding The process of building bridges from prior knowledge as a baseline and moving students beyond that point.

scan converter A device that displays a computer image output by converting a digital (computer) signal to an analog (video) signal.

scan/read systems Systems that combine the use of a computer, scanner, optical character recognition software, and speech output to read aloud printed text while providing a visually enhanced display on a computer monitor.

scanner An input device that captures and then translates printed text, images, or photographs into digital data.

school and classroom management support software (see classroom management support software)

screen magnification software Assistive device that can magnify a display supporting students with limited vision.

screen readers Assistive devices that support students with very poor vision or ones that get fatigued from screen magnification.

search engine A special program on the Internet that allows the user to type in key words to locate online material that contains those words or topics.

Second Life A rich and complex virtual reality world where participants use an avatar to explore and partake of its many offerings.

semantic web A view of the web where difficult problems can be solved via technology's ability to process and connect vast and diverse bits of information that would take people many years to interrelate.

server A powerful computer that provides services and enables sharing resources for computers on a network, such as email, program sharing, data storage and access, and printer sharing.

shared administrative tools, data, programs Applications and/or data installed on a server and made available to authorized users/workstations.

shareware Software that is offered to users for a small fee, usually paid on the honor system after the user has had a chance to try out the software and determine whether it is indeed useful for the user's purposes.

sheet-fed scanner A scanner that allows the user to manually feed multiple pages into a scanner. Many scanners can now "sheet-feed," use a document feeder so that the user does not have to feed multiple sheets manually.

simulations Software packages that present to the user a model or situation in a computerized or virtual format.

single switch with scanning Assistive device, for students with limited motor control. If they can control a single movement such as flexing a fist, turning their head side to side, or pressing a foot, they can access a computer via single switch with scanning.

site license Purchased rights to use a single copy of a software application for multiple computers/users as defined by the license. Normally cheaper to buy and support than individual copies of the software.

site map An outline of all the pages included on a web site, usually with a description of the type of information that can be located on each page.

smartboard A large interactive whiteboard that uses touch technology to detect user input. Used in conjunction with a computer and projector, it can become a giant touch screen.

smartphone A mobile phone that also includes capabilities found on a PDA or computer, such as email, web access and software applications.

soft copy Data that are still in an electronic form within the computer. Soft copy is volatile; it will disappear when power to the machine is cut off.

software Computer programs created to accomplish specific tasks or perform specific functions.

software bundle An interrelated collection (suite) of popular applications offered by some software manufacturers. An example is Microsoft's Office for Windows or Mac OS, which bundles Word, Excel, PowerPoint, and Outlook.

sound field amplification system A teacher's voice is amplified through classroom speakers.

speaker An audio output device to amplify the sound generated by a computer program, a CD, or other sound device.

speakerphone Telephone technology usually equipped with an omnidirectional microphone designed to pick up voices from anywhere in the room that allows all participants in a room to communicate using a single, specially equipped phone.

special needs software Software specifically designed to address the needs of learners with special needs as the result of a variety of physical or learning impairments.

stakeholders Representatives from all groups that will be affected by a strategic plan who, as a result, are selected and actively participate together in the strategic planning process.

stickykeys A feature that allows students to press keys sequentially to executive functions that typically require pressing keys simultaneously.

stimulus-response A stimulus is the initial action directed to the organism, and the response is the organism's reaction to that action.

storage A nonvolatile, electronic space on a magnetic or optical disc that the computer can use to store instructions and data for use at a later time.

strategic planning A process that includes a series of several distinct steps, each of which helps to focus the stakeholders and institution participating in the process in a single, clearly articulated direction.

strategies Components of the strategic plan, statements that describe how the plan's objectives can be accomplished.

streaming audio An audio technology for the web that sends audio in a continuous stream or flow to allow the user to listen to the audio as it is received by the browser, rather than waiting until its fully downloaded.

streaming video A video technology that compresses and plays back digital video that is sent in a continuous stream, allowing the user to view the video clip while it is being downloaded from the Internet, rather than waiting until it's fully downloaded.

students with special needs and students with exceptionalities Refers both to students who have disabilities that interfere with learning and students who are gifted and may need instructional strategies to help them meet their potential.

summative feedback Data that are returned at the end of a process.

switch A piece of equipment that offers a series of centralized connections to enable multiple computers to connect to a network.

SWOT analysis An acronym for "strengths, weaknesses, opportunities, threats." During this component of a strategic plan, participants brainstorm all of the factors, both positive and negative, that will affect the potential success of the plan they are developing.

synchronous A method of instructional delivery that occurs at the same time, although typically not in the same place.

synchronous communication A method of communicating in which the participants interact at the same (or in real) time.

system unit Contains the heart of a computer system: the circuit board (motherboard) with the CPU (central processing unit), memory (temporary storage), hard drive (longer term storage), and usually CD/DVD drive.

systems approach A model that specifies a methodical approach to the analysis and design of instruction, including a statement of observable learning objectives and the use of a systematic process that includes the specific evaluation techniques and instructional experiences.

tablet PC A personal computer that is similar in size to a traditional laptop, but allows the user to write on the surface of the screen with a stylus "pen." The text is then converted into a word-processing or graphics file.

TAGS Talented and gifted students, in addition to students with disabilities, that are also special needs students.

talking book A dramatization of a play or the recorded reading of a book, play, or short stories usually recorded on cassette tape or CD-ROM.

talking spell checkers Included in some word-processing programs that offer text-to-speech features. They can read aloud misspelled words and read a list of suggested correct words.

talking word-processing programs These assistive programs offer speaking text aloud and other spoken aloud editing features that can support the special needs of students with physical challenges.

TCP/IP The agreed-on transmission protocol that is used on the Internet and on networks so that communications between diverse computers can be understood.

TEACH (Technology Education and Copyright Harmonization) Act Became law in 2001 and clarified many guidelines relating to fair use for distance education, but many issues remain.

teacher licensure/certification Professional standards requiring educators to demonstrate specific skill and knowledge proficiencies in teaching. Certification standards are determined by each state's Department of Education.

teaching strategies The techniques or methods a teacher uses to present information to students. The teaching strategies can take student learning styles into account by providing different approaches to the same topic.

teaching style Typically, a teacher's personal preferences as to how to teach, frequently influenced by the way the teacher previously found effective for his or her own learning.

technical support Support personnel for distance or alternative delivery systems who are available when systems fail and/or who provide technical assistance to users so that instructional delivery can continue.

technologists Those whose primary responsibilities relate to the management of equipment, or educational technology.

Technology Standards for School Administrators (TSSA) A foundational document of the ISTE stressing administrators' obligation to use their leadership positions to promote technological literacy.

telecommunication Electronic communication between computers via telephone lines or cable.

telephone Traditional synchronous voice technology that allows two people to communicate orally via phone lines.

telephony The transmission of sounds between widely removed points with or without connecting wires. Telephony with computers uses the speakers and microphone of two or more computers connected to the Internet to transmit audio conversation across the Internet.

template A document that has been preformatted for a specific use but contains no data.

terrestrial A land-based component of a broadcast system.

test generator Software that creates tests by either randomly selecting questions within the database of questions or allowing the user to select the questions to be included.

text-to-speech software Programs that can read aloud what a student has typed.

theories Scientists' statements of their beliefs about an event or a cause usually supported by a large amount of experimental or observational evidence.

theory of multiple intelligences Howard Gardner theorized that each individual has multiple types of intelligences, only a few of which can be measured by IQ tests. These intelligences (or talents) include the verbal-linguistic, mathematical-logical, musical, visual-spatial, bodily-kinesthetic, interpersonal, intrapersonal, naturalistic, and existential intelligences.

time-lapse video Video whose playback has been sped up to give the appearance of altering time so that what may have taken days to occur can be viewed in the space of a few minutes.

touch screen A display that responds to human touch. Touch screen software usually displays a series of graphics or icons. Rather than using a mouse or a pointer, the icon on the screen is touched.

transparency A visual created on a thin sheet of transparent acetate for projection on an overhead projector.

True Knowledge A semantic search engine that can interpret questions and then seek the answer from all online sources.

tutorial software Software that presents new content in a carefully planned sequence with frequent opportunities for review and practice. It may also provide additional content or appropriate correction depending on student responses.

twisted-pair wire An inexpensive, flexible type of cable similar to telephone wire that is made up of a pair of copper wires twisted around each other.

Twitter A social networking vehicle, in essence a micro-blog, that allows "followers" to stay abreast of those they "follow" by reading their brief, up to 140 character, "tweets," text-based short messages, relating to what they are doing.

UD (Universal Design) Principles that were originally developed by architects and designers to ensure that access to buildings and products was not restricted for those with disabilities.

UDL (Universal Design for Learning) Offers educators a set of parameters for instructional design that considers what all students, regardless of the ways in which they are diverse, need to ensure learning success.

uplink A data link by which signals are transmitted from a terrestrial system to a satellite so that they can be bounced back down to another point on the globe.

upload To transfer data from a computer to another computer, typically one that is connected to the Internet.

USB (Universal Serial Bus) Common method of connecting devices to a computer.

USB flash (jump) drives Using 1.1 or 2.0 interface, they use flash memory (no moving parts) to store data. Faster, smaller, and hold more data than floppy drives.

URL (uniform resource locator) The address for a web pages (designations for a specific location) on the World Wide Web. A URL typically begins with "http://www" and then a domain name.

utility program Specialized programs that manage, improve, or oversee computer operations.

VCR (video cassette recorder) A device that plays back or records on video tape, the formats: VHS, Hi-8, or Beta.

VHS tape A relatively inexpensive type of magnetic recording videotape that can contain up to 120 minutes of recording at the standard playing (SP) speed or up to six or eight hours at slower speeds with lower quality.

video camera recorder A camera that records sound and images on magnetic tape that can be played back by using a VCR. Also called a camcorder (camera and recorder).

video capture card A component that can be added to a computer to allow for the conversion of traditional analog video into its digital equivalent.

videoconferencing software Enables users at either end of the connection to both see and hear each other, can range from low-tech webcams to high-definition studio-quality cameras and support equipment.

video study guide A study guide that accompanies a video and usually provides the viewer with a series of brief questions on key ideas presented in the same sequence as that in which they are presented in the video.

videocassette recorder (VCR) Recorder that uses VHS magnetic tape for recording video and can also record video as it is being received for delayed playback. Prerecorded tapes can be played in class and stopped for discussion, even backed up and replayed as desired.

videoconferencing A combination of software and hardware that enables users at either end of a synchronous connection not only to hear each other, but to see video images of each other as well. The audio and video may be transmitted over the Internet via ISDN or regular phone lines by being compressed at the sending end and decompressed at the receiving end.

virtual environments Fully rendered three-dimensional representations of real or imagined environments that allow the user to become fully immersed there.

virtual reality (VR) A combination of hardware and/or software that together create a three-dimensional digital environment within which the user can interact.

virus A program written specifically to disrupt computers and/or destroy data. They can copy themselves and infect computers. Often erroneously referred to as viruses are: malware, adware, and spyware.

visual communication Encoding and decoding information so that a message is communicated through visual elements.

visual literacy A type of literacy that enables the viewer to accurately interpret the visuals necessary for functioning effectively in our society.

voice mail Asynchronous voice recording technology that allows teachers and students to leave each other messages even when none of the participants is available to communicate via phone at the same time.

voice technology Technology that enables the computer to accept voice commands and dictation of data.

WAV file The digital version of analog audio. WAV files maintain the quality of the original sound, but the file size can be very large.

wearable computers A future technology that will provide devices built into clothing or small enough to wear or be pinned on to clothing.

Web 2.0 The term "Web 2.0" is commonly associated with web applications that facilitate interactive information sharing, interoperability, user-centered design, and collaboration on the World Wide Web.

Web 3.0 A predicted future evolution of the Web that will focus on fully supporting the mobile handheld computer.

web authoring systems/tools Software tools that assist in creating web pages by automatically generating HTML code making it reasonably easy to create a web site.

web browser A program that translates web page language, HTML (hypertext markup language), into an image on a computer's screen.

web hosting A service by which the user can upload the pages of a web site to the web host server, usually via an FTP program, which then makes the site available on the web; such services can be free or charge a monthly or annual fee.

web page A document written in HTML that displays information for use on the web and may contain a series of hyperlinks to other resources on the web.

web site A specific location on the Internet that houses a single or a collection of related web pages.

webcam A digital camera, normally with a built-in microphone, connected to a computer than can capture and/or transmit still and video images and sound and enable one-on-one or group communications.

weblogs (see blogs)

WEbook A web site that offers the opportunity to write, collaborate, review, and even publish online.

what-if analysis A capability of spreadsheets that allows the user to ask a "what-if?" question and then change the value in one or more cells to see how those changes will affect the outcome.

whiteboard A successor to the blackboard, it provides a slick, white surface on which a variety of specially formulated dry-erasable colored markers can be used. Whiteboards also provide a flat surface on which self-stick flip chart sheets can be hung. Additionally, some whiteboards have a metal backing that will support magnetic displays (see also electronic whiteboards).

wide area network (WAN) Networks that connect computers across a wide area, such as all of the schools in a district or all of the districts in a state.

wiki A web site in which content is written collaboratively so that anyone with a computer and Internet access can edit and add to the information posted.

Wikipedia One of the largest wikis, an online encyclopedia, it is published by the Wikipedia Foundation. There are also Wikitionary, Wikibooks, Wikinews, and Wikiquote wikis.

WiFi (wireless fidelity) A technology that uses radio frequency to connect WiFi-enabled computers and other digital devices to wirelessly connect to networks at high speeds.

WiMax (Worldwide Interoperability for Microwave Access) A telecommunications technology that enables remote wireless connection for computers.

Windows An operating system from Microsoft used by certain types of personal computers that tells the computer how to work. It is primarily a graphical user interface but also includes typed-in (text) commands, choices from preset menus, and icons.

wireless devices Devices that use wireless communications technology (e.g., microwave) to send and receive voice and digital data.

wireless network/networking A network in which information is transmitted wirelessly via infrared, radio wave, or microwave technology rather than through wires that are directly connected to computers.

wizard A miniprogram that creates a customized template by asking a series of questions about the desired format. It can help you create sophisticated documents without knowing how to issue complex commands.

word prediction software Programs that can make an educated guess about the word a student is typing based on the first few letters. It can help reduce the number of keystrokes required.

word-processing software Software that is used for text-oriented tasks such as creating, editing, and printing documents. It has all but replaced typewriters. Word processing can be a powerful support tool for students who are physically challenged.

workstation An intelligent terminal or personal computer that is connected to a computer network.

World Wide Web The most popular part of the Internet. It uses a graphical user interface and hypertext links between different addresses to allow easier navigation from one site of interest to another.

WYSIWYG ("What You See Is What You Get") A feature of many word-processing and web-authoring programs that allows the user to preview a document and see exactly what it will look like before it is printed or posted to the web.

YouTube A very popular and rapidly growing Internet video site and resource, now owned by Google. Originally meant for user-generated videos, it now includes movie, television, music, and commercial business–oriented clips and full-length videos as well. From an education standpoint, it offers both potential and peril.

REFERENCES

Abaya, B. 2000. Brisbane. Retrieved September 2, 2000, from www.wested.org/tie/dlrn/k12de.html.

Abdullah, M. H. 1998. Guidelines for evaluating web sites. Eric Digest. Retrieved May 12, 2002, from www.ed.gov.databases/ERIC_Digests/ed426440.html.

Acceptable Use Policies: Bangor, Michigan Public Schools/ Bangor Computer Network. 2001. Retrieved July 31, 2001, from www.bangorvikings.org/BTS/aup.

Acceptable Use Policies—A handbook. 2001. Retrieved June 21, 2001, from www.pen.k12.va.us/go/VDOE/Technology/AUP/home.shtml.

Acceptable Use Policy: Bellingham, Washington Schools. 2001. Retrieved July 31, 2001, from www.rice.edu/armadillo/About/bellingham.html.

Accessing challenging math curriculum. 2003. Retrieved June 22, 2003, from http://www.ldonline.org/ld_indepth-technology/opening_the_door_mike.html.

AECT home page. Retrieved March 22, 1999, from www.aect.org.

AECT. 1994. Instructional Technology: The Definition and Domains of the Field. Bloomington, IN: AECT.

Alliance for Technology Access. 2002. Retrieved April 20, 2002 from http://ataccess.org/community/successes/successes.html.

American Montessori Society. n.d. The Montessori method of education. Retrieved May 18, 2001, from www.amshq.org.

American Psychological Association. 1997. *Publication manual of the American Psychological Association*, 4th ed. Washington, DC: American Psychological Association.

Andrews, J. F., & Jordan, D. L. 1998. Multimedia stories for deaf children. *Teaching Exceptional Children* (May/June): 29.

Andrews, K., & Marshall, K. 2000. Making learning connections through telelearning. *Educational Leadership* 58(October): 53–56.

Archambault, R. D. ed. 1974. *John Dewey in education*. Chicago: University of Chicago.

Artificial intelligence (AI). 2001. Retrieved June 26, 2001, from www.britannica.com/original?content_id=1209.

ASPIN: Innovative K–12 Connectivity with CATV: Enhancing math and science through technology. 2001. Retrieved June 27, 2001, from http://aspin.asu.edu/projects/catv.

Association for Supervision and Curriculum Development. 1995. *Constructivism: Facilitator's guide*. Alexandria, VA: Association for Supervision and Curriculum Development.

Ausubel, D. P., J. D. Novak, & H. Hanesian. 1978. *Educational psychology: A cognitive view*. 2nd ed. New York: Holt, Rinehart & Winston.

Ayres, K., & Langone, J. 2005. Evaluation of software for functional skills instruction: Blending best practice with technology. *Technology in Action, Technology and Media Division, 1*(5): 1–8.

Banathy, B. H. 1995. Developing a systems view of education. *Educational Technology* 35:55.

Bandura, A. 1971. Analysis of modeling processes. In *Psychological modeling: Conflicting theories* (pp. 1–62), edited by A. Bandura. Chicago: Aldine Atherton.

Bandura, A. 1976. *Social learning theory*. Englewood Cliffs, NJ: Prentice-Hall.

Barlow, J. A. 1963. Programmed instruction in perspective: Yesterday, today, and tomorrow. In *Prospectus in programming: Proceedings of the 1962 Center for Programmed Instruction*, edited by R. T. Filer. New York: Macmillan.

Barrios, B. 2002. The subtle knife: Blog*diss: Blogs in the classroom. Retrieved May 8, 2003, from http://www.barclaybarrios.com/tsk/blog/classroom.html.

Bates, A. W. 1995. Technology, open learning and distance education (London: Routledge). Retrieved December 27, 2000, from www.ed.gov/databases/ERIC_Digests/ed395214.html.

BBC Online. 2000. Audio/video: The best of BBC in sound and pictures. Retrieved July 6, 2000, from www.bbc.co.uk/audiovideo.

Behrmann, M. M. 1998. Assistive technology for young children in special education. In *Learning with technology: ASCD yearbook 1998* (p. 90), edited by C. Dede. Alexandria, VA: Association for Supervision and Curriculum Development.

Berlo, D. K., & Reiser, R. A. 1987. Instructional technology: A history. In *Instructional technology: Foundations* (p. 16), edited by R. M. Gagné. Hillsdale, NJ: Erlbaum.

Bernard, J. Cotter High School's virtual school. Retrieved April 15, 2000, from www.rrr.net.

Bloom, B. 1956. *Taxonomy of educational objectives: The classification of educational goals*, 1st ed. New York: David McKay.

Bloom's taxonomy. Learning Skills Program. Retrieved May 8, 1999, from www.coun.vic.ca/learn/program/hndouts/bloom.html.

Boerner, G. 1999. Videoconferencing skills to maximize student learning. *School Executive* (January/February): 6–7.

Boettcher, J.V. 2001. The spirit of invention: Edging our way to 21st century teaching. *Syllabus* (June): 14, 10–11.

Bogue, B. 2003. Spokane Public Schools. Retrieved October 3, 2003, from http://www.palmone.com/us/education/studies/study53.html.

Bolton, T. Cognitive flexibility theory. Retrieved April 21, 1999, http://alcor.concordia.ca?~tbolton/edcomp/mod10b.html.

Bolze, S. 1998. Spin city. *Instructor* 108(November/December): 20.

Boswell, S. 2006, May 23. Sound field systems on the rise in schools: Improved test scores cited as benefit. *The ASHA Leader, 11*(7): 1, 32–33.

Boyce, A. 2002. Using cars to build Internet search skills. Retrieved January 10, 2002, from http://www.nea.org/cet/wired/index.html.

Boyle, E. A., Washburn, S. G., Rosenberg, M. S., Connelly, V. J., Brinckerhoff, L. C., & Banerjee, M. 2002. Reading's SLiCK with new audio texts and strategies. *Teaching Exceptional Children*, 35(2): 50–55.

Brangwin, N. 1999. Carmen Sandiego: A fifth-grader discovers a special tutor. Retrieved December 4, 1999, from www.techlearning.com/db_area/archives/WCE/archives/brangwin.htm.

Bransford, J. D., Brown, A. L., & Cocking, R. R. (Eds.). 2000. *How people learn: Brain, mind, experience, and school* (Expanded Ed.). Washington, DC: National Academies Press.

Brewer, W. R., & Kallick, B. 1996. Technology's promise for reporting student learning. In *Communicating student learning: ASCD yearbook 1996* (pp. 181–182), edited by T. R. Guskey. Alexandria, VA: Association for Supervision and Curriculum Development.

Bruner, J. S. 1962. *On knowing*. Cambridge, MA: Harvard University Press.

Bruner, J. S. 1966. *Toward a theory of instruction*. Cambridge, MA: Harvard University Press.

Bruner, J. S. 1969. *The relevance of education*. New York: W. W. Norton.

Bump, K. 2000. Creating healthy classrooms. *Classroom Leadership* 3(6): 7.

Burgstahler, Sheryl. 2008. Universal design in education: Principles and applications. Retrieved June 16, 2009, from http://www.washington.edu/doit/Brochures/PDF/ud_edu.pdf.

Burton, Mrs. 2003. KinderKonnect web page. Retrieved November 2, 2003, from http://www.kinderkonnect.com.

Butler, M. 1994. *How to use the Internet*. Emeryville, CA: Ziff-Davis Press.

Butler, S. 2002. Project Groundhog. Retrieved January 5, 2003, from http://www.ciconline.com/Enrichment/Teaching/learningwithtechnology/expertadvice/default.htm.

Cain, C. 1999. Networking classroom workstations. *School Executive* (November/December): 8.

Caine, R., & Caine, G. 1994. *Making connections: Teaching and the human brain*. New York: Addison-Wesley.

Caine, R., & Caine, G. 2000. Brain/mind learning principles. Retrieved July 9, 2000, from www.cainelearning.com/bbl/bbl2.htm.

Campbell, R. 2000. Leadership: Getting it done. Retrieved July 4, 2000, from www.ssu.missouri.edu/faculty/Rcampbell/Leadership/chapter6.htm.

Campion, C., & Mizell, A. P. 1999. SAXophone events [and] SAXophone schools. Retrieved July 31, 1999, from www.mhrcc.org/sax/saxevent.html and www.mhrcc.org/sax/saxskool.html.

Cannings, T., & Finkel, L. 1993. *The technology age classroom*. Wilsonville, OR: Franklin, Beedle, and Associates.

Center for Applied Special Technologies. 2007. Summary of 2007 national summit on universal design for learning working groups. Retrieved June 24, 2009, from http://www.cast.org/publications/bycast/index.html.

Center for Universal Design. 1997. *The principles of universal design, Version 2.0*. Raleigh, NC: North Carolina State University. Retrieved June 20, 2009, from http://www.design.ncsu.edu/cud/about_ud/udprincipleshtmlformat.html.

Certification requirements for the 50 states. University of Kentucky College of Education. Retrieved August 30, 2006 http://www.uky.edu/Education/TEP/usacert.html.

Civello, C. 1999. "Move over, please": The decentralization of the teacher in the computer-based classroom. *English Journal* (March): 92–94.

Clark, S. 2002. #2556. Cars. Retrieved May 20, 2003, from http://www.teachers.net/lessons/posts/2566.html.

Collaborative for Technology Standards for School Administrators. Retrieved August 31, 2006 http://cnets.iste.org/tssa/pdf/tssa.pdf.

Compressed video for instruction: Operations and applications. Washington, DC: Association for Educational Communications and Technology.

The Computer Ethics Institute. The Ten Commandments for Computer Ethics. Retrieved August 27, 2002, from http://www.brook.edu/its/cei/cei_hp.htm.

Conley, E. 2003. Movie night. Retrieved June 2, 2003, from http://www.nea.org/helpfrom/growing/works4me/tech/equip.html.

Cronin, G. 1999. Running a business. Retrieved August 7, 1999, from www.teachers.net/lessons/posts/1004.html.

Cross, K. P., & Angelo, T. A. 1998. *Classroom assessment techniques: A handbook for faculty*. Ann Arbor, MI: The University of Michigan.

Crotty, T. 2000. Constructivist theory unites distance learning and teacher education. Retrieved August 11, 2000, from http://edie.cprost.sfu.ca/it/constructivistlearning and www.hseidensticker.de/476.htm.

Crowder, N. A. 1963. A theorem in number theory [Presentation]. Intrinsic programming: Facts, fallacies, and future. In *Prospectus in programming: Proceedings of the 1962 Center for Programmed Instruction* (pp. 90–92), edited by R. T. Filer. New York: Macmillan.

Cummins, J. 2001. *Language, power, and pedagogy: Bilingual children in the crossfire*. Philadelphia: Multilingual Matters.

Cummins, J., Brown, K., & Sayers, D. 2007. *Literacy, technology, and diversity: Technology for success in changing times*. Boston: Allyn and Bacon.

Cyrs, T. E. 1976. Modular approach in curriculum design using the systems approach. In *Instructional media and technology: A professional's resource* (pp. 115–121), edited by P. J. Sleeman & D. M. Rockwell. Stroudsburg, PA: Dowden, Hutchinson, & Ross.

Davidson, H. 1999. The educators' lean and mean no-fat guide to fair use. *Technology & Learning* 20(September): 58–60, 62, 66.

Davidson, K. 1998. Education on the Internet: Linking theory to reality. Retrieved January 5, 2000, from www.oise.ca/~kdavidson/cons.html. Also in Mergel, B. 1998. Instructional design & learning theory. Retrieved January 8, 2000, from www.usask.ca/education/coursework/802papers/mergel/brenda.htm.

Davis, A. 2003. Elementary writers learn to love their weblogs. Retrieved October 31, 2003, from http://www97.intel.com/education/odyssey/day_300/day_300.htm.

Davis, D. 2002. Using assistive technology to help students write. *Media & Methods* (September/October) 39 (1), 14.

Debate over copyright protection in the Digital Age. Retrieved May 10, 2002, from http://groton.k12.ct.us/mts/eg15.htm.

Dede, C. 1995. The evolution of learning devices: Smart objects, information infrastructures, and shared synthetic environments. The Future of Networking Technologies for Learning. Retrieved June 12, 2001, from www.ed.gov/Technology/Futures/index.html.

Dede, C. 1996. Emerging technologies in distance education for business. Retrieved December 27, 2000, from www.ed.gov/databases/ERIC_Digests/ed395214.html.

Dede, C. 2000. Emerging technologies and distributed learning in higher education. Retrieved December 27, 2000, from http://virtual.gmu.edu/SS_research/cdpapers/index.htm.

DeKorne, C., & T. Y. Chin. 2002. Links to the missing: Exploring how technology is used in locating missing persons. Retrieved May 4, 2002, from http://www.nytimes.com/learning/teachers/lessons/20020425thursday_print.html.

Delisio, E. R. 2002. Research at the river links two schools. Retrieved April 3, 2003, from http://www.education-world.com/a_tech/tech122.shtml.

Denofrio, S. 1999. Technology notebook. *Instructor* 108(April): n.p.

DeVillar R. A. 2000. Literacy and the role of technology: Toward a framework for equitable schooling In J. V. Tinajero, R. A. DeVillar (Eds.), *The power of two languages 2000: Effective dual-language use across the curriculum*. New York: McGraw-Hill.

DeVillar R. A., Faltis C. J., & Cummins J. P. 1994. *Cultural diversity in schools: From rhetoric to practice*. Albany, NY: State University of New York Press.

Dewey, J. 1944. *Democracy and education*. New York: Macmillan.

Dewey, J. 1998. My pedagogic creed. In *Kaleidoscope: Readings in education* (pp. 280–285), edited by K. Ryan & J. Cooper. Boston: Houghton Mifflin. [Original work published in 1899.]

Diamant, R., & Bearison, D. 1991. Development of formal reasoning during successive peer interactions. *Developmental Psychology* 27: 277–284.

Diamond, J. 1999. [Abuzz question]. Retrieved September 20, 1999, from http://questions.nytimes.com.

Diaz, C. J. 2001. [No title]. Retrieved January 9, 2001, from www.nea.org/cet/wired/index.html.

Dickman, J. 2000. A student perspective. *Curriculum/Technology Quarterly* 9(Spring): 1–2.

Dodd, J. 2000. Music & MP3. *PC Tricks* 6: 95–98.

Dodge, P. 2002. Fixing grammar with technology. Retrieved February 13, 2003, from http://www.teachers.net/lessons/posts/2584.html.

Dodson, J. 1999. Using electronic sketchbooks in the classroom. *Media & Methods* (March/April): 10.

DO-IT. 2004. Disabilities, opportunities, internetworking, and technology. Retrieved May 20, 2009, from http://www.washington.edu/doit/faculty.

Donahue, B. 2000. Brenda Donahue's class: Centennial Education Center, Santa Ana, CA. Retrieved December 27, 2000, from www.otan.dni.us/webfarm/emailproject/cec.htm.

Drucker, P. 1999. Beyond the information revolution. *Atlantic Monthly* 284(October): 54, 57.

D'Souza, Q. 2006. RSS ideas for educators. Retrieved May 10, 2009, from http://www.teachinghacks.com/wp-content/uploads/2006/01/RSS%20Ideas%20for%20Educators111.pdf.

Dudzik, J. 1999. A marriage made in heaven. *Instructor* (September): 16.

Dudzik, J. 1999. E-pals. *Instructor* 109(October): 73.

Dudzik, J. 1999. Technology notebook. *Instructor* 108(April): n.p.

Duffy, M. 1999, June. [Interview].

Dunn, R. 1999. How do we teach them if we don't know how they learn? *Teaching K–8* 29(7), 50–52.

Dunn, R., & Dunn, K. 1992. *Teaching elementary students through their individual learning styles*. Boston: Allyn & Bacon.

Dunn, R., & Greggs, S. A. 1988. *Learning styles: Quiet revolution in American secondary schools*. Reston, VA: National Association of Secondary School Principals.

Dunn, R., Krimsky, J. S., Murray, J. B., & Quinn, P. J. 1985. Light up their lives: A review of research on the effects of lighting in children's achievement and behavior. *The Reading Teacher* 38: 863–869.

Dwight, V. 1998. [no title]. *Family PC* (September): 60.

Eagle Eye News. 2002. Retrieved May 15, 2002, from http://www.sisd.k12.ak.us/content/schools/pa/news%20letter/webmake.html.

Edling, J. V., Hamreus, D. G., Schalock, H. D., Beaird, J. H., Paulson, C. F., & Crawford, J. (1972). *The cognitive domain*. Washington, DC: Gryphon House.

EDUCAUSE. 2007. 7 things you should know series: Citizen journalism. Retrieved May 1, 2009, from http://net.educause.edu/ir/library/pdf/ELI7031.pdf.

EDUCAUSE. 2007. 7 things you should know series: Facebook II. Retrieved May 1, 2009, from http://net.educause.edu/ir/library/pdf/ELI7031.pdf.

EDUCAUSE. 2007. 7 things you should know series: Twitter. Retrieved May 1, 2009, from http://net.educause.edu/ir/library/pdf/ELI7031.pdf.

Educational computing: How are we doing? 1997. Retrieved February 17, 1999, from www.thejournal.com/magazine/97/jun/feature4.html.

Educational standards, what are they? Retrieved August 25, 2006 http://www.education-world.com/standards/national/index.shtml.

Fairhurst, A. M., & Fairhurst, L. L. 1995. *Effective teaching effective learning: Making the personality connection in your classroom*. Palo Alto, CA: Davies-Black.

Felder, R. M., & Soloman, B. A. Learning styles and strategies. Retrieved April 22, 1999, from www.crc4mse.org/ILS/ILS_ explained.html.

Ficklen, E., & Muscara, C. 2001, Fall. Harnessing technology in the classroom. *American Educator*, 25(3): 22–29.

Filipczak, B. 1995. Putting the learning in distance learning. Retrieved December 27, 2000, from www.ed.gov/databases/ERIC_Digests/ed395214.html.

FitzRoy, M. 2003, Sept. 6. Newest TV dateline: Landrum classroom. Retrieved September 8, 2003, from http://cgi.jacksonville.com.

Fry, E. 2003. Rural schools look to online courses. Juneau Express (June 25). Retrieved July 1, 2003, from http://www.juneauempire.com/stories/062503/loc_webschool.shtml.

Future technology. 1999. *PC Magazine* (June 22): 104, 113, 116, 119.

Gagné, R. M. 1985. *The conditions of learning*. 4th ed. New York: Holt, Rinehart & Winston.

Gagné, R. M., Briggs, L. J., & Wager, W. W. 1988. *Principles of instructional design*, 3rd ed. New York: Holt, Rinehart & Winston.

Ganesh, T. G., & Middleton, J. A. 2006. Challenges in linguistically and culturally diverse elementary settings with math instruction using learning technologies. *Urban Review: Issues and Ideas in Public Education*, 38(2): 101–143.

Garden State Pops Youth Orchestra. 1997. Learn and hear about different instruments. Retrieved July 6, 2000, from www.gspyo.com/education/html/instr-intro.html.

Gardner, H. 1988. Mobilizing resources for individual-centered education. In *Technology in education: Looking toward 2020*, edited by R. S. Nicerson & P. P. Zodihiates. Hillsdale, NJ: Erlbaum.

Gardner, H. 1993. *Multiple intelligences: The theory in practice (a reader)*. New York: Basic Books.

Gardner, H. 1999. A multiplicity of intelligences. *Scientific American* 9(Winter): 23.

Gardner, H. 1999. *Intelligence reframed: Multiple intelligences for the 21st century*. New York: Basic Books.

Gardner, H. 1999. Who owns intelligence? *The Atlantic Monthly* 283(February): 67–76.

Gates, B., October 28, 1999, Microsoft Corporation, Speech at the New York Institute of Technology, New York, NY. Retrieved May 5, 2002, from www.microsoft.com/billgates/speeches/10-28genl.asp.

Gazin, A. 2000. Focus on autobiography. *Instructor* 109 (January/February): 49.

Gold Ridge Elementary School web site. Retrieved November 2, 2003, from http://www.sonic.net/kargo/parent.htm.

Goldberg, L. 2002. Web pages to the rescue. *Instructor* (August), 112 (1), 27–28, 78.

Good, R. 2007. Master news media: Blog usage statistics and trends: Technorati state of the blogosphere—Q4 2006. Retrieved May 1, 2009, from http://www.masternewmedia.org/news/2007/04/06/blog_usage_statistics_and_trends.htm

Gore, A. 1998. Speech to the 15th International ITU Conference, October 12.

Grabe, M., & Grabe, C. 2004. *Integrating technology for meaningful learning* (4th ed.). New York: Houghton Mifflin.

Guenter, C. 2003. Student teaching electronic portfolio. Retrieved October 5, 2003, from http://www.csuchico.edu/educ/estport.htm.

Guerriero, A. 1999. [Abuzz question]. Retrieved September 22, 1999, http://questions.nytimes.com.

Guerriero, A. 1999. [Abuzz question]. Retrieved September 28, 1999, http://questions.nytimes.com.

Hackbarth, S. 1996. *The educational technology handbook: A comprehensive guide*. Englewood Cliffs, NJ: Educational Technology Publications.

Hakes, B. T., Cochenour, J. J., Rezabek, L. L., & Sachs, S. G. 1995.

Hall, T. 2002. *Differentiated instruction*. Wakefield, MA: National Center on Accessing the General Curriculum. Retrieved June 16, 2009, from http://www.cast.org/publications/ncac/ncac_diffinstruc.html.

Hardy, D. W. 2000. Algebra across the wire. Retrieved September 2, 2000, from http://wested.org/tie/dlrn/k12de.html.

Harper, G. 1998. Fair use guidelines for educational multimedia: The Copyright Act of 1976, as amended. Updated August 4, 1998. Retrieved July 19, 2000, from www.utsystem.edu/OGC/IntellectualProperty/ccmcquid.htm.

Harris, J. 1998. *Design tools for the Internet-supported classroom*. Alexandria, VA: Association for Supervision and Curriculum Development.

Harris, S. L. 1995. *The relationship between learning theory and curriculum development*. Unpublished manuscript, Florida International University at Miami, Florida.

Harrison, C. 2002. The WKEY Morning News. *Learning & Leading with Technology* (October), 30 (2), 40–43.

Harrison, J. L. 1999. [AT&T's virtual classroom]. Retrieved October 29, 1999, from www.nea.org/cet/wired/index.html.

Harrison, S. 2000. TEAMS distance learning. Retrieved August 9, 2000, from www.nea.org/cet/wired/index.html.

Hecker, L., Burns, L., Katz, L., Elkind, J., & Elkind, K. 2002. Benefits of assistive reading software for students with attention disorders. *Annals of Dyslexia*, 52: 243–272.

Heese, V. 1999. [No title]. Retrieved November 6, 1999, from www.techlearning.com/db_area_archives/WCE/archives/heese.htm.

Heese, V. 1999. Simple methods of integrating technology into primary classrooms. Retrieved November 5, 1999, from www.techlearning.com/db_area/archives/WCE/archives/heesepri.htm.

Heimdal, J. 2001. Rates on your life insurance go up last month? Retrieved January 10, 2002, from http://www.lessonplanspage.com/printables/PCIOMDDevFamilyBudgetOn-Spreadsheet812.html.

Higgins, K. J. 1999. School system broadcasts video with ATM/LANE. *Network Computing* 10(7): 72.

Hill, B. 1998. Senior project. Retrieved December 22, 1998, from www.intel.com/education/technology/mec/case_studies.htm.

Hirsch, S. 1999. A comparative study: San Diego, California, and Biarritz, France. Retrieved July 26, 1999, from www.edweb.sdsu.edu/triton/SDBiarritz/SDBiarritzUnit.html.

Hirschbuhl, J. J. (Ed). 1998. *Computers in education*. Guilford, CT: Dushkin.

History and emergence of universal design in education curriculum. 2009. Retrieved June 23, 2009, from http://www.k8accesscenter.org/training_resources/UniversalDesign.asp.

History of inventions. 2001. Retrieved June 26, 2001, from www.cbc4kids.ca/general/the-lab/history-of-invention/calendar.html.

History pen pals. 2002. Retrieved April 10, 2003, from http://www.nea.org/helpfrom/growing/works4me/tech/techclas.html.

Hoban, C. F., Sr., Hoban, C. F., Jr., & Zissman, S. B. 1937. *Visualizing the curriculum*. New York: The H. W. Wilson Co.

Hoffman, E. 1999. The dark side of the Internet: Controls of student access. *Syllabus: High School Edition* 1(1): 14–16.

Hofstetter, F. T., & Fox, P. 1997. *Multimedia literacy*. New York: McGraw-Hill.

Holloway, J. H. 2000. The digital divide. *Educational Leadership* 58(2): 90.

Holzberg, C. 2001. Yes, you can build a web site. *Instructor* 110(May/June): 62.

Hudson, M. & A. Cooley. 2003. Digital video camera use in classrooms. *Media & Methods* (February), 39 (4), 6.

Hughes, S. 2002. Cutting costs. Retrieved April 10, 2003, from http://www.nea.org/helpfrom/growing/works4me/tech/technclas.html.

Huitt, W. 1998. Bloom et al.'s taxonomy of the cognitive domain. Educational psychology interactive: The cognitive domain. Retrieved January 24, 2000, from www.valdosta.peachnet.edu/~whuitt/psy702/cogsys/bloom/html.

Hunt, M. 1993. *The story of psychology*. New York: Doubleday.

Huschak, I. H. 1999. Digital archaeology: Uncovering a city's past. Retrieved May 12, 2000, from http://techlearning.com/db_area/archives/WCE/archives/huschak.htm.

A Hypertext History of Instructional Design. Retrieved October 3, 2003, from http://www.coe.uh.edu/courses/cuin6373/idhistory/index.html.

Ideas for using video conferencing in the classroom. 2003. Retrieved June 13, 2003, from http://k-12.pisd.edu/distance_learning/uses.htm.

IDG. 1995. *Internet and the World Wide Web*. Foster City, CA: International Data Group Company.

Indiana's K-12 Plan for Technology. Retrieved August 30, 2006 http://www.doe.state.in.us/olr/techplan/.

Instructional event with lesson activity. Retrieved August 2, 1999, from www.seas/gwu.edu/sbraxton/ISD/GIFS/lesson_gagne.gif.

Integration via a browser-based intranet. 2002. Retrieved June 11, 2003, from http://www.nps.k12.va.us/infodiv/it/techconf/integbrw.htm.

The International Society for Technology in Education. 2000. *ISTE National Educational Technology Standards for Teachers*. Eugene, OR: ISTE.

The International Society for Technology in Education (ISTE). Retrieved August 25, 2006 from http://www.iste.org.

Internet Business. 2009. Number of new blogs. Retrieved May 1, 2009, from http://www.internet-business.com/number-of-new-blogs-per-day/.

James, S. 2003. One digital future. Retrieved November 9, 2003, from http://www.ldresources.com/articles/one_digital_future.html.

Jarvinen, E. M. 1988. The Lego/logo learning environment in technology education: An experiment in a Finnish context. *Journal of Technology Education* 9. Retrieved June 5, 1999, from http://scholar.lib.ft.edu/ejournals/JTE/v9n2/jrvinen.html.

Johnson, D. 2006. Seven things all adults should know about MySpace. Retrieved May 5, 2009, from http://www.educationworld.com/a_tech/columnists/johnson/johnson009.shtml.

Johnson, E. 1998. Making geography come alive with technology. *Media & Methods* (March/April): 14–16.

Johnson, S. R., & Johnson, R. B. 1971. *Assuring learning with self-instructional packages, or up the up staircase*. Chapel Hill, NC: Self-Instructional Packages.

Jonassen, D., Carr, C., & Yueh, H. 1998. Computers as mindtools for engaging learners in critical thinking. *Tech Trends*, 43(2): 24–32.

Jung, C. G. 1990. *Psychological types*. Rev. ed., translated by H. G. Baynes. Princeton, NJ: Princeton University Press.

Kekkonen-Moneta, S., & G. Moneta. 2001. E-learning in Hong Kong: Comparing learning outcomes in online multimedia and lecture versions of an introductory computing course. *British Journal of Educational Technology*, 33 (4), 2002, 423–433.

Kelly, E. J., & Partin, R. M. 1999. Mexico City earthquake. Retrieved August 17, 1999, from http://nardac.mip.berkeley.edu/tmp/browse_equis_res_14284.3html.

Kemp, J. E., & Smellie, D. C. 1989. *Planning, producing, and using instructional media.* New York: Harper & Row.

Kerka, S. 1996. Distance learning, the Internet, and the World Wide Web. ERIC Digest. Retrieved December 27, 2000, from www.ed.hov/databases/ERIC_Digests/ed395214.html.

Kindler, A. L. 2002. *Survey of the states' limited English proficient students and available educational programs and services, 2000–2001 summary report.* Washington, DC: U.S. Department of Education; Office of English Language Acquisition, Language Enhancement and Academic Achievement for Limited English Proficient Students.

Kinzie, M., Strauss, R., & Foss, J. 1994. Interactive frog dissection: An on-line tutorial. Retrieved December 26, 2000, from http://curry.edschool.virginia.edu/go/frog.

Knapps, K. J. 2000. Art and life in Africa project. Retrieved June 15, 2000, from www.uiowa.edu/~africart/teachers/lessons/036.html.

Kozma, R., & Schank, P. 1998. Connecting with the 21st century: Technology in support of educational reform. In *ASCD Yearbook 1998* (pp. 73–74), edited by C. Dede. Alexandria, VA: Association for Curriculum and Development.

Krantz, M. 2006. The guys behind MySpace. Retrieved May 11, 2009, from http://www.usatoday.com/money/companies/management/2006-02-12-myspace-usat_x.htm.

Krashen, S. 1991. Bilingual education and second language acquisition theory. In C. F. Leyba (Ed.), *Schooling and language minority students: A theoretical framework* (pp. 51–79). Los Angeles: Evaluation, Dissemination and Assessment Center, CSULA.

Krech, B. 1999. Show, don't tell. *Instructor* (October): n.p.

Kriwox, J. 2003. Quilting and geometry-patterns for living. Retrieved October 5, 2003, from http://ali.apple.com/ali_sites/deli/exhibits/1000077.

Krug, C. 1999. Video editing techniques in schools. *Media & Methods* (May/June): 55–56.

Kultgen, S. 1999. Computer portfolios. *Arts and Activities* (May): 20–21.

Laird, L. (1999). NEA CET: Wired classroom. Retrieved January 5, 2000, from www.nea.org/cet/wired/index.html.

Landon, A. 2003. How do you measure up? Retrieved October 4, 2003, from http://pegasus.cc.ucf.edu/~ucfcasio/measure.htm.

Laurino, B. 1999. Using chunks from class readers. Retrieved July 5, 2000, from www.ncte.org/teach/Laurino14954.html.

Le, P. 2003, September 16. Online coursework appeals to teenagers. Retrieved September 18, 2003, from http://www.indystar.com/print/articles/9/074716-3989-P.html.

LEARN NC. 2003, March. Student teachers and high school seniors beam the Internet. Retrieved April 2, 2003, from http://www.learnnc.org/Index.nsf/printView.

Learning styles. 1998. Retrieved August 15, 1999, from www.funderstanding.com/learning_theory_how6.html.

Lee, J. 1998. Web-based instruction. Retrieved January 28, 2000, from http://www.dsmt.org/exlee.

Lee, P. 1999. Tech learning. Retrieved December 15, 1999, from www.techlearning.com/db_area_archives/WCE/archives/paulalee.htm.

Lehmann, K. 1998. Travel and tour guide unit. In Wired Classroom: Etools Weekly Tip. National Education Association. Retrieved December 30, 1998, from www.nea.org/cet/wired/.

Leo, L. 1999. Picture perfect lessons. *Instructor* (March): 80–81.

Lever-Duffy, J. (2000). The evolution of distance education (pp. 251–274). In *Taking a big picture look at technology, learning, and the community college,* edited by Mark Milliron & Cindy Miles. Mission Viejo, CA: League for Innovation in the Community College.

Lewis, A. 2001. Sell yourself. Retrieved May 15, 2001, from www.successlink.org/great/g163.html.

Lopez, A. M., Jr., & Donlon, J. 2001. Knowledge engineering and education. *Educational Technology* 41(2): 45–50.

Lopez, W. J. 2003, August. Content delivery for a virtual high school. *T.H.E. Journal,* 31 (1), 32.

Lutkenhaus, K. 2000. [E-mail]. Retrieved March 4, 2000, from www.nea.org/cet/wired/index.html.

MacArthur, C. A. 1996. Using technology to enhance the writing processes of students with learning disabilities. *Journal of Learning Disabilities,* 29(4).

MacArthur, C. A. 2000. New tools for writing: Assistive technology for students with writing difficulties. *Topics in Language Disorders,* 20(4): 85–100.

MacArthur, C. A., Ferretti, R. P., Okolo, C. M., & Cavalier, A. R. 2001. Technology applications for students with literacy problems: A critical review. *The Elementary School Journal, 101*(3): 273–301.

Mahoney, M. J. 1994. *Human change processes.* New York: Basic Books.

Makled, C. 2002. Pilot program: Paddock project to aid in reading assessment. Retrieved May 21, 2003, from http://www.wirelessgeneration.com/web/print_milan.html (reprint from the *Milan News-Leader,* April 18, 2002).

Maple Lake School District: 1998. Acceptable use policy on district provided access to electronic information, services, and networks. Retrieved June 27, 2001, from http://www.maplelake.k12.mn.us/districtinfo/AUP.html.

Maran, R. 1998. *Computers Simplified,* 4th ed. Foster City, CA: IDG Books.

March, T. 2003. Eyes on art. Retrieved May 6, 2003, from http://www.kn.pacbell.com/wired/art2/guide/guide.html.

Martin, C. R. 2002. Looking at type: The fundamentals. Retrieved March 22, 2002, from www.knowyourtype.com/enfp.html.

Martin, S. 2000. Greece and Rome: A CBT project. Retrieved August 2, 2000, from www.techlearning.com/db_area/archives/WCE/archives.smartin.htm.

Maryland digital schools project: Field trips and interactives. 2003. Retrieved July 1, 2003, from http://www.thinkport.org/classroom/oftinteractive/default.tp.

Mater, J. A. 2001. My dream room. Retrieved May 25, 2001, from www.lessonplanspage.com/CILAPostersWithWordFormattingGrammar4.8.htm.

Mattingly, L. 1999. Integrating technology in the classroom. Retrieved August 26, 1999, from www.siec.K12.in.us/~west/slides/integrate/sld024.htm.

Maze, B. 1999, May. [Interview].

McDonald, B. 1999, May. [Interview].

McDonald, E. J. B. 1973. The development and evaluation of a set of multi-media self-instructional learning activity packages for use in remedial English at an urban community college (Doctoral dissertation, University of Memphis, 1973). *Dissertation Abstracts International* 34:04A.

McDonald, J. 1996. The paperless composition: Computer-assisted writing. *Innovation Abstracts* XVIII(October 18): n.p.

McGoogan, G. 2002. Around the world in 24 hours. *Educational Leadership* (October), 60 (2), 44–46.

McGowan, K. 1999. [Beehive question]. Retrieved September 28, 1999, from http://questions.nytimes.com.

McKibben, B. 2000. The world streaming in. *The Atlantic Monthly* 286 (July): 78.

McLean, M., & Miller, S. 1997. Importing video stills into computer documents. *Media & Methods* (September/ October): 12.

McLuhan, M. 1998. *Understanding media: The extensions of man.* Cambridge, MA: The Massachusetts Institute of Technology Press.

McLuhan, M., & Fiore, Q. 1967. *The medium is the message*. New York: Bantam Books.

McLuhan, M., & Fiore, Q. 1996. *The medium is the message: An inventory of effects,* renewed by J. Agel. San Francisco, CA: HardWired.

Medina-Jerez, W., Clark, D. B., Medina, A., & Ramirez-Marin, F. 2007. Science for ELLs: Rethinking our approach. *The Science Teacher,* 74(3): 52–56.

Meiers, V. 1999. Into the next millennium. Retrieved August 23, 1999, from http://cnets.iste.org/ss_68_1_done.html.

Mergel, B. 1998. Instructional design & learning theory. Retrieved January 8, 2000, from www.usask.ca/education/coursework/802papers/mergel/brenda.htm.

Merrimack Valley School District. 2001. Acceptable use policy. Retrieved June 27, 2001, from http://www.mv.k12.nh.us/schools/mvms/acceptable_use_policy.htm.

Meyer, A., & Rose, D. 2000. Universal design for individual differences. *Educational Leadership* 58(3): 39–43.

Michigan's Educational Technology Plan. Retrieved on August 30, 2006 http://www.techplan.org/STP2006ProposedMar032006.doc.

Microsoft in Education: new Teachers Corner. 2000. Lifesavers: How to find your way on the web. Retrieved May 20, 2002, from www.microsoft.com/education.mctn/newteacher/lifesavers/52001saver.asp.

Milici, J. (2003). Foreign studies. Retrieved October 23, 2003, from http://www.nea.org.

Miller, C. 2007. Some enlightening Internet video statistics: YouTube. Retrieved May 25, 2009, from http://churchcommunicationspro.com/2007/03/20/some-enlightening-internet-video-statistics-youtube/.

Miller, E. B. 1996. *The Internet resource directory*. Englewood, CO: Libraries Unlimited.

Miller, S. 1999. Greece and Rome: A CBT project. Retrieved May 12, 1999, from www.techlearning.com/db_area/archives/WCE/archives/smiller.htm.

Miller, S. P. 2009. *Validated practices for teaching students with diverse needs and abilities* (2nd ed.). Upper Saddle River, NJ: Pearson.

Millspaw, E. 1996–1997. Student team designs and maintains internet/intranet web sites. *The High School Magazine* (December/January): 58–59.

Milone, M. 1999. Enterprise computing. *Technology & Learning* 20(September): 31–32.

Milstein, M. 1999. The sound of dinosaurs. Retrieved July 5, 2000, from www.discovery.com/exp/fossilzone/sounds/dinosaurs.html.

Minsky, Marvin. 1988. Papert's principle. Retrieved September 28, 2001, from www.papert.org/articles/PapertsPrinciple.html.

Mir, S. 2002. Art exchange. Retrieved April 10, 2003, from http://www.nea.org/helpfrom/growing/works4me/tech/techclas.html.

Mitchell, L. 1999, April. [Interview]. South Elementary School, Pinson, TN.

Moore, J. Branksome Hall. Retrieved July 15, 1999, from www.branksome.on.ca/main.html.

Moore, K. 1999. *Volcanoes: A multi-media unit for cross-curricular instruction in the junior high school.* Henderson, TN: Chester County Junior High School.

Moore, K. April 1999. [Interview].

Moore, S. 2002. Creating tests with Microsoft Word. *Instructor* (September), 112 (3), 16.

Morgan, A. 1995. Research into student learning in distance education. Victoria, Australia: In Distance education at a glance: Guide #9: Strategies for distance learning, edited by B. Willis. Retrieved November 11, 2000, from http://www.uidaho.edu/evo/dist9.html.

Morris, P. (Developer). 21st century schoolhouse: Lesson plans. Retrieved February 27, 1999, from www.coedu.usf.edu/~morris/acsi_1p2.html.

"Mrs. Claus's Workshop," prepared by Mrs. Slaven's class at Elementary West in Loogootee, Indiana, http://www.siec.k12.in.us.

Multiple intelligences survey. Retrieved September 23, 1999, from http://familyeducation.com/article/print/0,1303,4-3201.00html?obj_gra.

Murphy, M. 1999. Expanding your classroom. Retrieved July 15, 1999, from www.techlearning.com/db_area/archives/WCE/archives/muggs2.htm.

Murphy, M. 2000. Expanding your classroom. Retrieved February 25, 2000, from http://www.techlearning.com/db_area/archives/WCE/archives/muggs2.htm.

Naisbitt, J. 1982. Megatrends. New York: Warner Communications.

National Board for Professional Teaching Standards. Their mission. Retrieved August 30, 2006 from http://www.nbpts.org/about_us/background/mission.

National Council for Accreditation of Teacher Education. 2008. 2008 NCATE unit standards. Retrieved June 2, 2009, from http://www.ncate.org/documents/boeMaterials/ncate_unit_stnds_%20summary2008.pdf.

National Education Association. 1996. Technology and portfolio assessment. NEA: Technology Brief No. 4. Retrieved May 5, 2002, from www.nea.org/cet/BRIEFS/brief4.html.

National Educational Technology Standards for Teachers. Retrieved March 29, 2002, from http://cnets.iste.org/pdf/page24–25.pdf.

National Reading Panel. 2007. *Report of the National Reading Panel: Teaching children to read. Reports of the subgroups* (NIH Publication 00-4754). Washington, DC: U.S. Government Printing Office.

National School Board Association. 2007. Creating & connecting// Research and guidelines on online social—and educational—networking. Retrieved May 11, 2009, from http://www.nsba.org/site/docs/41400/41340.pdf.

National Telecommunications and Information Administration. 2000. *Falling through the Net*. Washington, DC: Author.

NCATE and ISTE. Retrieved August 30, 2006. http://cnets.iste.org/ncate/n_unit.html.

Negroponte, N. 1996. *Being digital.* New York: Vintage Books/ Random House, p. 230.

Nellen, T. (2000). Cyber short stories. Retrieved August 21, 2000, from www.techlearning.com/db_area/archive/WCE/archives/tnellen.htm.

Newport, Stuart (ed). (2005) Largest Computation. *Guiness World Records.* Retrieved October 12, 2006.

Newton, D. A., & Dell, A. G. 2009. Issues in assistive technology implementation: Resolving AT/IT conflicts. *Journal of Special Education Technology,* 24(1): 51–56.

Nielson Company. 2009. Global faces and networked places: A Nielsen report on social networking's new global footprint. Retrieved May 6, 2009, from http://server-uk.imrworldwide.com/pdcimages/Global_Faces_and_Networked_Places-A_Nielsen_Report_on_Social_Networkings_New_Global_Footprint.pdf.

Niess, M. 1999. Integrating technology into math instruction. *Media & Methods* (January/February): 26–27.

Nix, D., & Spiro, R. J. (Eds.). 1990. *Cognition, education, and multimedia: Exploring ideas in high technology*. Hillsdale, NJ: Erlbaum.

Norris, B. 2000. [Gaggle.net]. Retrieved January 14, 2000, from www.nea.org/cet/wired/index.html.

Notebloom, R. 2000. One teacher's view. *Curriculum/Technology Quarterly* 9(Spring): 1–2.

Novak, J. D. 2001. The theory underlying concept maps and how to construct them. Retrieved May 5, 2002, from http://cmap.coginst.uwf.edu/info.

Novelli, D., S. Edmunds, & D. Gurwicz. Screen-saver stories. *Instructor* (May/June 2001) 110 (8), 74.

NTTI video utilization strategies. 2002. Retrieved November 30, 2003, from http://www.thirteen.org/edonline/ntti/resources/video2.html.

Nunes-Turcotte, O. 1998, November/December. Electronic learning in your classroom [Project page]. *Instructor,* n.p.

Nunley, K. 2000. How to layer your curriculum. Retrieved July 9, 2000, from www.brains.org/layered.htm.

Ocean in view. 2002. Retrieved May 12, 2003, from http://www97.intel.com/education/odyssey/day_289/day_289.htm.

Office of Technology Assessment. U.S. Congress. 1995. *Teachers and technology: Making the connection*. Washington, DC: U.S. Government Printing Office.

Oh, P. 1999. Back to basics: No-frills, but super, drill-and-practice software. *Instructor* 108(March): 74–76.

O'Reilly, T. 2005. What is Web 2.0: Design patterns and business models for the next generation of software. Retrieved May 6, 2009, from http://www.oreillynet.com/pub/a/oreilly/tim/news/2005/09/30/what-is-web-20.html.

Oros, L., Finger, A., & Morenegg, J. 1998, January/February. Creating digital portfolios. *Media & Methods*, 15.

Paivio, A. 2001. Dual coding theory. Retrieved October 4, 2001, from http://tip.psychology.org/paivio.html.

Papert, S. 1992. *The children's machine: Rethinking school in the age of the computer*. New York: Basic Books.

Papert, S. 1999. Papert on Piaget. Retrieved October 5, 2001, from www.papert.org/articles/Papertonpiaget.html.

Papert, S., & Harel, I. 1991. Situating constructionism. Retrieved September 28, 2001, from www.papert.org/articles/Situating Construtionism.html.

Parker, R. C. 1988. *Looking good in print.* Chapel Hill, NC: Ventana Press.

Parry, D. 2006. The technology of reading and writing in the digital space: Why RSS is crucial for a blogging classroom. Retrieved May 10, 2009, from http://blogsforlearning.msu.edu/articles/view.php?id=6.

Pavlov, I. P. 1927. *Conditioned reflexes*. London: Oxford University Press.

Payán, R. M., & Nettles, M. T. n.d. Current state of English-language learners in the U.S. K-12 student population. Washington, DC: Educational Testing Service. Retrieved May 11, 2009, from www.ets.org/Media/Conferences_and_Events/pdf/ELLsymposium/ELL_factsheet.pdf.

Payton, T. Traveling buddies. Retrieved July 15, 1999, from www.techlearning.com/db_area/archives/WCE/archives/tpayton.html.

Pearson, G. 2006. *Ask NCELA No. 1: How many school-aged English language learners (ELLs) are there in the U.S.?* Washington, DC: National Clearing House for English Language Acquisition and Language Instruction.

Pearson Education Development Group. (2003). Authentic assessment overview. Retrieved October 5, 2003, from http://teachervision.fen.com/lesson-plans/lesson-4911.html.

Peters, T. 1998. *Thriving on chaos: Handbook for management revolution.* New York: Alfred Knopf.

Piaget, J. 1952. *The origins of intelligence in children*. New York: International Universities.

Piaget, J. 1960. *Psychology of intelligence*. Paterson, NJ: Littlefield, Adams, & Co.

Piaget, J. 1970. *Science of education and the psychology of the child,* translated by D. Coltman. New York: Orion.

Piaget, J. 1976. *The grasp of consciousness: Action and concept in the young child,* translated by S. Wedgwood. Cambridge, MA: Harvard University Press.

Picture-perfect lessons. 1999. *Instructor* (March): 80–81.

Platt, P. Projects. Retrieved June 14, 2000, from http://gsh.lightspan.com/pr/_cfm/GetDetail.cfm?pID=593.

Popham, W. J., & Baker, E. L. 1970. *Establishing instructional goals*. Englewood Cliffs, NJ: Prentice-Hall.

Potter, B. 1999. *Parent power: Energizing home-school communication.* Portsmouth, NH: Heinemann.

Price, D. 1999, June. [Interview].

Price, S. D. 2001. Techie teacher takes prize/She gets Thinkquest Fellowship [Cathie Thomley]. *The Commercial Appeal* (February 13): n.p.

Prochelo, D., & Kmiec, B. 1998. Speech with advanced technology. Retrieved January 2, 1999, from www.ncrel.org/cw/availabl.htm.

Pruett, H. 2002. Having students learn basic grammar through technology. Retrieved May 23, 2003, from http://www.techlearning.com/db_area/archives/WCE/archives/hpruett.html.

Rahmani, L. 1973. *Soviet psychology: Philosophical, theoretical, and experiential issues*. New York: International Universities.

Railsback, K. 2001. Peering into the future. *InfoWorld* 22(42): 85–95.

Raskauskas, N. 2000. Interactive sports guides. Retrieved December 29, 2000, from http://henson.austin.apple.com/edres/shlessons/sports.shtml.

Rasmussen, K. 1999. Partners in education: How schools and homeschoolers work together. *Education Update* 41(June): 1–4, 5.

Re: Pido datos biográficos de Benjamin Bloom. I ask Benjamin Bloom's biography. Retrieved August 12, 1999, from www.funderstanding.com/messages/1138.htm.

Recipe for the classroom: 1 ideal computer learning station. 1998. *Children's Software Review* (September/October): 27.

Reed, J., & Woodruff, M. 1995. Videoconferencing: Using videoconferencing technology for teaching. Retrieved December 30, 2000, from http://www.pacbell.com/wired/vidconf/Using.html.

Rehak, M. 1999. Questions for John Ashbery: A child in time. *The New York Times Magazine*, April 4:15.

Reiser, R. A. 1987. Instructional technology. A history. In *Instructional technology: Foundations* (pp. 12–20), edited by R. M. Gagné. Hillsdale, NJ: Erlbaum.

Renner-Smith, S. 2002. "Fontastic" idea! *Creative Classroom* (March/April), 26.

Richardson, W. 2003. High school journalists use weblogs to mentor young writers. Retrieved October 31, 2003, from http://www97.intel.com/education/odyssey/day_301/day_301.htm.

Richardson, W. 2005. RSS: A quick start guide for educators. Retrieved May 10, 2009, from http://weblogg-ed.com/RSS_for_ed.

Richey, R. 2006. Reflections on the 2008 AECT definitions of the field. Retrieved June 1, 2009, from http://www.springerlink.com/content/88p665mv0p527470/fulltext.pdf.

Richey, Rita. 2008. Reflections on the 2008 AECT definitions of the field. *Tech Trends,* 52(1): 24–25.

Rivera, J. 2002. School on a postcard. Retrieved May 29, 2003, from http://www.ciconline.com/Enrichment/Teaching/learningwithtechnology/expertadvice/default.htm.

Roche, E. 1998. #258. Cooperative learning, technology, science, language. Retrieved August 17, 1999, from www.teachers.net/lessons/posts/258.html.

Rohfield, R. W., & Hiemstra, R. 1995. Moderating discussions in the electronic classroom. Retrieved December 27, 2000, from http:// www.ed.gov/databases/ERIC_Digests/ed395214.html.

Rose, D. H., & Meyer, A. 2002. *Teaching every student in the digital age: Universal design for learning*. Alexandria, VA: Association for Supervision and Curriculum Development.

Roth, M. K. 2003. Palm pilots beaming lessons. Retrieved October 3, 2003, from http://www.pdaed.com/vertical/features/Beaming.xml.

Rowling, D. 1999. Introducing the geometer's sketchpad to the classroom. Retrieved December 16, 1999, from www.techlearning.com/db_area/archives/WCE/archives/rowling.htm.

Royal, K. W. 1999. If you had computers in your classroom, what would you do with them? Retrieved May 12, 1999, from www.techlearning.com/db_area/archives/WCE/archives/royal.htm.

Russell Elementary School. 2001. Wade through the wondrous wetlands. Retrieved May 17, 2001, from http://applecom.

Saettler, P. 1968. A history of instructional technology. New York: McGraw-Hill.

Saettler, P. 1990. *The evolution of American educational technology*. Englewood, CO: Libraries Unlimited.

Sagan, C. 1998. *Billions and billions: Thoughts of life and death at the brink of the millennium*. New York: Ballantine.

Santo, C. 1998. An Internet day. *Family PC* (October): 54.

Santo, C. 1999. The Malverne method. *Family PC* (August): 101.

Santo, C. 1999. The way we were. *Family PC* (May): 119.

Schrock, K. 2000a. The ABCs of web site evaluation. Retrieved May 15, 2002, from www.kathyschrock.net/abcevol/index.htm.

Schrock, K. 2000b. Kathy Schrock's guide for educators. Retrieved May 20, 2002, from http://school.discovery.com/schrockguide/edtools.html.

Seavey, E. 2002. A team approach to oral history. Retrieved February 14, 2003, from http://www.col-ed.org/cur/sst/sst45.text.

Sharer, S. 2000. Videoconferencing and distance learning. *School Executive* (November/December): 6.

Sharp, W. 2001. Becoming a wireless campus: A student initiative. *T.H.E. Journal* 28(10): 60–66.

Shasha, D., & Lazere, C. 1998. *Out of their minds*. New York: Copernicus.

Shelly, G., Cashman, T., Waggoner, G., & Waggoner, W. 1998. *Discovering computers 98: A link to the future*. Cambridge, MA: Course Technologies.

Short, D. D. 1994. *Enhancing instructional effectiveness: A strategic approach*. Norwalk, CT: IBM Higher Education.

Skinner, B. F. 1953. *Science and human behavior.* New York: Macmillan.

Skinner, B. F. 1958. Teaching machines. *Science* 128: 969–977.

Skinner, B. F. 1971. *Beyond freedom and dignity*. New York: Alfred A. Knopf.

Skinner, B. F. 1974. *About behaviorism*. New York: Alfred A. Knopf.

Slaven, K. 1998. Mrs. Claus's workshop. Retrieved November 20, 1998, from www.siec.K12inu;.s./~west/proj/claus/facts1.htm.

Small wires, big learning: A Britannica online success story. 1999. *T.H.E. Journal* (January): 38.

SMART whiteboards. 2002. Retrieved April 20, 2002, from www.smarttech.com/profilees/charyk.asp.

Smith, S., Tyler, J. M., & Benacote, A. Internet supported teaching: Advice from the trenches. Retrieved January 9, 2001, from http://www.usdla.org/ED_magazine/illuniactive/JAN00_Issue/Internet.htm.

Solomon, G. 2000. A home (page) of your own. *Technology & Learning* 20(March): 46.

Sonoma County Department of Education. 2000. Twelve principles for brain-based learning. Retrieved July 9, 2000, from http://talkingpage.org/artic011.html.

Sorrentino, L. 1999. [Abuzz question]. Retrieved September 28, 1999, from http://questions.nytimes.com.

Sprenger, M. 1999. *Learning and memory: The brain in action*. Alexandria, VA: ASCD.

Stanford-Binet intelligence scale. Retrieved September 13, 1999, from www.richmond.edu/~capc/Binetmain.html.

Starr, L. 2000. Meet Bernie Dodge—the Frank Lloyd Wright of learning environments! Retrieved June 1, 2003, from http://www.education-world.com/a_tech/tech020.shtml.

Stein, C., & Driggs, L. 1999. Freedom of the press: Where should it end? Retrieved April 12, 1999, from www.nytimes.com/learning.

Stembor, E. 2000. University of Connecticut. Retrieved September 2, 2000, from http://www.wested.org/tie/dlrn/k12de.html.

Stephens, D. 2000. Timber Ridge Middle School travel brochures. Retrieved April 16, 2000, from www.timberridgemagnet.net/ad/tchpg.htm.

Sternberg, R. J. 1999. How intelligent is intelligence testing? *Scientific American* 9(Winter): 14.

Stetler, J. 2002. Internet exchange concert. Retrieved April 10, 2003, from http://www.nea.org/helpfrom/growing/works4me/tech/techclas.html.

Stowe, E. 1999. [Abuzz question]. Retrieved September 21, 1999, from http://questions.nytimes.com.

Sturgeon, K., & Lemen, D. 2001. Magnolia Elementary School: Policy and leadership. Retrieved June 27, 2001, from http://www.esc6.net/tiftrain.student/magnoliaelem/p1.html.

Suzanne. 2000. Farm sound. Retrieved July 4, 2000, from www.alfy.lycos.com/teachers/teach/lesson_bui/overView.asp?LessonId=95&saveVal=ye.

Submission process for NBPTS. Retrieved August 25, 2006 http://www.nbpts.org/for_candidates/the_portfolio.

Svedkauskaite, A., Reza-Hernandez, L., & Clifford, M. 2003. Critical issue: Using technology to support limited-English-proficient (LEP) students' learning experiences. Retrieved May 28, 2009, from www.ncrel.org/sdrs/areas/issues/methods/technlgy/te900.htm.

Sweaty palms, circa 1914. 1998. *The Wall Street Journal,* March 31, p. R8.

Sylvester, R. 1995. *A celebration of neurons: An educator's guide to the human brain.* Alexandria, VA: ASCD.

Tapia, S. T. 2000. Online classes moving into O. C. high schools. Retrieved November 30, 2000, from http://www.ocregister.com/education/online01130.cci.shtml.

Taverna, P., & Hongell, T. 2000. Meet Harriet Tubman: The story of a web site. *Learning and Leading with Technology* 27(March 20): 43–45, 62.

Teaching our youngest: A guide for preschool teachers and child care and family providers: Developing listening and speaking skills. 2002. Retrieved January 27, 2003, from http://www.ed.gov/offices/OESE/teachingouryoungest/developing.html.

Teaching with EPals. 2000. Retrieved May 17, 2002, from www.epals.com/curriculum_connections/index_en.html.

TEAMS distance learning: For all K–12 educators. Retrieved December 26, 2000, from http://teams.lacoe.edu.

Teleconferencing. 1999. Retrieved September 2, 2000, from http://www.wested.org/tie/dlrn/teleconferencing.html.

Tener, M. 2002. Learning with lyrics. *Creative Classroom* (November/December), 17 (3), 27.

The eight intelligences. Retrieved July 29, 1999, from http://familyeducation.com/article/print/0,1303,4-3201,00.html?obj_gra.

The Monster Exchange. 1998. *Family PC* (November): 194.

Thorndike, E. L., & Woodworth, R. S. 1901. Education as science. *Psychological Review* 8:247–261, 384–395, 553–564.

Thorndike, R. L. 1911. *Animal intelligence.* New York: Macmillan.

Tiene, D., & Ingram, A. 2001. *Exploring current issues in educational technology.* New York: McGraw Hill.

Tietz, H. 2002. Savoring expository writing through PowerPoint. Retrieved June 10, 2003, from http://www.techlearning.com/db_area/archives/WCE/archives/htietz.html.

TLC project showrooms: Networking. 2001. Retrieved June 27, 2001, from http://web.nysed.gov/technology/projects/oswegocs.html.

Turner, J. 2000. Cyberschool. Retrieved September 2, 2000, from http://www.wested.org/tie/dlrn/k12de.html.

Turner, M. A. 1999. [No title]. Retrieved April 23, 1999, from www.nea.org/cet/wired/index.html.

U.S. Department of Commerce. 2000. Digital divide. Retrieved June 27, 2001, from http://www.digitaldivide.gov.

U.S. Department of Education. 1994. *Strong families, strong schools: A research base for family involvement in learning from the United States Department of Education.* Washington, DC: U.S. Department of Education.

U.S. Department of Education Office of the Secretary *Benefits of Technology Use.* Retrieved August 25, 2006 http://www.ed.gov/about/offices/list/os/technology/plan/national/benefits.html.

U.S. Department of Education Office of the Secretary *Educational Technology Fact Sheet.* Retrieved August 25, 2006 (www.ed.gov/about/offices/list/os/technology/facts.html).

Use of NETS by State, Retrieved August 25, 2006 http://cnets.iste.org/docs/States_using_NETS.pdf.

Vaughn, K. 1999. [TeleMath]. Retrieved November 20, 1999, from www.nea.org/cet/wired/index.html.

Velez, L. 2003. Postcards from abroad. Retrieved May 14, 2003, from http://teachersnetwork.org/teachnetnyc/lvelez/postcards.htm.

Video conferencing in Plano ISD. 2003. Retrieved June 13, 2003, from http://k-12.pisd.edu/distance_learning/vidconf.htm.

Vitaska, D. 2002. The new language classroom: Bringing French to the U.S. *Media and Methods* (September/October) 39 (1), 10.

VMSTV 2003. Retrieved August 12, 2003, from http://www.vmstv.com.

Vygotsky, L. S. 1978. *Mind in society: The development of higher psychological processes.* Cambridge, MA: Harvard University Press.

Vygotsky, L. S. 1981. *Thought and language,* translated by E. Hanfmann & G. Vakar. Cambridge, MA: The MIT Press.

Vygotsky, L. S. 1987. *The collected works of L. S. Vygotsky.* Vol. 1. New York: Plenum.

Vygotsky, L. S. 1987. *Thinking and speech,* translated by N. Minck. New York: Plenum.

Wallace, L. 2002. Using projection technology to enhance teaching. *Media & Methods* (September/October), 39 (1), 6.

Wanderman, R. 2000. How computers change the writing process for people with learning disabilities (First Person Feature). Retrieved May 14, 2009, from http://www.ldonline.org.

Watson, J. B. 1962. *Behaviorism.* Chicago: University of Chicago Press.

Wehmeyer, M., Smith, S., Palmer, S., & Davies, D. 2004. Technology use by students with intellectual disabilities: An overview. *Journal of Special Education Technology,* 19(4): 7–21.

Weiger, E. 1999. [No title]. Retrieved July 20, 1999, from www.nea.org/cet/wired/index.html.

Wenglinsky, H. 1999. Teacher classroom practices and student performance: How schools can make a difference. Retrieved May 5, 2002, from www.ets.org/research/dload/RIBRR-01-19.pdf.

Wertheimer, M. 1945. *Productive thinking.* New York: Harper.

What to do with digital cameras. 1997. *Media & Methods* (November): 2, 8.

White, R. 1993. *How computers work.* Emeryville, CA: Ziff-Davis Press.

Wilkes, D. 2001. Wireless laptops in the classroom. *Media & Methods* 37(February): 33.

Willard, N. E. 2006. A briefing for educators: Online social networking communities and youth risk. Retrieved May 5, 2009, from http://csriu.org/documents/docs/youthriskonlinealert.pdf.

Williams, B. 2000. More than an exception to the rule. In M. Fried-Oken & H. Bersani, (Eds.), *Speaking up and spelling it out* (pp. 245–254). Baltimore: Paul Brookes.

Williams, P. 2000. In-school broadcasting: Capturing the excitement. *Media & Methods* (May/June): 6.

Willig, B. 2000. Schoolwide comprehensive courseware: An update. *Media & Methods* (January/February): 24, 26.

Willis, B. 1995. *Guide #2: Strategies for teaching at a difference and strategies for teaching at a glance; Guide #4: Evaluation for distance educators; Guide #6: Instructional audio; Guide #7; Computers in distance education: Guide #9: Strategies for distance learning; Guide #10: Distance education research; Guide #11: Interactive videoconferencing in distance education.* Retrieved November 11, 2000, from http://www.uidaho.edu/evo.html.

Windschitl, M. 1999. The challenges of sustaining constructivist classroom culture. *Phi Delta Kappan* 80: 751–755.

Wohlert, H. 2000. German by satellite. Retrieved June 17, 2000, from http://www.syllabus.com/casestudies/o.html.

Wolfe, B. 1999. Using technology as a tool for teaching across the curriculum. Retrieved July 15, 1999, from www.techlearning.com/db_area/archives/WCE/archives/bwolfe.htm.

Wood, J. M. 2001. Virtual art, real learning. *Instructor* 110(January/February): 80.

Wood, S. 1998–1999. *Computer projects.* Jackson, TN: Northeast Middle School.

Wrenn, E., S. Udell, & S. Sorensen. 2003. If I were president. Retrieved May 16, 2003, from http://www.apple.com.

Yam, P. 1999. Intelligence considered. *Scientific American* 9(Winter): 12–17.

Yarnell, K. 2002. Intranets: Repositories of school data. *School Executive* (September/October), 39 (1), 28.

Zehler, A. M., Fleischman, H. L., Hopstock, P. J., Stephenson, T. G., Pendzick, M. L., & Sapru, S. 2003. *Descriptive study of services to LEP students and LEP students with disabilities, Volume 1A: Research report*. Arlington, VA: Development Associates.

Zimbalist, A., & Driggs, L. 1999. Fan(tom) of the opera: Applying the plots of famous operas to modern life: A music genre appreciation lesson. Retrieved September 10, 1999, from http://www.nytimes.com/learning.

Zimbalist, A., & Driggs, L. 1999. When Moore is less for microprocessors: Examining how computer chips work and the Moore's Law prediction: A technology lesson. Retrieved July 1, 1999, from www.nytimes.com/learning.

Zora, D., 2003. A living alphabet. Retrieved May 16, 2003, from http:// www.apple.com.

INDEX